Microsoft

Excel 2002

Comprehensive Concepts and Techniques

Gary B. Shelly
Thomas J. Cashman
James S. Quasney

Contributing Author
Jeffrey J. Quasney

THOMSON
COURSE TECHNOLOGY

COURSE TECHNOLOGY
25 THOMSON PLACE
BOSTON MA 02210

SHELLY
CASHMAN
SERIES®

Australia • Canada • Denmark • Japan • Mexico • New Zealand • Philippines • Puerto Rico • Singapore
South Africa • Spain • United Kingdom • United States

THOMSON

COURSE TECHNOLOGY

COPYRIGHT © 2002 Course Technology, a division of Thomson Learning.
Printed in the United States of America

Asia (excluding Japan)
Thomson Learning
5 Shenton Way #01-01
UIC Building
Singapore 068808

Latin America
Thomson Learning
Seneca, 53
Colonia Polanco
11560 Mexico D.F. Mexico

Canada
Nelson/Thomson Learning
1120 Birchmount Road
Scarborough, Ontario
Canada M1K 5G4

Japan
Thomson Learning
Nihonjisyo Brooks Bldg 3-F
1-4-1 Kudankita, Chiyoda-Ku
Tokyo 102-0073 Japan

South Africa
Thomson Learning
15 Brookwood Street
P.O. Box 1722
Soverset West 7120
South Africa

UK/Europe/Middle East
Thomson Learning
Berkshire House
168-173 High Holborn
London, WC1V 7AA United Kingdom

Australia/New Zealand
Nelson/Thomson Learning
102 Dodds Street
South Melbourne, Victoria 3205
Australia

Spain
Thomson Learning
Calle Magallanes, 25
28015-MADRID
ESPANA

APPROVED COURSEWARE

"Microsoft and the Microsoft Office User Specialist Logo are registered trademarks of Microsoft Corporation in the United States and other countries. Course Technology is an independent entity from Microsoft Corporation, and not affiliated with Microsoft Corporation in any manner. This textbook may be used in assisting students to prepare for a Microsoft Office User Specialist Exam. Neither Microsoft Corporation, its designated review company, nor Course Technology warrants that use of this textbook will ensure passing the relevant Exam.
"Use of the Microsoft Office User Specialist Approved Courseware Logo on this product signifies that it has been independently reviewed and approved in complying with the following standards: 'Acceptable coverage of all content related to the Microsoft Office Exam entitled "Microsoft Excel 2002 Core Exam," and sufficient performance-based exercises that relate closely to all required content, based on sampling of text.'"

PHOTO CREDITS: Microsoft Excel 2002 *Project 2, page E 2.02-03* L.A.T.E. Ride brochure cover, Courtesy of Friends of the Parks, Chicago; *Project 3, pages E 3.02-03* Coins, man working on notebook computer, money, Courtesy of PhotoDisc, Inc.; house and car, lightbulb, telephone, television and radio, Courtesy of Corel; *Project 4, pages E 4.02-03* Woman with notebook computer, Courtesy of PhotoDisc, Inc.; Home, man at work desk, money, keyboard, Courtesy of Corel; *Project 5, pages E 5.02-03* Man holding glasses, woman writing, business meeting around a table, people meeting standing, Courtesy of PhotoDisc, Inc.; *Project 6, pages E 6.02-03* Business meeting, woman picking up dry cleaning, food market check-out, woman working on calculator, money, Courtesy of PhotoDisc, Inc.; *Project 7, pages E 7.02-03* Young couple, Courtesy of Dynamic Graphics, Inc.; people at piano, Courtesy of Corel Professional Photos; *Project 8, pages E 8.02-03* Woman chef, Courtesy of PhotoDisc, Inc.; child eating, volunteer servers, Courtesy of Union Rescue Mission, Los Angeles, California; baby in overalls, Courtesy of Digital Stock.

ISBN 0-7895-6279-0

4 5 6 7 8 9 10   BC   06 05 04 03 02

Microsoft
Excel 2002
Comprehensive Concepts and Techniques

Contents

3 PROJECT THREE

WHAT-IF ANALYSIS, CHARTING, AND WORKING WITH LARGE WORKSHEETS

■ WEB FEATURE

CREATING STATIC AND DYNAMIC WEB PAGES USING EXCEL

4 PROJECT FOUR

FINANCIAL FUNCTIONS, DATA TABLES, AMORTIZATION SCHEDULES, AND HYPERLINKS

Preface

The Shelly Cashman Series® offers the finest textbooks in computer education. We are proud of the fact that our series of Microsoft Office 4.3, Microsoft Office 95, Microsoft Office 97, and Microsoft Office 2000 textbooks have been the most widely used books in education. With each new edition of our Office books, we have made improvements based on the software and comments made by the instructors and students. The *Microsoft Office XP* books continue with the innovation, quality, and reliability that you have come to expect from the Shelly Cashman Series.

Office XP is the most significant upgrade ever to the Office suite. It provides a much smarter work experience for users. Microsoft has enhanced Office XP in the following areas: (1) streamlined user interface; (2) smart tags and task panes to help simplify the way people work; (3) speech and handwriting recognition; (4) an improved Help system; (5) enhanced Web capabilities; and (6) application-specific features. Each one of these enhancements is part of Microsoft Excel 2002 and is discussed in detail.

In this *Microsoft Excel 2002* book, you will find an educationally sound and easy-to-follow pedagogy that combines a step-by-step approach with corresponding screens. All projects and exercises in this book are designed to take full advantage of the Excel 2002 enhancements. The popular Other Ways and More About features offer in-depth knowledge of Excel 2002. The new Learn It Online page presents a wealth of additional exercises to ensure your students have all the reinforcement they need. The project openers provide a fascinating perspective of the subject covered in the project. The project material is developed carefully to ensure that students will see the importance of learning Excel for future coursework.

Objectives of This Textbook

Microsoft Excel 2002: Comprehensive Concepts and Techniques is intended for a three-unit course that presents in-depth coverage of Microsoft Excel 2002. No experience with a computer is assumed, and no mathematics beyond the high school freshman level is required. The objectives of this book are:

- To teach the fundamentals of Excel 2002
- To expose students to practical examples of the computer as a useful tool
- To acquaint students with the proper procedures to create workbooks suitable for course work, professional purposes, and personal use
- To develop an exercise-oriented approach that allows learning by doing
- To introduce students to new input technologies
- To encourage independent study, and help those who are working alone
- To assist students preparing to take the Microsoft Office User Specialist examination for both the Microsoft Excel 2002 Core level and Microsoft Excel 2002 Expert level.

Approved by Microsoft as Courseware
for the Microsoft Office User Specialist Program
Expert Level and Core Level

Microsoft Excel 2002: Comprehensive Concepts and Techniques has been approved by Microsoft as courseware for the Microsoft Office User Specialist (MOUS) program. After completing the projects and exercises in this book, students will be prepared to take both the Expert-level and Core-level Microsoft Office User Specialist Exams for Microsoft Excel 2002. The Excel 2002 Core-level skill set is presented in the first six projects. See Appendix E for additional information on the MOUS program and for Expert-level and Core-level tables that include the Excel 2002 MOUS skill set and corresponding page numbers on which a skill is discussed and practiced in the book, or visit the Web site mous.net.

By passing the certification exam for a Microsoft software program, students demonstrate their proficiency in that program to employers. This exam is offered at participating centers, participating corporations, and participating employment agencies. To purchase a Microsoft Office User Specialist certification exam, visit certiport.com.

The Shelly Cashman Series Microsoft Office User Specialist Center Web page (Figure 1) has more than fifteen Web pages you can visit to obtain additional information on the MOUS Certification program. The Web page scsite.com/offxp/cert.htm includes links to general information on certification, choosing an application for certification, preparing for the certification exam, and taking and passing the certification exam.

FIGURE 1   The Shelly Cashman Series Microsoft Office User Specialist Center Web Page

The Shelly Cashman Approach

Features of the Shelly Cashman Series *Microsoft Excel 2002* books include:

- **Project Orientation:** Each project in the book presents a practical problem and complete solution in an easy-to-understand approach.
- **Step-by-Step, Screen-by-Screen Instructions:** Each of the tasks required to complete a project is identified throughout the project. Full-color screens accompany the steps.
- **Thoroughly Tested Projects:** Every screen in the book is correct because it is produced by the author only after performing a step, resulting in unprecedented quality.
- **Other Ways Boxes and Quick Reference Summary:** The Other Ways boxes displayed at the end of most of the step-by-step sequences specify the other ways to do the task completed in the steps. Thus, the steps and the Other Ways box make a comprehensive reference unit.
- **More About Feature:** These marginal annotations provide background information and tips that complement the topics covered, adding depth and perspective.
- **Integration of the World Wide Web:** The World Wide Web is integrated into the Excel 2002 learning experience by (1) More About annotations that send students to Web sites for up-to-date information and alternative approaches to tasks; (2) a MOUS information Web page so students can prepare for the MOUS Certification examinations; (3) an Excel 2002 Quick Reference Summary Web page that summarizes the ways to complete tasks (mouse, menu, shortcut menu, and keyboard); and (4) the Learn It Online page at the end of each project, which has project reinforcement exercises, learning games, and other types of Web-based student activities.

Other Ways

1. Press ALT+D, D, D
2. In Voice Command mode, say "Data, Import External Data, Import Data"

More About

File Protection

Once you have protected your workbook with a password, it is important to write the password down or memorize it for future reference. Once you have saved the file with a password, it always will be a password-protected file; no way exists to bypass the requirement for a password.

Organization of This Textbook

Microsoft Excel 2002: Comprehensive Concepts and Techniques provides detailed instruction on how to use Excel 2002. The material is divided into nine projects, two Web Features, an Integration Feature, five appendices, and a Quick Reference Summary.

Project 1 – Creating a Worksheet and Embedded Chart In Project 1, students are introduced to Excel terminology, the Excel window, speech recognition and speech playback, and the basic characteristics of a worksheet and workbook. Topics include starting and quitting Excel; customizing Excel, entering text and numbers; selecting a range; using the AutoSum button; copying using the fill handle; changing font size and color; formatting in bold; centering across columns; using the AutoFormat command; charting using the ChartWizard; saving and opening a workbook; editing a worksheet; using the AutoCalculate area; and using the Excel Help system.

Project 2 – Formulas, Functions, Formatting, and Web Queries In Project 2, students use formulas and functions to build a worksheet and learn more about formatting and printing a worksheet. Topics include entering dates and formulas; using functions; verifying formulas; changing fonts; formatting text and numbers; conditional formatting; drawing borders; changing the widths of columns and rows; spell checking; changing sheet names; previewing a worksheet; printing a section of a worksheet; and displaying and printing the formulas in a worksheet. This project also introduces students to accessing real-time data using Web Queries and sending the open workbook as an e-mail attachment directly from Excel.

Project 3 – What-If-Analysis, Charting, and Working with Large Worksheets In Project 3, students learn how to work with larger worksheets, how to create a worksheet based on assumptions, how to use the IF function and absolute cell references, charting techniques, and how to perform what-if analysis. Topics include assigning global formats; rotating text; using the fill handle to create a series; deleting, inserting, copying, and moving data on a worksheet; displaying and formatting the system date; displaying and docking toolbars; creating a 3-D Pie chart on a chart sheet, enhancing a 3-D Pie chart; freezing titles; changing the magnification of worksheets; displaying different parts of the worksheet using panes; and simple what-if analysis and goal seeking.

Web Feature – Creating Static and Dynamic Web Pages Using Excel In this Web Feature, students are introduced creating a new folder, and creating static Web pages (noninteractive pages that do not change) and dynamic Web pages (interactive pages that offer Excel functionality). Topics include, saving and previewing an Excel workbook as a Web page; viewing and manipulating a Web page created in Excel using a browser; and using the Commands and Options dialog box.

Project 4 – Financial Functions, Data Tables, Amortization Schedules, and Hyperlinks In Project 4, students learn how to use financial functions and learn more about analyzing data in a worksheet. Topics include applying the PMT function to determine a monthly payment; the PV function to determine the amount due on a loan at the end of a year; adding a hyperlink to a Web page; using names to reference cells; protecting a worksheet; setting print options; conditional formatting; error checking; page setup; and analyzing data by creating a data table and an amortization schedule.

Project 5 – Creating, Sorting, and Querying a Worksheet Database In Project 5, students learn how to create, sort, and filter a database. Topics include using a data form to create and maintain a database; applying computational fields to a database; expanding the range of the database to include additional fields; creating subtotals; finding, extracting, and deleting records that pass a test; outlining a worksheet; and applying database and lookup functions.

Project 6 – Creating Templates and Working with Multiple Worksheets and Workbooks In Project 6, students learn to create a template and consolidate data into one worksheet. Topics include building and copying a template; multiple worksheets; 3-D cell references; customized formats; styles; charting; WordArt; adding text boxes and arrows; adding notes to a cell; adding a header and footer; creating and modifying lines and objects; changing margins; finding and replacing data; searching for files on disk; creating a workspace; and consolidating data by linking workbooks.

Integration Feature – Linking an Excel Worksheet to a Word Document and Web Discussions In this Integration Feature, students are introduced to linking a worksheet to a Word document and Web discussions. Topics include an explanation of the differences among copying and pasting, copying and embedding, and copying and linking; opening multiple applications; linking a worksheet to a Word document; saving and printing a document with a linked worksheet; and editing a linked worksheet in a Word document. Finally, students are introduced to using the Web to discuss a document using a discussion server.

Project 7 – Using Macros and Visual Basic for Applications (VBA) with Excel In Project 7, students learn how to automate tasks by incorporating VBA into their workbooks. Topics include protecting worksheets with passwords; using the macro recorder; executing macros; security; adding buttons to toolbars and commands to menus; creating a user interface by adding controls to a worksheet; setting properties; writing VBA code; using the Visual Basic Editor; validating incoming data; and using event-driven programs.

Project 8 – Formula Auditing, Data Validation, and Complex Problem Solving In Project 8, students learn how to go about solving complex problems. Topics include: using the Formula Auditing toolbar; using data validation; goal seeking; using Solver to solve multiple problems; saving multiple scenarios with Scenario Manager; analysis of Solver answers and multiple scenarios; and workbook properties.

Project 9 – Importing Data, Routing Changes, PivotCharts, PivotTables, and Trendlines In Project 9, students learn how to import data into an Excel workbook, collaboration techniques, and advanced data analysis techniques. Topics include importing data from a text file, an Access database, a Web page, and an XML file; turning tracking changes on and off; accepting and rejecting changes; serially routing a workbook to recipients; creating a PivotChart and PivotTable; analyzing a worksheet database using a PivotChart and PivotTable; sharing and merging workbooks; and creating a trendline on a chart.

Web Feature – Creating a PivotTable List Web Page using Excel In this Web Feature, students learn how to create and manipulate a PivotTable list. Topics include saving a worksheet database as a PivotTable list; viewing the PivotTable list using a browser; changing the view of the PivotTable list; adding summary totals; sorting columns of data; filtering techniques; removing fields and adding fields to a PivotTable list; and improving the appearance of a PivotTable list.

Appendices The book includes five appendices. Appendix A presents an introduction to the Microsoft Excel Help system. Appendix B describes how to use the speech and handwriting recognition capabilities of Excel 2002. Appendix C explains how to publish Web pages to a Web server. Appendix D shows how to reset the menus and toolbars. Appendix E introduces students to the Microsoft Office User Specialist (MOUS) Certification program.

Quick Reference Summary In Microsoft Excel 2002, you can accomplish a task in a number of ways, such as using the mouse, menu, shortcut menu, and keyboard. The Quick Reference Summary at the back of the book provides a quick reference to each task presented.

End-of-Project Student Activities

A notable strength of the Shelly Cashman Series *Microsoft Excel 2002* books is the extensive student activities at the end of each project. Well-structured student activities can make the difference between students merely participating in a class and students retaining the information they learn. The activities in the Shelly Cashman Series *Microsoft Excel 2002* books include the following:

- **What You Should Know** A listing of the tasks completed within a project together with the pages on which the step-by-step, screen-by-screen explanations appear.
- **Learn It Online** Every project features a Learn It Online page comprised of ten exercises. These exercises include True/False, Multiple Choice, Short Answer, Flash Cards, Practice Test, Learning Games, Tips and Tricks, Newsgroup usage, Expanding Your Horizons, and Search Sleuth.

- **Apply Your Knowledge** This exercise usually requires students to open and manipulate a file on the Data Disk. To obtain a copy of the Data Disk, follow the instructions on the inside back cover of this textbook.
- **In the Lab** Three in-depth assignments per project require students to apply the knowledge gained in the project to solve problems on a computer.
- **Cases and Places** Up to seven unique real-world case-study situations.

Shelly Cashman Series Teaching Tools

The three basic ancillaries that accompany this textbook are: Teaching Tools (ISBN 0-7895-6323-1), Course Presenter (ISBN 0-7895-6466-1), and MyCourse.com. These ancillaries are available to adopters through your Course Technology representative or by calling one of the following telephone numbers: Colleges and Universities, 1-800-648-7450; High Schools, 1-800-824-5179; Private Career Colleges, 1-800-477-3692; Canada, 1-800-268-2222; and Corporations and Government Agencies, 1-800-340-7450.

Teaching Tools

The contents of the Teaching Tools CD-ROM are listed below.

- **Instructor's Manual** The Instructor's Manual includes the following for each project: project objectives; project overview; detailed lesson plans with page number references; teacher notes and activities; answers to the end-of-project exercises; a test bank of 110 questions for every project (25 multiple-choice, 50 true/false, and 35 fill-in-the-blank) with page number references; and transparency references. The transparencies are available through the Figures in the Book. The test bank questions are the same as in ExamView and Course Test Manager.
- **Figures in the Book** Illustrations for every screen and table in the textbook are available in electronic form. Use this ancillary to present a slide show in lecture or to print transparencies for use in lecture with an overhead projector.
- **ExamView** ExamView is a state-of-the-art test builder that is easy to use. With ExamView, you quickly can create printed tests, Internet tests, and computer (LAN-based) tests. You can enter your own test questions or use the test bank that accompanies ExamView. The test bank is the same as the one described in the Instructor's Manual section. Instructors who want to continue to use our earlier generation test builder, Course Test Manager, rather than ExamView, can call Customer Service at 1-800-648-7450 for a copy of the Course Test Manager database for this book.
- **Course Syllabus** Any instructor who has been assigned a course at the last minute knows how difficult it is to come up with a course syllabus. For this reason, sample syllabi are included that can be customized easily to a course.
- **Lecture Success System** Lecture Success System files are used to explain and illustrate the step-by-step, screen-by-screen development of a project in the textbook without entering large amounts of data.
- **Instructor's Lab Solutions** Solutions and required files for all the In the Lab assignments at the end of each project are available. Solutions also are available for any Cases and Places assignment that supplies data.
- **Lab Tests/Test Outs** Tests that parallel the In the Lab assignments are supplied for the purpose of testing students in the laboratory on the material covered in the project or testing students out of the course.

- **Project Reinforcement** True/false, multiple choice, and short answer questions.
- **Student Files** All the files that are required by students to complete the Apply Your Knowledge exercises are included.
- **Interactive Labs** Eighteen completely updated, hands-on Interactive Labs that take students from ten to fifteen minutes each to step through help solidify and reinforce mouse and keyboard usage and computer concepts. Student assessment is available.

Course Presenter

Course Presenter is a lecture presentation system that provides PowerPoint slides for each project. Presentations are based on the projects' objectives. Use this presentation system to present well-organized lectures that are both interesting and knowledge-based. Course Presenter provides consistent coverage at schools that use multiple lecturers in their applications courses.

MyCourse 2.0

MyCourse 2.0 offers instructors and students an opportunity to supplement classroom learning with additional course content. You can use MyCourse 2.0 to expand on traditional learning by completing readings, tests, and other assignments through the customized, comprehensive Web site. For additional information, visit mycourse.com and click the Help button.

SAM XP

SAM XP is a powerful skills-based testing and reporting tool that measures your students' proficiency in Microsoft Office applications through real-world, performance-based questions. SAM XP is available for a minimal cost.

Acknowledgments

The Shelly Cashman Series would not be the leading computer education series without the contributions of outstanding publishing professionals. First, and foremost, among them is Becky Herrington, director of production and designer. She is the heart and soul of the Shelly Cashman Series, and it is only through her leadership, dedication, and tireless efforts that superior products are made possible.

Under Becky's direction, the following individuals made significant contributions to these books: Doug Cowley, production manager; Ginny Harvey, series specialist and developmental editor; Ken Russo, senior Web and graphic designer; Mike Bodnar, associate production manager; Mark Norton, Web designer; Betty Hopkins and Richard Herrera, interior design; Michelle French, Christy Otten, Kellee LaVars, Stephanie Nance, Chris Schneider, Sharon Lee Nelson, Sarah Boger, Amanda Lotter, Michael Greco, and Ryan Ung, graphic artists; Jeanne Black and Betty Hopkins, Quark layout artists; Lyn Markowicz, Nancy Lamm, Kim Kosmatka, Pam Baxter, Eva Kandarpa, Ellana Russo, and Marilyn Martin, copy editors/proofreaders; Cristina Haley, proofreader/indexer; Sarah Evertson of Image Quest, photo researcher; and Ginny Harvey, Rich Hansberger, Kim Clark, and Nancy Smith, contributing writers.

Finally, we would like to thank Richard Keaveny, associate publisher; Cheryl Ouellette, managing editor; Jim Quasney, series consulting editor; Alexandra Arnold, product manager; Erin Runyon, associate product manager; Francis Schurgot and Marc Ouellette, Web product managers; Rachel VanKirk, marketing manager; and Reed Cotter, editorial assistant.

Gary B. Shelly
Thomas J. Cashman
James S. Quasney
Jeffrey J. Quasney

Shelly Cashman Series – Traditionally Bound Textbooks

The Shelly Cashman Series presents the following computer subjects in a variety of traditionally bound textbooks. For more information, see your Course Technology representative or call 1-800-648-7450. For Shelly Cashman Series information, visit Shelly Cashman Online at **scseries.com**

COMPUTERS	
Computers	Discovering Computers 2002: Concepts for a Digital World, Web Enhanced, Complete Edition
	Discovering Computers 2002: Concepts for a Digital World, Web Enhanced, Introductory Edition
	Discovering Computers 2002: Concepts for a Digital World, Web Enhanced, Brief Edition
	Teachers Discovering Computers: Integrating Technology in the Classroom 2e
	Exploring Computers: A Record of Discovery 4e
	Study Guide for Discovering Computers 2002: Concepts for a Digital World, Web Enhanced
	Essential Introduction to Computers 4e (32-page)

WINDOWS APPLICATIONS	
Microsoft Office	Microsoft Office XP: Essential Concepts and Techniques (5 projects)
	Microsoft Office XP: Brief Concepts and Techniques (9 projects)
	Microsoft Office XP: Introductory Concepts and Techniques (15 projects)
	Microsoft Office XP: Advanced Concepts and Techniques (11 projects)
	Microsoft Office XP: Post Advanced Concepts and Techniques (11 projects)
	Microsoft Office 2000: Essential Concepts and Techniques (5 projects)
	Microsoft Office 2000: Brief Concepts and Techniques (9 projects)
	Microsoft Office 2000: Introductory Concepts and Techniques, Enhanced Edition (15 projects)
	Microsoft Office 2000: Advanced Concepts and Techniques (11 projects)
	Microsoft Office 2000: Post Advanced Concepts and Techniques (11 projects)
Integration	Integrating Microsoft Office XP Applications and the World Wide Web: Essential Concepts and Techniques
PIM	Microsoft Outlook 2002: Essential Concepts and Techniques
Microsoft Works	Microsoft Works 6: Complete Concepts and Techniques[1] • Microsoft Works 2000: Complete Concepts and Techniques[1] • Microsoft Works 4.5[1]
Microsoft Windows	Microsoft Windows 2000: Complete Concepts and Techniques (6 projects)[2]
	Microsoft Windows 2000: Brief Concepts and Techniques (2 projects)
	Microsoft Windows 98: Essential Concepts and Techniques (2 projects)
	Microsoft Windows 98: Complete Concepts and Techniques (6 projects)[2]
	Introduction to Microsoft Windows NT Workstation 4
	Microsoft Windows 95: Complete Concepts and Techniques[1]
Word Processing	Microsoft Word 2002[2] • Microsoft Word 2000[2] • Microsoft Word 97[1] • Microsoft Word 7[1]
Spreadsheets	Microsoft Excel 2002[2] • Microsoft Excel 2000[2] • Microsoft Excel 97[1] • Microsoft Excel 7[1] Microsoft Excel 5[1]
Database	Microsoft Access 2002[2] • Microsoft Access 2000[2] • Microsoft Access 97[1] • Microsoft Access 7[1]
Presentation Graphics	Microsoft PowerPoint 2002[2] • Microsoft PowerPoint 2000[2] • Microsoft PowerPoint 97[1] Microsoft PowerPoint 7[1]
Desktop Publishing	Microsoft Publisher 2002[1] • Microsoft Publisher 2000[1]

PROGRAMMING	
Programming	Microsoft Visual Basic 6: Complete Concepts and Techniques[1] • Programming in QBasic Java Programming: Complete Concepts and Techniques[1] • Structured COBOL Programming 2e

INTERNET	
Browser	Microsoft Internet Explorer 5: An Introduction • Microsoft Internet Explorer 4: An Introduction Netscape Navigator 6: An Introduction • Netscape Navigator 4: An Introduction
Web Page Creation and Design	Web Design: Introductory Concepts and Techniques • HTML: Complete Concepts and Techniques[1] Microsoft FrontPage 2002: Essential Concepts and Techniques • Microsoft FrontPage 2002[2] Microsoft FrontPage 2000[1] • JavaScript: Complete Concepts and Techniques[1]

SYSTEMS ANALYSIS	
Systems Analysis	Systems Analysis and Design 4e

DATA COMMUNICATIONS	
Data Communications	Business Data Communications: Introductory Concepts and Techniques 3e

[1] Also available as an Introductory Edition, which is a shortened version of the complete book
[2] Also available as an Introductory Edition, which is a shortened version of the complete book and also as a Comprehensive Edition, which is an extended version of the complete book

2002

Microsoft

EXCEL

Microsoft Excel 2002

PROJECT

1

Creating a Worksheet and Embedded Chart

You will have mastered the material in this project when you can:

O B J E C T I V E S

- Start Excel
- Describe the Excel worksheet
- Describe the speech recognition capabilities of Excel
- Select a cell or range of cells
- Enter text and numbers
- Use the AutoSum button to sum a range of cells
- Copy a cell to a range of cells using the fill handle
- Bold font, change font size, and change font color
- Center cell contents across a series of columns
- Apply the AutoFormat command to format a range
- Use the Name box to select a cell
- Create a Column chart using the Chart Wizard
- Save a workbook
- Print a worksheet
- Quit Excel
- Open a workbook
- Use the AutoCalculate area to determine totals
- Correct errors on a worksheet
- Use the Excel Help system to answer your questions

Smaller Is Smarter
Smart Card Technology
in Your Wallet

I t withdraws funds from your bank, opens your dorm room door, pays for telephone calls, and much more. You carry it in a pocket, purse, or wallet. What is it? It is a smart card.

It looks like an ordinary credit-card-sized piece of plastic, but instead of a magnetic strip on the back, it has an embedded microprocessor chip in it. For both individuals and businesses, smart cards provide convenience and security.

Students are familiar with the card. An increasing number of colleges and universities across the United States participate in smart card programs for campus IDs, as well as many foreign colleges and universities in Canada, Europe, Australia, and Israel. Close to one million smart cards are estimated to be in use in the college market, representing one in seventeen students.

Central Michigan University (CMU) uses the Chip Card for student, faculty, and staff identification and access to many of the university resources including computer labs and the campus library. In addition, if individuals opt for certain plans, they can use their cards to store a dollar amount for convenient use on campus, at selected businesses, and for ATM and debit cards.

In January 2001, the Smart Card Industry Association (SCIA) and the Smart Card Forum (SCF) combined their two organizations to form the Smart Card Alliance (the Alliance). The Alliance is the largest smart card-oriented, nonprofit group in the world with more than 225 member organizations, serving the smart card industry in the

SMART CARD

MAGGIE BLACK
AGE: 29
7429 LYON ST.
TRAVERSE CITY, MI
ID: 5428 4732 4732

United States (smartcardalliance.org). Members represent a cross-section of technology experts and smart card users in the government, private, and education sectors. Applications include telephony, financial, IT, government, identification, transportation, and health care.

Some visionaries predict 3.75 billion smart cards will be issued by 2005, with owners using them to make 25 billion transactions yearly. The cost to manufacture one card ranges from 80 cents to 15 dollars depending on the application and complexity.

Two types of smart cards are available. One is a memory card. The memory card contains a stored value that the owner can spend on transactions such as paying bus fare or making a call from a public telephone. When the value is depleted, the card is useless.

The second is an intelligent smart card. The intelligent card contains a processor that can store data and make decisions. Owners begin with a set monetary value, such as $100, and then they can make a purchase that does not exceed this figure. If the amount is insufficient, they can add money to the balance. These functions are similar to the activities you will perform using Microsoft Excel in this project for the Dynamite Music company, where you will enter numbers in predefined storage areas, or cells, and then calculate a sum.

The smart card originated in 1974 when Roland Moreno, a reporter and self-taught inventor, secured a chip on an epoxy card. His vision was for merchants to accept electronic payments by inserting three cards in his Take the Money and Run (TMR) machine. One card identified the merchant, the second contained the customer's electronic money, and the third had a list of deadbeat accounts that could not be used to make a transaction. Pictures and descriptions of Moreno's invention and other smart card developments are found in the Smart Card Museum (cardshow.com).

Today, chips for the cards are manufactured by such industry leaders as Motorola, Gemplus, and Schlumberger. These companies are working to meet the demand for the cards, which is increasing at a rate of 30 percent annually. With an ever-growing global marketplace, smart cards are smarter.

Microsoft Excel 2002

Creating a Worksheet and Embedded Chart

Three years ago while in college, Nadine Mitchell and four of her friends came up with the idea of starting a company that sold music to young adults through store outlets in malls. After graduation, they invested $5,000 each and started their dream company, Dynamite Music.

The friends opened their first music store in Boston. Initially, they sold compact discs, cassettes, and rare records (vintage vinyls). As sales grew, they opened additional outlets in Chicago, Denver, and Phoenix. Last year, they started selling their products on the Web. Rather than use a central Web site for Web sales, they decided to maintain Web sites for each store. This year they began to sell music by allowing customers to download music to their personal computers.

As sales continue to grow, the management at Dynamite Music has realized it needs a better tracking system for sales by quarter. As a result, the company has asked you to prepare a fourth quarter sales worksheet that shows the sales for the fourth quarter.

In addition, Nadine has asked you to create a graphical representation of the fourth quarter sales because she finds it easier to work with than lists of numbers.

What Is Microsoft Excel?

Microsoft Excel is a powerful spreadsheet program that allows you to organize data, complete calculations, make decisions, graph data, develop professional looking reports, publish organized data to the Web, and access real-time data from Web sites. The four major parts of Excel are:

- **Worksheets** Worksheets allow you to enter, calculate, manipulate, and analyze data such as numbers and text. The term worksheet means the same as spreadsheet.
- **Charts** Charts pictorially represent data. Excel can draw a variety of two-dimensional and three-dimensional charts.
- **Databases** Databases manage data. For example, once you enter data onto a worksheet, Excel can sort the data, search for specific data, and select data that satisfy a criteria.
- **Web Support** Web support allows Excel to save workbooks or parts of a workbook in HTML format so they can be viewed and manipulated using a browser. You also can access real-time data using Web queries.

Project One — Dynamite Music Fourth Quarter Sales

From your meeting with Dynamite Music's management, you have determined the following: needs, source of data, calculations, and chart requirements.

Needs: An easy-to-read worksheet (Figure 1-1) that shows Dynamite Music's fourth quarter sales for each of the product groups (Cassettes, Compact Discs, Vintage Vinyls, and Web Downloads) by store (Boston, Chicago, Denver, and Phoenix). The worksheet also should include total sales for each product group, each store, and total company sales for the fourth quarter.

Microsoft Excel - Dynamite Music 4th Quarter Sales

File Edit View Insert Format Tools Data Window Help

Type a question for help

Arial   10   B I U

H21

	A	B	C	D	E	F	G	H	I
1	**Dynamite Music**								
2		**Fourth Quarter Sales**							
3		*Boston*	*Chicago*	*Denver*	*Phoenix*	*Total*			
4	Cassettes	$ 53,465.30	$ 47,917.35	$ 31,913.75	$ 62,350.10	$195,646.50			
5	Compact Discs	92,023.75	70,392.10	86,140.55	83,450.75	332,007.15			
6	Vintage Vinyls	35,482.56	30,976.25	48,612.75	34,092.75	149,164.31			
7	Web Downloads	78,526.12	67,626.60	67,420.20	56,732.80	270,305.72			
8	*Total*	$ 259,497.73	$ 216,912.30	$ 234,087.25	$ 236,626.40	$ 947,123.68			

data in worksheet

3-D Column chart

$100,000.00
$80,000.00
$60,000.00
$40,000.00
$20,000.00
$-

Boston   Chicago   Denver   Phoenix

■ Cassettes
■ Compact Discs
□ Vintage Vinyls
□ Web Downloads

Sheet1 Sheet2 Sheet3

Ready

Start   Microsoft Excel - Dyn...   EN 1:01 PM

FIGURE 1-1

Source of Data: The data for the worksheet is available at the end of the fourth quarter from the chief financial officer (CFO) of Dynamite Music.

Calculations: You have determined that the following calculations must be made for the worksheet: (a) total fourth quarter sales for each of the four product groups; (b) total fourth quarter sales for each of the four stores; and (c) fourth quarter sales for the company.

Chart Requirements: Below the worksheet, construct a 3-D Column chart that compares the amount of sales for each product group within each store.

Starting and Customizing Excel

To start Excel, Windows must be running. Perform the steps on the next page to start Excel, or ask your instructor how to start Excel for your system.

Excel 2002

With its smart tags, speech recognition, shortcut menus, toolbars, what-if analysis tools, Web capabilities, hundreds of functions, and speech playback, Excel 2002 is one of the easiest, and yet most powerful, worksheet packages available. Its powerful analytical features make it possible to answer complicated what-if questions. Its Web capabilities allow you to create, publish, view, and analyze data on an intranet or the World Wide Web.

Steps **To Start Excel**

1 **Click the Start button on the Windows taskbar, point to Programs on the Start menu, and then point to Microsoft Excel on the Programs submenu.**

The commands on the Start menu display above the Start button and the Programs submenu displays (Figure 1-2). If the Office Speech Recognition software is installed on your computer, then the Language bar may display somewhere on the desktop.

FIGURE 1-2

2 **Click Microsoft Excel.**

Excel starts. After several seconds, a blank workbook titled Book1 displays in the Excel window (Figure 1-3).

3 **If the Excel window is not maximized, double-click its title bar to maximize it.**

Other Ways

1. Double-click Excel icon on desktop
2. Right-click Start button, click Open All Users, double-click New Office Document, click General tab, double-click Blank Workbook icon
3. Click Start button, click New Office Document, click General tab, double-click Blank Workbook icon

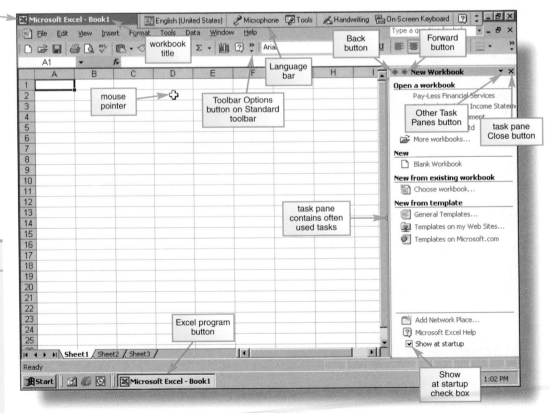

FIGURE 1-3

The screen in Figure 1-3 shows how the Excel window looks the first time you start Excel after installation on most computers. If the Office Speech Recognition software is installed on your system, then when you start Excel either the Language bar expands to include the functions available in Excel (shown at the top of Figure 1-3) or the language indicator displays on the right side of the Windows taskbar (Figure 1-7 on page E 1.11). In this book, the Language bar will be kept minimized until it is used. For additional information about the Language bar, see page E 1.16 and Appendix B.

Notice also that a task pane displays on the screen, and that the buttons on the toolbar display on a single row. A **task pane** is a separate window that enables users to carry out some Excel tasks more efficiently. In this book, to allow the maximum number of columns to display in Excel, a task pane should not display. For more efficient use of the buttons, they should display on two separate rows instead of sharing a single row. Perform the following steps to close the New Workbook task pane, minimize the Language bar, and display the buttons on two separate rows.

More About

The Excel Help System

Need Help? It is no further away than the Ask a Question box in the upper-right corner of the window. Click the box that contains the text, Type a question for help (Figure 1-4), type help, and then press the ENTER key. Excel will respond with a list of items you can click to learn about obtaining help on any Excel-related topic. To find out what is new in Excel 2002, type what's new in Excel in the Ask a Question box.

More About

Task Panes

You can drag a task pane title bar (Figure 1-3) to float the pane in your work area or dock it on either the left or right side of a screen, depending on your personal preference.

Steps To Customize the Excel Window

1 **If the New Workbook task pane displays in your Excel window, click the Show at startup check box to remove the check mark and then click the Close button in the upper-right corner of the task pane (Figure 1-3). If the Language bar displays, point to its Minimize button.**

Excel removes the check mark from the Show at startup check box. With the check mark removed, Excel will not display the New Workbook task pane the next time Excel starts. The New Workbook task pane closes resulting in additional columns displaying (Figure 1-4).

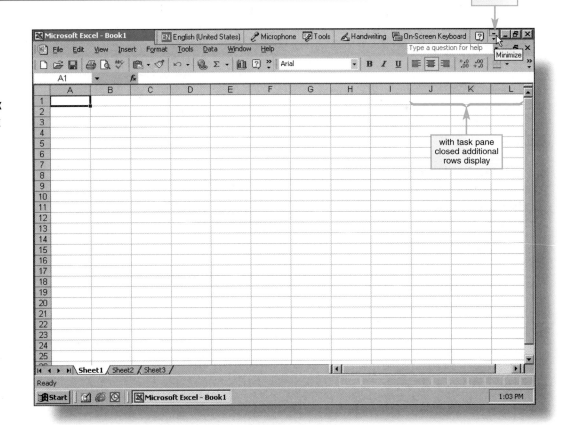

FIGURE 1-4

2 **Click the Minimize button on the Language bar. If the toolbars display positioned on the same row, click the Toolbar Options button and then point to Show Buttons on Two Rows.**

The Toolbar Options list displays showing the buttons that do not fit on the toolbars when buttons display on one row (Figure 1-5).

FIGURE 1-5

3 **Click Show Buttons on Two Rows.**

Excel displays the buttons on two separate rows (Figure 1-6). The Toolbar Options list shown in Figure 1-5 is empty because all of the buttons display on two rows.

FIGURE 1-6

As you work through creating a worksheet, you will find that certain Excel operations result in displaying a task pane. Besides the New Workbook task pane shown in Figure 1-3 on page E 1.08, Excel provides three additional task panes: the Clipboard task pane, the Search task pane, and the Insert Clip Art task pane. These task panes are discussed when they are used. You can display or hide a task pane by clicking the **Task Pane command** on the **View menu**. You can activate additional task panes by clicking the down arrow to the left of the Close button on the task pane title bar (Figure 1-3) and then selecting a task pane in the list. Using the Back and Forward buttons on the left side of the task pane title bar, you can switch between task panes.

The Excel Worksheet

When Excel starts, it creates a new blank workbook, called Book1. The **workbook** (Figure 1-7) is like a notebook. Inside the workbook are sheets, called **worksheets**. Each sheet name displays on a **sheet tab** at the bottom of the workbook. For example, Sheet1 is the name of the active worksheet displayed in the workbook called Book1. A new workbook opens with three worksheets. If necessary, you can add additional worksheets to a maximum of 255. If you click the tab labeled Sheet2, Excel displays the Sheet2 worksheet. This project uses only the Sheet1 worksheet.

More About

Worksheet Development

The key to developing a useful worksheet is careful planning. Careful planning can reduce your effort significantly and result in a worksheet that is accurate, easy to read, flexible, and useful. When analyzing a problem and designing a worksheet solution, you should follow these steps: (1) define the problem, including need, source of data, calculations, charting and Web or special requirements; (2) design the worksheet; (3) enter the data and formulas; and (4) test the worksheet.

FIGURE 1-7

The Worksheet

The worksheet is organized into a rectangular grid containing columns (vertical) and rows (horizontal). A column letter above the grid, also called the **column heading**, identifies each column. A row number on the left side of the grid, also called the **row heading**, identifies each row. With the screen resolution set to 800 × 600, 12 columns (A through L) and 24 rows (1 through 24) of the worksheet display on the screen when the worksheet is maximized as shown in Figure 1-7.

The intersection of each column and row is a cell. A **cell** is the basic unit of a worksheet into which you enter data. Each worksheet in a workbook has 256 columns and 65,536 rows for a total of 16,777,216 cells. The column headings begin with A and end with IV. The row headings begin with 1 and end with 65,536. Only a small fraction of the active worksheet displays on the screen at one time.

A cell is referred to by its unique address, or **cell reference**, which is the coordinates of the intersection of a column and a row. To identify a cell, specify the column letter first, followed by the row number. For example, cell reference C5 refers to the cell located at the intersection of column C and row 5 (Figure 1-7).

One cell on the worksheet, designated the **active cell**, is the one into which you can enter data. The active cell in Figure 1-7 is A1. The active cell is identified in three ways. First, a heavy border surrounds the cell; second, the active cell reference displays immediately above column A in the **Name box**; and third, the column heading A and row heading 1 are highlighted so it is easy to see which cell is active (Figure 1-7).

More About

The Worksheet Size and Window

256 columns and 65,536 rows make for a huge worksheet that you might imagine takes up the entire wall of a large room. Your computer screen, by comparison, is a small window that allows you to view only a minute area of the worksheet at one time. While you can't see the entire worksheet, you can move the window over the worksheet to view any part of it. To display the last row in a blank worksheet, press the END key and then press the DOWN ARROW key. Press CTRL+HOME to return to the top of the worksheet.

The Mouse Pointer

The mouse pointer can change to one of more than fifteen different shapes, such as an arrow, cross hair, or chart symbol, depending on the task you are performing in Excel and the mouse pointer's location on the screen.

The horizontal and vertical lines on the worksheet itself are called **gridlines**. Gridlines make it easier to see and identify each cell in the worksheet. If desired, you can turn the gridlines off so they do not display on the worksheet, but it is recommended that you leave them on.

The mouse pointer in Figure 1-7 on the previous page has the shape of a block plus sign. The mouse pointer displays as a **block plus sign** whenever it is located in a cell on the worksheet. Another common shape of the mouse pointer is the block arrow. The mouse pointer turns into the **block arrow** whenever you move it outside the worksheet or when you drag cell contents between rows or columns. The other mouse pointer shapes are described when they display on the screen.

Worksheet Window

You view the portion of the worksheet displayed on the screen through a **worksheet window** (Figure 1-7). Below and to the right of the worksheet window are **scroll bars**, **scroll arrows**, and **scroll boxes** that you can use to move the window around to view different parts of the active worksheet. To the right of the sheet tabs at the bottom of the screen is the **tab split box**. You can drag the tab split box (Figure 1-7) to increase or decrease the view of the sheet tabs. When you decrease the view of the sheet tabs, you increase the length of the horizontal scroll bar, and vice versa.

The menu bar, Standard toolbar, Formatting toolbar, formula bar, and Ask a question box display at the top of the screen, just below the title bar (Figure 1-8a).

Menu Bar

The **menu bar** is a special toolbar that includes the menu names (Figure 1-8a). Each **menu name** represents a menu of commands that you can use to retrieve, store, print, and manipulate data on the worksheet. When you point to a menu name on the menu bar, the area of the menu bar containing the name changes to a button. To display a menu, such as the Edit menu, click the Edit menu name on the menu bar (Figures 1-8b and 1-8c). A **menu** is a list of commands. If you point to a command on the menu with an arrow to its right, a **submenu** displays from which you can choose a command.

When you click a menu name on the menu bar, a **short menu** displays listing the most recently used commands (Figure 1-8b). If you wait a few seconds or click the arrows at the bottom of the short menu, the full menu displays. The **full menu** lists all the commands associated with a menu (Figure 1-8c). You also can display a full menu immediately by double-clicking the menu name on the menu bar. In this book, when you display a menu, always display the full menu using one of the following techniques.

Increasing the Viewing Area

If you want to increase the size of the viewing area to see more of the worksheet, click Full Screen on the View menu. You can also increase the viewing area by changing to a higher resolution. You change to a higher resolution by right-clicking the Windows desktop, clicking Properties, clicking the Settings tab, and increasing the Screen area.

1. Click the menu name on the menu bar and then wait a few seconds.
2. Click the menu name and then click the arrows at the bottom of the short menu.
3. Click the menu name and then point to the arrows at the bottom of the short menu.
4. Double-click the menu name.

Both short and full menus display some **dimmed commands** that appear gray, or dimmed, instead of black, which indicates they are not available for the current selection. A command with a dark gray shading to the left of it on a full menu is called a **hidden command** because it does not display on a short menu. As you use Excel, it automatically personalizes the short menus for you based on how often you use commands. That is, as you use hidden commands, Excel *unhides* them and places them on the short menu.

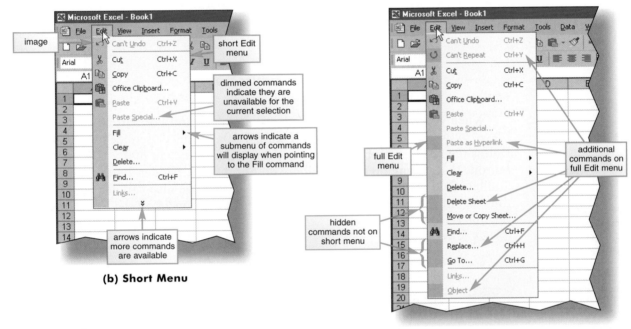

(c) Full Menu

FIGURE 1-8

The menu bar can change to include other menu names depending on the type of work you are doing in Excel. For example, if you are working with a chart sheet rather than a worksheet, the Chart menu bar displays with menu names that reflect charting commands.

Standard Toolbar and Formatting Toolbar

The **Standard toolbar** and the **Formatting toolbar** (Figure 1-8a) contain buttons and list boxes that allow you to perform frequent tasks more quickly than when using the menu bar. For example, to print a worksheet, you click the Print button on the Standard toolbar. Each button has a picture on the button face that helps you remember the button's function. Also, when you move the mouse pointer over a button or box, the name of the button or box displays below it in a **ScreenTip**.

Figures 1-9a and 1-9b on the next page illustrate the Standard and Formatting toolbars and describe the functions of the buttons. Each of the buttons and boxes will be explained in detail when they are used.

More About

Toolbars

You can move a toolbar to any location on the screen. Drag the move handle (Figure 1-10a on page E 1.14) to the desired location. Once the toolbar is in the window area, drag the title bar to move it. Each side of the screen is called a dock. You can drag a toolbar to a dock so it does not clutter the window.

(a) Standard Toolbar

(b) Formatting Toolbar

FIGURE 1-9

More About

Resetting Toolbars

If your toolbars have a different set of buttons than shown in Figure 1-10c, it probably means that a previous user added or deleted buttons. To reset the toolbars to their default, see Appendix D.

When you first install Excel, both the Standard and Formatting toolbars are preset to display on the same row (Figure 1-10a), immediately below the menu bar. Unless the resolution of your display device is greater than 800 × 600, many of the buttons that belong on these toolbars do not display. Hidden buttons display in the Toolbar Options list (Figure 1-10b). In this mode, you also can display all the buttons on either toolbar by double-clicking the **move handle** on the left of each toolbar (Figure 1-10a).

(a) Standard and Formatting Toolbars on One Row

(b) Toolbar Options List

(c) Standard and Formatting Toolbars on Two Rows

FIGURE 1-10

In this book, the Standard and Formatting toolbars are shown on two rows, one under the other so that all buttons display (Figure 1-10c). You show the two toolbars on two rows by clicking the **Show Buttons on Two Rows command** in the Toolbar Options list (Figure 1-10b).

Formula Bar

Below the Standard and Formatting toolbars is the formula bar (Figure 1-11). As you type, the data displays in the **formula bar**. Excel also displays the active cell reference on the left side of the formula bar in the Name box.

Status Bar

Immediately above the Windows taskbar at the bottom of the screen is the status bar. The **status bar** displays a brief description of the command selected (highlighted) in a menu, the function of the button the mouse pointer is pointing to, or the mode of Excel. **Mode indicators**, such as Enter and Ready, display on the status bar and specify the current mode of Excel. When the mode is Ready, Excel is ready to accept the next command or data entry. When the mode indicator reads Enter, Excel is in the process of accepting data through the keyboard into the active cell.

In the middle of the status bar is the AutoCalculate area. The **AutoCalculate area** can be used in place of a calculator to view the sum, average, or other types of totals of a group of numbers on the worksheet. The AutoCalculate area is discussed in detail later in this project.

Keyboard indicators, such as CAPS (Caps Lock), NUM (Num Lock), and SCRL (Scroll) show which keys are engaged. Keyboard indicators display on the right side of the status bar within the small rectangular boxes (Figure 1-11).

Sizing Toolbar Buttons

If you have difficulty seeing the small buttons on the toolbars, you can increase their size by clicking View on the menu bar, pointing to Toolbars, clicking Customize on the Toolbars submenu, clicking the Options tab, clicking the Large icons checkbox, and clicking the Close button.

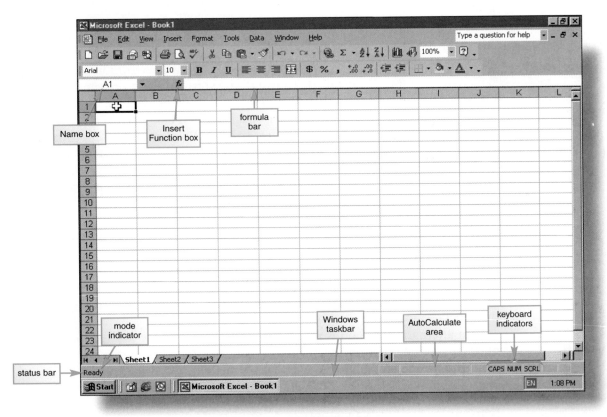

FIGURE 1-11

Speech Recognition and Speech Playback

With the **Office Speech Recognition software** installed and a microphone, you can speak the names of toolbar buttons, menus, menu commands, list items, alerts, and dialog box controls, such as OK and Cancel. You also can dictate cell entries, such as text and numbers. To indicate whether you want to speak commands or dictate cell entries, you use the **Language bar** (Figure 1-12a). You can display the Language bar in two ways: (1) click the Language Indicator button in the taskbar tray status area by the clock, and then click Show the Language bar on the menu (Figure 1-12b); or (2) point to the **Speech command** on the **Tools menu** and then click the **Speech Recognition command** on the **Speech submenu**.

(a) Language Bar

(b) Language Bar Menu

FIGURE 1-12

If the Language Indicator button does not display in the tray status area, and if the Speech command is dimmed on the Tools menu, the Office Speech Recognition software is not installed. To install the software, you first must start Word and then click Speech on the Tools menu.

If you have speakers, you can instruct the computer to read a worksheet to you. By selecting the appropriate option, you can have the worksheet read in a male or female voice.

Additional information on the speech recognition and speech playback capabilities in Excel is available in Appendix B.

Selecting a Cell

To enter data into a cell, you first must select it. The easiest way to **select a cell** (make it active) is to use the mouse to move the block plus sign to the cell and then click.

An alternative method is to use the **arrow keys** that are located just to the right of the typewriter keys on the keyboard. An arrow key selects the cell adjacent to the active cell in the direction of the arrow on the key.

You know a cell is selected (active) when a heavy border surrounds the cell (cell A1 in Figure 1-11 on the previous page) and the active cell reference displays in the Name box on the left side of the formula bar.

More About

Selecting a Cell

You can select any cell by entering the cell reference, such as b4, in the Name box on the left side of the formula bar.

Entering Text

In Excel, any set of characters containing a letter, hyphen (as in a telephone number), or space is considered **text**. Text is used to place titles on the worksheet, such as worksheet titles, column titles, and row titles. In Project 1 (Figure 1-13), the worksheet title, Dynamite Music, identifies the worksheet. The worksheet subtitle, Fourth Quarter Sales, identifies the type of report. The column titles in row 3 (Boston, Chicago, Denver, Phoenix, and Total) identify the numbers in each column. The row titles in column A (Cassettes, Compact Discs, Vintage Vinyls, Web Downloads, and Total) identify the numbers in each row.

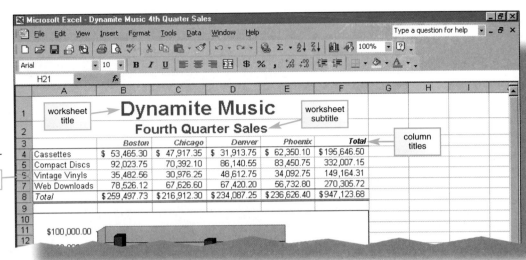

FIGURE 1-13

Entering the Worksheet Titles

The following steps show how to enter the worksheet titles in cells A1 and A2. Later in this project, the worksheet titles will be formatted so it displays as shown in Figure 1-13. Perform the following steps to enter the worksheet tiles.

 To Enter the Worksheet Titles

 Click cell A1.

Cell A1 becomes the active cell and a heavy border surrounds it (Figure 1-14).

FIGURE 1-14

 Type Dynamite Music **in cell A1.**

The title displays in the formula bar and in cell A1. The text in cell A1 is followed by the insertion point (Figure 1-15). The insertion point is a blinking vertical line that indicates where the next typed character will display.

FIGURE 1-15

3 **Point to the Enter box (Figure 1-16).**

When you begin typing a cell entry, Excel displays two additional boxes in the formula bar: the Cancel box and the Enter box.

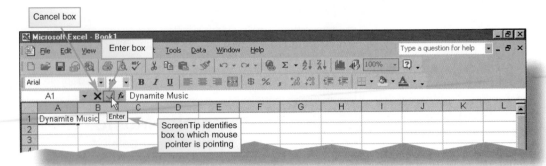

FIGURE 1-16

4 **Click the Enter box to complete the entry.**

Excel enters the worksheet title in cell A1 (Figure 1-17).

FIGURE 1-17

5 **Click cell A2 to select it. Type** Fourth Quarter Sales **as the cell entry. Click the Enter box to complete the entry.**

Excel enters the worksheet subtitle in cell A2 (Figure 1-18).

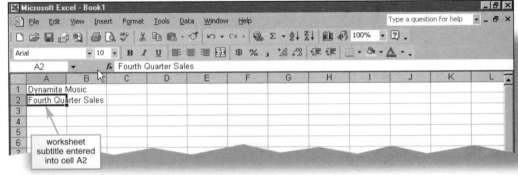

FIGURE 1-18

Other **Ways**

1. To complete entry, click any cell other than active cell
2. To complete entry, press ENTER key
3. To complete entry, press HOME, PAGE UP, PAGE DOWN, or END key
4. In Voice Command mode say, "Enter" to complete entry

In Steps 3 and 4, clicking the **Enter box** completes the entry. Clicking the **Cancel box** cancels the entry.

When you complete a text entry into a cell, a series of events occurs. First, Excel positions the text left-aligned in the cell. **Left-aligned** means the cell entry is positioned at the far left in the cell. Therefore, the D in the worksheet title, Dynamite Music, begins in the leftmost position of cell A1.

Second, when the text is longer than the width of a column, Excel displays the overflow characters in adjacent cells to the right as long as these adjacent cells contain no data. In Figure 1-17, the width of cell A1 is approximately nine characters. The text consists of 14 characters. Therefore, Excel displays the overflow characters from cell A1 in cell B1 because this cell is empty. If cell B1 contained data, only the first nine characters in cell A1 would display on the worksheet. Excel would hide the overflow characters, but they still would remain stored in cell A1 and display in the formula bar whenever cell A1 is the active cell.

Third, when you complete an entry by clicking the Enter box, the cell in which the text is entered remains the active cell.

Correcting a Mistake While Typing

If you type the wrong letter and notice the error before clicking the Enter box or pressing the ENTER key, use the BACKSPACE key to erase all the characters back to and including the one that is wrong. To cancel the entire entry before entering it into the cell, click the Cancel box in the formula bar or press the ESC key. If you see an error in a cell, select the cell and retype the entry. Later in this project, additional error-correction techniques are discussed.

AutoCorrect

The **AutoCorrect feature** of Excel works behind the scenes, correcting common mistakes when you complete a text entry in a cell. AutoCorrect makes three types of corrections for you:

1. Corrects two initial capital letters by changing the second letter to lowercase.
2. Capitalizes the first letter in the names of days.
3. Replaces commonly misspelled words with their correct spelling. For example, it will change the misspelled word *recieve* to *receive* when you complete the entry. AutoCorrect will correct the spelling automatically of more than 400 commonly misspelled words.

Entering Column Titles

To enter the column titles in row 3, select the appropriate cell and then enter the text, as described in the following steps.

 To Enter Column Titles

1 **Click cell B3.**

Cell B3 becomes the active cell. The active cell reference in the Name box changes from A2 to B3 (Figure 1-19).

FIGURE 1-19

2 **Type** Boston **in cell B3.**

Excel displays Boston in the formula bar and in cell B3 (Figure 1-20).

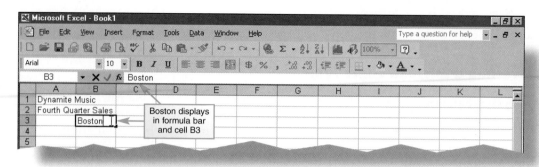

FIGURE 1-20

3 **Press the RIGHT ARROW key.**

Excel enters the column title, Boston, in cell B3 and makes cell C3 the active cell (Figure 1-21).

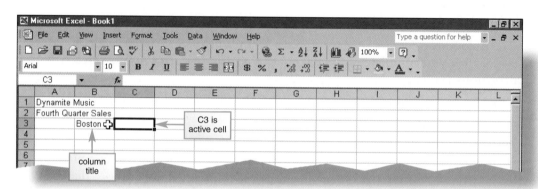

FIGURE 1-21

4 **Repeat Steps 2 and 3 for the remaining column titles in row 2. That is, enter** Chicago **in cell C3,** Denver **in cell D3,** Phoenix **in cell E3, and** Total **in cell F3. Complete the last entry in cell F3 by clicking the Enter box in the formula bar.**

The column titles display left-aligned as shown in Figure 1-22.

FIGURE 1-22

If the next entry is in an adjacent cell, use the arrow keys to complete the entry in a cell. When you press an arrow key to complete an entry, the adjacent cell in the direction of the arrow (up, down, left, or right) becomes the active cell. If the next entry is in a non-adjacent cell, click the next cell in which you plan to enter data, or click the Enter box or press the ENTER key and then click the appropriate cell for the next entry.

Entering Row Titles

The next step in developing the worksheet in Project 1 is to enter the row titles in column A. This process is similar to entering the column titles and is described in the following steps.

Steps **To Enter Row Titles**

1 **Click cell A4. Type**
Cassettes **and
then press the DOWN ARROW
key.**

*Excel enters the row title,
Cassettes, in cell A4, and
cell A5 becomes the active
cell (Figure 1-23).*

FIGURE 1-23

2 **Repeat Step 1 for
the remaining row
titles in column A. Enter**
Compact Discs **in cell A5,**
Vintage Vinyls **in cell
A6,** Web Downloads **in cell
A7, and** Total **in cell A8.**

*The row titles display as
shown in Figure 1-24.*

FIGURE 1-24

In Excel, text is left-aligned in a cell unless you change it by realigning it. Excel treats any combination of numbers, spaces, and nonnumeric characters as text. For example, the following entries are text:

401AX21, 921-231, 619 321, 883XTY

Entering Numbers

In Excel, you can enter numbers into cells to represent amounts. Numbers can contain only the following characters:

0 1 2 3 4 5 6 7 8 9 + - ( ) , / . $ % E e

If a cell entry contains any other keyboard character (including spaces), Excel interprets the entry as text and treats it accordingly. The use of the special characters is explained when they are used in the project.

In Project 1, the Dynamite Music Fourth Quarter numbers are summarized to the right in Table 1-1. These numbers, which represent fourth quarter sales for each of the stores and product groups, must be entered in rows 4, 5, 6, and 7. Perform the steps on the next page to enter these values one row at a time.

Table 1-1 Dynamite Music Fourth Quarter Data				
	BOSTON	**CHICAGO**	**DENVER**	**PHOENIX**
Cassettes	53465.30	47917.35	31913.75	62350.10
Compact Discs	92023.75	70392.10	86140.55	83450.75
Vintage Vinyls	35482.56	30976.25	48612.75	34092.75
Web Downloads	78526.12	67626.60	67420.20	56732.80

Steps **To Enter Numeric Data**

1 **Click cell B4. Type** 53465.30 **and then press the RIGHT ARROW key.**

Excel enters the number 53465.30 in cell B4 and changes the active cell to cell C4 (Figure 1-25). Excel does not display the insignificant zero. The zero will reappear when the numbers are formatted with dollar signs and commas later in this project.

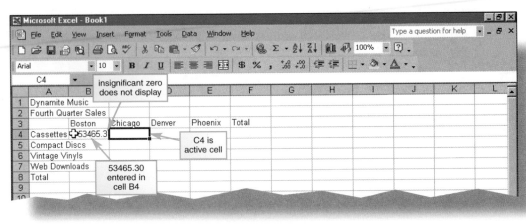

FIGURE 1-25

2 **Enter** 47917.35 **in cell C4,** 31913.75 **in cell D4, and** 62350.10 **in cell E4.**

Row 4 now contains the fourth quarter sales by store for the product group Cassettes (Figure 1-26). The numbers in row 4 are right-aligned, which means Excel displays the cell entry to the far right in the cell.

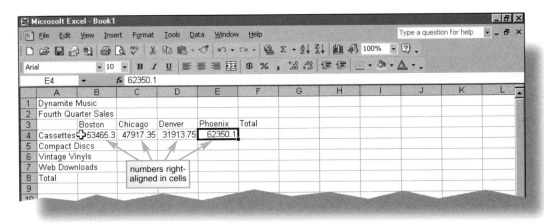

FIGURE 1-26

3 **Click cell B5. Enter the remaining fourth quarter sales provided in Table 1-1 on the previous page for each of the three remaining product groups in rows 5, 6, and 7.**

The fourth quarter sales display as shown in Figure 1-27.

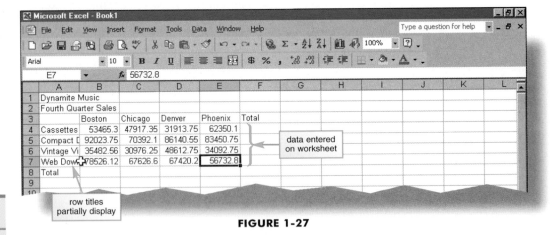

FIGURE 1-27

Entering Numbers as Text

There are times when you will want Excel to treat numbers, such as zip codes and telephone numbers, as text. To enter a number as text, start the entry with an apostrophe (').

As you can see in Figure 1-27, when you enter data into the cell in column B, the row titles in column A partially display. Later when the worksheet is formatted, the row titles will display in their entirety.

Steps 1 through 3 complete the numeric entries. You are not required to type dollar signs, commas, or trailing zeros. As shown in Figure 1-27, trailing zeros do not display. When you enter a number that has cents, however, you must add the decimal point and the numbers representing the cents when you enter the number. Later in this project, dollar signs, commas, and trailing zeros will be added to improve the appearance and readability of the numbers.

More About

Number Limits

In Excel, a number can be between approximately -1×10^{308} and 1×10^{308}. That's a negative 1 followed by 308 zeros or a positive 1 followed by 308 zeros. To enter a number such as 7,500,000,000,000 you can type it as shown or you can type 7.5E12, which stands for 7.5×10^{12}.

Calculating a Sum

The next step in creating the worksheet is to determine the total fourth quarter sales for the Boston store in column B. To calculate this value in cell B8, Excel must add the numbers in cells B4, B5, B6, and B7. Excel's **SUM function** provides a convenient means to accomplish this task.

To use the SUM function, first you must identify the cell in which the sum will be stored after it is calculated. Then, you can use the **AutoSum button** on the Standard toolbar to enter the SUM function as shown in the following steps.

Steps To Sum a Column of Numbers

1 **Click cell B8 and then point to the AutoSum button on the Standard toolbar.**

Cell B8 becomes the active cell (Figure 1-28).

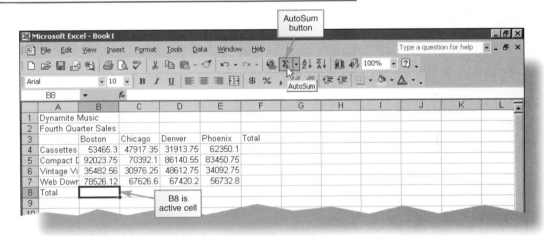

FIGURE 1-28

2 **Click the AutoSum button.**

*Excel responds by displaying =SUM(B4:B7) in the formula bar and in the active cell B8 (Figure 1-29). A ScreenTip displays below the active cell. The B4:B7 within parentheses following the function name SUM is Excel's way of identifying the cells B4 through B7. Excel also surrounds the proposed cells to sum with a moving border, called a **marquee**.*

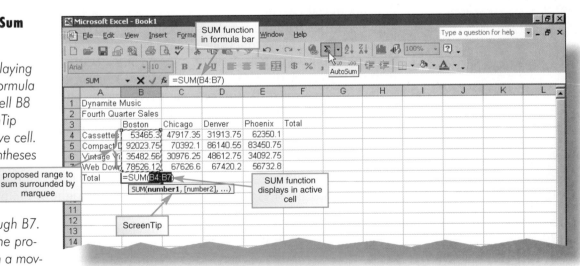

FIGURE 1-29

3 **Click the AutoSum button a second time.**

Excel enters the sum of the fourth quarter sales in cell B8 (Figure 1-30). The SUM function assigned to cell B8 displays in the formula bar when cell B8 is the active cell.

FIGURE 1-30

Other Ways

1. Click Insert Function button in formula bar, select SUM in Select a function list, click OK button, select range, click OK button
2. On Insert menu click Function, select SUM in Select a function list, click OK button, select range, click OK button
3. Press ALT+EQUAL SIGN (=) twice
4. In Voice Command mode say, "AutoSum, Sum, Enter"

When you enter the SUM function using the AutoSum button, Excel automatically selects what it considers to be your choice of the group of cells to sum. The group of adjacent cells B4, B5, B6, and B7 is called a **range**. A range is a series of two or more adjacent cells in a column or row or a rectangular group of cells. Many Excel operations, such as summing numbers, take place on a range of cells.

When proposing the range to sum, Excel first looks for a range of cells with numbers above the active cell and then to the left. If Excel proposes the wrong range, you can drag through the correct range anytime prior to clicking the AutoSum button a second time. You also can enter the correct range by typing the beginning cell reference, a colon (:), and the ending cell reference.

If you click the AutoSum button arrow on the right side of the AutoSum button, Excel displays a list of often used functions from which you can choose. The list includes functions that allow you to determine the average, the minimum value, and the maximum value of a range of numbers.

Using the Fill Handle to Copy a Cell to Adjacent Cells

Excel also must calculate the totals for Chicago in cell C8, Denver in cell D8, and for Phoenix in cell E8. Table 1-2 illustrates the similarities between the entry in cell B8 and the entries required for the totals in cells C8, D8, and E8.

To place the SUM functions in cells C8, D8, and E8, you can follow the same steps shown previously in Figures 1-28 through 1-30. A second, more efficient method is to copy the SUM function from cell B8 to the range C8:E8. The cell being copied is called the **source area** or **copy area**. The range of cells receiving the copy is called the **destination area** or **paste area**.

Although the SUM function entries are similar in Table 1-2, they are not exact copies. The range in each SUM function entry to the right of cell B8 uses cell references that are one column to the right of the previous column. When you copy cell references, Excel automatically adjusts them for each new position, resulting in the SUM function entries illustrated in Table 1-2. Each adjusted cell reference is called a **relative reference**.

Table 1-2	Function Entries in Row 8	
CELL	**SUM FUNCTION ENTRIES**	**REMARK**
B8	=SUM(B4:B7)	Sums cells B4, B5, B6, and B7
C8	=SUM(C4:C7)	Sums cells C4, C5, C6, and C7
D8	=SUM(D4:D7)	Sums cells D4, D5, D6, and D7
E8	=SUM(E4:E7)	Sums cells E4, E5, E6, and E7

The easiest way to copy the SUM formula from cell B8 to cells C8, D8, and E8 is to use the fill handle. The **fill handle** is the small black square located in the lower-right corner of the heavy border around the active cell. Perform the following steps to use the fill handle to copy cell B8 to the adjacent cells C8:E8.

Steps **To Copy a Cell to Adjacent Cells in a Row**

1 **With cell B8 active, point to the fill handle.**

The mouse pointer changes to a cross hair (Figure 1-31).

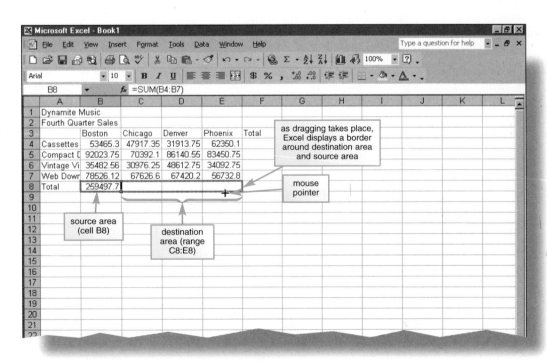

FIGURE 1-31

2 **Drag the fill handle to select the destination area, range C8:E8.**

Excel displays a shaded border around the destination area, range C8:E8, and the source area, cell B8 (Figure 1-32).

FIGURE 1-32

3 **Release the mouse button.**

Excel copies the SUM function in cell B8 to the range C8:E8 (Figure 1-33). In addition, Excel calculates the sums and enters the results in cells C8, D8, and E8. The Auto Fill Options button displays to the right and below the destination area.

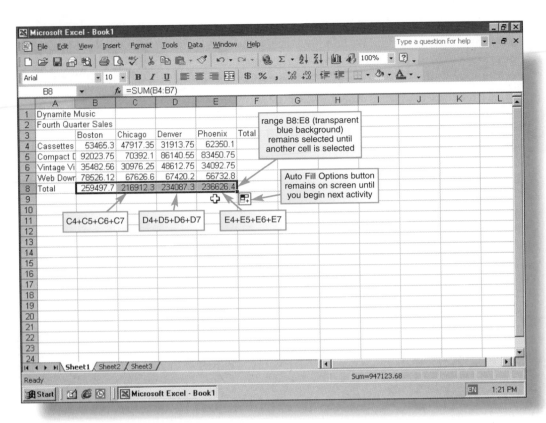

FIGURE 1-33

Once the copy is complete, Excel continues to display a heavy border and transparent (blue) background around cells B8:E8. The heavy border and transparent background indicate a selected range. Cell B8, the first cell in the range, does not display with the transparent background be cause it is the active cell. If you click any cell, Excel will remove the heavy border and transparent background. The heavy border and transparent (blue) background is called **see-through view**.

When you copy one range to another, Excel displays an Auto Fill Options button to the right and below the destination area (Figure 1-33). The **Auto Fill Options button** allows you choose whether you want to copy the value in the price area with formatting, without formatting, or only copy the format. To list the selections, click the Auto Fill Options button. The Auto Fill Options button disappears when you begin another activity.

Determining Row Totals

The next step in building the worksheet is to determine totals for each product group and total fourth quarter sales for the company in column F. Use the SUM function in the same manner as you did when the sales by store were totaled in row 8. In this example, however, all the rows will be totaled at the same time. The following steps illustrate this process.

Steps **To Determine Multiple Totals at the Same Time**

1 **Click cell F4.**

Cell F4 becomes the active cell (Figure 1-34).

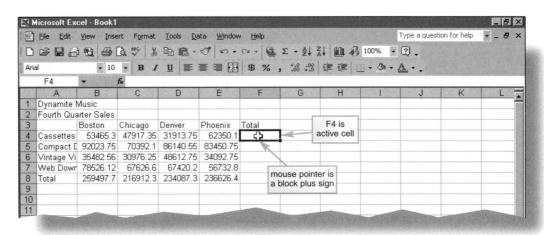

FIGURE 1-34

2 **With the mouse pointer in cell F4 and in the shape of a block plus sign, drag the mouse pointer down to cell F8.**

Excel highlights the range F4:F8 (Figure 1-35).

FIGURE 1-35

3 **Click the AutoSum button on the Standard toolbar.**

Excel assigns the appropriate SUM functions to cell F4, F5, F6, F7, and F8, and then calculates and displays the sums in the respective cells (Figure 1-36).

4 **Select cell A9 to deselect the range F4:F8.**

FIGURE 1-36

Summing Columns and Rows

A more efficient way to determine the totals in row 8 and column F in Figure 1-36 is to select the range (B4:F8) and then click the AutoSum button. The range B4:F8 includes the numbers to sum plus an additional row (row 8) and an additional column (column F), in which the totals will display.

If each cell in the selected range is next to a row of numbers, Excel assigns the SUM function to each cell in the selected range when you click the AutoSum button. Thus, five SUM functions with different ranges were assigned to the selected range, one for each row. This same procedure could have been used earlier to sum the columns. That is, rather than selecting cell B8, clicking the AutoSum button twice, and then copying the SUM function to the range C8:E8, you could have selected the range B8:E8 and then clicked the AutoSum button once.

Formatting the Worksheet

The text, numeric entries, and functions for the worksheet now are complete. The next step is to format the worksheet. You **format** a worksheet to emphasize certain entries and make the worksheet easier to read and understand.

Figure 1-37a shows the worksheet before formatting. Figure 1-37b shows the worksheet after formatting. As you can see from the two figures, a worksheet that is formatted not only is easier to read, but also looks more professional.

(a) Before Formatting

(b) After Formatting

FIGURE 1-37

To change the unformatted worksheet in Figure 1-37a to the formatted worksheet in Figure 1-37b, the following tasks must be completed:

1. Bold, enlarge, and change the color of the worksheet titles in cells A1 and A2.

2. Center the worksheet titles in cells A1 and A2 across columns A through F.

3. Format the body of the worksheet. The body of the worksheet, range A3:F8, includes the column titles, row titles, and numbers. Formatting the body of the worksheet results in numbers represented in a dollars-and-cents format, dollar signs in the first row of numbers and the total row, underlining that emphasizes portions of the worksheet, and modified column widths.

The process required to format the worksheet is explained in the remainder of this section. Although the format procedures will be carried out in the order described above, you should be aware that you can make these format changes in any order.

Fonts, Font Color, Font Size, and Font Style

Characters that display on the screen are a specific shape, size, color, and style. The **font type** defines the appearance and shape of the letters, numbers, and special characters. The **font size** specifies the size of the characters on the screen. Font size is gauged by a measurement system called points. A single point is about 1/72 of one inch in height. Thus, a character with a **point size** of 10 is about 10/72 of one inch in height.

Font style indicates how the characters are formatted. Common font styles include regular, bold, underlined, or italicized. The font also can display in a variety of colors.

When Excel begins, the preset font type for the entire workbook is Arial with a size and style of 10-point regular black. Excel allows you to change the font characteristics in a single cell, a range of cells, the entire worksheet, or the entire workbook.

Bolding a Cell

You **bold** an entry in a cell to emphasize it or make it stand out from the rest of the worksheet. Perform the following steps to bold the worksheet title in cell A1.

Steps To Bold a Cell

1   Click cell A1 and then point to the Bold button on the Formatting toolbar.

The ScreenTip displays immediately below the Bold button to identify the function of the button (Figure 1-38).

FIGURE 1-38

2   Click the Bold button.

Excel applies a bold format to the worksheet title, Dynamite Music (Figure 1-39).

FIGURE 1-39

When the active cell is bold, the Bold button on the Formatting toolbar displays with a transparent blue background (Figure 1-39). Clicking the Bold button a second time removes the bold format.

Increasing the Font Size

Increasing the font size is the next step in formatting the worksheet title. You increase the font size of a cell so the entry stands out and is easier to read. Perform the steps on the next page to increase the font size of the worksheet title in cell A1.

Steps | To Increase the Font Size of a Cell Entry

1 **With cell A1 selected, click the Font Size box arrow on the Formatting toolbar and then point to 24 in the Font Size list.**

The Font Size list displays as shown in Figure 1-40.

FIGURE 1-40

2 **Click 24. The font size of the characters in the worksheet title in cell A1 increase from 10 point to 24 point (Figure 1-41).**

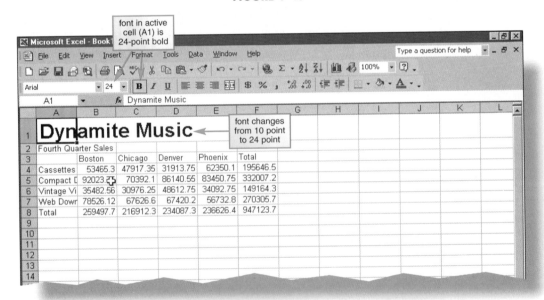

FIGURE 1-41

Other **Ways**

1. On Format menu click Cells, click Font tab, select font size in Size box, click OK button
2. Right-click cell, click Format Cells on shortcut menu, click Font tab, select font size in Size box, click OK button
3. InVoice Command mode say, "Font Size, [desired font size]"

An alternative to clicking a font size in the Font Size list is to click the Font Size box, type the font size, and then press the ENTER key. With cell A1 selected (Figure 1-41), the Font Size box shows the new font size 24 and the transparent blue Bold button shows the active cell is bold.

Changing the Font Color of a Cell

The next step is to change the color of the font in cell A1 from black to violet. Perform the following steps to change the color of the font.

To Change the Font Color of a Cell

1 With cell A1 selected, click the Font Color button arrow on the Formatting toolbar. Point to the color Violet (column 7, row 3) on the Font Color palette.

The Font Color palette displays (Figure 1-42).

FIGURE 1-42

2 Click Violet.

The font in the worksheet title in cell A1 changes from black to violet (Figure 1-43).

FIGURE 1-43

You can choose from 40 different font colors in the Font Color palette in Figure 1-42. Your Font Color palette may have more or fewer colors, depending on color settings of your operating system. When you choose a color, Excel changes the Font Color button on the Formatting toolbar to the chosen color. Thus, to change the font color of the text in another cell to the same color, you need only select the cell and click the Font Color button.

Centering the Worksheet Title across Columns

The final step in formatting the worksheet title is to center it across columns A through F. Centering a worksheet title across the columns used in the body of the worksheet improves the worksheet's appearance. Perform the steps on the next page to center the worksheet title.

Other Ways

1. On Format menu, click Cells, click Font tab, click Color button, select color, click OK button

2. Right-click cell, click Format Cells on shortcut menu, click Font tab, click Color button, select color, click OK button

3. In Voice Command mode say, "Font Color, [desired color]"

Steps **To Center a Cell's Contents across Columns**

1 **With cell A1 selected, drag to cell F1. Point to the Merge and Center button on the Formatting toolbar.**

Excel highlights the selected cells (Figure 1-44).

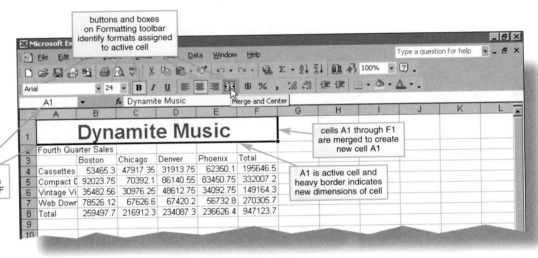

FIGURE 1-44

2 **Click the Merge and Center button.**

Excel merges the cells A1 through F1 to create a new cell A1 and centers the contents of cell A1 across columns A through F (Figure 1-45). After the merge, cells B1 through F1 no longer exist on the worksheet.

FIGURE 1-45

Other Ways

1. On Format menu click Cells, click Alignment tab, select Center Across Selection in Horizontal list, click OK button

2. Right-click cell, click Format Cells on shortcut menu, click Alignment tab, select Center Across Selection in Horizontal list, click OK button

3. In Voice Command mode say, "Merge and Center"

Excel not only centers the worksheet title across the range A1:F1, but it also merges cells A1 through F1 into one cell, cell A1. The alternative to merging cells is **splitting a cell**. You split a merged cell by selecting it and clicking the Merge and Center button. For example, if you click the Merge and Center button a second time in Step 2, it will change cell A1 to cells A1, B1, C1, D1, E1, and F1. For the Merge and Center button to work properly, all the cells except the leftmost cell in the range of cells must be empty.

Most formats assigned to a cell will display on the Formatting toolbar when the cell is selected. For example, with cell A1 selected in Figure 1-45 the font type and font size display in their appropriate boxes. Transparent blue buttons indicate an assigned format. To determine if less frequently used formats are assigned to a cell, point to the cell and right-click. Next, click Format Cells, and then click each of the tabs in the Format Cells dialog box.

Formatting the Worksheet Subtitle

The worksheet subtitle in cell A2 is to be formatted the same as the worksheet title in cell A1, except that the font size should be 16 rather than 24. Perform the following steps to format the worksheet subtitle in cell A2.

TO FORMAT THE WORKSHEET SUBTITLE

1 Select cell A2.

2 Click the Bold button on the Formatting toolbar.

3 Click the Font Size arrow on the Formatting toolbar and click 16.

4 Click the Font Color button.

5 Select the range A2:F2 and then click the Merge and Center button on the Formatting toolbar.

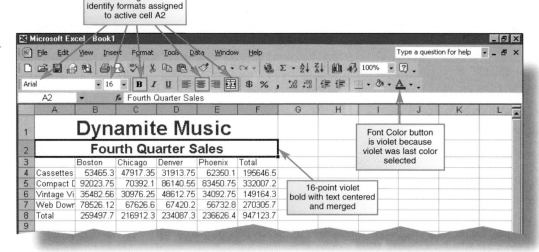

FIGURE 1-46

The worksheet subtitle in cell A2 display as shown in Figure 1-46.

With cell A2 selected, the buttons and boxes on the Formatting toolbar describe the primary formats assigned to cell A2. The steps used to format the worksheet subtitle in cell A2 were the same as the steps used to assign the formats to the worksheet title in cell A1, except for assigning the font color. To color the worksheet title font in cell A1 violet, the Font Color arrow and Font Color palette were used. To color the worksheet subtitle in cell A2 violet, the Font Color button was used. Recall that the Font Color button is assigned the last font color used, which was violet.

Using AutoFormat to Format the Body of a Worksheet

Excel has several customized format styles called **table formats** that allow you to format the body of the worksheet. Using table formats can give your worksheet a professional appearance. Follow these steps to format the range A3:F8 automatically using the **AutoFormat command** on the **Format menu**.

Steps **To Use AutoFormat to Format the Body of a Worksheet**

1 **Select cell A3, the upper-left corner cell of the rectangular range to format. Drag the mouse pointer to cell F8, the lower-right corner cell of the range to format.**

Excel highlights the range to format with a heavy border and transparent blue background (Figure 1-47).

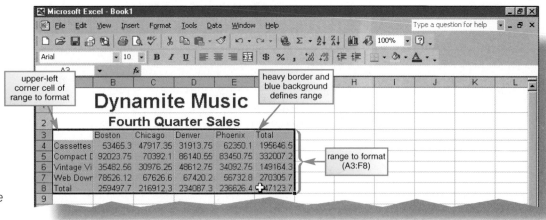

FIGURE 1-47

2   **Click Format on the menu bar and then point to AutoFormat.**

The Format menu displays (Figure 1-48).

FIGURE 1-48

3   **Click AutoFormat. Click the Accounting 1 format in the AutoFormat dialog box. Point to the OK button.**

The AutoFormat dialog box displays with a list of customized formats (Figure 1-49). Each format illustrates how the body of the worksheet will display if it is chosen.

FIGURE 1-49

4   **Click the OK button. Select cell A10 to deselect the range A3:F8.**

Excel displays the worksheet with the range A3:F8 using the customized format, Accounting 1 (Figure 1-50).

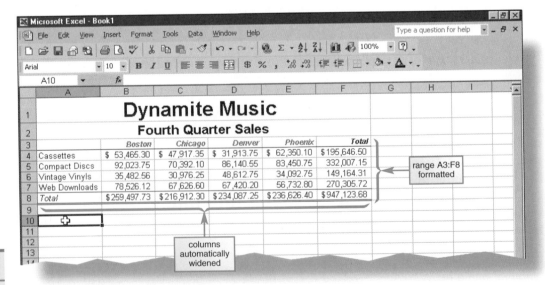

FIGURE 1-50

Other **Ways**

1. Press ALT+O, A
2. In Voice Command mode say, "Format, AutoFormat, [desired AutoFormat], OK"

The formats associated with Accounting 1 include bold, italic, right-aligned column titles; numbers displayed as dollars and cents with comma separators; numbers aligned on the decimal point; dollar signs in the first row of numbers and in the total row; and top and bottom rows display with borders. The width of column A also has been increased so the longest row title in cell A7, Web Downloads, just fits in the column. The widths of columns B through F have been increased so that the formatted numbers will fit in the cells.

The AutoFormat dialog box shown in Figure 1-49 includes 17 table formats and five buttons. Use the vertical scroll bar in the dialog box to view the 11 table formats that do not display. Each one of these table formats offers a different look. The one you choose depends on the worksheet you are creating. The last table format in the list, called None, removes all formats.

The five buttons in the dialog box allow you to cancel, complete the entries, get Help, and adjust a customized format. The **Close button** terminates current activity without making changes. You also can use the **Cancel button**, immediately below the **OK button**, for this purpose. Use the **Question Mark button**, to obtain Help on any box or button located in the dialog box. The **Options button** allows you to select additional formats to assign as part of the selected customized format.

The worksheet now is complete. The next step is to chart the fourth quarter sales for the four product groups by store. To create the chart, you must select the cell in the upper-left corner of the range to chart (cell A3). Rather than clicking cell A3 to select it, the next section describes how to use the Name box to select the cell.

Using the Name Box to Select a Cell

The Name box is located on the left side of the formula bar. To select any cell, click the Name box and enter the cell reference of the cell you want to select. Perform the following steps to select cell A3.

Steps **To Use the Name Box to Select a Cell**

1 **Click the Name box in the formula bar. Type** a3 **in the Name box.**

Even though cell A10 is the active cell, the Name box displays the typed cell reference a3 (Figure 1-51).

FIGURE 1-51

2 **Press the ENTER key.**

Excel changes the active cell from cell A10 to cell A3 (Figure 1-52).

A3 is active cell

Dynamite Music

Fourth Quarter Sales

	Boston	Chicago	Denver	Phoenix	Total
Cassettes	$ 53,465.30	$ 47,917.35	$ 31,913.75	$ 62,350.10	$195,646.50
Compact Discs	92,023.75	70,392.10	86,140.55	83,450.75	332,007.15
Vintage Vinyls	35,482.56	30,976.25	48,612.75	34,092.75	149,164.31
Web Downloads	78,526.12	67,626.60	67,420.20	56,732.80	270,305.72
Total	$ 259,497.73	$216,912.30	$234,087.25	$236,626.40	$947,123.68

FIGURE 1-52

As you will see in later projects, besides using the Name box to select any cell in a worksheet, you also can use it to assign names to a cell or range of cells.

Excel supports several additional ways to select a cell, as summarized in Table 1-3.

More About

Naming Cells and Ranges

If you repeatedly select certain cells in a worksheet, consider naming the cells in the Name box. Select the cells one at a time and then type in a name in the Name box for each, such as Company Total for cell F8 in Figure 1-52. Then, when you want to select one of the named cells, click the Name box arrow and then click the cell name in the Name box list. You can also name ranges the same way.

More About

Navigation

For more information on selecting cells that contain certain entries, such as constants or formulas, visit the Excel 2002 More About Web page (scsite.com/ex2002/ more.htm) and click Using Go To Special.

Table 1-3 Selecting Cells in Excel

KEY, BOX, OR COMMAND	FUNCTION
ALT+PAGE DOWN	Selects the cell one window to the right and moves the window accordingly.
ALT+PAGE UP	Selects the cell one window to the left and moves the window accordingly.
ARROW	Selects the adjacent cell in the direction of the arrow on the key.
CTRL+ARROW	Selects the border cell of the worksheet in combination with the arrow keys and moves the window accordingly. For example, to select the rightmost cell in the row that contains the active cell, press CTRL+RIGHT ARROW. You also can press the END key, release it, and then press the arrow key to accomplish the same task.
CTRL+HOME	Selects cell A1 or the cell one column and one row below and to the right of frozen titles and moves the window accordingly.
Find command on Edit menu	Finds and selects a cell that contains specific contents that you enter in the Find dialog box. If necessary, Excel moves the window to display the cell. You can press SHIFT+F5 or CTRL+F to display the Find dialog box.
F5 or Go To command on Edit menu	Selects the cell that corresponds to the cell reference you enter in the Go To dialog box and moves the window accordingly. You can press CTRL+G to display the Go To dialog box.
HOME	Selects the cell at the beginning of the row that contains the active cell and moves the window accordingly.
Name box	Selects the cell in the workbook that corresponds to the cell reference you enter in the Name box.
PAGE DOWN	Selects the cell down one window from the active cell and moves the window accordingly.
PAGE UP	Selects the cell up one window from the active cell and moves the window accordingly.

Adding a 3-D Column Chart to the Worksheet

The 3-D Column chart in Figure 1-53 is called an **embedded chart** because it is drawn on the same worksheet as the data.

For the Boston store, the light blue column represents the fourth quarter sales for the Cassettes product group ($53,465.30); the purple column represents the fourth quarter sales for Compact Discs ($92,023.75); the light yellow column represents the fourth quarter sales for Vintage Vinyls ($35,482.56); and the turquoise column represents the fourth quarter sales for Web Downloads ($78,526.12). For the stores Chicago, Denver, and Phoenix, the columns follow the same color scheme to represent the comparable fourth quarter sales. The totals from the worksheet are not represented because the totals were not in the range specified for charting.

Excel derives the scale along the vertical axis (also called the **y-axis** or **value axis**) of the chart on the basis of the values in the worksheet. For example, no value in the range B4:E7 is less than zero or greater than $100,000.00. Excel also determines the $20,000.00 increments along the y-axis automatically. The format used by Excel for the numbers along the y-axis includes representing zero (0) with a dash (Figure 1-53).

With the range to chart selected, you click the **Chart Wizard button** on the Standard toolbar to initiate drawing the chart. The area on the worksheet where the chart displays is called the **chart location**. The chart location is the range A10:F20, immediately below the worksheet data.

Follow the steps below to draw a 3-D Column chart that compares the fourth quarter sales by product group for the four stores.

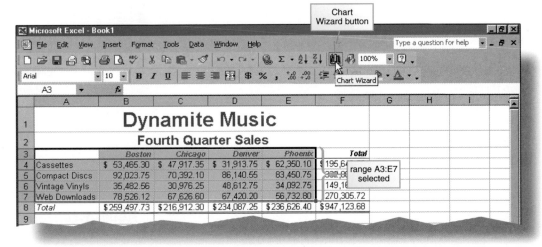

FIGURE 1-53

Steps **To Add a 3-D Column Chart to the Worksheet**

1 **With cell A3 selected, position the block plus sign mouse pointer within the cell's border and drag the mouse pointer to the lower-right corner cell (cell E7) of the range to chart (A3:E7). Point to the Chart Wizard button on the Standard toolbar.**

Excel highlights the range to chart (Figure 1-54).

FIGURE 1-54

2 **Click the Chart Wizard button.**

The Chart Wizard - Step 1 of 4 - Chart Type dialog box displays.

3 **With Column selected in the Chart type list, click the 3-D Column chart sub-type (column 1, row 2) in the Chart sub-type area. Point to the Finish button.**

Column is highlighted in the Chart type list and Clustered column with a 3-D visual effect is highlighted in the Chart sub-type area (Figure 1-55).

FIGURE 1-55

4 **Click the Finish button. If the chart toolbar displays, click its Close button. When the chart displays, point to an open area in the lower-right section of the Chart Area so the ScreenTip, Chart Area, displays.**

Excel draws the 3-D Clustered column chart (Figure 1-56). The chart displays in the middle of the window in a selection rectangle. The small sizing handles at the corners and along the sides of the selection rectangle indicate the chart is selected.

FIGURE 1-56

5 **Drag the chart down and to the left to position the upper-left corner of the dotted line rectangle over the upper-left corner of cell A10 (Figure 1-57).**

Excel displays a dotted line rectangle showing the new chart location. As you drag the selected chart, the mouse pointer changes to a cross hair with four arrowheads.

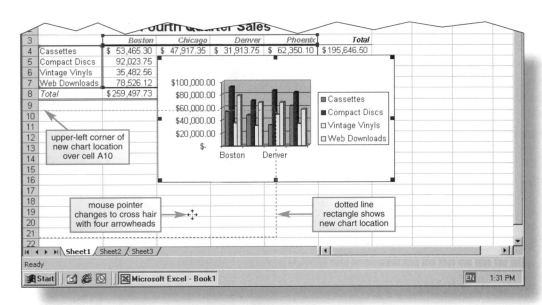

FIGURE 1-57

6 **Release the mouse button. Point to the middle sizing handle on the right edge of the selection rectangle.**

The chart displays in a new location (Figure 1-58). The mouse pointer changes to a horizontal line with two arrowheads when it points to a sizing handle.

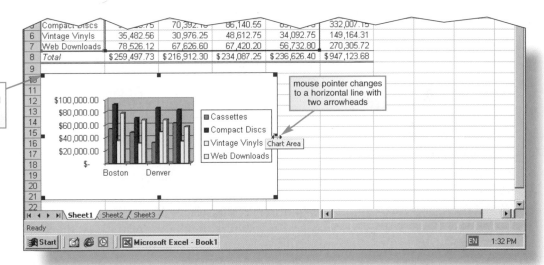

FIGURE 1-58

7 **While holding down the ALT key, drag the sizing handle to the right edge of column F. Release the mouse button.**

While you drag, the dotted line rectangle shows the new chart location (Figure 1-59). Holding down the ALT key while you drag a chart snaps (aligns) the new border to the worksheet gridlines.

FIGURE 1-59

8 If necessary, hold down the ALT key and drag the lower-middle sizing handle down to the bottom border of row 21. Click cell H21 to deselect the chart.

The new chart location extends from the top of cell A10 to the bottom of cell F21 (Figure 1-60).

FIGURE 1-60

The embedded 3-D Column chart in Figure 1-60 compares the fourth quarter sales for the four product groups within each store. It also allows you to compare fourth quarter sales among the stores.

Excel automatically selects the entries in the topmost row of the range (row 3) as the titles for the horizontal axis (also called the **x-axis** or **category axis**) and draws a column for each of the 16 cells in the range containing numbers. The small box to the right of the column chart in Figure 1-55 on page E 1.38 contains the legend. The **legend** identifies each bar in the chart. Excel automatically selects the leftmost column of the range (column A) as titles within the legend. As indicated earlier, it also automatically scales the y-axis on the basis of the magnitude of the numbers in the chart range.

Excel offers 14 different chart types (Figure 1-55 on page E 1.38). The **default chart type** is the chart Excel draws if you click the Finish button in the first Chart Wizard dialog box. When you install Excel on a computer, the default chart type is the 2-D (two-dimensional) Column chart.

Saving a Workbook

While you are building a workbook, the computer stores it in memory. If the computer is turned off or if you lose electrical power, the workbook is lost. Hence, you must save on a floppy disk or hard disk any workbook that you will use later. A saved workbook is referred to as a **file**. The following steps illustrate how to save a workbook on a floppy disk in drive A using the Save button on the Standard toolbar.

Steps To Save a Workbook

1 **With a floppy disk in drive A, click the Save button on the Standard toolbar.**

The Save As dialog box displays (Figure 1-61). The preset Save in folder is Documents and Settings (your Save in folder may be different), the preset file name is Book1, and the file type is Microsoft Excel Workbook. The buttons on the top and on the side are used to select folders and change the display of file names and other information.

FIGURE 1-61

2 **Type** Dynamite Music 4th Quarter Sales **in the File name box. Point to the Save in box arrow.**

The new file name replaces Book1 in the File name text box (Figure 1-62). A file name can be up to 255 characters and can include spaces.

FIGURE 1-62

3 **Click the Save in box arrow and then point to 3½ Floppy (A:).**

A list of available drives and folders displays (Figure 1-63).

FIGURE 1-63

4 **Click 3½ Floppy (A:) and then point to the Save button in the Save As dialog box.**

Drive A becomes the selected drive (Figure 1-64).

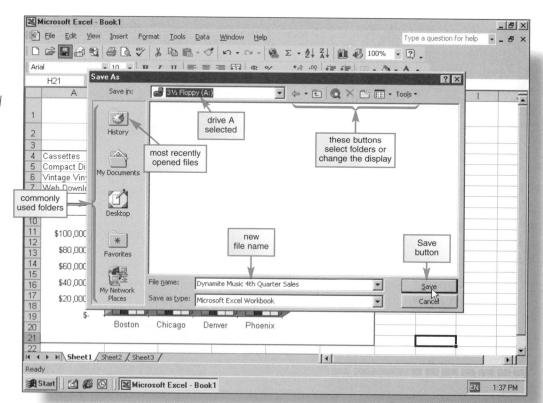

FIGURE 1-64

5 **Click the Save button.**

Excel saves the workbook on the floppy disk in drive A using the file name, Dynamite Music 4th Quarter Sales. Excel automatically appends the extension .xls to the file name you entered in Step 2, which stands for Excel workbook. Although the workbook is saved on a floppy disk, it also remains in memory and displays on the screen (Figure 1-65). The new file name displays on the title bar.

FIGURE 1-65

While Excel is saving the workbook, it momentarily changes the word Ready on the status bar to Saving. It also displays a horizontal bar on the status bar indicating the amount of the workbook saved. After the save operation is complete, Excel changes the name of the workbook in the title bar from Book1 to Dynamite Music 4th Quarter Sales (Figure 1-65).

The seven buttons at the top and to the right in the Save As dialog box in Figure 1-64 and their functions are summarized in Table 1-4.

When you click the **Tools button** in the Save As dialog box, a list displays. The **General Options command** in the list allows you to save a backup copy of the workbook, create a password to limit access to the workbook, and carry out other functions that are discussed later. Saving a backup workbook means that each time you save a workbook, Excel copies the current version of the workbook on disk to a file with the same name, but with the words, Backup of, appended to the front of the file name. In the case of a power failure or some other problem, use the backup version to restore your work.

You also can use the General Options command on the Tools list to assign a password to a workbook so others cannot open it. A password is case-sensitive and can be up to 15 characters long. **Case-sensitive** means Excel can differentiate between uppercase and lowercase letters. If you assign a password and forget the password, you cannot access the workbook.

Other Ways

1. On File menu click Save As, type file name, select drive or folder, click OK button
2. Press CTRL+S, type file name, select drive or folder, click OK button
3. In Voice Command mode say, "File, Save As, [type desired file name], Save"

Table 1-4 Save As Dialog Box Toolbar Buttons

BUTTON	BUTTON NAME	FUNCTION
	Default File Location	Displays contents of default file location
	Up One Level	Displays contents of next level up folder
	Search the Web	Starts browser and displays search engine
	Delete	Deletes selected file or folder
	Create New Folder	Creates new folder
	Views	Changes view of files and folders
Tools	Tools	Lists commands to print or modify file names and folders

The five buttons on the left of the Save As dialog box in Figure 1-64 on page E 1.42 allow you to select frequently used folders. The **History button** displays a list of shortcuts (pointers) to the most recently used files in a folder titled Recent. You cannot save workbooks to the Recent folder.

Printing a Worksheet

Once you have created the worksheet, you might want to print it. A printed version of the worksheet is called a **hard copy** or **printout**.

You might want a printout for several reasons. First, to present the worksheet and chart to someone who does not have access to a computer, it must be in printed form. A printout, for example, can be handed out in a management meeting about fourth quarter sales. In addition, worksheets and charts often are kept for reference by people other than those who prepare them. In many cases, worksheets and charts are printed and kept in binders for use by others. Perform the following steps to print the worksheet.

More About

Saving Workbooks

Excel allows you to save a workbook in over 30 different file formats. You choose the file format by clicking the Save as type box arrow at the bottom of the Save As dialog box (Figure 1-64 on page E 1.42). Microsoft Excel Workbook is the default file format. But you can, for example, save a workbook in Web Page format so you can publish it to the World Wide Web.

Steps — To Print a Worksheet

1 Ready the printer according to the printer instructions. Point to the Print button on the Standard toolbar (Figure 1-66).

FIGURE 1-66

2 Click the Print button. When the printer stops printing the worksheet and the chart, retrieve the printout.

Excel sends the worksheet to the printer, which prints it (Figure 1-67).

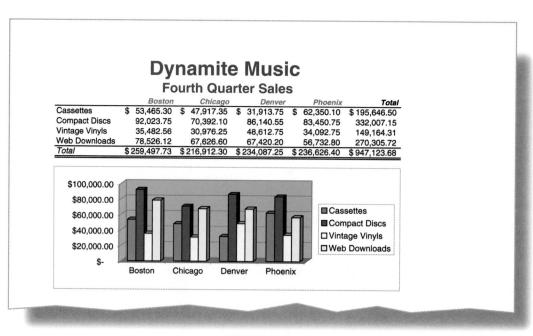

FIGURE 1-67

Other Ways

1. On File menu click Print, click OK button
2. Right-click workbook Control-menu icon on menu bar, click Print on shortcut menu, click OK button
3. Press CTRL+P, click OK button
4. In Voice Command mode say, "Print"

Prior to clicking the Print button, you can select which columns and rows in the 44worksheet to print. The range of cells you choose to print is called the **print area**. If you do not select a print area, as was the case in the previous set of steps, Excel automatically selects a print area on the basis of used cells. As you will see in future projects, Excel has many different print options, such as allowing you to preview the printout on the screen to see if the printout is satisfactory before sending it to the printer.

Quitting Excel

After you build, save, and print the worksheet and chart, Project 1 is complete. To quit Excel, complete the following steps.

Steps **To Quit Excel**

1 **Point to the Close button on the right side of the title bar (Figure 1-68).**

FIGURE 1-68

2 **Click the Close button.**

If you made changes to the workbook, the Microsoft Excel dialog box displays the question, Do you want to save the changes you made to 'Dynamite Music 4th Quarter Sales.xls'? (Figure 1-69). Clicking the Yes button saves the changes before quitting Excel. Clicking the No button quits Excel without saving the changes. Clicking the Cancel button cancels the exit and returns control to the worksheet.

3 **Click the No button.**

FIGURE 1-69

In Figure 1-68 on the previous page, you can see that two Close buttons and two Control-menu icons display. The Close button and Control-menu icon on the title bar close Excel. The Close button and Control-menu icon on the menu bar close the workbook, but not Excel.

Starting Excel and Opening a Workbook

Once you have created and saved a workbook, you often will have reason to retrieve it from a floppy disk. For example, you might want to review the calculations on the worksheet and enter additional or revised data on it. The following steps assume Excel is not running.

 To Start Excel and Open a Workbook

1 **With your floppy disk in drive A, click the Start button on the taskbar and then point to Open Office Document (Figure 1-70).**

FIGURE 1-70

2 **Click Open Office Document. If necessary, click the Look in box arrow and then click 3½ Floppy (A:) in the Look in list.**

The Open Office Document dialog box displays (Figure 1-71).

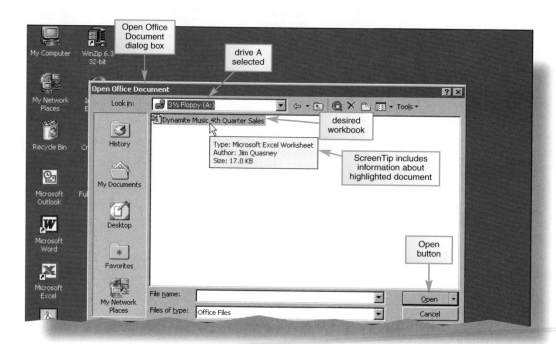

FIGURE 1-71

3 **Double-click the file name Dynamite Music 4th Quarter Sales.**

Excel starts, opens the workbook Dynamite Music 4th Quarter Sales.xls from drive A, and displays it on the screen (Figure 1-72). An alternative to double-clicking the file name is to click it and then click the Open button in the Open Office Document dialog box.

FIGURE 1-72

AutoCalculate

You easily can obtain a total, an average, or other information about the numbers in a range by using the AutoCalculate area on the status bar. All you need do is select the range of cells containing the numbers you want to check. Next, right-click the AutoCalculate area to display the shortcut menu (Figure 1-73 on the next page). The check mark to the left of the active function (Sum) indicates that the sum of the selected range displays. The function commands on the AutoCalculate shortcut menu are described in Table 1-5.

Table 1-5	AutoCalculate Shortcut Menu Commands
COMMAND	**FUNCTION**
None	No value displays in the AutoCalculate area
Average	Displays the average of the numbers in the selected range
Count	Displays the number of nonblank cells in the selected range
Count Nums	Displays the number of cells containing numbers in the selected range
Max	Displays the highest value in the selected range
Min	Displays the lowest value in the selected range
Sum	Displays the sum of the numbers in the selected range

The steps on the next page show how to display the average fourth quarter sales by store for the Cassettes product group.

Steps | To Use the AutoCalculate Area to Determine an Average

1 **Select the range B4:E4. Right-click the AutoCalculate area on the status bar.**

The sum of the numbers in the range B4:E4 displays ($195,646.50) as shown in Figure 1-73 because Sum is active in the AutoCalculate area. You may see a total other than the sum in your AutoCalculate area. The shortcut menu listing the various types of functions displays above the AutoCalculate area.

FIGURE 1-73

2 **Click Average on the shortcut menu.**

The average of the numbers in the range B4:E4 displays in the AutoCalculate area (Figure 1-74).

3 **Right-click the AutoCalculate area and then click Sum on the shortcut menu.**

The AutoCalculate area displays the sum as shown earlier in Figure 1-73.

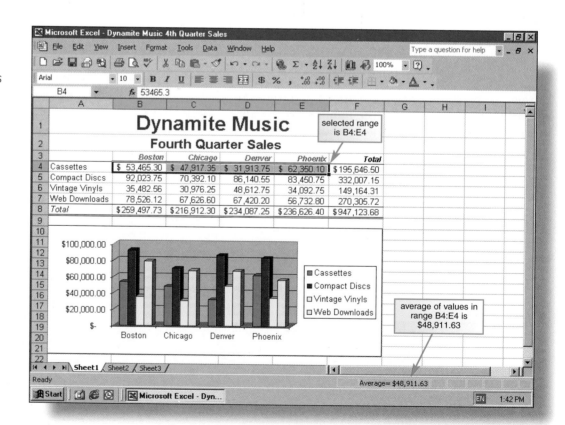

FIGURE 1-74

To change to any one of the other five functions for the range B4:E4, right-click the AutoCalculate area, then click the desired function.

The selection None at the top of the AutoCalculate shortcut menu in Figure 1-73 turns off the AutoCalculate area. Thus, if you select None, then no value will show in the AutoCalculate area when you select a range.

Correcting Errors

You can correct errors on a worksheet using one of several methods. The method you choose will depend on the extent of the error and whether you notice it while typing the data or after you have entered the incorrect data into the cell.

Correcting Errors While You Are Typing Data into a Cell

If you notice an error while you are typing data into a cell, press the BACKSPACE key to erase the portion in error and then type the correct characters. If the error is a major one, click the Cancel box in the formula bar or press the ESC key to erase the entire entry and then reenter the data from the beginning.

In-Cell Editing

If you find an error in the worksheet after entering the data, you can correct the error in one of two ways:

1. If the entry is short, select the cell, retype the entry correctly, and click the Enter box or press the ENTER key. The new entry will replace the old entry.

2. If the entry in the cell is long and the errors are minor, the **Edit mode** may be a better choice. Use the Edit mode as described below.

   a. Double-click the cell containing the error. Excel switches to Edit mode, the active cell contents display in the formula bar, and a flashing insertion point displays in the active cell (Figure 1-75). This editing procedure is called **in-cell editing** because you can edit the contents directly in the cell. The active cell contents also display in the formula bar.

   b. Make your changes, as indicated below.

      (1) To insert between two characters, place the insertion point between the two characters and begin typing. Excel inserts the new characters at the location of the insertion point.

      (2) To delete a character in the cell, move the insertion point to the left of the character you want to delete and then press the DELETE key, or place the insertion point to the right of the character you want to delete and then press the BACK-SPACE key. You also can use the mouse to drag through the character or adjacent characters you want to delete and then press the DELETE key or click the **Cut button** on the Standard toolbar.

      (3) When you are finished editing an entry, click the Enter box or press the ENTER key.

FIGURE 1-75

Editing the Contents of a Cell

Rather than using in-cell editing, you can select the cell and then click the formula bar to edit the contents.

When Excel enters the Edit mode, the keyboard usually is in Insert mode. In **Insert mode**, as you type a character, Excel inserts the character and moves all characters to the right of the typed character one position to the right. You can change to Overtype mode by pressing the INSERT key. In **Overtype mode**, Excel overtypes, or replaces, the character to the right of the insertion point. The INSERT key toggles the keyboard between Insert mode and Overtype mode.

While in Edit mode, you may have reason to move the insertion point to various points in the cell, select portions of the data in the cell, or switch from inserting characters to overtyping characters. Table 1-6 summarizes the more common tasks used during in-cell editing.

Table 1-6   Summary of In-Cell Editing Tasks

TASK	MOUSE	KEYBOARD
Move the insertion point to the beginning of data in a cell	Point to the left of the first character and click	Press HOME
Move the insertion point to the end of data in a cell	Point to the right of the last character and click	Press END
Move the insertion point anywhere in a cell	Point to the appropriate position and click the character	Press RIGHT ARROW or LEFT ARROW
Highlight one or more adjacent characters	Drag the mouse pointer through adjacent characters	Press SHIFT+RIGHT ARROW or SHIFT+LEFT ARROW
Select all data in a cell	Double-click the cell with the insertion point in the cell	
Delete selected characters	Click the Cut button on the Standard toolbar	Press DELETE
Delete characters to the left of insertion point		Press BACKSPACE
Toggle between Insert and Overtype modes		Press INSERT

Escaping an Activity

When it comes to canceling the current activity, the most important key on the keyboard is the ESC (Escape) key. Whether you are entering data into a cell or responding to a dialog box, pressing the ESC key cancels the current activity.

Undoing the Last Entry

Excel provides the **Undo command** on the **Edit menu** and the **Undo button** on the Standard toolbar (Figure 1-76) that you can use to erase the most recent worksheet entries. Thus, if you enter incorrect data in a cell and notice it immediately, click the Undo command or Undo button and Excel changes the cell contents to what they were prior to entering the incorrect data.

FIGURE 1-76

If Excel cannot undo an action, then the Undo button is inoperative. Excel remembers the last 16 actions you have completed. Thus, you can undo up to 16 previous actions by clicking the Undo button arrow to display the Undo list and clicking the action to be undone (Figure 1-76). You can drag through several actions in the Undo list to undo all of them at once.

Next to the Undo button on the Standard toolbar is the Redo button. The **Redo button** allows you to repeat previous actions. You also can click Redo on the Edit menu rather than using the Redo button.

Clearing a Cell or Range of Cells

If you enter data into the wrong cell or range of cells, you can erase, or clear, the data using one of several methods. *Never press the SPACEBAR to clear a cell.* Pressing the SPACEBAR enters a blank character. A blank character is text and is different from an empty cell, even though the cell may appear empty.

Excel provides four methods to clear the contents of a cell or a range of cells, which are discussed below.

TO CLEAR CELL CONTENTS USING THE FILL HANDLE

1. Select the cell or range of cells and point to the fill handle so the mouse pointer changes to a cross hair.
2. Drag the fill handle back into the selected cell or range until a shadow covers the cell or cells you want to erase. Release the mouse button.

TO CLEAR CELL CONTENTS USING THE SHORTCUT MENU

1. Select the cell or range of cells to be cleared.
2. Right-click the selection.
3. Click Clear Contents on the shortcut menu.

TO CLEAR CELL CONTENTS USING THE DELETE KEY

1. Select the cell or range of cells to be cleared.
2. Press the DELETE key.

TO CLEAR CELL CONTENTS USING THE CLEAR COMMAND

1. Select the cell or range of cells to be cleared.
2. Click Edit on the menu bar and then point to Clear.
3. Click All on the Clear submenu.

You also can select a range of cells and click the Cut button on the Standard toolbar or click Cut on the Edit menu. Be aware, however, that the Cut button or Cut command not only deletes the contents from the range, but also copies the contents of the range to the Office Clipboard.

Clearing the Entire Worksheet

Sometimes, everything goes wrong. If this happens, you may want to clear the worksheet entirely and start over. To clear the worksheet, follow the steps on the next page.

More About

The Undo Button

The Undo button can undo far more complicated worksheet activities than just removing the latest entry from a cell. In fact, most commands can be undone if you click the Undo button before you make another entry or issue another command. You cannot undo a save or print, but, as a general rule, the Undo button can restore the worksheet data and settings to what they were the last time Excel was in Ready mode. With Excel 2002, you have multiple-level undo and redo capabilities.

More About

Getting Back to Normal

If you accidentally assign unwanted formats to a range of cells, you can use the Clear command on the Edit menu to delete the formats of a selected range. Doing so changes the format to Normal style. To view the characteristics of the Normal style, click Style on the Format menu or press ALT+APOSTROPHE (').

TO CLEAR THE ENTIRE WORKSHEET

1 Click the Select All button on the worksheet (Figure 1-76 on page E 1.50).

2 Press the DELETE key or click Edit on the menu bar, point to Clear and then click All on the Clear submenu.

More About

Quick Reference

For a table that lists how to complete the tasks covered in this book using the mouse, menu, shortcut menu, and keyboard, see the Quick Reference Summary at the back of this book or visit the Shelly Cashman Series Office XP Web page (scsite.com/offxp/qr.htm) and then click Microsoft Excel 2002.

The **Select All button** selects the entire worksheet. Instead of clicking the Select All button, you also can press CTRL+A. You also can clear an unsaved workbook by clicking the workbook's Close button or by clicking the **Close command** on the File menu. If you close the workbook, click the **New button** on the Standard toolbar or click the **New command** on the File menu to begin working on the next workbook.

To delete an embedded chart, complete the following steps.

TO DELETE AN EMBEDDED CHART

1 Click the chart to select it.

2 Press the DELETE key.

Excel Help System

At any time while you are using Excel, you can get answers to questions using the Excel Help system. You can activate the Excel Help system by using the Ask a Question box on the menu bar, the Microsoft Excel Help button on the Standard toolbar, or the Help menu (Figure 1-77). Used properly, this form of online assistance can increase your productivity and reduce your frustrations by minimizing the time you spend learning how to use Excel.

The following section shows how to get answers to your questions using the Ask a Question box. Additional information on using the Excel Help system is available in Appendix A and Table 1-7 on page E1.54.

More About

The Excel Help System

The best way to become familiar with the Excel Help system is to use it. Appendix A includes detailed information on the Excel Help system and exercises that will help you gain confidence in using it.

Obtaining Help Using the Ask a Question Box on the Menu Bar

The **Ask a Question box** on the right side of the menu bar lets you type free-form questions such as. *how do I save* or *how do I create a Web page*, or you can type in terms such as, *copy*, *save*, or *formatting*. Excel responds by displaying a list of topics related to what you entered. The following steps show how to use the Ask a Question box to obtain information on formatting a worksheet.

Steps **To Obtain Help Using the Ask a Question Box**

1 **Type** formatting **in the Ask a Question box on the right side of the menu bar (Figure 1-77).**

FIGURE 1-77

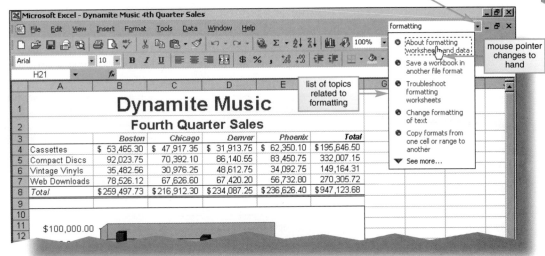

FIGURE 1-78

2 Press the ENTER key. When the list of topics displays below the Ask a Question box, point to the topic, About formatting worksheets and data.

A list of topics displays relating to the term, formatting. The mouse pointer changes to a hand indicating it is pointing to a link (Figure 1-78).

3 Click About formatting worksheets and data. When the Microsoft Excel Help window displays, double-click its title bar to maximize it.

Excel opens a Microsoft Excel Help window that provides Help information about worksheet formatting (Figure 1-79).

4 Click the Close button on the Microsoft Excel Help window title bar.

The Microsoft Excel Help window closes and the worksheet is active.

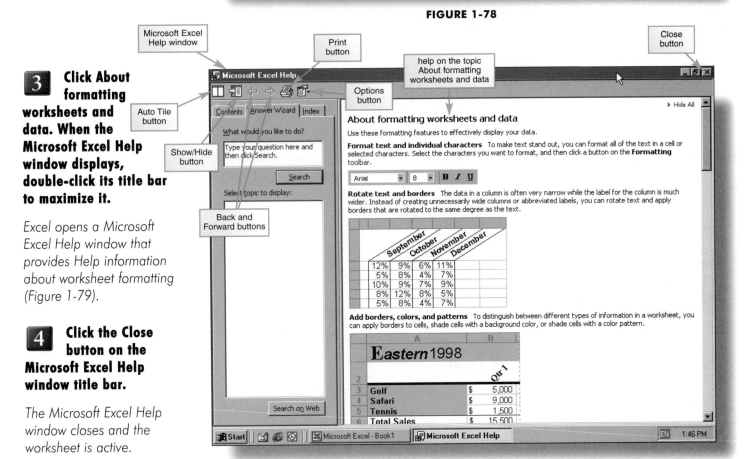

FIGURE 1-79

Use the buttons in the upper-left corner of the Microsoft Excel Help window (Figure 1-79) to navigate through the Help system, change the display, and print the contents of the window.

As you enter questions and terms in the Ask a Question box, Excel adds them to its list. Thus, if you click the Ask a Question box arrow (Figure 1-78), a list of previously asked questions and terms will display.

Table 1-7 summarizes the 11 categories of Help available to you. Because of the way the Excel Help system works, be sure to review the rightmost column of Table 1-7 if you have difficulties activating the desired category of Help. Additional information on using the Excel Help system is available in Appendix A.

Table 1-7 Excel Help System		
TYPE	**DESCRIPTION**	**HOW TO ACTIVATE**
Answer Wizard	Answers questions or searches for terms that you type in your own words.	Click the Microsoft Excel Help button on the Standard toolbar. Click the Answer Wizard tab.
Ask a Question box	Answers questions or searches for terms that you type in your own words.	Type a question or term in the Ask a Question box on the menu bar and then press the ENTER key.
Contents sheet	Groups Help topics by general categories. Use when you know only the general category of the topic in question.	Click the Microsoft Excel Help button on the Standard toolbar. Click the Contents tab.
Detect and Repair	Automatically finds and fixes errors in the application.	Click Detect and Repair on the Help menu.
Hardware and Software Information	Shows Product ID and allows access to system information and technical support information.	Click About Microsoft Excel on the Help menu and then click the appropriate button.
Help for Lotus 1-2-3 Users	Used to assist Lotus 1-2-3 users who are learning Microsoft Excel.	Click Lotus 1-2-3 Help on the Help menu.
Index sheet	Similar to an index in a book. Use when you know exactly what you want.	Click the Microsoft Excel Help button on the Standard toolbar. If necessary, maximize the Help window by double-clicking its title bar. Click the Index tab.
Office Assistant	Similar to the Ask a Question box in that the Office Assistant answers questions that you type in your own words, offers tips, and provides help for a variety of Excel features.	Click the Office Assistant icon. If the Office Assistant does not display, click Show the Office Assistant on the Help menu.
Office on the Web	Used to access technical resources and download free product enhancements on the Web.	Click Office on the Web on the Help menu.
Question Mark button	Used to identify unfamiliar items in a dialog box.	Click the Question Mark button in the title bar of a dialog box and then click an item in the dialog box.
What's This? command	Used to identify unfamiliar items on the screen.	Click What's This? on the Help menu, and then click an item on the screen.

Quitting Excel

To quit Excel, complete the following steps.

TO QUIT EXCEL

1. Click the Close button on the right side of the title bar (see Figure 1-68 on page E 1.45).

2. If the Microsoft Excel dialog box displays, click the No button.

More About

Quitting Excel

Do not forget to remove your floppy disk from drive A after quitting Excel, especially if you are working in a laboratory environment. Nothing can be more frustrating than leaving all of your hard work behind on a floppy disk for the next user.

CASE PERSPECTIVE SUMMARY

The worksheet created in this project allows the management of Dynamite Music to examine fourth quarter sales for the four key product groups. Furthermore, the 3-D Column chart should meet the needs of Nadine Mitchell, who as you recall, would rather view the numbers graphically.

Project Summary

In creating the Dynamite Music Fourth Quarter Sales worksheet and chart in this project, you gained a broad knowledge of Excel. First, you were introduced to starting Excel. You learned about the Excel window and how to enter text and numbers to create a worksheet. You learned how to select a range and how to use the AutoSum button to sum numbers in a column or row. Using the fill handle, you learned how to copy a cell to adjacent cells.

Once the worksheet was built, you learned how to change the font size of the title, bold the title, and center the title across a range using buttons on the Formatting toolbar. Using the steps and techniques presented in the project, you formatted the body of the worksheet using the AutoFormat command, and you used the Chart Wizard to add a 3-D Column chart. After completing the worksheet, you saved the workbook on disk, printed the worksheet and chart, and then quit Excel. You learned how to start Excel by opening an Excel document, use the AutoCalculate area, and edit data in cells. Finally, you learned how to use the Excel Help system to answer your questions.

What You Should Know

Having completed this project, you now should be able to perform the following tasks:

- Add a 3-D Column Chart to the Worksheet *(E 1.37)*
- Bold a Cell *(E 1.29)*
- Center a Cell's Contents across Columns *(E 1.32)*
- Change the Font Color of a Cell *(E 1.31)*
- Clear Cell Contents Using the Clear Command *(E 1.51)*
- Clear Cell Contents Using the DELETE Key *(E 1.51)*
- Clear Cell Contents Using the Fill Handle *(E 1.51)*
- Clear Cell Contents Using the Shortcut Menu *(E 1.51)*
- Clear the Entire Worksheet *(E 1.52)*
- Copy a Cell to Adjacent Cells in a Row *(E 1.25)*
- Customize the Excel Window *(E 1.09)*
- Delete an Embedded Chart *(E 1.52)*
- Determine Multiple Totals at the Same Time *(E 1.27)*
- Enter Column Titles *(E 1.19)*
- Enter Numeric Data *(E 1.22)*
- Enter Row Titles *(E 1.21)*
- Enter the Worksheet Titles *(E 1.17)*
- Format the Worksheet Subtitle *(E 1.33)*
- Increase the Font Size of a Cell Entry *(E 1.30)*
- Obtain Help Using the Ask a Question Box *(E 1.52)*
- Print a Worksheet *(E 1.44)*
- Quit Excel *(E 1.45, E 1.54)*
- Save a Workbook *(E 1.41)*
- Start Excel *(E 1.08)*
- Start Excel and Open a Workbook *(E 1.46)*
- Sum a Column of Numbers *(E 1.23)*
- Use AutoFormat to Format the Body of a Worksheet *(E 1.33)*
- Use the AutoCalculate Area to Determine an Average *(E 1.48)*
- Use the Name Box to Select a Cell *(E 1.35)*

More About

Microsoft Certification

The Microsoft Office User Specialist (MOUS) Certification program provides an opportunity for you to obtain a valuable industry credential — proof that you have the Excel 2002 skills required by employers. For more information, see Appendix E or visit the Shelly Cashman Series MOUS Web page at scsite.com/offxp/cert.htm.

Learn It Online

Instructions: To complete the Learn It Online exercises, start your browser, click the Address bar, and then enter scsite.com/offxp/exs.htm. When the Office XP Learn It Online page displays, follow the instructions in the exercises below.

1 Project Reinforcement TF, MC, and SA

Below Excel Project 1, click the Project Reinforcement link. Print the quiz by clicking Print on the File menu. Answer each question. Write your first and last name at the top of each page, and then hand in the printout to your instructor.

2 Flash Cards

Below Excel Project 1, click the Flash Cards link. When Flash Cards displays, read the instructions. Type 20 (or a number specified by your instructor) in the Number of Playing Cards text box, type your name in the Name text box, and then click the Flip Card button. When the flash card displays, read the question and then click the Answer box arrow to select an answer. Flip through Flash Cards. Click Print on the File menu to print the last flash card if your score is 15 (75%) correct or greater and then hand it in to your instructor. If your score is less than 15 (75%) correct, then redo this exercise by clicking the Replay button.

3 Practice Test

Below Excel Project 1, click the Practice Test link. Answer each question, enter your first and last name at the bottom of the page, and then click the Grade Test button. When the graded practice test displays on your screen, click Print on the File menu to print a hard copy. Continue to take practice tests until you score 80% or better. Hand in a printout of the final practice test to your instructor.

4 Who Wants to Be a Computer Genius?

Below Excel Project 1, click the Computer Genius link. Read the instructions, enter your first and last name at the bottom of the page, and then click the Play button. Hand in your score to your instructor.

5 Wheel of Terms

Below Excel Project 1, click the Wheel of Terms link. Read the instructions, and then enter your first and last name and your school name. Click the Play button. Hand in your score to your instructor.

6 Crossword Puzzle Challenge

Below Excel Project 1, click the Crossword Puzzle Challenge link. Read the instructions, and then enter your first and last name. Click the Play button. Work the crossword puzzle. When you are finished, click the Submit button. When the crossword puzzle redisplays, click the Print button. Hand in the printout.

7 Tips and Tricks

Below Excel Project 1, click the Tips and Tricks link. Click a topic that pertains to Project 1. Right-click the information and then click Print on the shortcut menu. Construct a brief example of what the information relates to in Excel to confirm you understand how to use the tip or trick. Hand in the example and printed information.

8 Newsgroups

Below Excel Project 1, click the Newsgroups link. Click a topic that pertains to Project 1. Print three comments. Hand in the comments to your instructor.

9 Expanding Your Horizons

Below Excel Project 1, click the Articles for Microsoft Excel link. Click a topic that pertains to Project 1. Print the information. Construct a brief example of what the information relates to in Excel to confirm you understand the contents of the article. Hand in the example and printed information to your instructor.

10 Search Sleuth

Below Excel Project 1, click the Search Sleuth link. To search for a term that pertains to this project, select a term below the Project 1 title and then use the Google search engine at google.com (or any major search engine) to display and print two Web pages that present information on the term. Hand in the printouts to your instructor.

online

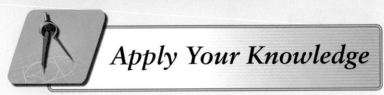

Apply Your Knowledge

1 Marco Polo's Travel Bookstore 1st Quarter Sales Worksheet

Instructions: Start Excel. Open the workbook Magellan's Travel Bookstore 1st Quarter Sales from the Data Disk. See the inside back cover of this book for instructions for downloading the Data Disk or see your instructor for information on accessing the files required in this book.

Make the changes to the worksheet described in Table 1-8 so it appears as shown in Figure 1-80. As you edit the values in the cells containing numeric data, watch in the totals in row 8, the totals in column G, and the chart change. When you enter a new value, Excel automatically recalculates the formulas. After you have successfully made the changes listed in the table, the total sales in cell G8 should be $1,486,082.12.

Table 1-8 New Worksheet Data	
CELL	**CHANGE CELL CONTENTS TO**
A1	Marco Polo's Travel Bookstore
B4	78,221.46
C4	69,789.50
D6	74,943.13
F6	86,699.98
F7	98,421.43

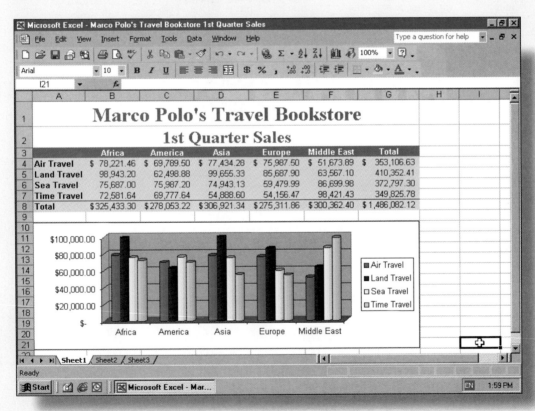

FIGURE 1-80

To learn how to split cells, click cell A1 and then click the Merge and Center button to split cell A1 into cells A1, B1, C1, D1, E1, F1, and G1. To re-merge the cells into one, select the range A1:G1 and click the Merge and Center button.

Enter your name, course, laboratory assignment number, date, and instructor name in cells A24 through A28. Save the workbook. Use the file name, Marco Polo's Travel Bookstore 1st Quarter Sales. Print the revised worksheet and hand in the printout to your instructor.

In the Lab

1 Madonna's Virtual Sojourn Annual Sales Analysis Worksheet

Problem: The president of Madonna's Virtual Sojourn, a travel agency that courts college age students, needs a sales analysis worksheet similar to the one shown in Figure 1-81. Your task is to develop the worksheet.

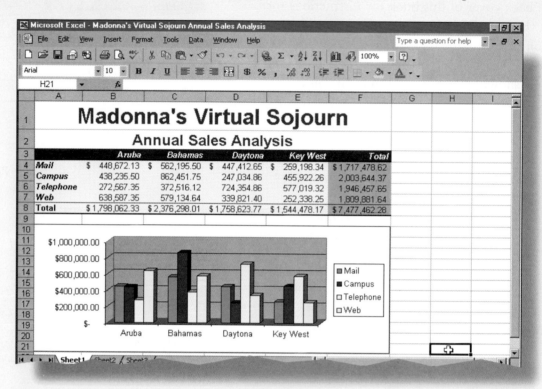

FIGURE 1-81

Instructions: Perform the following tasks.

1. Create the worksheet shown in Figure 1-81 using the sales amounts and categories in Table 1-9.

Table 1-9	Madonna's Virtual Sojourn Annual Sales Data			
	ARUBA	*BAHAMAS*	*DAYTONA*	*KEY WEST*
Mail	448,672.13	562,195.50	447,412.65	259,198.34
Campus	438,235.50	862,451.75	247,034.86	455,922.26
Telephone	272,567.35	372,516.12	724,354.86	577,019.32
Web	638,587.35	579,134.64	339,821.40	252,338.25

2. Determine the totals for the types of sales channels, travel destinations, and company totals.
3. Format the worksheet title, Madonna's Virtual Sojourn, to 26-point Arial, bold brown font, centered across columns A through F. Do not be concerned if the edges of the worksheet title do not display.
4. Format the worksheet subtitle, Annual Sales Analysis, to 18-point Arial, bold brown font, centered across columns A through F.

In the Lab

5. Format the range A3:F8 using the AutoFormat command on the Format menu as follows: (a) Select the range A3:F8 and then apply the table format Accounting 1; and (b) with the range A3:F8 still selected, apply the table format Colorful 2. Excel appends the formats of Colorful 2 to the formats of Accounting 1.

6. Select the range A3:E7 and then use the Chart Wizard button on the Standard toolbar to draw a Clustered column with a 3-D visual effect chart (column 1, row 2 in Chart sub-type list). Move the chart to the upper-left corner of cell A10 and then drag the lower-right corner of the chart location to cell F21. If all the labels along the horizontal axis do not display as shown in Figure 1-81, select a cell in column F, click Format on the menu bar, point to Column on the Format menu, click Width on the Column submenu, increase the column width by two or more units, and then click the OK button.

7. Enter your name, course, laboratory assignment number, date, and instructor name in cells A24 through A28.

8. Save the workbook using the file name Madonna's Virtual Sojourn Annual Sales Analysis.

9. Print the worksheet.

10. Make the following two corrections to the sales amounts: $596,321.75 for Bahamas sales by telephone (cell C6), $157,390.58 for Key West sales by mail (cell E4). After you enter the corrections, the company totals should equal $7,599,460.15 in cell F8.

11. Print the revised worksheet. Close the workbook without saving the changes.

2 Razor Sharp Scooter 3rd Quarter Expenses Worksheet

Problem: As the chief accountant for Razor Sharp Scooter, Inc., the vice president has asked you to create a worksheet to analyze the 3rd quarter expenses for the company by department and expense category (Figure 1-82). The expenses for the 3rd quarter are shown in Table 1-10.

Table 1-10 Razor Sharp Scooter 3rd Quarter Expenses					
	FINANCE	HELP DESK	MARKETING	SALES	SYSTEMS
Benefits	12378.23	11934.21	15823.10	10301.60	4123.89
Travel	23761.45	15300.89	6710.35	18430.15	6510.25
Wages	18001.27	13235.50	17730.58	12000.45	20931.53
Other	6145.20	3897.21	4910.45	8914.34	1201.56

Instructions: Perform the following tasks.

1. Create the worksheet shown in Figure 1-82 on the next page using the data in Table 1-10.

2. Direct Excel to determine totals expenses for the five departments, the totals for each expense category, and the company total.

3. Format the worksheet title, Razor Sharp Scooter, in 24-point Arial bold violet font, and center it across columns A through G.

4. Format the worksheet subtitle, 3rd Quarter Expenses, in 18-point Arial bold violet font, and center it across columns A through G.

(continued)

In the Lab

Razor Sharp Scooter 3rd Quarter Expenses Worksheet *(continued)*

FIGURE 1-82

5. Use the AutoFormat command on the Format menu to format the range A3:G8. Use the table format Accounting 2.

6. Use the ChartWizard button on the Standard toolbar to draw the 3-D Cone chart (column 1, row 1 in the Chart sub-type list), as shown in Figure 1-82. Chart the range A3:F7 and use the chart location A10:G21. If all the labels along the horizontal axis do not display as shown in Figure 1-82, select a cell in column G, click Format on the menu bar, point to Column on the Format menu, click Width on the Column submenu, increase the column width by two or more units, and then click the OK button.

7. Enter your name, course, laboratory assignment number, date, and instructor name in cells A24 through A28.

8. Save the workbook using the file name, Razor Sharp Scooter 3rd Quarter Expenses. Print the worksheet.

9. Two corrections to the expenses were sent in from the accounting department. The correct expenses are $22,537.43 for wages in the Finance department and $21,962.75 for travel in the Sales department. After you enter the two corrections, the company total should equal $240,310.97 in cell G8. Print the revised worksheet.

10. Use the Undo button to change the worksheet back to the original numbers in Table 1-10. Use the Redo button to change the worksheet back to the revised state.

11. Hand in all printouts to your instructor. Close the workbook without saving the changes.

In the Lab

3 College Cash Flow Analysis Worksheet

Problem: Attending college is an expensive proposition and your resources are limited. To plan for your four-year college career, you have decided to organize your anticipated resources and expenses in a worksheet. The data required to prepare your worksheet is shown in Table 1-11.

Part 1 Instructions: Using the numbers in Table 1-11, follow the steps below to create the worksheet shown in columns A through F in Figure 1-83 on the next page.

Table 1-11 College Cash Flow Analysis

RESOURCES	FRESHMAN	SOPHOMORE	JUNIOR	SENIOR
Financial Aid	5,025.00	5326.50	5646.09	5984.86
Job	1,525.00	1616.50	1713.49	1816.30
Parents	2,600.00	2756.00	2921.36	3096.64
Savings	1,100.00	1166.00	1235.96	1310.12
EXPENSES	**FRESHMAN**	**SOPHOMORE**	**JUNIOR**	**SENIOR**
Clothes	540.00	572.40	606.74	643.15
Entertainment	725.00	768.50	814.61	863.49
Miscellaneous	355.00	376.30	398.88	422.81
Room & Board	3480.00	3688.80	3910.13	4144.74
Tuition & Books	5150.00	5459.00	5786.54	6133.73

1. Enter the worksheet title in cell A1 and the section titles, Resources and Expenses, in cells A2 and A9, respectively.
2. Use the AutoSum button to calculate the totals in rows 8 and 16 and column F.
3. Increase the font in the worksheet title to 24 and change its color to red. Center the worksheet title in cell A1 across columns A through F. Increase the font size in the table titles in cells A2 and A9 to 18 and change their color to green.
4. Format the range A3:F8 using the AutoFormat command on the Format menu as follows: (a) Select the range A3:F8 and then apply the table format Accounting 1; and (b) with the range A3:F8 still selected, apply the table format List 1. Format the range A10:F16 using the AutoFormat command on the Format menu as follows: (a) Select the range A10:F16 and then apply the table format Accounting 1; and (b) with the range A3:F8 still selected, apply the table format List 1.
5. Enter your name in cell A19 and your course, laboratory assignment number, date, and instructor name in cells A20 through A23. Save the workbook using the file name, College Resources and Expenses.
6. Print the worksheet in landscape orientation. You print in landscape orientation by clicking Landscape on the Page tab in the Page Setup dialog box. Click Page Setup on the File menu to display the Page Setup dialog box. Click the Save button on the Standard toolbar to save the workbook with the new print settings.
7. All Junior-year expenses in column D increased by $500. Re-enter the new Junior-year expenses. Change the financial aid for the Junior year by the amount required to cover the increase in expenses. The totals in cells F8 and F16 should equal $47,339.82. Print the worksheet. Close the workbook without saving changes. Hand in the two printouts to your instructor.

(continued)

In the Lab

College Cash Flow Analysis Worksheet *(continued)*

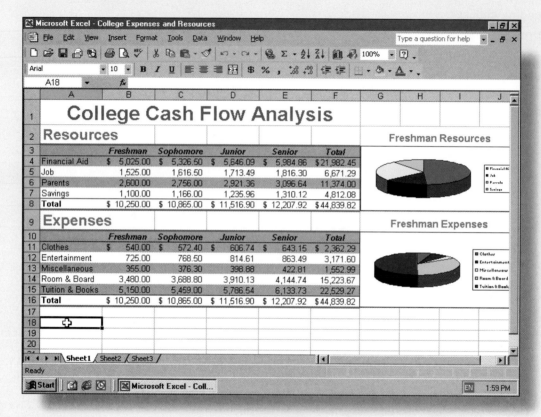

FIGURE 1-83

Part 2 Instructions: Open the workbook College Resources and Expenses created in Part 1. Draw a 3-D Pie chart in the range G3:J8 that shows the contribution of each category of resource for the freshman year. Chart the range A4:B7. Add the Pie chart title shown in cell G2 in Figure 1-83. Change the Pie chart title's font to 12-point, bold green. Center the Pie chart title over the range G2:J2. Draw a 3-D Pie chart in the range G10:J16 that shows the contribution of each category of expense for the Freshman year. Chart the range A11:B15. Add the Pie chart title shown in cell G9 in Figure 1-83. Change the Pie chart title's font to 12-point, bold green. Center the Pie chart title over the range G9:J9. Save the workbook using the file name, College Resources and Expenses 2. Print the worksheet. Hand in the printout to your instructor.

Part 3 Instructions: Open the workbook College Resources and Expenses 2 created in Part 2. A close inspection of Table 1-11 on the previous page shows a 6% increase each year over the previous year. Use the Ask a Question box on the menu bar to learn how to enter the data for the last three years using a formula and the Copy command. For example, the formula to enter in cell C4 is =B4 * 1.06. Enter formulas to replace all the numbers in the range C4:E7 and C11:E15. If necessary, reformat the tables as described in Part 1. The worksheet should appear as shown in Figure 1-83, except that some of the totals will be off by 0.01 due to round-off errors. Save the worksheet using the file name, College Resources and Expenses 3. Print the worksheet. Press CTRL+ACCENT (`) to display the formulas. Print the formulas version. Hand in both printouts to your instructor.

Cases and Places

The difficulty of these case studies varies:
▶ are the least difficult; ▶▶ are more difficult; and ▶▶▶ are the most difficult.

1 ▶ You work part time for Kylie's Pet Shop. Your primary responsibilities include caring for the pets. Your manager, Elma Presley, recently learned that you are enrolled in a computer class. She has asked you to prepare a worksheet and chart to help her analyze the 3rd quarter sales by store and by pet (Table 1-12). Use the concepts and techniques presented in this project to create the worksheet and chart.

Table 1-12   Kylie's Pet Shop 3rd Quarter Sales

	BOSTON	CLEVELAND	SAN DIEGO	DALLAS
Birds	16734	17821	24123	17989
Cats	15423	12134	16574	33401
Dogs	13495	26291	17345	27098
Fish	25462	22923	28034	25135

2 ▶ Computer Discount Sales sells computers throughout the state of Indiana. The number of servers, desktop computers, notebook computers, and handheld computers sold has increased each year from 1998 through 2002, as indicated in Table 1-13. Create a worksheet and 3-D Column chart that illustrates these increases. Use the concepts and techniques presented in this project to create the worksheet and chart.

Table 1-13   Computer Discount Sales 1998-2002

	SERVERS	DESKTOPS	NOTEBOOKS	HANDHELDS
1998	7323	22231	6125	225
1999	7498	32356	26315	1257
2000	7615	38489	36727	13313
2001	7734	42501	46501	24407
2002	7944	52578	56623	26761

3 ▶ As a newspaper reporter, you are preparing an article on the coming election based on a recent survey of the electorate, arranged by age of those polled (Table 1-14). You have been asked to produce a worksheet to accompany your article. Use the concepts and techniques presented in this project to create the worksheet and an embedded Column chart.

Table 1-14   Valley Heights Mayoral Race Election Poll Results

	18-29	30-41	42-53	54-65	66+
Groen	625	301	512	440	205
Sabol	235	279	357	213	410
Walker	462	732	433	176	399
Webb	724	521	321	835	276

Cases and Places

4 ▶ Alyssa's Boutique on 5th Avenue in New York sells costume jewelry to an exclusive clientele. The company is trying to decide whether it is feasible to open another boutique in the Boston area. You have been asked to develop a worksheet totaling all the revenue received last year from customers living in the Boston area. The revenue from customers living in the Boston area by quarter is: Quarter 1, $104,561.38; Quarter 2, $91,602.55; Quarter 3, $258,220.10; and Quarter 4, $333,725.25. Create a 3-D Pie chart to illustrate Boston-area revenue contribution by quarter. Use the AutoCalculate area to find the average quarterly revenue.

5 ▶▶ The Virtual Reality Theater is a movie house that shows virtual reality movies at weekday evening, weekend matinee, and weekend evening screenings. Three types of tickets are sold at each presentation: general admission, senior citizen, and children. The theater management has asked you to prepare a worksheet, based on the revenue from a typical week, that can be used in reevaluating its ticket structure. During an average week, weekday evening shows generate $9,835 from general admission ticket sales, $5,630 from senior citizen ticket sales, and $1,675 from children ticket sales. Weekend matinee shows make $7,250 from general admission ticket sales, $2,345 from senior citizen ticket sales, and $3,300 from children ticket sales. Weekend evening shows earn $9,230 from general admission ticket sales, $8,125 from senior citizen ticket sales, and $1,600 from children ticket sales. Use the concepts and techniques presented in this project to prepare a worksheet that includes total revenues for each type of ticket and for each presentation time, and a Bar chart illustrating ticket revenues.

6 ▶▶▶ Athletic footwear stores must track carefully the sales of their different shoe brands so they can restock their inventory promptly. Visit an athletic shoe store and make a list of the top five brands of running shoes. Find out how many of each brand was sold each of the last three months. Using this information, create a worksheet showing the number of each brand sold each month, the total number of running shoes sold each month, the total number of each brand sold over three months, and a total number of all running shoes sold over three months. Include a 3-D Column chart to illustrate the data.

7 ▶▶▶ Visit the Registrar's office at your school and obtain the ages of students majoring in at least five different academic departments this semester. Separate the ages of the students in the departments by four different age groups. Using this information, create a worksheet showing the number of attending students by age group in each department. Include totals and a 3-D Column chart.

Microsoft Excel 2002

PROJECT

2

Formulas, Functions, Formatting, and Web Queries

You will have mastered the material in this project when you can:

O B J E C T I V E S

- Enter multiple lines of text in the same cell
- Enter a formula using the keyboard
- Enter formulas using Point mode
- Identify the arithmetic operators +, –, *, /, %, and ^
- Recognize smart tags
- Apply the AVERAGE, MAX, and MIN functions
- Determine a percentage
- Verify a formula using Range Finder
- Change the font of a cell
- Color the characters and background of a cell
- Add borders to a range
- Format numbers using the Format Cells dialog box
- Add conditional formatting to a range of cells
- Align text in cells
- Change the width of a column and height of a row
- Check the spelling of a worksheet
- Preview how a printed copy of the worksheet will look
- Distinguish between portrait and landscape orientation
- Print a partial or complete worksheet
- Display and print the formulas version of a worksheet
- Print to fit
- Use a Web query to get real-time data from a Web site
- Rename sheets
- E-mail the active workbook from within Excel

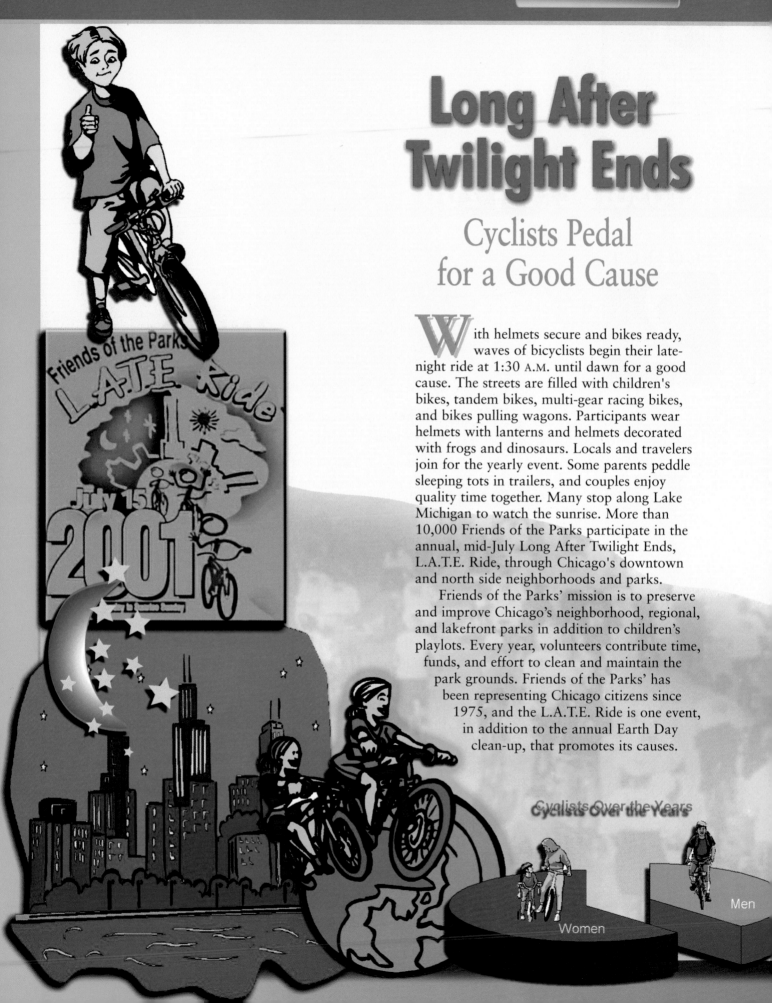

Long After Twilight Ends

Cyclists Pedal for a Good Cause

With helmets secure and bikes ready, waves of bicyclists begin their late-night ride at 1:30 A.M. until dawn for a good cause. The streets are filled with children's bikes, tandem bikes, multi-gear racing bikes, and bikes pulling wagons. Participants wear helmets with lanterns and helmets decorated with frogs and dinosaurs. Locals and travelers join for the yearly event. Some parents peddle sleeping tots in trailers, and couples enjoy quality time together. Many stop along Lake Michigan to watch the sunrise. More than 10,000 Friends of the Parks participate in the annual, mid-July Long After Twilight Ends, L.A.T.E. Ride, through Chicago's downtown and north side neighborhoods and parks.

Friends of the Parks' mission is to preserve and improve Chicago's neighborhood, regional, and lakefront parks in addition to children's playlots. Every year, volunteers contribute time, funds, and effort to clean and maintain the park grounds. Friends of the Parks' has been representing Chicago citizens since 1975, and the L.A.T.E. Ride is one event, in addition to the annual Earth Day clean-up, that promotes its causes.

Cyclists Over the Years											
	1989	1990	1991	1992	1993	1994	1995	1996	19		2000
Women	125	350	600	1,300	1,550	2,250	2,700	3,010	3,		,900
Men	200	400	650	1,800	1,750	2,075	2,900	3,0			3,8

So how does the Friends of the Parks' organization attempt to manage and organize information about the more than 10,000 participants who take part in the L.A.T.E. Ride event each year? Staff, many of whom volunteer their time and expertise, use worksheets to organize, chart, and present all types of data with relative ease. They analyze and manipulate data; specifically, they input numbers and enter formulas to determine averages and percentages, as well as find the minimum and maximum numbers in a series. In addition, they create traditional Pie charts, Column charts, and other chart forms to represent the data visually.

If they want to determine the demographics of the L.A.T.E. bike riders, they input participants' ages taken from a Friends of the Parks' survey and let the worksheet generate Pie charts depicting the age breakdowns. Moreover, they can create a Column chart showing the number of participants from year to year. The Friends of the Parks' also can track how many participants live in Chicago, the suburbs, or other states and the number of male and female cyclists.

You will perform similar tasks in this project when you create a worksheet for the Greenback Stock Club. You will enter formulas, use the AVERAGE, MAX, and MIN functions, and then verify the formulas for accuracy.

The L.A.T.E. Ride was established in 1989 with 350 cyclists; today more than 10,000 bike riders have participated. It is not by sheer coincidence that the numbers have escalated dramatically. Once the staff at the Friends of the Parks' collects survey data, they then input the numbers into worksheets using ranges of numbers, enter formulas, and apply formats for appropriate charts. Such data is important to determine marketing strategies or finalize the total number of glow-in-the-dark T-shirts and number tags needed for the participants to don for the ride.

Join the people of the Windy City who pedal for the parks in Chicago's only 25-mile nocturnal bicycling event by visiting The L.A.T.E. Ride Web site at lateride.org

Microsoft Excel 2002

Formulas, Functions, Formatting, and Web Queries

CASE PERSPECTIVE

Several years ago, while in college, Abby Lane and five of her friends started Greenback Stock Club. The friends decided to focus on researching and investing in well established companies. Every month, they invested $25 each, researched an assigned company, and came to the meeting with their buy and sell recommendations.

All have graduated from college, are married, and are living in different parts of the country. They still invest in the stock market and have increased their monthly contributions to $100 each.

The value of the club's portfolio, or group of investments, recently surpassed the $300,000.00 mark. As a result, the members voted unanimously to purchase a new computer and a copy of Microsoft Office XP for Abby, the club's permanent treasurer. With Excel, she plans to create a worksheet summarizing the club's stock activities that she can e-mail to the club members. She wants to use its Web query capabilities to access real-time stock quotes. Abby has asked you to show her how to create the workbook and access real-time stock quotes over the Internet using Excel.

Introduction

In Project 1, you learned how to enter data, sum values, make the worksheet easier to read, and draw a chart. You also learned about online Help and saving, printing, and opening a workbook from a floppy disk. This project continues to emphasize these topics and presents some new ones.

The new topics include formulas, smart tags, verifying formulas, changing fonts, adding borders, formatting numbers and text, conditional formatting, changing the widths of columns and heights of rows, spell checking, e-mailing from within an application, and alternative types of worksheet displays and printouts. One alternative display and printout shows the formulas rather than the values in the worksheet. When you display the formulas in the worksheet, you see exactly what text, data, formulas, and functions you have entered into it. Finally, this project covers Web queries to obtain real-time data from a Web site.

Project Two — Greenback Stock Club

The summary notes from your meeting with Abby include the following: need, source of data, calculations, and Web requirements.

Need: An easy-to-read worksheet that summarizes the club's investments (Figure 2-1a). For each stock, the worksheet is to include the stock name, stock symbol, date acquired, number of shares, initial price per share, initial cost, current price per share, current value, gain/loss, and percent gain/loss. Abby also has requested that the worksheet include totals and the average, highest value, and lowest value for each column of numbers. Finally, Abby wants to use Excel to access real-time stock quotes using Web queries (Figure 2-1b).

(a) Worksheet

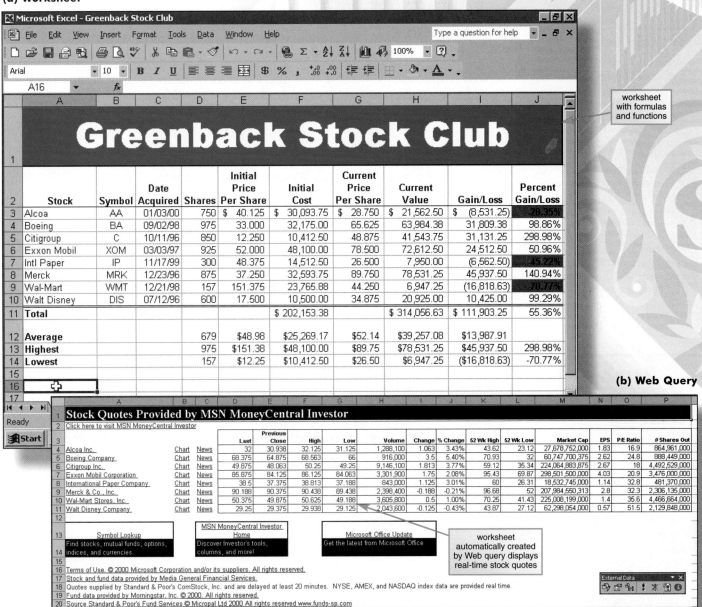

worksheet
with formulas
and functions

(b) Web Query

worksheet
automatically created
by Web query displays
real-time stock quotes

FIGURE 2-1

Source of Data: The data supplied by Abby includes the stock names, symbols, dates acquired, number of shares, initial price per share, and current price per share. This data is shown in Table 2-1.

Calculations: The following calculations must be made for each of the stocks:

1. Initial Cost = Shares × Initial Price Per Share
2. Current Value = Shares × Current Price Per Share
3. Gain/Loss = Current Value − Initial Cost
4. Percent Gain/Loss = $\dfrac{\text{Gain/Loss}}{\text{Initial Cost}}$
5. Compute the totals for initial cost, current value, and gain/loss.
6. Use the AVERAGE function to determine the average for the number of shares, initial price per share, initial cost per share, current price per share, current value, and gain/loss.
7. Use the MAX and MIN functions to determine the highest and lowest values for the number of shares, initial price per share, initial cost per share, current price per share, current value, gain/loss, and percent gain/loss.

Web Requirements: Use the Web query feature of Excel to get real-time stock quotes for the stocks owned by Greenback Stock Club (Figure 2-1b on the previous page).

Starting and Customizing Excel

To start and customize Excel, Windows must be running. Perform the following steps to start Excel. Once the Excel window opens, steps 3 through 5 close the task pane, minimize the Language bar, and ensure that the Standard and Formatting toolbars display on two rows.

TO START AND CUSTOMIZE EXCEL

1 Click the Start button on the Windows taskbar, point to Programs on the Start menu, and then click Microsoft Excel on the Programs submenu.

2 If the Excel window is not maximized, double-click its title bar to maximize it.

3 If the New Workbook task pane displays, click the Show at startup check box at the bottom of the task pane to remove the check mark and then click the Close button in the upper-right corner to close the task pane.

4 If the Language bar displays, click its Minimize button.

5 If the Standard and Formatting toolbars display on one row, click the Toolbar Options button on the right side of either toolbar and then click Show Buttons on Two Rows on the Toolbar Options menu.

The Excel window with the Standard and Formatting toolbars on two rows displays as shown in Figure 2-1a on the previous page.

Entering the Titles and Numbers into the Worksheet

The worksheet title in Figure 2-1a on the previous page is centered across columns A through J in row 1. Because the centered text first must be entered into the left-most column of the area across which it is centered, it will be entered into cell A1, as shown in the following steps.

TO ENTER THE WORKSHEET TITLE

1 Select cell A1. Type Greenback Stock Club in the cell.

2 Press the DOWN ARROW key.

The worksheet title displays in cell A1 as shown in Figure 2-2 on page E 2.09.

The column titles in row 2 begin in cell A2 and extend through cell J2. As shown in Figure 2-1a, the column titles in row 2 include multiple lines of text. To start a new line in a cell, press ALT+ENTER after each line, except for the last line, which is completed by clicking the Enter box, pressing the ENTER key, or pressing one of the arrow keys. When you see ALT+ENTER in a step, while holding down the ALT key, press the ENTER key and then release both keys.

The stock names and the row titles Total, Average, Highest, and Lowest in column A begin in cell A3 and continue down to cell A14.

The stock club's investments are summarized in Table 2-1. These numbers are entered into rows 3 through 10. The steps required to enter the column titles, stock names and symbols, total row titles, and numbers as shown in Figure 2-2 on page E 2.09 are explained in the remainder of this section.

Table 2-1 Greenback Stock Club Portfolio					
STOCK	*SYMBOL*	*DATE ACQUIRED*	*SHARES*	*INITIAL PRICE PER SHARE*	*CURRENT PRICE PER SHARE*
Alcoa	AA	01/03/2000	750	40.125	28.75
Boeing	BA	09/02/1998	975	33.00	65.625
Citigroup	C	10/11/1996	850	12.25	48.875
Exxon Mobil	XOM	03/03/1997	925	52.00	78.5
Intl Paper	IP	11/17/1999	300	48.375	26.5
Merck	MRK	12/23/1996	875	37.25	89.75
Wal-Mart	WMT	12/21/1998	157	151.375	44.25
Walt Disney	DIS	07/12/1996	600	17.50	34.875

TO ENTER THE COLUMN TITLES

1 With cell A2 selected, type Stock and then press the RIGHT ARROW key.

2 Type Symbol and then press the RIGHT ARROW key.

3 Type Date and then press ALT+ENTER. Type Acquired and then press the RIGHT ARROW key.

4 Type Shares and then press the RIGHT ARROW key.

5 Type Initial and then press ALT+ENTER. Type Price and then press ALT+ENTER. Type Per Share and then press the RIGHT ARROW key.

6 Type Initial and then press ALT+ENTER. Type Cost and then press the RIGHT ARROW key.

7 Type Current and then press ALT+ENTER. Type Price and then press ALT+ENTER. Type Per Share and then press the RIGHT ARROW key.

8 Type Current and then press ALT+ENTER. Type Value and then press the RIGHT ARROW key.

9 Type Gain/Loss and press the RIGHT ARROW key.

10 Type Percent and then press ALT+ENTER. Type Gain/Loss and then click cell A3.

The column titles display as shown in row 2 of Figure 2-2. When you press ALT+ENTER to add more lines to a cell, Excel automatically increases the height of the entire row.

The stock data in Table 2-1 on the previous page includes a date on which each stock was acquired. Excel considers a date to be a number and, therefore, displays it right-aligned in the cell.

The following steps describe how to enter the stock data shown in Table 2-1 on the previous page, which includes dates. The dates in column C will be formatted later in this project to a two-digit year.

TO ENTER THE STOCK DATA

1 With cell A3 selected, type Alcoa and then press the RIGHT ARROW key. Type AA and then press the RIGHT ARROW key.

2 With cell C3 selected, type 01/03/2000 and then press the RIGHT ARROW key. Type 750 and then press the RIGHT ARROW key.

3 With cell E3 selected, type 40.125 and then press the RIGHT ARROW key twice. Type 28.75 and then press the ENTER key.

4 Click cell A4. Enter the data in Table 2-1 for the seven remaining stocks in rows 4 through 10.

The stock data displays in rows 3 through 10 as shown in Figure 2-2.

TO ENTER THE TOTAL ROW TITLES

1 Click cell A11. Type Total and then press the DOWN ARROW key. With cell A12 selected, type Average and then press the DOWN ARROW key.

2 With cell A13 selected, type Highest and then press the DOWN ARROW key. With cell A14 selected, type Lowest and then press the ENTER key. Click cell F3.

The total row titles display as shown in Figure 2-2.

More *About*

Two-Digit Years

When you enter a two-digit year value, and the Short date format under Regional Options in Control Panel is set to M/dd/yyyy, Excel changes a two-digit year prior to 30 to 20xx and a two-digit year of 30 and greater to 19xx. Use four-digit years to ensure that Excel interprets year values the way you intend.

More *About*

Entering Numbers into a Range

An efficient way to enter data into a range of cells, is first to select a range. Enter the number that you want to assign to the upper-left cell of the range. Excel responds by entering the value and moving the active cell selection down one cell. When you enter the last value in the first column, Excel moves to the top of the next column.

Entering Formulas

The initial cost for each stock, which displays in column F, is equal to the number of shares in column D times the initial price per share in column E. Thus, the initial cost for Alcoa in cell F3 is obtained by multiplying 750 (cell D3) times 40.125 (cell E3).

One of the reasons Excel is such a valuable tool is that you can assign a **formula** to a cell and Excel will calculate the result. Consider, for example, what would happen if you had to multiply 750 × 40.125 and then manually enter the result, 30093.75, in cell F3. Every time the values in cells D3 and E3 changed, you would have to recalculate the product and enter the new value in cell F3. By contrast, if you enter a formula in cell F3 to multiply the values in cells D3 and E3, Excel recalculates the product whenever new values are entered into those cells and displays the result in cell F3. Complete the following steps to enter the initial cost formula in cell F3 using the keyboard.

FIGURE 2-2

 To Enter a Formula Using the Keyboard

More *About*

Automatic Recalculation

Every time you enter a value into a cell in the worksheet, Excel recalculates all formulas. You can change to manual recalculation by clicking Options on the Tools menu and then clicking Manual on the Calculation sheet. In manual calculation mode, press F9 to recalculate.

1 **With cell F3 selected, type =d3*e3 in the cell.**

The formula displays in the formula bar and in cell F3 (Figure 2-3). Excel displays colored borders around the cells referenced in the formula.

FIGURE 2-3

2 **Press the RIGHT ARROW key twice to select cell H3.**

Instead of displaying the formula in cell F3, Excel completes the arithmetic operation indicated by th e formula and displays the result, 30093.75 (Figure 2-4).

Microsoft Excel - Book1

File Edit View Insert Format Tools Data Window Help

Type a question for help

value of formula (750 x 40.125)

100%

Arial 10 B I U $ %

H3

	A	B	C	D	E	F	G	H	I	J	K	L
1	Greenback Stock Club											
2	Stock	Symbol	Date Acquired	Shares	Initial Price Per Share	Initial Cost	Current Price Per Share	Current Value	Gain/Loss	Percent Gain/Loss		
3	Alcoa	AA	1/3/2000	750	40.125	30093.75	28.75					
4	Boeing	BA	9/2/1998	975	33		65.625					
5	Citigroup	C	10/11/1996	850	12.25		48.875					
6	Exxon Mol	XOM	3/3/1997	925	52		78.5					
7	Intl Paper	IP	11/17/1999	300	48.375		26.5					
8	Merck	MRK	12/23/1996	875	37.25		89.75					
9	Wal-Mart	WMT	12/21/1998	157	151.375		44.25					
10	Walt Disne	DIS	7/12/16	600								

active cell is H3 after typing formula and pressing RIGHT ARROW key twice

FIGURE 2-4

The equal sign (=) preceding d3*e3 is an important part of the formula: it alerts Excel that you are entering a formula or function and not text. Because the most common error is to mistakenly reference the wrong cell in a formula, Excel colors the borders of the cells selected to visually show which cells you are referencing. The coloring helps in the reviewing process to ensure the cell references are correct.

The asterisk (*) following d3 is the arithmetic operator that directs Excel to perform the multiplication operation. The valid Excel arithmetic operators are described in Table 2-2.

Table 2-2 Summary of Arithmetic Operators

ARITHMETIC OPERATOR	MEANING	EXAMPLE OF USAGE	MEANING
−	Negation	−95	Negative 95
%	Percentage	=65%	Multiplies 65 by 0.01
^	Exponentiation	=3 ^ 4	Raises 3 to the fourth power, which in this example is equal to 81
*	Multiplication	=12.4 * D5	Multiplies the contents of cell D5 by 12.4
/	Division	=J2 / J4	Divides the contents of cell J2 by the contents of cell J4
+	Addition	=2 + 6	Adds 2 and 6
−	Subtraction	=H12 − 29	Subtracts 29 from the contents of cell H12

You can enter the cell references in formulas in uppercase or lowercase, and you can add spaces before and after arithmetic operators to make the formulas easier to read. That is, =d3*e3 is the same as =d3 * e3, =D3 * e3, or =D3 * E3.

Order of Operations

When more than one operator is involved in a formula, Excel follows the same basic order of operations that you use in algebra. Moving from left to right in a formula, the **order of operations** is as follows: first negation (−), then all percentages (%), then all exponentiations (^), then all multiplications (*) and divisions (/), and finally, all additions (+) and subtractions (−).

You can use **parentheses** to override the order of operations. For example, if Excel follows the order of operations, 5 * 6 − 2 equals 28. If you use parentheses, however, to change the formula to 5 * (6 − 2), the result is 20, because the parentheses instruct Excel to subtract 2 from 6 before multiplying by 5. Table 2-3 illustrates several examples of valid formulas and explains the order of operations.

The first formula (=d3*e3) in the worksheet was entered into cell F3 using the keyboard. The next section shows you how to enter the formulas in cells H3 and I3 using the mouse to select cell references in a formula.

Table 2-3	Examples of Excel Formulas
FORMULA	**REMARK**
=K3	Assigns the value in cell K3 to the active cell.
=24 + − 4^2	Assigns the sum of 24 + 16 (or 40) to the active cell.
=4 * D4 or =D4 * 4 or =(4 * D4)	Assigns four times the contents of cell D4 to the active cell.
=25% * 8	Assigns the product of 0.25 times 8 (or 2) to the active cell.
= − (Q5 * Z17)	Assigns the negative value of the product of the values contained in cells Q5 and Z17 to the active cell.
=3 * (M3 − P2)	Assigns the product of three times the difference between the values contained in cells M3 and P2 to the active cell.
=K5 / Y7 − D6 * L9 + W4 ^ V10	From left to right: first exponentiation (W4 ^ V10), then division (K5 / Y7), then multiplication (D6 * L9), then subtraction (K5 / Y7) − (D6 * L9), and finally addition (K5 / Y7 − D6 * L9) + (W4 ^ V10). If cells K5 = 10, D6 = 6, L9 = 2, W4 = 5, V10 = 2, and Y7 = 2, then Excel assigns the active cell the value 18; that is, 10 / 2 − 6 * 2 + 5 ^ 2 = 18.

Entering Formulas Using Point Mode

In the worksheet shown in Figure 2-1a on page E 2.05, the current value of each stock displays in column H. The current value for Alcoa in cell H3 is equal to the number of shares in cell D3 times the current price per share in cell G3. The gain/loss for Alcoa in cell I3 is equal to the current value in cell H3 minus the initial cost in cell F3. The percent gain/loss for Alcoa in cell J3 is equal to the gain/loss in cell I3 divided by the initial cost in cell F3.

Instead of using the keyboard to enter the formulas =D3*G3 in cell H3, =H3 − F3 in cell I3, and =I3/F3 in cell J3, you can use the mouse and Point mode to enter these three formulas. **Point mode** allows you to select cells for use in a formula by using the mouse. Perform the following steps to enter formulas using Point mode.

More About

Using Point Mode

Point mode allows you to create formulas using the mouse. You can use the on-screen keyboard and mouse to enter the arithmetic operators. The on-screen keyboard is available through the Language bar (see Appendix B). Thus, with Excel you can enter entire formulas without ever touching the keyboard.

Steps **To Enter Formulas Using Point Mode**

1 **With cell H3 selected, type = (equal sign) to begin the formula and then click cell D3.**

Excel surrounds cell D3 with a marquee and appends D3 to the equal sign (=) in cell H3 (Figure 2-5).

FIGURE 2-5

2 **Type * (asterisk) and then click cell G3.**

Excel surrounds cell G3 with a marquee and appends G3 to the asterisk (*) in cell H3 (Figure 2-6).

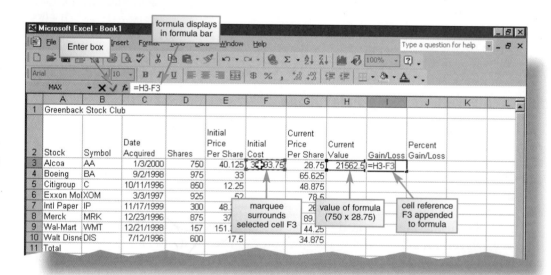

FIGURE 2-6

3 **Click the Enter box. Click cell I3. Type = (equal sign) and then click cell H3. Type – (minus sign) and then click cell F3.**

Excel determines the product of =D3*G3 and displays the result, 21562.5, in cell H3. The formula =H3 – F3 displays in cell I3 and in the formula bar (Figure 2-7).

FIGURE 2-7

4 **Click the Enter box. Click cell J3. Type = (equal sign) and then click cell I3. Type / (division sign) and then click cell F3. Click the Enter box.**

The Gain/Loss for Alcoa, -8531.25, displays in cell I3 and the Percent Gain/Loss for Alcoa, -0.28349, displays in cell J3 (Figure 2-8). The -0.28349 represents approximately -28.35%.

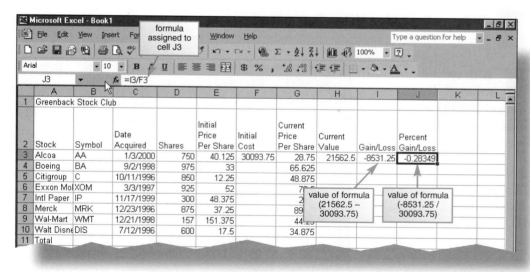

FIGURE 2-8

Depending on the length and complexity of the formula, using Point mode to enter formulas often is faster and more accurate than using the keyboard. In some instances, you may want to combine the keyboard and mouse when entering a formula in a cell. You can use the keyboard to begin the formula, for example, and then use the mouse to select a range of cells.

The true value assigned by Excel to cell J3 from the division operation in Step 4 is -0.283489097. While all the decimal places do not display in Figure 2-8, Excel maintains all of them for computational purposes. Thus, if cell J3 is referenced in a formula, the value used for computational purposes is -0.283489097, not -0.28349. Excel displays the value in cell J3 as -0.28349 because the width of the cell will hold only 7 digits, the minus sign, and the decimal point. If you increase the width of column J, then the true value -0.283489097 displays. It is important to recognize this difference between the displayed value and the actual value to better understand why in some cases the sum of a column is a penny off from the expected value.

Copying the Formulas Using the Fill Handle

The four formulas for Alcoa in cells F3, H3, I3, and J3 now are complete. You could enter the same four formulas one at a time for the seven remaining stocks, Boeing, Citigroup, Exxon Mobil, International Paper, Merck, Wal-Mart, and Walt Disney. A much easier method of entering the formulas, however, is to select the formulas in row 3 and then use the fill handle to copy them through row 10. Recall from Project 1 that the fill handle is a small rectangle in the lower-right corner of the active cell. Perform the following steps to copy the formulas.

More About

Formulas

To change a formula to a number (constant), select the cell, click the Copy button on the Standard toolbar, click the Past button arrow on the Standard toolbar, click Paste Special, click Values, and click the OK button.

 To Copy Formulas Using the Fill Handle

1 Click cell F3 and then point to the fill handle. Drag the fill handle down through cell F10 and continue to hold down the mouse button.

A border surrounds the source and destination areas (range F3:F10) and the mouse pointer changes to a cross hair (Figure 2-9).

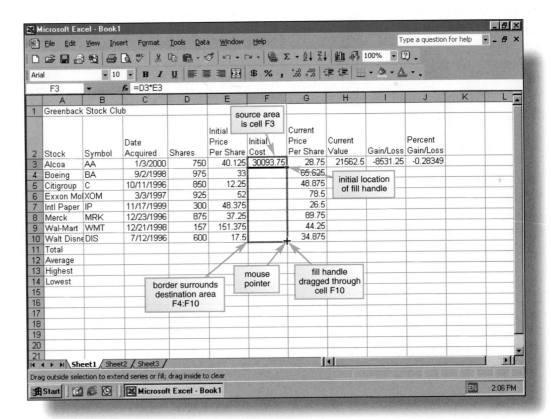

FIGURE 2-9

2 **Release the mouse button. Select the range H3:J3 and then point to the fill handle.**

Excel copies the formula =D3*E3 to the range F4:F10 and displays the initial costs for the remaining seven stocks. The range H3:J3 is selected (Figure 2-10). The Auto Fill Options button displays, which allows you to refine the copy.

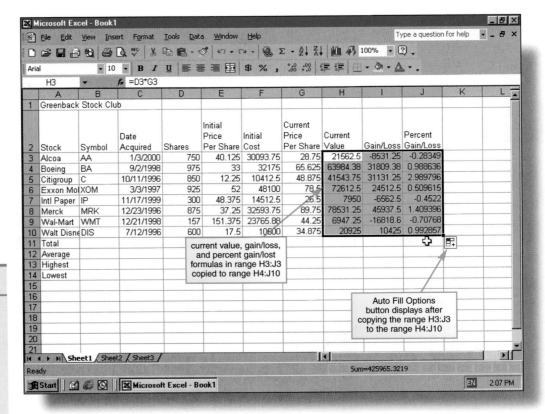

FIGURE 2-10

3 **Drag the fill handle down through the range H4:J10.**

Excel copies the three formulas =D3*G3 in cell H3, =H3-F3 in cell I3, and =I3/F3 in cell J3 to the range H4:J10 and displays the current value, gain/loss, and percent gain/loss for the remaining seven stocks (Figure 2-11).

Other Ways

1. Select source area, click Copy button on Standard toolbar, select destination area, click Paste button on Standard toolbar

2. Select source area, on Edit menu click Copy, select destination area, on Edit menu click Paste

3. Select source area, right-click source area, click Copy on shortcut menu, select destination area, right-click destination area, click Paste on shortcut menu

4. Select source area, in Voice Command mode say, "Copy," select destination area, in Voice Command mode say, "Paste"

FIGURE 2-11

Recall that when you copy a formula, Excel adjusts the cell references so the new formulas contain references corresponding to the new location and performs calculations using the appropriate values. Thus, if you copy downward, Excel adjusts the row portion of cell references. If you copy across, then Excel adjusts the column portion of cell references. These cell references are called **relative references**.

Smart Tags

A **smart tag** is a button that automatically appears on the screen, such as the Auto Fill Options button in Figures 2-10 and 2-11. Table 2-4 summarizes the smart tags available in Excel. When you see a smart tag, click it to display a menu of options that you can choose from to modify the previous operation or obtain additional information.

With some of the smart tags, such as the Trace Error and Smart Tag Actions, Excel notifies you that it is available by displaying a smart tag indicator in a cell. A smart tag indicator is a small triangle located in one of the corners of the cell. If you select a cell with a smart tag indicator, the smart tag button displays.

Table 2-4	Smart Tags in Excel	
BUTTON	**NAME**	**MENU FUNCTION**
	Auto Fill Options	Gives options for how to fill cells following a fill operation, such as dragging the fill handle
	AutoCorrect Options	Undoes an automatic correction, stops future automatic corrections of this type, or displays the AutoCorrect Options dialog box
	Insert Options	Lists formatting options following an insert of cells, rows, or columns
	Paste Options	Specifies how moved or pasted items should display, e.g., with original formatting, without formatting, or with different formatting
	Smart Tag Actions	Lists information options for a cell containing data recognized by Excel, such as a stock symbol (see In the Lab 3, Part 4 on Page E 2.77)
	Trace Error	Lists error checking options following the assignment of an invalid formula to a cell

Determining the Totals Using the AutoSum Button

The next step is to determine the totals in row 11 for the initial cost in column F, current value in column H, and gain/loss in column I. To determine the total initial cost in column F, you must sum cells F3 through F10. To do so, you can enter the function =sum(f3:f10) in cell F11, or you can select cell F11 and then click the AutoSum button on the Standard toolbar twice. Similar SUM functions or the AutoSum button can be used in cells H11 and I11 to determine total current value and total gain/loss, respectively. Recall from Project 1 that when you select one cell and use the AutoSum button, you must click the button twice. If you select a range, then you need only click the AutoSum button once.

TO DETERMINE TOTALS USING THE AUTOSUM BUTTON

1 Select cell F11. Click the AutoSum button twice. (Do not double-click.)

2 Select the range H11:I11. Click the AutoSum button.

The three totals display in row 11 as shown in Figure 2-12.

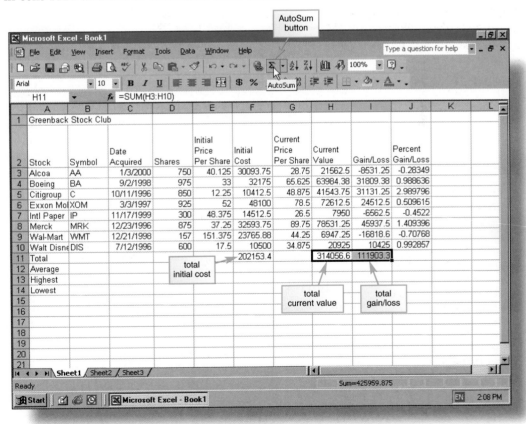

FIGURE 2-12

More About

Selecting a Range

If you dislike dragging to select a range, press F8 and use the arrow keys to select one corner of the range and then the cell diagonally opposite it in the proposed range. Make sure you press F8 to turn selection off after you are finished with the range or you will continue to select ranges.

Rather than using the AutoSum button to calculate column totals individually, you can select all three cells before clicking the AutoSum button to calculate all three column totals at one time. To select the nonadjacent range F11, H11, and I11, select cell F11, and then, while holding down the CTRL key, drag through the range H11:I11. Next, click the AutoSum button.

Determining the Total Percent Gain/Loss

With the totals in row 11 determined, you can copy the percentage gain/loss formula in cell J10 to cell J11 as shown in the following steps.

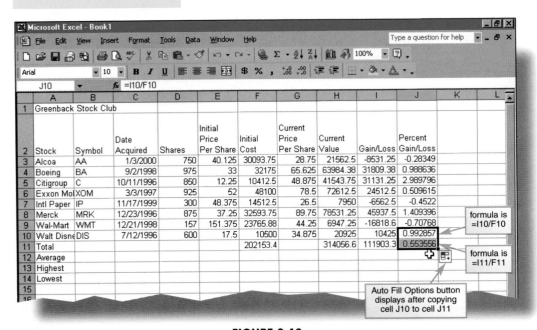

FIGURE 2-13

TO DETERMINE THE TOTAL PERCENT GAIN/LOSS

1 Select cell J10 and then point to the fill handle.

2 Drag the fill handle down through cell J11.

The formula, =I10/F10, in cell J10 is copied to cell J11. The resultant formula in cell J11 is =I11/F11, which shows a total club gain on the club's holdings of 0.553556 or 55.3556% (Figure 2-13).

The formula was not copied to cell J11 when cell J3 was copied to the range J4:J10 because both cells involved in the computation (I11 and F11) were blank, or zero, at the time. A **blank cell** in Excel has a numerical value of zero, which would have resulted in an error message in cell J11. Once the totals were determined, both cells I11 and F11 (especially F11, because it is the divisor) had non-zero numerical values.

More About

Formulas and Functions

For more information on entering formulas and functions, visit the Excel 2002 More About Web page (scsite.com/ex2002/more.htm) and click using Formulas and Functions.

Using the AVERAGE, MAX, and MIN Functions

The next step in creating the Greenback Stock Club worksheet is to compute the average, highest value, and lowest value for the number of shares in the range D12:D14 using the AVERAGE, MAX, and MIN functions. Once the values are determined for column D, the entries can be copied across to the other columns.

Excel includes prewritten formulas called **functions** to help you compute these statistics. A function takes a value or values, performs an operation, and returns a result to the cell. The values that you use with a function are called **arguments**. All functions begin with an equal sign and include the arguments in parentheses after the function name. For example, in the function =AVERAGE(D3:D10), the function name is AVERAGE, and the argument is the range D3:D10.

With Excel, you can enter functions using one of six methods: (1) the keyboard or mouse; (2) the Insert Function box on the formula bar; (3) the AutoSum menu; (4) the Function command on the Insert menu; (5) type equal sign in cell and then select function from Name box area in formula bar (Figure 2-14); and (6) Voice Command mode. The method you choose will depend on your typing skills and whether you can recall the function name and required arguments. In the following pages, each of the first three methods will be used. The keyboard and mouse will be used to determine the average number of shares (cell D12). The AutoSum menu will be used to determine the highest number of shares (cell D13). The Insert Function button on the formula bar will be used to determine the lowest number of shares (cell D14).

Determining the Average of a Range of Numbers

The AVERAGE function sums the numbers in the specified range and then divides the sum by the number of non-zero cells in the range. To determine the average of the numbers in the range D3:D10, use the AVERAGE function, as shown in the following steps.

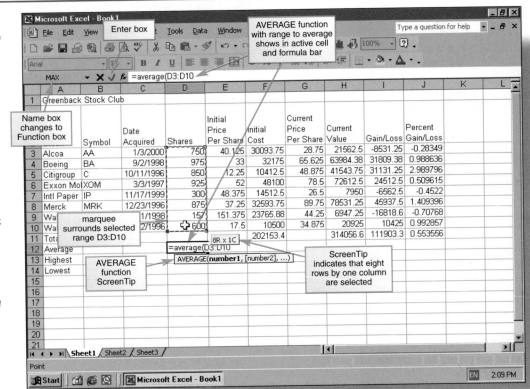

> **More About**
>
> ### Statistical Functions
>
> A blank cell usually is considered to be equal to zero. The statistical functions, however, ignore blank cells. Thus, in Excel, the average of three cells with values of 7, blank, and 5 is 6 or (7 + 5) / 2 and not 4 or (7 + 0 + 5) /3.

To Determine the Average of a Range of Numbers Using the Keyboard and Mouse

Steps

1 **Select cell D12. Type** =average(**in the cell. Click cell D3, the first endpoint of the range to average. Drag through cell D10, the second endpoint of the range to average.**

A marquee surrounds the range D3:D10. When you click cell D3, Excel appends cell D3 to the left parenthesis in the formula bar and surrounds cell D3 with a marquee. When you begin dragging, Excel appends to the argument a colon (:) and the cell reference of the cell where the mouse pointer is located (Figure 2-14).

FIGURE 2-14

2 Click the Enter box.

Excel computes the average of the eight numbers in the range D3:D10 and displays the result, 679, in cell D12 (Figure 2-15). Thus, the average number of shares owned in the eight companies is 679.

FIGURE 2-15

Other Ways

1. Click Insert Function box in formula bar, click AVERAGE function
2. Click AutoSum button arrow on Standard toolbar, click AVERAGE function
3. On Insert menu click Function, click AVERAGE function
4. In Voice Command mode say, "Insert, Function," [select Statistical category], in Voice Command mode say, "AVERAGE, OK"

The AVERAGE function requires that the range (the argument) be included within parentheses following the function name. Excel automatically appends the right parenthesis to complete the AVERAGE function when you click the Enter box or press the ENTER key. When you use Point mode, as in the previous steps, you cannot use the arrow keys to complete the entry. While in Point mode, the arrow keys change the selected cell reference in the range you are selecting.

Determining the Highest Number in a Range of Numbers

The next step is to select cell D13 and determine the highest (maximum) number in the range D3:D10. Excel has a function called the **MAX function** that displays the highest value in a range. Although you could enter the MAX function using the keyboard and Point mode as described in the previous steps, an alternative method to entering the function is to use the Insert Function box on the formula bar, as shown in the following steps.

To Determine the Highest Number in a Range of Numbers
Steps ## Using the Insert Function Box

1 **Select cell D13. Click the Insert Function box on the formula bar. When the Insert Function dialog box displays, click MAX in the Select a function box. Point to the OK button.**

The Insert Function dialog box displays (Figure 2-16).

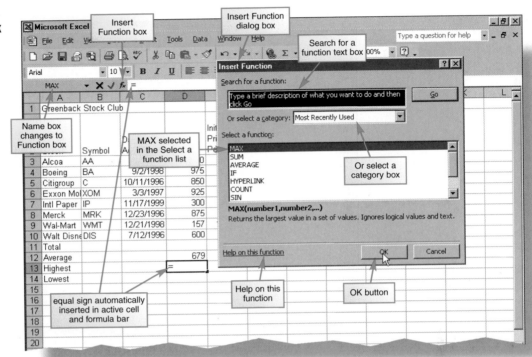

FIGURE 2-16

2 **Click the OK button. When the Function Arguments dialog box displays, type** d3:d10 **in the Number 1 box. Point to the OK button.**

The Function Arguments dialog box displays with the range d3:d10 entered in the Number 1 box (Figure 2-17). The completed MAX function displays in the formula bar, and the end of the function displays in the active cell, D13.

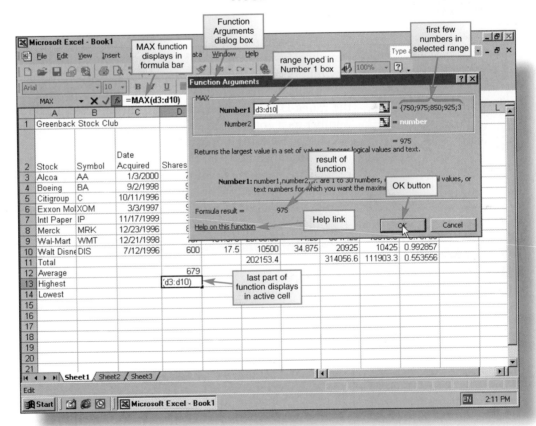

FIGURE 2-17

3   **Click the OK button.**

Excel determines that the highest value in the range D3:D10 is 975 (value in cell D4) and displays it in cell D13 (Figure 2-18).

FIGURE 2-18

Other Ways

1. Click Insert Function box in formula bar, click MAX function
2. On Insert menu click Function, click MAX function
3. Type MAX function in cell
4. In Voice Command mode say, "Insert, Function," [select Statistical category], in Voice Command mode say, "MAX, OK"

As shown in Figure 2-17 on the previous page, the Function Arguments dialog box displays the value the MAX function will return to cell D13. It also lists the first few numbers in the selected range, next to the Number 1 box.

In this example, rather than entering the MAX function, you easily could scan the range D3:D10, determine that the highest number of shares is 975, and enter the number as a constant in cell D13. The display would be the same as Figure 2-18. Because it contains a constant, cell D13 will continue to display 975, even if the values in the range D3:D10 change. If you use the MAX function, however, Excel will recalculate the highest value in the range D3:D10 each time a new value is entered into the worksheet. Manually determining the highest value in the range also would be more difficult if the club owned more stocks.

Determining the Lowest Number in a Range of Numbers

The next step is to enter the MIN function in cell D14 to determine the lowest (minimum) number in the range D3:D10. Although you can enter the MIN function using either of the methods used to enter the AVERAGE and MAX functions, the following steps show an alternative using the AutoSum menu on the Standard toolbar.

The Formula Palette

In Figure 2-17 on the previous page, you can drag the Function Arguments dialog box out of the way and drag through the desired range. You can also click the Collapse Dialog button to the right of the Number 1 box to hide the Formula Palette. After selecting the range, click the Collapse Dialog button a second time to display the Formula Palette.

To Determine the Lowest Number in a Range of Numbers
Steps Using the AutoSum Menu

1 Select cell D14. Click the AutoSum button arrow on the Standard toolbar. When the AutoSum menu displays, point to Min.

The AutoSum menu displays (Figure 2-19).

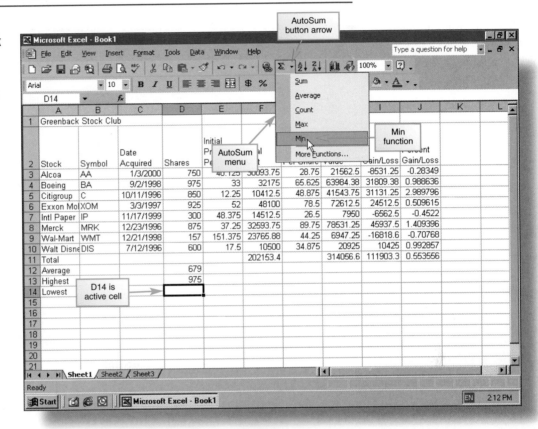

FIGURE 2-19

2 Click Min.

The function =MIN (D12:D13) displays in the formula bar and in cell D14. A marquee surrounds the range D12:D13 (Figure 2-20). The range D12:D13 automatically selected by Excel is not correct.

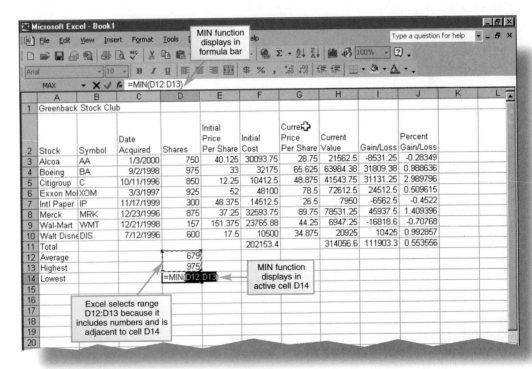

FIGURE 2-20

3 | **Click cell D3 and then drag through cell D10.**

The function in the formula bar and in cell D14 displays with the new range D3:D10 (Figure 2-21).

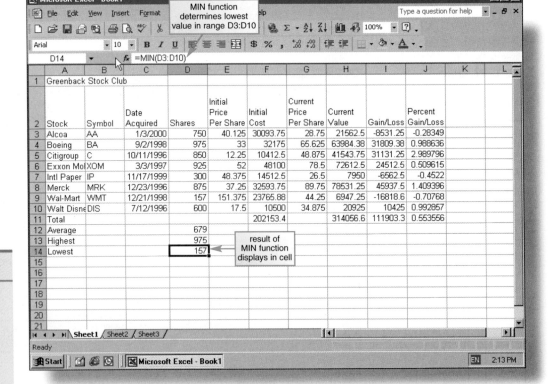

FIGURE 2-21

4 | **Click the Enter box.**

Excel determines that the lowest value in the range D3:D10 is 157 and displays it in cell D14 (Figure 2-22).

Other Ways

1. Click Insert Function box in formula bar, click MIN function
2. On Insert menu click Function, click MIN function
3. Type MIN function in cell
4. In Voice Command mode say, "Insert, Function," [select Statistical category], in Voice Command mode say, "MIN, OK"

FIGURE 2-22

You can see from the previous example that using the AutoSum menu allows you to enter one of the often-used functions into a cell easily without requiring you to memorize its name or the required arguments. If you need to use a function not available in the AutoSum menu and can not remember its name, then click More Functions in the list or click the Insert Function box on the formula bar.

Thus far, you have learned to use the SUM, AVERAGE, MAX, and MIN functions. In addition to these four functions, Excel has more than 400 additional functions that perform just about every type of calculation you can imagine. These functions are categorized in the Insert Function dialog box in Figure 2-16 on page E 2.19. To view the categories, click the Or select a category box arrow. To obtain a description of a selected function, select its name in the Insert Function dialog box. The description displays below the Select a function list in the dialog box.

Copying the AVERAGE, MAX, and MIN Functions

The next step is to copy the AVERAGE, MAX, and MIN functions in the range D12:D14 to the range E12:J14. The fill handle again will be used to complete the copy. The following steps illustrate this procedure.

More About

Functions

To obtain a summary list of all the functions available by category in Excel, click the Help button on the Standard toolbar, click the Index tab on the left side of the window, type function in the Type keywords text box, click the Search button, click Worksheet functions listed by category in the Choose a topic list. Click each category on the right side of the window. Click the Print button for a printed copy.

 Steps

To Copy a Range of Cells across Columns to an Adjacent Range Using the Fill Handle

1 **Select the range D12:D14. Drag the fill handle in the lower-right corner of the selected range through cell J14 and continue to hold down the mouse button.**

Excel displays an outline around the source and destination areas (range D12:J14) as shown in Figure 2-23.

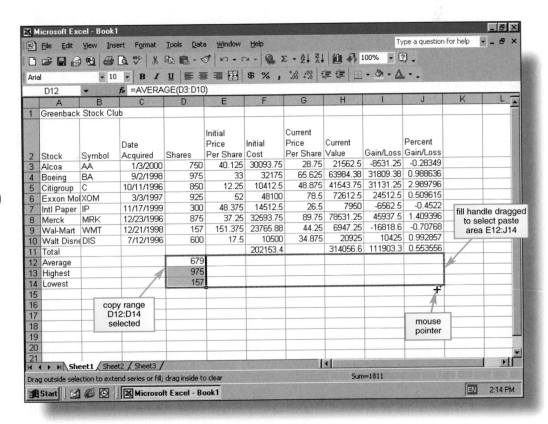

FIGURE 2-23

2 Release the mouse button.

Excel copies the three functions to the range E12:J14 (Figure 2-24). The Auto Fill Options button displays, which allows you to refine the copy.

AVERAGE, MAX, and MIN functions in range D12:D14 copied to range E12:J14

Auto Fill Options button

FIGURE 2-24

3 Select cell J12 and press the DELETE key to delete the average of the percent gain/loss.

Cell J12 is blank (Figure 2-25).

percents in range J3:J10 cannot be averaged

FIGURE 2-25

Other Ways

1. Select source area and point to border of range, while holding down CTRL key, drag copy area to destination area
2. Select source area, on Edit menu click Copy, select destination area, on Edit menu click Paste
3. Right-click source area, click Copy on shortcut menu, right-click destination area, click Paste
4. Select source area, press CTRL+C, select destination area, press CTRL+V
5. Select source area, in Voice Command mode say, "Copy," [select destination area], in Voice Command mode say, "Paste"

The average of the percent gain/loss in cell J12 was deleted in Step 3 because an average of percents of this type is mathematically invalid.

Remember that Excel adjusts the ranges in the copied functions so each function refers to the column of numbers above it. Review the numbers in rows 12 through 14 in Figure 2-24. You should see that the functions in each column return the appropriate values, based on the numbers in rows 3 through 10 of that column.

Saving the Workbook

With the data and formulas entered into the workbook, the next step is to save the workbook using the file name Greenback Stock Club.

TO SAVE THE WORKBOOK

1 Click the Save button on the Standard toolbar.

2 When the Save As dialog box displays, type Greenback Stock Club in the File name text box.

3 If necessary, click 3½ Floppy (A:) in the Save in list. Click the Save button in the Save As dialog box.

Excel saves the workbook on the floppy disk in drive A using the file name Greenback Stock Club.

This concludes entering the data and formulas into the worksheet. After saving the file, the worksheet remains on the screen with the file name, Greenback Stock Club, on the title bar.

More About

File Types

Excel lets you save a workbook in over 30 different file formats, such as Microsoft Excel Workbook, text, Web page, XML Spreadsheet, Unicode Text, Lotus 1-2-3 format, dBASE format, Text (Macintosh), and many more. You choose the file format from the Save as type list at the bottom of the Save As dialog box. The different formats come in handy when you need to transfer the data in a workbook to another application package or to non-PC hardware.

Verifying Formulas Using Range Finder

One of the more common mistakes made with Excel is to include a wrong cell reference in a formula. An easy way to verify that a formula references the cells you want it to reference is to use Excel's Range Finder. **Range Finder** can be used to check which cells are being referenced in the formula assigned to the active cell. Range Finder allows you to make immediate changes to the cells referenced in a formula.

To use Range Finder to verify that a formula contains the intended cell references, double-click the cell with the formula you want to check. Excel responds by highlighting the cells referenced in the formula so you can check that the correct cells are being used. The following steps use Range Finder to check the formula in cell J3.

Steps To Verify a Formula Using Range Finder

1 **Double-click cell J3.**

Excel responds by displaying the cells in the worksheet referenced by the formula in cell J3 using different color borders (Figure 2-26). The different colors allow you to see easily which cells are being referenced by the formula in cell J3.

2 **Press the ESC key to quit Range Finder. Select cell A16.**

FIGURE 2-26

More About

Auditing Formulas

An alternative to using the Range Finder is to use the Formula Auditing command on the Tools menu. The Formula Auditing command displays a menu of auditing commands that give a more detailed analysis of formulas and offer different ways to view formulas. Another useful command on the Tools menu is the Error Checking command, which checks all formulas in a workbook to ensure they are referencing valid data.

Not only does Range Finder show you the cells referenced in the formula in cell J3, but you can drag the colored borders to other cells and Excel will change the cell references in the formula to the newly selected cells. If you use Range Finder to change cells referenced in a formula, press the ENTER key to complete the edit.

Formatting the Worksheet

Although the worksheet contains the appropriate data, formulas, and functions, the text and numbers need to be formatted to improve their appearance and readability.

In Project 1, you used the AutoFormat command to format the majority of the worksheet. This section describes how to change the unformatted worksheet in Figure 2-27a to the formatted worksheet in Figure 2-27b using the Formatting toolbar and Format Cells command.

(a) **Unformatted Worksheet**

(b) **Formatted Worksheet**

FIGURE 2-27

The following outlines the type of formatting that is required in Project 2:

1. Worksheet title
   a. Font type — bold Arial Black
   b. Font size — 36
   c. Font style — bold
   d. Alignment — center across columns A through J and center vertically
   e. Background color (range A1:J1) — green
   f. Font color — white
   g. Border — thick box border around range A1:J1

2. Column titles
   a. Font style — bold
   b. Alignment — center
   c. Border — bottom border on row 2

3. Data
   a. Alignment — center data in column B
   b. Format dates in column C to the mm/dd/yy format
   c. Numbers in top row (columns E through I in row 3) — Currency style
   d. Numbers below top row (rows 4 through 10) — Comma style
   e. Border — bottom double border on row 10

4. Total line
   a. Row title in cell A11 font Style — bold
   b. Numbers — Currency style with floating dollar sign

5. Function lines
   a. Row titles in range A12:A14 font style — bold
   b. Numbers — Currency style with floating dollar sign in columns E through I

6. Percentages in column J
   a. Numbers — Percentage style with two decimal places; if a cell in range J3:J10 is less than zero, then bold font and color background of cell red

7. Column widths
   a. Column A — 14.00 characters
   b. Columns B through E — best fit
   c. Columns F, H, and I — 12.00 characters
   d. Column G and J — 9.43

8. Row heights
   a. Row 1 — 61.50 points
   b. Rows 2 — 42.00 points
   c. Row 12 — 24.00 points
   d. Remaining rows — default

Except for vertically centering the worksheet title in row 1, the Date format assigned to the dates in column C, the Currency style assigned to the functions in rows 12 through 14, and the conditional formatting in column J, all of the listed formats can be assigned to cells using the Formatting toolbar and mouse.

Changing the Font and Centering the Worksheet Title

When developing presentation-quality worksheets, different fonts often are used in the same worksheet. Excel allows you to change the font of individual characters in a cell or all the characters in a cell, in a range of cells, or in the entire worksheet. To emphasize the worksheet title in cell A1, the font type, size, and style are changed and the worksheet title is centered as described in the steps on the next page.

More About

Choosing Colors

Knowing how people perceive colors helps you emphasize parts of your worksheet. Warmer colors (red and orange) tend to reach toward the reader. Cooler colors (blue, green, and violet) tend to pull away from the reader. Bright colors jump out of a dark background and are easiest to see. White or yellow text on a dark blue, green, purple, or black background is ideal.

More About

Toolbars

You can remove a button from a toolbar by holding down the ALT key and dragging it off the toolbar. See Appendix D to reset a toolbar to its default settings.

More About

Font Colors

Excel has the Cycle Font Color button that cycles through the font colors in the selected cell. Click the button and the color of the font changes in the active cell. Keep clicking, and eventually the font colors repeat. To add the Cycle Font Color button to a toolbar, right-click a toolbar, click Customize, click the Commands tab, click Format in the Categories list, scroll down to the Cycle Font Color button in the Commands list, and drag it to a toolbar.

Steps | **To Change the Font and Center the Worksheet Title**

1 **Click cell A1. Click the Font box arrow on the Formatting toolbar. Point to Arial Black (or Impact if your system does not have Arial Black).**

The Font list displays with Arial Black highlighted (Figure 2-28).

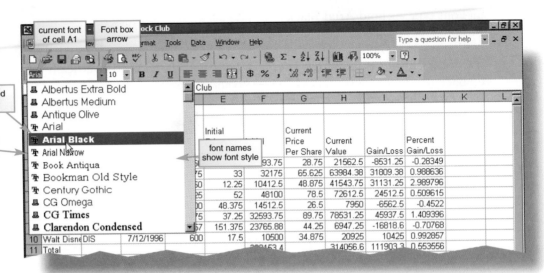

FIGURE 2-28

2 **Click Arial Black (or Impact). Click the Font Size box arrow on the Formatting toolbar and click 36 on the Font Size list. Click the Bold button.**

The text in cell A1 displays in 36-point Arial Black bold font. Excel automatically increases the height of row 1 so that the larger characters fit in the cells (Figure 2-29).

FIGURE 2-29

3 **Select the range A1:J1. Right-click the selection. Point to Format Cells on the shortcut menu.**

The shortcut menu displays (Figure 2-30).

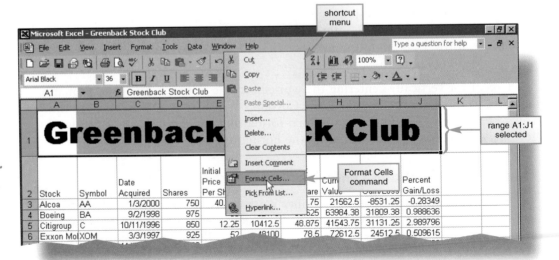

FIGURE 2-30

4 **Click Format Cells on the shortcut menu. When the Format Cells dialog box displays, click the Alignment tab. Click the Horizontal box arrow and select Center in the Horizontal list. Click the Vertical box arrow and select Center in the Vertical list. Click the Merge cells check box in the Text control area. Point to the OK button.**

The Format Cells dialog box displays as shown in Figure 2-31.

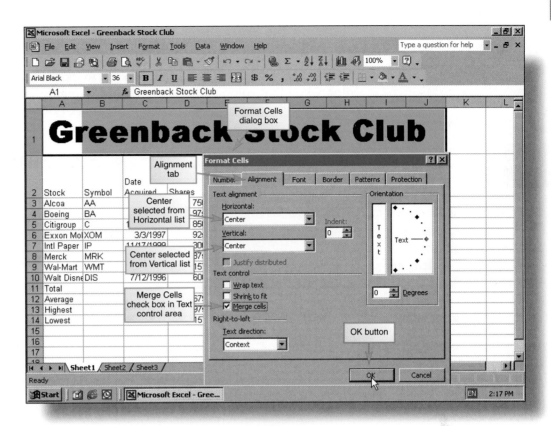

FIGURE 2-31

5 **Click the OK button.**

Excel merges the cells A1 through J1 to create a new cell A1 and centers the worksheet title across columns A through J and centers it vertically in row 1 (Figure 2-32).

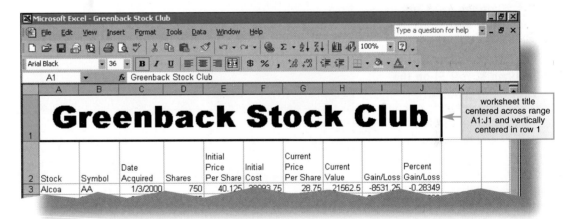

FIGURE 2-32

You can change a font type, size, or style at any time while the worksheet is active. Some Excel users prefer to change fonts before they enter any data. Others change the font while they are building the worksheet or after they have entered all the data.

In Project 1, the Merge and Center button on the Formatting toolbar was used to center the worksheet title across columns. Instead, Step 4 used the Alignment tab in the Format Cells dialog box, because the project also called for vertically centering the worksheet title in row 1.

Other Ways

1. On Format menu click Cells, click appropriate tab, select formats, click OK button

2. Right-click cell, click Format Cells on shortcut menu, click appropriate tab, select formats, click OK button

3. Press CTRL+1, click appropriate tab, select formats, click OK button

4. In Voice Command mode say, "Format, Cells, [desired tab], [desired format], OK"

Changing the Worksheet Title Background and Font Colors and Applying an Outline Border

The final formats to be assigned to the worksheet title are the green background color, white font color, and thick box border (Figure 2-27b on page E 2.26). Perform the following steps to complete the formatting of the worksheet title.

Steps | **To Change the Title Background and Font Colors and Apply an Outline Border**

1 **With cell A1 selected, click the Fill Color button arrow on the Formatting toolbar and then point to the color Green (column 4, row 2) on the Fill Color palette.**

The Fill Color palette displays (Figure 2-33).

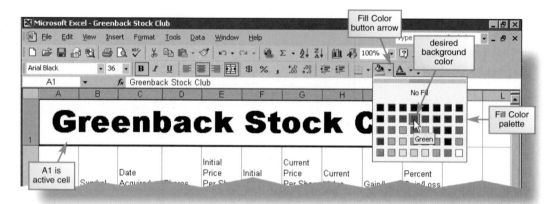

FIGURE 2-33

2 **Click the color Green. Click the Font Color button arrow on the Formatting toolbar. Point to the color White (column 8, row 5) on the Font Color palette.**

The background color of cell A1 changes from white to green, and the Font Color palette displays (Figure 2-34).

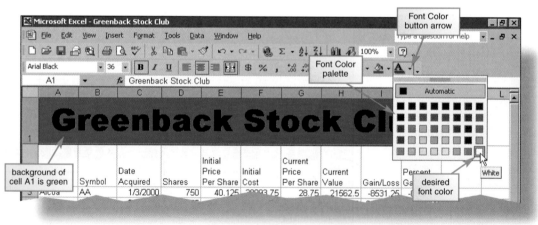

FIGURE 2-34

3 **Click the color White. Click the Borders button arrow on the Formatting toolbar and then point to the Thick Box Border button (column 4, row 3) on the Borders palette.**

The font in the worksheet title changes from black to white, and the Borders palette displays (Figure 2-35).

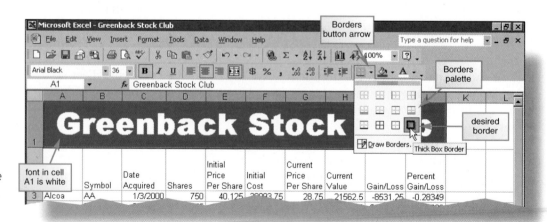

FIGURE 2-35

4 Click the Thick Box Border button. Click cell A2 to deselect cell A1.

Excel displays a thick box border around cell A1 (Figure 2-36).

FIGURE 2-36

Other Ways

1. On Format menu click Cells, click appropriate tab, click desired format, click OK button
2. Right-click range, click Format Cells on shortcut menu, click appropriate tab, click desired format, click OK button
3. Press CTRL+1, click appropriate tab, click desired format, click OK button
4. In Voice Command mode say, "Format, Cells, [desired tab], [desired format], OK"

You can remove borders, such as the thick box border around cell A1, by selecting the range and clicking the No Border button on the Borders palette. You can remove a background color by selecting the range, clicking the Fill Color button arrow on the Formatting toolbar, and clicking No Fill on the Fill Color palette. The same technique allows you to change the font color back to Excel's default, except you use the Font Color button arrow and click Automatic.

Applying Formats to the Column Titles

According to Figure 2-27b on page E 2.26, the column titles are bold, centered, and have a bottom border (underline). The following steps assign these formats to the column titles.

 Steps To Bold, Center, and Underline the Column Titles

1 Select the range A2:J2. Click the Bold button on the Formatting toolbar. Click the Center button on the Formatting toolbar. Click the Borders button arrow on the Formatting toolbar and then point to the Bottom Border button (column 2, row 1) on the Borders palette.

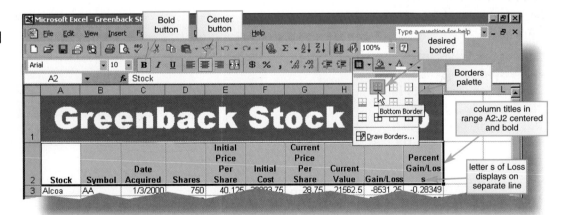

FIGURE 2-37

The column titles in row 2 are bold and centered (Figure 2-37). The Borders palette displays. The column titles in columns E and G display on four lines and the column title in J2 displays with the letter s from the word Loss on a line by itself. These column titles will be fixed later by increasing the column widths.

2 Click the Bottom Border button (column 2 row 1) on the Borders palette.

Excel adds a bottom border to the range A2:J2.

Other Ways

1. Same as 1 to 3 in the above Other Ways box
2. In Voice Command mode say, "Bold, Center, Borders, Bottom Border"

You can align the contents of cells in several different ways. Left alignment, center alignment, and right alignment are the more frequently used alignments. In fact, these three alignments are used so often that Excel has Align Left, Center, and Align Right buttons on the Formatting toolbar. In addition to aligning the contents of a cell horizontally, you also can align the contents of a cell vertically as shown earlier. In addition, you can rotate the contents of a cell to various angles (see the Format Cells dialog box in Figure 2-31 on page E 2.29).

Centering the Stock Symbols and Formatting the Dates and Numbers in the Worksheet

With the column titles formatted, the next step is to center the stock symbols in column B and format the dates in column C. If a cell entry is short, such as the stock symbols in column B, centering the entries within their respective columns improves the appearance of the worksheet. The following steps center the data in cells B3 to B10 and formats the dates in cells C3 to C10.

Adding Colors and Borders

Colors and borders can change a boring worksheet into an interesting and easy-to-read worksheet. Colors and borders can also be used to make important information stand out.

 Steps To Center Data in Cells and Format Dates

1 **Select the range B3:B10. Click the Center button on the Formatting toolbar.**

The stock symbols in column B are centered.

2 **Select the range C3:C10. Right-click the selected range and click Format Cells. When the Format Cells dialog box displays, click the Number tab, click Date in the Category list, click 03/14/01 in the Type list, and then point to the OK button.**

The Format Cells dialog box displays as shown in Figure 2-38.

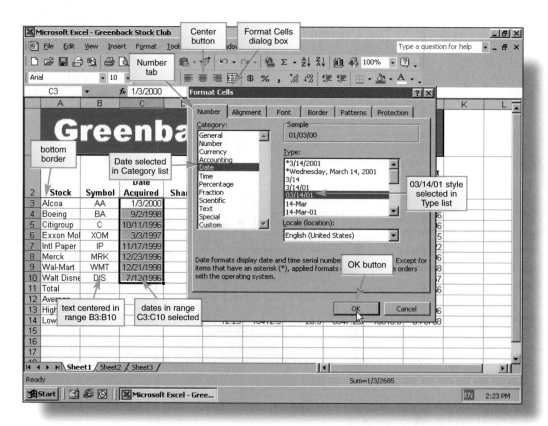

FIGURE 2-38

3 **Click the OK button. Select cell E3 to deselect the range C3:C10.**

The dates in column C display using the date format style mm/dd/yy (Figure 2-39).

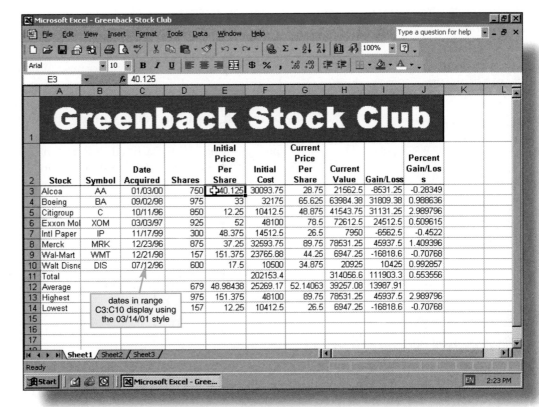

dates in range C3:C10 display using the 03/14/01 style

FIGURE 2-39

Rather than selecting the range B3:B10 in Step 1, you could have clicked the column B heading immediately above cell B1, and then clicked the Center button on the Formatting toolbar. In this case, all cells in column B down to cell B65536 would have been assigned center alignment. This same procedure could have been used to format the dates in column C.

Formatting Numbers Using the Formatting Toolbar

You can use the buttons on the Formatting toolbar to format numbers as dollar amounts, whole numbers with comma placement, and percentages. Customized numeric formats also can be assigned using the **Cells command** on the Format menu or the Format Cells command on the shortcut menu.

As shown in Figure 2-27(b) on page E 2.26, the worksheet is formatted to resemble an accounting report. For example, in columns E through I, the first row of numbers (row 3), the totals (row 11), and the rows below the totals (rows 13 and 14) display with dollar signs, while the remaining numbers (rows 4 through 10) in these columns do not. To display a dollar sign in a number, you should use the Currency style format.

Other **Ways**

1. On Format menu click Cells, click appropriate tab, click desired format, click OK button

2. Right-click range, click Format Cells on shortcut menu, click appropriate tab, click desired format, click OK button

3. Press CTRL+1, click appropriate tab, click desired format, click OK button

4. In Voice Command mode say, "Format, Cells, [desired tab], [desired format], OK"

Rotating and Fitting Text in Cells

Besides aligning text horizontally and vertically in a cell, you can rotate text and shrink text to fit in a cell. To rotate text or shrink text to fit in a cell, click Format Cells on the shortcut menu, click the Alignment tab, and then select the type of text control you want.

The **Currency style format** displays a dollar sign to the left of the number, inserts a comma every three positions to the left of the decimal point, and displays numbers to the nearest cent (hundredths place). The **Currency Style button** on the Formatting toolbar assigns the desired Currency style format. When you use the Currency Style button, Excel displays a **fixed dollar sign** to the far left in the cell, often with spaces between it and the first digit. To assign a **floating dollar sign** that displays immediately to the left of the first digit with no spaces, you must use the Cells command on the Format menu or the Format Cells command on the shortcut menu. The project specifications call for a fixed dollar sign to be assigned to the numbers in columns E through I in rows 3 and 11, and a floating dollar sign to be assigned to the monetary amounts in columns E through I in rows 12 through 14.

To display monetary amounts with commas and no dollar signs, you will want to use the Comma style format. The **Comma style format** inserts a comma every three positions to the left of the decimal point and displays numbers to the nearest hundredths (cents).

The following steps show how to assign formats using the Currency Style button and the Comma Style button on the Formatting toolbar. These steps also underline row 10 and bold the total row titles.

Steps — To Apply a Currency Style Format and Comma Style Format Using the Formatting Toolbar

1 Select the range E3:I3. While holding down the CTRL key, select the nonadjacent range F11:I11. Point to the Currency Style button on the Formatting toolbar.

The nonadjacent ranges display as shown in Figure 2-40.

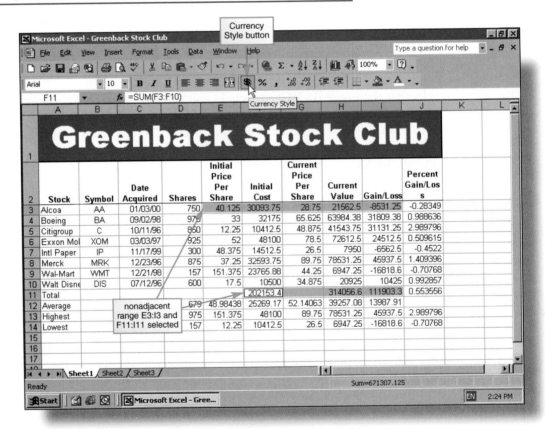

FIGURE 2-40

2 **Click the Currency Style button. Select the range E4:I10 and then point to the Comma Style button on the Formatting toolbar.**

Excel automatically increases the width of columns F, H, and I to best fit, so the numbers assigned the Currency style format will fit in the cells (Figure 2-41). The range E4:I10 is selected.

FIGURE 2-41

3 **Click the Comma Style button.**

Excel assigns the Comma style format to the range E4:I10.

4 **Click cell E3. Click the Increase Decimal button on the Formatting toolbar. Do the same to cell G3. Select the range E4:E10. Click the Increase Decimal button on the Formatting toolbar. Do the same to the range G4:G10. Click cell A10 to deselect the range G4:G10.**

The initial prices and current prices display with three decimal positions (Figure 2-42).

FIGURE 2-42

The **Increase Decimal button** on the Formatting toolbar is used to display additional decimal places in a cell. Each time you click the Increase Decimal button, Excel adds a decimal place to the selected cell. The **Decrease Decimal button** removes a decimal place from the selected cell each time it is clicked.

More About

Formatting Numbers as You Enter Them

You can format numbers when you enter them by entering a dollar sign ($), comma (,), or percent sign (%) as part of the number. For example, if you enter 1500, Excel displays 1500. However, if you enter $1500, Excel displays $1,500.

The Currency Style button assigns a fixed dollar sign to the numbers in the ranges E3:I3 and F11:I11. In each cell in these ranges, the dollar sign displays to the far left with spaces between it and the first digit in the cell. Excel automatically rounds a number to fit the selected format.

Underlining the Row above the Title Row and Bolding the Total Row Titles

The following steps add a bottom double border to row 10 and bolds the total row titles.

TO UNDERLINE THE ROW ABOVE THE TITLE ROW AND BOLD THE TOTAL ROW TITLES

1. Select the range A10:J10, click the Borders button arrow on the Formatting toolbar, and then click the Bottom Double Border (column 1, row 2) on the Borders palette.

2. Select the range A11:A14, click the Bold button on the Formatting toolbar. Select cell E12.

The row immediately above the total row has a double underline, signifying the last stock in the worksheet. The row titles in the range A11:A14 are bold (Figure 2-43).

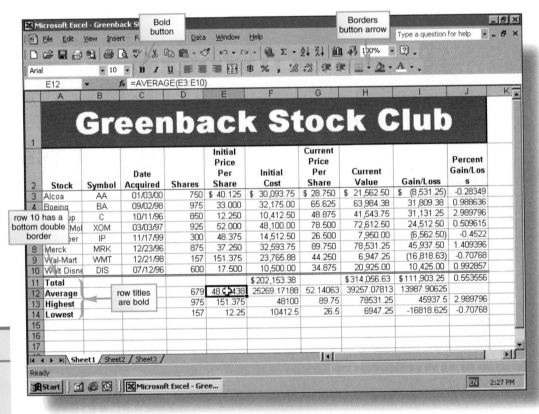

FIGURE 2-43

More About

Formatted Numbers in Calculations

The numbers you see on your screen may not be the same ones used in calculations. When a number has more decimal places than are showing on the screen because you formatted it, the actual number and not the displayed number is used in the computation.

Formatting Numbers Using the Format Cells Command on the Shortcut Menu

The following steps show you how to use the Format Cells command on the shortcut menu to apply the Currency style format with a floating dollar sign to the totals in the range E12:I14.

To Apply a Currency Style Format with a Floating Dollar Sign Using the Format Cells Command

1 **Select the range E12:I14. Right-click the selected range. Point to Format Cells on the shortcut menu.**

The shortcut menu displays (Figure 2-44).

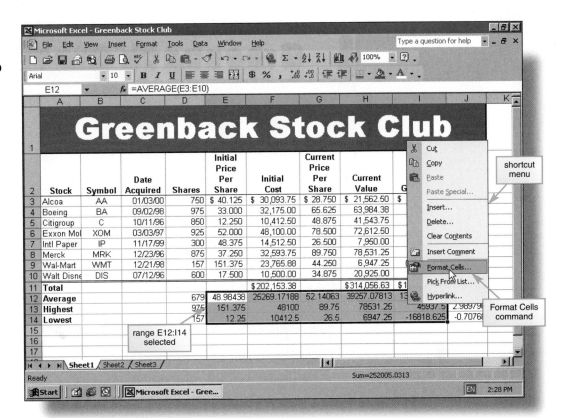

FIGURE 2-44

2 **Click Format Cells. Click the Number tab in the Format Cells dialog box. Click Currency in the Category list, click the third style ($1,234.10) in the Negative numbers list, and then point to the OK button.**

The Format Cells dialog box displays (Figure 2-45).

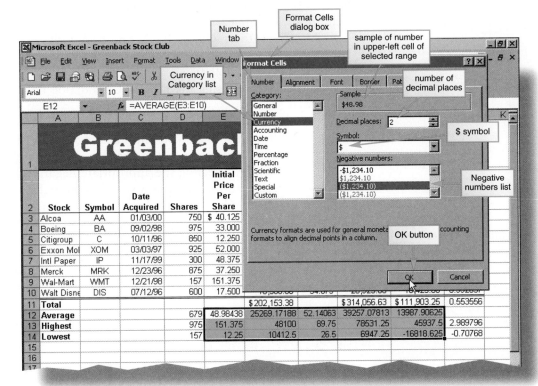

FIGURE 2-45

3 **Click the OK button.**

The worksheet displays with the totals in rows 12 through 14 assigned the Currency style format with a floating dollar sign (Figure 2-46).

FIGURE 2-46

Recall that a floating dollar sign always displays immediately to the left of the first digit, and the fixed dollar sign always displays on the left side of the cell. Cell E3, for example, has a fixed dollar sign, while cell E12 has a floating dollar sign. Also recall that, while cells E3 and E12 both were assigned a Currency style format, the Currency style was assigned to cell E3 using the Currency Style button on the Formatting toolbar. The result is a fixed dollar sign. The Currency style was assigned to cell E12 using the Format Cells dialog box and the result is a floating dollar sign.

As shown in Figure 2-45 on the previous page, you can choose from 12 categories of formats. Once you select a category, you can select the number of decimal places, whether or not a dollar sign should display, and how negative numbers should display. Selecting the appropriate negative numbers format in Step 2 is important, because doing so adds a space to the right of the number (as do the Currency Style and Comma Style buttons). Some of the available negative number formats do not align the numbers in the worksheet on the decimal points.

The negative number format selected in the previous set of steps displays in cell I14, which has a negative entry. The third selection in the Negative numbers list (Figure 2-45) purposely was chosen to agree with the negative number format assigned to cell I9 using the Comma Style button.

Formatting Numbers Using the Percent Style Button and Increase Decimal Button

The last entry in the worksheet that needs to be formatted is the percent gain/loss in column J. Currently, the numbers in column J display as a decimal fraction (-0.28349 in cell J3). Follow these steps to change to the Percent style format with two decimal places.

 Steps **To Apply a Percent Style Format**

1 **Select the range J3:J14. Click the Percent Style button on the Formatting toolbar.**

The numbers in column J display as a rounded whole percent.

2 **Click the Increase Decimal button on the Formatting toolbar twice.**

The numbers in column J display with two decimal places (Figure 2-47).

FIGURE 2-47

The **Percent Style button** on the Formatting toolbar is used to display a value determined by multiplying the cell entry by 100, rounding the result to the nearest percent, and adding a percent sign. For example, when cell J3 is formatted using the Percent Style and Increase Decimal buttons, the actual value -0.283489097 displays as -28.35%.

Other Ways

1. On Format menu click Cells, click Number tab, click Percentage in Category list, select format, click OK button

2. Right-click range, click Format Cells on shortcut menu, click Number tab, click Percentage in Category list, select format, click OK button

3. Press CTRL+1, click Number tab, click Percentage in Category list, select format, click OK button

4. Press CTRL+SHIFT+PERCENT SIGN (%)

5. In Voice Command mode say, "Format, Cells, Number, Percentage, OK"

Conditional Formatting

The last formatting requirement is to emphasize the negative percents in column J by formatting them in bold with a red background. The **Conditional Formatting command** on the Format menu will be used to complete this task.

Excel lets you apply formatting that appears only when the value in a cell meets conditions that you specify. This type of formatting is called **conditional formatting**. You can apply conditional formatting to a cell, a range of cells, the entire worksheet, or the entire workbook. Usually, you apply it to a range of cells that contains values you want to highlight if conditions warrant. For example, you can instruct Excel to bold and change the color of the background of a cell if the value in the cell meets a condition, such as being less than zero. Assume you assign the range J3:J10 the following condition:

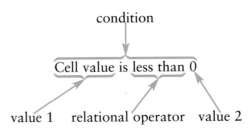

A **condition**, which is made up of two values and a relational operator, is true or false for each cell in the range. If the condition is true, then Excel applies the formatting. If the condition is false, then Excel suppresses the formatting. What makes conditional formatting so powerful is that the cell's appearance can change as you enter new values in the worksheet.

The following steps show how to assign conditional formatting to the range J3:J10. In this case, any cell value less than zero will cause the number in the cell to display in bold with a red background.

Steps **To Apply Conditional Formatting**

1 **Select the range J3:J10. Click Format on the menu bar and then point to Conditional Formatting.**

The Format menu displays (Figure 2-48).

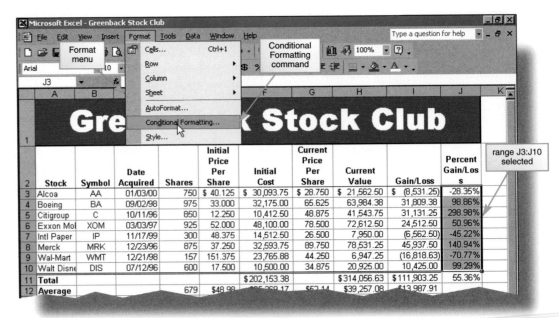

FIGURE 2-48

2 Click Conditional Formatting. When the Conditional Formatting dialog box displays, if necessary, click the leftmost text box arrow and then click Cell Value Is. Click the middle text box arrow and then click less than. Type 0 in the rightmost text box. Point to the Format button.

The Conditional Formatting dialog box displays as shown in Figure 2-49.

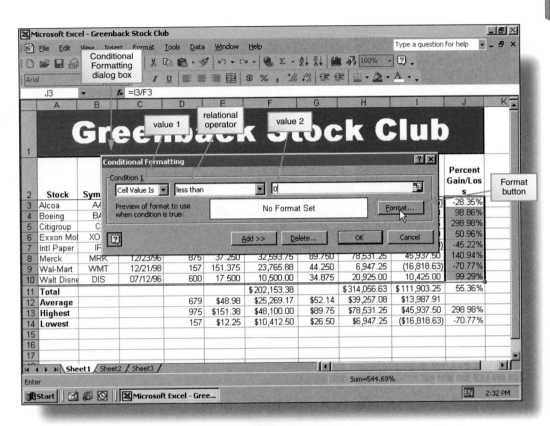

FIGURE 2-49

3 Click the Format button. When the Format Cells dialog box displays, click the Font tab and then click Bold in the Font style list. Click the Patterns tab. Click the color Red (column 1, row 3). Point to the OK button.

The Patterns sheet in the Format Cells dialog box displays as shown in Figure 2-50.

FIGURE 2-50

4 **Click the OK button. When the Conditional Formatting dialog box displays, point to the OK button.**

The Conditional Formatting dialog box displays as shown in Figure 2-51. In the middle of the dialog box, Excel displays a preview of the format to use when the condition is true.

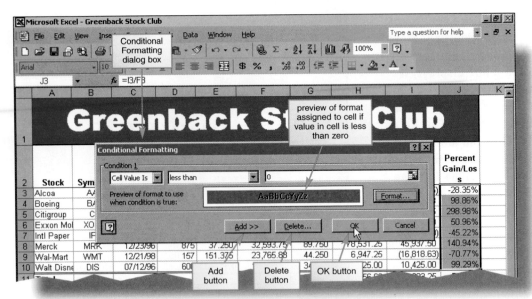

FIGURE 2-51

5 **Click the OK button. Click cell A16 to deselect the range J3:J10.**

Excel assigns the conditional format to the range J3:J10. Any negative value in this range displays in bold with a red background (Figure 2-52).

FIGURE 2-52

Other Ways

1. Press ALT+O, D
2. In Voice Command mode say, "Format, Conditional Formatting"

In Figure 2-51, the **preview box** in the Conditional Formatting dialog box shows the format that will be assigned to all cells in the range J3:J10 that have a value less than zero. This preview allows you to modify the format before you click the OK button. The **Add button** in the Conditional Formatting dialog box allows you to add up to two additional conditions. The **Delete button** allows you to delete one or more active conditions.

The middle text box in the Conditional Formatting dialog box contains the relational operator. The eight different relational operators from which you can choose are summarized in Table 2-5.

With the number formatting complete, the next step is to change the column widths and row heights to make the worksheet easier to read.

Table 2-5 Summary of Conditional Formatting Relational Operators	
RELATIONAL OPERATOR	**DESCRIPTION**
Between	Cell value is between two numbers
Not between	Cell value is not between two numbers
Equal to	Cell value is equal to a number
Not equal to	Cell value is not equal to a number
Greater than	Cell value is greater than a number
Less than	Cell value is less than a number
Greater than or equal to	Cell value is greater than or equal to a number
Less than or equal to	Cell value is less than or equal to a number

Changing the Widths of Columns and Heights of Rows

When Excel starts and the blank worksheet displays on the screen, all of the columns have a default width of 8.43 characters, or 64 pixels. A **character** is defined as a letter, number, symbol, or punctuation mark in 10-point Arial font, the default font used by Excel. An average of 8.43 characters in this font will fit in a cell. Another measure is pixels, which is short for picture element. A **pixel** is a dot on the screen that contains a color. The size of the dot is based on your screen's resolution. At a common resolution of 800 × 600, 800 pixels display across the screen and 600 pixels display down the screen for a total of 480,000 pixels. It is these 480,000 pixels that form the font and other items you see on the screen.

The default row height in a blank worksheet is 12.75 points (or 17 pixels). Recall from Project 1 that a point is equal to 1/72 of an inch. Thus, 12.75 points is equal to about one-sixth of an inch. You can change the width of the columns or height of the rows at any time to make the worksheet easier to read or to ensure that an entry displays properly in a cell.

Changing the Widths of Columns

When changing the column width, you can set the width manually or you can instruct Excel to size the column to best fit. **Best fit** means that the width of the column will be increased or decreased so the widest entry will fit in the column. Sometimes, you may prefer more or less white space in a column than best fit provides. Excel thus allows you to change column widths manually.

When the format you assign to a cell causes the entry to exceed the width of a column, Excel automatically changes the column width to best fit. This happened earlier when the Currency style format was used (Figure 2-41 on page E 2.35). If you do not assign a cell in a column a format, the width will remain 8.43 characters, as is the case in columns A and B. To set a column width to best fit, double-click the right boundary of the column heading above row 1.

The following changes will be made to the column widths: column A to 14.00 characters; B through D to best fit; columns E, G and J to 9.43 characters columns; and F, H, and I to 12.00 characters. Perform the steps on the next page to change the column widths.

More About

Painting Formats

Painting is not an envious chore. In Excel, however, if you know how to paint you can save yourself time and effort when formatting a worksheet. For example, if you see a cell that has the format you want to assign to another cell or range of cells, click the cell with the desired format, click the Format Painter button on the Standard toolbar, and then click the cell or drag through the cells you want to paint the format with.

More About

Best Fit

Although Excel automatically increases the width of a column or the height of a row when you assign a format to a cell, it will not increase the column width or row height when a cell contains a formula and you change the value of a cell that is referenced in the formula. For example, if you change the number of shares in cell D3 from 750 to 100,000, Excel will recalculate the formulas and display number signs (#) for the initial cost, gain/lost, and current value because the results of the formulas have more digits than can fit in the cell. You can fix the problem by double-clicking the right boundary of the column heading to change to best fit.

Steps | To Change the Widths of Columns

1 **Point to the boundary on the right side of the column A heading above row 1. When the mouse pointer changes to a split double arrow, drag to the right until the ScreenTip, Width: 14.00 (103 pixels), displays.**

A dotted line shows the proposed right border of column A (Figure 2-53).

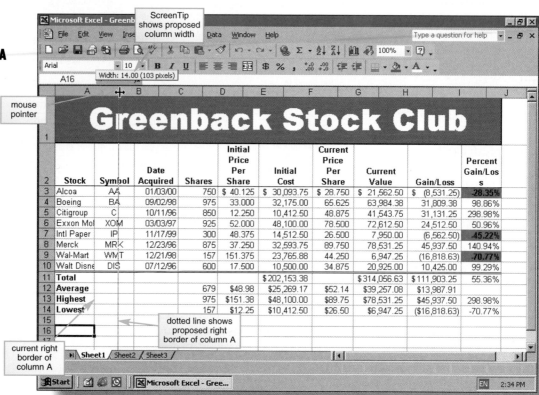

FIGURE 2-53

2 **Release the mouse button. Drag through column headings B through D above row 1. Point to the boundary on the right side of column heading D.**

The mouse pointer becomes a split double arrow (Figure 2-54).

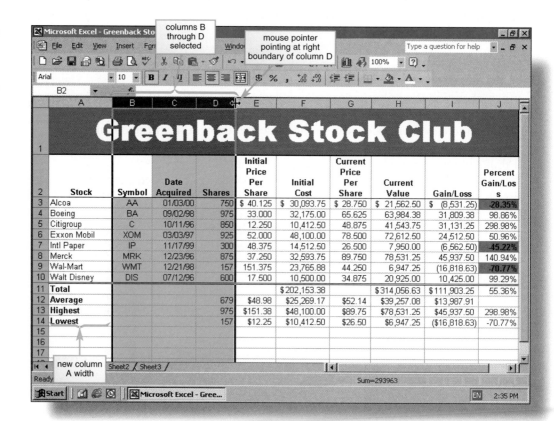

FIGURE 2-54

3 Double-click the right boundary of column heading D to change the width of columns B, C, and D to best fit. Click the column E heading above row 1. While holding down the CTRL key, click the column G heading and then the column J heading above row 1 so that columns E, G, and J are selected. Point to the boundary on the right side of the column J heading above row 1. Drag to the right until the ScreenTip, Width: 9.43 (71 pixels), displays.

A dotted line shows the proposed right border of column J (Figure 2-55).

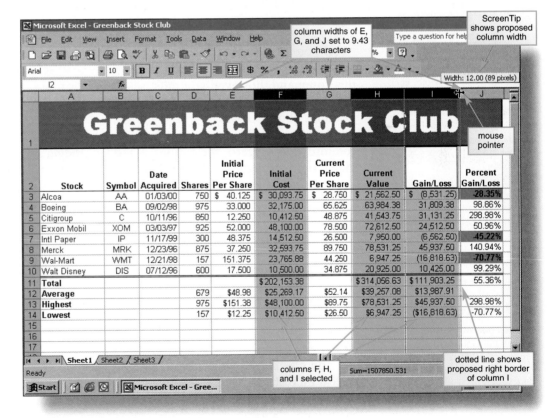

FIGURE 2-55

4 Release the mouse button. Click the column F heading above row 1 to select column F. While holding down the CTRL key, click the column H and I headings above row 1 so that columns F, H, and I are selected. Point to the boundary on the right side of the column I heading above row 1. Drag to the right until the ScreenTip, Width: 12.00 (89 pixels), displays.

A dotted line shows the proposed right border of column I (Figure 2-56).

FIGURE 2-56

5 **Release the mouse button. Click cell A16 to deselect columns F, H, and I.**

The worksheet displays with the new columns widths (Figure 2-57).

width of column A set to 14.00 characters

width of columns B through D set to best fit

width of columns E, G, and J set to 9.43 characters

width of columns F, H, and I set to 12.00 characters

Greenback Stock Club

Stock	Symbol	Date Acquired	Shares	Initial Price Per Share		Current Price Per Share	Current Value	Gain/Loss	Percent Gain/Loss
Alcoa	AA	01/03/00	750	$ 40.125	$ 30,093.75	$ 28.750	$ 21,562.50	$ (8,531.25)	-28.35%
Boeing	BA	09/02/98	975	33.000	32,175.00	65.625	63,984.38	31,809.38	98.86%
Citigroup	C	10/11/96	850	12.250	10,412.50	48.875	41,543.75	31,131.25	298.98%
Exxon Mobil	XOM	03/03/97	925	52.000	48,100.00	78.500	72,612.50	24,512.50	50.96%
Intl Paper	IP	11/17/99	300	48.375	14,512.50	26.500	7,950.00	(6,562.50)	-45.22%
Merck	MRK	12/23/96	875	37.250	32,593.75	89.750	78,531.25	45,937.50	140.94%
Wal-Mart	WMT	12/21/98	157	151.375	23,765.88	44.250	6,947.25	(16,818.63)	-70.77%
Walt Disney	DIS	07/12/96	600	17.500	10,500.00	34.875	20,925.00	10,425.00	99.29%
Total					$ 202,153.38		$ 314,056.63	$ 111,903.25	55.36%
Average			679	$48.98	$25,269.17	$52.14	$39,257.08	$13,987.91	
Highest			975	$151.38	$48,100.00	$89.75	$78,531.25	$45,937.50	298.98%
Lowest			157	$12.25	$10,412.50	$26.50	$6,947.25	($16,818.63)	-70.77%

FIGURE 2-57

If you want to increase or decrease the column width significantly, you can use the **Column Width command** on the shortcut menu to change a column's width. To use this command, however, you must select one or more entire columns. As shown in the previous set of steps, you select entire columns by dragging through the column headings above row 1.

A column width can vary from zero (0) to 255 characters. If you decrease the column width to zero, the column is hidden. **Hiding** is a technique you can use to hide data that might not be relevant to a particular report or sensitive data that you do not want others to see. When you print a worksheet, hidden columns do not print. To display a hidden column, position the mouse pointer to the right of the column heading boundary where the hidden column is located and then drag to the right.

Changing the Heights of Rows

When you increase the font size of a cell entry, such as the title in cell A1, Excel automatically increases the row height to best fit so the characters display properly. Recall that Excel did this earlier when you entered multiple lines in a cell in row 2 (see Figure 2-2 on page E 2.09).

You also can increase or decrease the height of a row manually to improve the appearance of the worksheet. The following steps show how to improve the appearance of the worksheet by increasing the height of row 1 to 61.50 points, decreasing the height of row 2 to 42.00 points, and increasing the height of row 12 to 24.00 points. Perform the following steps to change the heights of these three rows.

Steps To Change the Height of a Row by Dragging

1 **Point to the boundary below row heading 1. Drag down until the ScreenTip, Height: 61.50 (82 pixels), displays.**

The mouse pointer changes to a split double arrow (Figure 2-58). The distance between the dotted line and the top of row 1 indicates the proposed row height for row 1.

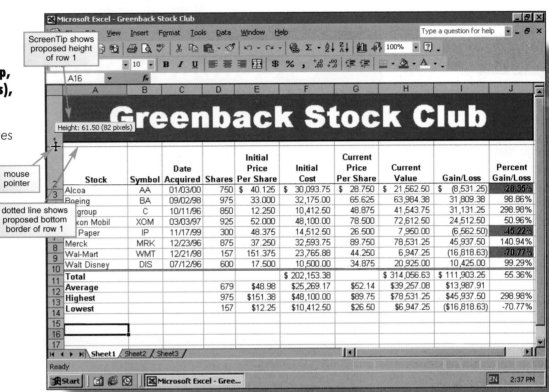

FIGURE 2-58

2 **Release the mouse button. Point to the boundary below row heading 2. Drag up until the ScreenTip, Height: 42.00 (56 pixels), displays.**

Excel displays a horizontal dotted line (Figure 2-59). The distance between the dotted line and the top of row 2 indicates the proposed height for row 2.

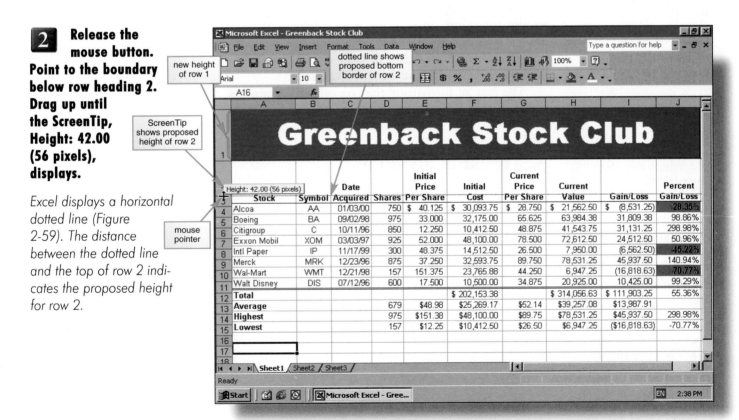

FIGURE 2-59

3 Release the mouse button. Point to the boundary below row heading 12. Drag down until the ScreenTip, Height: 24.00 (32 pixels), displays. Release the mouse button. Click cell A16.

The Total row and the Average row have additional white space between them, which improves the appearance of the worksheet (Figure 2-60). The formatting of the worksheet is complete.

FIGURE 2-60

The row height can vary between zero (0) and 409 points. As with column widths, when you decrease the row height to zero, the row is hidden. To display a hidden row, position the mouse pointer just below the row heading boundary where the row is hidden and then drag down. To set a row height to best fit, double-click the bottom boundary of the row heading.

The task of formatting the worksheet is complete. The next step is to check the spelling of the worksheet.

Checking Spelling

Excel has a **spell checker** you can use to check the worksheet for spelling errors. The spell checker looks for spelling errors by comparing words on the worksheet against words contained in its standard dictionary. If you often use specialized terms that are not in the standard dictionary, you may want to add them to a custom dictionary using the **Spelling dialog box**.

When the spell checker finds a word that is not in either dictionary, it displays the word in the Spelling dialog box. You then can correct it if it is misspelled.

To illustrate how Excel responds to a misspelled word, the word, Symbol, in cell B2 is misspelled purposely as the word, Simbol, as shown in Figure 2-61.

Steps **To Check Spelling on the Worksheet**

1 Select cell B2 and enter Simbol to misspell the word Symbol. Select cell A1. Click the Spelling button on the Standard toolbar. When the spell checker stops on cell B2 and with the word, Symbol, highlighted in the Suggestions list, point to the Change button.

When the spell checker identifies the misspelled word, Simbol, the Spelling dialog box displays (Figure 2-61).

FIGURE 2-61

2 Click the Change button. As the spell checker checks the remainder of the worksheet, click the Ignore All and Change buttons as needed.

The spell checker changes the misspelled word, Simbol, to the correct word, Symbol, and continues spell checking the worksheet. When the spell checker is finished, it displays the Microsoft Excel dialog box with a message indicating that the spell check is complete (Figure 2-62).

3 Click the OK button.

FIGURE 2-62

Other **Ways**

1. On Tools menu click Spelling
2. Press F7
3. In Voice Command mode say, "Spelling"

When the spell checker identifies that a cell contains a word not in its standard or custom dictionary, it selects that cell as the active cell and displays the Spelling dialog box. The Spelling dialog box (Figure 2-61 on the previous page) lists the word not found in the dictionary, a suggested correction, and a list of alternative suggestions. If one of the words in the Suggestions list is correct, click it and then click the Change button. If none of the suggestions is correct, type the correct word in the Not in Dictionary text box and then click the Change button. To change the word throughout the worksheet, click the **Change All button** instead of the Change button. To skip correcting the word, click the **Ignore Once button**. To have Excel ignore the word for the remainder of the worksheet, click the **Ignore All button**.

Consider these additional guidelines when using the spell checker:

- To check the spelling of the text in a single cell, double-click the cell to make the formula bar active and then click the Spelling button on the Standard toolbar.
- If you select a single cell so that the formula bar is not active and then start the spell checker, Excel checks the remainder of the worksheet, including notes and embedded charts.
- If you select a range of cells before starting the spell checker, Excel checks the spelling of the words only in the selected range.
- To check the spelling of all the sheets in a workbook, click Select All Sheets on the sheet tab shortcut menu and then start the spell checker. To display the sheet tab shortcut menu, right-click the sheet tab.
- If you select a cell other than cell A1 before you start the spell checker, a dialog box will display when the spell checker reaches the end of the worksheet, asking if you want to continue checking at the beginning.
- To add words to the dictionary, click the **Add to Dictionary button** in the Spelling dialog box (Figure 2-61) when Excel identifies the word as not in the dictionary.
- Click the **AutoCorrect button** (Figure 2-61) to add the misspelled word and the correct version of the word to the AutoCorrect list. For example, suppose you misspell the word, do, as the word, dox. When the Spelling dialog box displays the correct word, do, in the Change to box, click the AutoCorrect button. Then, anytime in the future that you type the word, dox, Excel automatically will change it to the word, do.

Saving a Workbook a Second Time Using the Same File Name

Earlier in this project, you saved an intermediate version of the workbook using the file name, Greenback Stock Club. To save the workbook a second time using the same file name, click the Save button on the Standard toolbar as shown in the following step.

TO SAVE A WORKBOOK A SECOND TIME USING THE SAME FILE NAME

1 Click the Save button on the Standard toolbar.

Excel saves the workbook on the floppy disk in drive A using the file name Greenback Stock Club.

Excel automatically stores the latest version of the workbook using the same file name, Greenback Stock Club. When you save a workbook a second time using the same file name, Excel will not display the Save As dialog box as it does the first time you save the workbook. You also can click **Save** on the File menu or press SHIFT+F12 or CTRL+S to save a workbook again.

If you want to save the workbook using a new name or on a different drive, click Save As on the File menu. Some Excel users, for example, use the Save button to save the latest version of the workbook on the default drive. Then, they use the Save As command to save a copy on another drive.

Previewing and Printing the Worksheet

In Project 1, you printed the worksheet without first previewing it on the screen. By previewing the worksheet, however, you see exactly how it will look without generating a printout. Previewing allows you to see if the worksheet will print on one page in portrait orientation. **Portrait orientation** means the printout is printed across the width of the page. **Landscape orientation** means the printout is printed across the length of the page. Previewing a worksheet using the **Print Preview command** on the File menu or **Print Preview button** on the Standard toolbar can save time, paper, and the frustration of waiting for a printout only to discover it is not what you want.

Perform the following steps to preview and then print the worksheet.

Steps **To Preview and Print a Worksheet**

1 **Point to the Print Preview button on the Standard toolbar (Figure 2-63).**

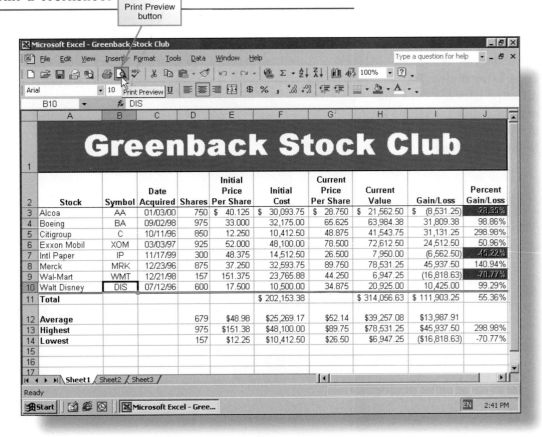

FIGURE 2-63

2 Click the Print Preview button. When the Preview window opens, point to the Setup button.

Excel displays a preview of the worksheet in portrait orientation, because portrait is the default orientation. In portrait orientation, the worksheet does not fit on one page (Figure 2-64).

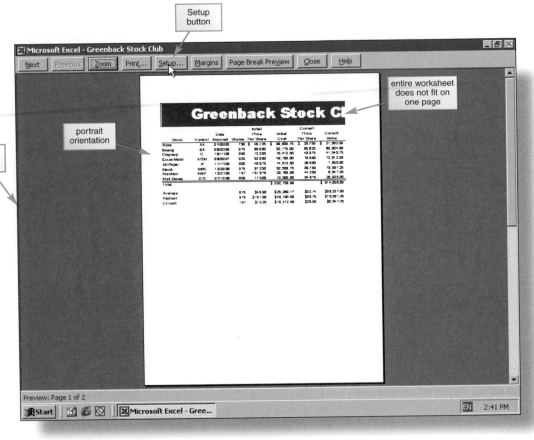

FIGURE 2-64

3 Click the Setup button. When the Page Setup dialog box displays, click the Page tab and then click Landscape in the Orientation area. Point to the OK button.

The Page Setup dialog box displays. The Orientation area contains two option buttons, Portrait and Landscape (Figure 2-65).

FIGURE 2-65

4 **Click the OK button. Point to the Print button at the top of the Preview window.**

The worksheet displays in the Preview window in its entirety in landscape orientation (Figure 2-66).

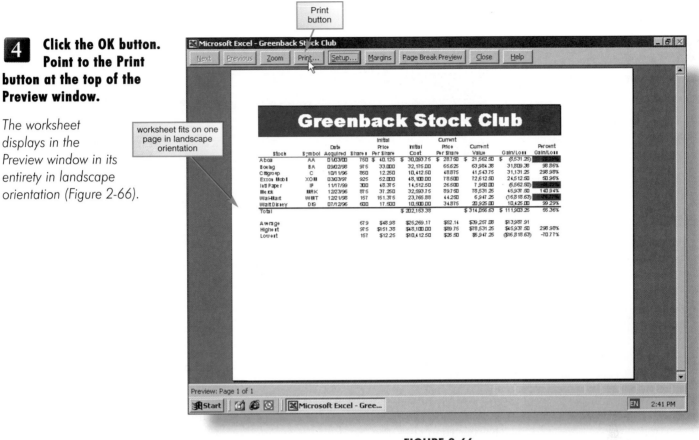

FIGURE 2-66

5 **Click the Print button. When the Print dialog box displays, point to the OK button.**

The Print dialog box displays as shown in Figure 2-67.

FIGURE 2-67

6 **Click the OK button. Click the Save button on the Standard toolbar.**

Excel prints the worksheet (Figure 2-68). The workbook is saved with the landscape orientation.

landscape orientation

Greenback Stock Club

Stock	Symbol	Date Acquired	Shares	Initial Price Per Share	Initial Cost	Current Price Per Share	Current Value	Gain/Loss	Percent Gain/Loss
Alcoa	AA	01/03/00	750	$ 40.125	$ 30,093.75	$ 28.750	$ 21,562.50	$ (8,531.25)	-28.35%
Boeing	BA	09/02/98	975	33.000	32,175.00	65.625	63,984.38	31,809.38	98.86%
Citigroup	C	10/11/96	850	12.250	10,412.50	48.875	41,543.75	31,131.25	298.98%
Exxon Mobil	XOM	03/03/97	925	52.000	48,100.00	78.500	72,612.50	24,512.50	50.96%
Intl Paper	IP	11/17/99	300	48.375	14,512.50	26.500	7,950.00	(6,562.50)	-45.22%
Merck	MRK	12/23/96	875	37.250	32,593.75	89.750	78,531.25	45,937.50	140.94%
Wal-Mart	WMT	12/21/98	157	151.375	23,765.88	44.250	6,947.25	(16,818.63)	-70.77%
Walt Disney	DIS	07/12/96	600	17.500	10,500.00	34.875	20,925.00	10,425.00	99.29%
Total					$ 202,153.38		$ 314,056.63	$ 111,903.25	55.36%
Average			679	$48.98	$25,269.17	$52.14	$39,257.08	$13,987.91	
Highest			975	$151.38	$48,100.00	$89.75	$78,531.25	$45,937.50	298.98%
Lowest			157	$12.25	$10,412.50	$26.50	$6,947.25	($16,818.63)	-70.77%

FIGURE 2-68

Other Ways

1. On File menu click Print Preview
2. On File menu click Page Setup, click Print Preview button
3. On File menu click Print, click Entire Workbook, click Preview button
4. In Voice Command mode say, "Print Preview"

Once you change the orientation and save the workbook, it will remain until you change it. When you open a new workbook, Excel sets the orientation to portrait.

Several buttons are at the top of the Preview window (see Figure 2-66 on the previous page). The functions of these buttons are summarized in Table 2-6.

Rather than click the Next and Previous buttons to move from page to page as described in Table 2-6, you can press the PAGE UP and PAGE DOWN keys. You also can click the previewed page in the Preview window when the mouse pointer shape is a magnifying glass to carry out the function of the Zoom button.

The Page Setup dialog box in Figure 2-65 on page E 2.52 allows you to make changes to the default settings for a printout. For example, on the Page tab, you can set the orientation as was done in the previous set of steps, scale the printout so it fits on one page, and set the page size and print quality. Scaling is an alternative to changing the orientation to fit a wide worksheet on one page. This technique will be discussed shortly. The Margins tab, Header/Footer tab, and Sheet tab in the Page Setup dialog box allow even more control of the way the printout will appear. These tabs will be discussed when they are used.

The Print dialog box shown in Figure 2-67 on the previous page displays when you use the Print command on the File menu or a Print button in a dialog box or Preview window. It does not display when you use the Print button on the Standard toolbar, as was the case in Project 1. The Print dialog box allows you to select a printer, instruct Excel what to print, and indicate how many copies of the printout you want.

Printing a Section of the Worksheet

You might not always want to print the entire worksheet. You can print portions of the worksheet by selecting the range of cells to print and then clicking the Selection option button in the Print what area in the Print dialog box. The following steps show how to print the range A2:F14.

Table 2-6	Print Preview Buttons
BUTTON	**FUNCTION**
Next	Previews the next page
Previous	Previews the previous page
Zoom	Magnifies or reduces the print preview
Print...	Prints the worksheet
Setup...	Displays the Print Setup dialog box
Margins	Changes the print margins
Page Break Preview	Previews page breaks
Close	Closes the Preview window
Help	Displays Help about the Preview window

Steps **To Print a Section of the Worksheet**

1 **Select the range A2:F14. Click File on the menu bar and then click Print. Click Selection in the Print what area. Point to the OK button.**

The Print dialog box displays (Figure 2-69). Because the Selection option button is selected, Excel will print only the selected range.

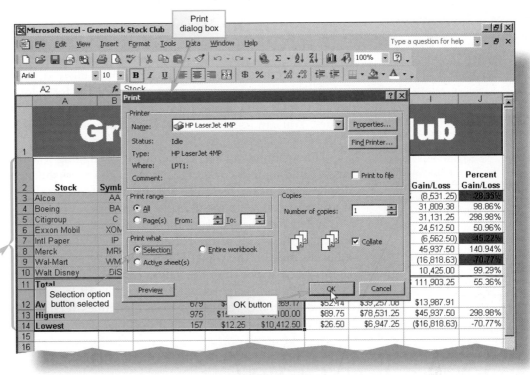

FIGURE 2-69

2 **Click the OK button. Click cell A16 to deselect the range A2:F14.**

Excel prints the selected range of the worksheet on the printer (Figure 2-70).

only selected range prints

		Date		Initial Price	Initial
Stock	**Symbol**	**Acquired**	**Shares**	**Per Share**	**Cost**
Alcoa	AA	01/03/00	750	$ 40.125	$ 30,093.75
Boeing	BA	09/02/98	975	33.000	32,175.00
Citigroup	C	10/11/96	850	12.250	10,412.50
Exxon Mobil	XOM	03/03/97	925	52.000	48,100.00
Intl Paper	IP	11/17/99	300	48.375	14,512.50
Merck	MRK	12/23/96	875	37.250	32,593.75
Wal-Mart	WMT	12/21/98	157	151.375	23,765.88
Walt Disney	DIS	07/12/96	600	17.500	10,500.00
Total					$ 202,153.38
Average			679	$48.98	$25,269.17
Highest			975	$151.38	$48,100.00
Lowest			157	$12.25	$10,412.50

FIGURE 2-70

Three option buttons display in the Print what area in the Print dialog box (Figure 2-69). As shown in the previous steps, the **Selection option button** instructs Excel to print the selected range. The **Active sheet(s) option button** instructs Excel to print the active sheet (the one displaying on the screen) or the selected sheets. Finally, the **Entire workbook option button** instructs Excel to print all the sheets with content in the workbook.

Other **Ways**

1. Select range to print, on File menu click Print Area, click Set Print Area, click Print button on the Standard toolbar; on File menu click Print Area, click Clear Print Area

2. Select range to print, in Voice Command mode say, "File, Print Area, Set Print Area"

Displaying and Printing the Formulas Version of the Worksheet

More About

Printing

To avoid wasting ink, print worksheets with color in black and white. You print in black and white by clicking Page Setup on the File menu prior to printing. When the Page Setup dialog box displays, click the Sheet tab, click Black and White in the Print area, and click the OK button. Then, click the Print button.

Thus far, you have been working with the **values version** of the worksheet, which shows the results of the formulas you have entered, rather than the actual formulas. Excel also allows you to display and print the **formulas version** of the worksheet, which displays the actual formulas you have entered, rather than the resulting values. You can toggle between the values version and formulas version by pressing CTR+ACCENT MARK (`) to the left of the number 1 key.

The formulas version is useful for debugging a worksheet. **Debugging** is the process of finding and correcting errors in the worksheet. Because the formula version displays and prints formulas and functions, rather than the results, it is easier to see if any mistakes were made in the formulas.

When you change from the values version to the formulas version, Excel increases the width of the columns so the formulas and text do not overflow into adjacent cells on the right. The formulas version of the worksheet thus usually is significantly wider than the values version. To fit the wide printout on one page, you can use landscape orientation and the **Fit to option** on the Page tab in the Page Setup dialog box. To change from the values version to the formulas version of the worksheet and print the formulas on one page, perform the following steps.

Steps: To Display the Formulas in the Worksheet and Fit the Printout on One Page

1 Press CTRL+ACCENT MARK (`). Click the right horizontal scroll arrow until column J displays.

Excel changes the display of the worksheet from values to formulas (Figure 2-71). The formulas in the worksheet display showing unformatted numbers, formulas, and functions that were assigned to the cells. Excel automatically increases the column widths.

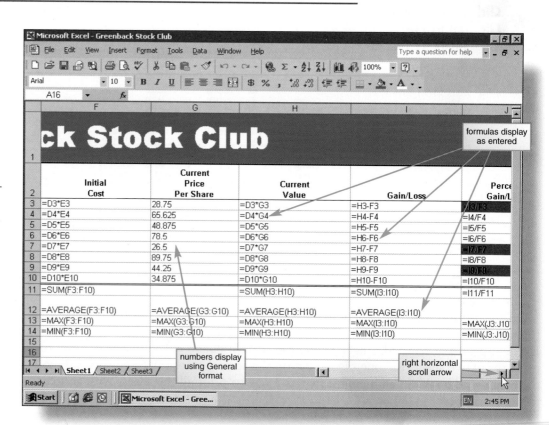

FIGURE 2-71

2 **Click File on the menu bar and then click Page Setup. When the Page Setup dialog box displays, click the Page tab. If necessary, click Landscape to select it, and then click Fit to in the Scaling area. Point to the Print button in the Page Setup dialog box.**

Excel displays the Page Setup dialog box with the Landscape and Fit to option buttons selected (Figure 2-72.

FIGURE 2-72

3 **Click the Print button. When the Print dialog box displays, click the OK button. When you are done viewing and printing the formulas version, press CTRL+ACCENT MARK (`) to display the values version.**

Excel prints the formulas in the worksheet on one page in landscape orientation (Figure 2-73). Excel displays the values version of the worksheet.

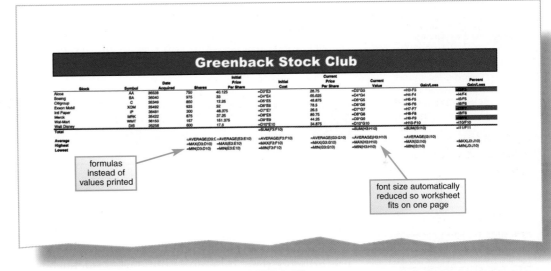

FIGURE 2-73

Other Ways

1. On Tools menu click Options, click View tab, click Formulas check box, click OK button
2. In Voice Command mode say, "Tools, Options, View, Formulas, OK"

Although the formulas version of the worksheet was printed in the previous example, you can see from Figure 2-71 that the display on the screen also can be used for debugging the worksheet.

Changing the Print Scaling Option Back to 100%

Depending on your printer driver, you may have to change the Print Scaling option back to 100% after using the Fit to option. Complete the steps on the next page to reset the Print Scaling option so future worksheets print at 100%, instead of being squeezed on one page.

TO CHANGE THE PRINT SCALING OPTION BACK TO 100%

1 Click File on the menu bar and then click Page Setup.

2 Click the Page tab in the Page Setup dialog box. Click Adjust to in the Scaling area.

3 If necessary, type 100 in the Adjust to box.

4 Click the OK button.

The print scaling is set to normal.

The **Adjust to box** allows you to specify the percentage of reduction or enlargement in the printout of a worksheet. The default percentage is 100%. When click the Fit to option, this percentage automatically changes to the percentage required to fit the printout on one page.

Importing External Data from a Web Source Using a Web Query

One of the major features of Excel is its capability of importing external data from sites on the World Wide Web. To import external data from a World Wide Web site, you must have access to the Internet. You then can import data stored on a World Wide Web site using a **Web query**. When you run a Web query, Excel imports the external data in the form of a worksheet. As described in Table 2-7, three Web queries are available when you first install Excel. All three Web queries relate to investment and stock market activities.

Table 2-7 Excel Web Queries	
QUERY	*EXTERNAL DATA RETURNED*
MSN MoneyCentral Investor Currency Rates	Currency rates
MSN MoneyCentral Investor Major Indices	Major indices
MSN MoneyCentral Investor Stock Quotes	Up to 20 stocks of your choice

The data returned by the stock-related Web queries is real-time in the sense that it is no more than 20 minutes old during the business day. The steps below show how to get the most recent stock quotes for the eight stocks owned by the Greenback Stock Club — Alcoa, Boeing, Citigroup, Exxon Mobil, International Paper, Merck, Wal-Mart, and Walt Disney. Although you can have a Web query return data to a blank workbook, the following steps have the data returned to a blank worksheet in the Greenback Stock Club workbook.

To Import Data from a Web Source Using a Web Query

1 **With the Greenback Stock Club workbook open, click the Sheet2 tab at the bottom of the window. Click cell A1. Click Data on the menu bar, point to Import External Data and then point to Import Data on the Import External Data submenu.**

The Import External Data submenu displays as shown in Figure 2-74.

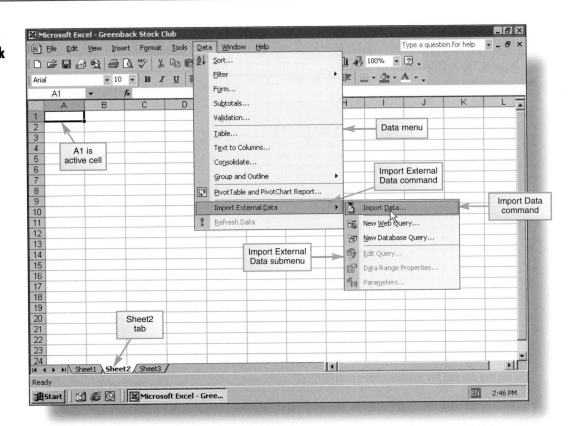

FIGURE 2-74

2 **Click Import Data. When the Select Data Source dialog box displays, click MSN MoneyCentral Investor Stock Quotes. Point to the Open button.**

The Select Data Source dialog box displays (Figure 2-75). If your display is different, ask your instructor for the folder location of the Web queries.

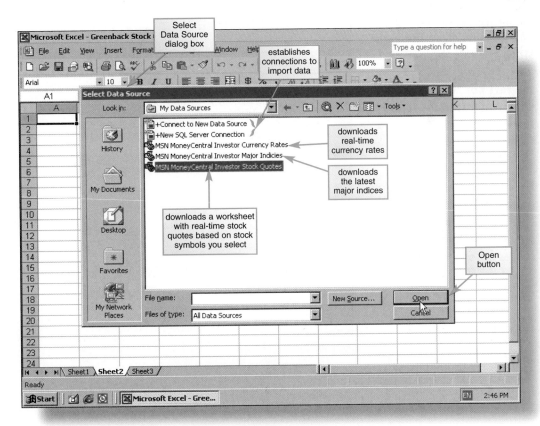

FIGURE 2-75

3 Click the Open button. When the Import Data dialog box displays, if necessary, click Existing worksheet to select it. Point to the OK button.

The Import Data dialog box displays (Figure 2-76).

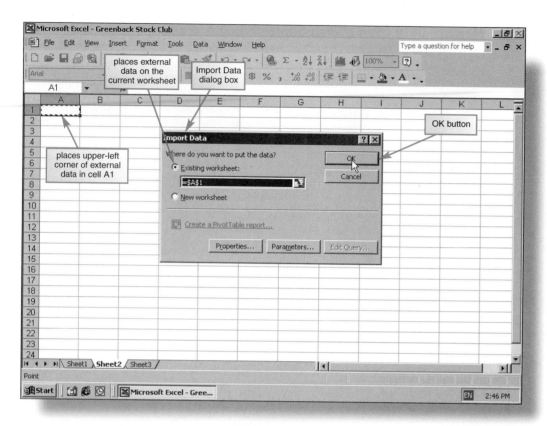

FIGURE 2-76

4 Click the OK button. When the Enter Parameter Value dialog box displays, type the eight stock symbols aa ba c xom ip mrk wmt dis **in the text box. Click Use this value/reference for future refreshes to select it. Point to the OK button.**

The Enter Parameter Value dialog box displays (Figure 2-77). You can enter up to 20 stock symbols separated by spaces (or commas).

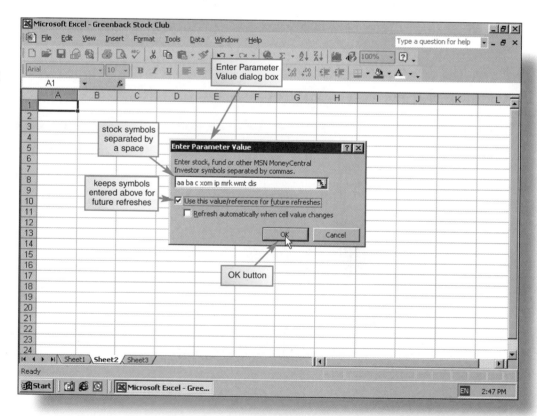

FIGURE 2-77

5 **Click the OK button.**

Once your computer connects to the Internet, a message displays to inform you that Excel is getting external data. After a short period, Excel displays a new worksheet with the desired data (Figure 2-78). A complete display of the worksheet is shown in Figure 2-1b on page E 2.05.

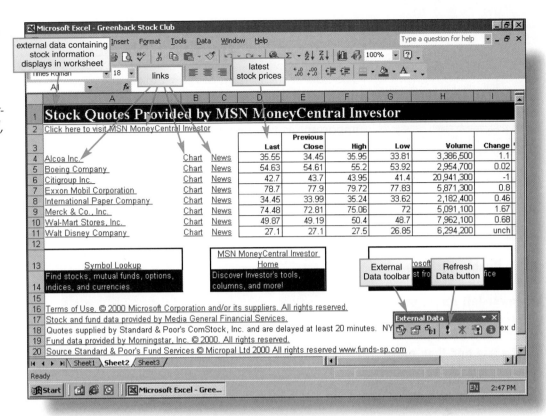

FIGURE 2-78

As shown in Figure 2-78, Excel displays the data returned from the Web query in an organized, formatted worksheet, which has a worksheet title, column titles, and a row of data for each stock symbol entered. Other than the first column, which contains the stock name and stock symbol, you have no control over the remaining columns of data returned. The latest price of each stock displays in column D.

Once the worksheet displays, you can refresh the data as often as you want. To refresh the data for all the stocks, click the **Refresh All button** on the **External Data toolbar** (Figure 2-79). Because the Use this value/reference for future refreshes check box was selected (Figure 2-77), Excel will continue to use the same stock symbols each time it refreshes. You can change the symbols by clicking the **Query Parameters button** on the External Data toolbar.

If the External Data toolbar does not display, right-click any toolbar and then click External Data. Rather than use the External Data toolbar, you also can invoke any Web query command by right-clicking the returned worksheet to display a shortcut menu.

This section gives you an idea of the potential of Web queries by having you use just one of Excel's Web queries. To reinforce the topics covered here, work through In the Lab 3 on page E 2.74.

The workbook is nearly complete. The final step is to change the names of the sheets located on the sheet tabs at the bottom of the Excel window.

Other Ways

1. Press ALT+D, D, D
2. In Voice Command mode say, "Data, Import External Data, Import Data"

FIGURE 2-79

Changing the Sheet Names

The tabs at the bottom of the window allow you to display any sheet in the workbook. You click the tab of the sheet you want to display. The names of the sheets are preset to Sheet1, Sheet2, and so on. These names become increasingly important as you move towards more sophisticated workbooks, especially those in which you reference cells between sheets. The following steps show how to rename sheets by double-clicking the sheet tabs.

Steps **To Rename the Sheets**

1 **Double-click the tab labeled Sheet2 in the lower-left corner of the window. Type** Real-Time Stock Quotes **as the sheet name and then press the ENTER key.**

The new sheet name displays on the tab (Figure 2-80).

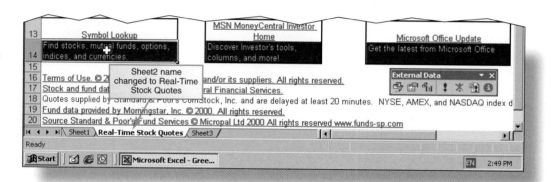

FIGURE 2-80

2 **Double-click the tab labeled Sheet1 in the lower-left corner of the window. Type** Investment Analysis **as the sheet name and then press the ENTER key.**

The sheet name changes from Sheet1 to Investment Analysis (Figure 2-81).

	Stock	Symbol	Date Acquired	Shares	Initial Price Per Share	Initial Cost	Current Price Per Share	Current Value	Gain/Loss	Percent Gain/Loss
3	Alcoa	AA	01/03/00	750	$ 40.125	$ 30,093.75	$ 28.750	$ 21,562.50	$ (8,531.25)	-28.35%
4	Boeing	BA	09/02/98	975	33.000	32,175.00	65.625	63,984.38	31,809.38	98.86%
5	Citigroup	C	10/11/96	850	12.250	10,412.50	48.875	41,543.75	31,131.25	298.98%
6	Exxon Mobil	XOM	03/03/97	925	52.000	48,100.00	78.500	72,612.50	24,512.50	50.96%
7	Intl Paper	IP	11/17/99	300	48.375	14,512.50	26.500	7,950.00	(6,562.50)	-45.22%
8	Merck	MRK	12/23/96	875	37.250	32,593.75	89.750	78,531.25	45,937.50	140.94%
9	Wal-Mart	WMT	12/21/98	157	151.375	23,765.88	44.250	6,947.25	(16,818.63)	-70.77%
10	Walt Disney	DIS	07/12/96	600	17.500	10,500.00	34.875	20,925.00	10,425.00	99.29%
11	**Total**					$ 202,153.38		$ 314,056.63	$ 111,903.25	55.36%
12	**Average**			9	$48.98	$25,269.17	$52.14	$39,257.08	$13,987.91	
13	**Highest**			5	$151.38	$48,100.00		$78,531.25	$45,937.50	298.98%
14	**Lowest**			7	$12.25	$10,412.50		$6,947.25	($16,818.63)	-70.77%

FIGURE 2-81

Sheet names can be up to 31 characters (including spaces) in length. Longer sheet names, however, mean that fewer tabs will display. To display more sheet tabs, you can drag the tab split box (Figure 2-81) to the right. This will reduce the size of the scroll bar at the bottom of the screen. Double-click the tab split box to reset it to its normal position.

You also can use the tab scrolling buttons to the left of the sheet tabs (Figure 2-81) to move between sheets. The leftmost and rightmost scroll buttons move to the first or last sheet in the workbook. The two middle scroll buttons move one sheet to the left or right.

E-Mailing a Workbook from within Excel

The most popular service on the Internet is electronic mail, or e-mail. Using **e-mail**, you can converse with friends across the room or on another continent. One of the features of e-mail is the ability to attach Office files, such as Word documents or Excel workbooks, to an e-mail and send it to a co-worker. In the past, if you wanted to send a workbook you saved it, closed the file, launched your e-mail program, and then attached the workbook to the e-mail before sending it. With Excel you have the capability of e-mailing the worksheet or workbook directly from within Excel. For these steps to work properly, you must have an e-mail address and one of the following as your e-mail program: Outlook, Outlook Express, Microsoft Exchange Client, or another 32-bit e-mail program compatible with Messaging Application Programming Interface. The following steps show how to e-mail the workbook from within Excel to Abby Lane. Assume her e-mail address is lane_abby@hotmail.com.

More About

E-Mail

Several Web sites are available that allow you to sign up for free e-mail. For more information on signing up for free e-mail, visit the Excel 2002 More About Web page (scsite.com/ex2002/more.htm) and click Signing Up for E-mail.

More About

Quick Reference

For a table that lists how to complete the tasks covered in this book using the mouse, menu, shortcut menu, and keyboard, see the Quick Reference Summary at the back of this book or visit the Shelly Cashman Series Office XP Web page site (scsite.com/offxp/qr.htm) and then click Excel 2002.

Steps **To E-Mail a Workbook from within Excel**

1 **With the Greenback Stock Club workbook open, click File on the menu bar, point to Send To, and then point to Mail Recipient (as Attachment) on the Send To submenu.**

The File menu and Send To submenu display as shown in Figure 2-82.

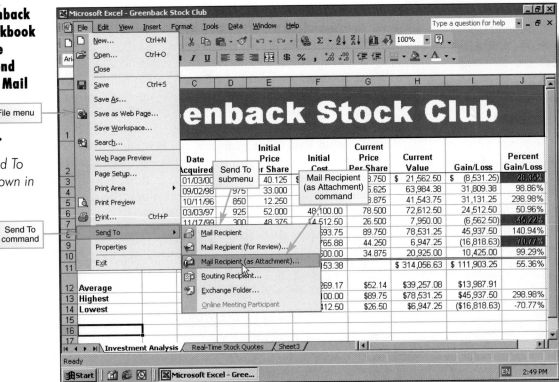

FIGURE 2-82

2 **Click Mail Recipient (as Attachment). When the e-mail Message window opens, type** lane_abby@hotmail.com **in the To text box. Type the message shown in the message area in Figure 2-83. Point to the Send button.**

Excel displays the e-mail Message window (Figure 2-83).

3 **Click the Send button.**

The e-mail with the attached workbook is sent to lane_abby@hotmail.com.

FIGURE 2-83

Because the workbook was sent as an attachment, Abby Lane can double-click the attachment in the e-mail to open it in Excel, or she can save it to disk and then open it at a later time. The worksheet also could have been sent as part of the Word document by using the **E-mail button** on the Standard toolbar or by clicking the **Mail Recipient command** on the File menu. In this case, Abby would be able to read the worksheet in the e-mail message, but would not be able to open it in Excel.

Many more options are available that you can choose when you send an e-mail from within Excel. For example, the Bcc and From buttons on the toolbar in the Message window give you the same capabilities as an e-mail program. The Options button on the toolbar allows you to send the e-mail to a group of people in a particular sequence and get responses along the route.

Quitting Excel and Saving the Workbook

After completing the workbook and related activities, you can quit Excel by performing the following steps.

TO QUIT EXCEL AND SAVE THE WORKBOOK

1 Click the Investment Analysis tab.

2 Click the Close button on the upper-right corner of the title bar.

3 When the Microsoft Excel dialog box displays, click the Yes button to quit Excel and save the changes to the workbook on disk.

Project Summary

In creating the Greenback Stock Club workbook, you learned how to enter formulas, calculate an average, find the highest and lowest numbers in a range, verify formulas using Range Finder, change fonts, draw borders, format numbers, change column widths and row heights, and add conditional formatting to a range of numbers. You learned how to spell check a worksheet, preview a worksheet, print a worksheet, print a section of a worksheet, and display and print the formulas in the worksheet using the Fit to option. You also learned how to complete a Web query to generate a worksheet using external data obtained from the World Wide Web and rename sheet tabs. Finally, you learned how to send an e-mail directly from within Excel with the opened workbook attached.

What You Should Know

Having completed this project, you now should be able to perform the following tasks:

- Apply a Currency Style Format and Comma Style Format Using the Formatting Toolbar (E 2.34)
- Apply a Currency Style Format with a Floating Dollar Sign Using the Format Cells Command (E 2.37)
- Apply a Percent Style Format (E 2.39)
- Apply Conditional Formatting (E 2.40)
- Bold, Center, and Underline the Column Titles (E 2.31)
- Center Data in Cells and Format Dates (E 2.32)
- Change the Font and Center the Worksheet Title (E 2.28)
- Change the Height of a Row by Dragging (E 2.47)
- Change the Print Scaling Option Back to 100% (E 2.58)
- Change the Title Background and Font Colors and Apply an Outline Border (E 2.30)
- Change the Widths of Columns (E 2.44)
- Check Spelling on the Worksheet (E 2.49)
- Copy a Range of Cells across Columns to an Adjacent Range Using the Fill Handle (E 2.23)
- Copy Formulas Using the Fill Handle (E 2.13)
- Determine the Average of a Range of Numbers Using the Keyboard and Mouse (E 2.17)
- Determine the Highest Number in a Range of Numbers Using the Insert Function Box (E 2.19)
- Determine the Lowest Number in a Range of Numbers Using the AutoSum Menu (E 2.21)
- Determine the Total Percent Gain/Loss (E 2.16)
- Determine Totals Using the AutoSum Button (E 2.15)
- Display the Formulas in the Worksheet and Fit the Printout on One Page (E 2.56)
- E-Mail a Workbook from within Excel (E 2.63)
- Enter a Formula Using the Keyboard (E 2.09)
- Enter Formulas Using Point Mode (E 2.11)
- Enter the Column Titles (E 2.07)
- Enter the Stock Data (E 2.08)
- Enter the Total Row Titles (E 2.08)
- Enter the Worksheet Title (E 2.07)
- Import Data from a Web Source Using a Web Query (E 2.59)
- Preview and Print a Worksheet (E 2.51)
- Print a Section of the Worksheet (E 2.55)
- Quit Excel and Save the Workbook (E 2.64)
- Rename the Sheets (E 2.62)
- Save a Workbook a Second Time Using the Same File Name (E 2.50)
- Save the Workbook (E 2.25)
- Start and Customize Excel (E 2.06)
- Underline the Row above the Title Row and Bold the Total Row Titles (E 2.36)
- Verify a Formula Using Range Finder (E 2.25)

Learn It Online

Instructions: To complete the Learn It Online exercises, start your browser, click the Address bar, and then enter scsite.com/offxp/exs.htm. When the Office XP Learn It Online page displays, follow the instructions in the exercises below.

1 Project Reinforcement TF, MC, and SA

Below Excel Project 2, click the Project Reinforcement link. Print the quiz by clicking Print on the File menu. Answer each question. Write your first and last name at the top of each page, and then hand in the printout to your instructor.

2 Flash Cards

Below Excel Project 2, click the Flash Cards link. When Flash Cards displays, read the instructions. Type 20 (or a number specified by your instructor) in the Number of Playing Cards text box, type your name in the Name text box, and then click the Flip Card button. When the flash card displays, read the question and then click the Answer box arrow to select an answer. Flip through Flash Cards. Click Print on the File menu to print the last flash card if your score is 15 (75%) correct or greater and then hand it in to your instructor. If your score is less than 15 (75%) correct, then redo this exercise by clicking the Replay button.

3 Practice Test

Below Excel Project 2, click the Practice Test link. Answer each question, enter your first and last name at the bottom of the page, and then click the Grade Test button. When the graded practice test displays on your screen, click Print on the File menu to print a hard copy. Continue to take practice tests until you score 80% or better. Hand in a printout of the final practice test to your instructor.

4 Who Wants to Be a Computer Genius?

Below Excel Project 2, click the Computer Genius link. Read the instructions, enter your first and last name at the bottom of the page, and then click the Play button. Hand in your score to your instructor.

5 Wheel of Terms

Below Excel Project 2, click the Wheel of Terms link. Read the instructions, and then enter your first and last name and your school name. Click the Play button. Hand in your score to your instructor.

6 Crossword Puzzle Challenge

Below Excel Project 2, click the Crossword Puzzle Challenge link. Read the instructions, and then enter your first and last name. Click the Play button. Work the crossword puzzle. When you are finished, click the Submit button. When the crossword puzzle redisplays, click the Print button. Hand in the printout.

7 Tips and Tricks

Below Excel Project 2, click the Tips and Tricks link. Click a topic that pertains to Project 2. Right-click the information and then click Print on the shortcut menu. Construct a brief example of what the information relates to in Excel to confirm you understand how to use the tip or trick. Hand in the example and printed information.

8 Newsgroups

Below Excel Project 2, click the Newsgroups link. Click a topic that pertains to Project 2. Print three comments. Hand in the comments to your instructor.

9 Expanding Your Horizons

Below Excel Project 2, click the Articles for Microsoft Excel link. Click a topic that pertains to Project 2. Print the information. Construct a brief example of what the information relates to in Excel to confirm you understand the contents of the article. Hand in the example and printed information to your instructor.

10 Search Sleuth

Below Excel Project 2, click the Search Sleuth link. To search for a term that pertains to this project, select a term below the Project 2 title and then use the Google search engine at google.com (or any major search engine) to display and print two Web pages that present information on the term. Hand in the printouts to your instructor.

o n l i n e

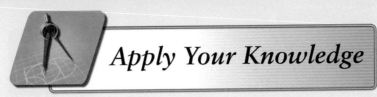

1 Buy It Online Profit Analysis Worksheet

Instructions: Start Excel. Open the workbook Buy It Online from the Data Disk. See the inside back cover of this book for instructions for downloading the Data Disk or see your instructor for information on accessing the files required in this book. The purpose of this exercise is to open a partially completed workbook, enter formulas and functions, copy the formulas and functions, and then format the numbers. As shown in Figure 2-84, the completed worksheet analyzes profits by product.

Buy It Online
Profit Analysis

Product	Description	Unit Cost	Unit Profit	Units Sold	Total Sales	Total Profit	% Total Profit
1H34	Hard Disk	$ 92.95	$ 19.75	32,435	$ 3,655,424.50	$ 640,591.25	17.524%
1J76	Monitor	175.99	45.65	16,534	3,664,595.76	754,777.10	20.596%
2L98	Printer	110.60	62.50	32,102	5,556,856.20	2,006,375.00	36.106%
2Q78	Scanner	160.50	55.25	43,910	9,473,582.50	2,426,027.50	25.608%
3K03	Stereo Speakers	121.35	38.75	34,391	5,505,999.10	1,332,651.25	24.204%
3A04	System Unit	200.23	95.15	23,910	7,062,535.80	2,275,036.50	32.213%
4P01	PDA	50.65	12.85	45,219	2,871,406.50	581,064.15	20.236%
4T43	Tax Software	34.20	14.35	63,213	3,068,991.15	907,106.55	29.557%
5W34	FTP Software	43.00	12.75	52,109	2,905,076.75	664,389.75	22.870%
9C31	Game Software	38.25	13.00	76,145	3,902,431.25	989,885.00	25.366%
Totals				419,968	$ 47,666,899.51	$ 12,577,904.05	
Lowest		$34.20	$12.75	16,534	$2,871,406.50	$581,064.15	17.524%
Highest		$200.23	$95.15	76,145	$9,473,582.50	$2,426,027.50	36.106%
Average		$102.77	$37.00	41,997	$4,766,689.95	$1,257,790.41	

FIGURE 2-84

Perform the following tasks.

1. Complete the following entries in row 3:
   a. Total Sales (cell F3) = Units Sold * (Unit Cost + Unit Profit) or =E3 * (C3+D3)
   b. Total Profit (cell G3) = Unit Profit * Units Sold or = D3 * E3
   c. % Total Profit (cell H3) = Total Profit / Total Sales or = G3 / F3
2. Use the fill handle to copy the three formulas in the range F3:H3 to the range F4:H12. After the copy is complete, click the Fill Options button and click the Fill Without Formatting option to maintain the bottom double border in the range F12:H12.
3. Determine totals for the Units Sold, Total Sales, and Total Profit in row 13.
4. In the range C14:C16, determine the lowest value, highest value, and average value, respectively for the range C3:C12. Use the fill handle to copy the three functions to the range D14:H16. Delete the average from cell H16, because you cannot average percents. *(continued)*

Apply Your Knowledge

Buy It Online Profit Analysis Worksheet *(continued)*

5. Use the Currency Style button on the Formatting toolbar to format the numbers in the ranges C3:D3, F3:G3, and F13:G13. Use the Comma Style button on the Formatting toolbar to format the numbers in cell E3, the range C4:G12, and the range E13:E16. Use the Decrease Decimal button on the Formatting toolbar to display the numbers in the range E3:E16 as whole numbers. Use the Percent Style and the Increase Decimal buttons on the Formatting toolbar to format the range H3:H15. Increase the decimal positions in this range to 3. Use the Format Cells command on the shortcut menu to format the numbers in the ranges C14:D16 and F14:G16 to a floating dollar sign.

6. Use Range Finder to verify the formula in cell G3.

7. Enter your name, course, laboratory assignment number (Apply 2-1), date, and instructor name in the range A20:A24.

8. Preview and print the worksheet in landscape orientation. Save the workbook. Use the file name, Buy It Online 2.

9. Print the range A1:H13. Print the formulas version (press CTRL+ACCENT MARK (`) to display the formulas version of the worksheet in landscape orientation on one page (Figure 2-85) using the Fit to option in the Page sheet in the Page Setup dialog box. Press CTRL+ACCENT MARK (`) to display the values version.

10. In column D, use the keyboard to add manually $2.00 to the profit of each product with a Unit Profit less than $30.00; else add $3.00. You should end up with $13,568,687.05 in cell G13. Print the worksheet. Do not save the workbook.

11. Hand in the four printouts to your instructor.

Report

Buy It Online
Profit Analysis

Product	Description	Unit Cost	Unit Profit	Units Sold	Total Sales	Total Profit	% Total Profit
1H34	Hard Disk	92.95	19.75	32435	=E3*(C3+D3)	=E3*D3	=G3/F3
1J76	Monitor	175.99	45.65	16534	=E4*(C4+D4)	=E4*D4	=G4/F4
2L96	Printer	110.8	62.5	32102	=E5*(C5+D5)	=E5*D5	=G5/F5
2Q78	Scanner	160.5	55.25	43910	=E6*(C6+D6)	=E6*D6	=G6/F6
3K03	Stereo Speakers	121.35	38.75	34391	=E7*(C7+D7)	=E7*D7	=G7/F7
3A04	System Unit	300.23	95.15	23910	=E8*(C8+D8)	=E8*D8	=G8/F8
4P01	PDA	50.65	12.65	45219	=E9*(C9+D9)	=E9*D9	=G9/F9
4T43	Tax Software	34.2	14.35	63213	=E10*(C10+D10)	=E10*D10	=G10/F10
5W34	FTP Software	43	12.75	52109	=E11*(C11+D11)	=E11*D11	=G11/F11
9C31	Game Software	38.25	13	76145	=E12*(C12+D12)	=E12*D12	=G12/F12
Totals					=SUM(E3:E12)	=SUM(F3:F12)	=SUM(G3:G12)
Lowest		=MIN(C3:C12)	=MIN(D3:D12)	=MIN(E3:E12)	=MIN(F3:F12)	=MIN(G3:G12)	=MIN(H3:H12)
Highest		=MAX(C3:C12)	=MAX(D3:D12)	=MAX(E3:E12)	=MAX(F3:F12)	=MAX(G3:G12)	=MAX(H3:H12)
Average		=AVERAGE(C3:C12)	=AVERAGE(D3:D12)	=AVERAGE(E3:E12)	=AVERAGE(F3:F12)	=AVERAGE(G3:G12)	

FIGURE 2-85

In the Lab

1 Ray's Ready Mix Concrete Weekly Payroll Worksheet

Problem: Ray's Ready Mix Concrete has hired you as an intern in its software applications department. Because you took an Excel course last semester, the assistant manager has asked you to prepare a weekly payroll report for the six employees listed in Table 2-8.

Table 2-8 Ray's Ready Mix Concrete Weekly Payroll Data

EMPLOYEE	RATE	HOURS	DEPENDENTS
Sanchez, Edgar	32.25	49.50	6
Wright, Felix	23.50	28.00	1
Wreath, Christy	22.40	70.00	4
Elamain, Al	29.75	18.00	5
Pedal, Rose	21.35	36.00	4
Space, Si	16.25	42.00	2

FIGURE 2-86

Instructions: Perform the following tasks to create a worksheet similar to the one shown in Figure 2-86.

1. Enter the worksheet title Ray's Ready Mix Concrete in cell A1. Enter the column titles in row 2, the data from Table 2-8 in columns A through D, and the row titles in the range A9:A12.

(continued)

In the Lab

Ray's Ready Mix Concrete Weekly Payroll Worksheet *(continued)*

2. Use the following formulas to determine the gross pay, federal tax, state tax, and net pay for the first employee:
   a. Gross Pay (cell E3) = Rate*Hours or =B3*C3.
   b. Federal Tax (cell F3) = 20% * (Gross Pay – Dependents * 38.46) or =20% *(E3 – D3 * 38.46)
   c. State Tax (cell G3) = 3.2% * Gross Pay or =3.2% * E3
   d. Net Pay (cell H3) = Gross Pay – (Federal Tax + State Tax) or =E3 – (F3 + G3)
   Copy the formulas for the first employee to the remaining employees.
3. Calculate totals for hours, gross pay, federal tax, state tax, and net pay in row 9.
4. Use the appropriate functions to determine the average, highest, and lowest values of each column in rows 10 through 12.
5. Use Range Finder to verify each of the formulas entered in row 3.
6. Change the worksheet title to 26-point Arial Black bold orange font (or a font of your choice). Center the worksheet title across columns A through H. Vertically center the worksheet title. Use buttons on the Formatting toolbar to assign the Comma style with two decimal places to the range B3:H12. Bold, italicize, and assign a bottom border (column 2, row 1 on the Borders palette) to the range A2:H2. Align right the column titles in the range B2:H2. Bold and italicize the range A9:A12. Assign a top and thick bottom border (column 1, row 3 on the Borders palette) to the range A9:H9.
7. Change the width of column A to 18.00 characters. If necessary, change the widths of columns B through H to best fit. Change the heights of row 1 to 39.75 points and rows 2 and 10 to 30.00 points.
8. Use the Conditional Formatting command on the Format menu to display bold white font on an orange background for any net pay less than $550.00 in the range H3:H8.
9. Enter your name, course, laboratory assignment number (Lab 2-1), date, and instructor name in the range A14:A18.
10. Spell check the worksheet. Save the workbook using the file name Ray's Ready Mix Concrete.
11. Preview and then print the worksheet.
12. Press CTRL+ACCENT MARK (`) to change the display from the values version to the formulas version. Print the formulas version of the worksheet in landscape orientation using the Fit to option on the Page tab in the Page Setup dialog box. After the printer is finished, press CTRL+ACCENT MARK (`) to reset the worksheet to display the values version. Reset the Scaling option to 100% by clicking the Adjust to option button in the Page sheet in the Page Setup dialog box and then setting the percent value to 100%.
13. Use the keyboard to increase manually the number of hours worked for each employee by 16 hours. The total net pay in cell H9 should equal $6,418.42. If necessary, increase the width of column F to best fit to view the new federal tax total. Preview and print the worksheet with the new values. Hand in the printouts to your instructor.
14. Click cell A1. Try to click cells B1 through H1. You can't because cells B1 through H1 were merged into cell A1 in Step 6. With cell A1 selected, click the Merge and Center button to split cell A1 into cells A1, B1, C1, D1, E1, F1, G1, and H1. Now click cells B1 through H1. Close the workbook without saving changes.

In the Lab

2 Emelyne's Secret Emporium Monthly Accounts Receivable Balance Sheet

Problem: You are a consultant to the Accounting department of Emelyne's Secret Emporium, a popular Manhattan-based merchandise company with several outlets along the East coast. You have been asked to use Excel to generate a report (Figure 2-87) that summarizes the monthly accounts receivable balance. A graphic breakdown of the data also is desired. The customer accounts receivable data in Table 2-9 is available for test purposes.

Table 2-9	Emelyne's Secret Emporium Accounts Receivable Data				
CUSTOMER ID	**CUSTOMER NAME**	**BEGINNING BALANCE**	**PURCHASES**	**PAYMENTS**	**CREDITS**
C3451110	Stone, Emerald	16548.30	2691.70	4012.00	435.10
G2343865	Skiles, L'Triece	8340.10	5000.80	6000.00	0.00
G9147655	Juarez, Louis	3401.65	750.30	1050.00	25.00
K3433390	Wong, Ho-Young	18761.60	5560.00	2200.00	35.25
M6104458	Patel, Radjika	2098.20	1596.10	1200.00	189.95
S3918744	Penn, Shem	8231.80	200.20	1375.00	67.00
T6501934	Jasmine, Zo	2090.00	1080.00	500.00	35.00

FIGURE 2-87

(continued)

In the Lab

Emelyne's Secret Emporium Monthly Accounts Receivable Balance Sheet *(continued)*

Instructions Part 1: Create a worksheet similar to the one shown in Figure 2-87 on the previous page. Include all seven customers in Table 2-9 on the previous page in the report, plus a service charge and a new balance for each customer. Assume no negative unpaid monthly balances. Perform the following tasks.

1. Click the Select All button (to the left of column heading A) and then click the Bold button on the Standard toolbar to bold the entire worksheet.
2. Assign the worksheet title, Emelyne's Secret Emporium, to cell A1. Assign the worksheet subtitle, Monthly Accounts Receivable Balance, to cell A2.
3. Enter the column titles in the range A3:H3 as shown in Figure 2-87.
4. Enter the customer numbers and row titles in column A. Enter the remaining data in Table 2-9.
5. Use the following formulas to determine the monthly service charge in column G and the new balance in column H for customer C3451110. Copy the two formulas down through the remaining customers.
   a. Service Charge = 2.25% * (Beginning Balance – Payments – Credits)
   b. New Balance = Beginning Balance + Purchases – Payments – Credits + Service Charge
6. Calculate totals for beginning balance, purchases, payments, credits, service charge, and new balance in row 11.
7. Assign cell C12 the appropriate function to calculate the average value in the range C4:C10. Copy cell C12 to the range D12:H12.
8. Assign cell C13 the appropriate function to calculate the maximum value in the range C4:C10. Copy cell C13 to the range D13:H13.
9. Assign cell C14 the appropriate function to calculate the minimum value in the range C4:C10. Copy cell C14 to the range D14:H14.
10. Change the worksheet title in cell A1 to 36-point Impact font (or a similar font). Format the worksheet subtitle in cell A2 to 20-point CG Times font. Center the worksheet titles in cells A1 and A2 vertically and across column A through H. Change the width of column A to 12.00 characters. Change the widths of columns B through H to best fit. Change the height of row 1 to 53.25 points. Change the heights of rows 2, 3, and row 12 to 27.75 points.
11. Select the range A1:H2 and then change the background color to Blue (column 6, row 2) on the Fill Color palette. Change the font color in the range A1:H2 to White (column 8, row 5) on the Font Color palette.
12. Italicize the column titles in row 3. Use the Borders button to add a bottom border to the column titles in row 3. Center the column titles in the range B3:H3. Italicize the titles in the range A11:A14. Use the Borders button to add a top and double bottom border (column 4, row 2 on the Borders palette) to the range A11:H11.
13. Use the Format Cells command on the shortcut menu to assign the Currency style with a floating dollar sign to the cells containing numeric data in row 4 and rows 11 through 14. Use the same command to assign the Comma style (currency with no dollar sign) to the range C5:H10. The Format Cells command is preferred over the Comma Style button because the worksheet specifications call for displaying zero as 0.00 rather than as a dash (-), as shown in Figure 2-87.
14. Use the Conditional Formatting command on the Format menu to change the font to white bold on a blue background in any cell in the range H4:H10 that contains a value greater than or equal to 10000.
15. Change the widths of columns C through H to best fit again, if necessary.

16. Rename the sheet Accounts Receivable.

17. Enter your name, course, laboratory assignment number (Lab 2-2), date, and instructor name in the range A16:A20.

18. Spell check the worksheet. Save the workbook using the file name Emelyne's Secret Emporium.

19. Preview and then print the worksheet. Print the range A3:C14. Press CTRL+ACCENT MARK (`) to change the display from the values version to the formulas version and then print the worksheet to fit on one page in landscape orientation. After the printer is finished, press CTRL+ACCENT MARK (`) to reset the worksheet to display the values version. Reset the Scaling option to 100% by clicking the Adjust to option button on the Page tab in the Page Setup dialog box and then setting the percent value to 100%. Hand in the three print-outs to your instructor.

Instructions Part 2: This part requires that you use the Chart Wizard button on the Standard toolbar to draw a 3-D Bar chart. If necessary, use the Ask a Question box on the menu bar to obtain information on drawing a Bar chart.

Draw the 3-D Bar chart showing each customer's total new balance as shown in Figure 2-88. Select the nonadjacent chart ranges B4:B10 and H4:H10. That is, select the range B4:B10 and then hold down the CTRL key and select the range H4:H10. The category names in the range B4:B10 will identify the bars, while the data series in the range H4:H10 will determine the length of the bars. Click the Chart Wizard button on the Standard toolbar. Draw the 3-D Bar chart on a new chart sheet. Use the Bar chart sub-type Clustered Bar with 3-D visual effect (column 1, row 2).

Click the Next button to display the next dialog box. Add the chart title Accounts Receivable.

Rename the Chart1 sheet Bar Chart. Drag the Accounts Receivable tab to the left of the Bar Chart tab. Save the workbook using the same file name as in Part 1. Preview and print the chart. Hand in the printout to your instructor.

FIGURE 2-88

In the Lab

Emelyne's Secret Emporium Monthly Accounts Receivable Balance Sheet *(continued)*

Instructions Part 3: Change the following purchases: account number G9147655 to $5000.00; account number T6501934 to $2500.00. The total new balance in cell H11 should equal $65,848.97. Select both sheets by holding down the SHIFT key and clicking the Bar Chart tab. Preview and print the selected sheets. Hand in the printouts to your instructor.

Instructions Part 4: With your instructor's permission, e-mail the workbook with the changes indicated in Part 3 as an attachment to your instructor. Close the workbook without saving the changes.

3 Equity Web Queries

Problem: Francis Florida, president of Live Snakes and Gators, Inc., recently attended a Microsoft Office seminar at the local community college and learned that Excel can connect to the World Wide Web, download real-time stock data into a worksheet, and then refresh the data as often as needed. Because you have had courses in Excel and the Internet, he has hired you as a consultant to develop a stock analysis workbook. His portfolio is listed in Table 2-10.

Table 2-10 Francis Florida's Stock Portfolio	
COMPANY	STOCK SYMBOL
Caterpillar	CAT
General Electric	GE
Microsoft	MSFT
Pfizer	PFE
Sun Microsystems	SUNW
Wal-Mart	WMT

Instructions Part 1: If necessary, connect to the Internet. Open a new Excel workbook and select cell A1. Perform the following steps to run a Web query to obtain multiple stock quotes, using the stock symbols in Table 2-10.

1. Point to Import External Data on the Data menu and then click Import Data.
2. Double-click MSN MoneyCentral Investor Stock Quotes in the Select Data Source dialog box. If the Web queries do not display, see your instructor for their location.
3. Click the OK button in the Import Data dialog box.
4. When the Enter Parameter Value dialog box displays, enter the stock symbols in Table 2-10 into the text box, being sure to separate them with a comma or space. Click the Use this value/reference for future refreshes check box, click the Refresh automatically when cell value changes, and then click the OK button. After several seconds, the stock data returned by the Web query displays in a worksheet as shown in Figure 2-89. Because the stock data returned is real-time, the numbers on your worksheet may be different.

In the Lab

5. Enter your name, course, laboratory assignment number (Lab 2-3a), date, and instructor name in the range A22:A26.
6. Rename the sheet Multiple Quotes. Save the workbook using the file name Francis Florida's Equities Online. Preview and then print the worksheet in landscape orientation using the Fit to option.
7. Click the following links and print each: Click here to visit MSN MoneyCentral Investor; Pfizer Inc; and Pfizer Inc News. Also, print the latest news item regarding Pfizer from the Pfizer Inc News page. After printing each Web page, close the browser. If necessary, click the Microsoft Excel button on the taskbar to activate Excel. Hand in the printouts to your instructor.

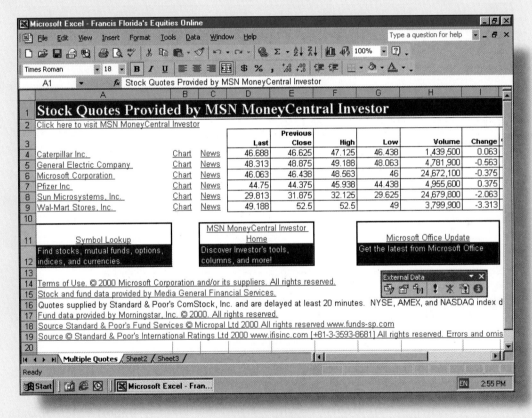

FIGURE 2-89

Instructions Part 2: Perform the following tasks to create a worksheet listing the major indices and their current values as shown in Figure 2-90 on the next page.

1. With the workbook created in Part 1 open, click the Sheet2 tab. Point to Import External Data on the Data menu and then click Import Data.
2. Double-click MSN MoneyCentral Investor Major Indices in the Select Data Source dialog box.
3. Click the OK button in the Import Data dialog box, starting the data in cell A1 of the existing worksheet.
4. The Web query returns the worksheet shown in Figure 2-90 on the next page. Your results may differ.
5. Enter your name, course, laboratory assignment number (Lab 2-3b), date, and instructor name in the range A26:A30.

(continued)

In the Lab

Equity Web Queries *(continued)*

6. Rename the sheet Major Indices. Save the workbook using the same file as in Part 1. Preview and then print the worksheet in landscape orientation using the Fit to option. Hand in the printout to your instructor.

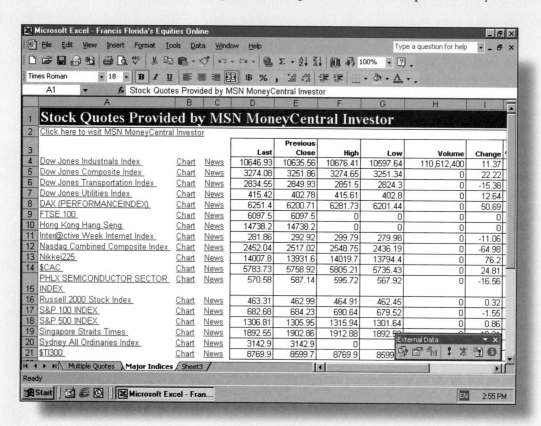

FIGURE 2-90

Instructions Part 3: Create a worksheet showing the latest currency rates (Figure 2-91).

1. With the workbook created in Part 1 open, click the Sheet3 tab. Point to Import External Data on the Data menu and then click Import Data.
2. Double-click MSN MoneyCentral Investor Currency Rates in the Select Data Source dialog box.
3. Click the OK button in the Import Data dialog box, starting the data in cell A1 of the existing worksheet.
4. The Web query returns the worksheet shown in Figure 2-91. Your results may differ.
5. Enter your name, course, laboratory assignment number (Lab 2-3c), date, and instructor name in the range A68:A72.
6. Rename the sheet Currency Rates. Save the workbook using the same file as in Part 1. Preview and then print the worksheet in portrait orientation using the Fit to option. Hand in the printout to your instructor.

In the Lab

FIGURE 2-91

Instructions Part 4: Excel recognizes certain types of data in a cell, such as stock symbols, that it labels with **smart tags**. Excel inserts a **smart tag indicator** (a small purple triangle) in the lower right corner of any cell to indicate that it recognizes the data. If you click the cell with the smart tag indicator, Excel displays the Smart Tag Actions button. If you click the Smart Tag Actions button, Excel displays a menu (Figure 2-92) that can be used to gain instant access to information about the data.

Do the following:

1. Click the New button on the Standard toolbar to display a new workbook. To ensure smart tags is enabled, click AutoCorrect Options on the Tools menu and when the AutoCorrect dialog box displays, click the Smart Tags tab. If necessary, add check marks to the Label data with smart tags, Smart tags list, and Embed smart tags in this workbook check boxes. Click the OK button.

2. Enter the column title Stock Symbols in cell A1. Enter the three stock symbols AMD (Advanced Micro Device), CSCO (Cisco Systems), and INTC (Intel) in the range A2:A4 (Figure 2-92). Save the workbook using the file name Smart Tags.

3. Click cell A4. When the Smart Tag Actions button displays, click it to display the Smart Tag Action list (Figure 2-92). One at a time, click the first four commands under Financial Symbol. Insert the refreshable stock price on a new worksheet. Print the new worksheet and the Web pages that display when you invoke the other three commands. Hand the printouts in to your instructor.

4. Repeat Step 3 for the stock symbols in cells A2 and A3.

FIGURE 2-92

Cases and Places

The difficulty of these case studies varies:
▶ are the least difficult; ▶▶ are more difficult; and ▶▶▶ are the most difficult.

1 ▶   You are the chairman of the fund-raising committee for the computer club. You want to compare various fund-raising ideas to determine which will give you the best profit. You obtain information from six businesses about their products (Table 2-11). Using this data, produce a worksheet to share the information with your committee. Write formulas for the percent profit and the profit per 100 sales. Show the minimum and maximum values for the four numeric columns in Table 2-11. Use the concepts and techniques presented in this project to create and format the worksheet.

Table 2-11	Fund-Raising Data				
COMPANY	PRODUCT	SELLING PRICE	PROFIT	PERCENT PROFIT	PROFIT PER 100 SALES
Stickum	Stickers	$2.50	$0.75		
Granny's Best	Cookies	2.00	1.00		
Write Stuff	Stationary	1.75	0.40		
Best Candy	Candy Bars	1.60	0.35		
Gum-It	Gum	1.75	0.50		
Dip-N-Donuts	Donuts	2.60	0.45		

2 ▶   Occasionally, you buy magazines for you and your family members. In an effort to save money, you are considering subscribing to some of these magazines, even though every issue will not be read. To help you decide which magazines to subscribe to, you make the list shown in Table 2-12 showing the magazines you purchase frequently, the newsstand price, how many times you purchase the magazine each year, and the annual subscription cost. Use the concepts and techniques presented in this project to prepare a worksheet to compare your yearly expenditure for each magazine to the cost of an annual subscription. Include annual newsstand cost and the difference between the annual subscription cost and the annual newsstand cost for each magazine. Determine the maximum, minimum, and average for each numeric column.

Table 2-12	Magazine Subscription Data				
MAGAZINE NAME	NEWSSTAND PRICE	ISSUES PURCHASED EACH YEAR	ANNUAL SUBSCRIPTION PRICE	ANNUAL NEWSSTAND PRICE	SUBSCRIPTION LESS NEWSSTAND
Country Living Gardner	$3.95	4	$12.00		
Disney Adventures	2.99	3	11.85		
Fitness	2.75	4	13.75		
Fortune	5.95	10	35.00		
Newsweek	3.75	25	28.50		
Parenting	2.85	4	12.97		
Sports Illustrated	2.99	30	42.00		
T.V. Guide	1.95	28	49.50		

Cases and Places

3 ▶ In order to determine the effectiveness of their endangered species recovery plan, the Fish and Wildlife Department traps and releases red wolves in selected areas and records how many are pregnant. To obtain a representative sample, the department tries to trap approximately 20% of the population. The sample for five sections is shown in Table 2-13.

Use the following formula to determine the total red wolf population for each section:

Wolves in a Section = 5 * (Total Catch + Pregnant Wolves) – 5 * Death Rate * (Total Catch + Pregnant Wolves)

Use the concepts and techniques presented in this project to create the worksheet. Determine appropriate totals. Finally, estimate the total state red wolf population if 898 sections are in the state.

Table 2-13	Red Wolf Catch Data		
SECTION	WOLVES CAUGHT	WOLVES PREGNANT	ANNUAL DEATH RATE
1	5	2	51%
2	6	1	67%
3	7	2	54%
4	4	2	13%
5	2	1	51%

4 ▶ You and your three room-mates have just received the monthly electric bill for $545, and they have accused you of driving up the total by burning the midnight oil. You are convinced your late-night studying has little effect on the total amount due. You obtain a brochure from the electric company that lists the typical operating costs of appliance s based on average sizes and local electricity rates (Table 2-14). With this data, you produce a worksheet to share with your roommates. Use the concepts and techniques presented in this project to create and format the worksheet.

Table 2-14	Typical Electrical Operating Costs of Appliances			
APPLIANCE	COST PER HOUR	HOURS USED DAILY	TOTAL COST PER DAY	TOTAL COST PER MONTH (30 DAYS)
Clothes dryer	$0.9222	3		
Iron	$0.2157	2.5		
Light bulb (150 watt)	$0.0420	6		
Personal computer	$0.0524	4		
Radio	$0.0095	3		
Stereo	$0.0101	6.5		
Television	$0.0267	4		
VCR	$0.0065	1		

5 ▶▶ Mortimer's Furniture uses a formula to determine the selling price of an item based on that item's wholesale cost. The formula is Selling Price = Wholesale Cost / (1 – Margin). Use this formula to determine the selling price for margins of 60%, 65%, and 70% for the following items and their costs: Sofa, $350; Lamp, $125; End Table, $225; Chair, $215; Rug, $425; Picture, $100. Prepare a professional-looking worksheet showing each item's wholesale cost, selling price for the three margins, and the retailer's profit for each of the three margins. Show totals, averages, maximums, and minimums. Include a chart illustrating what part of the profit is represented by each item when all six items are sold.

Cases and Places

6 ▶▶ Use the concepts and techniques described in this project to run the Web queries titled MSN MoneyCentral Investor Major Indices and Microsoft MoneyCentral Investor Currency Rates on separate worksheets shortly after the stock market opens. Print each worksheet to fit on one page in landscape orientation. Refresh the worksheets later in the day near the stock market close. Print the worksheets and compare them.

7 ▶▶▶ Computer Discount Sales has decided to pay a 2.5% commission to its salespeople to stimulate sales. The company currently pays each employee a base salary. The management has projected each employee's sales for the next quarter. This information — employee name, employee base salary, and projected sales — follows: Balast, Jack, $8,000.00, $325,557.00; Franks, Ed, $9,500.00, $464,188.00; Hass, Tim, $7,000.00, $199,250.00; Moore, Renee, $5,320.00, $398,450.00; Lister, Bob, $9,250.00, $832,897.00.

With this data, you have been asked to develop a worksheet calculating the amount of commission and the projected quarterly salary for each employee. The following formulas can be used to obtain this information:

Commission Amount = 2.5% x Projected Sales
Quarterly Salary = Employee Base Salary + Commission Amount

Include a total, average value, highest value, and lowest value for employee base salary, commission amount, and quarterly salary. Create a 3-D Pie chart illustrating the portion each employee's quarterly salary contributes to the total quarterly salary. Use the concepts and techniques presented in this project to create and format the worksheet. Use the Excel Help system to create a professional-looking 3-D Pie chart with title and data labels.

Microsoft Excel 2002

PROJECT

3

What-If Analysis, Charting, and Working with Large Worksheets

You will have mastered the material in this project when you can:

OBJECTIVES

- Rotate text in a cell
- Create a series of month names
- Use the Format Painter button to format cells
- Copy and paste
- Insert and delete cells
- Use smart tags
- Format numbers using format symbols
- Freeze titles
- Display and format the system date
- Use absolute cell references in a formula
- Use the IF function to perform a logical test
- Copy absolute cell references
- Display and dock toolbars
- Add a drop shadow to a range of cells
- Create a 3-D Pie chart on a separate chart sheet
- Color worksheet tabs
- Rearrange sheets in a workbook
- Preview and print multiple sheets
- Use the Zoom box to change the worksheet view
- View different parts of the worksheet through window panes
- Use Excel to answer what-if questions
- Goal seek

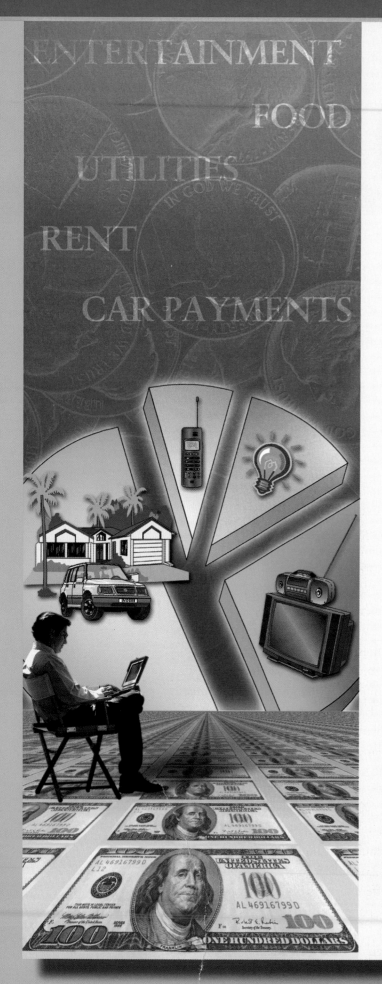

Cash in on Financial Advice

Make Money Management Count

Coinage in America dates back to the eighteenth century when Congress created the United States Mint on April 2, 1792. To ensure that the Nation could conduct its trade and commerce, the U.S. Mint produced a sufficient quantity of circulating coinage. Traditionally, between 14 and 20 billion coins are circulated annually. Recently, the introduction of the 50 States Commemorative Quarter and the Golden Dollar has increased annual Mint production to more than 27 billion coins.

In a single room in the basement of the main United States Treasury building, two men and four women separated and sealed by hand $1 and $2 United States Notes, which had been printed by private bank note companies. This event led to the establishment of the Bureau of Engraving and Printing on August 29, 1862, with the first currency being printed by the Bureau in the fall of 1863.

Counting currency today is an automated process, but imagine if you were asked to count one trillion Golden Dollar coins. At a rate of one per second, twenty-four hours a day, it would require 32,000 years; an impossible feat.

The current U.S. national debt exceeds five trillion dollars ($5,000,000,000,000) with projected annual interest payments of more than $235 billion. Italy, Japan, and Australia also face debts in trillions of dollars. It is no wonder that financial counselors encourage sound fiscal control and budgeting to avoid deficit spending or debt. People who borrow are

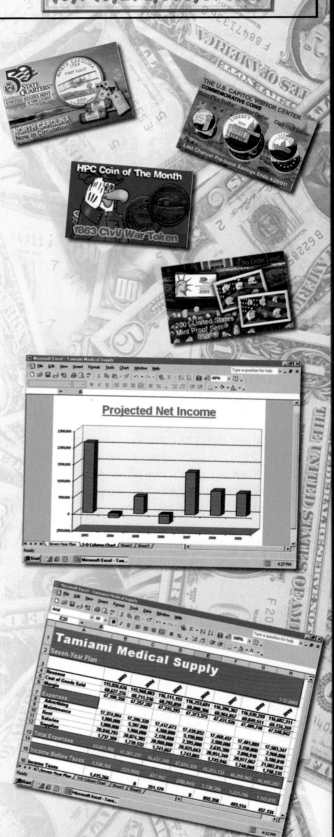

expected both to be able and willing to pay back what they owe along with an appropriate amount of interest.

When working with any sum of money — whether an individual's thousands, the more than 125 American billionaires' billions, or even the nation's trillions — creating a realistic budget indeed can be difficult. Budgets provide a sense of perspective that makes it possible to keep debt at a minimum. Although you are not responsible for preparing a national $1.64 trillion budget, knowing where your money goes is the first step in planning a sound personal budget.

Budgeting using worksheets helps reconcile income and expenses. For example, based on a loan calculation and a budget, you can determine a reasonable monthly car payment. Your living expenses may include rent, food, utilities, car and loan payments, credit card payments, and entertainment. Developing a solid budget for these expenses can help you determine if you will be able to buy a future home. Budgets track your income, expenses, net worth, and cash flow, while organizing your financial data in a logical format. Using electronic spreadsheet software makes it easy to show exactly how you spend money.

In this project, you will use Excel's automatic recalculation feature to complete what-if analysis. It is a powerful tool used to analyze worksheet data. It allows you to scrutinize the impact of changing values in cells that are referenced by a formula in another cell. What if you need to know how much money to put down on a home loan in order to find a manageable monthly payment? What if your income changes or you add a new expense or pay a final payment? These questions and more can be answered easily with Excel's what-if capabilities. Excel not only recalculates all the formulas in a worksheet when new data is entered, it also redraws any associated charts.

Although seemingly restrictive at times, a personal financial plan allows you to examine line by line how your money is spent. Because monetary problems can happen to anyone, regardless of income, sensible use of credit cards, budgeting, and family money management are key components for maintaining an average debt-to-asset ratio of 30 percent. When a situation looks bleak, cash in on financial advice: use credit-counseling services to help with credit repair and education.

Microsoft Excel 2002

What-If Analysis, Charting, and Working with Large Worksheets

PROJECT

3

C A S E   P E R S P E C T I V E

Maria Cianti is the chief executive officer (CEO) of Awesome Intranets, a computer company that specializes in the installation of intranets worldwide. Twice a year, Maria submits a plan to her senior staff to show projected revenues, expenses, and net income for the next six months.

Last June, Maria used pencil, paper, and a calculator to complete the report and draw a 3-D Pie chart. When she presented her report, one of her managers asked for the effect on the projected net income if the marketing expense allocation was changed. While her management team waited impatiently, Maria took several minutes to calculate the answers. Once she changed the projected expenses, the 3-D Pie chart no longer matched the projections. Maria now wants to use a computer and spreadsheet software to address what-if questions so she can take advantage of its instantaneous recalculation feature. As lead spreadsheet specialist for Awesome Intranets, you are to meet with Maria, determine her needs, and create the worksheet and chart.

Introduction

This project introduces you to techniques that will enhance your abilities to create worksheets and draw charts. You will learn about other methods for entering values in cells and formatting these values. You also will learn how to use absolute cell references and how to use the IF function to assign a value to a cell based on a logical test.

In the previous projects, you learned how to use the Standard and Formatting toolbars. Excel has several other toolbars that can make your work easier. One such toolbar is the **Drawing toolbar**, which allows you to draw shapes and arrows and add drop shadows to cells you want to emphasize.

Worksheets normally are much larger than those created in the previous projects, often extending beyond the size of the window (Figure 3-1a). Because you cannot see the entire worksheet on the screen at one time, working with a large worksheet can be difficult. For this reason, Excel provides several commands that allow you to change the display on the screen so you can view critical parts of a large worksheet at one time. One command lets you freeze the row and column titles so they always display on the screen. Another command splits the worksheet into separate window panes so you can view different parts of a worksheet.

From your work in Project 1, you are aware of how easily charts can be created. This project covers additional charting techniques that allow you to convey your message in a dramatic pictorial fashion (Figure 3-1b).

When you set up a worksheet, you should use as many cell references in formulas as possible, rather than constant values. The cell references in a formula are called assumptions. **Assumptions** are values in cells you can change to determine new values for formulas. This project emphasizes the use of assumptions and introduces you to answering what-if questions such as, what if you decrease the marketing expenses assumption (cell B21 in Figure 3-1a) by 5% — how would the decrease affect the projected six-month net income (cell H14 in Figure 3-1a)? Being able to quickly analyze the effect of changing values in a worksheet is an important skill in making business decisions.

(a) Worksheet

(b) 3-D Pie Chart

FIGURE 3-1

Project Three — Awesome Intranets' Six-Month Financial Projections

You took the following notes about the required worksheet and chart in your meeting with the CEO, Maria Cianti.

Need: A worksheet (Figure 3-1a on the previous page) and 3-D Pie chart (Figure 3-1b on the previous page) are required. The worksheet is to show Awesome Intranets' projected monthly revenue, expenses, and net income for a six-month period. The 3-D Pie chart is to show the contribution of each projected month's net income to the projected six-month total net income.

Source of Data: The six projected monthly revenues (row 4 of Figure 3-1a) and the seven assumptions (range B17:B23) that are used to determine the projected monthly expenses are based on the company's historical data. All the remaining numbers in Figure 3-1a are determined from these 13 numbers using formulas.

Calculations: Each of the projected monthly expenses in the range B7:G12 of Figure 3-1a — administrative, bonus, commission, equipment, marketing, and technical support — is determined by taking an assumed percentage of the corresponding projected monthly revenue in row 4. The assumptions in the range B17:B23 are as follows:

1. The projected monthly administrative expenses (row 7) are 11.75% (cell B17) of the projected monthly revenue (row 4).

2. The projected monthly bonus (row 8) is $60,000.00 (cell B18) if the projected monthly revenue (row 4) exceeds the revenue for bonus (cell B22) to be awarded; otherwise, the projected monthly bonus is zero. The revenue for bonus value is in cell B22 ($6,500,000.00).

3. The projected monthly commission expenses (row 9) are 2.25% (cell B19) of the projected monthly revenue (row 4).

4. The projected monthly equipment expenses (row 10) are 27.75% (cell B20) of the projected monthly revenue (row 4).

5. The projected monthly marketing expenses (row 11) are 15.35% (cell B21) of the projected monthly revenue (row 4).

6. The projected monthly technical support expenses (row 12) are 31.50% (cell B23) of the projected monthly revenue (row 4).

The projected total monthly expenses in row 13 of Figure 3-1a are the sum of the corresponding projected monthly expenses in rows 7 through 12. The projected monthly net income in row 14 is equal to the corresponding projected monthly revenue (row 4) minus the projected monthly total expenses (row 13).

Because the projected expenses in rows 7 through 12 are dependent on the assumptions in the range B17:B23, you can use the what-if capability of Excel to determine the impact of changing these assumptions on the projected monthly total expenses in row 13 and the projected monthly net income in row 14.

Chart Requirements: A 3-D Pie chart is required on a separate sheet (Figure 3-1b) that shows the contribution of each month to the projected net income for the six-month period.

Starting and Customizing Excel

To start Excel, Windows must be running. Perform the following steps to start and customize Excel. Once the Excel window opens, steps 4 and 5 close the task pane and ensure that the Standard and Formatting toolbars display on two rows.

More About

Correctness

Studies have shown that over 25% of all business worksheets have errors. If you are not careful entering data and formulas, then your worksheet is prone to errors. You can ensure correctness in your formulas by carefully checking them using Range Finder and the Error Checking command on the Tools menu. The Auditing command on the Tools menu can also be helpful when verifying formulas.

More About

Large Worksheets

The automatic recalculation feature of Excel can become annoying when working with large worksheets with many formulas. You can easily grow impatient waiting for the recalculation to take place each time you complete an entry. You can switch Excel to manual recalculation by clicking Tools on the menu bar, clicking Options, clicking the Calculation tab, and then clicking the Manual option button. You then press F9 to recalculate when you are done entering all the values.

TO START AND CUSTOMIZE EXCEL

1 Click the Start button on the Windows taskbar, point to Programs on the Start menu, and then click Microsoft Excel on the Programs submenu.

2 If the Excel window is not maximized, double-click its title bar to maximize it.

3 If the New Workbook task pane displays, click the Show at startup check box at the bottom of the task pane to remove the check mark and then click the Close button in the upper-right corner to close the task pane.

4 If the Language bar displays, click its Minimize button.

5 If the Standard and Formatting toolbars display on one row, click the Toolbar Options button on the right side of either toolbar and then click Show Buttons on Two Rows in the Toolbar Options list.

The Excel window with the Standard and Formatting toolbars on two rows displays as shown in Figure 3-2 on the next page.

If your toolbars display differently than those shown in Figure 3-2, see Appendix D for additional information on resetting the toolbars and menus.

Changing the Font of the Entire Worksheet to Bold

After starting Excel, the next step is to change the font of the entire worksheet to bold so all entries will be emphasized.

TO BOLD THE FONT OF THE ENTIRE WORKSHEET

1 Click the Select All button immediately above row heading 1 and to the left of column heading A.

2 Click the Bold button on the Formatting toolbar.

No immediate change takes place on the screen. As you enter text and numbers into the worksheet, however, Excel will display them in bold.

Entering the Worksheet Titles

The worksheet contains two titles, one in cell A1, and another in cell A2. In the previous projects, titles were centered across the worksheet. With large worksheets that extend beyond the size of a window, it is best to enter titles in the upper-left corner as shown in Figure 3-1a on page E 3.05. Perform the following steps to enter the worksheet titles.

TO ENTER THE WORKSHEET TITLES

1 Select cell A1 and then enter `Awesome Intranets` as the worksheet title.

2 Select cell A2 and then enter `Six-Month Financial Projections` as the worksheet subtitle.

Excel responds by displaying the worksheet titles in cells A1 and A2 in bold as shown in Figure 3-2 on the next page.

More About

The Startup Submenu

Any application on the Startup submenu starts automatically when you turn your computer on. To add Excel to the Startup submenu, do the following: 1) Click Start on the Windows taskbar, point to Programs, and then point to Startup on the Programs submenu; 2) Right drag Microsoft Excel from the Programs submenu to the Startup submenu; 3) When the shortcut menu displays, click Copy. The next time you turn your computer on, Excel will automatically start.

More About

Eliminating Eyestrain

Bolding the entire worksheet makes it easier for users to read the worksheet. An alternative is to increase the font size of the entire worksheet to 12- or 14-point or increase the percentage in the Zoom box, especially if users have less than average eyesight.

More *About*

Positioning Data in a Cell

In Excel, you use the Alignment sheet shown in Figure 3-3 to position data in a cell by centering, left-aligning, right-aligning, indenting, aligning at the top, bottom, or center, and rotating. If you enter 90° in the Degrees box, the text will display vertically and read from bottom to top in the cell.

Rotating Text and Using the Fill Handle to Create a Series

When you first enter text, its angle is zero degrees (0°), and it reads from left to right in a cell. You can **rotate text** counterclockwise by entering a number between 1° and 90° on the Alignment sheet in the Format Cells dialog box.

In Projects 1 and 2, you used the fill handle to copy a cell or a range of cells to adjacent cells. You also can use the fill handle to create a series of numbers, dates, or month names automatically. Perform the following steps to enter the month name, January, in cell B3, format cell B3 (including rotating the text), and then enter the remaining month names in the range C3:G3 using the fill handle.

Steps **To Rotate Text and Use the Fill Handle to Create a Series of Month Names**

1 **Select cell B3. Type** January **as the cell entry and then click the Enter box. Click the Font Size box arrow on the Formatting toolbar and then click 11 in the Font Size list. Click the Borders button arrow and then click the Bottom Border button on the Borders palette. Right-click cell B3 and then point to Format Cells on the shortcut menu.**

The text, January, displays in cell B3 using the assigned formats (Figure 3-2). The shortcut menu displays.

FIGURE 3-2

2 **Click Format Cells. When the Format Cells dialog box displays, click the Alignment tab. Click the 45° point in the Orientation area and point to the OK button.**

The Alignment sheet in the Format Cells dialog box displays. The Text hand in the Orientation area points to the 45° point and 45 displays in the Degrees box (Figure 3-3).

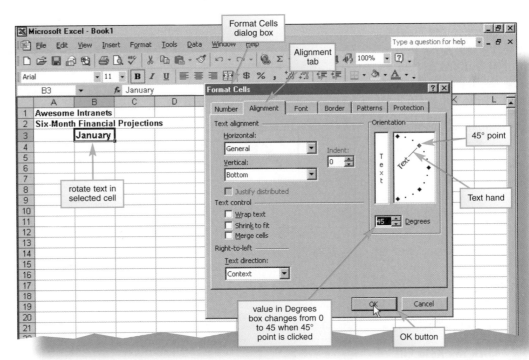

FIGURE 3-3

3 **Click the OK button. Point to the fill handle on the lower-right corner of cell B3.**

The text, January, in cell B3 displays at a 45° angle (Figure 3-4). Excel automatically increases the height of row 3 to best fit to display the rotated text. The mouse pointer changes to a cross hair.

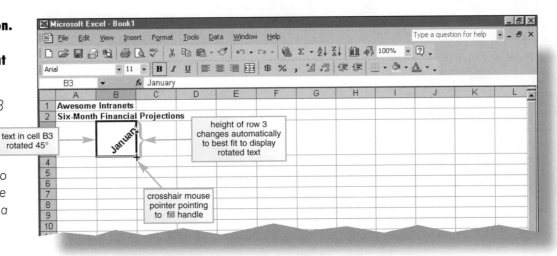

FIGURE 3-4

4 **Drag the fill handle to the right to select the range C3:G3.**

Excel displays a light border that surrounds the selected range (Figure 3-5). A ScreenTip displays indicating the month of the last cell in the selected range.

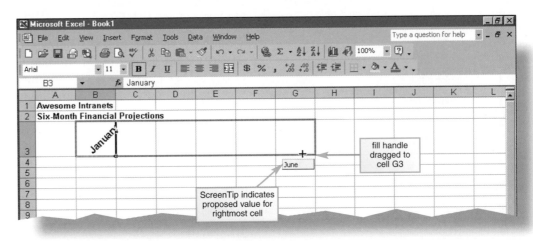

FIGURE 3-5

5 Release the mouse button. Click the Auto Fill Options button below the lower-right corner of the fill area.

Using January in cell B3 as the basis, Excel creates the month name series February through June in the range C3:G3 (Figure 3-6). The formats assigned to cell B3 earlier in Step 1 (11-point font, bottom border, text rotated 45°) also are copied to the range C3:G3. The Auto Fill Options menu displays the fill options available.

6 Click the Auto Fill Options button to hide the Fill Options list.

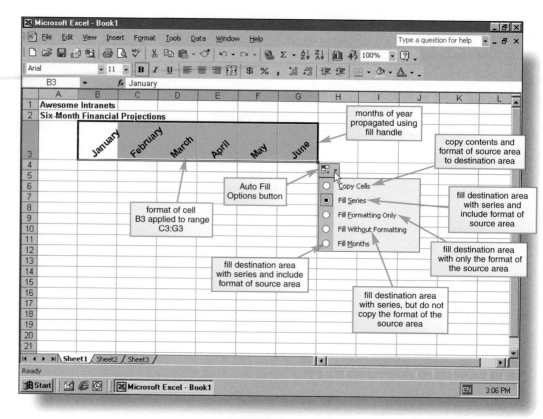

FIGURE 3-6

Other Ways

1. Enter start month in cell, right-drag fill handle in direction to fill, click Fill Months on shortcut menu
2. Select range to fill, in Voice Command mode say, "Edit, Fill, Series, Auto Fill"

Besides creating a series of values, the fill handle also copies the format of cell B3 to the range C3:G3. With some fill operations, you may not want to duplicate the formats of the cell with the initial value. If this is the case, then after the range fills, click the Auto Fill Options button (Figure 3-6) and select the option you desire from the Auto Fill Options menu. As shown in Figure 3-6, the Fill Series option is the default. That is, this is the option Excel uses to fill the area. If you choose another option in the Auto Fill Options menu, then Excel immediately changes the contents of the fill area. The Auto Fill Options button remains active until you begin the next Excel operation.

You can use the fill handle to create longer series than the one shown in Figure 3-6. If you drag the fill handle past cell G3 in Step 4, Excel continues to increment the months and logically will repeat January, February, and so on, if you extend the range far enough to the right.

You can create several different types of series using the fill handle. Table 3-1 illustrates several examples. Notice in examples 4 through 7 that, if you use the fill handle to create a series of numbers or non-sequential

Table 3-1	Examples of Series Using the Fill Handle	
EXAMPLE	CONTENTS OF CELL(S) COPIED USING THE FILL HANDLE	NEXT THREE VALUES OF EXTENDED SERIES
1	4:00	5:00, 6:00, 7:00
2	Qtr2	Qtr3, Qtr4, Qtr1
3	Quarter 3	Quarter 4, Quarter 1, Quarter 2
4	Jan-2003, Apr-2003	Jul-2003, Oct-2003, Jan-2004
5	2003, 2004	2005, 2006, 2007
6	1, 2	3, 4, 5
7	780, 760	740, 720, 700
8	Mon	Tue, Wed, Thr
9	Monday, Wednesday	Friday, Sunday, Tuesday
10	2nd Section	3rd Section, 4th Section, 5th Section
11	-101, -103	-105, -107, -109

months, you must enter the first item in the series in one cell and the second item in the series in an adjacent cell. Next, select both cells and drag the fill handle through the destination area.

Copying a Cell's Format Using the Format Painter Button

Because Total, the last column title, is not part of the series, it must be entered separately in cell H3 and formatted to match the other column titles. Imagine how many steps it would take, however, to assign the formatting of the other column titles to this cell — first, you have to change the font to 11 point, then add a bottom border, and finally, rotate the text 45°. Using the **Format Painter button** on the Standard toolbar, however, you can format a cell quickly by copying a cell's format to another cell. The following steps enter the column title, Total, in cell H3 and format the cell using the Format Painter button.

More About

The Mighty Fill Handle

If you drag the fill handle to the left or up, Excel will decrement the series rather than increment the series. To use the fill handle to copy a potential series initiator, like the word January, to a destination area, hold down the CTRL key while you drag. If you drag the fill handle back into the middle of a cell, Excel erases the contents.

Steps To Copy a Cell's Format Using the Format Painter Button

1 **Click cell H3. Type** Total **and then press the LEFT ARROW key. With cell G3 selected, click the Format Painter button on the Standard toolbar. Point to cell H3.**

The mouse pointer changes to a block plus sign with a paint brush (Figure 3-7).

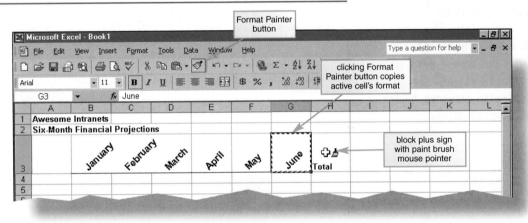

FIGURE 3-7

2 **Click cell H3 to assign the format of cell G3 to cell H3. Click cell A4.**

Excel copies the format of cell G3 (11-point font, bottom border, text rotated 45°) to cell H3 (Figure 3-8). Cell A4 is now the active cell.

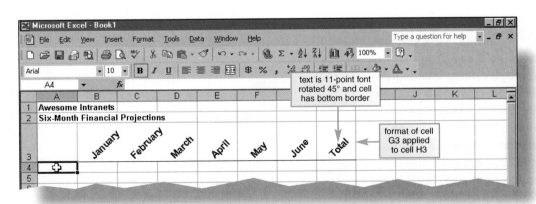

FIGURE 3-8

Other Ways

1. Select cell with desired format, in Voice Command mode say, "Format Painter," select cell or range of cells

The Format Painter button also can be used to copy the formats of a cell to a range of cells. To copy formats to a range of cells, select the cell or range with the desired format, click the Format Painter button on the Standard toolbar, and then drag through the range to which you want to paste the formats.

Increasing the Column Widths and Entering Row Titles

In Project 2, the column widths were increased after the values were entered into the worksheet. Sometimes, you may want to increase the column widths before you enter the values and, if necessary, adjust them later. The following steps increase the column widths and add the row titles in column A down to Assumptions in cell A16.

Steps To Increase Column Widths and Enter Row Titles

1 Move the mouse pointer to the boundary between column heading A and column heading B so that the mouse pointer changes to a split double arrow. Drag the mouse pointer to the right until the ScreenTip displays, Width: 25.00 (180 pixels).

The ScreenTip and distance between the left edge of column A and the vertical dotted line below the mouse pointer shows the proposed column width (Figure 3-9).

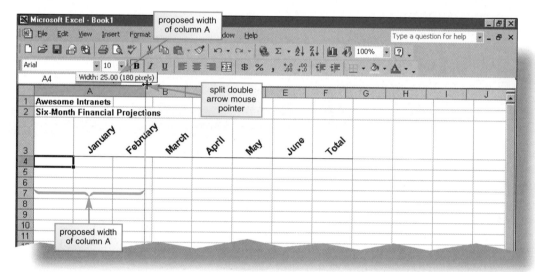

FIGURE 3-9

2 Release the mouse button. Click column heading B and drag through column heading G to select columns B through G. Move the mouse pointer to the boundary between column headings B and C and then drag the mouse to the right until the ScreenTip displays, Width: 13.00 (96 pixels).

The distance between the left edge of column B and the vertical line below the mouse pointer shows the proposed width of columns B through G (Figure 3-10).

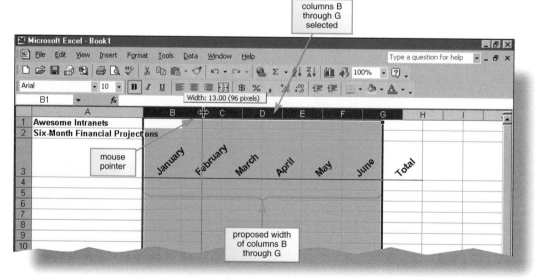

FIGURE 3-10

3 Release the mouse button. Use the technique described in Step 1 to increase the width of column H to 15.00. Enter Revenue in cell A4, Expenses in cell A6, Administrative in cell A7, Bonus in cell A8, Commission in cell A9, Equipment in cell A10. Enter Marketing in cell A11, Technical Support in cell A12, Total Expenses in cell A13, Net Income in cell A14, and Assumptions in cell A16. Select the range A7:A12. Click the Increase Indent button on the Formatting toolbar. Click cell A17.

The row titles display as shown in Figure 3-11.

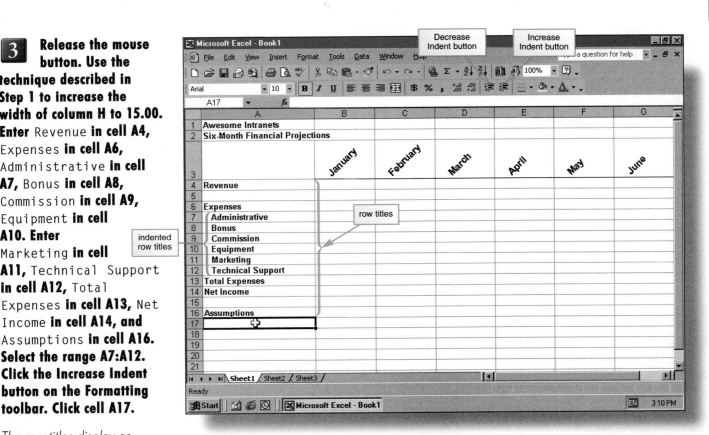

FIGURE 3-11

The **Increase Indent button** indents the contents of a cell to the right by three spaces each time you click it. The **Decrease Indent button** decreases the indent by three spaces each time you click it.

Copying a Range of Cells to a Nonadjacent Destination Area

As shown in Figure 3-1a on page E 3.05, the row titles in the Assumptions table in the range A17:A23 are the same as the row titles in the range A7:A12, with the exception of the additional entry in cell A22. Hence, you can create the Assumptions table row titles by copying the range A7:A12 to the range A17:A22 and inserting a row for the additional entry in cell A22. The range to copy (range A7:A12) is not adjacent to the destination area (range A17:A22). In the first two projects, you used the fill handle to copy a range of cells to an adjacent destination area. To copy a range of cells to a nonadjacent destination area, however, you cannot use the fill handle.

A more versatile method of copying a cell or range of cells is to use the Copy button and Paste button on the Standard toolbar. You can use these two buttons to copy a range of cells to an adjacent or nonadjacent destination area.

Other **Ways**

1. To indent, right-click range, click Format Cells, click Alignment tab, click Left (Indent) in Horizontal list, type number of spaces to indent in Indent text box, click OK button

2. To indent, in Voice Command mode say, "Increase Indent"

More **About**

Shrink to Fit

An alternative to increasing the column widths is to shrink the characters in the cell to fit the current width of the column. To shrink to fit, click Format on the menu bar, click Cells, click the Alignment tab, and click the Shrink to fit check box in the Text control area.

More About

Copying Across Workbooks

You can copy a range of cells in one workbook to another by opening the source workbook, selecting the range, clicking the Copy button to place the range of cells on the Office Clipboard, activating the destination workbook, selecting the destination area, and clicking the Paste button.

When you click the **Copy button**, it copies the contents and format of the selected range and places the copy on the Office Clipboard. The **Copy command** on the Edit menu or shortcut menu works the same as the Copy button. The **Office Clipboard** allows you to collect up to 24 different items from any Office application. When you have one item on the Office clipboard and then copy a second item, Excel automatically displays the **Clipboard task pane** on the left side of the screen showing its contents. You can display the Clipboard task pane at anytime by clicking the **Task Pane command** on the **View menu**. If the Workbook or Search task pane displays, click the **Other Task Panes arrow** on the Task Pane title bar and click Clipboard.

The **Paste button** copies the newest item on the Office Clipboard to the destination area. The **Paste command** on the Edit menu or shortcut menu works the same as the Paste button. If you want to copy an older item on the Office Clipboard, click the icon representing the item on the Clipboard task pane. The following steps use the Copy and Paste buttons to copy a range of cells to a nonadjacent destination area.

Steps **To Copy a Range of Cells to a Nonadjacent Destination Area**

1 **Select the range A7:A12 and then click the Copy button on the Standard toolbar. Click cell A17, the top cell in the destination area. Point to the Paste button.**

Excel surrounds the range A7:A12 with a marquee when you click the Copy button (Figure 3-12). Excel also copies the values and formats of the range A7:A12 onto the Office Clipboard.

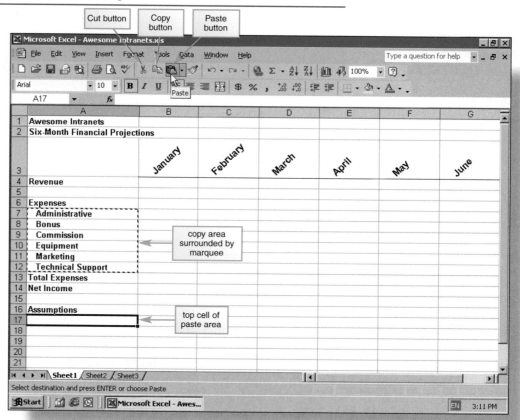

FIGURE 3-12

2 **Click the Paste button on the Standard toolbar. Click the Paste Options button to the right of the destination area to view the paste options available.**

Excel copies the values and formats of the last item placed on the Office Clipboard (range A7:A12) to the destination area A17:A22 (Figure 3-13). The Paste Options menu displays showing the available paste options. The default option is Keep Source Formatting, which means both the contents and format are copied.

3 **After reviewing the Paste Options menu, press the ESC key twice.**

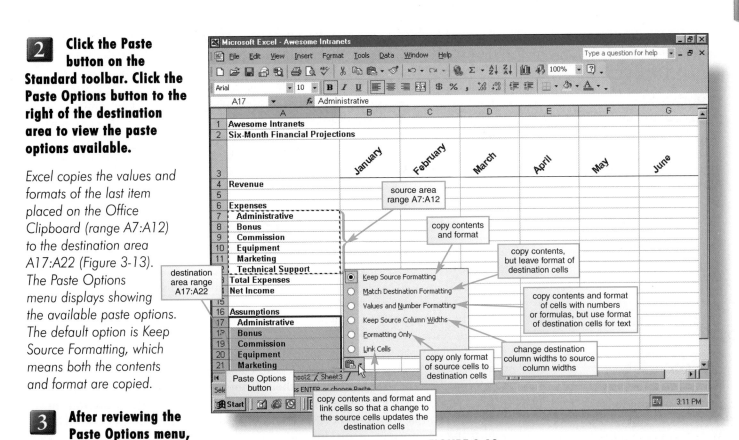

FIGURE 3-13

The first time you press the ESC key, Excel hides the Paste Options menu. The second time you press the ESC key, it removes the marquee from the source area and disables the Paste button on the Standard toolbar.

In Step 1 and Figure 3-12, you can see that you are not required to select the entire destination area (range A17:A22) before clicking the Paste button. Because the destination area is exactly the same size as the source area, you have to select only the upper-left cell of the destination area. In the case of a single column range such as A17:A22, the top cell of the destination area (cell A17) also is the upper-left cell of the destination area.

When you complete a copy, the values and formats in the destination area are replaced with the values and formats of the latest item placed on the Office Clipboard. Any data contained in the destination area prior to the copy and paste is lost. If you accidentally delete valuable data, immediately click the Undo button on the Standard toolbar or click the **Undo Paste command** on the Edit menu to undo the paste.

The Paste Options menu in Figure 3-13 shows the paste options available immediately after clicking the Paste button. If you select an option, Excel modifies the most recent paste operation to agree with your selection. The default is to copy the contents and formats of the cells. In the previous set of steps, it was not necessary to click the Paste Options button. It was clicked in Step 2 to show the paste options available following a copy and paste operation.

Other **Ways**

1. Select source area, on Edit menu click Copy, select destination area, on Edit menu click Paste

2. Right-click source area, click Copy on shortcut menu, right-click destination area, click Paste on shortcut menu

3. Select source area and point to border of range; while holding down the CTRL key, drag source area to destination area

4. Select source area, press CTRL+C, select destination area, press CTRL+V

5. Select source area, in Voice Command mode say, "Copy," select destination area, in Voice Command mode say, "Paste"

Copying versus Moving

You may hear someone say, "move it or copy it , its all the same." No, it's not the same! When you move cells, the original location is blanked and the format is reset to the default. When you copy cells, the copy area remains intact. In short, copy cells to duplicate and move cells to rearrange.

The Cut Command

When you cut a cell or range of cells using the Cut command or Cut button, it is copied to the Office Clipboard but it is not removed from the worksheet until you paste it in the destination area by clicking the Paste button or pressing the ENTER key. When you complete the paste, the entry and its formats are removed from the source area.

Inserting Multiple Rows

If you want to insert multiple rows, you have two choices. First, you can insert a single row by using the Insert command on the shortcut menu and then press F4 repeatedly to keep inserting rows. The second method involves selecting rows before inserting. For instance, if you want to insert five rows, select five existing rows in the worksheet and then click Insert on the shortcut menu.

The Paste button on the Standard toolbar (Figure 3-12 on page E 3.14) includes an arrow, which displays a list of advanced paste options (Formulas, Values, No Borders, Transpose, Paste Link, Paste Special). These options will be discussed when they are used.

An alternative to clicking the Paste button is to press the ENTER key. The ENTER key completes the paste operation, removes the marquee from the source area, and disables the Paste button so that you cannot paste to other destination areas. The ENTER key was not used in the previous set of steps so that the capabilities of the Paste Options button could be discussed. The Paste Options button does not display when you use the ENTER key to complete the paste operation.

Using Drag and Drop to Move or Copy Cells

You also can use the mouse to move or copy cells. First, you select the source area and point to the border of the cell or range. You know you are pointing to the border of the cell or range when the mouse pointer changes to a **block arrow**. To move the selected cell or cells, drag the selection to the destination area. To copy a selection, hold down the CTRL key while dragging the selection to the destination area. Be sure to release the mouse button before you release the CTRL key. Using the mouse to move or copy cells is called **drag and drop**.

Another way to move cells is to select them, click the Cut button on the Standard toolbar (Figure 3-12) to remove them from the worksheet and copy them to the Office Clipboard, select the destination area, and then click the Paste button on the Standard toolbar or press the ENTER key. You also can use the Cut command on the Edit menu or shortcut menu, instead of the Cut button.

Inserting and Deleting Cells in a Worksheet

At anytime while the worksheet is on the screen, you can insert cells to enter new data or delete cells to remove unwanted data. You can insert or delete individual cells, a range of cells, entire rows, entire columns, or entire worksheets.

Inserting Rows

The **Rows command** on the Insert menu or the **Insert command** on the shortcut menu allows you to insert rows between rows that already contain data. In the Assumptions table at the bottom of the worksheet, a row must be inserted between rows 21 and 22 so the Revenue for Bonus assumption can be added (shown in Figure 3-1a on page E 3.05). The following steps show how to accomplish the task of inserting a new row into the worksheet.

Steps **To Insert a Row**

1 **Right-click row heading 22 and then point to Insert on the shortcut menu.**

Row 22 is selected, and the shortcut menu displays (Figure 3-14).

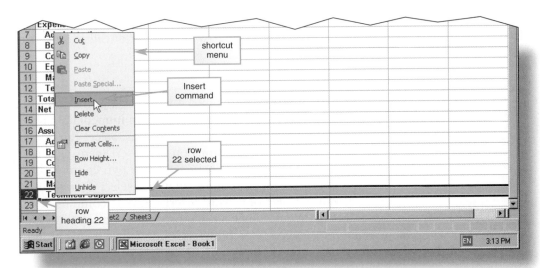

FIGURE 3-14

2 **Click Insert.**

Excel inserts a new row in the worksheet by shifting down the selected row 22 and all rows below it (Figure 3-15). Excel selects the new row. The Insert Options button displays just above the row inserted.

FIGURE 3-15

Other **Ways**

1. On Insert menu, click Rows
2. Click row heading, press CTRL+SHIFT+PLUS SIGN
3. Select number of rows to insert, in Voice Command mode say, "Insert, Rows"

To insert adjacent rows, select as many rows as you want by dragging through the row headings immediately below where you want the new rows inserted, and then right-click the selected rows.

When you insert a row, Excel automatically copies the format from the row above the inserted row. You can change this by clicking the **Insert Options button** that displays immediately above the inserted row (Figure 3-15). Following the insertion of a row, the Insert Options button lets you select from the following: (1) Format Same As Above; (2) Format Same As Below; and (3) Clear Formatting. The Format Same as Above option is the default. The Insert Options button remains active until you begin the next Excel operation.

If the rows that are shifted down include any formulas, Excel adjusts the cell references to the new locations. Thus, if a formula in the worksheet references a cell in row 22 before the insert, then the cell reference in the formula is adjusted to row 23 after the insert.

Moving, Copying, and Inserting

You can move and insert between existing cells by holding down the SHIFT key while you drag the selection to the gridline where you want to insert. You can also copy and insert by holding down the CTRL and SHIFT keys while you drag the selection to the desired gridline.

The Insert Options Button

When inserting columns or rows, the Insert Options button only displays if there are formats assigned to the leftmost column or top row of the selection.

Undoing What You Did

Copying, deleting, inserting, and moving have the potential to render a worksheet useless. Carefully review these actions before continuing on to the next task. If your not sure the action is correct, click the Undo button on the Standard toolbar.

The primary difference between the Insert command on the shortcut menu and the Rows command on the Insert menu is that the Insert command on the shortcut menu requires that you select an entire row (or rows) in order to insert a row (or rows). The Rows command on the Insert menu requires that you select a single cell in a row to insert one row or a range of cells to insert multiple rows.

Inserting Columns

You insert columns into a worksheet in the same way you insert rows. To insert columns, begin your column selection immediately to the right of where you want Excel to insert the new blank columns. Select the number of columns you want to insert. Next, click Columns on the Insert menu or click Insert on the shortcut menu. The primary difference between these two commands is this: The **Columns command** on the Insert menu requires that you select a single cell in a column to insert one column or a range of cells to insert multiple columns. The Insert command on the shortcut menu, however, requires that you select an entire column (or columns) to insert a column (or columns). Following the insertion of a column, Excel displays the Insert Options button, which allows you to modify the insertion in a fashion similar to that discussed earlier when inserting rows.

Inserting Individual Cells or a Range of Cells

The Insert command on the shortcut menu or the **Cells command** on the Insert menu allows you to insert a single cell or a range of cells. You should be aware that if you shift a single cell or a range of cells, however, they no longer may be lined up with their associated cells. To ensure that the values in the worksheet do not get out of order, it is recommended that you insert only entire rows or entire columns. If you insert a single cell or a range of cells, the Insert Options button allows you to modify the insert the same as for inserting rows and columns.

Deleting Columns and Rows

The Delete command on the Edit menu or shortcut menu removes cells (including the data and format) from the worksheet. Deleting cells is not the same as clearing cells. The Clear command, which was described earlier in Project 1 on page E 1.51, clears the data from the cells, but the cells remain in the worksheet. The **Delete command** removes the cells from the worksheet and shifts the remaining rows up (when you delete rows) or shifts the remaining columns to the left (when you delete columns). If formulas located in other cells reference cells in the deleted row or column, Excel does not adjust these cell references. Excel displays the error message **#REF!** in those cells to indicate a cell reference error. For example, if cell A7 contains the formula =A4+A5 and you delete row 5, Excel assigns the formula =A4+#REF! to cell A6 (originally cell A7) and displays the error message #REF! in cell A6. It also displays an Error Options button when you select the cell containing the value #REF!, which allows you to select options to determine the nature of the problem.

Deleting Individual Cells or a Range of Cells

Although Excel allows you to delete an individual cell or range of cells, you should be aware that if you shift a cell or range of cells on the worksheet, they no longer may be lined up with their associated cells. For this reason, it is recommended that you delete only entire rows or entire columns.

Entering Numbers with a Format Symbol

The next step in creating the Six-Month Financial Projections worksheet is to enter the row title, Revenue for Bonus, in cell A22 and enter the assumption values in the range B17:B23. You can enter the assumption numbers and then format them later, as you did in Projects 1 and 2, or you can enter them with format symbols. When you enter a number with a **format symbol**, Excel immediately displays the number with the assigned format. Valid format symbols include the dollar sign ($), comma (,), and percent sign (%).

If you enter a whole number, it displays without any decimal places. If you enter a number with one or more decimal places and a format symbol, Excel displays the number with two decimal places. Table 3-2 illustrates several examples of numbers entered with format symbols. The number in parentheses in column 4 indicates the number of decimal places.

The following steps describe how to complete the entries in the Assumptions table.

Table 3-2	Numbers Entered with Format Symbols		
FORMAT SYMBOL	**TYPED IN FORMULA BAR**	**DISPLAYS IN CELL**	**COMPARABLE FORMAT**
,	5,435	5,435	Comma (0)
	2,164.7	2,164.70	Comma (2)
$	$812	$812	Currency (0)
	$7723.82	$7,723.82	Currency (2)
	$96,291.4	$96,291.40	Currency (2)
%	78%	78%	Percent (0)
	38.5%	38.50%	Percent (1)
	29.83%	29.83%	Percent (2)

Steps   To Enter a Number with a Format Symbol

1 Click cell A22 and enter the row title Revenue for Bonus **in the cell.**

decimal and percent sign entered with number instructs Excel to format cell to Percent style with two decimal places

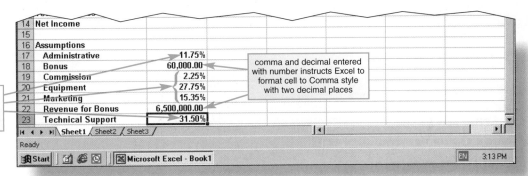

comma and decimal entered with number instructs Excel to format cell to Comma style with two decimal places

FIGURE 3-16

2 Enter 11.75% **in cell B17,** 60,000.00 **in cell B18,** 2.25% **in cell B19,** 27.75% **in cell B20,** 15.35% **in cell B21,** 6,500,000.00 **in cell B22, and** 31.5% **in cell B23.**

The entries display in a format based on the format symbols entered with the numbers (Figure 3-16).

Saving the Workbook

The next step is to save the workbook using the file name, Awesome Intranets.

Other Ways

1. Right-click range, click Format Cells on shortcut menu, click Number tab, click desired category in Category list, [select desired format], click OK button

2. Press CTRL+1, click Number tab, click category in Category list, [desired format], click OK button

3. In Voice Command mode say, "Format, Cells, Number, [desired category and format], OK"

More About

Freezing Titles

If you only want to freeze column headings, select the appropriate cell in column A before you click Freeze Panes on the Window menu. If you only want to freeze row titles, then select the appropriate cell in row 1. To freeze both column and row titles, select the cell that is the intersection of the column and row titles.

TO SAVE THE WORKBOOK

1 Click the Save button on the Standard toolbar.

2 When the Save As dialog box displays, type Awesome Intranets in the File name text box.

3 If necessary, click 3½ Floppy (A:) in the Save in list. Click the Save button in the Save As dialog box.

Excel saves the workbook on the floppy disk in drive A using the file name, Awesome Intranets.

Freezing Worksheet Titles

Freezing worksheet titles is a useful technique for viewing large worksheets that extend beyond the window. For example, when you scroll down or to the right, the column titles in row 3 and the row titles in column A that define the numbers no longer display on the screen. This makes it difficult to remember what the numbers represent. To alleviate this problem, Excel allows you to freeze the titles so they display on the screen no matter how far down or to the right you scroll.

Complete the following steps to freeze the worksheet title and column titles in rows 1, 2, and 3, and the row titles in column A using the **Freeze Panes command** on the **Window menu**.

Steps **To Freeze Column and Row Titles**

1 Press CTRL+HOME to select cell A1 and ensure that row 1 and column 1 display on the screen. Click cell B4, the cell below the column headings you want to freeze and to the right of the row titles you want to freeze. Click Window on the menu bar and then point to Freeze Panes.

The Window menu displays (Figure 3-17).

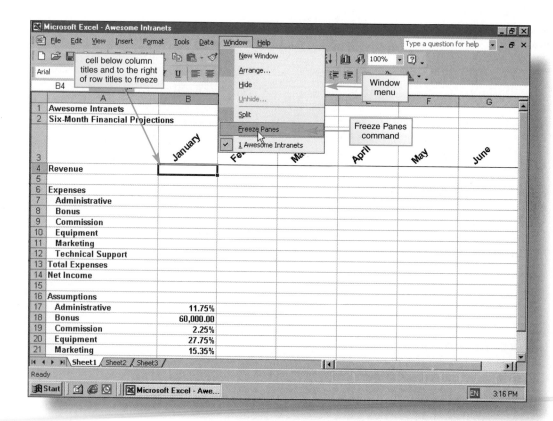

FIGURE 3-17

2 Click Freeze Panes on the Window menu.

Excel displays a thin black border on the right side of column A indicating the split between the frozen row titles in column A and the rest of the worksheet. It also displays a thin black line below row 3 indicating the split between the frozen column titles in rows 1 through 3 and the rest of the worksheet (Figure 3-18).

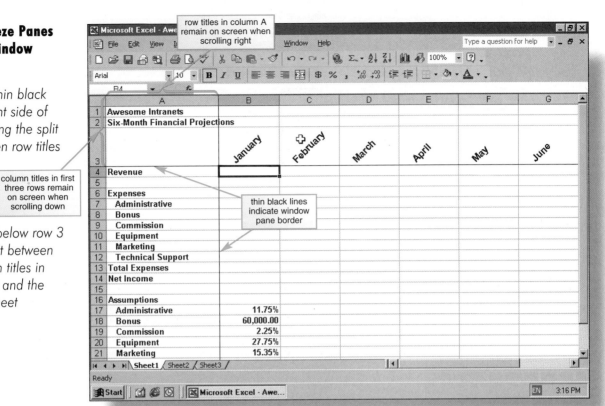

FIGURE 3-18

Once frozen, the row titles in column A will remain on the screen even when you scroll to the right to display column H. The titles remain frozen until you unfreeze them. You unfreeze the titles by clicking the **Unfreeze Panes command** on the Window menu. Later steps in this project show you how to use the Unfreeze Panes command.

It is important that you display the upper-left corner of the screen before you freeze the titles. For example, if in Step 1, cell B4 was selected without first selecting cell A1 to ensure the upper-left corner of the screen displayed, then Excel would have frozen the titles and also hidden rows 1 and 2. That is, you would not be able to display rows 1 and 2 until you unfreeze the titles.

Entering the Projected Revenue

The next step is to enter the projected monthly revenue in row 4 and compute the projected six-month total revenue in cell H4. Enter these numbers without any format symbols as shown in the following steps.

TO ENTER THE PROJECTED REVENUE

1. Enter 6692019 in cell B4, 5039219 in cell C4, 6929671 in cell D4, 6124450 in cell E4, 4919023 in cell F4, and 7327012 in cell G4.

2. Click cell H4 and then click the AutoSum button on the Standard toolbar twice.

The projected six-month total revenue (37031394) displays in cell H4 (Figure 3-19 on the next page). Columns B and C have scrolled off the screen, but column A remains because it was frozen earlier.

Other Ways

1. Press ALT+W, F
2. In Voice Command mode say, "Window, Freeze Panes"

More About

Freezing Titles

If any columns to the left or rows at the top of the worksheet are scrolled off the screen when you freeze titles, then you will not be able to view these columns or rows until you unfreeze titles.

FIGURE 3-19

The Number of Days

How many days have you been alive? Enter today's date (i.e., 12/5/2003) in cell A1. Next, enter your birth date (i.e., 6/22/1986) in cell A2. Select cell A3 and enter the formula =A1 - A2. Format cell A3 to the General style using the Cells command on the Format menu. Cell A3 will display the number of days you have been alive.

Updating the Date and Time

If the system date displays in a cell and changes while the workbook is active, then the date and time in the cell will not change until an entry is made into another cell or you complete some other activity, such as undoing a previous activity or pressing function key F9.

Recall from Projects 1 and 2 that if you select a single cell below or to the right of a range of numbers, you must click the AutoSum button twice to display the sum. If you select a range of cells below or to the right of a range of numbers, you need to click the AutoSum button only once to display the sums.

Displaying the System Date

The worksheet in Figure 3-1a on page E 3.05 includes a date stamp in cell H2. A **date stamp** shows the system date of which your computer keeps track. If the computer's system date is set to the current date, which normally it is, then the date stamp is equivalent to the current date.

In information processing, a report often is meaningless without a date stamp. For example, if a printout of the worksheet in this project were distributed to the company's analysts, the date stamp would show when the six-month projections were made.

To enter the system date in a cell in the worksheet, use the **NOW function**. The NOW function is one of 14 date and time functions available in Excel. When assigned to a cell, the NOW function returns a number that corresponds to the date and time beginning with December 31, 1899. For example, January 1, 1900 equals 1, January 2, 1900 equals 2, and so on. Noon equals .5. Thus, noon on January 1, 1900 equals 1.5 and 6 P.M. on January 1, 1900 equals 1.75.

Excel automatically formats the date stamp to the date and time format, mm/dd/yy hh:mm, where the first mm is the month, dd is the day of the month, yy is the last two digits of the year, hh is the hour of the day, and mm is the minutes past the hour.

The following steps show how to enter the NOW function and change the format from mm/dd/yy hh:mm to mm/dd/yyyy. With the recent turn of the century, it is recommended that you display all dates with a four-digit year.

Steps **To Enter and Format the System Date**

1 **Click cell H2 and then click the Insert Function box on the formula bar. When the Insert Function dialog box displays, click the Or select a category box arrow, and select Date & Time in the list. Scroll down in the Select a function list and then click NOW. Point to the OK button.**

Excel displays an equal sign in the active cell and in the formula bar. The Insert Function dialog box displays as shown in Figure 3-20.

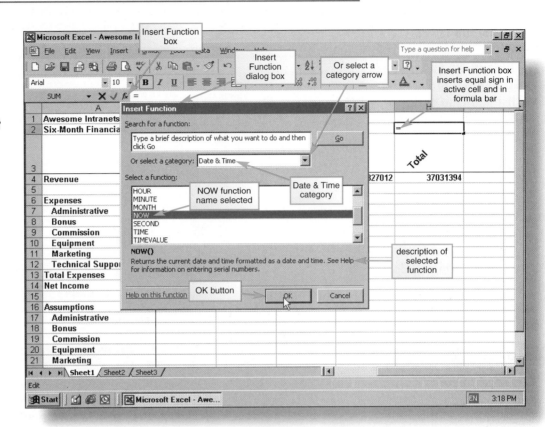

FIGURE 3-20

2 **Click the OK button. When the Function Arguments dialog box displays, click the OK button. Right-click cell H2 and point to Format Cells.**

Excel displays the system date and time in cell H2 using the default date and time format m/d/yy hh:mm. The system date on your computer may be different. The shortcut menu displays (Figure 3-21).

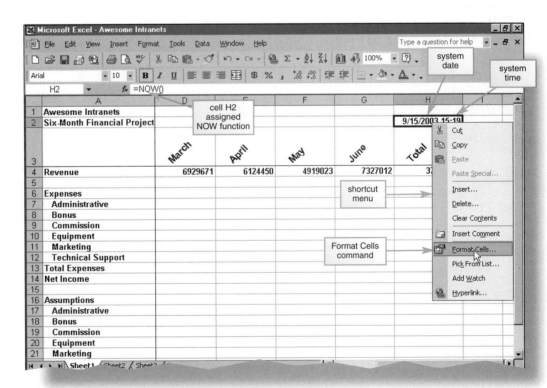

FIGURE 3-21

3 **Click Format Cells on the shortcut menu. If necessary, click the Number tab in the Format Cells dialog box. Click Date in the Category list. Scroll down in the Type list and then click 3/14/2001. Point to the OK button.**

Excel displays the Format Cells dialog box with Date selected in the Category list and 3/14/2001 (mm/dd/yyyy) selected in the Type list (Figure 3-22). A sample of the format using the data in the active cell (H2) displays in the Sample area.

FIGURE 3-22

4 **Click the OK button.**

Excel displays the system date in the form m/d/yyyy (Figure 3-23).

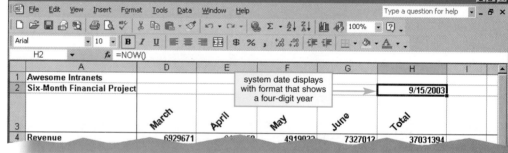

FIGURE 3-23

In Figure 3-23, the date displays right-aligned in the cell because Excel treats a date as a number. If you assign the **General format** (Excel's default format for numbers) to a date in a cell, the date displays as a number. For example, if the system time and date is 6:00 P.M. on June 29, 2003 and the cell containing the NOW function is assigned the General format, then Excel displays the following number in the cell:

$$37801.75$$

number of days since December 31, 1899   time of day is 6:00 P.M. (¾ of day complete)

The whole number portion of the number (37801) represents the number of days since December 31, 1899. The decimal portion .75 represents the time of day (6:00 P.M.). To assign the General format to a cell, click General in the Category list in the Format Cells dialog box (Figure 3-22).

Absolute Versus Relative Addressing

The next step is to enter the formulas that calculate the projected monthly expenses in the range B7:G13 and the net incomes in row 14 (Figure 3-1a on page E 3.05). The projected monthly expenses are based on the projected monthly revenue in row 4 and the assumptions in the range B17:B23. The formulas for each column (month) are the same, except for the reference to the projected monthly revenues in row 4, which varies according to the month (B4 for January, C4 for February, and so on). Thus, the formulas can be entered for January in column B and copied to columns C through G. The formulas for determining the projected January expenses and net income in column B are shown in Table 3-3.

If you enter the formulas shown in the third column in Table 3-3 in column B for January and then copy them to columns C through G (February through June) in the worksheet, Excel will adjust the cell references for each column automatically. Thus, after the copy, the February administrative expense in cell C7 would be =C17*C4. While the cell reference C4 (February Revenue) is correct, the cell reference C17 references an empty cell. The formula for cell C7 should read =B17*C4 rather than =C17*C4. In this instance, you need a way to keep a cell reference in a formula the same when it is copied.

> **More About**
>
> **Absolute Referencing**
>
> Absolute referencing is one of the most difficult worksheet concepts to understand. One point to keep in mind is that the paste operation is the only one affected by an absolute cell reference. An absolute cell reference instructs the paste operation to keep the same cell reference as it copies a formula from one cell to another.

Table 3-3   Formulas for Determining January Expenses and Net Income

CELL	EXPENSE/INCOME	FORMULA	COMMENT
B7	Administrative	=B17 * B4	Administrative % times January revenue
B8	Bonus	=IF(B4 >= B22, B18, 0)	Bonus equals value in B18 or zero
B9	Commission	=B19 * B4	Commission % times January revenue
B10	Equipment	=B20 * B4	Equipment % times January revenue
B11	Marketing	=B21 * B4	Marketing % times January revenue
B12	Technical Support	=B23 * B4	Technical Support % times January revenue
B13	Total Expenses	=SUM(B7:B12)	Sum of January expenses
B14	Net Income	=B4 - B13	January Revenue minus January Expenses

To keep a cell reference constant when it copies a formula or function, Excel uses a technique called **absolute referencing**. To specify an absolute reference in a formula, enter a dollar sign ($) before any column letters or row numbers you want to keep constant in formulas you plan to copy. For example, $B$17 is an absolute reference, while B17 is a relative reference. Both reference the same cell. The difference becomes apparent when they are pasted into a destination area. A formula using the absolute reference $B$17 instructs Excel to keep the cell reference B17 constant (absolute) as it is pastes the formula to a new location. A formula using the relative cell reference B17 instructs Excel to adjust the cell reference as it pastes. Table 3-4 gives some additional examples of absolute references. A cell reference with only one dollar sign before either the column or the row is called a **mixed cell reference**.

Table 3-4   Additional Examples of Absolute References

CELL REFERENCE	TYPE OF REFERENCE	MEANING
$B$17	Absolute reference	Both column and row references remain the same when you copy this cell reference because they are absolute.
B$17	Mixed reference	This cell reference is mixed. The column reference changes when you copy this cell reference to another column because it is relative. The row reference does not change because it is absolute.
$B17	Mixed reference	This cell reference is mixed. The row reference changes when you copy this cell reference to another row because it is relative. The column reference does not change because it is absolute.
B17	Relative reference	Both column and row references are relative. When copied to another row and column, both the row and column in the cell reference are adjusted to reflect the new location.

Entering a Formula Containing Absolute Cell References

The following steps show how to enter the Administrative formula (=$B$17*B4) in cell B7 using Point mode. To enter an absolute reference, you can type the dollar sign ($) as part of the cell reference or with the insertion point in or to the right of the cell reference you want to change to absolute, press F4.

Steps **To Enter a Formula Containing Absolute Cell References**

1 **Press CTRL+HOME and then click cell B7. Type = (equal sign) and then click cell B17. Press F4 to change B17 to an absolute reference in the formula. Type * (asterisk) and then click cell B4.**

*The formula =$B$17*B4 displays in cell B7 and in the formula bar (Figure 3-24). A marquee surrounds cell B4.*

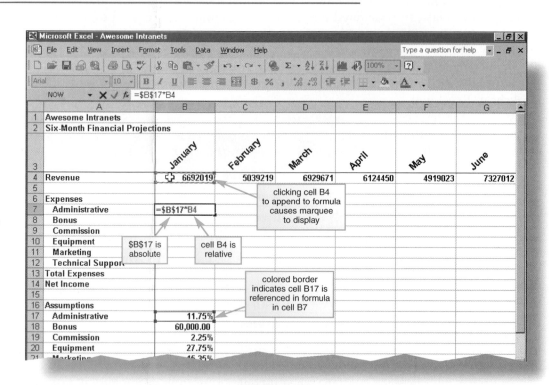

FIGURE 3-24

2 **Click the Enter box on the formula bar.**

Excel displays the result, 786312.2325, of the formula in cell B7 (Figure 3-25). With cell B7 selected, the formula assigned to it displays in the formula bar.

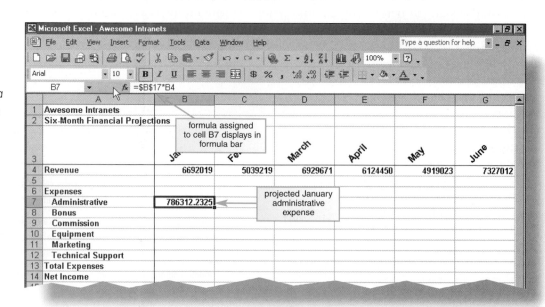

FIGURE 3-25

Making Decisions — The IF Function

If the projected January revenue in cell B4 is greater than or equal to the revenue for bonus in cell B22 (6,500,000.00), then the projected January bonus in cell B8 is equal to the amount in cell B18 (60,000.00); otherwise, cell B8 is equal to zero. One way to assign the projected monthly bonus in row 8 is to check each month individually to see if the projected revenue in row 4 equals or exceeds the revenue for bonus amount in cell B22 and, if so, then to enter 60,000.00 in row 8 for the corresponding month. Because the data in the worksheet changes each time you prepare the report or adjust the figures, however, you will find it preferable to have Excel assign the projected monthly bonus to the entries in the appropriate cells automatically. To do so, you need a formula or function in cell B8 that displays 60,000.00 or 0.00 (zero), depending on whether the projected January revenue in cell B4 is greater than or equal to or less than the number in cell B22.

The Excel **IF function** is useful when the value you want to assign to a cell is dependent on a logical test. For example, assume you assign cell B8 the IF function:

$$=IF(B4>=\$B\$22,\$B\$20,0)$$

logical_test   value_if_true   value_if_false

If the projected January revenue in cell B4 is greater than or equal to the value in cell B22, then the value in cell B18, 60000, displays in cell B8. If the projected January revenue in cell B4 is less than the value in cell B22, then cell B8 displays 0 (zero).

The general form of the IF function is:

$$=IF(logical\_test, value\_if\_true, value\_if\_false)$$

The argument, value_if_true, is the value you want displayed in the cell when the logical test is true. The argument, value_if_false, is the value you want displayed in the cell when the logical test is false.

The leftmost entry in the general form of the IF function, **logical_test**, is made up of two expressions and a comparison operator. Each expression can be a cell reference, a number, text, a function, or a formula. Valid **comparison operators**, their meaning, and examples of their use in IF functions are shown in Table 3-5.

The steps on the next page assign the IF function =IF(B4>=$B$22,$B$18,0) to cell B8. This IF function will determine whether or not the worksheet assigns a bonus for January.

More **About**

Nested IF functions

Nested IF functions include one or more IF functions in the value_if_true or value_if_false arguments. Assume you want to set cell A10 to the value 100 if cell B1 is equal to 1, 200 if cell B1 is equal to 2, and 300 if cell B1 is equal to any other value. The following IF function assigned to cell A10 would solve the problem: =IF(B1 = 1, 100, IF(B1 = 2, 200, 300)).

Table 3-5 Comparison Operators		
COMPARISON OPERATOR	**MEANING**	**EXAMPLE**
=	Equal to	=IF(D4 = K6, T15 ^ S4, K7 + K3)
<	Less than	=IF(D29 * G2 < 398, $F$3, U23 - 3)
>	Greater than	=IF(MAX(F3:F5) > 90, 0, 1)
>=	Greater than or equal to	=IF(L9 >= $H$6, A8 * X4, 5)
<=	Less than or equal to	=IF(Z6 + W2 <= 43, $B10, 25 * V17)
<>	Not equal to	=IF(R3 <> B$4, "Yes","No")

Steps To Enter an IF Function

1 **Click cell B8. Type** `=if(b4>=$b$22, $b$18,0` **in the cell. Click the Insert Function box on the formula bar to display the Function Arguments dialog box to view the function arguments. Point to the OK button.**

The IF function displays in the formula bar and in the active cell B8. The Function Arguments dialog box displays showing the logical_test, value_if_true, value_if_false, results of each part of the IF function, and the value that will be assigned to the cell based on the logical test (Figure 3-26).

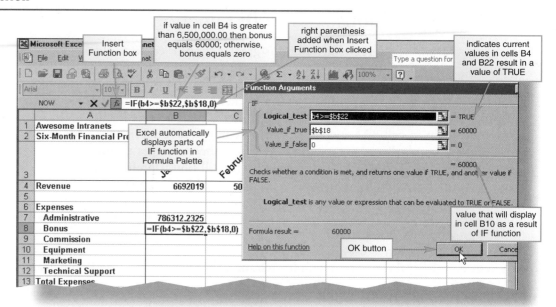

FIGURE 3-26

2 **Click the OK button.**

Excel displays 60000 in cell B8 because the value in cell B4 (6692019) is greater than or equal to the value in cell B22 (6,500,000.00) (Figure 3-27).

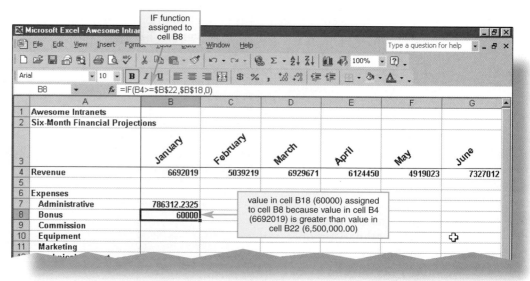

FIGURE 3-27

In Step 1, you could have clicked the Enter box or pressed the ENTER key to complete the entry rather than clicking the Edit Formula box. The Edit Formula box was clicked so you could see the IF function arguments in the Function Arguments dialog box before assigning the function to cell B8.

The value that Excel displays in cell B8 depends on the values assigned to cells B4, B18, and B22. For example, if the projected revenue in cell B4 is reduced below 6,500,000.00, then the IF function in cell B8 will change the display to zero. If you change the bonus in cell B18 and the revenue is large enough, it will change the results in cell B8. Finally, increasing the revenue for bonus in cell B22 so that it exceeds the projected monthly revenue will change the results in cell B8.

Entering the Remaining Projected Expense and Net Income Formulas for January

The projected January commission expense in cell B9 is equal to the commission assumption in cell B19 (2.25%) times the projected January revenue in cell B4. The projected January equipment expense in cell B10 is equal to the equipment assumption in cell B20 (27.75%) times the projected January revenue in cell B4. Similar formulas determine the projected January marketing expense in cell B11 and the January technical support expense in cell B12.

The projected total expenses for January in cell B13 is equal to the sum of the January expenses in the range B7:B12. The projected January net income in cell B14 is equal to the projected January revenue in cell B4 minus the projected January expenses in cell B13. The formulas are short, and therefore they are typed in the following steps, rather than entered using Point mode.

TO ENTER THE REMAINING PROJECTED JANUARY EXPENSE AND NET INCOME FORMULAS

1 Click cell B9. Type =b19*b4 and then press the down arrow key. Type =b20*b4 and then press the down arrow key. Type =b21*b4 and then press the down arrow key. Type =b23*b4 and then press the down arrow key. With cell B13 selected, click the AutoSum button on the Standard toolbar twice. Click cell B14. Type =b4-b13 and then press the ENTER key.

2 Press CTRL+ACCENT MARK(`).

3 When you are finished viewing the formulas version, press CTRL+ACCENT MARK(`) to display the values version.

The projected January expenses, total expenses, and net income display (Figure 3-28a). Excel displays the formulas version of the worksheet (Figure 3-28b).

(a) Values Version

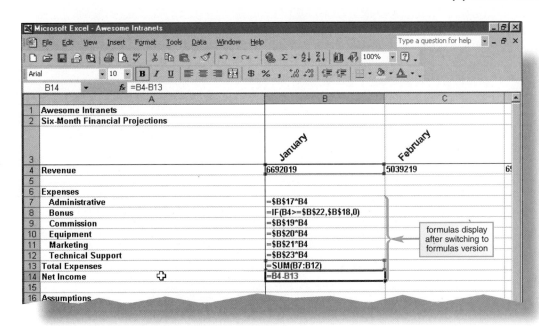

(b) Formulas Version

FIGURE 3-28

Microsoft **Excel 2002**

Viewing the formulas version (Figure 3-28b on the previous page) of the worksheet allows you to check the formulas assigned to the range B7 through B14. You can see that Excel converts all the formulas to uppercase.

Copying the Projected January Expenses and Net Income Formulas to the Other Months

To copy the projected expenses and totals for January to the other five months, complete the following steps using the fill handle.

 To Copy the Projected January Expenses and Net Income Using the Fill Handle

1 Select the range B7:B14. Point to the fill handle in the lower-right corner of cell B14.

The range B7:B14 is selected and the mouse pointer changes to a cross hair (Figure 3-29).

FIGURE 3-29

2 Drag the fill handle to select the destination area C7:G14. Release the mouse button.

Excel copies the formulas in the range B7:B14 to the destination area C7:G14 and displays the calculated amounts (Figure 3-30). The Auto Fill Options button displays below the fill area.

FIGURE 3-30

Determining the Projected Total Expenses by Category and Total Net Income

Follow the steps below to determine the total projected expenses by category and net income in the range H7:H14.

TO DETERMINE THE PROJECTED TOTAL EXPENSES BY CATEGORY AND TOTAL NET INCOME

1 Select the range H7:H14.

2 Click the AutoSum button on the Standard toolbar.

The projected total expenses by category and total net income display in the range H7:H14 (Figure 3-31).

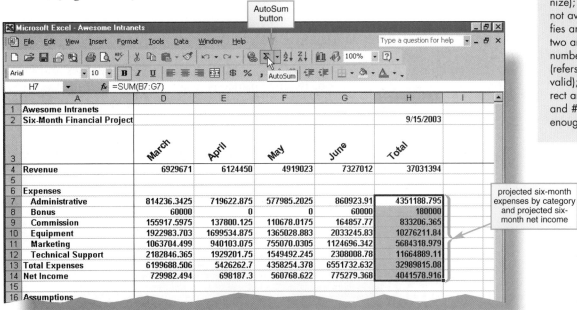

FIGURE 3-31

Unfreezing Worksheet Titles and Saving the Workbook

All the text, data, and formulas have been entered into the worksheet. The next step is to improve the appearance of the worksheet. Before modifying the worksheet's appearance, complete the following steps to unfreeze the titles and save the workbook using its current file name, Awesome Intranets.

TO UNFREEZE THE WORKSHEET TITLES AND SAVE THE WORKBOOK

1 Click cell B4 to clear the range selection from the previous steps.

2 Click Window on the menu bar and then point to Unfreeze Panes (Figure 3-32 on the next page).

3 Click Unfreeze Panes.

4 Click the Save button on the Standard toolbar.

Excel unfreezes the titles so that column A scrolls off the screen when you scroll to the right and the first three rows scroll off the screen when you scroll down. The latest changes to the workbook are saved on disk using the file name, Awesome Intranets.

Microsoft **Excel 2002**

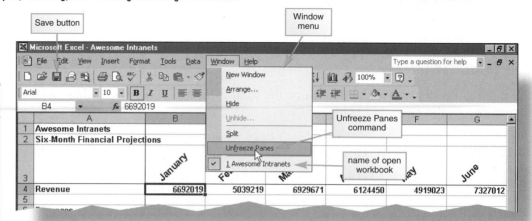

FIGURE 3-32

More About

Work Days

Assume that you have two dates: one in F3 and the other in F4. The date in F3 is your starting date and the date in F4 is the ending date. To calculate the work days between the two dates (excludes weekends), use the following formula: =NETWORKDAYS(F3, F4). For this function to work, make sure the Analysis Tool-Pak add-in is installed. You can install it by clicking Add-In on the Tools menu.

Formatting the Worksheet

The worksheet created thus far determines the projected monthly expenses and net incomes for the six-month period. Its appearance is uninteresting, however, even though some minimal formatting (bolding worksheet, formatting assumptions' numbers, changing the column widths, and formatting the date) was performed earlier. This section will complete the formatting of the worksheet to make the numbers easier to read and to emphasize the titles, assumptions, categories, and totals. The worksheet will be formatted in the following manner so it appears as shown in Figure 3-33: (1) format the numbers; (2) format the worksheet title, column title, row titles, and net income row; and (3) format the assumptions table.

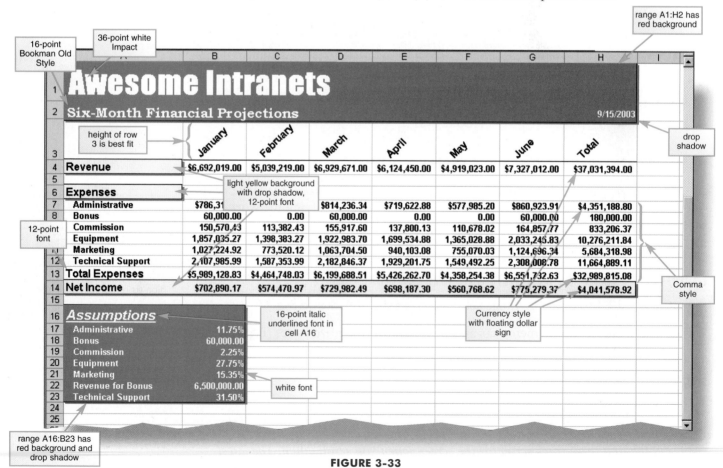

FIGURE 3-33

Formatting the Numbers

The projected monthly revenue and expenses in the range B4:H13 are to be formatted as follows:

1. Assign the Currency style with a floating dollar sign to rows 4, 7, 13, and 14.
2. Assign a customized Comma style to rows 8 through 12.

To assign a Currency style with a floating dollar sign, you must use the Format Cells command rather than the Currency Style button on the Formatting toolbar, which assigns a fixed dollar sign. The Comma style also must be assigned using the Format Cells command, because the Comma Style button on the Formatting toolbar displays a dash (-) when a cell has a value of zero. The specifications for this worksheet call for displaying a value of zero as 0.00 (see cell C8 in Figure 3-33), rather than as a dash. To create a Comma style using the Format Cells command, you can assign a Currency style with no dollar sign. The following steps format the numbers in rows 4 and 7 through 14.

More About

Nonadjacent Ranges

One of the more difficult tasks to learn is selecting nonadjacent ranges. To complete this task, do not hold down the CTRL key when you select the first range because Excel will consider the current active cell to be the first selection. Once the first range is selected, hold down the CTRL key and drag through the ranges. If a desired range is not in the window, use the scroll arrows to move the window over the range. It is not necessary to hold down the CTRL key while you scroll.

 Steps To Assign Formats to Nonadjacent Ranges

1 Select the range B4:H4. While holding down the CTRL key, select the nonadjacent ranges B7:H7 and B13:H14. Use the horizontal scroll button to display cells to select, if necessary. Release the CTRL key. Right-click the selected range and then point to Format Cells on the shortcut menu.

Excel highlights the selected nonadjacent ranges, and the shortcut menu displays as shown in Figure 3-34.

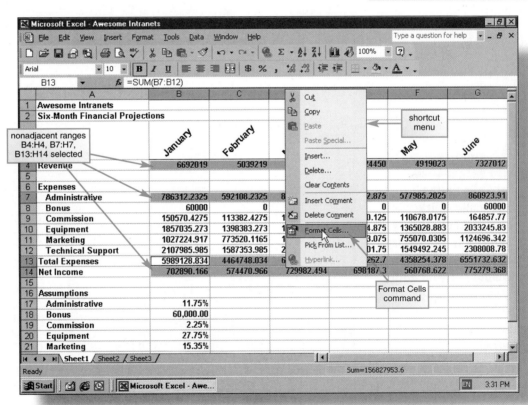

FIGURE 3-34

2 Click Format Cells. When the Format Cells dialog box displays, click the Number tab, click Currency in the Category list, select 2 in the Decimal places box, click $ in the Symbol list to ensure a dollar sign displays, and click ($1,234.10) in the Negative numbers list. Point to the OK button.

The cell format settings display in the Number sheet of the Format Cells dialog box (Figure 3-35).

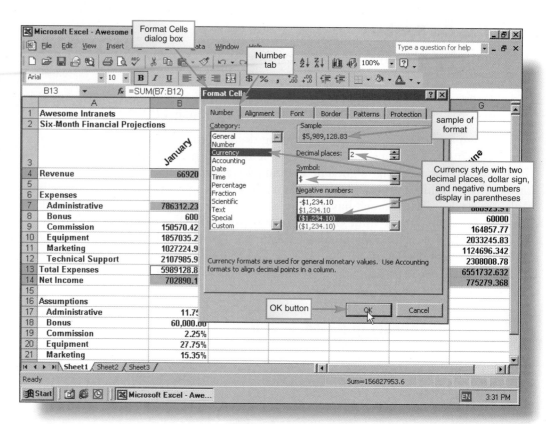

FIGURE 3-35

3 Click the OK button. Select the range B8:H12. Right-click the selected range. Click Format Cells on the shortcut menu. Click Currency in the Category list, select 2 in the Decimal places box, click None in the Symbol list so a dollar sign does not display, click (1,234.10) in the Negative numbers list. Point to the OK button.

The format settings display in the Format Cells dialog box as shown in Figure 3-36.

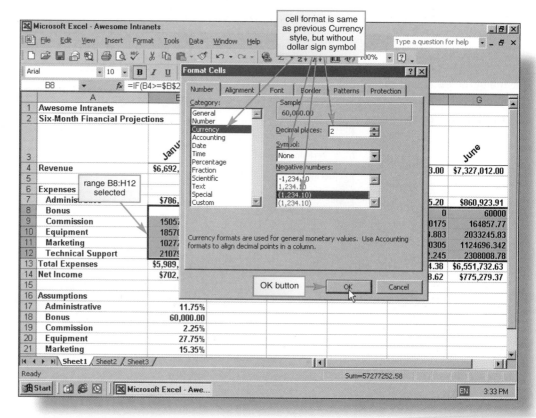

FIGURE 3-36

4 **Click the OK button. Select cell A1 to deselect the range B8:H12.**

The cell formats display as shown in Figure 3-37.

FIGURE 3-37

In accounting, negative numbers often are displayed with parentheses surrounding the value rather than with a negative sign preceding the value. Thus, in Step 3 the format (1,234.10) in the Negative numbers list was clicked. The data being used in this project contains no negative numbers. You must, however, select a format for negative numbers, and you must be consistent if you are choosing different formats in a column, otherwise the decimal points may not line up.

Instead of selecting Currency in the Category list in Step 3 (Figure 3-36), you could have selected Accounting to generate the same format. You should review the formats available below each category title. Thousands of combinations of format styles can be created using the options in the Format Cells dialog box.

Formatting the Worksheet Titles

To emphasize the worksheet titles in cells A1 and A2, the font type, size, and color are changed as described in the steps on the next page.

Other Ways

1. On Format menu click Cells, click Number tab, click category in Category list, select format, click OK button
2. Right-click range, click Format Cells on shortcut menu, click Number tab, click category in Category list, select format, click OK button
3. Press CTRL+1, click Number tab, click category in Category list, select format, click OK button
4. In Voice Command mode say, "Format, Cells, Number, [desired category], OK"

Microsoft Excel 2002

Steps To Format the Worksheet Titles

1 With cell A1 selected, click the Font box arrow on the Formatting toolbar. Scroll down and point to Impact (or a similar font) in the Font list.

The Font list displays as shown in Figure 3-38. The names of the fonts in the Font list display in the font style they represent, allowing you to view the style before you assign it to a cell or range of cells.

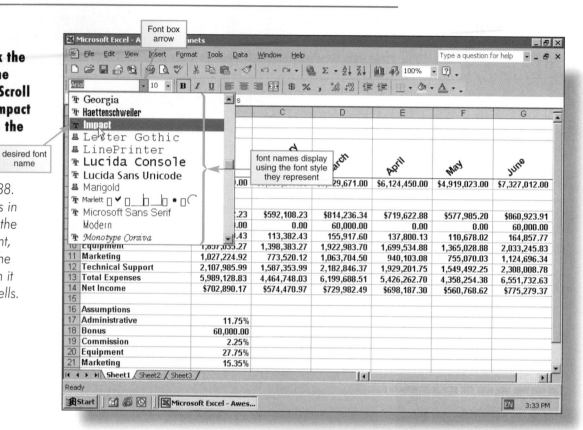

FIGURE 3-38

2 Click Impact. Click the Font Size box arrow on the Formatting toolbar and then click 36.

3 Click cell A2. Click the Font box arrow. Click Bookman Old Style (or a similar font) in the Font list. Click the Font Size box arrow and then click 16 in the Font Size list.

The worksheet titles in cells A1 and A2 display as shown in Figure 3-39.

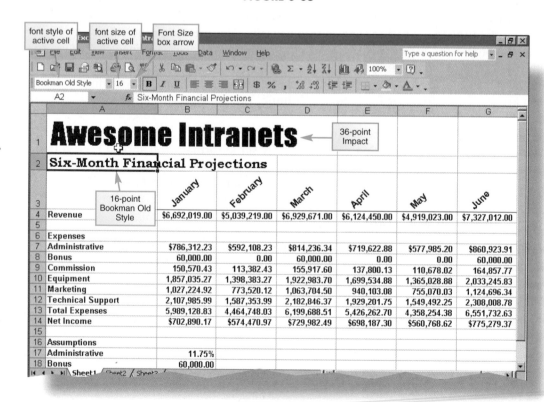

FIGURE 3-39

4   **Select the range A1:H2. Click the Fill Color button arrow on the Formatting toolbar. Click Red (column 1, row 3) on the Fill Color palette. Click the Font Color button arrow on the Formatting toolbar. Point to White (column 8, row 5) on the Font Color palette.**

Excel assigns a red background to the selected range and the Font Color palette displays (Figure 3-40).

5   **Click White.**

Excel changes the color of the font in the range A1:H2 from black to white (see Figure 3-33 on page E 3.32).

FIGURE 3-40

The next step is to add a drop shadow to the selected range A1:H2 using the Shadow button on the Drawing toolbar. First, the Drawing toolbar must display on the screen. The following section describes how to display an inactive (hidden) toolbar and then dock it.

Displaying the Drawing Toolbar

Excel has hundreds of toolbar buttons, most of which display on 19 built-in toolbars. Two of these 19 built-in toolbars are the Standard toolbar and Formatting toolbar, which usually display at the top of the screen. Another built-in toolbar is the Drawing toolbar. The **Drawing toolbar** provides tools that can simplify adding lines, boxes, and other geometric figures to a worksheet. You also can create customized toolbars containing the buttons that you use often.

You can use the shortcut menu that displays when you right-click a toolbar or the **Toolbars command** on the View menu to display or hide any Excel toolbar. The Drawing toolbar also can be displayed or hidden by clicking the Drawing button on the Standard toolbar. Perform the step on the next page to display the Drawing toolbar.

Other Ways

1. On Format menu click Cells, click Patterns tab to color background (or click Font tab to color font), click OK button

2. Right-click range, click Format Cells on shortcut menu, click Patterns tab to color background (or click Font tab to color font), click OK button

3. Press CTRL+1, click Patterns tab to color background (or click Font tab to color font), click OK button

4. In Voice Command mode say, "Format, Cells, Patterns (or Font), [desired color], OK"

Steps **To Display the Drawing Toolbar**

1 **Click the Drawing button on the Standard toolbar.**

The Drawing toolbar displays (Figure 3-41). Excel displays the Drawing toolbar on the screen in the same location and with the same shape as it displayed the last time it was used.

FIGURE 3-41

When a toolbar displays in the middle of the screen as shown in Figure 3-41, the toolbar includes a title bar. The Toolbar Options button and Close button display on the right side of the title bar.

Moving and Docking a Toolbar

The Drawing toolbar in Figure 3-41 is called a **floating toolbar** because it displays in its own window and can be moved anywhere in the Excel window. You move the toolbar by pointing to the toolbar title bar or to a blank area within the toolbar window (not a button) and then dragging the toolbar to its new location. As with any window, you also can resize the toolbar by dragging the toolbar window borders. To hide a floating toolbar, click the Close button on the toolbar title bar. Sometimes a floating toolbar gets in the way no matter where you move it or how you resize it. Hiding the toolbar is one solution. At times, however, you will want to keep the toolbar available for use. For this reason, Excel allows you to position toolbars on the edge of its window. If you drag the toolbar close to the edge of the window, Excel positions the toolbar in a **toolbar dock**.

Excel has four toolbar docks, one on each of the four sides of the window. You can add as many toolbars to a dock as you want. Each time you dock a toolbar, however, the Excel window slightly decreases in size to compensate for the room occupied by the toolbar. The following steps show how to dock the Drawing toolbar at the bottom of the screen below the scroll bar.

Steps To Dock a Toolbar at the Bottom of the Screen

1 **Point to the Drawing toolbar title bar or to a blank area in the Drawing toolbar.**

2 **Drag the Drawing toolbar over the status bar at the bottom of the screen.**

Excel docks the Drawing toolbar at the bottom of the screen (Figure 3-42).

Drawing toolbar docked horizontally across bottom of window

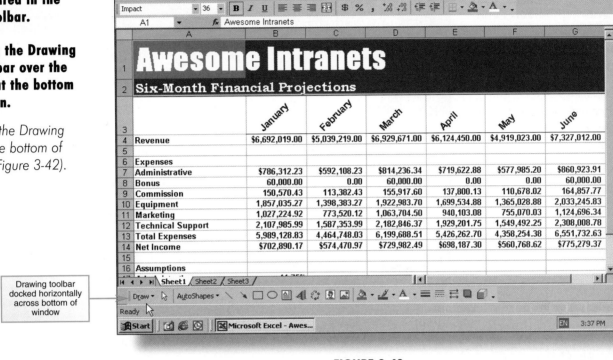

FIGURE 3-42

Compare Figure 3-42 with Figure 3-41. Excel automatically resizes the Drawing toolbar to fit across the window and between the scroll bar and status bar. Also notice that the heavy window border that surrounded the floating toolbar has changed to a light border. To move a toolbar to any of the other three docks, drag the toolbar from its current position to the desired side of the window. To move a docked toolbar, it is easiest to point to the move handle and when the mouse pointer changes to a cross with four arrowheads, drag it to the desired locator.

Adding a Drop Shadow to the Title Area

With the Drawing toolbar docked at the bottom of the screen, the next step is to add the drop shadow to the range A1:H2, as shown in the steps on the next page.

More About

Docking Toolbars

If you dock a toolbar on the left or right edge of the window that includes a box or a button with a list, the list will not be available.

More About

Toolbars

You can create your own toolbar and assemble the buttons you want on it by using the Customize command on the shortcut menu that displays when you right-click a toolbar. When the Customize dialog box displays, click the Toolbars tab, click the New button, name the toolbar, click the Commands tab, drag buttons to the new toolbar.

Steps **To Add a Drop Shadow**

1 With the range A1:H2 selected, click the Shadow Style button on the Drawing toolbar. Point to Shadow Style 14 (column 2, row 4) on the Shadow Style palette.

Excel displays the Shadow Style palette of drop shadows with varying shadow depths (Figure 3-43).

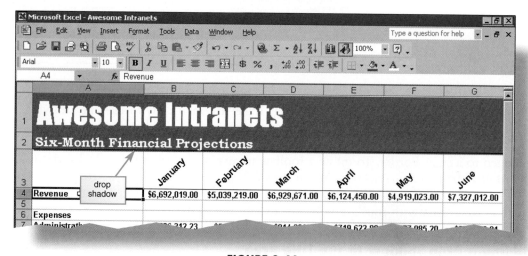

FIGURE 3-43

2 Click Shadow Style 14. Click cell A4 to deselect the drop shadow.

Excel adds a drop shadow to the range A1:H2 (Figure 3-44).

FIGURE 3-44

Other **Ways**

1. In Voice Command mode say, "Drawing, Shadow Style, Shadow Style 14"

When you add a drop shadow to a range of cells, Excel selects the drop shadow and surrounds it with handles. To deselect the drop shadow, select any cell, as described in Step 2 above.

Formatting the Category Row Titles and Net Income Row

The following steps change the font size in cells A4, A6, A13, and A14 to 12 point; and then adds the light yellow background color and drop shadows to cells A4, A6, and the range A14:H14.

To Change Font Size, Add Background Colors, and Add Drop Shadows to Nonadjacent Selections

Steps

1 With cell A4 selected, hold down the CTRL key, click cells A6, A13, and A14. Click the Font Size box arrow on the Formatting toolbar and then click 12 in the Font Size list.

The font size in cells A4, A6, A13, and A14 changes to 12 point.

2 Click cell A4. While holding down the CTRL key, click cell A6 and then select the range A14:H14. Click the Fill Color button arrow on the Formatting toolbar. Click Light Yellow (column 3, row 5) on the Fill Color palette. Click the Shadow Style button on the Drawing toolbar and point to Shadow Style 14 (column 2, row 4) on the Shadow palette.

The nonadjacent ranges are selected and the background color is changed to yellow (Figure 3-45). The Shadow Style palette displays.

3 Click Shadow Style 14.

Excel adds a drop shadow to cells A4, A6, and the range A14:H14 (Figure 3-46).

FIGURE 3-45

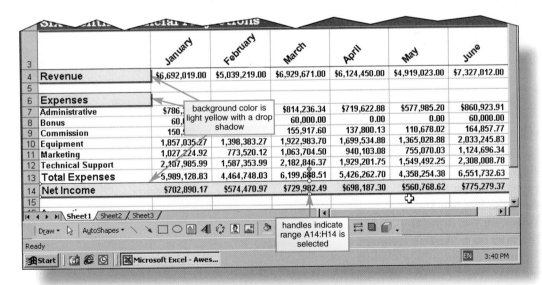

FIGURE 3-46

An alternative to formatting all three areas (cell A4, cell A6, and the range A14:H14) at once is to select each one separately and apply the formats.

Formatting the Assumptions Table

The last step to improving the appearance of the worksheet is to format the Assumptions table in the range A16:B23. The specifications in Figure 3-33 on page E 3.32 require a 16-point italic underlined font for the title in cell A16. The range A16:B23 has a red background color, white font, and a drop shadow that surrounds it. The following steps format the Assumptions table.

Steps **To Format the Assumptions Table**

1 **Scroll down so rows 16 through 23 display. Click cell A16. Click the Font Size box arrow on the Formatting toolbar and then click 16 in the Font Size list. Click the Italic button and then the Underline button on the Formatting toolbar. Select the range A16:B23. Click the Fill Color button arrow on the Formatting toolbar. Point to Red (column 1, row 3) on the Fill Color palette.**

The Assumptions table heading displays with the new formats. The range A16:B23 is selected and the Fill Color palette displays (Figure 3-47).

FIGURE 3-47

2 **Click Red on the Fill Color palette. Click the Font Color button on the Formatting toolbar to change the font in the selected range to white. Click the Shadow Style button on the Drawing toolbar. Click Shadow Style 14 on the Shadow Style palette. Select cell D23 to deselect the range A16:B23.**

The Assumptions table displays as shown in Figure 3-48.

FIGURE 3-48

The previous steps introduced you to two new formats, italic and underline. When you assign the **italic** font style to a cell, Excel slants the characters slightly to the right as shown in cell A16 in Figure 3-47. The **underline** format underlines only the characters in the cell rather than the entire cell as is the case when you assign a cell a bottom border.

Hiding the Drawing Toolbar and Saving the Workbook

The formatting of the worksheet is complete. The following steps hide the Drawing toolbar and save the workbook.

TO HIDE THE DRAWING TOOLBAR AND SAVE THE WORKBOOK

1. Click the Drawing button on the Standard toolbar.

2. Click the Save button on the Standard toolbar

Excel hides the Drawing toolbar (Figure 3-49) and saves the workbook using the file name Awesome Intranets.

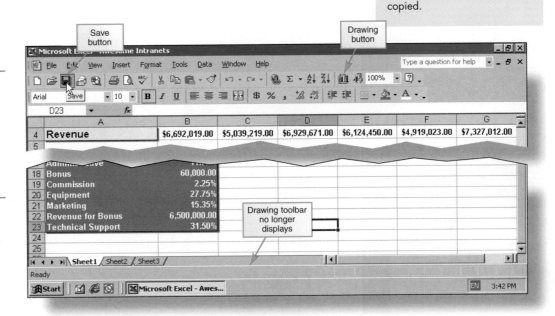

FIGURE 3-49

Adding a 3-D Pie Chart to the Workbook

The next step in the project is to draw the 3-D Pie chart on a separate sheet in the workbook Awesome Intranets, as shown in Figure 3-50 on the next page. A **Pie chart** is used to show the relationship or proportion of parts to a whole. Each slice (or wedge) of the pie shows what percent that slice contributes to the total (100%). The 3-D Pie chart in Figure 3-50 shows the contribution of each projected month's net income to the projected six-month net income. The Pie chart makes it easy to evaluate January's contribution to the projected six-month net income in comparison to the other months.

Unlike the 3-D Column chart in Project 1, the 3-D Pie chart in Figure 3-50 is not embedded in the worksheet. This Pie chart resides on a separate sheet called a **chart sheet.**

The ranges in the worksheet to chart are the nonadjacent ranges B3:G3 (month names) and B14:G14 (monthly net incomes). The month names in the range B3:G3 will identify the slices; these entries are called **category names.** The range B14:G14 contains the data that determines the size of the slices in the pie; these entries are called the **data series.** Because there are six months, the 3-D Pie chart contains six slices.

This project also calls for emphasizing the January contribution to the projected total net income by offsetting its slice from the main portion. A Pie chart with one or more slices offset is called an **exploded Pie chart.**

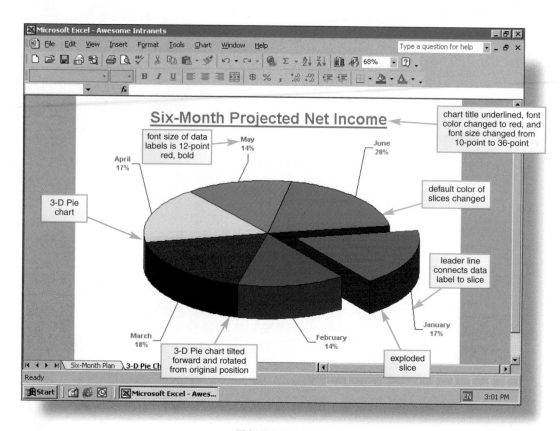

FIGURE 3-50

As shown in Figure 3-50, the default 3-D Pie chart also has been enhanced by rotating and tilting the pie forward, changing the colors of the slices, and modifying the chart title and labels that identify the slices.

Drawing a 3-D Pie Chart on a Separate Chart Sheet

The following steps show how to draw the 3-D Pie chart on a separate chart sheet using the Chart Wizard button on the Standard toolbar.

 To Draw a 3-D Pie Chart on a Separate Chart Sheet

1 Select the range B3:G3. While holding down the CTRL key, select the range B14:G14. Point to the Chart Wizard button on the Standard toolbar.

The nonadjacent ranges are selected (Figure 3-51).

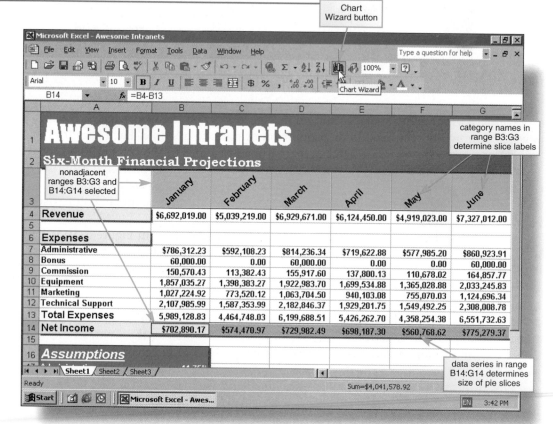

FIGURE 3-51

2 Click the Chart Wizard button on the Standard toolbar. When the Chart Wizard - Step 1 of 4 - Chart Type dialog box displays, click Pie in the Chart type list and then click the 3-D Pie chart (column 2, row 1) in the Chart sub-type box. Point to the Next button.

The Chart Wizard - Step 1 of 4 - Chart Type dialog box displays, which allows you to select one of the 14 types of charts available in Excel (Figure 3-52).

FIGURE 3-52

3 Click the Next button.

The Chart Wizard - Step 2 of 4 - Chart Source Data dialog box displays showing a sample of the 3-D Pie chart and the chart data range. A marquee surrounds the nonadjacent ranges on the worksheet (Figure 3-53).

FIGURE 3-53

4 **Click the Next button. When the Chart Wizard - Step 3 of 4 - Chart Options dialog box displays, type** Six-Month Projected Net Income **in the Chart title text box. Point to the Legend tab.**

Excel redraws the sample 3-D Pie chart with the chart title, Six-Month Projected Net Income (Figure 3-54). Excel automatically bolds the chart title.

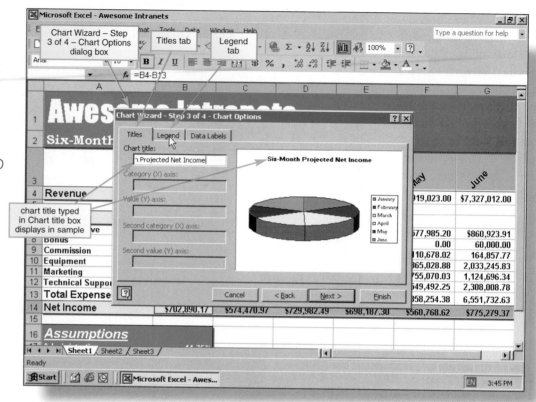

FIGURE 3-54

5 **Click the Legend tab and then click Show legend to remove the check mark from its check box. Point to the Data Labels tab.**

The Legend tab displays. Excel redraws the sample 3-D Pie chart without the legend. (Figure 3-55).

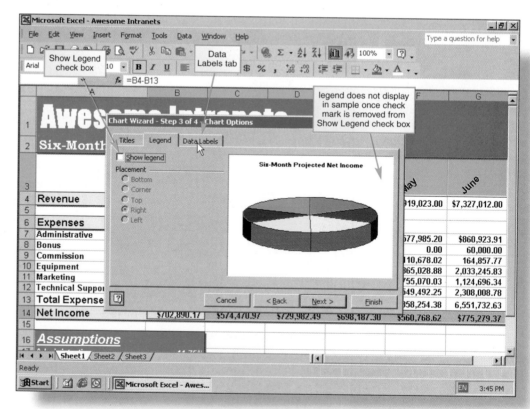

FIGURE 3-55

6 **Click the Data Labels tab. In the Label Contains area, click Category name and click Percentage to add check marks to their respective check boxes. Click Show leader lines to add a check mark to its check box. Point to the Next button.**

The Data Labels sheet displays. Excel redraws the sample 3-D Pie chart with data labels and percentages (Figure 3-56).

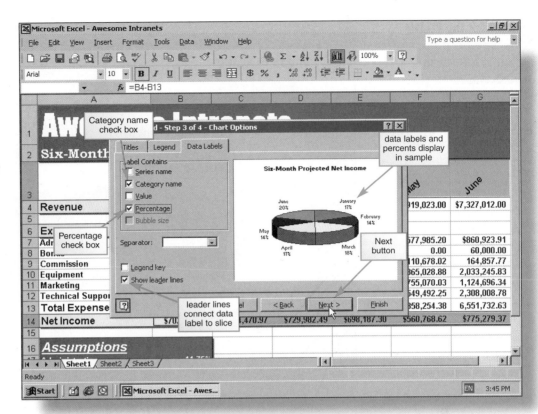

FIGURE 3-56

7 **Click the Next button. When the Chart Wizard - Step 4 of 4 - Chart Location dialog box displays, click As new sheet. Point to the Finish button.**

The Chart Wizard - Step 4 of 4 - Chart Location dialog box gives you two chart location options: to draw the chart on a new sheet in the workbook or to draw it as an object in a worksheet (Figure 3-57).

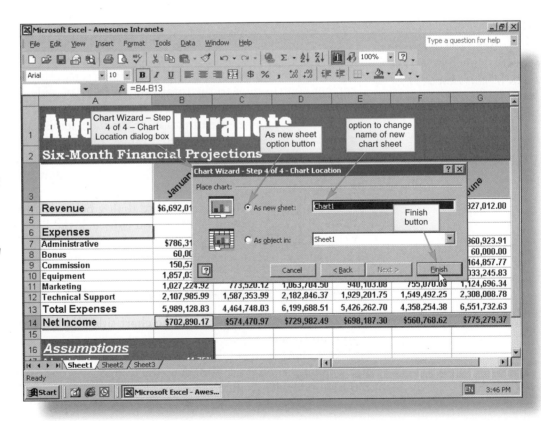

FIGURE 3-57

8 **Click the Finish button. If the Chart toolbar displays, click it's Close button.**

Excel draws the 3-D Pie chart on a separate chart sheet (Chart1) in the Awesome Intranets workbook (Figure 3-58).

FIGURE 3-58

Other Ways

1. Select range to chart, press F11

2. Select range to chart, press ALT+I, H

3. Select range to chart, in Voice Command mode say, "Chart Wizard, [desired chart type]"

Each slice of the 3-D Pie chart in Figure 3-58 represents one of the six months – January, February, March, April, May, and June. The names of the months and the percent contribution to the total value display outside the slices. The chart title, Six-Month Projected Income, displays immediately above the 3-D Pie chart.

Excel determines the direction of the data series range (down a column or across a row) on the basis of the selected range. Because the selection for the 3-D Pie chart is across the worksheet (ranges B3:G3 and B14:G14), Excel automatically selects the Rows option button in the Data Range sheet as shown in Figure 3-53 on page E 3.45.

In any of the four Chart Wizard dialog boxes (Figure 3-52 through Figure 3-57 on page E 3.45 through E 3.47), you can click the Back button to return to the previous Chart Wizard dialog box. You also can click the Finish button in any of the dialog boxes to create the chart with the options selected up to that point.

Formatting the Chart Title and Data Labels

The next step is to format the chart title and labels that identify the slices. Before you can format a **chart item**, such as the chart title or data labels, you must select it. Once a chart item is selected, you can format it using the Formatting toolbar, shortcut menu, or the Format menu. The following steps use the Formatting toolbar to format chart items much like cell entries were formatted earlier.

Steps **To Format the Chart Title and Data Labels**

1 Click the chart title. On the Formatting toolbar, click the Font Size box arrow, click 28 in the Font Size list, click the Underline button, click the Font Color button arrow, and then point to Red (column 1, row 3) on the Font Color palette.

Excel displays a selection rectangle around the chart title, increases the font size of the chart title, and underlines the chart title (Figure 3-59). The Font Color palette displays.

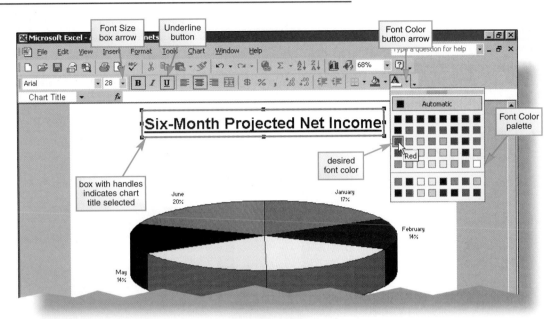

FIGURE 3-59

2 Click Red. Click one of the five data labels that identify the slices. On the Formatting toolbar, click the Font Size box arrow, click 12 in the Font Size list, click the Bold button, and then click the Font Color button to change the font to the color red.

The chart title and data labels display in red as shown in Figure 3-60. The data labels are selected.

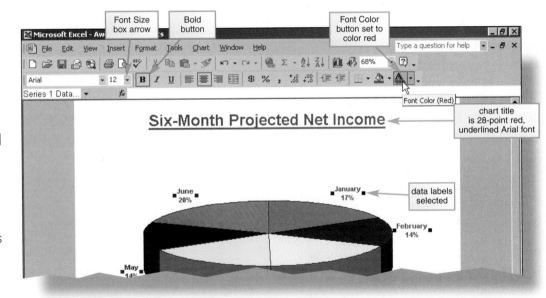

FIGURE 3-60

If you compare Figure 3-60 with Figure 3-58, you can see that the labels and chart title are easier to read and make the chart sheet look more professional.

Changing the Colors of the Slices

The next step is to change the colors of the slices of the pie. The colors shown in Figure 3-60 are the default colors Excel uses when you first create a 3-D Pie chart. Project 3 requires that the colors be changed to those shown in Figure 3-50 on page E 3.44. To change the colors of the slices, select them one at a time and use the Fill Color button arrow on the Formatting Toolbar as shown in the steps on the next page.

Other **Ways**

1. Right-click title or labels, click Format Chart Title or click Format Data Labels on shortcut menu
2. Press CTRL+B to bold
3. Press CTRL+U to underline
4. In Voice Command mode say, "Bold" or say, "Underline"

Steps To Change the Colors of the Pie Slices

1 Click the January slice twice. (Do not double-click.) Click the Fill Color button arrow on the Formatting toolbar and then point to Green (column 4, row 2) on the Fill Color palette.

Excel displays sizing handles around the January slice, and the Fill Color palette displays (Figure 3-61).

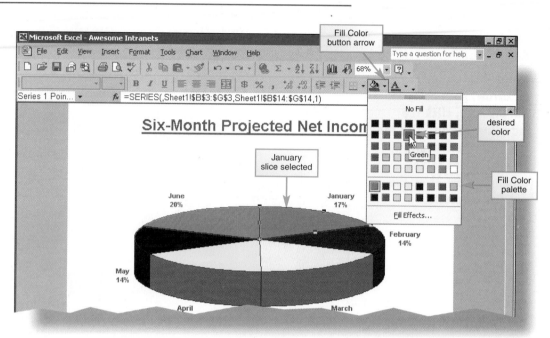

FIGURE 3-61

2 Click Green. One at a time, click the remaining slices and then use the Fill Color button arrow on the Formatting toolbar to change each slice to the following colors: June – Red (column 1, row 3); May – Orange (column 2, row 2); April – Yellow (column 3, row 4); March – Plum (column 7, row 4); and February – Blue (column 6, row 2). Click outside the Chart Area.

The chart displays with colors assigned to the slices as shown in Figure 3-62.

Other Ways

1. Click slice twice, right-click selected slice, click Format Data Point on shortcut menu, click Patterns tab, click color, click OK button

2. Click slice twice, in Voice Command mode say, "Format, Selected Data Point, Patterns, [desired color], OK"

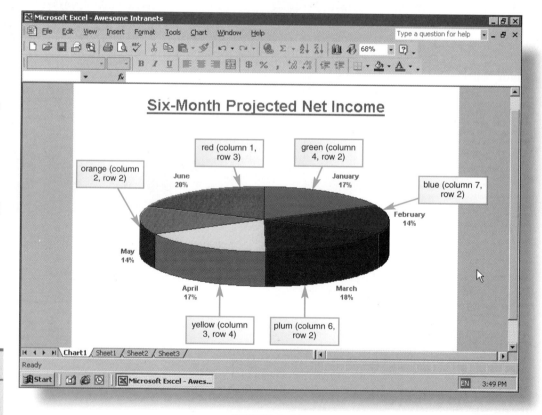

FIGURE 3-62

Exploding the 3-D Pie Chart

The next step is to emphasize the slice representing January by offsetting, or exploding, it from the rest of the slices so that it stands out. Perform the following steps to explode a slice of the 3-D Pie chart.

 To Explode the 3-D Pie Chart

1 **Click the slice labeled January twice. (Do not double-click.)**

Excel displays sizing handles around the January slice.

2 **Drag the slice to the desired position and then release the mouse button.**

Excel redraws the 3-D Pie chart with the January slice offset from the rest of the slices (Figure 3-63).

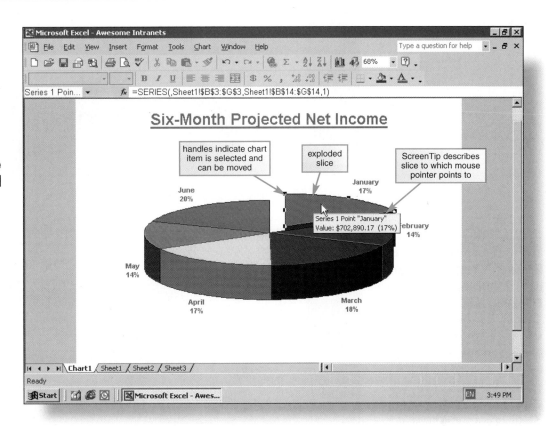

FIGURE 3-63

You can offset as many slices as you want, but remember that the reason for offsetting a slice is to emphasize it. Offsetting multiple slices tends to reduce the impact on the reader and reduces the overall size of the pie chart.

Rotating and Tilting the 3-D Pie Chart

With a three-dimensional chart, you can change the view to better display the section of the chart you are trying to emphasize. Excel allows you to control the rotation angle, elevation, perspective, height, and angle of the axes by using the **3-D View command** on the Chart menu.

To obtain a better view of the offset January slice, you can rotate the 3-D Pie chart 80° to the left. The rotation angle of the 3-D Pie chart is defined by the line that divides the January and June slices. When Excel initially draws a pie chart, it always points one of the dividing lines between two slices to 12 o'clock (or zero degrees). Besides rotating the 3-D Pie chart, the steps on the next page also change, or tilt, the elevation so the 3-D Pie chart is at less of an angle to the viewer.

 More About

Exploding a 3-D Pie Chart

If you click the 3-D Pie Chart so that all the slices are selected, you can drag one of the slices to explode all of the slices.

Steps **To Rotate and Tilt the 3-D Pie Chart**

1 **With the January slice selected, click Chart on the menu bar and then point to 3-D View.**

The Chart menu displays (Figure 3-64).

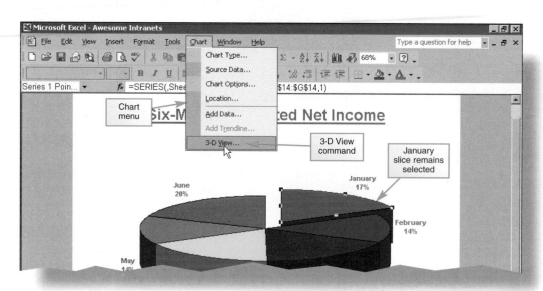

FIGURE 3-64

2 **Click 3-D View. Click the up arrow button in the 3-D View dialog box until 25 displays in the Elevation box.**

The 3-D View dialog box displays (Figure 3-65). A sample of the 3-D Pie chart displays in the dialog box. The result of increasing the elevation of the 3-D Pie chart is to tilt it forward.

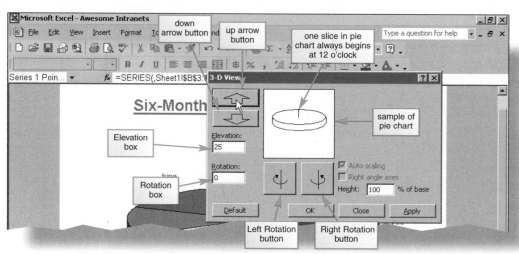

FIGURE 3-65

3 **Rotate the Pie chart by clicking the Left Rotation button until the Rotation box displays 80. Point to the OK button.**

The new rotation setting (80) displays in the Rotation box as shown in Figure 3-66. A sample of the rotated pie chart displays in the dialog box.

FIGURE 3-66

4 **Click the OK button.**
Click outside the
chart area.

Excel displays the 3-D Pie
chart tilted forward and
rotated to the left, which
makes the space between the
January slice and the main
portion of the pie more
prominent (Figure 3-67).

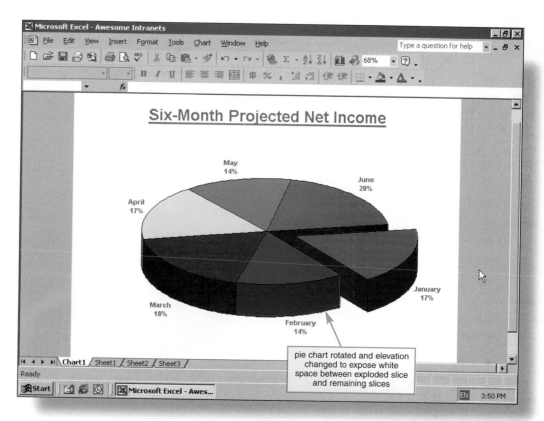

FIGURE 3-67

Compare Figure 3-67 with Figure 3-64. The offset of the January slice is more noticeable in Figure 3-67 because the pie chart has been tilted and rotated to expose the white space between the January slice and the main portion of the 3-D Pie chart.

In addition to controlling the rotation angle and elevation, you also can control the thickness of the 3-D Pie chart by entering a percent smaller or larger than the default 100% in the **Height text box** (Figure 3-66).

Adding Leader Lines to the Data Labels

If you drag the data labels away from each slice, Excel draws thin **leader lines** that connect each data label to its corresponding slice. If the leader lines do not display, click Chart Options on the Chart menu, click the Data Labels tab, and click the Show leader lines option button (Figure 3-56 on page E 3.47). Perform the steps on the next page to add leader lines to the data labels.

More About

Changing a Pie Chart's Perspective

You can increase or decrease the base height (thickness) of the Pie chart by changing the height to base ratio in the Format 3-D View dialog box.

Steps **To Add Leader Lines to the Data Labels**

1 **Click the January data label twice. (Do not double-click.)**

Excel displays a box with handles around the January data label.

2 **Point to the upper-left sizing handles on the box border and drag the January data label away from the January slice. Select and drag the remaining data labels away from their corresponding slices as shown in Figure 3-68. Click outside the chart area.**

The data labels display with leader lines as shown in Figure 3-68.

FIGURE 3-68

You also can select and format individual labels by clicking a specific data label after all the data labels have been selected. Making an individual data label larger or a different color, for example, helps you emphasize a small or large slice in a pie chart.

Renaming and Reordering the Sheets and Coloring Their Tabs

The final step in creating the workbook is to adjust the tabs at the bottom of the screen. The following steps show you how to rename the sheets, color the tabs, and reorder the sheets so the worksheet precedes the chart sheet.

Steps **To Rename and Reorder the Sheets, and Color Their Tabs**

1 **Double-click the tab labeled Chart1 at the bottom of the screen. Type** 3-D Pie Chart **as the new tab label. Press the ENTER key. Right-click the tab and point to Tab Color on the shortcut menu.**

The label on the Chart1 tab changes to 3-D Pie Chart (Figure 3-69). The shortcut menu displays.

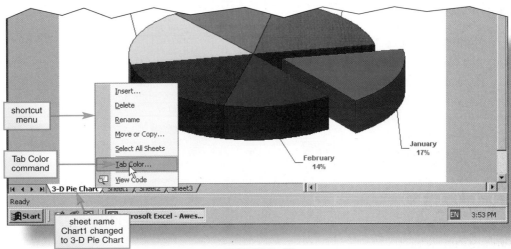

shortcut menu

Tab Color command

sheet name Chart1 changed to 3-D Pie Chart

FIGURE 3-69

2 **Click Tab Color. When the Format Tab Color dialog box displays, click Red (column 1, row 3) in the Tab Color area. Point to the OK button.**

The Format Tab Color dialog box displays as shown in Figure 3-70.

Format Tab Color dialog box

desired color

OK button

FIGURE 3-70

3 **Click the OK button.**

Excel displays the name on the tab with a red underline (Figure 3-71). The red underline indicates the sheet is active. When the sheet is inactive, the tab will display with a red background.

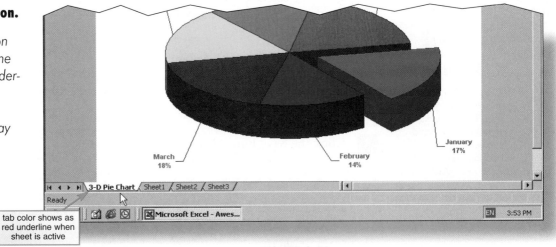

tab color shows as red underline when sheet is active

FIGURE 3-71

4 Double-click the tab labeled Sheet1 at the bottom of the screen. Type Six-Month Plan as the new sheet name and then press the ENTER key. Right-click the tab and click Tab Color on the shortcut menu. When the Format Tab Color dialog box displays, click Light Yellow (column 3, row 5) in the Tab Color area, and then click the OK button.

Excel displays the name on the tab with a yellow underline.

	January	February	March	April	May	June
3						
4 Revenue	$6,692,019.00	$5,039,219.00	$6,929,671.00	$6,124,450.00	$4,919,023.00	$7,327,012.00
5						
6 Expenses						
7 Administrative	$786,312.23	$592,108.23	$814,236.34	$719,622.88	$577,985.20	$860,923.91
	60,000.00	0.00	60,000.00	0.00	0.00	60,000.00
	150,570.43	113,382.43	155,917.60	137,800.13	110,678.02	164,857.77
	1,857,035.27	1,398,383.27	1,922,983.70	1,699,534.88	1,365,028.88	2,033,245.83
	1,027,224.92	773,520.12	1,063,704.50	940,103.08	755,070.03	1,124,696.34
12 Technical Support	2,	7,353.99	2,182,846.37	1,929,201.75	1,549,492.25	2,308,008.78
13 Total Expenses	5,	4,748.03	6,199,688.51	5,426,262.70	4,358,254.38	6,551,732.63
14 Net Income	$702,890.17	$574,470.97	$729,982.49	$698,187.30	$560,768.62	$775,279.37
15						
16 Assumptions						

Sheet1 sheet renamed Six-Month Plan, colored light yellow and moved ahead of 3-D Pie Chart sheet

3-D Pie Chart tab colored red

◄ ► ►┃ \ **Six-Month Plan** ╱ 3-D Pie Chart ╱ Sheet2 ╱ Sheet3 ╱

Ready

Start · Microsoft Excel - Awes... · EN · 4:01 PM

FIGURE 3-72

5 Drag the Six-Month Plan tab to the left in front of the 3-D Pie Chart tab. Click cell D16 to deselect the chart ranges.

Excel rearranges the sequence of the sheets and displays the worksheet (Figure 3-72).

Other Ways

1. To rename sheet, right-click sheet tab, click Rename on shortcut menu
2. To move sheet, on Edit menu click Move or Copy
3. To move sheet, right-click sheet tab, click Move or Copy on shortcut menu
4. To move sheet, in Voice Command mode say, "Edit, Move" or "Edit, Copy"

More About

Checking Spelling

Unless a range of cells or an object is selected when you check spelling, Excel checks the selected worksheet, including all cell values, cell comments, embedded charts, text boxes, buttons, and headers and footers.

Checking Spelling, Saving, Previewing, and Printing the Workbook

With the workbook complete, the next series of steps checks spelling, saves, previews, and prints the workbook. Each sequence of steps concludes with saving the workbook to ensure that the latest changes are saved on disks.

Checking Spelling in Multiple Sheets

The spell checker checks the spelling only in the selected sheets. It will check all the cells in the selected sheets unless you select a range of two or more cells. Before checking the spelling, select the 3-D Pie Chart sheet as described in the following steps.

TO CHECK SPELLING IN MULTIPLE SHEETS

1 With the Six-Month Plan sheet active, hold down the CTRL key and then click the 3-D Pie Chart tab.

2 Click the Spelling button on the Standard toolbar. Correct any errors.

3 Click the Save button on the Standard toolbar.

Previewing and Printing the Workbook

After checking the spelling, the next step is to preview and print the sheets. As with spelling, Excel previews and prints only selected sheets. Also, because the worksheet is too wide to print in portrait orientation, the orientation must be changed to landscape. Perform the following steps to preview and print the workbook.

TO PREVIEW AND PRINT THE WORKBOOK IN LANDSCAPE ORIENTATION

1 Ready the printer. If both sheets are not selected, hold down the CTRL key and then click the tab of the inactive sheet.

2 Click File on the menu bar and then click Page Setup. Click the Page tab and then click Landscape.

3 Click the Print Preview button in the Page Setup dialog box. When the preview of the first of the selected sheets displays, click the Next button to view the next sheet. Click the Previous button to redisplay the first sheet.

4 Click the Print button at the top of the Print Preview window. When the Print dialog box displays, click the OK button.

5 Right-click the Six-Month Plan tab. Click Ungroup Sheets on the shortcut menu to deselect the 3-D Pie Chart tab.

6 Click the Save button on the Standard toolbar.

The worksheet and 3-D Pie chart print as shown in Figures 3-73(a) and 3-73(b).

More *About*

Printing in Black and White

You can speed up the printing process and save ink if you do the following before printing: click File on the menu bar, click Page Setup, click the Sheet tab, click the Black and white check box.

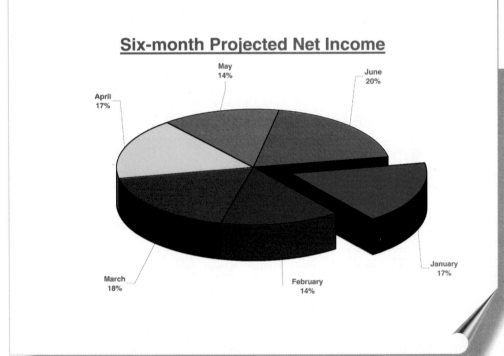

Awesome Intranets Six-Month Financial Projections							9/15/2003
	January	February	March	April	May	June	Total
Revenue	$6,592,019.00	$5,039,219.00	$6,929,571.00	$6,124,450.00	$4,919,023.00	$7,327,012.00	$37,031,394.00
Expenses							
Administrative	$786,312.23	$592,108.23	$814,236.34	$719,622.88	$577,985.20	$860,923.91	$4,351,188.80
Bonus	60,000.00	0.00	60,000.00	0.00	0.00	60,000.00	180,000.00
Commission	150,570.43	113,382.43	155,917.60	137,800.13	110,678.02	164,857.77	833,206.37
Equipment	1,857,035.27	1,398,383.27	1,922,983.70	1,699,534.88	1,365,026.88	2,033,245.83	10,276,211.84
Marketing	1,027,224.92	773,520.12	1,063,704.50	940,103.08	755,070.03	1,124,696.34	5,684,318.98
Technical Support	2,107,985.99	1,587,353.99	2,182,846.37	1,929,201.75	1,549,492.25	2,308,008.76	11,664,889.11
Total Expenses	5,989,128.83	4,464,748.03	6,199,688.51	5,426,262.70	4,358,254.38	6,551,732.63	32,989,815.08
Net Income	$702,890.17	$574,470.97	$729,982.49	$698,187.30	$560,768.62	$775,279.37	$4,041,578.92

Assumptions	
Administrative	11.75%
Bonus	60,000.00
Commission	2.25%
Equipment	27.75%
Marketing	15.35%
Revenue for Bonus	6,500,000.00
Technical Support	31.50%

(a) Worksheet

Six-month Projected Net Income

May 14%
June 20%
April 17%
January 17%
March 18%
February 14%

(b) 3-D Pie Chart

FIGURE 3-73

Changing the View of the Worksheet

With Excel, you easily can change the view of the worksheet. For example, you can magnify or shrink the worksheet on the screen. You also can view different parts of the worksheet through **window panes**.

Shrinking and Magnifying the View of a Worksheet or Chart

You can magnify (zoom in) or shrink (zoom out) the display of a worksheet or chart by using the **Zoom box** on the Standard toolbar. When you magnify a worksheet, the characters on the screen become larger, and fewer columns and rows display. Alternatively, when you shrink a worksheet, more columns and rows display. Magnifying or shrinking a worksheet affects only the view; it does not change the window size or printout of the worksheet or chart. Perform the following steps to shrink and magnify the view of the worksheet.

Steps **To Shrink and Magnify the View of a Worksheet or Chart**

1 **Click the Zoom box arrow on the Standard toolbar. Point to 75% in the Zoom list.**

A list of percentages displays (Figure 3-74).

FIGURE 3-74

2 **Click 75%.**

Excel shrinks the display of the worksheet to 75% of its normal display (Figure 3-75). With the worksheet zoomed out to 75%, you can see more rows and columns than you did at 100% magnification. Many of the numbers, however, display as a series of number signs (#) because the columns are not wide enough to display the formatted numbers.

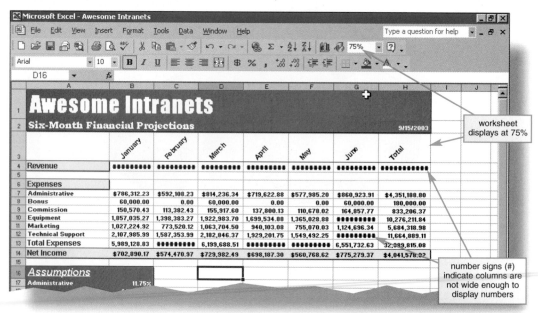

FIGURE 3-75

3   **Click the Zoom box arrow on the Standard toolbar and then click 100%.**

Excel returns to the default display of 100%.

4   **Click the 3-D Pie Chart tab at the bottom of the screen. Click the Zoom box arrow on the Standard toolbar and then click 100%.**

Excel changes the magnification of the chart from 68% (shown in Figure 3-68 on page E 3.54) to 100% (Figure 3-76). The chart displays at the same size as the printout of the chart.

5   **Enter 68 in the Zoom box to return the chart to its original magnification.**

FIGURE 3-76

Excel normally displays a chart at approximately 70% magnification at 800 × 600 resolution so that the entire chart displays on the screen. By changing the magnification to 100%, you can see only a part of the chart, but at a magnification that corresponds with the chart's size on a printout. Excel allows you to enter a percent magnification in the Zoom box between 10 and 400 for worksheets and chart sheets.

Splitting the Window into Panes

Previously in this project, you used the Freeze Panes command to freeze worksheet titles on a large worksheet so they always would display on the screen. When working with a large worksheet, you also can split the window into two or four window panes to view different parts of the worksheet at the same time. To split the window into four panes, select the cell where you want the four panes to intersect. Next, click the Split command on the Window menu. Follow the steps on the next page to split the window into four panes.

Other Ways

1. On View menu click Zoom, click desired percent magnification, click OK button

2. Type desired percent magnification in Zoom box on Standard toolbar

3. Press ALT+V, Z

4. In Voice Command mode say, "Zoom [desired percent magnification]"

Steps To Split a Window into Four Panes

1 **Click the Six-Month Plan tab. Click cell D5, the intersection of the four proposed panes. Click Window on the menu bar and then point to Split.**

The Window menu displays (Figure 3-77).

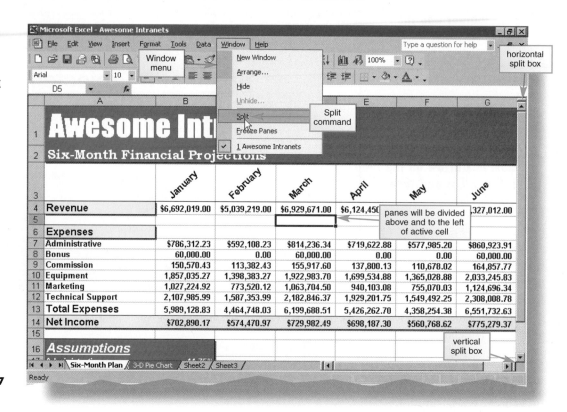

FIGURE 3-77

2 **Click Split. Use the scroll arrows to display the four corners of the worksheet.**

Excel divides the window into four panes, and the four corners of the worksheet display (Figure 3-78).

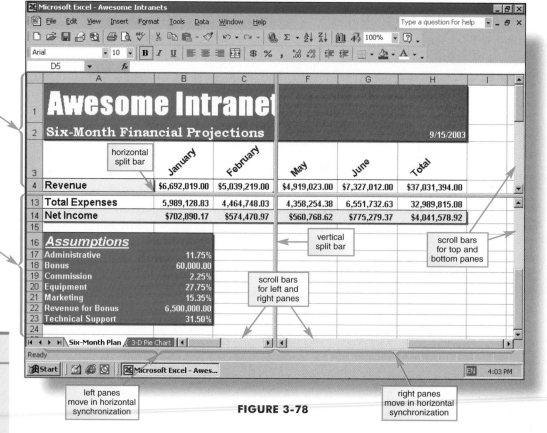

FIGURE 3-78

Other Ways

1. Drag horizontal split box and vertical split box to desired locations
2. In Voice Command mode say, "Window, Split"

The four panes in Figure 3-78 are used to display the following: (1) the upper-left pane displays the range A1:C4; (2) the upper-right pane displays the range F1:I4; (3) the lower-left pane displays the range A13:C24; and (4) the lower-right pane displays the range F13:I24.

The vertical bar going up and down the middle of the window is called the **vertical split bar**. The horizontal bar going across the middle of the window is called the **horizontal split bar**. If you use the scroll bars below the window and to the right of the window to scroll the window, you will see that the panes split by the horizontal split bar scroll together vertically. The panes split by the vertical split bar scroll together horizontally. To resize the panes, drag either split bar to the desired location in the window.

You can change the values of cells in any of the four panes. Any change you make in one pane also takes effect in the other panes. To remove one of the split bars from the window, drag the split box to the edge of the window or double-click the split bar. Follow these steps to remove both split bars.

TO REMOVE THE FOUR PANES FROM THE WINDOW

1 Position the mouse pointer at the intersection of the horizontal and vertical split bars.

2 Double-click the split four-headed arrow.

Excel removes the four panes from the window.

What-If Analysis

The automatic recalculation feature of Excel is a powerful tool that can be used to analyze worksheet data. Using Excel to scrutinize the impact of changing values in cells that are referenced by a formula in another cell is called **what-if analysis** or **sensitivity analysis**. Excel not only recalculates all formulas in a worksheet when new data is entered, but also redraws any associated charts.

In Project 3, the projected monthly expenses and net incomes in the range B7:G14 are dependent on the assumptions in the range B17:B23. Thus, if you change any of the assumption values, Excel immediately recalculates the projected monthly expenses in rows 7 through 12, and the projected monthly expenses and net incomes in rows 13 and 14. Finally, because the projected monthly net incomes in row 14 change, Excel redraws the 3-D Pie chart, which is based on these numbers.

A what-if question for the worksheet in Project 3 might be, what if the Bonus, Equipment, and Marketing assumptions in the Assumptions table are changed as follows: Bonus $60,000.00 to $40,000.00; Equipment 27.75% to 15.50%; Marketing 15.35% to 10.00% — how would these changes affect the projected six-month total net income in cell H14? To answer a question like this, you need to change only the second, fourth, and fifth values in the Assumptions table. Excel instantaneously recalculates the worksheet and redraws the 3-D Pie chart to answer the question regarding the projected six-month total net income in cell H14.

The steps on the next page change the three assumptions as indicated in the previous paragraph and determine the new projected six-month total net income in cell H14. To ensure that the Assumptions table and the projected six-month total net income in cell H14 display on the screen at the same time, the steps also divide the window into two vertical panes.

More About

Window Panes

If you want to split the window into two panes, rather than four, drag the vertical split box or horizontal split box (Figure 3-77) to the desired location. You can also drag the center of the four panes in any direction to change the size of the panes.

More About

What-If Analysis

Besides manually changing assumptions in a worksheet, Excel has additional methods for answering what-if questions, including Goal Seeking, Solver, Pivot Tables, Scenario Manager, and the Analysis ToolPak. For more information, enter each of these what-if tools in the Ask a Question box on the menu bar.

Steps To Analyze Data in a Worksheet by Changing Values

1 Use the vertical scroll bar to move the window so cell A4 is in the upper-left corner of the screen.

2 Drag the vertical split box (see Figure 3-77 on page E 3.60) from the lower-right corner of the screen to the left so that the vertical split bar is positioned in the middle of column F. Use the right scroll arrow to display the totals in column H in the right pane. Click cell B18 in the left pane.

Excel divides the window into two vertical panes and shows the totals in column H in the pane on the right side of the window (Figure 3-79).

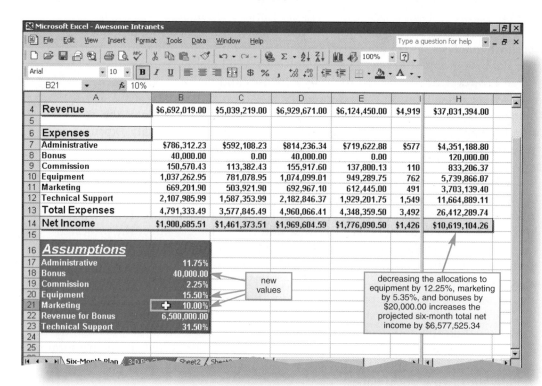

FIGURE 3-79

3 Enter 40000 in cell B18, 15.5 in cell B20, and 10 in cell B21.

Excel immediately recalculates all the formulas in the worksheet, including the projected six-month total net income in cell H14 (Figure 3-80).

FIGURE 3-80

Each time you enter a new assumption, Excel recalculates the worksheet and redraws the 3-D Pie chart. This process usually takes less than one second, depending on how many calculations must be performed and the speed of your computer. Compare the projected six-month total net incomes in cell H14 in Figures 3-79 and 3-80. By changing the values of the three assumptions (Figure 3-80), the projected six-month total net income in cell H14 increases from $4,041,578.92 to $10,619,104.26. This translates into an increase of $6,577,525.34 for the projected six-month total net income.

Goal Seeking

If you know the result you want a formula to produce, you can use **goal seeking** to determine the value of a cell on which the formula depends. The following steps close and reopen the Awesome Intranets workbook and use the **Goal Seek command** on the Tools menu to determine what projected technical support percentage in cell B23 will yield a projected six-month total net income of $6,000,000.00 in cell H14, rather than $4,041,578.92.

More About

Undo

The Undo button is ideal for returning the worksheet to its original state after you have changed the values in a worksheet to answer a what-if question. To display the original worksheet after answering a what-if question, click the Undo button for each value you changed.

 To Goal Seek

1 **Close the Awesome Intranets workbook without saving changes. Click the Open button on the Standard toolbar and then reopen Awesome Intranets.**

2 **Drag the vertical split box to the middle of column F. Scroll down so row 4 is at the top of the screen. Display column H in the right pane. Click cell H14, the cell that contains the projected six-month total net income. Click Tools on the menu bar and then point to Goal Seek.**

The vertical split bar displays in the middle of column F, and the Tools menu displays (Figure 3-81).

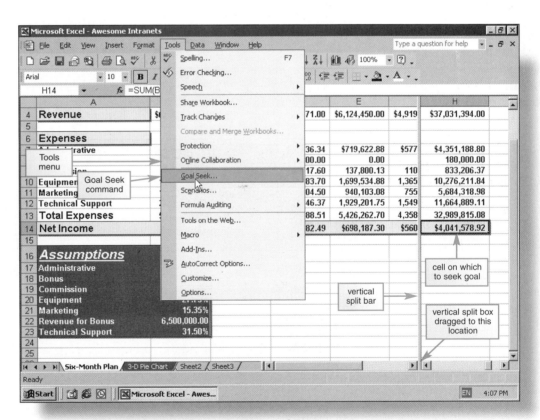

FIGURE 3-81

3 **Click Goal Seek.**

The Goal Seek dialog box displays. The Set cell box is assigned the cell reference of the active cell in the worksheet (cell H14) automatically.

4 **Click the To value text box. Type 6,000,000 and then click the By changing cell box. Click cell B23 on the worksheet and then point to the OK button.**

The Goal Seek dialog box displays as shown in Figure 3-82. A marquee displays around cell B23.

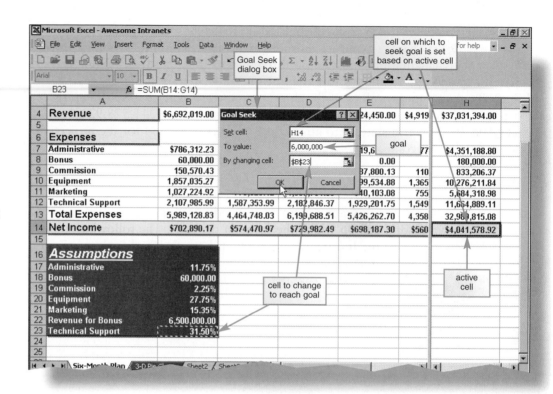

FIGURE 3-82

5 **Click the OK button.**

Excel immediately changes cell H14 from $4,041,578.92 to the desired value of $6,000,000.00. More importantly, Excel changes the technical support assumption in cell B23 from 31.50% to 26.21% (Figure 3-83). Excel also displays the Goal Seek Status dialog box. If you click the OK button, Excel keeps the new values in the worksheet. If you click the Cancel button, Excel redisplays the original values.

6 **Click the Cancel button in the Goal Seek Status dialog box.**

Other Ways

1. Press ALT+T, G
2. In Voice Command mode say, "Tools, Goal Seek," enter desired values, in Voice Command mode say, "OK"

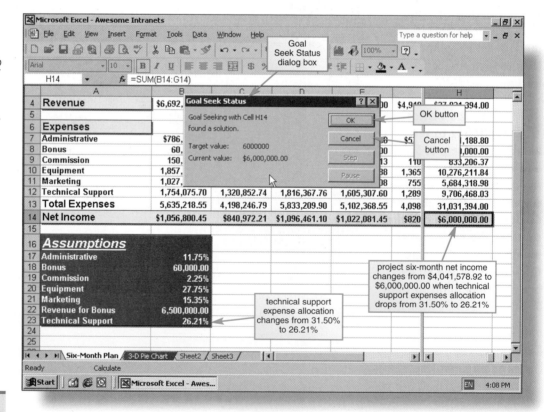

FIGURE 3-83

Goal seeking assumes you can change the value of only one cell referenced directly or indirectly. In this example, to change the projected six-month total net income in cell H14 to $6,000,000.00, the technical support percentage in cell B23 must decrease by 5.29% from 31.50% to 26.21%.

You can see from this goal seeking example that the cell to change (cell B23) does not have to be referenced directly in the formula or function. For example, the projected six-month total net income in cell H14 is calculated by the function =SUM(B14:G14). Cell B23 is not referenced in the function. Instead, cell B23 is referenced in the formulas in rows 7 through 12, on which the projected monthly net incomes in row 14 are based. Excel is capable of goal seeking on the projected six-month total net income by varying the technical support assumption.

Quitting Excel

To quit Excel, complete the following steps.

TO QUIT EXCEL

1 Click the Close button on the title bar.

2 If the Microsoft Excel dialog box displays, click the No button.

More About

Goal Seeking

Goal seeking is a methodology in which you know what answer you want a formula in a cell to be, but you do not know the value to place in a cell that is involved in the formula. You can goal seek by changing the value in a cell that is indirectly used in the formula as illustrated in Figures 3-82 and 3-83.

CASE PERSPECTIVE SUMMARY

With the worksheet and chart developed in this project, the CEO of Awesome Intranets, Maria Cianti, easily can respond to any what-if questions brought up by her senior management team the next time she presents her semi-annual plan. Questions that took several minutes to answer with paper and pencil now can be answered in a few seconds. Furthermore, computational errors are less likely to occur.

Project Summary

In creating the Awesome Intranets workbook, you learned how to work with large worksheets that extend beyond the window and how to use the fill handle to create a series. You learned to display hidden toolbars, dock a toolbar at the bottom of the screen, and hide an active toolbar. You learned about the difference between absolute cell references and relative cell references and how to use the IF function. You also learned how to rotate text in a cell, generate a series, freeze titles, change the magnification of the worksheet, display different parts of the worksheet through panes, create a 3-D Pie chart, and improve the appearance of a 3-D Pie chart. Finally, this project introduced you to using Excel to do what-if analysis by changing values in cells and goal seeking.

More About

The Quick Reference

For a table that lists how to complete the tasks covered in this book using the mouse, menu, shortcut menu, and keyboard, see the Quick Reference Summary at the back of this book or visit the Shelly Cashman Series Office site (scsite.com/offxp/qr.htm) and click the application name.

What You Should Know

Having completed this project, you now should be able to perform the following tasks:

- Add a Drop Shadow (E 3.40)
- Add Leader Lines to the Data Labels (E 3.54)
- Analyze Data in a Worksheet by Changing Values (E 3.62)
- Assign Formats to Nonadjacent Ranges (E 3.33)
- Bold the Font of the Entire Worksheet (E 3.07)
- Change Font Size, Add Background Colors, and Add Drop Shadows to Nonadjacent Selections (E 3.41)
- Change the Colors of the Pie Slices (E 3.50)
- Check Spelling in Multiple Sheets (E 3.56)
- Copy a Cell's Format Using the Format Painter Button (E 3.11)
- Copy a Range of Cells to a Nonadjacent Destination Area (E 3.14)
- Copy the Projected January Expenses and Net Income Using the Fill Handle (E 3.30)
- Determine the Projected Total Expenses by Category and Total Net Income (E 3.31)
- Display the Drawing Toolbar (E 3.38)
- Dock a Toolbar at the Bottom of the Screen (E 3.39)
- Draw a 3-D Pie Chart on a Separate Chart Sheet (E 3.44)
- Enter a Formula Containing Absolute Cell References (E 3.26)
- Enter a Number with a Format Symbol (E 3.19)
- Enter an IF Function (E 3.28)
- Enter and Format the System Date (E 3.23)

- Enter the Projected Revenue (E 3.21)
- Enter the Remaining Projected January Expense and Net Income Formulas (E 3.29)
- Enter the Worksheet Titles (E 3.07)
- Explode the 3-D Pie Chart (E 3.51)
- Format the Assumptions Table (E 3.42)
- Format the Chart Title and Data Labels (E 3.49)
- Format the Worksheet Titles (E 3.36)
- Freeze Column and Row Titles (E 3.20)
- Goal Seek (E 3.53)
- Hide the Drawing Toolbar and Save the Workbook (E 3.43)
- Increase Column Widths and Enter Row Titles (E 3.12)
- Insert a Row (E 3.17)
- Preview and Print the Workbook in Landscape Orientation (E 3.57)
- Quit Excel (E 3.65)
- Remove the Four Panes from the Window (E 3.61)
- Rename and Reorder the Sheets, and Color Their Tabs (E 3.55)
- Rotate and Tilt the 3-D Pie Chart (E 3.52)
- Rotate Text and Use the Fill Handle to Create a Series of Month Names (E 3.08)
- Save the Workbook (E 3.20)
- Shrink and Magnify the View of a Worksheet or Chart (E 3.58)
- Split a Window into Four Panes (E 3.60)
- Start and Customize Excel (E 3.07)
- Unfreeze the Worksheet Titles and Save the Workbook (E 3.31)

More About

Microsoft Certification

The Microsoft Office User Specialist (MOUS) Certification program provides an opportunity for you to obtain a valuable industry credential - proof that you have the Excel 2002 skills required by employers. For more information, see Appendix E or visit the Shelly Cashman Series MOUS Web page at scsite.com/offxp/cert.htm.

Learn It Online

Instructions: To complete the Learn It Online exercises, start your browser, click the Address bar, and then enter scsite.com/offxp/exs.htm. When the Office XP Learn It Online page displays, follow the instructions in the exercises below.

1 Project Reinforcement TF, MC, and SA

Below Excel Project 3, click the Project Reinforcement link. Print the quiz by clicking Print on the File menu. Answer each question. Write your first and last name at the top of each page, and then hand in the printout to your instructor.

2 Flash Cards

Below Excel Project 3, click the Flash Cards link. When Flash Cards displays, read the instructions. Type 20 (or a number specified by your instructor) in the Number of Playing Cards text box, type your name in the Name text box, and then click the Flip Card button. When the flash card displays, read the question and then click the Answer box arrow to select an answer. Flip through Flash Cards. Click Print on the File menu to print the last flash card if your score is 15 (75%) correct or greater and then hand it in to your instructor. If your score is less than 15 (75%) correct, then redo this exercise by clicking the Replay button.

3 Practice Test

Below Excel Project 3, click the Practice Test link. Answer each question, enter your first and last name at the bottom of the page, and then click the Grade Test button. When the graded practice test displays on your screen, click Print on the File menu to print a hard copy. Continue to take practice tests until you score 80% or better. Hand in a printout of the final practice test to your instructor.

4 Who Wants to Be a Computer Genius?

Below Excel Project 3, click the Computer Genius link. Read the instructions, enter your first and last name at the bottom of the page, and then click the Play button. Hand in your score to your instructor.

5 Wheel of Terms

Below Excel Project 3, click the Wheel of Terms link. Read the instructions, and then enter your first and last name and your school name. Click the Play button. Hand in your score to your instructor.

6 Crossword Puzzle Challenge

Below Excel Project 3, click the Crossword Puzzle Challenge link. Read the instructions, and then enter your first and last name. Click the Play button. Work the crossword puzzle. When you are finished, click the Submit button. When the crossword puzzle redisplays, click the Print button. Hand in the printout.

7 Tips and Tricks

Below Excel Project 3, click the Tips and Tricks link. Click a topic that pertains to Project 3. Right-click the information and then click Print on the shortcut menu. Construct a brief example of what the information relates to in Excel to confirm you understand how to use the tip or trick. Hand in the example and printed information.

o n l i n e

8 Newsgroups

Below Excel Project 3, click the Newsgroups link. Click a topic that pertains to Project 3. Print three comments. Hand in the comments to your instructor.

9 Expanding Your Horizons

Below Excel Project 3, click the Articles for Microsoft Excel link. Click a topic that pertains to Project 3. Print the information. Construct a brief example of what the information relates to in Excel to confirm you understand the contents of the article. Hand in the example and printed information to your instructor.

10 Search Sleuth

Below Excel Project 3, click the Search Sleuth link. To search for a term that pertains to this project, select a term below the Project 3 title and then use the Google search engine at google.com (or any major search engine) to display and print two Web pages that present information on the term. Hand in the printouts to your instructor.

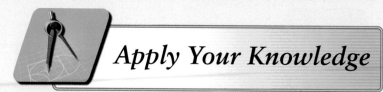

Apply Your Knowledge

1 Understanding the IF Function and Absolute Referencing

Instructions: Fill in the correct answers.

1. Determine the truth value (true or false) of the following logical tests, given the following cell values: X4 = 40; Y3 = 49; K7 = 120; Z2 = 10; and Q9 = 25. Enter true or false.
   a. Y3 < X4   Truth value: _____
   b. Q9 = K7   Truth value: _____
   c. X4 + 15 * Z2 / 5 <> K7   Truth value: _____
   d. K7 / Z2 > X4 – Y3   Truth value: _____
   e. Q9 * 2 – 42 < (X4 + Y3 - 8) / 9   Truth value: _____
   f. K7 + 300 <= X4 * Z2 + 10   Truth value: _____
   g. Q9 + K7 > 2 * (Q9 + 25)   Truth value: _____
   h. X4 + Z2 <> 2 * (Q9 / 5)   Truth value: _____

2. Write an IF function for cell G7 that assigns the value of cell B7 to cell G7 if the value in cell K6 is greater than the value in cell H7; otherwise, have the IF function assign zero (0) to cell G7.
   Function: _____

3. Write an IF function for cell J8 that assigns the text "OK" if the value in cell L9 is three times greater than the value in cell M6; otherwise, have the IF function assign the text "Not OK" to cell J8.
   Function: _____

4. A nested IF function is an IF function that contains another IF function in the value_if_true or value_if_false arguments. For example, =IF(A1 = "NY","Region 1", IF(A1 = "MI", "Region 2", "Not Applicable")) is a valid nested IF function. Start Excel and enter this IF function in cell B1 and then use the fill handle to copy the function down through cell B7. Enter the following data in the cells in the range A1:A7 and then write down the results that display in cells B1 through B7 for each set. Set 1: A1 = IL; A2 = NY; A3 = NY; A4 = MI; A5 = NY; A6 = MI; A7 = NY. Set 2: A1= WI; A2 = KY; A3 = NY; A4 = IL; A5 = NY; A6 = NY; A7 = IL.
   Set 1 Results: _____
   Set 2 Results: _____

5. Write cell X49 as a relative reference, absolute reference, mixed reference with the row varying, and mixed reference with the column varying.

   _____   _____   _____   _____

6. Write the formula for cell J8 that divides cell K4 by the sum of cells M7 through M10. Write the formula so that when it is copied to cells K8 and L8, cell K4 remains absolute.
   Formula: _____

7. Write the formula for cell T5 that divides cell V5 by the sum of cells C4, D4, and E4. Write the formula so that when it is copied to cells T6, T7, and T8, cell V5 remains absolute.
   Formula: _____

8. Write the formula for cell A2 that multiplies cell U4 by the sum of cells M7 through M12. Write the formula so that when it is copied to cells A2 and A3, Excel adjusts all the cell references according to the new location.
   Formula: _____

In the Lab

1 Tamiami Medical Supply Seven-Year Financial Plan

Problem: As the spreadsheet specialist at Tamiami Medical Supply, you have been asked to create a worksheet that will project the revenue, expenses, taxes, and income for the next seven years based on the assumptions in Table 3-6. The desired worksheet is shown in Figure 3-84.

Table 3-6 Data for Assumptions	
Units Sold in Year 2002	9,492,016
Unit Cost	7.23
Annual Sales Growth	5.95%
Annual Price Decrease	5.50%
Margin	40.75%

Microsoft Excel - Tamiami Medical Supply

File   Edit   View   Insert   Format   Tools   Data   Window   Help

Type a question for help

Arial   10   B I U $ % , .00 .00

A29

Tamiami Medical Supply

Seven-Year Plan   1/3/2003

	2003	2004	2005	2006	2007	2008	2009
Revenue	115,826,626	115,968,803	116,111,155	116,253,681	116,396,382	116,539,259	116,682,311
Cost of Goods Sold	68,627,276	68,711,516	68,795,859	68,880,306	68,964,857	69,049,511	69,134,269
Margin	47,199,350	47,257,287	47,315,295	47,373,375	47,431,526	47,489,748	47,548,042
Expenses							
Advertising	17,374,994	17,396,320	17,417,673	17,439,052	17,460,457	17,481,889	17,503,347
Maintenance	1,900,000	5,397,000	4,200,000	5,150,000	2,500,000	3,150,000	2,960,000
Rent	1,800,000	1,980,000	2,178,000	2,395,800	2,635,380	2,898,918	3,188,810
Salaries	20,848,793	20,874,385	20,900,008	20,925,663	20,951,349	20,977,067	21,002,816
Supplies	1,737,399	1,739,532	1,741,667	1,743,805	1,745,946	1,748,089	1,750,235
Total Expenses	43,661,186	47,387,237	46,437,348	47,654,320	45,293,132	46,255,962	46,405,207
Income Before Taxes	3,538,164	(129,950)	877,947	(280,945)	2,138,394	1,233,786	1,142,835
Income Taxes	1,415,266	0	351,179	0	855,358	493,514	457,134
Net Income	2,122,898	(129,950)	526,768	(280,945)	1,283,036	740,271	685,701
Assumptions							
Units Sold in Year 2002	9,492,016						
Unit Cost	$7.23						
Annual Sales Growth	5.95%						
Annual Price Decrease	5.50%						
Margin	40.75%						

Seven-Year Plan / 3-D Column Chart / Sheet2 / Sheet3 /

Ready

Start   Microsoft Excel - Tam...   EN   4:27 PM

FIGURE 3-84

Instructions Part 1: Complete the following steps to create the worksheet shown in Figure 3-84.

1. Use the Select All button and Bold button to bold the entire worksheet. Enter the worksheet titles in cells A1 and A2. Enter the system date in cell H2 using the NOW function. Format the date to the 3/14/2001 style.

(continued)

In the Lab

Tamiami Medical Supply Seven-Year Financial Plan *(continued)*

2. Enter the seven column titles 2003 through 2009 in the range B3:H3 by entering 2003 in cell B3, formatting it, and using the fill handle. Format cell B3 as follows: a) change the number in cell B3 to text by assigning it the format Text in the Format Cells dialog box; b) center and italicize cell B3; c) rotate its contents 45°. Use the Format Painter button to copy the format assigned to cell B3 to the range C3:H3.

3. Enter the row titles in the range A4:A24. Change the font size in cells A7, A13, A15, and A17 to 12 point. Change the font size in cell A19 to 14 point and underline the characters in the cell. Add a heavy bottom border to the range A3:H3.

4. Change the following column widths: A = 23.43; B through H = 11.00. Change the heights of rows 7, 13, 15, 16, and 17 to 24.00.

5. Enter the assumptions values in Table 3-6 in the range B20:B24. Use format symbols.

6. Assign the Comma style format with no decimal places to the range B4:H17.

7. Complete the following entries:
   a. 2003 Revenue (cell B4) = Units Sold 2002 * (Unit Cost / (1 – Margin)) or =B20 * (B21 / (1 – B24))
   b. 2004 Revenue (cell C4) = 2003 Revenue * (1 + Annual Sales Growth) * (1 – Annual Price Decrease) or =B4 * (1 + $B$22) * (1 – $B$23)
   c. Copy cell C4 to the range D4:H4.
   d. 2003 Cost of Goods Sold (cell B5) = 2003 Revenue – (2003 Revenue * Margin) or =B4 * (1 - $B$24)
   e. Copy cell B5 to the range C5:H5.
   f. 2003 Margin (cell B6) = 2003 Revenue – 2003 Cost of Goods Sold or =B4 – B5
   g. Copy cell B6 to the range C6:H6.
   h. 2003 Advertising (cell B8) = 1000 + 15% * 2003 Revenue or =1000 + 15% * B4
   i. Copy cell B8 to the range C8:H8.
   j. Maintenance (row 9): 2003 = 1,900,000; 2004 = 5,397,000; 2005 = 4,200,000; 2006 = 5,150,000; 2007 = 2,500,000; 2008 = 3,150,000; 2009 = 2,960,000
   k. 2003 Rent (cell B10) = 1,800,000
   l. 2004 Rent (cell C10) = 2003 Rent + 10% * 2003 Rent or =B10 + (10% * B10)
   m. Copy cell C10 to the range D10:H10.
   n. 2003 Salaries (cell B11) = 18% * 2003 Revenue or =18% * B4
   o. Copy cell B11 to the range C11:H11.
   p. 2003 Supplies (cell B12) = 1.5% * 2003 Revenue or =1.5% * B4
   q. Copy cell B12 to the range C12:H12.
   r. 2003 Total Expenses (cell B13) = SUM(B8:B12)
   s. Copy cell B13 to the range C13:H13.
   t. 2003 Income Before Taxes (cell B15) = 2003 Margin – 2003 Total Expenses or =B6 – B13
   u. Copy cell B15 to the range C15:H15.
   v. 2003 Income Taxes (cell B16): If 2003 Income Before Taxes is less than zero, then 2003 Income Taxes equal zero; otherwise 2003 Income Taxes equal 40% * 2003 Income Before Taxes or =IF(B15 < 0, 0, 40% * B15)
   w. Copy cell B16 to the range C16:H16.
   x. 2003 Net Income (cell B17) = 2003 Income Before Taxes – 2003 Income Taxes or =B15 – B16
   y. Copy cell B17 to the range C17:H17.

In the Lab

8. Change the font in cell A1 to 26-point Arial Black (or a similar font). Change the font in cell A2 to 16-point Arial Narrow (or a similar font). Change the font in cell H2 to 10-point Century Gothic (or a similar font). Change the background and font colors and add drop shadows as shown in Figure 3-84 on page E 3.69.

9. Enter your name, course, laboratory assignment (Lab 3-1), date, and instructor name in the range A27:A31. Save the workbook using the file name, Tamiami Medical Supply.

10. Use the Page Setup command on the File menu to fit the printout on one page in portrait orientation. Preview and print the worksheet. Preview and print the formulas version (CTRL+ACCENT MARK) of the worksheet in landscape orientation using the Fit to option button in the Page Setup dialog box. After printing the formulas version, reset the print scaling to 100%. Press CTRL+ACCENT MARK to display the values version of the worksheet. Save the workbook again.

11. Zoom to: (a) 200%; (b) 75%; (c) 25%; (d) 100%.

Instructions Part 2: Draw a 3-D Column chart (Figure 3-85) that compares the projected net incomes for the years 2003 through 2009. Use the nonadjacent ranges B3:H3 and B17:H17. Add the chart title and format it as shown in Figure 3-85. To change the color of the columns, right-click a column and then click Format Data Series. To change the color of the walls behind and to the left of the columns, right-click a wall and then click Format Walls. Rename and rearrange the sheets, and color their tabs as shown in Figure 3-85. Save the workbook using the same file name (Tamiami Medical Supply) as defined in Part 1. Print both sheets.

FIGURE 3-85

(continued)

In the Lab

Tamiami Medical Supply Seven-Year Financial Plan *(continued)*

Instructions Part 3: If the 3-D Column chart is on the screen, click the Seven-Year Plan tab to display the worksheet. Divide the window into two panes by dragging the horizontal split bar between rows 6 and 7. Use the scroll bars to display both the top and bottom of the worksheet.

Using the numbers in columns 2 and 3 of Table 3-7, analyze the effect of changing the annual sales growth (cell B22) and annual price decrease (cell B23) on the annual net incomes in row 17. The resulting answers are in column 4 of Table 3-7. Print both the worksheet and chart for each case.

Close the workbook without saving it, and then reopen it. Use the Goal Seek command to determine a margin (cell B24) that would result in a net income in 2009 of $5,000,000 (cell H17). You should end up with a margin of 45.85% in cell B24. After you complete the goal seeking, print only the worksheet. Do not save the workbook with the latest changes.

Table 3-7 Data to Analyze and Results

CASE	ANNUAL SALES GROWTH	ANNUAL PRICE DECREASE	2009 RESULTING NET INCOME
1	16.50%	3.50%	$5,079,297
2	19.75%	-3.75%	$12,284,399
3	32.15%	11.65%	$7,312,377

2 Sun-N-Fun Resort and Spa Indirect Expense Allocation

Problem: You are a summer intern at the elegant five-star Sun-N-Fun Resort and Spa. Your work-study advisor at school and your supervisor at Sun-N-Fun Resort and Spa have agreed on a challenging Excel project for you to do. They want you to create an indirect expense allocation worksheet (Figure 3-86) that will help the resort and spa administration better evaluate the profit centers described in Table 3-8.

Table 3-8 Sun-N-Fun Resort and Spa Worksheet Data

	RESTAURANT	BANQUET ROOM	LOUNGE	SPA	BUSINESS CENTER	CONFERENCE ROOMS	GIFT SHOP	CHILDREN'S GAME ROOM
Revenue	625900	478350	392775	53230	133125	78450	85350	17435
Cost of Sales	213450	123900	105630	34945	12600	42500	34000	8550
Direct Expenses	145750	62000	48460	12500	6345	18750	30200	6200
Square Footage	2250	4650	1400	2350	600	5500	500	600

In the Lab

FIGURE 3-86

	Restaurant	Banquet Room	Lounge	Spa	Business Center	Conference Rooms	Gift Shop	Children's Game Room	Total
Revenue	$625,900.00	$478,350.00	$392,775.00	$53,230.00	$133,125.00	$78,450.00	$85,350.00	$17,435.00	$1,864,615.00
Cost of Sales	213,450.00	123,900.00	105,630.00	34,945.00	12,600.00	42,500.00	34,000.00	8,550.00	575,575.00
Direct Expenses	145,750.00	62,000.00	48,460.00	12,500.00	6,345.00	18,750.00	30,200.00	6,200.00	330,205.00
Indirect Expenses									
Administrative	$24,336.26	$18,599.21	$15,271.89	$2,069.69	$5,176.17	$3,050.29	$3,318.58	$677.91	$72,500.00
Depreciation	7,720.59	15,955.88	4,803.92	8,063.73	2,058.82	18,872.55	1,715.69	2,058.82	61,250.00
Energy	15,440.94	11,800.88	9,689.75	1,313.18	3,284.19	1,935.36	2,105.58	430.12	46,000.00
Insurance	1,575.63	3,256.30	980.39	1,645.66	420.17	3,851.54	350.14	420.17	12,500.00
Maintenance	3,277.31	6,773.11	2,039.22	3,422.97	873.95	8,011.20	728.29	873.95	26,000.00
Marketing	17,538.89	13,404.26	11,006.29	1,491.60	3,730.41	2,198.32	2,391.67	488.56	52,250.00
Total Indirect Expenses	$69,889.61	$69,789.65	$43,791.45	$18,006.83	$15,543.71	$37,919.26	$10,609.95	$4,949.53	$270,500.00
Net Income	$196,810.39	$222,660.35	$194,893.55	($12,221.83)	$98,636.29	($20,719.26)	$10,540.05	($2,264.53)	$688,335.00
Square Footage	2,250	4,650	1,400	2,350	600	5,500	500	600	17,850
Planned Indirect Expenses									
Administrative	$72,500.00								
Depreciation	$61,250.00								
Energy	$46,000.00								
Insurance	$12,500.00								
Maintenance	$26,000.00								
Marketing	$52,250.00								

Sun-N-Fun Resort and Spa
Indirect Expenses of Profit Centers — 12/8/2003

Instructions Part 1: Do the following to create the worksheet shown in Figure 3-86.

1. Use the Select All button and Bold button to bold the entire worksheet. Enter the worksheet titles Sun-N-Fun Resort and Spa in cell A1 and Indirect Expenses of Profit Centers in cell A2. Enter the system date in cell J2 using the NOW function. Format the date to the 3/14/2001 format style.

2. Enter the first four rows of data in Table 3-8 in rows 3 through 6. In row 3, use ALT+ENTER to display the column titles on two lines in a cell. Select the range J4:J6 and click the AutoSum button. Add a bottom border to the range B3:J3. Center the column headings in the range B3:J3.

3. Enter the Square Footage row in Table 3-8 in row 16 using the Comma format symbol. Select cell J16 and use the AutoSum button to determine the sum of the values in the range B16:I16. Vertically center the range A16:J16.

4. Change the following column widths: A = 26.00; B through I = 12.00, and J = 13.00. Change the height of row 16 to 39.00.

5. Enter the remaining row titles in the range A7:A17 as shown in Figure 3-86. Use the Indent button on the Formatting toolbar to indent the row titles in the range A8:A13. Increase the font size to 12 in cells A7, A14, and A15.

6. Copy the range A8:A13 to the range A18:A23. Enter the numbers shown in the range B18:B23 of Figure 3-86 with format symbols.

(continued)

In the Lab

Sun-N-Fun Resort and Spa Indirect Expense Allocation *(continued)*

7. The planned indirect expenses in the range B18:B23 are to be prorated across the profit center as follows: Administrative (row 8), Energy (row 10), and Marketing (row 13) on the basis of revenue volume; Depreciation (row 92), Insurance (row 11), and Maintenance (row 12) on the basis of square feet. Use the following formulas to accomplish the prorating:

   a. Restaurant Administrative (cell B8) = Administrative Expenses * Restaurant Revenue / Total Revenue or =$B$18 * B4 / $J$4

   b. Restaurant Depreciation (cell B9) = Depreciation Expenses * Restaurant Square Feet / Total Square Feet or =$B$19 * B16 / $J$16

   c. Restaurant Energy (cell B10) = Energy Expenses * Restaurant Revenue / Total Revenue or =$B$20 * B4 / $J$4

   d. Restaurant Insurance (cell B11) = Insurance Expenses * Restaurant Square Feet / Total Square Feet or =$B$21 * B16 / $J$16

   e. Restaurant Maintenance (cell B12) = Maintenance Expenses * Restaurant Square Feet / Total Square Feet or =$B$22 * B16 / $J$16

   f. Restaurant Marketing (cell B13) = Marketing Expenses * Restaurant Revenue / Total Revenue or =$B$23 * B4 / $J$4

   g. Restaurant Total Indirect Expenses (cell B14) = SUM(B8:B13)

   h. Restaurant Net Income (cell B15) = Revenue – (Cost of Sales + Direct Expenses + Indirect Expenses) or =B4 – (B5 + B6 + B14)

   i. Use the fill handle to copy the range B8:B15 to the range C8:I15.

   j. Select the range J8:J15 and click the AutoSum button on the Standard toolbar.

8. Add a bottom border to the range B13:J13. Use the Format Cells dialog box to assign the Currency style with two decimal places and display negative numbers in parentheses to the following ranges: B4:J4; B8:J8; and B14:J15. Assign the format Comma style with two decimal places and display negative numbers in parentheses to the following ranges: B5:J6 and B9:J13.

9. Change the font in cell A1 to 48-point Arial Black (or a similar font). Change the font in cell A2 to 26-point Arial Black (or a similar font). Change the font in cell A17 to 14-point italic and underlined.

10. Use the background color Blue (column 6, row 2) on the Fill Color palette, the font color White (column 8, row 5) on the Font Color palette, and a drop shadow (Shadow Style 14) for the following ranges: A1:J2; A7; A15:J15; and A17:B23. The Shadow Style button is on the Drawing toolbar.

11. Rename the Sheet1 sheet, Indirect Expenses, and color its tab blue.

12. Enter your name, course, laboratory assignment (Lab 3-2), date, and instructor name in the range A27:A31. Save the workbook using the file name, Sun-N-Fun Resort and Spa.

13. Use the Page Setup command on the File menu to change the orientation to landscape. Preview and print the worksheet. Preview and print the formulas version (CTRL+ACCENT MARK) of the worksheet in landscape orientation using the Fit to option button in the Page Setup dialog box. After printing the formulas version, reset the print scaling to 100%. Press CTRL+ACCENT MARK to display the values version of the worksheet. Save the workbook again.

14. Divide the window into four panes and display the four corners of the worksheet. Remove the four panes.

In the Lab

Instructions Part 2: Draw a 3-D Pie chart (Figure 3-87) that shows the contribution of each category of indirect expense to the total indirect expenses. That is, chart the nonadjacent ranges A8:A13 (category names) and J8:J13 (data series). Show labels and percents. Do not show the legend. Make the following changes to the 3-D Pie chart:

1. Add the chart title and format it to 36-point Arial blue underlined font.
2. Explode the Administrative slice.
3. Select a slice and use the 3-D View command on the shortcut menu to change the elevation to 35° and the rotation to 80°.
4. Change the color of the slices as shown in Figure 3-87. Change the data labels to bold 12 point. Color the data labels the same as the slice they represent.
5. Drag the data labels away from the 3-D Pie chart so the leader lines from the data labels to the corresponding slices display.
6. Rename the Chart1 sheet 3-D Pie Chart and color its tab red. Rearrange the sheets so the Indirect Expenses sheet is to the left of the 3-D Pie Chart sheet. Click the Indirect Expenses tab.
7. Save the workbook using the file name Sun-N-Fun Resort and Spa. Preview and print both sheets.

FIGURE 3-87

(continued)

In the Lab

Sun-N-Fun Resort and Spa Indirect Expense Allocation *(continued)*

Instructions Part 3: Using the numbers in Table 3-9, analyze the effect of changing the planned indirect expenses in the range B18:B23 on the net incomes for each profit center. Print the worksheet for each case. You should end with the following totals in cell J15: Case 1 = $611,835.00 and Case 2 = $724,585.00

Table 3-9	What-IF Data	
	CASE 1	CASE 2
Administrative	95,000.00	63,500.00
Depreciation	76,500.00	61,000.00
Energy	52,000.00	29,500.00
Insurance	22,500.00	12,250.00
Maintenance	39,000.00	18,000.00
Marketing	62,000.00	50,000.00

3 Modifying Ray's Ready Mix Concrete Weekly Payroll Worksheet

Problem: Your supervisor in the Payroll department has asked you to modify the payroll workbook developed in Exercise 1 of the Project 2 In the Lab section on page E 2.69, so that it displays as shown in Figure 3-88. If you did not complete Exercise 1 in Project 2, ask your instructor for a copy of the Ray's Ready Mix Concrete workbook or complete that exercise before you begin this one.

Ray's Ready Mix Concrete

	A	B	C	D	E	F	G	H	I	J	K	L
2	Weekly Payroll Report for	9/15/2003										
3	Employee	Rate	Hours	Dep.	YTD Soc. Sec.	Gross Pay	Soc. Sec.	Medicare	Fed. Tax	State Tax	Net Pay	
4	Sanchez, Edgar	32.25	49.50	6	4,974.00	1,749.56	108.47	25.37	303.76	55.99	1,255.97	
5	Wright, Felix	12.00	28.00	10	5,540.20	336.00	13.70	4.87	0.00	10.75	306.68	
6	Wreath, Christy	22.40	70.00	4	4,254.00	1,904.00	118.05	27.61	350.03	60.93	1,347.38	
7	Elamain, Al	29.75	18.00	5	5,553.90	535.50	0.00	7.76	68.64	17.14	441.96	
8	Space, Si	16.25	42.00	2	4,825.50	698.75	43.32	10.13	124.37	22.36	498.57	
9	Tuf, Chang	22.15	48.00	6	4,825.50	1,151.80	71.41	16.70	184.21	36.86	842.62	
10	Knob, Doris	29.15	36.25	4	5,553.90	1,056.69	0.00	15.32	180.57	33.81	826.98	
11	Totals		291.75			35,527.00	7,432.30	354.95	107.77	1,211.58	237.83	5,520.17
12												
13	Social Security Tax	6.20%										
14	Medicare Tax	1.45%										
15	Maximum Social Security	$5,553.90										
16												
17												
18												
19												

FIGURE 3-88

The major modifications requested by your supervisor include: (1) reformatting the worksheet; (2) adding computations of time-and-a-half for hours worked greater than 40; (3) removing the conditional formatting assigned to the range E3:E8; (4) charging no federal tax in certain situations; (5) adding Social Security and Medicare deductions; (6) adding and deleting employees; and (7) changing employee information.

In the Lab

Instructions Part 1: Open the workbook, Ray's Ready Mix Concrete, created in Project 2. Perform the following tasks.

1. Select the range A2:H12. Point to Clear on the Edit menu and use the Format command on the Clear submenu to clear all formats. Change the worksheet title font to the color red.
2. Delete rows 10 through 12. Select rows 2 through 15 by dragging through the row headings and click the Bold button. Insert a row above row 2, click the Insert Options button that displays immediately below the new row 2, and select the Format Same As Below option. Enter the worksheet subtitle Weekly Payroll Report for in cell A2.
3. Insert a new column between columns D and E by right-clicking the column E heading and inserting a column. Enter the new column E title, YTD Soc. Sec, in cell E3. Insert two new columns between columns F and G. Enter the new column G title Soc. Sec. in cell G3. Enter the new column H title Medicare in cell H3. Freeze the panes (titles) in column A and rows 1 through 3.
4. Change the column widths and row heights as follows: A = 25.00; B = 9.43; C = 6.43; D = 6.00; E = 13.14; F through K = 9.71; and row 3 = 18.00. Right-align the column titles in the range B3:K3. Assign the NOW function to cell B2 and format it to the 3/14/2001 style.
5. Delete row 8 (Pedal, Rose). Change Felix Wright's rate of pay to 12 and number of dependents to 10.
6. In column E, enter the YTD Social Security values listed in Table 3-10.
7. Insert two new rows immediately above the Totals row. Add the new employee data as listed in Table 3-11.
8. Use the Format Cells dialog box to assign a Comma style and two decimal places to the ranges B4:C11 and E4:K11. Center the range D4:D10.
9. Enter the Social Security and Medicare tax information headings in the range A13:A15. Enter the values in the range B13:B15. Use format symbols to format the numbers as shown in Figure 3-88.
10. Change the formulas to determine the gross pay in column F and the federal tax in column I.

   a. In cell F4, enter an IF function that applies the following logic:

   If Hours <= 40, then Gross Pay = Rate * Hours, otherwise Gross Pay = Rate * Hours + 0.5 * Rate * (Hours − 40)

   b. Copy the IF function in cell F4 to the range F5:F10.
   c. In cell I4, enter the IF function that applies the following logic:

   **If (Gross Pay − Dependents * 38.46) > 0, then Federal Tax = 20% *
(Gross Pay − Dependents * 38.46), otherwise Federal Tax = 0**

   d. Copy the IF function in cell I4 to the range I5:I10.

Table 3-10	YTD Social Security Values
NAME	*YTD SOC. SEC.*
Sanchez, Edgar	4,974.00
Wright, Felix	5,540.20
Wreath, Christy	4,254.00
Elamain, Al	5,553.90
Space, Si	4,825.50

Table 3-11	New Employee Data			
EMPLOYEE	*RATE*	*HOURS*	*DEPENDENTS*	*YTD SOC. SEC.*
Tuf, Chang	22.15	48	6	4,825.50
Knob, Doris	29.15	36.25	4	5,553.90

(continued)

In the Lab

Modifying Ray's Ready Mix Concrete Weekly Payroll Worksheet *(continued)*

11. An employee pays Social Security tax only if his or her YTD Social Security is less than the maximum Social Security in column E. Use the following logic to determine the Social Security tax for Edgar Sanchez in cell G4:

If Soc. Sec. Tax * Gross Pay + YTD Soc. Sec. > Maximum Soc. Sec.,
then Maximum Soc. Sec. – YTD Soc. Sec., otherwise Soc. Sec. Tax * Gross Pay

12. Make sure references to the values in the social security tax table (B13:B15) are absolute, and then copy the IF function to the range G5:G10.

13. In cell H4, enter the following formula and then copy it to the range H5:H10:

Medicare = Medicare Tax * Gross Pay

14. Copy the state tax in cell J4 to the range J5:J10.

15. In cell K4, enter the following formula and copy it to the range K5:K10:

Gross Pay – (Soc. Sec. + Medicare + Fed. Tax + State Tax)

16. Determine any new totals as shown in row 11 of Figure 3-88.

17. Enter your name, course, laboratory assignment (Lab 3-3), date, and instructor name in the range A18:A22.

18. Unfreeze the panes (titles). Save the workbook using the file name Ray's Ready Mix Concrete 2.

19. Use the Zoom box on the Standard toolbar to change the view of the worksheet. One by one, select all the percents in the Zoom list. When you are done, return the worksheet to 100% magnification.

20. Use the Page Setup command on the File menu to change the orientation to landscape. Preview the worksheet. If number signs display in place of numbers in any columns, adjust the column widths. Print the worksheet. Save the worksheet using the same file name.

21. Preview and print the formulas version (CTRL+ACCENT MARK) in landscape orientation using the Fit to option button in the Page Setup dialog box. Close the worksheet without saving the latest changes.

Instructions Part 2: Using the numbers in Table 3-12, analyze the effect of changing the Social Security tax in cell B13 and the Medicare tax in cell B14. Print the worksheet for each case. The first case should result in a total Social Security tax in cell G11 of $509.07. The second case should result in a total Social Security tax of $632.91.

Instructions Part 3: Hand in your handwritten results for this exercise to your instructor. Start Excel and open Ray's Ready Mix Concrete 2.

Table 3-12 Social Security and Medicare Taxes		
CASE	SOCIAL SECURITY TAX	MEDICARE TAX
1	9%	3.25%
2	11.25%	2.75%

1. Select cell F4. Write down the formula that displays in the formula bar. Select the range C4:C10. Point to the border surrounding the range and drag the selection to the range D13:D19. Click cell F4, and write down the formula that displays in the formula bar below the one you wrote down earlier. Compare the two formulas. What can you conclude about Excel when you move cells involved in a formula? Click the Undo button on the Standard toolbar.

2. Right-click the range C4:C10 and click Delete. When the Delete dialog box displays, click Shift cells left. What displays in cell F4? Use the Excel Help system to find a definition of the display in cell F4. Write the definition down. Click the Undo button on the Standard toolbar.

3. Right-click the range C4:C10 and click Insert. When the Delete dialog box displays, click Shift cell right. What displays in the formula bar when you click cell F4? What displays in the formula bar when you click cell G4? What can you conclude about inserting cells? Close the workbook without saving the changes.

Cases and Places

The difficulty of these case studies varies:
▶ are the least difficult; ▶▶ are more difficult; and ▶▶▶ are the most difficult.

1 ▶ Rose's floral shop is open all year, but most of the shop's production revolves around four holidays: Valentine's Day (14,500 flowers), Sweetest Day (8,250 flowers), Mother's Day (11,500 flowers), and Memorial Day (5,975 flowers). On these days 42% of the store's output is roses, 18% is carnations, 31% is mums, and the remaining 9% is tulips. The roses sell for $5.00 each, the carnations for $1.95 each, the mums for $3.50 each, and the tulips for $2.50 each. Rose's management is considering revising its production figures. They have asked you to create a worksheet they can use in making this decision. The worksheet should show the total number of each flower ordered for each holiday, total flowers ordered for the four holidays, potential sales for each type of flower, total potential sales for each holiday, and total potential sales from each type of flower. Include an appropriate chart illustrating total potential sales for each flower type. Use the concepts and techniques presented in this project to create and format the worksheet.

2 ▶ You are the product manager for Class Publishers, a company that produces textbooks for the college market. One of your responsibilities is to submit income projections to your publisher for the books you plan to sign. The projected first year net sales for the books you plan to do are shown in Table 3-13. Also included in the table are the percent of net sales for payment of royalties and manufacturing costs. Use the concepts and techniques presented in this project to create and format a worksheet that shows the projected royalties, projected manufacturing cost, net income for each book, and totals for the four numeric columns in Table 3-13. The net income for a book is equal to the net sales minus the royalty and manufacturing costs.

Table 3-13	Projected 1st Year Net Sales				
BOOK	**NET SALES**	**ROYALTY**	**MANU. COSTS**	**NET INCOME**
A	2,453,345.75	—	—	—
B	1,372,915.50	—	—	—
C	945,238.25	—	—	—
TOTAL	—	—	—	—
ASSUMPTIONS				
ROYALTIES	16.25%			
MANU. COSTS	23.5%			

Your publisher reviewed your plan and returned it, requesting printouts of the worksheet for the following set of values: Set 1 – Royalty 12.5%; Manufacturing Costs 30.5%; Set 2 – Royalty 18.5%; Manufacturing Costs 32%.

Cases and Places

3 ▶ Nivo Power Company is the largest utility company in the Northeast. The company generates revenue from the sale of natural gas and electricity. A fixed percentage of this revenue is spent on marketing, payroll, equipment, production costs, and administrative expenses. Nivo Power's president has summarized the company's receipts and expenditures over the past year on a quarterly basis as shown in Table 3-14.

Table 3-14 Projected Revenue and Expenses				
REVENUES	**QUARTER 1**	**QUARTER 2**	**QUARTER 3**	**QUARTER 4**
NATURAL GAS	87,345,450	78,415,823	82,245,111	67,712,810
ELECTRICITY	72,631,781	61,712,992	75,312,643	61,324,912
EXPENDITURES				
MARKETING	15.25%			
PAYROLL	25.35%			
EQUIPMENT	19.25%			
PRODUCTION	9.75%			
ADMINISTRATIVE	12.25%			

With this data, you have been asked to prepare a worksheet similar to Figure 3-1a on page E 3.05 for the next shareholders' meeting. The worksheet should show total revenues, total expenditures, and net income for each quarterly period. Include a chart that illustrates quarterly net income. Use the concepts and techniques presented in this project to create and format the worksheet and chart. During the meeting, one shareholder lobbied to reduce marketing expenditures by 1.75% and payroll costs by 7.5%. Perform a what-if analysis reflecting the proposed changes in expenditures.

4 ▶▶ Your neighbors want to save enough money to send their son to a private school. They have job orders at their cabinet shop for the next six months: $1,200 in July, $975 in August, $1,900 in September, $1,175 in October, $675 in November, and $955 in December. Each month, they spend 37.25% of the job order income on material, 2.25% on patterns, 4.55% on their retirement account, and 43% on food and clothing. The remaining profits (orders – expenses) will be put aside for the boy's education. The husband's parents have agreed to provide an additional $25 whenever their monthly profit exceeds $150. Your neighbors have asked you to create a worksheet that shows orders, expenses, profits, bonuses, and savings for the next six months, and totals for each category. They would like you to (a) goal seek to determine what percentage of profits to spend on food and clothing if $800 is needed for the school, and (b) perform a what-if analysis to determine the effect of reducing the percentage spent on material to 25%. Use the concepts and techniques presented in this project to create and format the worksheet.

5 ▶▶▶ Balancing a budget is a significant challenge for many students attending college. Whether you work part-time or simply draw on a sum of money while going to school, you must equalize income and expenditures to maintain your budget. Use the concepts and techniques presented in this project to create and format a worksheet that reflects your monthly budget throughout the school year. Indicate the amount of money you have available each month. Hypothesize percentages for monthly expenditures (tuition, books, entertainment, and so on). On the basis of these assumptions, determine expenditures for each month. Include a row for occasional miscellaneous expenses (such as travel). Ascertain the amount of money remaining at the end of each month; this amount will become part or all of the money available for the subsequent month. Perform at least one what-if analysis to examine the effect of changing one or more of the values in the worksheet, and goal seek to determine how an expenditure must be modified to have an additional $500 available at the end of the school year.

Microsoft Excel 2002

Creating Static and Dynamic Web Pages Using Excel

CASE PERSPECTIVE

Quick Lube, an auto oil and lubrication commerce, has experienced explosive growth since its beginning three years ago. Thanks to the popularity of their guaranteed 15-minute turnaround, complimentary coffee and rolls, and overall service, the company has grown faster than anyone could have imagined.

John French is the national sales manager for Quick Lube. He has a workbook that he and his group use to analyze weekly sales. In the past, John printed the worksheet and chart, sent it out to duplicate it, and mailed it to his distribution list. He also made his computer available to members of his workgroup who did not have Excel, so they could analyze sales using the workbook.

John would like to save the Excel workbook (Figure 1a) on the company's intranet as a Web page (Figure 1b) so members on the distribution list could display it using their browser. He also suggested publishing the same workbook on the company's intranet as a dynamic (interactive) Web page (Figure 1c) so his workgroup could use its browser to manipulate the formulas and Bar chart without requiring Excel 2002.

Introduction

Excel provides fast, easy methods for saving workbooks as Web pages that can be stored on the World Wide Web, a company's intranet, or a local hard drive. A user then can display the workbook using a browser, rather than Excel.

You can save a workbook, or a portion of a workbook, as a static Web page or a dynamic Web page. A **static Web page**, also called a **noninteractive Web page** or **view-only Web page** is a snapshot of the workbook. It is similar to a printed report in that you can view it through your browser, but you cannot modify it. A **dynamic Web page**, also called an **interactive Web Page**, includes the interactivity and functionality of the workbook. For example, with a dynamic Web page you can enter formulas, re-format cells, and change values in the worksheet to do what-if analysis while displaying a copy of the worksheet in your browser. A user does not even need Excel on their computer to complete these tasks.

As shown in Figure 1 on the next page, this Web Feature shows you how to save a workbook (Figure 1a) as a static Web page (Figure 1b) and view it using your browser. Then it shows you how to take the same workbook and save it as a dynamic Web page (Figure 1c) and view it using your browser. After displaying the dynamic Web page in your browser, this Web Feature shows you how to change values to test the Web page's interactivity and functionality.

The Save as Web Page command on the File menu allows you to **publish** workbooks, which is the process of making them available to others; for example, on the World Wide Web or on a company's intranet. If you have access to a Web server, you can publish Web pages by saving them to a Web folder or to an FTP location. The procedures for publishing Web pages to a Web folder or FTP location using Microsoft Office applications are discussed in Appendix C.

This Web Feature shows you how to create and save the Web pages and associated folders on a floppy disk rather than to a Web server. Before creating the Web pages, this feature also shows you how to preview a workbook as a Web page and how to create a new folder through the Save As dialog box.

(a) **Workbook Viewed in Excel**

FIGURE 1

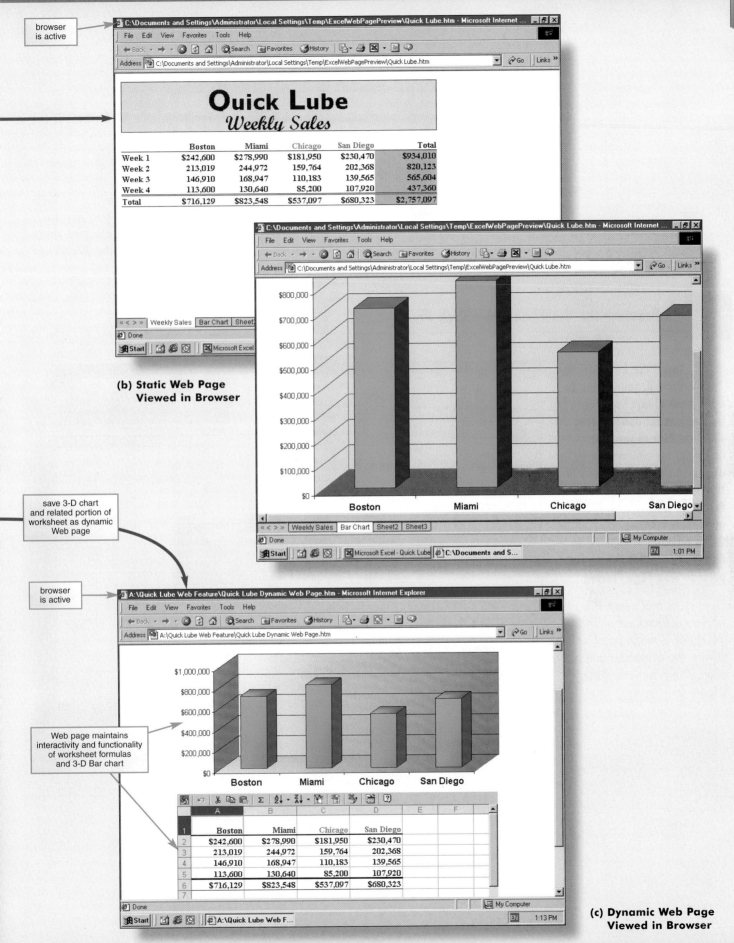

(b) Static Web Page Viewed in Browser

(c) Dynamic Web Page Viewed in Browser

Using Web Page Preview and Saving an Excel Workbook as a Static Web Page

Once you have created an Excel workbook, you can preview it as a Web page. If the preview is acceptable, then you can save the workbook as a Web page.

Web Page Preview

At anytime during the construction of a workbook, you can preview it as a Web page by using the **Web Page Preview command** on the File menu. When you invoke the Web Page Preview command, it starts your browser and displays the active sheet in the workbook as a Web page. The following steps show how to use the Web Page Preview command.

Steps **To Preview the Workbook as a Web Page**

1 **Insert the Data Disk in drive A. See the inside back cover of this book for instructions for downloading the Data Disk or see your instructor for information on accessing the files required in this book. Start Excel and then open the workbook, Quick Lube, on drive A. Click File on the menu bar and then point to Web Page Preview.**

Excel starts and opens the workbook Quick Lube. The workbook is made up of two sheets, the worksheet and a chart. The File menu displays (Figure 2).

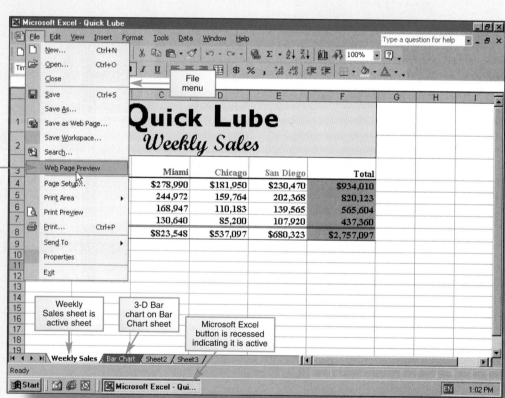

FIGURE 2

2 Click Web Page Preview.

Excel starts your browser and displays a Web page preview of the Weekly Sales sheet in the Quick Lube workbook (Figure 3). The Excel button on the taskbar is no longer recessed. A recessed browser button displays on the taskbar indicating it is active. A preview of the chart is available by clicking the Bar Chart tab at the bottom of the Web page. The Web page preview in the browser is nearly identical to the display of the worksheet in Excel.

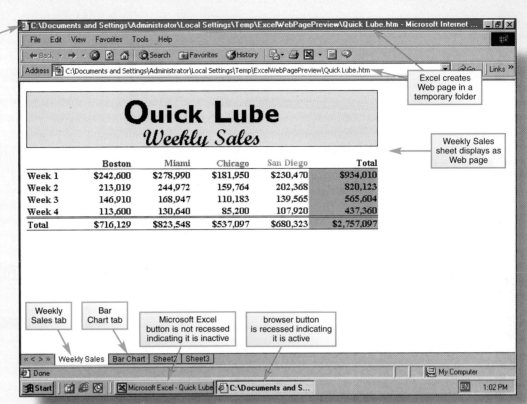

FIGURE 3

3 Click the Bar Chart tab at the bottom of the Web page.

The 3-D Bar chart displays in the browser (Figure 4).

4 When you are finished viewing the Web page preview of the Quick Lube workbook, click the Close button on the right side of the browser title bar.

The browser closes, Excel becomes active, and the worksheet displays.

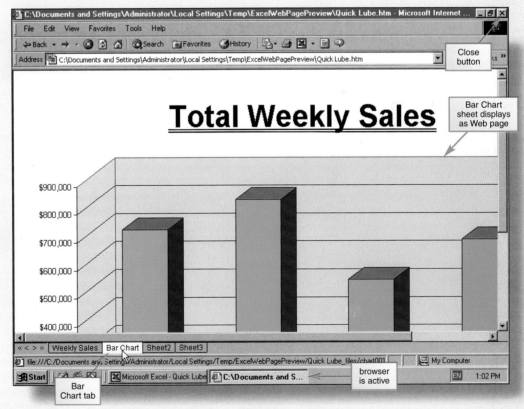

FIGURE 4

The Web Page preview shows that Excel has the capability to produce professional-looking Web pages from workbooks.

Saving a Workbook as a Static Web Page to a New Folder

Once the preview of the workbook as a Web page is acceptable, you can save it as a Web page so it can be viewed by others using a Web browser, such as Internet Explorer or Netscape. The file format that Excel saves the workbook in is called **HTML (hypertext markup language)**, which is a language browsers can interpret.

Experienced users organize their storage devices by creating folders. They then save related files to a common folder. Excel allows you to create folders in the Save As dialog box before saving a file. Perform the following steps to create a new folder on drive A and save the workbook as a static Web page to the new folder.

Publishing Web Pages

For more information on publishing Web pages using Excel, visit the Excel 2002 More About Web page (scsite.com/ex2002/more.htm) and click Publishing Web Pages using Excel.

Steps **To Save an Excel Workbook as a Static Web Page to a Newly Created Folder**

1 **With the workbook Quick Lube open, click File on the menu bar and then point to Save as Web Page.**

The File menu displays (Figure 5).

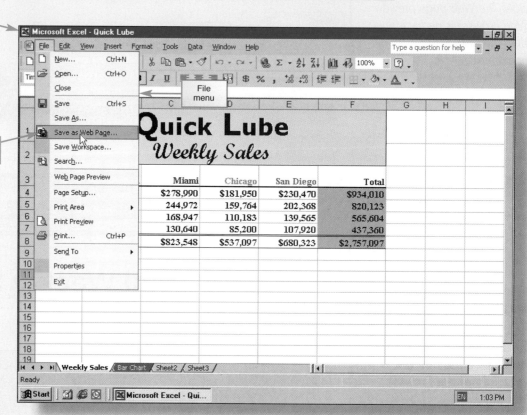

FIGURE 5

2 **Click Save as Web Page. When the Save As dialog box displays, type** Quick Lube Static Web Page **in the File name text box. Click the Save in box arrow and select 3½ Floppy (A:). Click the Create New Folder button. When the New Folder dialog box displays, type** Quick Lube Web Feature **in the Name box. Point to the OK button.**

The Save As dialog box and the New Folder dialog box display as shown in Figure 6.

FIGURE 6

3 **Click the OK button. Point to the Save button in the Save As dialog box.**

The Save As dialog box displays as shown in Figure 7.

4 **Click the Save button. Click the Close button on the right side of the title bar to close Excel.**

Excel saves the workbook in HTML format on drive A in the folder Quick Lube Web Feature using the file name Quick Lube Static Web Page.htm. Excel shuts down.

FIGURE 7

The Favorites Folder

To add a workbook to your Favorites folder, click Save As on the File menu, right-click the file in its original folder and choose Create Shortcut. Next, select the newly created shortcut in the same folder and choose Add To Favorites from the Tools menu (click the Tools arrow on the far right side in the Save As dialog box). To open the file at a later date, simply click the Favorites folder on the Places bar. If you prefer to store the shortcut in your default folder, just cut and paste the shortcut from one folder to another.

The Save As dialog box that displays when you use the Save as Web Page command is slightly different from the Save As dialog box that displays when you use the Save As command. When you use the Save as Web Page command, a **Save area** displays in the dialog box. Within the Save area are two option buttons, a check box, and a Publish button (Figure 7 on the previous page). You can select only one of the option buttons. The **Entire Workbook option button** is selected by default. This indicates Excel will save all the active sheets (Weekly Sales and Bar Chart) in the workbook as a static Web page if you click the Save button. The alternative is the **Selection Sheet option button**. If you select this option, Excel will save only the active sheet (the one that is displaying in the Excel window) in the workbook. If you add a check mark to the **Add interactivity check box**, then Excel saves the sheet as a dynamic Web page. If you leave the Add interactivity check box unchecked, Excel saves the active sheet as a static Web page.

The **Publish button** in the Save As dialog box in Figure 7 is an alternative to the Save button. It allows you to customize the Web page further. In the previous set of steps, the Save button was used to complete the save. Later in this feature, the Publish button will be used to explain further how you can customize a Web page.

If you have access to a Web server and it allows you to save files to a Web folder, then you can save the Web page directly to the Web server by clicking the **My Network Places button** in the lower left corner of the Save As dialog box (Figure 7). If you have access to a Web server that allows you to save to an FTP site, then you can select the FTP site under **FTP locations** in the Save in box just as you select any folder to save a file to. To save a workbook to a Web server, see Appendix C.

After Excel saves the workbook in Step 4, the HTML file (not the workbook) displays in the Excel window. Excel can continue to display the workbook in HTML format because within the HTML file that it created, it also saved the Excel formats that allow it to display the HTML file in Excel. This is referred to as **round tripping** the HTML file back to the application in which it was created.

It was not necessary to create a new folder in the previous set of steps. The Web page could have been saved to drive A in the same manner files were saved to drive A in the previous projects. Creating a new folder, however, allows you to organize your work. Whether you save the Web page to the drive A or to a folder on drive A, Excel automatically creates an additional folder which it uses to store the graphics required to display the Web page.

Another point concerning the new folder created in the previous set of steps is that Excel automatically inserts the new folder name in the Save in box when you click the OK button in the New Folder dialog box (Figure 7).

Viewing the Static Web Page Using Your Browser

With the static Web page saved to the folder Quick Lube Web Feature on drive A, the next step is to view it using your browser as shown in the following steps. You can use Microsoft Internet Explorer or Netscape to view a static Web page.

More About

Viewing Web Pages Created in Excel

To view static (noninteractive) Web pages created in Excel, you can use any browser. To view dynamic (interactive) Web pages created in Excel, viewers must have the Microsoft Office Web Components and Microsoft Internet Explorer 4.01 or later installed on your computer. The Microsoft Office Web Components come with Microsoft Office XP.

Steps **To View and Manipulate the Static Web Page Using Your Browser**

1 **If necessary, insert the Data Disk in drive A. Click the Start button on the taskbar, point to Programs, and then click Internet Explorer. When the Internet Explorer window displays, type** `a:\quick lube web feature\quick lube static web page.htm` **in the Address bar and then press the ENTER key.**

The Web page, Quick Lube Static Web Page.htm, displays with the Weekly Sales sheet active (Figure 8).

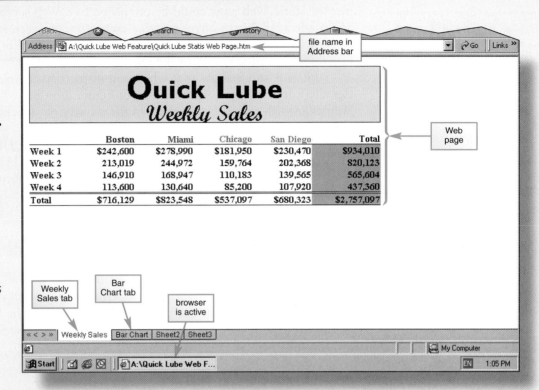

FIGURE 8

2 **Click the Bar Chart tab at the bottom of the window. Use the scroll arrows to display the lower portion of the chart.**

The 3-D Bar chart displays as shown in Figure 9.

3 **Click the Close button at the right side of the Internet Explorer title bar.**

The Internet Explorer window closes.

FIGURE 9

Viewing the Source Code

To view the HTML source code for the static Web page created in Excel, display the Web page in your browser, click View menu on the menu bar, and then click Source in Microsoft Internet Explorer or Page Source in Netscape Navigator. If you are familiar with HTML, you will notice additional XML (Extensible Markup Language) code. The XML code contains the Excel formats so you can open the HTML file in Excel.

You can see from Figures 8 and 9 on the previous page that the static Web page is an ideal media for distributing information to a large group of people. For example, the static Web page could be published to a Web server connected to the Internet and made available to anyone with a computer, browser, and the address of the Web page. Thus, publishing a static Web page of a workbook is an alternative to distributing printed copies of the workbook.

Figures 8 and 9 show that when you instruct Excel to save the entire workbook (see the Entire Workbook check box in Figure 7 on page EW 1.07), it creates a Web page with tabs for each sheet in the workbook. Clicking a tab displays the corresponding sheet.

If you want, you can use the Print command on the File menu in your browser to print the sheets one at a time. You can also view the HTML source created by Excel by clicking Source on the View menu in Internet Explorer or Page Source on the View menu in Netscape.

Saving an Excel Chart as a Dynamic Web Page

This section shows you how to publish a dynamic Web page that includes Excel functionality and interactivity. The objective is to publish the 3-D Bar chart that is on the Bar Chart sheet in the Quick Lube workbook. The following steps use the Publish button in the Save As dialog box, rather than the Save button, to illustrate the additional publishing capabilities of Excel.

Steps: To Save an Excel Chart as a Dynamic Web Page

1 Insert the Data Disk in drive A. Start Excel and then open the workbook, Quick Lube, on drive A. Click File on the menu bar and then point to Save as Web Page.

The File menu displays (Figure 10).

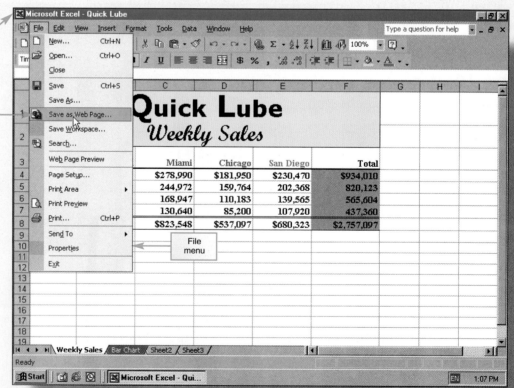

FIGURE 10

2 **Click Save as Web Page. When the Save As dialog box displays, type** Quick Lube Dynamic Web Page **in the File name text box. If necessary, click the Save in box arrow, select 3½ Floppy (A:) in the Save in list, and then select the folder Quick Lube Web Feature. Point to the Publish button.**

The Save As dialog box displays (Figure 11). When you use the Publish button, you do not have to concern yourself with the option buttons and check box in the Save area.

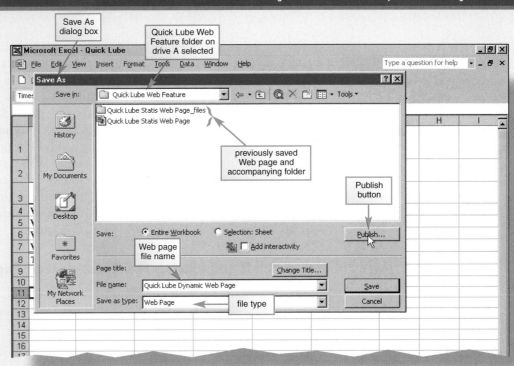

FIGURE 11

3 **Click the Publish button. When the Publish as Web Page dialog box displays, click the Choose box arrow and then click Items on Bar Chart. Click the Add interactivity with check box in the Viewing options area. If necessary, select Chart functionality in the list box in the Viewing options area. Point to the Publish button.**

The Publish as Web page dialog box displays (Figure 12). When you select Items on the Bar Chart, Excel immediately displays the Bar Chart sheet in the Excel window.

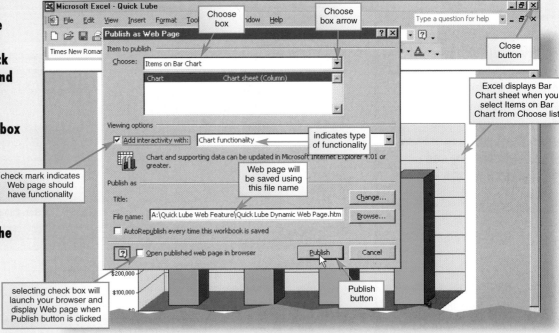

FIGURE 12

4 **Click the Publish button. Click the Close button on the right side of the Excel title bar to close Excel.**

Excel saves the dynamic Web page to the folder Quick Lube Web Feature on the Data Disk in drive A using the file name, Quick Lube Dynamic Web Page.htm. Excel shuts down.

Excel allows you to save an entire workbook, a sheet in the workbook, or a range on a sheet as a Web page. In Figure 11 on the pervious page, you have the option in the Save area to save the entire workbook or a sheet. These option buttons are used with the Save button. If you want to be more selective in what you save, then you can disregard the option buttons in the Save area in Figure 11 and click the Publish button as described in Step 3. The Choose box in the Publish as Web Page dialog box in Figure 12 on the previous page allows you more options in what to include on the Web page. You also may save the Web page as a dynamic Web page (interactive) or a static Web page (noninteractive) by selecting the appropriate options in the Viewing options area. The check box at the bottom of the dialog box gives you the opportunity to start your browser automatically and display the newly created Web page when you click the Publish button.

Viewing and Manipulating the Dynamic Web Page Using Your Browser

With the dynamic Web page saved to the folder Quick Lube Web Feature on drive A, the next step is to view and manipulate the dynamic Web page using your browser as shown in the following steps.

 To View and Manipulate the Dynamic Web Page Using Your Browser

1 **Click the Start button on the taskbar, point to Programs, and then click Internet Explorer. When the Internet Explorer window displays, type** a:\quick lube web feature\quick lube dynamic web page.htm **in the Address bar and then press the ENTER key.**

The Web page, Quick Lube Dynamic Web Page.htm, displays as shown in Figure 13. This Web page contains information from the Quick Lube workbook. The 3-D Bar chart displays with the rows and columns of the worksheet that determine the heights of the bars in the chart immediately below it.

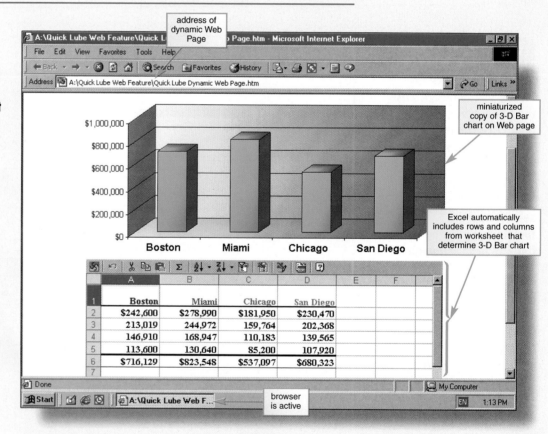

FIGURE 13

2 Click cell B4 and then enter 600000.

The 600,000 replaces the 168,947. The formulas in the worksheet portion are recalculated and the heights of the bars in the 3-D Bar chart and the scaling factor along the y-axis change to agree with the new totals in row 6 (Figure 14).

3 Click the Close button at the right side of the Internet Explorer title bar.

The Internet Explorer window closes.

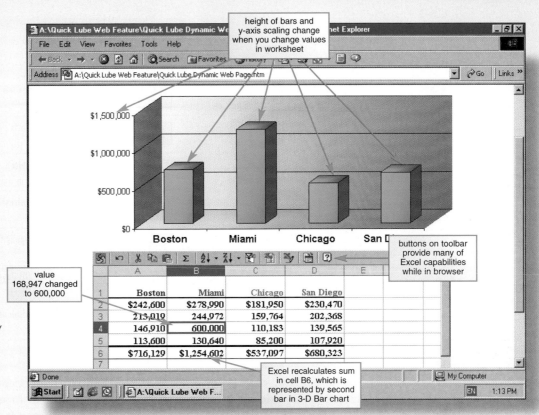

FIGURE 14

Figure 13 shows the result of saving the 3-D Bar chart as a dynamic Web page. Excel displays a miniature version of the 3-D Bar chart and automatically adds the columns and rows from the worksheet below the chart that affect the numbers charted. As shown in Figure 14, you can change the numbers in the worksheet that determine the heights of the bars in the chart and the Web page instantaneously recalculates all formulas and redraws the chart with a new scaling factor along the y-axis. When cell B4 is changed from 168,947 to 600,000, the Web page recalculates the totals in row 6. The bar representing Miami is based on the number in cell B6. Thus, when the number in cell B6 changes from 823,548 to 1,254,602 because of the change made to cell B4, the bar representing Miami changes to a much taller one in relation to the other bars. The interteractivity and functionality allow you to share a workbook's formulas and charts with others who may not have access to Excel, but do have access to a browser.

Modifying the Worksheet on a Dynamic Web Page

Immediately above the rows and columns in the worksheet in Figure 14 is a toolbar. The toolbar allows you to invoke the most commonly used worksheet commands. For example, you can select a cell immediately below a column of numbers and click the AutoSum button to sum the numbers in the column. Cut, copy, and paste capabilities also are available. The functions of the buttons on the toolbar in Figure 14 are summarized in Table 1 on the next page.

Table 1   Toolbar Options

BUTTON	NAME OF BUTTON	FUNCTION
	Office Logo	Displays information about the Microsoft Office Web component, including the version number installed
	Undo	Reverses the last command or action, or deletes the last entry typed
	Cut	Removes the selection and places it on the Office Clipboard
	Copy	Copy the selection to the Office Clipboard
	Paste	Inserts the most recent item placed on the Clipboard
	AutoSum	Inserts the SUM function in a cell and selects a range to sum

Table 1   Toolbar Options *(continued)*

BUTTON	NAME OF BUTTON	FUNCTION
	Sort Ascending	Sorts the selected items in ascending sequence
	Sort Descending	Sorts the selected items in descending sequence
	AutoFilter	Selects specific items you want to display in a list
	Refresh All	Refreshes data when connected to the Web
	Export to Excel	Opens the Web page as a workbook in Excel
	Commands and Options	Displays the Commands and Options dialog box
	Help	Displays Microsoft Spreadsheet Help

More About

Creating Links

You can add hyperlinks to an Excel workbook before you save it as a Web page. You can add hyperlinks that link to a Web page, a location in a Web page, or to an e-mail address that automatically starts the viewer's e-mail program.

In general, you can add formulas, format, sort, and export the Web page to Excel. Many additional Excel capabilities are available through the **Commands and Options dialog box** (Figure 15). You display the Commands and Options dialog box by clicking the **Commands and Options button** on the toolbar. When the Command and Options dialog box displays, click the Format tab. You can see in Figure 15, that many of the common formats, such as bold, italic, underline, font color, font style, and font size, are available through your browser for the purpose of formatting cells in the worksheet below the 3-D Bar chart on the Web page.

Modifying the dynamic Web page does not change the makeup of the original workbook or the Web page stored on disk, even if you use the Save As command on the browser's File menu. If you do use the Save As command in your browser, it will save the original htm file without any changes you might have made. You can, however, use the **Export to Excel button** on the Spreadsheet toolbar to create a workbook that will include any changes you made in your browser. The Export to Excel button only saves the worksheet and not the chart.

FIGURE 15

CASE PERSPECTIVE SUMMARY

John is excited with the two Web pages you created. By publishing the static Web page on the company's intranet, he no longer has to mail printouts of the Workbook to his distribution list. Furthermore, because he can make the worksheet and chart available as a dynamic Web page, members of his group no longer need to use his computer.

Web Feature Summary

This Web Feature introduced you to previewing a Web page, creating a new folder on disk, and publishing and viewing two types of Web pages: static and dynamic. Whereas the static Web page is a snapshot of the workbook, a dynamic Web page adds functionality and interactivity to the Web page. Besides changing the data and generating new results with a dynamic Web page, you also can add formulas and change the formats in your browser to improve the appearance of the Web page.

What You Should Know

Having completed this project, you now should be able to perform the following tasks:

▶ Preview the Workbook as a Web Page (EW 1.04)
▶ Save an Excel Chart as a Dynamic Web Page *(EW 1.10)*
▶ Save an Excel Workbook as a Static Web Page to a Newly Created Folder *(EW 1.06)*
▶ View and Manipulate the Dynamic Web Page Using Your Browser *(EW 1.12)*
▶ View and Manipulate the Static Web Page Using Your Browser *(EW 1.09)*

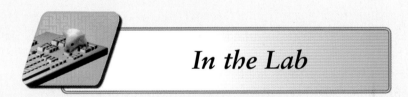

In the Lab

1 Web CD Club Web Page

Problem: You are a student employed part-time as a spreadsheet specialist by Web CD Club. Your supervisor has asked you to create a static Web page and dynamic Web page from the company's annual sales workbook.

Instructions Part 1: Start Excel and open the Web CD Club workbook from the Data Disk. Perform the following tasks:

1. Review the worksheet and chart so you have an idea of what the workbook contains. Preview the workbook as a Web page.
2. Save the workbook as a Web page to a new folder titled Web Feature 1 Exercises on drive A using the file name, Web CD Club Static Web Page. Make sure you select Entire Workbook in the Save area before you click the Save button. Close Excel.
3. Start your browser. Type a:\web feature 1 exercises\web cd club static web page.htm in the Address bar. When the Web page displays, click the tabs at the bottom of the window to view the sheets. As you view each sheet, print it in landscape orientation. Close your browser window.

(continued)

In the Lab

Web CD Club Web Page *(continued)*

Instructions Part 2: Start Excel and open the Web CD Club workbook from the Data Disk. Perform the following tasks:

1. Click File on the menu bar and then click Save as Web Page. Use the Publish button to save the workbook as a Web page to the folder Web Feature 1 Exercises on drive A using the file name, Web CD Club Dynamic Web Page. In the Publish as Web Page dialog box, select Items on Bar Chart in the Choose box, click the Add Interactivity with check box and add chart functionality. Click the Publish button. Quit Excel.

2. Start your browser. Type a:\web feature 1 exercises\web cd club dynamic web page.htm in the Address bar. When the Web page displays, click cell B6 and then click the AutoSum button on the toolbar twice. Cell B6 should equal $2,806,007. Print the Web page.

3. Enter the following gross sales: East = 235,000; North = 542,500; South = 300,500; West = 200,000; and International = 1,500,000. Cell B6 should equal $2,778,000. Print the Web page. Close the browser window.

2 Refurbished Computers Plus Web Page

Problem: You are the spreadsheet analyst for Refurbished Computers Plus. You have been asked to create a static Web page and dynamic Web page from the workbook that the company uses to project sales and payroll expenses.

Instructions Part 1: Start Excel and open the Refurbished Computers Plus workbook from the Data Disk. Perform the following tasks:

1. Display the 3-D Pie Chart sheet. Redisplay the Projected Expenses sheet. Preview the workbook as a Web page.

2. Save the workbook as a Web page to the folder Web Feature 1 Exercises on drive A using the file name, Refurbished Computers Plus Static Web Page. Make sure you select Entire Workbook in the Save area before you click the Save button. Quit Excel.

3. Start your browser. Type a:\web feature 1 exercises\refurbished computers plus static web page.htm in the Address bar. When the Web page displays, click the tabs at the bottom of the window to view the sheets. Print each sheet in landscape orientation. Quit your browser.

Instructions Part 2: Start Excel and open the Refurbished Computers Plus workbook from the Data Disk. Perform the following tasks:

1. Click File on the menu bar and then click Save as Web Page. Use the Publish button to save the workbook as a Web page to the folder Web Feature 1 Exercises on drive A using the file name, Refurbished Computers Plus Dynamic Web Page. In the Publish as Web Page dialog box, select Items on 3-D Pie Chart in the Choose box, click the Add Interactivity with check box and add chart functionality. Click the Publish button. Quit Excel.

2. Start your browser. Type a:\web feature 1 exercises\refurbished computers plus dynamic web page.htm in the Address bar. When the Web page displays, print it in landscape orientation.

3. Scroll down and change the values of the following cells: cell B15 = 28%; cell B16 = 4.5%; cell B17 = 25,000; cell B19 = 20.25%; and cell B20 = 7.75%. Cell H12 should equal $1,782,939.49. The 3-D Pie chart should change to display the new contributions to the projected payroll expenses.

Microsoft Excel 2002

PROJECT

Financial Functions, Data Tables, Amortization Schedules, and Hyperlinks

You will have mastered the material in this project when you can:

O B J E C T I V E S

- Control the color and thickness of outlines and borders
- Assign a name to a cell and refer to the cell in a formula by using the assigned name
- Determine the monthly payment of a loan using the financial function PMT
- Create a data table to analyze data in a worksheet
- Add a pointer to a data table
- Create an amortization schedule
- Determine a present value of a loan using the PV function
- Analyze worksheet data by changing values
- Add a hyperlink to a worksheet element
- Use names and the Set Print Area command to print sections of a worksheet
- Set print options
- Protect and unprotect cells in a worksheet
- Use the formula checking features of Excel

Financial Functions and What-If Analysis

Tools That Prove Useful for Potential Borrowers

The American Dream to which most people aspire is an ideal of a happy successful life, owning a home in a traditional neighborhood, with a warm sense of community. Only two percent of Americans have healthy financial outlooks, however, according to some financial planners. As college tuition fees increase exponentially, with some costing more than $1,000 per week, students may doubt whether career plans following graduation will be worth the money spent on education. With corporate downsizing, fluctuating interest rates, and job insecurity, as well as student loans, credit card debt, and other financial obligations, many individuals and families are finding it difficult to realize this dream.

Creative lending institutions, however, work with customers' purse strings to explore various mortgage options. They often use worksheets such as the Pay-Less Financial Services that you will create in this Excel project. The loan analysis in this project evaluates data by applying financial functions and an amortization schedule, and using an additional what-if tool, the data table, to guide consumers and help determine their ability to purchase a home. Another feature of Excel, allows you to add hyperlinks to a worksheet, making it possible to click a link in the worksheet to start your Web browser and display an associated Web page.

Citibank offers a variety of personal finance options including student and personal loans, equity loans, and mortgages. CitiMortgage, which uses online loan forms and question and answer Web pages, helps potential buyers ascertain whether they qualify for home loans.

Home shoppers, particularly first-time buyers, often do not know whether they have a sufficient down payment and adequate income to purchase a home. Then they need to know maximum sales prices of homes they can afford. To provide this information, the CitiMortgage Web pages provide tools that determine loan amounts based on annual income, credit history, and asset and debt information, and then establish down payments required to qualify for mortgage options. Using online forms, prospective buyers enter information, which in turn is evaluated using the home purchase analyzer. Behind this analysis is a worksheet that calculates monthly payments, varying interest rates, and loan amounts. Customers can apply online, talk to a CitiMortgage consultant who will walk them

through the process, or they can contact a sales center to complete the transaction in person.

After entering the information and current interest rates for particular loan amounts, financial functions determine the maximum loan amounts and monthly payments based on the data. If a client has an approximate sales price in mind, the figure is used to determine if the property is affordable. For example, if the home is priced at $150,000, the price, coupled with other property expenses, amounts to 35.73 percent of the total gross income.

These figures are examined to find the annual income required to obtain 30-year fixed, 15-year fixed, and adjustable-rate mortgages with down payments of 25, 20, 10, and 5 percent. For example, the client needs an annual income of $40,365 and a 25 percent down payment of $37,500 to obtain a 30-year fixed mortgage with an interest rate of 8.75 percent and monthly payments of $1,111. Additional analysis indicates that the client needs to earn $57,525 with a 10-percent down payment of $15,000 to obtain a 15-year fixed mortgage at 8.25 percent with monthly payments of $1,583.

Most lenders use worksheets as a starting point to help borrowers explore mortgage options and compare rates, terms, and monthly costs. With automatic recalculation, its wide array of financial functions, and powerful what-if capabilities, Excel makes this type of data analysis easy and uncomplicated. Buyers can use these tools to determine affordability and substantiate their monetary picture, bringing them closer to the American Dream.

Microsoft Excel 2002

Financial Functions, Data Tables, Amortization Schedules, and Hyperlinks

PROJECT

4

C A S E   P E R S P E C T I V E

Ethan Cromwell recently purchased Pay-Less Financial Services. His major goal during his first few months of ownership is to computerize the loan department so loan officers can generate instant loan information when a customer comes in for an interview. He has hired you as his technical consultant to help him achieve this goal.

Ethan attended a Microsoft seminar for business owners, during which he learned about Excel's many capabilities, including its financial functions and what-if tools. Ethan has asked you to create a workbook that will calculate loan payment information, display an amortization schedule, and display a table that shows loan payments for varying interest rates. He also wants loan officers to have the ability to print portions of the worksheet and display the Pay-Less Financial Services 2002 Statement of Condition using a browser.

To ensure that the loan officers do not delete the formulas in the worksheet, he has asked you to investigate the feasibility of protecting cells in the worksheet so they cannot be changed accidentally.

Introduction

Two of the most powerful aspects of Excel are its wide array of functions and its capability to organize answers to what-if questions. In this project you will learn about financial functions such as the PMT function, which allows you to determine a monthly payment for a loan (upper-left side of Figure 4-1a).

In earlier projects, you learned how to analyze data by using Excel's recalculation feature and goal seeking. This project introduces an additional what-if tool called data tables. You use a data table to automate your data analyses and organize the answers returned by Excel. The Data Table section on the lower-left in Figure 4-1a answers questions pertaining to the effect the 11 different interest rates in column B have on the monthly payment, total interest, and total cost of a loan.

Another important loan analysis tool is the Amortization Schedule section (right side of Figure 4-1a). An amortization schedule shows the beginning and ending balances and the amount of payment that applies to the principal and interest over a period of time.

A key feature of Excel is its capability to add hyperlinks to a worksheet. Hyperlinks are built-in links (file path names or URLs) to other Office documents or HTML files (Web pages). When you click the embedded graphic in Figure 4-1a, the browser starts and displays an HTML file (Figure 4-1b). The HTML file contains Pay-Less Financial Services 2002 Statement of Condition.

In previous projects, you learned how to print in a variety of ways. This project continues to introduce you to additional methods of printing by using names and the Set Print Area command.

Finally, this project introduces you to cell protection and formula checking. Cell protection ensures that users do not inadvertently change values that are critical to the worksheet. The formula checker checks the formulas in a workbook similar to the way the spell checker checks for misspelled words.

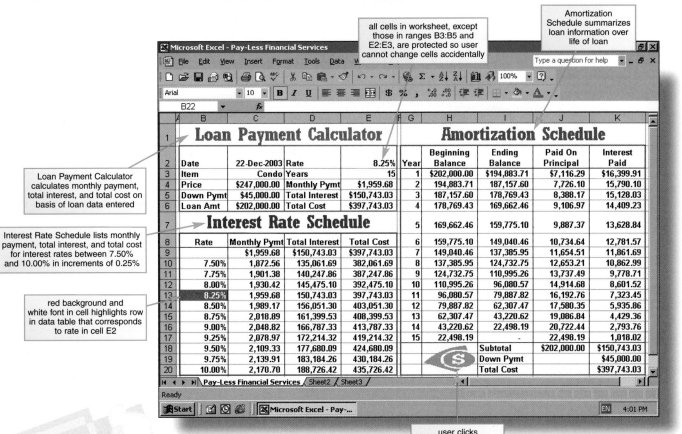

(a) Worksheet

(b) Web Page

FIGURE 4-1

Project Four — Pay-Less Financial Services Loan Analysis

From your meeting with Ethan Cromwell you have determined the following need, source of data, calculations, and special requirements.

Need: An easy-to-read worksheet (Figure 4-1a on the previous page) that determines the monthly payment, total interest, and total cost for a loan; a data table that answers what-if questions based on changing interest rates; an amortization schedule that shows annual summaries; and a hyperlink assigned to an object so that when you click the object, the Pay-Less Financial Services 2002 Statement of Condition displays (Figure 4-1b on the previous page).

Source of Data: The data (item, price of item, down payment, interest rate, and term of the loan in years) is determined by the loan officer and customer when they initially meet for the loan.

Calculations: The following calculations must be made for each loan:

1. Loan Amount = Price – Down Payment
2. Monthly Payment = PMT function
3. Total Interest = 12 × Years × Monthly Payment Loan Amount
4. Total Cost = 12 × Years x Monthly Payment + Down Payment

Use the Table command to create the data table. The amortization schedule involves the following calculations:

1. Beginning Balance = Loan Amount
2. Ending Balance = PV function (present value) or zero
3. Paid on Principal = Beginning Balance – Ending Balance
4. Interest Paid = 12 × Monthly Payment – Paid on Principal or zero
5. Column Totals = SUM function

Special Requirements:

1. Protect the worksheet in such a way that the loan officers cannot enter data mistakenly into wrong cells.
2. Add a hyperlink to an HTML file containing the company's 2002 Statement of Condition.
3. Assign names to the ranges of the three major sections of the worksheet and the worksheet itself, so that they can be used to print each section separately.

Starting and Customizing Excel

Perform the following steps to start and customize Excel. Once the Excel window opens, steps 3 through 5 close the task pane, minimize the Language bar, and ensure that the Standard and Formatting toolbars display on two rows.

TO START AND CUSTOMIZE EXCEL

1 Click the Start button on the Windows taskbar, point to Programs on the Start menu, and then click Microsoft Excel on the Programs submenu.

2 If the Excel window is not maximized, double-click its title bar to maximize it.

3 If the New Workbook task pane displays, click the Show at startup check box at the bottom of the task pane to remove the check mark and then click the Close button in the upper-right corner to close the task pane.

4 If the Language bar displays, click its Minimize button.

5 If the Standard and Formatting toolbars display on one row, click the Toolbar Options button on the right side of either toolbar and then click Show Buttons on Two Rows in the Toolbar Options list.

The Excel window with the Standard and Formatting toolbars on two rows displays as shown in Figure 4-1 on page E 4.05.

If your toolbars display differently than those shown in Figure 4-1, see Appendix D for additional information on resetting the toolbars and menus.

Changing the Font Style of the Entire Worksheet

The first step in this project is to change the font style of the entire worksheet to bold to ensure that the characters in the worksheet stand out.

TO CHANGE THE FONT STYLE OF THE ENTIRE WORKSHEET

1 Click the Select All button immediately above row heading 1 and to the left of column heading A.

2 Click the Bold button on the Formatting toolbar.

As you enter text and numbers in the worksheet, they will display in bold.

Entering the Section Title, Row Titles, and System Date

The next step is to enter the Loan Payment Calculator section title, row titles, and system date. To make the worksheet easier to read, the width of column A will be decreased to 0.50 characters and used as a separator between the loan analysis section and the row headings on the left. Using a column as a separator between sections on a worksheet is a common technique used by spreadsheet specialists. The width of columns B through E will be increased so the intended values fit. The heights of rows 1 and 2, which contain the titles, will be increased so they stand out. The worksheet title also will be changed to 22-point red Rockwell Condensed font.

Perform the following steps to enter the section title, row titles, and system date.

TO ENTER THE SECTION TITLE, ROW TITLES, AND SYSTEM DATE

1 Click cell B1. Type `Loan Payment Calculator` as the section title and then press the ENTER key. Select the range B1:E1. Click the Merge and Center button on the Formatting toolbar.

2 With cell B1 active, click the Font box arrow on the Formatting toolbar, scroll down in the Font list, and then click Rockwell Condensed (or Clarendon Condensed). Click the Font Size box arrow on the Formatting toolbar and then click 22. Click the Font Color button on the Formatting toolbar to change the color of the font to red.

3 Drag through row headings 1 and 2 and then position the mouse pointer on the bottom boundary of row heading 2. Drag down until the ScreenTip, Height: 27.00 (36 pixels), displays.

4 Click cell B2, type `Date` and then press the RIGHT ARROW key.

5 With cell C2 selected, type `=now()` and then press the ENTER key.

More About

Global Formatting

To assign formats to all the cells in all the worksheets in a workbook, click the Select All button, then right-click a tab and click Select All Sheets on the shortcut menu. Next, assign the formats. To deselect the sheets, hold down the SHIFT key and click the Sheet1 tab. You also can select a cell or a range of cells and then select all sheets to assign formats to a cell or a range of cells on all the sheets in a workbook.

More About

Designing Worksheets

Do not create worksheets with the idea that they are to be used only once. Instead, carefully design worksheets as if they will be on display and evaluated by your colleagues. Smart worksheet design starts with visualizing the results you need. For additional information on good worksheet design, visit the Excel 2002 More About Web page (scsite.com/ex2002/more.htm) and click Smart Spreadsheet Design.

6 Right-click cell C2 and then click Format Cells on the shortcut menu. When the Format Cells dialog box displays, click the Number tab, click Date in the Category list, scroll down in the Type list, and click 14-Mar-2001. Click the OK button.

7 Enter the following row titles:

CELL	ENTRY	CELL	ENTRY	CELL	ENTRY
B3	Item	B6	Loan Amt	D4	Monthly Pymt
B4	Price	D2	Rate	D5	Total Interest
B5	Down Pymt	D3	Years	D6	Total Cost

8 Position the mouse pointer on the right boundary of column heading A and then drag to the left until the ScreenTip, Width: 0.50 (6 pixels) displays.

9 Position the mouse pointer on the right boundary of column heading B and then drag to the right until the ScreenTip, Width: 10.14 (76 pixels) displays.

10 Click the column C heading to select it and then drag through column headings D through E. Position the mouse pointer on the right boundary of column heading C and then drag until the ScreenTip, Width: 12.29 (91 pixels), displays.

11 Double-click the Sheet1 tab, type Pay-Less Financial Services as the sheet name, and then click cell C2 to complete the entry. Right-click the tab and click Tab Color. Click red (column 1, row 3) and then click the OK button.

12 Click the Save button on the Standard toolbar. Save the workbook using the file name Pay-Less Financial Services to drive A.

The loan analysis section title, row titles, and system date display as shown in Figure 4-2.

More About

Concatenation

You can concatenate text, numbers, or text and numbers from two or more cells into a single cell. The ampersand (&) is the concatenation operator. For example, if cell A1 = AB, cell A2 = CD, cell A3 = 25, and you assigned cell A4 the formula =A1&A2&A3, then ABCD25 displays in cell A4.

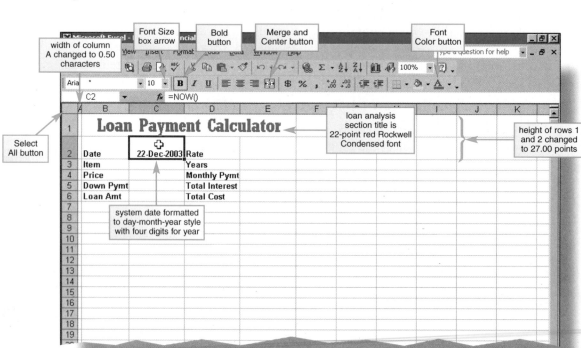

FIGURE 4-2

Adding Borders to a Range

In previous projects, you were introduced to outlining a range using the Borders button on the Formatting toolbar. To control the color and thickness of the outline and borders, use the Border tab in the Format Cells dialog box. The following steps outline the Loan Payment Calculator section. To further subdivide the row titles and numbers, light borders also are added within the section as shown in Figure 4-1a on page E 4.05.

More About

Shortcut Menus

Excel requires that you point to the object (cell, range, toolbar) on the screen when you right-click to display the corresponding shortcut menu. For example, if you select the range G6:J14, and right-click with the mouse pointer on cell A1, then the shortcut menu pertains to cell A1, and not the selected range G6:J14.

 To Add Borders to a Range

1 Select the range B2:E6. Right-click the selected range and then point to Format Cells on the shortcut menu (Figure 4-3).

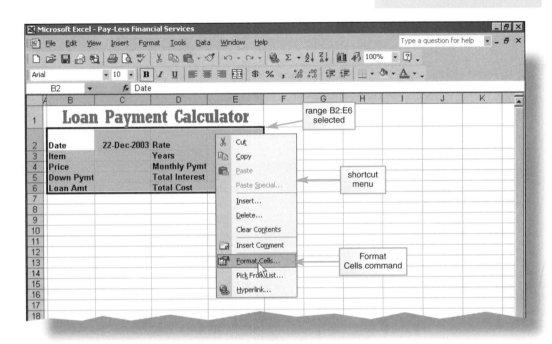

FIGURE 4-3

2 Click Format Cells. When the Format Cells dialog box displays, click the Border tab. Click the Color box arrow. Click the color Red (column 1, row 3) on the Color palette. Click the medium line style in the Style box (column 2, row 5). Click the Outline button in the Presets area.

Excel previews the red outline in the Border area (Figure 4-4).

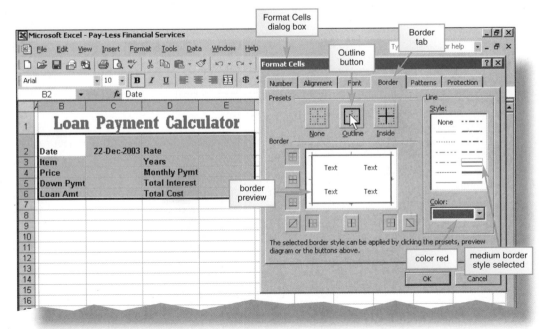

FIGURE 4-4

3 **Click the Color box arrow. Click Automatic (row 1) on the Color palette. Click the light border in the Style box (column 1, row 7). Click the Vertical Line button in the Border area and then point to the OK button.**

Excel previews the vertical border in the Border area (Figure 4-5).

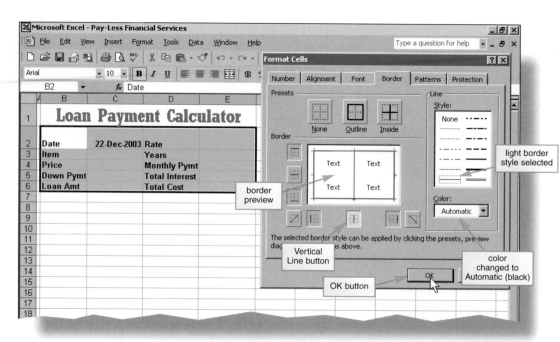

FIGURE 4-5

4 **Click the OK button. Select cell B8 to deselect the range B2:E6.**

Excel adds a red outline with vertical borders to the right side of each column in the range B2:E6 (Figure 4-6).

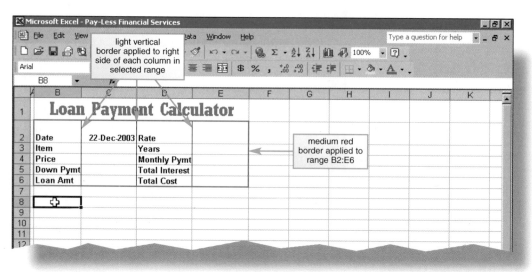

FIGURE 4-6

Other **Ways**

1. For black borders, click Borders button on Formatting toolbar
2. On Format menu click Cells, click Border tab
3. Click Format Cells on short-cut menu, click Border tab
4. In Voice command mode, say "Format, Cells, Border"

As shown in Figure 4-5, you can add a variety of borders with color to a cell or range of cells to improve its appearance. It is important that you select border characteristics in the order specified in the steps; that is, (1) choose the color; (2) choose the border line style; and (3) choose the border type. If you attempt to do these steps in any other order, you will not end up with the desired borders.

Formatting Cells Before Entering Values

While usually you format cells after you enter the values, Excel also allows you to format cells before you enter the values. The following steps assign the Currency style format with a floating dollar sign to the ranges C4:C6 and E4:E6 before the values are entered.

TO FORMAT CELLS BEFORE ENTERING VALUES

1 Select the range C4:C6. While holding down the CTRL key, select the nonadjacent range E4:E6. Right-click one of the selected ranges.

2 Click Format Cells on the shortcut menu. When the Format Cells dialog box displays, click the Number tab.

3 Click Currency in the Category list and then click the fourth format, ($1,234.10), in the Negative numbers list.

4 Click the OK button.

The ranges C4:C6 and E4:E6 are assigned the Currency style format with a floating dollar sign.

As you enter numbers into these cells, the numbers will display using the Currency style format. You also could have selected the range B4:E6 rather than the nonadjacent ranges and assigned the Currency style format to this range, which includes text. The Currency style format has no impact on text in a cell.

Entering the Loan Data

As shown in Figure 4-1a on page E 4.05, five items make up the loan data in the worksheet: the item to be purchased, the price of the item, the down payment, the interest rate, and the number of years until the loan is paid back (also called the term of the loan). These items are entered into cells C3 through C5 and cells E2 and E3. The steps below describe how to enter the following loan data: Item - Condo; Price - $247,000.00; Down Payment - $45,000.00; Interest Rate - 8.25%; and Years - 15.

TO ENTER THE LOAN DATA

1 Click cell C3. Type Condo and click the Enter box on the formula bar. With cell C3 still active, click the Align Right button on the Formatting toolbar. Click cell C4 and enter 247000 for the price of the condo. Click cell C5 and enter 45000 for the down payment.

2 Click cell E2. Enter 8.25% for the interest rate. Click cell E3 and enter 15 for the number of years.

The loan data displays in the worksheet as shown in Figure 4-7.

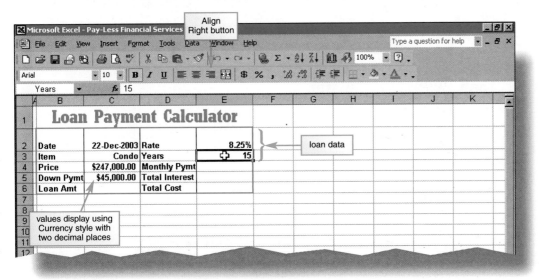

FIGURE 4-7

The values in cells C4 and C5 in Figure 4-7 on the previous page display using the Currency style with two decimal places, because this format was assigned to the cells prior to entering the values. Excel also automatically formats the interest rate to the Percent style with two decimal places, because the percent sign (%) was appended to 8.25 when it was entered into cell E2.

Calculating the four remaining entries in the loan analysis section of the worksheet — loan amount (cell C6), monthly payment (cell E4), total interest (cell E5), and total cost (cell E6) — require that you enter formulas that reference cells C4, C5, C6, E2, and E3. The formulas will be entered referencing names assigned to cells, such as Price, rather than cell references, such as C4, because names are easier to remember than cell references.

Creating Cell Names Based On Row Titles

Worksheets often have column titles at the top of each column and row titles to the left of each row that describe the data within the worksheet. You can use these titles within formulas when you want to refer to the related data by **name**. Names are created from column and row titles through the use of the **Name command** on the Insert menu. You also can use the same command to define descriptive names that are not column titles or row titles to represent cells, ranges of cells, formulas, or constants.

Naming a cell that you plan to reference in a formula helps make the formula easier to read and remember. For example, the loan amount in cell C6 is equal to the price in cell C4 less the down payment in cell C5. Therefore, according to what you learned in the earlier projects, you can write the loan amount formula in cell C6 as =C4 – C5. By assigning the corresponding row titles in column B as the names of cells C4 and C5, however, you can write the loan amount formula as =Price – Down_Pymt, which is clearer and easier to understand than =C4 – C5.

The following steps assign each row title in cells B4 through B6 to their adjacent cell in column C and assigns each row title in cells D2 through D6 to their adjacent cell in column E.

Steps **To Create Names Based on Row Titles**

1 **Select the range B4:C6. Click Insert on the menu bar. Point to Name and then point to Create on the Name submenu.**

Excel highlights the range B4:C6. The Insert menu and Name submenu display (Figure 4-8).

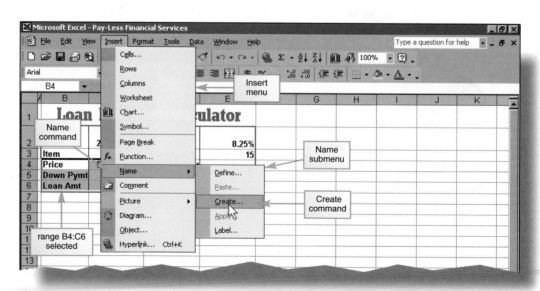

FIGURE 4-8

2 **Click Create. When the Create Names dialog box displays, point to the OK button.**

The Create Names dialog box displays (Figure 4-9). The Left column check box is selected automatically in the Create names in area because the direction of the cells containing text selected in Step 1 is downward.

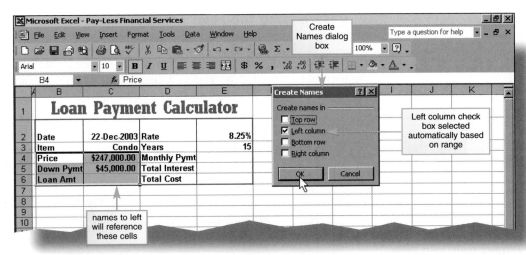

FIGURE 4-9

3 **Click the OK button. Select the range D2:E6. Click Insert on the menu bar, point to Name, and then click Create on the Name submenu. Click the OK button in the Create Names dialog box. Click cell B8 to deselect the range D2:E6.**

You now can use the names in the range B4:B6 and D2:D6 in formulas to reference the adjacent cells on the right. Excel is not case-sensitive with respect to names of cells. Hence, you can enter the names of cells in formulas in uppercase or lowercase letters. Some names, such as Down Pymt in cell B5, include a space because they are made up of two or more words. To use a name in a formula that is made up of two or more words, you replace any space with the **underscore character** (_). For example, Down Pymt is written as down_pymt when you want to reference the adjacent cell C5.

If you enter a formula using Point mode and click a cell that has a name, then Excel will insert the name of the cell rather than the cell reference.

Consider these additional points regarding the assignment of names to cells:

1. A name can be a minimum of one character to a maximum of 255 characters.
2. If you want to assign a name that is not a text item in an adjacent cell, use the **Define command** on the Name submenu (Figure 4-8) or select the cell or range and type the name in the Name box in the formula bar.
3. Names are absolute cell references. This is important to remember if you plan to copy formulas that contain names, rather than cell references.
4. The names display in alphabetical order in the Name box when you click the Name box arrow (Figure 4-10).
5. Names are **global** to the workbook. That is, a name assigned on one worksheet in a workbook can be used on other sheets in the same workbook to reference the associated cell or range of cells.

Spreadsheet specialists often assign names to a cell or range of cells so they can select them quickly. If you want to select a cell or range of cells that has been assigned a name, you can click the Name box arrow (Figure 4-10) and then click the name of the cell you want to select. This method is similar to using the Go To command on the Edit menu or the F5 key to select a cell, but it is much quicker. When you select a name in the Name list that references a range, Excel highlights the range on the worksheet.

Other Ways

1. Type name in Name box, press ENTER key
2. On Insert menu point to Names, click Define, enter name, click OK button
3. Press CTRL+SHIFT+F3
4. In Voice command mode, say "Insert, Name, Create, OK"

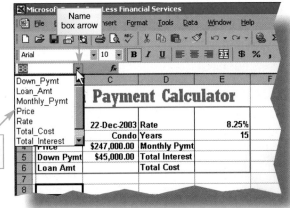

FIGURE 4-10

Determining the Loan Amount

To determine the loan amount in cell C6, subtract the down payment in cell C5 from the price in cell C4. As indicated earlier, you could do this by entering the formula =C4 – C5 or you can enter the formula = price – down_pymt or use Point mode as shown in the following steps.

 Steps To Enter the Loan Amount Formula Using Names

1 **Click cell C6. Type = (equal sign) and then click cell C4. Type – (minus sign) and then click cell C5. Point to the Enter box.**

The formula displays in cell C6 and in the formula bar using the names of the cells (Figure 4-11).

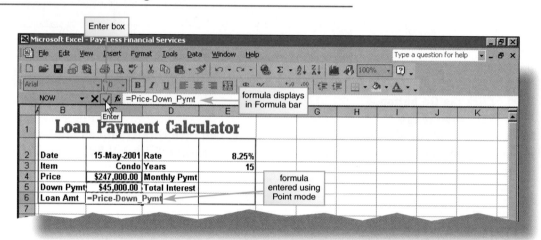

FIGURE 4-11

2 **Click the Enter box.**

Excel assigns the formula =Price – Down_Pymt to cell C6. The result of the formula ($202,000.00) displays in cell C6 using the Currency style format assigned earlier (Figure 4-12). With cell C6 active, its name (Loan_Amt) displays in the Name box in the formula bar.

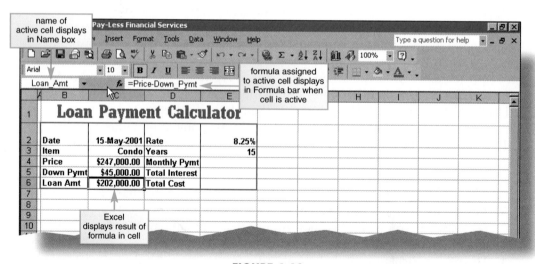

FIGURE 4-12

An alternative to creating names is to use labels. A **label** is a row title or column title, similar to the adjacent names created earlier. Any row title or column title can be used in formulas to reference corresponding cells. It is not necessary to enter commands to assign label names.

The major drawback to using labels in some applications is that they are **relative**, which means the label may very well reference a cell that is nonadjacent to the label. It also is important to note that Excel does not recognize labels in formulas unless you activate label usage. To activate **label usage**, click Tools on the menu bar, click Options, click the Calculation tab, and select Accept labels in formulas. Any row title or column title then can be used in formulas to reference corresponding cells.

Labels are different from names in the following ways: (1) labels are not absolute, they are relative; (2) they cannot be used on other worksheets in the workbook; (3) they do not display in the Name list (Figure 4-10 on page E 4.13); and (4) you can use them without entering underscores in place of spaces.

Determining the Monthly Payment

The next step is to determine the monthly payment for the loan. You can use Excel's **PMT function** to determine the monthly payment in cell E4. The PMT function has three arguments — rate, payment, and loan amount. Its general form is:

=PMT(rate, payment, loan amount)

where rate is the interest rate per payment period, payment is the number of payments, and loan amount is the amount of the loan.

In the worksheet shown in Figure 4-12, cell E2 displays the annual interest rate. Financial institutions, however, calculate interest on a monthly basis. Therefore, the rate value in the PMT function is rate / 12 (cell E2 divided by 12), rather than just rate (cell E2). The number of payments (or periods) in the PMT function is 12 * years (12 times cell E3) because there are 12 months, or 12 payments, per year.

Excel considers the value returned by the PMT function to be a debit and, therefore, returns a negative number as the monthly payment. To display the monthly payment as a positive number, you can enter a negative sign before the loan amount. Thus, the loan amount is equal to –loan_amt. The PMT function for cell E4 is:

=PMT(rate / 12, 12 * years, – loan_amt)

monthly interest rate   number of payments   loan amount

The following steps use the keyboard, rather than Point mode, to enter the PMT function to determine the monthly payment in cell E4.

 Steps To Enter the PMT Function

1 **Click cell E4.**
Type =pmt(rate / 12, 12 * years, -loan_amt **as the function.**
Point to the Enter box on the formula bar.

The PMT function displays in cell E4 and in the formula bar (Figure 4-13). The ScreenTip shows the general form of the PMT function. The arguments in brackets in the ScreenTip are optional and not required for the computation described here. Excel automatically adds the closing parenthesis to the function.

FIGURE 4-13

More About

Naming Cells

You can create row and column names at the same time if you have a worksheet with column titles and row titles. Simply select the column titles and row titles along with the cells to name. On the Insert menu, point to Name; on the Name submenu, click Create. In the Create Names dialog box, click both Top Row and Left Column, and then click the OK button. As a result, you can use the column title and row title separated by a space to refer to the intersecting cell.

More About

Closing Parenthesis

Excel does not require you to enter the closing parenthesis when assigning a function to a cell. See Figure 4-13 below.

2 Click the Enter box on the formula bar.

Excel displays the monthly payment $1,959.68 in cell E4, based on a loan amount of $202,000.00 (cell C6) with an annual interest rate of 8.25% (cell E2) for a term of 15 years (cell E3).

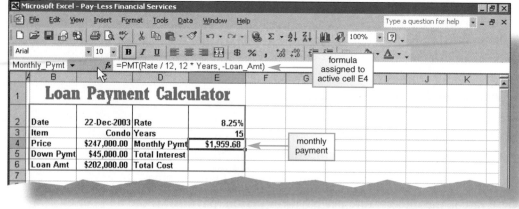

FIGURE 4-14

In addition to the PMT function, Excel provides more than 50 additional financial functions to help you solve the most complex finance problems. These functions save you from entering long, complicated formulas to obtain needed results. Table 4-1 summarizes three of the more frequently used financial functions.

Table 4-1 Financial Functions	
FUNCTION	**DESCRIPTION**
FV(rate, periods, payment)	Returns the future value of an investment based on periodic, constant payments, and a constant interest rate.
PMT(rate, periods, loan amount)	Calculates the payment for a loan based on constant payments and constant interest rate.
PV(rate, periods, payment)	Returns the present value of an investment. The present value is the total amount that a series of future payments is worth now.

Determining the Total Interest and Total Cost

The next step is to determine the total interest (company's gross profit on the loan) and the borrower's total cost of the item being purchased. The total interest (cell E5) is equal to the number of payments times the monthly payment, less the loan amount:

=12 * years * monthly_pymt – loan_amt

The total cost of the item to be purchased (cell E6) is equal to the number of payments times the monthly payment plus the down payment:

=12 * years * monthly_pymt + down_pymt

To enter the total interest and total cost formulas, perform the following steps.

TO DETERMINE THE TOTAL INTEREST AND TOTAL COST

1 Click cell E5. Use Point mode and the keyboard to enter the formula =12 * years * monthly_pymt - loan_amt to determine the total interest.

2 Click cell E6. Use Point mode and the keyboard to enter the formula =12 * years * monthly_pymt + down_pymt to determine the total cost.

3 Click cell B8 to deselect cell E6.

4 Click the Save button on the Standard toolbar to save the workbook using the file name Pay-Less Financial Services.

Excel displays a total interest (company's gross profit) of $150,743.03 in cell E5 and a total cost to the borrower of $397,743.03 in cell E6 for the condo (Figure 4-15). Excel saves the workbook.

With the loan analysis section of the worksheet complete, you can use it to determine the monthly payment, total interest, and total cost for any loan data.

Entering New Loan Data

Assume you want to purchase a Chevy van for $25,500.00. You have $3,750.00 for a down payment and you want the loan for a term of three years. Pay-Less Financial Services currently is charging 9% interest for a three-year auto loan. The following steps show how to enter the new loan data.

TO ENTER NEW LOAN DATA

1 Click cell C3. Type Chevy Van and then press the DOWN ARROW key.

2 In cell C4, type 25500 and then press the DOWN ARROW key.

3 In cell C5, type 3750 and then click cell E2.

4 In cell E2, type 9 and then press the DOWN ARROW key.

5 In cell E3, type 3 and then click cell B8.

Excel instantaneously recalculates the loan information in cells C6, E4, E5, and E6 (Figure 4-16).

FIGURE 4-15

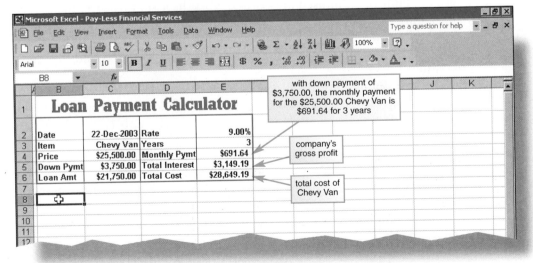

FIGURE 4-16

More *About*

Selecting Cells

If you double-click the top of the heavy border surrounding the active cell, Excel will make the first empty cell below any non-blank cell in the column the active cell. If you double-click the left side of the heavy border surrounding the active cell, Excel will make the first empty cell to the right of any non-blank cell in the row the active cell.

As you can see from Figure 4-16 on the previous page, the monthly payment for the Chevy van is $691.64. The total interest is $3,149.19. By paying for the car over a three-year period, you actually will pay a total cost of $28,649.19 for a $25,500.00 Chevy van.

The next step is to create the data table described earlier and shown in Figure 4-1 on page E 4.05. Before creating the data table, follow these steps to re-enter the original loan data.

TO ENTER THE ORIGINAL LOAN DATA

1 Click cell C3. Type Condo and then press the DOWN ARROW key.

2 In cell C4, type 247000 and then press the DOWN ARROW key.

3 In cell C5, type 45000 and then click cell E2.

4 In cell E2, type 8.25 and then press the DOWN ARROW key.

5 In cell E3, type 15 and then click cell B8.

Excel instantaneously recalculates all formulas in the worksheet each time you enter a value. The original loan information displays as shown in Figure 4-15 on the previous page.

More *About*

Data Tables

Data tables have one purpose, and that is to organize the answers to what-if questions. You can create two kinds of data tables. The first type involves changing one input value to see the resulting effect on one or more formulas. The second type involves changing two input values to see the resulting effect on one formula.

Using a Data Table to Analyze Worksheet Data

You already have seen that if you change a value in a cell, Excel immediately recalculates and displays the new results of any formulas that reference the cell directly or indirectly. But what if you want to compare the results of the formula for several different values? Writing down or trying to remember all the answers to the what-if questions would be unwieldy. If you use a data table, however, Excel will organize the answers in the worksheet for you automatically.

A **data table** is a range of cells that shows the answers generated by formulas in which different values have been substituted. The data table shown below the loan analysis section in Figure 4-17, for example, will display the resulting monthly payment, total interest, and total cost values based on different interest rates in column B.

Data tables are built in an unused area of the worksheet (in this case, the range B7:E20). Figure 4-17 illustrates the makeup of a one-input data table. With a **one-input data table**, you vary the value in one cell (in this worksheet, cell E2, the interest rate). Excel then calculates the results of one or more formulas and fills the table with the results.

An alternative to a one-input table is a two-input data table. A **two-input data table** allows you to vary the values in two cells, but you can apply it to only one formula. A two-input data table example is illustrated in In the Lab 1, Part 2 on page E 4.59.

The interest rates that will be used to analyze the loan formulas in this project range from 7.50% to 10.00%, increasing in increments of 0.25%. The one-input data table shown in Figure 4-18 illustrates the impact of varying the interest rate on three formulas: the monthly payment (cell E4), total interest paid (cell E5), and the total cost of the item to be purchased (cell E6). The series of interest rates in column B are called **input values**.

The first step in constructing the data table shown in Figure 4-18 is to enter the data table section title and column titles in the range B7:E8 and adjust the heights of rows 7 and 8.

FIGURE 4-17

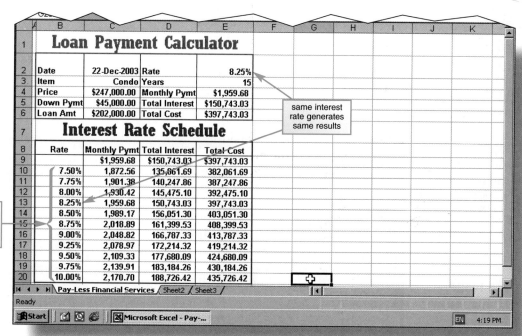

FIGURE 4-18

TO ENTER THE DATA TABLE TITLE AND COLUMN TITLES

1 Click cell B7. Enter Interest Rate Schedule as the data table section title.

2 Click cell B1. Click the Format Painter button on the Standard toolbar. Click cell B7 to copy the format of cell B1. Click the Font Color button arrow on the Formatting toolbar and then click Blue (column 6, row 2) on the Font Color palette.

3 Enter the column titles in the range B8:E8 as shown in Figure 4-19. Select the range B8:E8 and then click the Center button on the Formatting toolbar to center the column titles.

4 Position the mouse pointer on the bottom boundary of row heading 7. Drag up until the ScreenTip, Height: 26.25 (35 pixels), displays. Position the mouse pointer on the bottom boundary of row heading 8. Drag down until the ScreenTip, Height: 16.50 (22 pixels), displays. Click cell B10 to deselect the range B8:E8.

The data table title and column headings display as shown in Figure 4-19.

Creating a Percent Series Using the Fill Handle

The next step is to create the percent series in column B using the fill handle. These percents will serve as the input data for the data table.

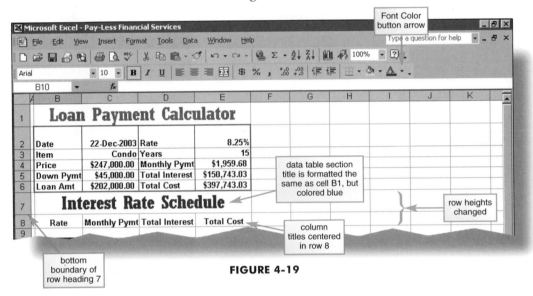

FIGURE 4-19

Steps **To Create a Percent Series Using the Fill Handle**

1 **With cell B10 selected, enter** 7.50% **as the first number in the series. Select cell B11 and enter** 7.75% **as the second number in the series.**

2 **Select the range B10:B11 and then point to the fill handle. Drag the fill handle through cell B20 and hold.**

Excel shades the border of the fill area (Figure 4-20). The ScreenTip, 10.00%, displays below the fill handle indicating the last value in the series. This value will display in cell B20.

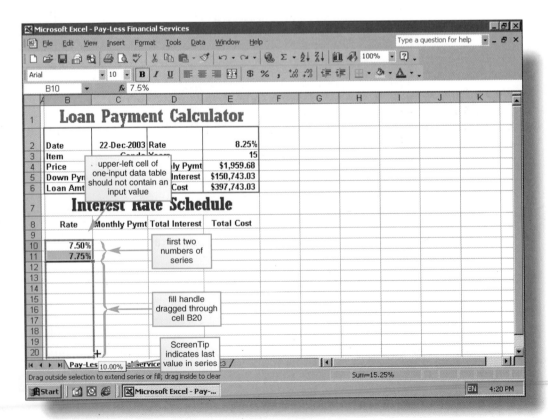

FIGURE 4-20

3 **Release the mouse button. Click cell C9 to deselect the range B10:B20.**

Excel generates the series of numbers from 7.50% to 10.00% in the range B10:B20 (Figure 4-21). The series increases in increments of 0.25%. The Auto Fill Options button displays to the right of the last cell filled.

	Rate	Monthly Pymt	Total Interest	Total Cost
8	Rate	Monthly Pymt	Total Interest	Total Cost
9				
10	7.50%			
11	7.75%			
12	8.00%			
13	8.25%			
14	8.50%			
15	8.75%			
16	9.00%			
17	9.25%			
18	9.50%			
19	9.75%			
20	10.00%			

C9 is active cell

Excel extends series to cell B20

Auto Fill Options button

FIGURE 4-21

Other **Ways**

1. Right-drag fill handle in direction to fill, click Fill Series on shortcut menu
2. In Voice command, say "Edit, Fill, Series, AutoFill,

Excel will use the percents in column B to calculate the formulas to be evaluated and entered at the top of the data table in row 9. This series begins in cell B10, not cell B9, because the cell immediately to the left of the formulas in a one-input data table should not include an input value.

Entering the Formulas in the Data Table

The next step in creating the data table is to enter the three formulas in cells C9, D9, and E9. The three formulas are the same as the monthly payment formula in cell E4, the total interest formula in cell E5, and the total cost formula in cell E6. The number of formulas you place at the top of a one-input data table depends on the application. Some one-input data tables will have only one formula, while others might have several. In this case, three formulas are affected when the interest rate changes.

Excel provides four ways to enter these formulas in the data table: (1) retype the formulas in cells C9, D9, and E9; (2) copy cells E4, E5, and E6 to cells C9, D9, and E9, respectively; (3) enter the formulas =monthly_pymt in cell C9, =total_interest in cell D9, and =total_cost in cell E9; or (4) enter the formulas =e4 in cell C9, =e5 in cell D9, and =e6 in cell E9.

The best alternative is the fourth one. That is, use the cell references preceded by an equal sign to define the formulas in the data table. This is the best method because: (1) it is easier to enter the cell references; and (2) if you change any of the formulas in the range E4:E6, the formulas at the top of the data table are updated automatically. Using the names of the cells in formulas is nearly as good an alternative. The reason why cell references are preferred over cell names is because if you use cell references, Excel assigns the format of the cell reference (Currency style format) to the cell. If you use cell names, Excel will not assign the format to the cell.

Perform the following steps to enter the formulas in the data table.

TO ENTER THE FORMULAS IN THE DATA TABLE

1 With cell C9 active, type =e4 and then press the RIGHT ARROW key.

2 Type =e5 in cell D9 and then press the RIGHT ARROW key.

3 Type =e6 in cell E9 and then click the Enter box.

The results of the formulas display in the range C9:E9 (Figure 4-22 on the next page). Excel automatically assigns the Currency style format to cells C9 through E9 based on the formats assigned to cells E4 through E6.

More **About**

Formulas in Data Tables

Any experienced Excel user will tell you that to enter the formulas at the top of the data table, you should enter the cell reference or name of the cell preceded by an equal sign (Figure 4-22). This ensures that if you change the original formula in the worksheet, Excel automatically will change the corresponding formula in the data table. If you use a cell reference, Excel also copies the format to the cell. If you use a name, Excel does not copy the format to the cell.

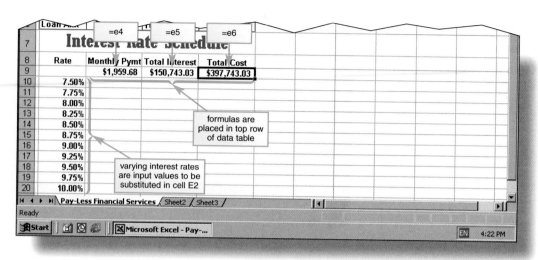

FIGURE 4-22

It is important to understand that the entries in the top row of the data table (row 9) refer to the formulas that the loan department wants to evaluate using the series of percentages in column B.

Defining the Data Table

After creating the interest rate series in column B and entering the formulas in row 9, the next step is to define the range B9:E20 as a data table. You use the **Table command** on the **Data menu** to define the range B4:E20 as a data table. Cell E2 is the **input cell**, the one you want to vary.

Steps **To Define a Range as a Data Table**

1 **Select the range B9:E20. Click Data on the menu bar and then point to Table.**

The Data menu displays (Figure 4-23). The range to be defined as the data table begins with the formulas in row 9. The section title and column headings in the range B7:E8 are not part of the data table, even though they identify the data table and columns in the table.

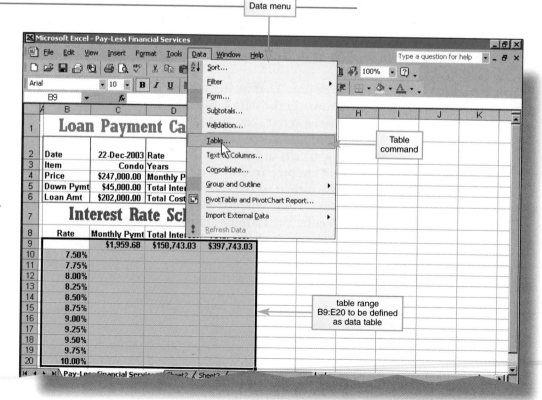

FIGURE 4-23

2 Click Table. When the Table dialog box displays, click the Column input cell text box. Click cell E2 in the Loan Payment Calculator section as the input cell and then point to the OK button.

A marquee surrounds the selected cell E2, indicating it will be the input cell in which values from column B in the data table are substituted in the formulas in row 9. $E$2 displays in the Column input cell text box in the Table dialog box (Figure 4-24).

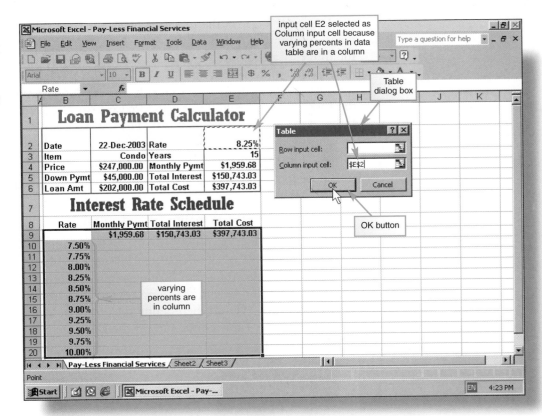

FIGURE 4-24

3 Click the OK button.

Excel calculates the results of the three formulas in row 9 for each interest rate in column B and immediately fills columns C, D, and E of the data table (Figure 4-25). The resulting values for each interest rate are displayed in the corresponding rows.

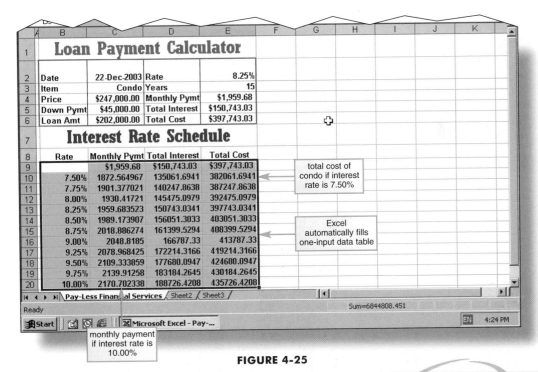

FIGURE 4-25

Other Ways

1. Select data table range, in Voice command mode, say "Data, Table, [select input cell], OK"

In Figure 4-25 on the previous page, the data table displays the monthly payment, total interest, and total cost for the interest rates in column B. For example, if the interest rate is 8.25% (cell E2), the monthly payment is $1,959.68 (cell E4). If, however, the interest rate is 10.00% (cell B20), the monthly payment is $2,170.70 rounded to the nearest cent (cell C20). If the interest rate is 7.50% (cell B10), then the total cost of the condo is $382,061.69 rounded to the nearest cent (cell E10), rather than $397,743.03 (cell E6). Thus, a 0.75% decrease from the interest rate of 8.25% results in a $15,681.34 decrease in the total cost of the house.

The following list details important points you should know about data tables:

1. The formula(s) you are analyzing must include a cell reference to the input cell.

2. You can have as many active data tables in a worksheet as you want.

3. While only one value can vary in a one-input data table, the data table can analyze as many formulas as you want.

4. To include additional formulas in a one-input data table, enter them in adjacent cells in the same row as the current formulas (row 9 in Figure 4-25) and then define the entire new range as a data table by using the Table command on the Data menu.

5. You delete a data table as you would delete any other item on a worksheet. That is, select the data table and press the DELETE key.

Formatting the Data Table

The next step is to format the data table to improve its readability, as shown in the following steps.

TO FORMAT THE DATA TABLE

1 Select the range B8:E20. Right-click the selected range and then click Format Cells on the shortcut menu. When the Format Cells dialog box displays, click the Border tab.

2 Click the Color box arrow. Select Blue (column 6, row 2) on the Color palette. Click the medium line style in the Style area (column 2, row 5). Click the Outline button in the Presets area.

3 Click the Color box arrow. Click Automatic (row 1) on the Color palette. Click the light line style in the Style area (column 1, row 7). Click the Vertical Border button in the Border area. Click the OK button.

4 Select the range B8:E8. Click the Borders button arrow on the Formatting toolbar and then click Bottom Border (column 2, row 1).

5 Select the range C10:E20. Click the Comma Style button on the Formatting toolbar. Click cell G20 to deselect the range C10:E20.

6 Click the Save button on the Standard toolbar to save the workbook using the file name Pay-Less Financial Services.

The worksheet displays as shown in Figure 4-26.

The data table is complete. Each time you enter new data into the Loan Payment Calculator section, Excel recalculates all formulas, including the data table.

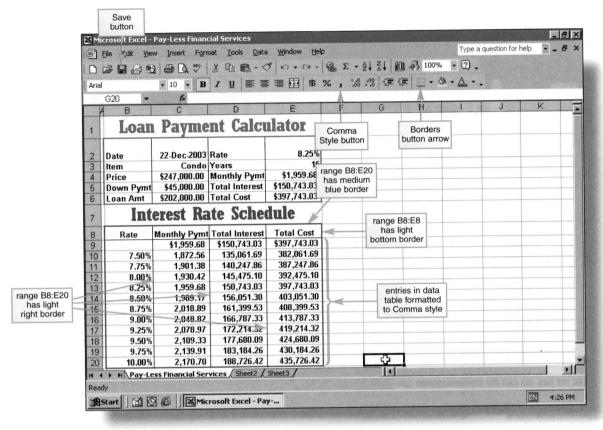

FIGURE 4-26

Adding a Pointer to the Data Table Using Conditional Formatting

If the interest rate in cell E2 is between 7.50% and 10.00% and its decimal portion is a multiple of 0.25 (such as 8.25%), then one of the rows in the data table agrees exactly with the monthly payment, interest paid, and total cost in the range E4:E6. For example, in Figure 4-26, row 13 (8.25%) in the data table agrees with the results in the range E4:E6, because the interest rate in cell B13 is the same as the interest rate in cell E2. Analysts often look for the row in the data table that agrees with the input cell results. To make this row stand out, you can use conditional formatting to make the cell in column B that agrees with the input cell (cell E2) stand out, as shown in the steps on the next page.

More About

Conditional Formatting

You can add up to three different conditions to a cell or range of cells. To specify additional conditions, click the Add button in the Conditional Formatting dialog box. If more than one condition is true for a cell, then Excel applies the format of the first condition that is true.

To Add a Pointer to the Data Table

1 Select the range B10:B20. Click Format on the menu bar and then point to Conditional Formatting.

The Format menu displays (Figure 4-27).

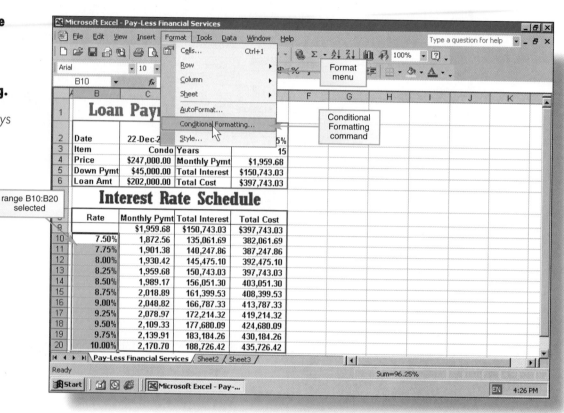

FIGURE 4-27

2 Click Conditional Formatting. When the Conditional Formatting dialog box displays, click Cell Value Is in the left list if necessary and then click equal to in the middle list. Type =$E$2 in the third box from the left. Click the Format button, click the Patterns tab, and then click Red (column 1, row 3) on the Color palette. Click the Font tab, click the Color arrow, and then click White (column 8, row 5) on the Color palette. Click Bold in the Font Style list. Click the OK button in the Format Cells dialog box.

The Conditional Formatting dialog box displays as shown in Figure 4-28.

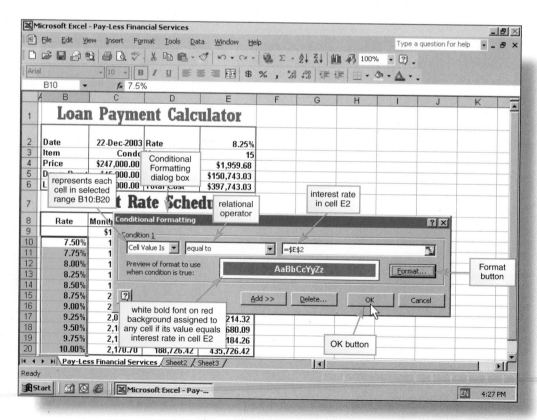

FIGURE 4-28

3 **Click the OK button in the Conditional Formatting dialog box. Click cell G20 to deselect the range B10:B20.**

Cell B13 in the data table, which contains 8.25%, displays with white bold font on a red background, because 8.25% is the same as the rate in cell E2 (Figure 4-29).

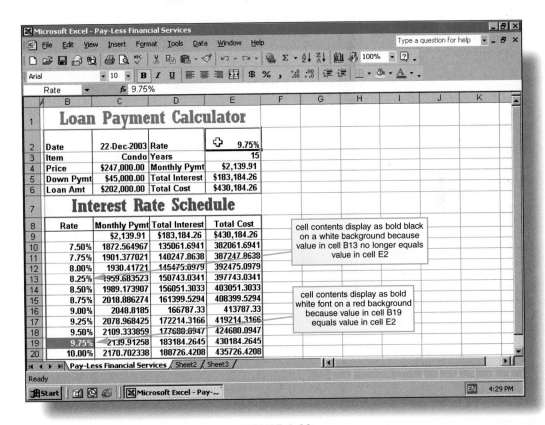

FIGURE 4-29

4 **Enter** 9.75 **in cell E2.**

Excel immediately displays cell B19 with a white bold font on a red background. Cell B13 displays with black bold font on a white background (Figure 4-30). Thus, the white bold font on a red background serves as a pointer in the data table to indicate the row that agrees with the input cell (cell E2).

5 **Enter** 8.25 **in cell E2 to return the Loan Payment Calculator section and Interest Rate Schedule section to their original states as shown in Figure 4-29.**

FIGURE 4-30

Other Ways

1. Press ALT+O, D
2. In Voice command mode, say "Format, Conditional Formatting"

When the loan officer using this worksheet enters a different percent in cell E2, the pointer will move or disappear. It will disappear whenever the interest rate in cell E2 is outside the range of the data table or its decimal portion is not a multiple of 0.25.

Creating an Amortization Schedule

The next step in this project is to create the Amortization Schedule shown on the right side of Figure 4-31. An **amortization schedule** shows the beginning and ending balances and the amount of payment that applies to the principal and interest for each year over the life of the loan. For example, if a customer wanted to pay off the loan after six years, the Amortization Schedule tells the loan officer what the payoff would be (cell I8 in Figure 4-31). The Amortization Schedule shown in Figure 4-31 will work only for loans of up to 15 years. You could, however, extend the table to any number of years. The Amortization Schedule also contains summaries in rows 18, 19, and 20. These summaries should agree exactly with the amounts in the Loan Payment Calculator section in the range B1:E6.

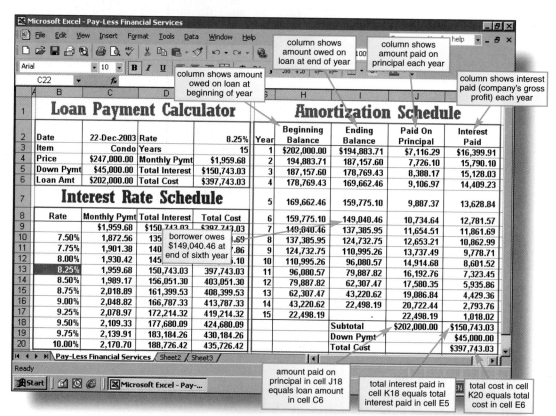

FIGURE 4-31

The following sections show how to construct the Amortization Schedule shown in Figure 4-31.

Changing Column Widths and Entering the Titles

The first step in creating the Amortization Schedule is to adjust the column widths and enter the Amortization Schedule section title and column titles, as shown in the following steps.

TO CHANGE COLUMN WIDTHS AND ENTER TITLES

1 Position the mouse pointer on the right boundary of column heading F and then drag to the left until the ScreenTip, Width: 0.50 (6 pixels) displays.

2 Position the mouse pointer on the right boundary of column heading G and then drag to the left until the ScreenTip, Width: 4.00 (33 pixels), displays.

3 Drag through column headings H through K to select them. Position the mouse pointer on the right boundary of column heading K and then drag to the right until the ScreenTip, Width: 12.14 (90 pixels) displays.

4 Click cell G1. Type Amortization Schedule as the section title. Press the ENTER key.

5 Click cell B1. Click the Format Painter button on the Standard toolbar. Click cell G1 to copy the format of cell B1. Click the Merge and Center button on the Formatting toolbar to split cell G1. Select the range G1:K1 and click the Merge and Center button on the Formatting toolbar.

6 Click the Font Color button arrow on the Formatting toolbar and then click Green (column 4, row 2) on the Color palette.

7 Enter the column titles in the range G2:K2 as shown in Figure 4-32. Where appropriate, press ALT+ENTER to enter the titles on two lines. Select the range G2:K2 and then click the Center button on the Formatting toolbar. Click cell G3.

The section title and column headings display as shown in Figure 4-32.

FIGURE 4-32

FIGURE 4-33

Creating a Series of Integers Using the Fill Handle

The next step is to create a series of numbers, using the fill handle, that represent the years during the life of the loan. The series begins with 1 (year 1) and ends with 15 (year 15).

TO CREATE A SERIES OF INTEGERS USING THE FILL HANDLE

1 With cell G3 active, enter 1 as the initial year. Click cell G4 and enter 2 to represents the next year.

2 Select the range G3:G4 and point to the fill handle. Drag the fill handle through cell G17.

Excel creates the series of integers 1 through 15 in the range G3:G17 (Figure 4-33).

As will be demonstrated shortly, the series of integers in the range G3:G17 play an important role in determining the ending balance and interest paid in the amortization schedule.

Entering the Formulas in the Amortization Schedule

The next step is to enter the four formulas in row 3 that form the basis of the amortization schedule. Later, these formulas will be copied through row 17. The formulas are summarized in Table 4-2.

Table 4-2	Formulas for the Amortization Schedule		
CELL	**DESCRIPTION**	**FORMULA**	**COMMENT**
H3	Beginning Balance	=C6	The beginning balance is the initial loan amount in cell C6.
I3	Ending Balance	=PV($E$2 /12, 12 * ($E$3 − G3), -$E$4)	The balance at the end of a year is equal to the present value of the payments paid over the remaining life of the loan.
J3	Paid on Principal	=H3 − I3	The amount paid on the principal is equal to the beginning balance (cell H3) less the ending balance (cell I3).
K3	Interest Paid	=12 * $E$4 − J3	The interest paid during the year is equal to 12 times the monthly payment (cell E4) less the amount paid on the principal (cell J3).

Of the four formulas in Table 4-2, the most difficult to understand is the PV function that will be assigned to cell I3. The **PV function** returns the present value of an annuity. An **annuity** is a series of fixed payments (such as the monthly payment in cell E4) made at the end of a fixed number of terms (months) at a fixed interest rate. You can use the PV function to determine how much the borrower of the loan still owes at the end of each year.

The PV function can determine the ending balance after the first year (cell I3) by using a term equal to the number of months the borrower still must make payments. For example, if the loan is for 15 years (180 months), then the borrower still owes 168 payments after the first year. The number of payments outstanding can be determined from the formula 12 * (E3 − G3) or 12 * (15 − 1), which equals 168. Recall that column G contains integers that represent the years of the loan. After the second year, the number of payments remaining is 156, and so on.

Annuities

For additional information on annuities, visit the Excel 2002 More About Web page (scsite.com/ex2002/more.htm) and click Annuities.

If you assign the PV function to cell I3 as shown in Table 4-2, and you copy it to the range I4:I17, the ending balances for each year will display properly. If, however, the loan is for less than 15 years, then the ending balances displayed for the years beyond the time the loan is due are invalid. For example, if a loan is taken out for five years, then the rows representing years 6 through 15 in the Amortization Schedule should be zero. The PV function, however, will display negative numbers even though the loan already has been paid off.

What is needed is a way to assign the PV function to the range I3:I17 as long as the corresponding year in column G is less than or equal to the number of years in cell E3. If the corresponding year in column G is greater than the number of years in cell E3, then the ending balance for that year and the remaining years should be zero. The following IF function displays the value of the PV function or zero in cell I3 depending on whether the corresponding value in column G is less than or equal to the number of years in cell E3. Recall that the dollar signs within the cell references indicate the cell reference is absolute and, therefore, will not change as you copy the function downward.

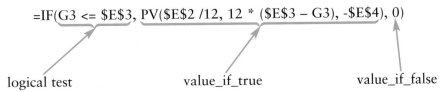

=IF(G3 <= $E$3, PV($E$2 /12, 12 * ($E$3 – G3), -$E$4), 0)

logical test   value_if_true   value_if_false

In the above formula, the logical test determines if the year in column G is less than or equal to the term of the loan in cell E3. If the logical test is true, then the IF function assigns the PV function to the cell. If the logical test is false, then the IF function assigns zero (0) to the cell.

The PV function in the IF function includes absolute cell references (cell references with dollar signs) to ensure that these cell references in column E do not change when the If function later is copied down the column. The following steps enter the four formulas shown in Table 4-2 into row 3. Row 3 represents year 1 of the loan.

More About

Present Value

For additional information on the present value of an investment, visit the Excel 2002 More About Web page (scsite.com/ex2002/more.htm) and click Present Value.

Steps **To Enter the Formulas in the Amortization Schedule**

1 **Select cell H3. Type** **=c6 and then press the RIGHT ARROW key to enter the beginning balance of the loan. Type** =if(g3 <= e3, pv(e2 / 12, 12 * (e3 - g3), -e4), 0) **as the entry for cell I3. Point to the Enter box.**

The loan amount displays in cell H3 as the first year's beginning balance using the same format as in cell C6. The IF function displays in cell I3 and in the formula bar (Figure 4-34).

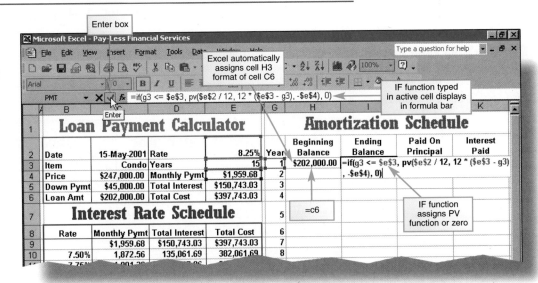

FIGURE 4-34

2 **Click the Enter box.**

Excel evaluates the IF function in cell I3 and displays the result of the PV function (194883.707) because the value in cell G3 (1) is less than or equal to the term of the loan in cell E3 (15). With cell I3 active, the formula displays in the formula bar (Figure 4-35). If the borrower wanted to pay off the loan after one year, the cost would be $194,883.71.

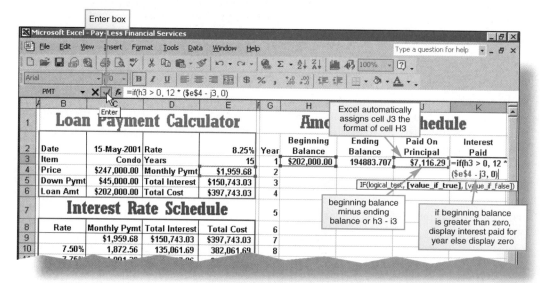

FIGURE 4-35

3 **Click cell J3. Type =h3 - i3 and then press the RIGHT ARROW key. Type =if(h3 > 0, 12 * e4 - j3, 0) in cell K3. Point to the Enter box.**

The amount paid on the principal after one year displays in cell J3 using the same format as in cell H3. The IF function displays in cell K3 and in the formula bar (Figure 4-36).

FIGURE 4-36

4 **Click the Enter box.**

The interest paid after one year (16399.90924) displays in cell K3 (Figure 4-37). Thus, the company's gross profit for the first year of the loan is $16,399.91.

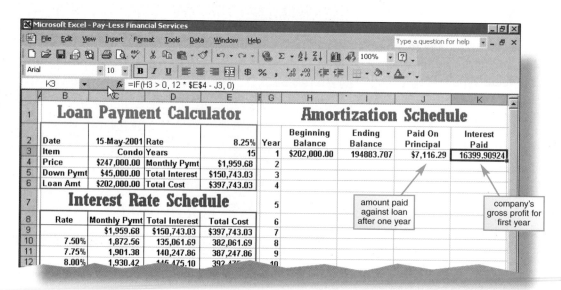

FIGURE 4-37

When you enter a formula in a cell, Excel assigns the cell the same format as the first cell reference in the formula. For example, when you enter =c6 in cell H3, Excel assigns the format in cell C6 to H3. The same applies to cell J3. Excel assigns the Currency style format to J3, because cell reference H3 is the first cell reference in the formula (=H3 − I3) assigned to cell J3 and cell H3 has a Currency style format. Although this method of formatting also works for most functions, it does not work for the IF function. Thus, the results of the IF functions in cells I3 and K3 display using the General format, which is the format of all cells when you open a new workbook.

With the formulas entered into the first row, the next step is to copy them to the remaining rows in the Amortization Schedule. The required copying is straightforward except for the beginning balance column. To obtain the next year's beginning balance (cell H4), you have to use last year's ending balance (I3). Once cell I3 is copied to cell H4, then H4 can be copied to the range H5:H17.

Perform the following steps to copy the formulas.

 To Copy the Formulas to Fill the Amortization Schedule

1 Select the range I3:K3 and then point to the fill handle. Drag the fill handle down through row 17.

The formulas in cells I3, J3, and K3 are copied to the range I4:K17 (Figure 4-38). Many of the numbers displayed are incorrect because most of the cells in column H do not contain beginning balances. The Auto Fill Options button displays below and to the right of the destination area.

FIGURE 4-38

2 **Select cell H4. Type =i3 and then click the Enter box.**

The ending balance for year 1 in cell I3 also displays as the beginning balance for year 2 in cell H4 (Figure 4-39).

FIGURE 4-39

3 **With cell H4 active, point to the fill handle. Drag the fill handle down through row 17.**

The formula in cell H4 (=I3) is copied to the range H5:H17 (Figure 4-40). Because the cell reference I3 in the formula in cell H4 is relative, Excel adjusts the row portion of the cell reference as it is copied downward. Thus, each new beginning balance in column H is equal to the ending balance of the previous year.

FIGURE 4-40

The numbers that display in the Amortization Schedule in Figure 4-40 are now correct, although they need to be formatted to make them easier to read. Cell I17 shows that at the end of the fifteenth year, the ending balance is zero, which is what it should be for a 15-year loan.

Entering the Total Formulas in the Amortization Schedule

The next step is to determine the amortization schedule totals in rows 18 through 20. These totals should agree with the totals in the Loan Payment Calculator section (range B1:E6). Perform the following steps to enter the total formulas in the Amortization Schedule.

To Enter the Total Formulas in the Amortization Schedule

1 **Click cell I18. Enter** Subtotal **as the row title. Select the range J18:K18. Click the AutoSum button on the Standard toolbar.**

The total amount paid on the principal and the total interest paid display in cells J18 and K18, respectively (Figure 4-41). These results in cells J18 and K18 agree exactly with the values in cells C6 and E5.

FIGURE 4-41

2 **Click cell I19. Type** Down Pymt **as the row title. Click cell K19 and enter** =c5 **as the down payment. Click cell I20. Type** Total Cost **as the row title. Click K20, type** =j18 + k18 + k19 **as the total cost and then click the Enter box.**

The amortization schedule totals display as shown in Figure 4-42.

FIGURE 4-42

The formula assigned to cell K20 sums the amounts paid on the principal (cell J18), the total interest paid (cell K18), and the down payment (cell K19).

Here again, Excel assigns the same format to cell J18 as in cell J3, because cell J3 is the first cell reference in =SUM(J3:J17). Furthermore, cell J18 was selected first when the range J18:K18 was selected to determine the sum. Thus, Excel assigned cell K18 the same format that was assigned to cell J18. Finally, cell K19 was assigned the Currency style format, because cell K19 was assigned the formula =c5, and cell C5 has a Currency style format. For the same reason, the value in cell K20 displays in Currency style format.

More About

Round-Off Errors

If you manually add the numbers in column K (range K3:K17) and compare it to the sum in cell K18, you will notice that the total interest paid is $0.01 off. This round-off error is due to the fact that some of the numbers involved in the computations have more decimal places than display in the cells. You can use the ROUND function on the formula entered into cell K3 to ensure the total is exactly correct. For information on the ROUND function, click the Insert Function box in the formula bar, click Math & Trig in the Function category list, scroll down in the Function name list, and then click ROUND.

Formatting New Loan Data

The final step in creating the amortization schedule is to format it so it is easier to read. The formatting is divided into two parts: (1) format the numbers; and (2) add borders.

When the beginning balance formula (=c6) was entered earlier into cell H3, Excel automatically copied the Currency style format along with the value from cell C6 to cell H3. The following steps use the Format Painter button to copy the Currency style format from cell H3 to the range I3:K3. Finally, the Comma Style button on the Formatting toolbar will be used to assign the Comma style format to the range H4:K17.

TO FORMAT THE NUMBERS IN THE AMORTIZATION SCHEDULE

1 Click cell H3. Click the Format Painter button on the Standard toolbar. Drag through the range I3:K3 to assign the Currency style format to the numbers.

2 Select the range H4:K17. Click the Comma Style button on the Formatting toolbar. Select cell H19 to deselect the range H4:K17.

The numbers in the amortization schedule display as shown in Figure 4-43.

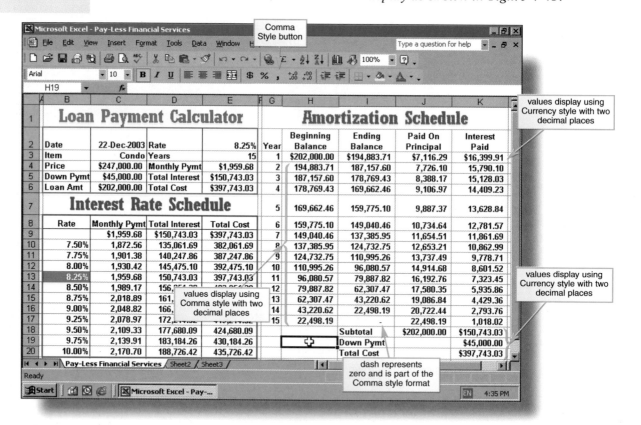

FIGURE 4-43

The Comma Style button on the Formatting toolbar was used purposely to format the body of the amortization schedule because it uses the dash to represent zero (see cell I17). If the term of a loan is for less than 15 years, the amortization schedule will include zeros in cells. The dash has a more professional appearance than columns of zeros.

The following steps add the borders to the amortization schedule.

TO ADD BORDERS TO THE AMORTIZATION SCHEDULE

1 Select the range G2:K20. Right-click the selected range and then click Format Cells on the shortcut menu.

2 When the Format Cells dialog box displays, click the Border tab.

3 Click the Color box arrow. Click Green (column 4, row 2) on the Color palette. Click the medium line style in the Style area (column 2, row 5). Click the Outline button in the Presets area.

4 Click the Color box arrow. Click Automatic (row 1) on the palette. Click the light line style in the Style area (column 1, row 7). Click the vertical line button in the Border area. Click the OK button.

5 Select the range G2:K2. Click the Borders button on the Formatting toolbar to assign the range a light bottom border.

6 Select the range G17:K17 and click the Borders button on the Formatting toolbar to assign the range a light bottom border. Click cell H19.

7 Click the Save button on the Standard toolbar to save the workbook using the file name, Pay-Less Financial Services.

The worksheet displays as shown in Figure 4-44.

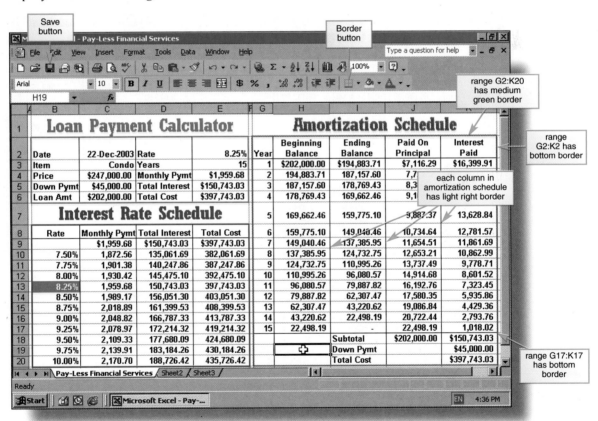

FIGURE 4-44

Entering New Loan Data

With the Loan Payment Calculator, Interest Rate Schedule, and Amortization Schedule sections of the worksheet complete, you can use them to generate new loan information. For example, assume you want to purchase a camper for $13,500.00. You have $5,600.00 for a down payment and want the loan for five years. Pay-Less Financial Services currently is charging 9.75% interest for a five-year loan.

The following steps show how to enter the new loan data.

TO ENTER NEW LOAN DATA

1 Click cell C3. Type Camper and then press the DOWN ARROW key.

2 In cell C4, type 13500 and then press the DOWN ARROW key.

3 In cell C5, type 5600 as the down payment.

4 Click cell E2, type 9.75 and then press the DOWN ARROW key.

5 In cell E3, type 5 and then press the DOWN ARROW key. Click cell H19.

Excel automatically recalculates the loan information in cells C6, E4, E5, E6, the data table in the range B7:E20, and the Amortization Schedule in the range G3:K20 (Figure 4-45).

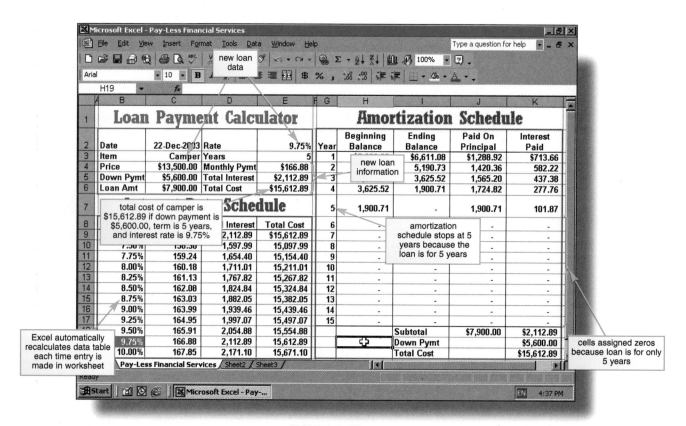

FIGURE 4-45

As shown in Figure 4-45, the monthly payment for the camper is $166.88 (cell E4). The total interest is $2,112.89 (cell E5). The total cost for the $13,500.00 Camper is $15,612.89 (cell E6). Because the term of the loan is for five years, the rows for years 6 through 15 in the Amortization Schedule section display a dash (-), which represents zero (0).

The following steps enter the original loan data.

TO ENTER THE ORIGINAL LOAN DATA

1 Click cell C3. Type `Condo` and then press the DOWN ARROW key.

2 In cell C4, type `247000` and then press the DOWN ARROW key.

3 In cell C5, type `45000` as the down payment.

4 Click cell E2, type `8.25` and then press the DOWN ARROW key.

5 In cell E3, type `15` and then click the Enter box or press the ENTER key. Click cell H19.

Excel automatically recalculates the loan information, the data table, and the amortization schedule as shown in Figure 4-46a.

Adding a Hyperlink to the Worksheet

A **hyperlink** points to the location of a computer on which a destination file is stored. With Excel, you easily can create hyperlinks (Figure 4-46a) to other files on your personal computer, your intranet, or the World Wide Web. The destination file (or hyperlinked file) can be any Office document or HTML file (Web page as shown in Figure 4-46b). Two primary worksheet elements exist to which you can assign a hyperlink:

1. **Text** — Enter text in a cell and make the text a hyperlink; text hyperlinks display in the color blue and are underlined.
2. **Embedded graphic** — Draw or insert a graphic, such as clip art, and then make the graphic a hyperlink.

You use the **Hyperlink command** on the shortcut menu to assign the hyperlink to the worksheet element.

(a) Worksheet

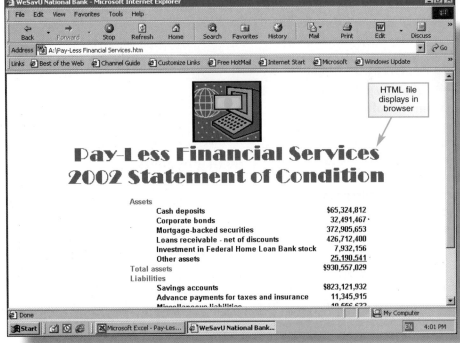

(b) Web Page

FIGURE 4-46

Microsoft **Excel 2002**

Assigning a Hyperlink to an Embedded Graphic

The following steps show how to assign a hyperlink to a graphic. The destination file is an HTML file (Web page) that contains the Pay-Less Financial Services 2002 Statement of Condition. The destination file, Pay-Less Financial Services.htm, is located on the Data Disk. If you do not have a copy of the Data Disk, see the inside back cover of this book.

Steps **To Assign a Hyperlink to an Embedded Graphic**

1 **With the Data Disk in drive A, click Insert on the menu bar, point to Picture, and then point to Clip Art on the Picture submenu.**

The Insert menu and Picture submenu display (Figure 4-47).

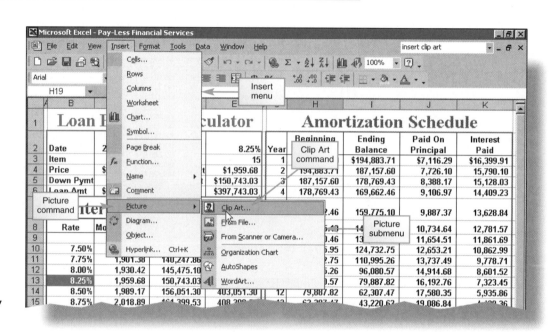

FIGURE 4-47

2 **Click Clip Art. When the Insert Clip Art task pane displays, click the Search in box arrow, and if necessary click the Everywhere checkbox to insert a check mark. Type** money **in the Search text text box and point to the Search button.**

The Insert Clip Art task pane displays as shown in Figure 4-48. Use the Tips for Finding Clips link at the bottom of the task pane to learn more about finding clip art.

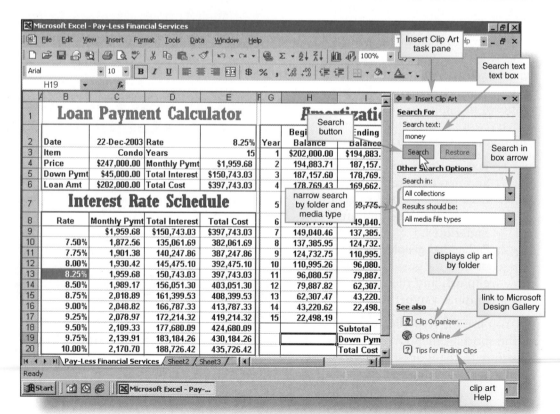

FIGURE 4-48

3 Click the Search button. When the Results display, point to the dollar sign graphic, then click the button arrow on its right side. When the shortcut menu displays, point to Insert.

The Results display in the task pane. A button arrow displays on the right side of the active graphic and a shortcut menu displays (Figure 4-49).

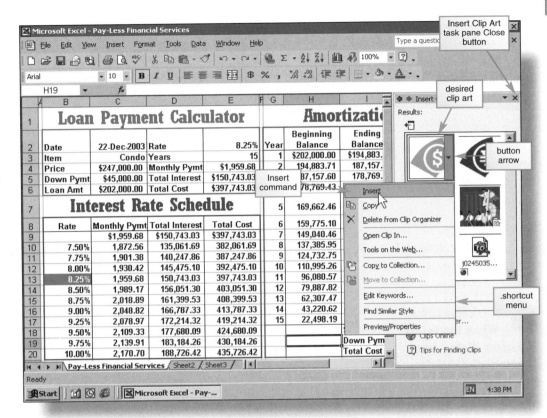

FIGURE 4-49

4 Click Insert. Click the Close button on the title bar of the Insert Clip Art task pane. Scroll down in the worksheet so the dollar sign graphic is fully visible.

Excel embeds the dollar sign graphic below the data in the worksheet (Figure 4-50).

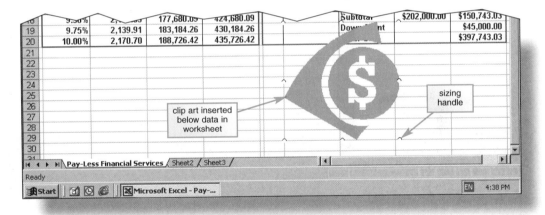

FIGURE 4-50

5 Drag the sizing handles to resize the graphic and then drag it so it displays in the range H18:H20.

The dollar sign graphic displays as shown in Figure 4-51.

	7.75%	1,901.38	140,247.86	387,247.86	9	124,732.75	110,995.26	13,737.49	9,778.71
11									
12	8.00%	1,930.42	145,475.10	392,475.10	10	110,995.26	96,080.57	14,914.68	8,601.52
13	8.25%	1,959.68	150,743.03	397,743.03	11	96,080.57	79,887.82	16,192.76	7,323.45
14	8.50%	1,989.17	156,051.30	403,051.30	12	79,887.82	62,307.47	17,580.35	5,935.86
15	8.75%	2,018.89	161,399.53	408,399.53	13	62,307.47	43,220.62	19,086.84	4,429.36
16	9.00%	2,048.82	166,787.33	413,787.33	14	43,220.62	22,498.19	20,722.44	2,793.76
17	9.25%	2,078.97	172,214.32	419,214.32	15	22,498.19	-	22,498.19	1,018.02
18	9.50%	2,109.33	177,680.09	424,680.09			Subtotal	$202,000.00	$150,743.03
19	9.75%	2,139.91	183,184.26	430,184.26			Down Pymt		$45,000.00
20	10.00%	2,170.70	188,726.42	435,726.42			Total Cost		$397,743.03

clip art resized and dragged to desired area on worksheet

clip art remains selected

FIGURE 4-51

6 With the graphic selected, right-click it and then point to Hyperlink on the shortcut menu (Figure 4-52).

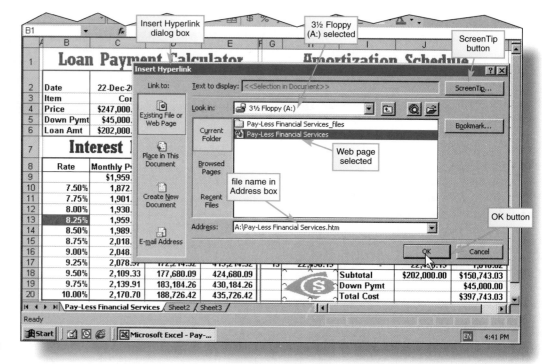

FIGURE 4-52

7 Click Hyperlink. When the Insert Hyperlink dialog box displays, click 3½ Floppy (A:) in the Look in list, and then click the file name titled Pay-Less Financial Services in the list of files. Point to the OK button.

The Insert Hyperlink dialog box displays as shown in Figure 4-53.

8 Click the OK button. Click cell J19 to deselect the graphic. Click the Save button on the Standard toolbar to save the workbook using the file name Pay-Less Financial Services.

FIGURE 4-53

Excel assigns the hyperlink, a:\Pay-Less Financial Services.htm, to the dollar sign graphic. Excel saves the workbook using the file name Pay-Less Financial Services.

To edit the hyperlink, right-click the dollar sign graphic to display the shortcut menu and then click **Edit Hyperlink.** You also can right-click the dollar sign graphic and click the Insert Hyperlink button on the Standard toolbar.

Displaying and Printing a Hyperlinked File

The next step is to display and print the hyperlinked file by clicking the dollar sign graphic on the worksheet and using the Print command in the browser. Once you assign a hyperlink to an element in your worksheet, you can position the mouse pointer on the element to display the hyperlink as a ScreenTip. Clicking the dollar sign graphic will display the hyperlinked file, as shown in the following steps.

More About

Personalized ScreenTips

You can add a personalized ScreenTip to a hyperlink by clicking the ScreenTip button in the Insert Hyperlink dialog box (Figure 4-53). If you add a personalized ScreenTip, it displays in place of the path of the file when you point to the hyperlink (Figure 4-54).

Steps: To Display and Print a Hyperlinked File

1 **With the Data Disk in drive A, point to the dollar sign graphic.**

The mouse pointer changes to a hand. A ScreenTip displays indicating the destination file to which the graphic is hyperlinked (Figure 4-54).

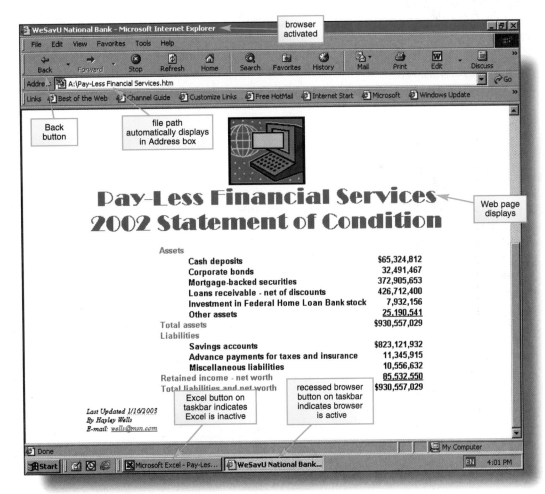

mouse pointer changes to hand when moved over hyperlink

ScreenTip indicates file path and name

FIGURE 4-54

2 **Click the dollar sign graphic. If the Language pack installation dialog box displays, click the check box and then click the Cancel button.**

Excel starts your browser and displays the HTML file (Web page) as shown in Figure 4-55. Both the Excel button and browser button display on the Windows taskbar.

3 **Click Print on the File menu in the browser window. When the Print dialog box displays, click the Print button. When you are finished viewing and printing the Web page, click the Back button to return to Excel.**

The browser closes and the loan analysis worksheet displays in the active window. The hyperlinked file prints on the printer.

FIGURE 4-55

If the hyperlink does not connect you to the destination file, make sure you selected the correct file in the list in the Insert Hyperlink dialog box (Figure 4-53 on page E 4.42). If you entered the hyperlink correctly and it still does not display, check to be sure the file exists on the Data Disk.

Printing Sections of the Worksheet

In Project 2, you learned to print a section of a worksheet by selecting it and using the Selection option in the Print dialog box (see page E 2.55). If you find yourself continually selecting the same range in a worksheet to print, you can make the range to print permanent by using the **Set Print Area command** on the Print Area submenu. You display the Print Area submenu by pointing to the **Print Area command** on the File menu. When you use the Set Print Area command, the system will continue to print only that range until you clear it using the **Clear Print command** on the Print Area submenu or set a new print area.

Setting Up to Print

Before printing, you should consider what print options you want to use. Up to this point you have been introduced to changing the orientation of a printed copy of a worksheet and the fit to option. This section describes additional print options available on the Sheet sheet in the Page Setup dialog box (Figure 4-57). These print options pertain to the way the worksheet will appear in the printed copy. One of the more important print options is the capability of printing in black and white. Printing in black and white not only speeds up the printing process, but also saves ink. This is especially true if you have a color printer and need only a black and white printed copy of the worksheet. Follow these steps to ensure any printed copy fits on one page and prints in black and white.

Steps **To Setup to Print**

1 **Click File on the menu bar and then click Page Setup. When the Page Setup dialog box displays, click the Page tab. Click Fit to in the Scaling area. Point to the Sheet tab.**

The Page sheet in the Page Setup dialog box displays as shown in Figure 4-56. The Fit to option will ensure that any printout will fit on one page in portrait orientation.

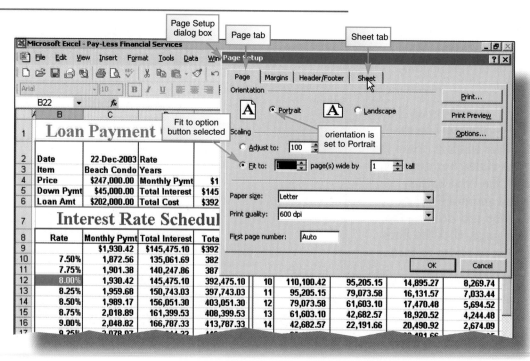

FIGURE 4-56

2 **Click the Sheet tab.**
Click Black and
white in the Print area.
Point to the OK button.

The Sheet sheet in the Page
Setup dialog box displays as
shown in Figure 4-57.

3 **Click the OK button.**

FIGURE 4-57

Other Ways

1. In Voice command mode, say "File, Page Setup, Page or Sheet, [select option],

Table 4-3 summarizes the print options available on the Sheet sheet in the Page Setup dialog box.

Table 4-3 Print Options Available Using the Sheet Sheet	
PRINT OPTION	**DESCRIPTION**
Print area text box	Excel prints from cell A1 to the last occupied cell in a worksheet unless you instruct it to print a selected area. You can select a range to print with the mouse, or you can enter a range in the Print area text box. The range can be a name. Nonadjacent ranges will print on a separate page.
Print titles area	This area is used to print row titles and column titles on each page of a worksheet that exceeds a page. You must specify a range, even if you are designating one column (i.e., 1:4 means the first four rows).
Gridlines check box	This check box determines whether gridlines will print.
Black and white check box	A check mark in this check box speeds up printing and saves ink if you have colors in a worksheet.
Draft quality check box	A check mark in this check box speeds up printing by ignoring formatting and not printing most graphics.
Row and column headings check box	A check mark in this check box instructs Excel to include the column headings (A, B, C, etc.) and row headings (1, 2, 3, etc.) in the printout.
Page order area	Determines the order in which multipage worksheets will print.

Printing a Section of a Worksheet Using the Set Print Area Command

The steps on the next page show how to print only the Loan Payment Calculator section by setting the print area to the range B1:E6.

Steps **To Set the Print Area**

1 Select the range B1:E6. Point to Print Area on the File menu and then point to Set Print Area on the Print Area submenu.

The File menu and Print Area submenu display (Figure 4-58).

FIGURE 4-58

2 Click Set Print Area. Point to the Print button on the Standard toolbar (Figure 4-59).

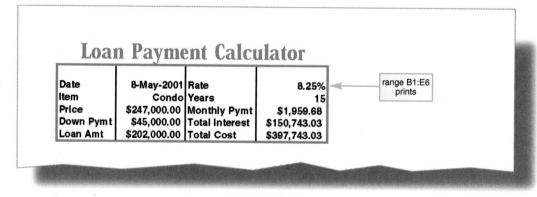

FIGURE 4-59

3 Click the Print button.

Excel prints the range B1:E6 (Figure 4-60).

4 Click Clear Print Area on the Print Area submenu (Figure 4-58) to reset the print area to the entire worksheet.

Loan Payment Calculator

Date	8-May-2001	Rate	8.25%
Item	Condo	Years	15
Price	$247,000.00	Monthly Pymt	$1,959.68
Down Pymt	$45,000.00	Total Interest	$150,743.03
Loan Amt	$202,000.00	Total Cost	$397,743.03

range B1:E6 prints

FIGURE 4-60

Other **Ways**

1. Press ALT+F, type T, S
2. In Voice command mode, say "File, Print Area, Set Print Area or Clear Print Area"

Once you set a print area, Excel will continue to print the specified range, rather than the entire worksheet. If you save the workbook with the print area set, then Excel will remember the settings the next time you open the workbook and print. To remove the print area so that the entire worksheet prints, click Clear Print Area on the Print Area submenu as described in Step 4.

Naming Print Areas

With some spreadsheet applications, you will want to print several different areas of a worksheet, depending on the request. Rather than using the Set Print Area command or manually selecting the range each time you want to print, you can name the ranges using the Name box on the formula bar, and then use one of the names to select an area before using the Set Print Area command or Selection option button. The following steps name the Loan Payment Calculator section, the Interest Rate Schedule section, the Amortization Schedule section, and the entire worksheet, and then prints each section using the Selection option button in the Print dialog box.

 Steps **To Name and Print Sections of a Worksheet**

1 Select the range B1:E6. Click the Name box and type Loan_Payment as the name of the range.

The name Loan_Payment displays in the Name box (Figure 4-61).

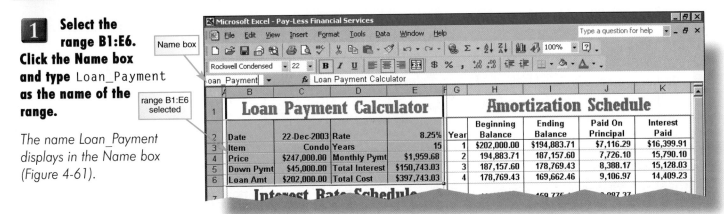

FIGURE 4-61

2 Press the ENTER key. Select the range B7:E20, click the Name box, and type Interest_Schedule as the name of the range and then press the ENTER key. Select the range G1:K20, click the Name box, and type Amortization_Schedule as the name of the range and then press the ENTER key. Select the range B1:K20, click the Name box, and type All_Sections as the name of the range and then press the ENTER key. Click any cell on the worksheet. Click the Name box arrow on the formula bar and point to Loan_Payment.

The new names display in the Name box (Figure 4-62).

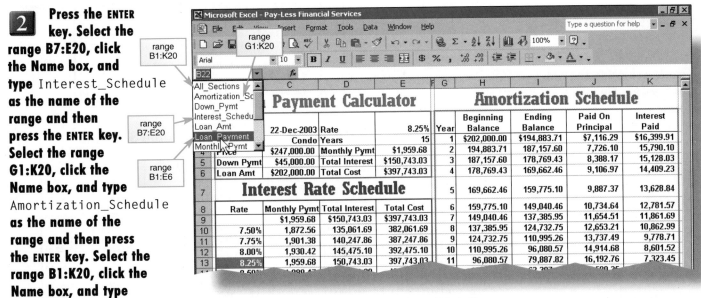

FIGURE 4-62

3 **Click Loan_Payment. Click File on the menu bar and then click Print. When the Print dialog box displays, click Selection in the Print what area, and then point to the OK button.**

The range named Loan_Payment is selected. The Print dialog box displays as shown in Figure 4-63.

FIGURE 4-63

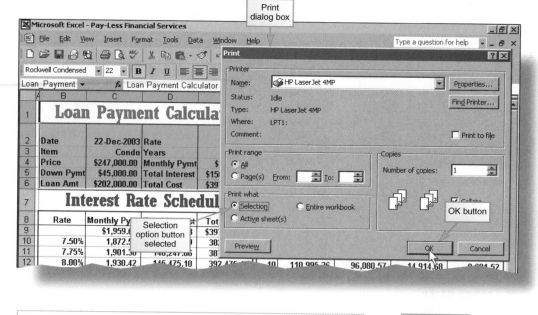

4 **Click the OK button. One at a time, use the Name box to select the names Interest_Schedule, Amortization_Schedule, and All_Sections and print them following the instructions in Step 3.**

The four areas of the worksheet print as shown in Figure 4-64.

5 **Click the Save button on the Standard toolbar to save the workbook using the file name Pay-Less Financial Services.**

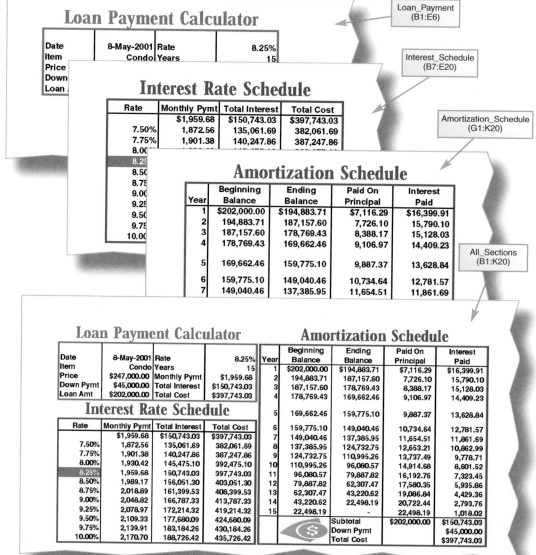

FIGURE 4-64

Other Ways

1. On Insert menu point to Names, click Define, type name, click OK button

2. In Voice command mode, say "Insert, Name, Define, [type name], OK"

Recall that the Fit to option was selected earlier (Figure 4-56 on page E 4.44). This selection ensures that the entire worksheet fits across the page in portrait orientation.

Protecting the Worksheet

When building a worksheet for novice users, you should protect the cells in the worksheet that you do not want changed, such as cells that contain text and formulas.

When you create a new worksheet, all the cells are assigned a locked status, but the lock is not engaged, which leaves cells unprotected. **Unprotected cells** are cells whose values you can change at anytime. **Protected cells** are cells that you cannot change.

You should protect cells only after the worksheet has been tested fully and displays the correct results. Protecting a worksheet is a two-step process:

1. Select the cells you want to leave unprotected and change their cell protection settings to an unlocked status.
2. Protect the entire worksheet.

At first glance, these steps may appear to be backwards. Once you protect the entire worksheet, however, you cannot change anything, including the locked status of individual cells.

In the loan analysis worksheet (Figure 4-65), the user should make changes to only five cells: the item in cell C3; the price in cell C4; the down payment in cell C5; the interest rate in cell E2; and the years in cell E3. These cells must remain unprotected so that users can enter amounts. The remaining cells and the embedded dollar sign graphic in the worksheet should be protected so they cannot be changed by the user.

The following steps show how to protect the loan analysis worksheet.

More *About*

Protecting Worksheets

You can move from one unprotected cell to another unprotected cell in a worksheet by using the TAB and SHIFT+TAB keys.

Steps **To Protect a Worksheet**

1 **Select the range C3:C5. Hold down the CTRL key and then select the nonadjacent range E2:E3. Right-click one of the selected ranges and then point to Format Cells on the shortcut menu.**

The shortcut menu displays (Figure 4-65).

FIGURE 4-65

2 **Click Format Cells. When the Format Cells dialog box displays, click the Protection tab. Click the Locked check box to remove the check mark. Point to the OK button.**

The Protection sheet in the Format Cells dialog box displays with the check mark removed from the Locked check box (Figure 4-66). This means the selected cells (C3:C5 and E2:E3) will not be protected when the Protect command later is invoked.

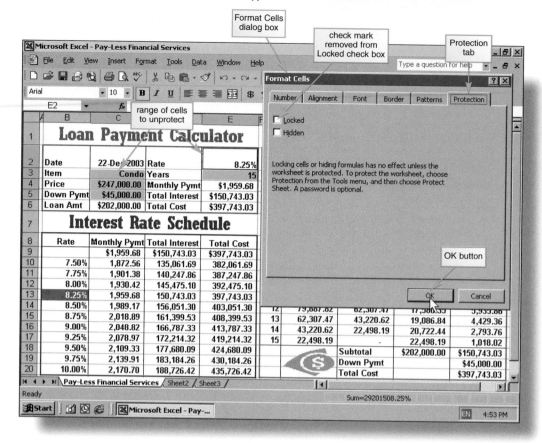

FIGURE 4-66

3 **Click the OK button. Click cell J19 to deselect the ranges C3:C5 and E2:E3. Click Tools on the menu bar. Point to Protection and then point to Protect Sheet on the Protection submenu.**

Excel displays the Tools menu and Protection submenu (Figure 4-67).

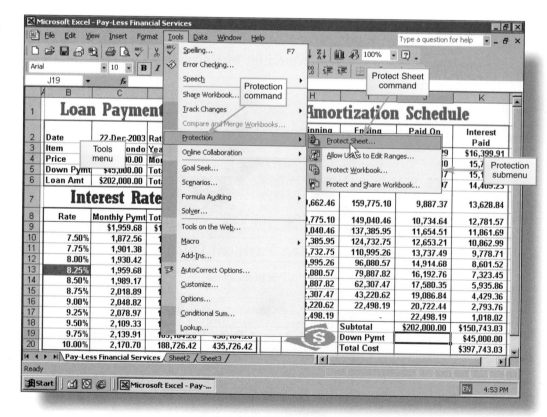

FIGURE 4-67

4 **Click Protect Sheet. When the Protect Sheet dialog box displays, make sure the Protect worksheet and contents of locked cells check box at the top of the dialog box and the first two check boxes in the list contain check marks. Point to the OK button.**

The Protect Sheet dialog box displays (Figure 4-68). All three check boxes are selected, thus protecting the worksheet from changes to contents (except the cells left unlocked). The two check boxes in the list allow the user to select any cell on the worksheet, but the user can change only unlocked cells.

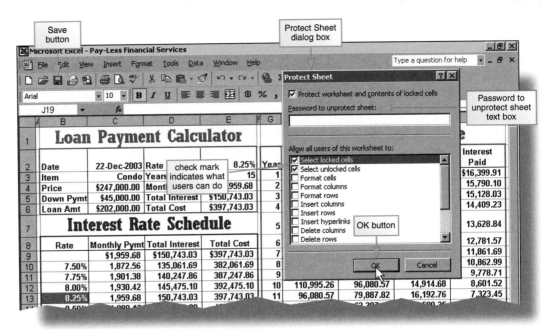

FIGURE 4-68

5 **Click the OK button. Click the Save button on the Standard toolbar to save the protected workbook using the file name, Pay-Less Financial Services.**

All the cells in the worksheet are protected, except for the ranges C3:C5 and E2:E3.

The **Protect Sheet dialog box** in Figure 4-68 lets you enter a password. You should create a **password** when you want to keep others from changing the worksheet from protected to unprotected. The check boxes in the list in the Protect Sheet dialog box also give you the option to modify the protection so that the user can make certain changes.

If you want to protect more than one sheet, select each one before you begin the protection process or click **Protect Workbook** on the **Protection submenu** that displays (Figure 4-67) when you point to **Protection** on the Tools menu.

If you want to unlock cells for specific users, you can use the **Allow Users to Edit Ranges command** on the Protection submenu. For additional information on unlocking cells for specific users, enter protect worksheet in the Ask a Question box on the right side of the menu bar.

When this workbook is submitted to the loan officers, they now will be able to enter data in only the unprotected cells. If they try to change any protected cell, such as the monthly payment in cell E4, Excel displays a dialog box with a diagnostic message as shown in Figure 4-69 on the next page. An alternative to displaying this dialog box is to remove the check mark from the Select unlocked cells check box in the Protect Sheet dialog box (Figure 4-68). With the check mark removed, the user can't select a locked cell.

Other Ways

1. In Voice command mode, say "Tools, Protection, Protect Sheet, [select desired options], OK"

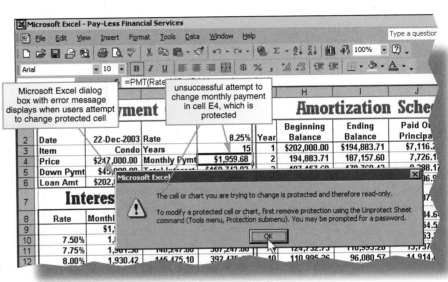

FIGURE 4-69

To unprotect the worksheet so that you can change cells in the worksheet such as titles or formulas, unprotect the document by pointing to Protection on the Tools menu and then clicking the **Unprotect Sheet command**.

Formula Checking

Similar to the spell checker, Excel has a **formula checker** that checks formulas in a worksheet for rule violations. You invoke the formula checker by clicking the **Error Checking command** on the Tools menu. Each time Excel encounters a cell with a formula that violates one of its rules, it displays a dialog box containing information about the formula and a suggestion on how to fix the formula. Table 4-4 lists Excel's formula checking rules. You can choose which rules you want Excel to use by enabling and disabling them on the Error Checking sheet in the Options dialog box shown in Figure 4-70.

Table 4-4	Formula Checking Rules	
RULE	**NAME OF RULE**	**DESCRIPTION**
1	Evaluates to error value	The cell contains a formula that does not use the expected syntax, arguments, or data types.
2	Text date with 2 digit years	The cell contains a text date with a two-digit year that can be misinterpreted as the wrong century.
3	Number stored as text	The cell contains numbers stored as text.
4	Inconsistent formula in region	The cell contains a formula that does not match the pattern of the formulas around it.
5	Formula omits cells in region	The cell contains a formula that does not include a correct cell or range reference.
6	Unlocked cells containing formulas	Cell with formula is unlocked in a protected worksheet.
7	Formulas referring to empty cells	Cells referred to in formula are empty.

Background Formula Checking

You can enable background formula checking. **Background formula checking** means that Excel will continually review the workbook for errors in formulas as you create or manipulate it. To enable background formula checking, do the following.

TO ENABLE BACKGROUND FORMULA CHECKING

1 Click Options on the Tools menu. When the Options dialog box displays, click the Error Checking tab.

2 Click the Enable background error checking check box if necessary to add a check mark.

3 Click any check box in the Rules area that does not contain a check mark.

4 Click the OK button.

Following Step 3, the Options dialog box displays as shown in Figure 4-70.

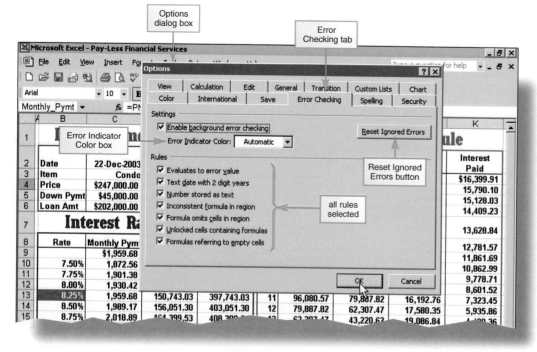

FIGURE 4-70

You can decide which rules you want the background formula checker to highlight by adding and removing check marks from the check boxes in the Rules area (Figure 4-70). If you add or remove check marks, then you should click the **Reset Ignored Errors button** to reset error checking.

When a formula fails to pass one of the rules and background formula checking is enabled, then Excel displays a small green triangle in the upper-left corner of the cell assigned the formula in question.

Assume for example, that background formula checking is enabled and that cell E4, which contains the PMT function in the Pay-Less Financial Services workbook is unlocked. Because rule 6 in Table 4-4 stipulates that a cell containing a formula must be locked, Excel displays a green triangle in the upper left corner of cell E4 (Figure 4-71).

When you select the cell with the green triangle, a Trace Error button displays next to the cell. If you click the **Trace Error button**, the Trace Error menu displays (Figure 4-71). The first item in the menu identifies the error (Unprotected Formula). The remainder of the menu lists commands from which you can choose. The first command locks the cell. Invoking the Lock Cell command fixes the problem so that the formula no longer violates the rule. The next to the last command displays the Options dialog box with the Error Checking sheet active (Figure 4-70).

The background formula checker can become annoying when you are creating certain types of worksheets that may violate the formula rules until referenced cells contain data. It is not unusual to end up with green triangles in cells throughout your worksheet. If this is the case, then disable background formula error checking (Figure 4-70) and use the Error Checking command on the Tools menu.

It is strongly recommended that you use background formula checking or the Error Checking command on the Tools menu during the testing phase to ensure the formulas in your workbook do not violate the rules listed in Table 4-4.

FIGURE 4-71

Quitting Excel

To quit Excel, follow the steps below.

TO QUIT EXCEL

1. Click the Close button on the right side of the title bar.

2. If a Microsoft Excel dialog box displays, click the No button.

More About

Quick Reference

For a table that lists how to complete the tasks covered in this book using the mouse, menu, shortcut menu, and keyboard, see the Quick Reference Summary at the back of this book or visit the Shelly Cashman Series Office XP Web page (scsite.com/offxp/qr.htm), and then click Microsoft Excel 2002.

More About

Closing Files

If you have multiple workbooks opened, you can close them all at the same time by holding down the SHIFT key when you click File on the menu bar. The Close command changes to the Close All command.

CASE PERSPECTIVE SUMMARY

The worksheet you developed in this project will handle all of Ethan Cromwell's requirements for his newly acquired company Pay-Less Financial Services. The Loan Payment Calculator, Interest Rate Schedule, and Amortization Schedule are easy to read in the protected worksheet, which will help with customer relations. The hyperlink associated with the dollar sign graphic gives the loan officer quick access to the bank's 2002 Statement of Condition to answer customer questions.

Project Summary

In this project you learned how to use names, rather than cell references, to enter formulas. You learned how to develop professional looking worksheets. You learned how to use financial functions, such as the PMT and PV functions. You also learned how to analyze data by creating a data table and amortization schedule. This project explained how to add a hyperlink to a worksheet. You learned how to set print options and print sections of a worksheet using names and the Set Print Area command. Finally, you learned how to protect a worksheet and how to check formulas for rule violations.

What You Should Know

Having completed this project, you now should be able to perform the following tasks:

- Add a Pointer to the Data Table *(E 4.26)*
- Add Borders to a Range *(E 4.09)*
- Add Borders to the Amortization Schedule *(E 4.36)*
- Assign a Hyperlink to an Embedded Graphic *(E 4.40)*
- Change Column Widths and Enter Titles *(E 4.29)*
- Change the Font Style of the Entire Worksheet *(E 4.07)*
- Copy the Formulas to Fill the Amortization Schedule *(E 4.33)*
- Create a Percent Series Using the Fill Handle *(E 4.20)*
- Create a Series of Integers Using the Fill Handle *(E 4.30)*
- Create Names Based on Row Titles *(E 4.12)*
- Define a Range as a Data Table *(E 4.22)*
- Determine the Total Interest and Total Cost *(E 4.16)*
- Display and Print a Hyperlinked File *(E 4.43)*
- Enable Background Formula Checking *(E 4.52)*
- Enter New Loan Data *(E 4.17 and E 4.38)*
- Enter the Data Table Title and Column Titles *(E 4.19)*
- Enter the Formulas in the Amortization Schedule *(E 4.31)*
- Enter the Formulas in the Data Table *(E 4.21)*
- Enter the Loan Amount Formula Using Names *(E 4.14)*
- Enter the Loan Data *(E 4.11)*
- Enter the Original Loan Data *(E 4.18 and E 4.39)*
- Enter the PMT Function *(E 4.15)*
- Enter the Section Title, Row Titles, and System Date *(E 4.07)*
- Enter the Total Formulas in the Amortization Schedule *(E 4.35)*
- Format Cells Before Entering Values *(E 4.11)*
- Format the Data Table *(E 4.24)*
- Format the Numbers in the Amortization Schedule *(E 4.36)*
- Name and Print Sections of a Worksheet *(E 4.47)*
- Protect a Worksheet *(E 4.49)*
- Quit Excel *(E 4.53)*
- Set the Print Area *(E 4.46)*
- Setup to Print *(E 4.44)*
- Start and Customize Excel *(E 4.06)*

More About

Microsoft Certification

The Microsoft Office User Specialist (MOUS) Certification program provides an opportunity for you to obtain a valuable industry credential — proof that you have the Excel 2002 skills required by employers. For more information, see Appendix E or visit the Shelly Cashman Series MOUS Web page at scsite.com/offxp/cert.htm.

Learn It Online

Instructions: To complete the Learn It Online exercises, start your browser, click the Address bar, and then enter scsite.com/offxp/exs.htm. When the Office XP Learn It Online page displays, follow the instructions in the exercises below.

1 Project Reinforcement TF, MC, and SA

Below Excel Project 4, click the Project Reinforcement link. Print the quiz by clicking Print on the File menu. Answer each question. Write your first and last name at the top of each page, and then hand in the printout to your instructor.

2 Flash Cards

Below Excel Project 4, click the Flash Cards link. When Flash Cards displays, read the instructions. Type 20 (or a number specified by your instructor) in the Number of Playing Cards text box, type your name in the Name text box, and then click the Flip Card button. When the flash card displays, read the question and then click the Answer box arrow to select an answer. Flip through Flash Cards. Click Print on the File menu to print the last flash card if your score is 15 (75%) correct or greater and then hand it in to your instructor. If your score is less than 15 (75%) correct, then redo this exercise by clicking the Replay button.

3 Practice Test

Below Excel Project 4, click the Practice Test link. Answer each question, enter your first and last name at the bottom of the page, and then click the Grade Test button. When the graded practice test displays on your screen, click Print on the File menu to print a hard copy. Continue to take practice tests until you score 80% or better. Hand in a printout of the final practice test to your instructor.

4 Who Wants to Be a Computer Genius?

Below Excel Project 4, click the Computer Genius link. Read the instructions, enter your first and last name at the bottom of the page, and then click the Play button. Hand in your score to your instructor.

5 Wheel of Terms

Below Excel Project 4, click the Wheel of Terms link. Read the instructions, and then enter your first and last name and your school name. Click the Play button. Hand in your score to your instructor.

6 Crossword Puzzle Challenge

Below Excel Project 4, click the Crossword Puzzle Challenge link. Read the instructions, and then enter your first and last name. Click the Play button. Work the crossword puzzle. When you are finished, click the Submit button. When the crossword puzzle redisplays, click the Print button. Hand in the printout.

7 Tips and Tricks

Below Excel Project 4, click the Tips and Tricks link. Click a topic that pertains to Project 4. Right-click the information and then click Print on the shortcut menu. Construct a brief example of what the information relates to in Excel to confirm you understand how to use the tip or trick. Hand in the example and printed information.

8 Newsgroups

Below Excel Project 4, click the Newsgroups link. Click a topic that pertains to Project 4. Print three comments. Hand in the comments to your instructor.

9 Expanding Your Horizons

Below Excel Project 4, click the Articles for Microsoft Excel link. Click a topic that pertains to Project 4. Print the information. Construct a brief example of what the information relates to in Excel to confirm you understand the contents of the article. Hand in the example and printed information to your instructor.

10 Search Sleuth

Below Excel Project 4, click the Search Sleuth link. To search for a term that pertains to this project, select a term below the Project 4 title and then use the Google search engine at google.com (or any major search engine) to display and print two Web pages that present information on the term. Hand in the printouts to your instructor.

online

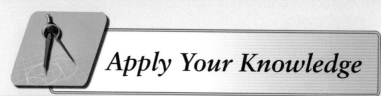

Apply Your Knowledge

1 Loan Payment Calculator

Instructions: Start Excel and perform the following tasks.

1. Start Excel. Open the workbook Loan Payment Calculator from the Data Disk. See the inside back cover of this book for instructions for downloading the Data Disk or see your instructor for information on accessing the files required in this book.

2. Use the Name command on the Insert menu to create names for cells in the range B3:B9 using the row titles in the range A3:A9.

3. Determine the loan amount in cell B8 by entering the formula: =Price – Down_Payment.

4. Determine the monthly payment in cell B9 by entering the function: =PMT(Interest_Rate/12, 12 * Years, – Loan_Amount).

5. In the data table, assign the formulas to the right to cells E4, F4, and G4.

CELL	FORMULA
E4	=B9
F4	=12 * B7 * B9 +B5
G4	=F4 – B4

6. Use the Table command on the Data menu to define the range D4:G16 as a one-input data table. Use cell B6 (interest rate) as the column input cell. Format the data table so that it appears as shown in Figure 4-72.

7. Add your name, course, computer laboratory assignment number (Apply Your Knowledge 4-1), date, and instructor name in column A beginning in cell A14.

8. Use the Page Setup command to select the Fit to and Black and white options. Use the Set Print Area command to select the range A1:G12 and then use the Print button on the Standard toolbar to print. Use the Clear Print Area command to clear the print area. Name the following ranges: A1:B9 – Calculator; D1:G16 – Rate_Schedule; and A1:G16 – All_Sections. Print each range by selecting the name in the Name box and using the Selection option in the Print dialog box.

9. Unlock the range B3:B7. Protect the worksheet. Only allow the user to select unlocked cells.

10. Press CTRL+ACCENT MARK (`) and print the formulas version in landscape. Press CTRL+ACCENT MARK (`) to display the values version.

11. Save the workbook using the file name, Loan Payment Calculator 2.

12. Determine the monthly payment and print the worksheet for each data set: (a) Item = Summer Cottage; Price = $213,000.00; Down Payment = $45,000.00; Interest Rate = 9.00%; Years = 10; (b) Item = 15' Boat; Price = $12,000.00; Down Payment = $0.00; Interest Rate = 10.50%; Years = 6. You should get the following monthly payment results: (a) $2,128.15; (b) $225.35.

FIGURE 4-72

In the Lab

1 BankOnline.com Retirement Investment Model

Problem: You are a part-time employee for BankOnline.com, a small start-up e-commerce banking company that hit it big when the company's investors took the company public. With the number of employees expected to reach 1,250 by the end of the year and the tight job market, the Benefits committee has developed several employee benefit plans to keep current employees and attract new employees. One of the new employee benefits is a 401(k) plan. The chairperson of the Benefits committee has asked you to develop a retirement investment model worksheet that will allow each current and prospective employee to see the effect (dollar accumulation) of investing a percent of his or her monthly salary over a period of years (Figure 4-73). The plan calls for the com-

pany to match an employee's investment dollar for dollar up to 2.50%. Thus, if an employee invests 4% of his or her annual salary, then the company matches the first 2.50%. If an employee invests only 2% of his or her annual salary, then the company matches the entire 2%. The chairperson wants a one-input data table to show the future value of the investment for different periods of time.

Instructions Part 1: With a blank worksheet on the screen, perform the following tasks.

1. Change the font of the entire worksheet to bold. Change the column widths to the following: A and D = 0.50; B = 20.00; C, F, and G = 13.00. Change the row heights to the following: 1 and 2 = 36.00; 3 = 4.50; and 4 = 26.25.

FIGURE 4-73

2. Enter the following worksheet titles: B1 = BankOnline.com; B2 = Retirement Savings Model. Change their font size to 26 point. One at a time, merge and center cells B1 and B2 across columns B through G. Change the background color of cells B1 and B2 to red. Change the font color to white. Draw a medium line style black border around cells B1 and B2.

3. Enter the row titles in column B, beginning in cell B4 as shown in Figure 4-73. Add the data in Table 4-5 to column C. Use the dollar and percent symbols to format the numbers in the range C5:C9.

4. Use the Create command on the Name submenu (Insert menu) to assign the row titles in column B (range B4:B14) to the adjacent cells in column C. Use these names to enter the following formulas in the range C11:C14. Step 4e formats the displayed results of the formulas.

   a. Employee Monthly Contribution (cell C11) = Annual_Salary * Percent_Invested / 12

   b. Employer Monthly Contribution (cell C12) = IF(Percent_Invested < Company_Match, Percent_Invested * Annual_Salary / 12; Company_Match * Annual_Salary / 12)

Table 4-5 Employee Data

ROW TITLE	ITEM
Employee Name	Rachel Love
Annual Salary	$68,500.00
Percent Invested	4.00%
Company Match	2.50%
Annual Return	7.50%
Years	20

(continued)

In the Lab

BankOnline.com Retirement Investment Model *(continued)*

  c. Total Monthly Contribution (cell C13) = SUM(C11:C12)

  d. Future Value (cell C14) = FV(Annual_Return/12, 12 * Years, -Total)

  e. If necessary, use the Format Painter button on the Standard toolbar to assign the Currency style format in cell C5 to the range C11:C14.

The **Future Value function** in Step 4d returns to the cell the future value of the investment. The **future value** of an investment is its value at some point in the future based on a series of payments of equal amounts made over a number of periods earning a constant rate of return.

5. Add borders to the range B4:C14 as shown in Figure 4-73 on the previous page.

6. Use the concepts and techniques developed in this project to add the data table in Figure 4-73 to the range E4:G15 as follows.

  a. Enter and format the table column titles in row 4.

  b. Use the fill handle to create the series of years beginning with 5 and ending with 50 in increments of 5 in column E, beginning in cell E6.

  c. In cells F5 and G5, use cell references to enter the formulas so Excel will copy the formats. That is, in cell F5, enter the formula =C14. In cell G5, enter the formula: =12 * C11 * C9.

  d. Use the Table command on the Data menu to define the range E5:G15 as a one-input data table. Use cell C9 as the column input cell.

  e. Format the numbers in the range F6:G15 to the Comma style format. Add borders as shown in Figure 4-73.

7. Use the Conditional Formatting command on the Format menu to add a red pointer to the data table in the Years column that shows the row that equals the years in cell C9.

8. Add your name, course, computer laboratory assignment number (Lab 4-1), date, and instructor name in column B beginning in cell B17.

9. Spell check and formula check the worksheet.

10. Use the Page Setup command to select the Fit to and Black and white options.

11. Print the worksheet. Press CTRL+ACCENT MARK (`) and print the formulas version. Press CTRL+ACCENT MARK (`) to display the values version.

12. Unlock the cells in the range C4:C9. Protect the worksheet. Allow users to select only unlocked cells.

13. Save the workbook using the file name BankOnline.

14. Determine the future value for the data in Table 4-6. Print the worksheet for each data set. The following Future Value results should display in cell C14: Data Set 1 = $652,462.77; Data Set 2 = $1,962,896.98; and Data Set 3 = $291,300.36. Close Excel without saving the workbook.

Table 4-6 Future Value Data			
	DATA SET 1	DATA SET 2	DATA SET 3
Employee Name	Jim Couples	Joan More	Connie Friend
Annual Salary	$105,000.00	$82,500.00	$34,500.00
Percent Invested	5.5%	7%	3.5%
Company Match	3%	4%	1.5%
Annual Return	7.5%	8.5%	5%
Years	25	35	45

Instructions Part 2: The chairperson of the Benefits committee has requested that you include a two-input data table (Figure 4-74) on the worksheet created in Part 1 that shows the future value for varying the employee investment (cell C6) and company match (cell C7). Complete the following tasks to create the two-input data table.

1. If necessary, open the workbook BankOnline created in Part 1. Unprotect the worksheet.

2. Enter the data table title and subtitle as shown in cells I1 and I2 in Figure 4-74. Merge and center the titles over columns I through S. Format the titles as shown.

Varying the Percent Invested and Company Match

Percent Invested in Left Column and Company Match in Top Row

future value formula

row of different company matching percentages

$205,457.17	1.50%	1.75%	2.00%	2.25%	2.50%	2.75%	3.00%	3.25%	3.50%	3.75%
2.00%	110,630.78	118,532.98	126,435.18	126,435.18	126,435.18	126,435.18	126,435.18	126,435.18	126,435.18	126,435.18
2.25%	118,532.98	126,435.18	134,337.38	142,239.58	142,239.58	142,239.58	142,239.58	142,239.58	142,239.58	142,239.58
2.50%	126,435.18	134,337.38	142,239.58	150,141.78	158,043.98	158,043.98	158,043.98	158,043.98	158,043.98	158,043.98
2.75%	134,337.38	142,239.58	150,141.78	158,043.98	165,946.18	173,848.38	173,848.38	173,848.38	173,848.38	173,848.38
3.00%	142,239.58	150,141.78	158,043.98	165,946.18	173,848.38	181,750.57	189,652.77	189,652.77	189,652.77	189,652.77
3.25%	150,141.78	158,043.98	165,946.18	173,848.38	181,750.57	189,652.77	197,554.97	205,457.17	205,457.17	205,457.17
3.50%	158,043.98	165,946.18	173,848.38	181,750.57	189,652.77	197,554.97	205,457.17	213,359.37	221,261.57	221,261.57
3.75%	165,946.18	173,848.38	181,750.57	189,652.77	197,554.97	205,457.17	213,359.37	221,261.57	229,163.77	237,065.97
4.00%	173,848.38	181,750.57	189,652.77	197,554.97	205,457.17	213,359.37	221,261.57	229,163.77	237,065.97	244,968.17
4.25%	181,750.57	189,652.77	197,554.97	205,457.17	213,359.37	221,261.57	229,163.77	237,065.97	244,968.17	252,870.36
4.50%	189,652.77	197,554.97	205,457.17	213,359.37	221,261.57	229,163.77	237,065.97	244,968.17	252,870.36	260,772.56

column of different percentages invested by employee

FIGURE 4-74

3. Enter =C14 in cell I4. For a two-input data table, the formula you are analyzing must be assigned to the upper-left cell in the range of the data table.
4. Use the fill handle to create the list of percents 2.00% through 4.50%, in increments of 0.25% in the range I5:I15 and 1.50% through 3.75% in increments of 0.25% in the range J4:S4.
5. Select the range I4:S15. Click Table on the Data menu. When the Table dialog box displays, enter cell C7 in the Row input cell and cell C6 in the Column input cell.
6. Format the two-input data table as shown in Figure 4-74.
7. Protect the worksheet so that the user can select only unlocked cells.
8. Change the print orientation to landscape. Print the worksheet. Print the formulas version of the worksheet.
9. Save the workbook using the file name BankOnline 2. Close Excel.

2 CashFast Loan Analysis and Amortization Schedule

Problem: Each student in your Office XP Applications course is assigned a real-world project that involves working with a local company. For your project, you are working with the CashFast Loan Company, a division of Pay-Less Financial Services. The manager of CashFast has asked you to create the loan analysis worksheet shown in Figure 4-75 on the next page. She also wants a hyperlink added to the worksheet that displays the Pay-Less Financial Services 2002 Statement of Condition. Finally, she wants you to demonstrate the goal seeking capabilities of Excel.

Instructions: With a blank worksheet on the screen, perform the following tasks to create the worksheet in Figure 4-75.

1. Select the entire worksheet by clicking the Select All button. Bold the entire worksheet and change all the columns to a width of 15.00.
2. Enter the worksheet title in cell B1 and change its font to 20-point dark red Arial Black (or a similar font style). Enter the worksheet subtitle in cell B2 and change its font to 12-point dark red Arial Black (or a similar font style). One at a time, merge and center cells B1 and B2 across columns B through F.
3. Enter the text in the ranges B3:B5 and E3:E5.

(continued)

In the Lab

CashFast Loan Analysis and Amortization Schedule *(continued)*

CashFast Loan Company
A Division of Pay-Less Financial Services

	Price	$232,500.00		Rate	9.25%
	Down Pymt	$48,250.00		Years	30
	Loan Amount	$184,250.00		Monthly Pymt	$1,515.78

Year	Beginning Balance	Ending Balance	Paid On Principal	Interest Paid
1	$184,250.00	$183,053.91	$1,196.09	$16,993.26
2	183,053.91	181,742.36	1,311.55	16,877.81
3	181,742.36	180,304.22	1,438.14	16,751.21
4	180,304.22	178,727.26	1,576.96	16,612.40
5	178,727.26	176,998.09	1,729.17	16,460.18
6	176,998.09	175,102.01	1,896.08	16,293.27
7	175,102.01	173,022.91	2,079.10	16,110.26
8	173,022.91	170,743.13	2,279.78	15,909.57
9	170,743.13	168,243.30	2,499.83	15,689.52
10	168,243.30	165,502.17	2,741.13	15,448.23
11	165,502.17	162,496.46	3,005.71	15,183.64
12	162,496.46	159,200.62	3,295.84	14,893.52
13	159,200.62	155,586.65	3,613.96	14,575.39
14	155,586.65	151,623.85	3,962.80	14,226.55
15	151,623.85	147,278.55	4,345.31	13,844.05
16	147,278.55	142,513.82	4,764.73	13,424.62
17	142,513.82	137,289.17	5,224.64	12,964.71
18	137,289.17	131,560.22	5,728.95	12,460.41
19	131,560.22	125,278.29	6,281.93	11,907.42
20	125,278.29	118,390.01	6,888.29	11,301.07
21	118,390.01	110,836.83	7,553.17	10,636.18
22	110,836.83	102,554.59	8,282.24	9,907.12
23	102,554.59	93,472.92	9,081.67	9,107.68
24	93,472.92	83,514.64	9,958.27	8,231.08
25	83,514.64	72,595.16	10,919.49	7,269.86
26	72,595.16	60,621.67	11,973.48	6,215.87
27	60,621.67	47,492.46	13,129.21	5,060.14
28	47,492.46	33,095.96	14,396.50	3,792.85
29	33,095.96	17,309.85	15,786.11	2,403.24
30	17,309.85	-	17,309.85	879.50
		Subtotal	$184,250.00	$361,430.61
		Down Pymt		$48,250.00
		Total Cost		$593,930.61

FIGURE 4-75

4. Enter 232500 (price) in cell C3, 48250 (down payment) in cell C4, 9.25% (interest rate) in cell F3, and 30 (years) in cell F4. Determine the loan amount by entering the formula =C3 - C4 in cell C5. Determine the monthly payment by entering the PMT function =PMT(F3 / 12, 12 * F4, -C5) in cell F5.

5. In the range B3:F5, color the background dark red, the font white, and add a thick black border to the range.

6. Enter the column titles for the amortization schedule in the range B6:F6. Center the column titles. Use the fill handle to generate the series of years in the range B7:B36 and center them.

7. Assign the formulas and functions to the cells indicated in Table 4-7.

8. Enter the total titles in the range D37:D39 as shown in Figure 4-75.

9. Copy cell C8 to the range C9:C36. Copy the range D7:F7 to the range D8:F36. Assign the Currency style format to the range C7:F7. Assign the Comma style format to the range C8:F36. Draw the borders shown in Figure 4-75.

10. Insert the businesswomen graphic shown in the range D3:D5. (Search in All collections for business.) Assign the hyperlink a:\Pay-Less Financial Services.htm to the clip art graphic. Display and print the HTML file (Web page). You must have the Data Disk in drive A to display the HTML file.

11. Change the tab name to Loan Analysis. Color it dark red.

12. Add your name, course, laboratory assignment number (Lab 4-3), date, and instructor name in column B beginning in cell B40.

13. Spell check and formula check the worksheet. Use Range Finder (double-click cell) to check all formulas listed in Table 4-7.

Table 4-7 Cell Assignments	
CELL	**FORMULA OR FUNCTION**
C7	=C5
D7	=IF(B7 <= $F$4, PV($F$3 / 12, 12 * ($F$4 – B7), -$F$5),0)
E7	=C7 – D7
F7	=IF(C7 > 0, 12 * $F$5 – E7, 0)
C8	=D7
E37	=SUM(E7:E36)
F37	=SUM(F7:F36)
F38	=C4
F39	=E37 + F37 + F38

In the Lab

14. Use the Page Setup command to select the Fit to and Black and white options.

15. Unlock the cells in the ranges C3:C4 and F3:F4. Protect the worksheet so that users can select any cell in the worksheet, but can only change the unlocked cells.

16. Save the workbook using the file name CashFast Loan Company.

17. Print the worksheet. Press CTRL+ACCENT MARK (`) and print the formulas version. Press CTRL+ACCENT MARK (`) to display the values version.

18. Use Excel's goal seeking capabilities to determine the down payment required for the loan data in Figure 4-75 if the monthly payment is set to $1,200.00. The down payment that results for a monthly payment of $1,200.00 is $86,634.45. Print the worksheet with the new monthly payment of $1,200.00. Close the workbook without saving changes.

3 Rodney's Gadgets Annual Income Statement and Break-Even Analysis

Problem: You are a consultant to Rodney's Gadgets, Inc. Your area of expertise is cost-volume-profit (CVP) (also called break-even analysis), which investigates the relationship among a product's expenses (cost), its volume (units sold), and the operating income (gross profit). Any money a company earns above the break-even point is called operating income, or gross profit (row 14 in the Break-Even Analysis table in Figure 4-76 on the next page). You have been asked to prepare an annual income statement and a data table that shows revenue, expenses, and income for units sold between 300,000 and 700,000 in increments of 25,000.

Instructions: With a blank worksheet on the screen, perform the following tasks.

1. Change the font of the entire worksheet to bold. Change the column widths to the following: A = 21.00; B = 26.00; C = 13.71; D = 0.50; E = 7.14; and F through H = 11.14. Change the heights of rows 1 and 2 to 27.00.

2. Enter the following worksheet titles: Rodney's Gadgets in cell A1; and Annual Income Statement in cell A2. Increase the font size in cell A1 and A2 to 20 points. One at a time, merge and center cells A1 and A2 across columns A through C. Change the background color of cells A1 and A2 to blue (column 6, row 2 on the Fill Color palette). Change the font color to white (column 8, row 5 on the Font Color palette). Add a medium blue outline to the range A1:A2.

3. Enter the row titles in columns A and B as shown in Figure 4-76. Change the row titles in column A to 12 point. Add the data shown in Table 4-8 on the next page in column C. Use the dollar sign ($) and comma symbol (,) to format the numbers in column C as you enter them.

4. Select the range B4:C18. Point to Name on the Insert menu to display the Name submenu. Use the Create command on the Name submenu to assign the row titles in column B to the adjacent cells in column C. Use these names to enter the following formulas in column C:
   a. Total Revenue (cell C6) = Units_Sold * Price_per_Unit (or =C4 * C5)
   b. Total Fixed Expenses (cell C12) = SUM(C8:C11)
   c. Total Material Cost (cell C15) = Units_Sold * Material_Cost_per_Unit (or =C4 * C14)
   d. Total Manufacturing Cost (cell C17) = Units_Sold * Manufacturing_Cost_per_Unit (or =C4 * C16)
   e. Total Variable Expenses (cell C18) = Total_Material_Cost + Total_Manufacturing_Cost (or =C15 + C17)
   f. Total Expenses (cell C20) = Total_Fixed_Expenses + Total_Variable_Expenses (or =C12 + C18)
   g. Operating Income (cell C21) = Total_Revenue – Total_Expenses (or =C6 – C20)

5. If necessary, use the Format Painter button on the Standard toolbar to assign the Currency style format in cell C8 to the unformatted dollar amounts in column C.

(continued)

In the Lab

Rodney's Gadgets Annual Income Statement and Break-Even Analysis *(continued)*

6. Add a thick black bottom border to the ranges B5:C5, B11:C11, and B17:C17 as shown in Figure 4-76.

7. Use the concepts and techniques presented in this project to add the data table to the range E1:H21 as follows:

   a. Add the data table titles Break-Even in cell E1 and Analysis in cell E2. Merge and center cells E1 and E2 across columns E through H. Increase the font size in cells E1 and E2 to 20 point. Format the background and font colors as shown in Figure 4-76. Enter and center the column titles in the range E3:H3.

   b. Use the fill handle to create the series of units sold in column E from 300,000 to 700,000 in increments of 25,000, beginning in cell E5.

   c. In cells F4, G4, and H4, use cell references to enter the formulas so Excel will copy the formats. That is, in cell F4, enter the formula =C6. In cell G4, enter the formula =C20. In cell H4, enter the formula =C21. Adjust the column widths if necessary.

   d. Use the Table command on the Data menu to define the range E4:H21 as a one-input data table. Use cell C4 (units sold) as the column input cell.

   e. Use the Format Cells command on the shortcut menu to format the range F5:H21 to the Comma style format with no decimal places and negative numbers in red with parentheses. Add a medium red outline and vertical light black borders to the range E1:H21.

8. Spell check and formula check the worksheet. Add your name, course, computer laboratory assignment number (Lab 4-2), date, and instructor name in column A beginning in cell A24.

9. Use the Page Setup command to select the Fit to and Black and white options.

10. Unlock the following cells: C4, C5, C14, and C16. Protect the workbook so the user can select only unlocked cells.

11. Save the workbook using the file name Rodney's Gadgets Income Statement.

12. Print the worksheet. Press CTRL+ACCENT MARK (`) and print the formulas version. Press CTRL+ACCENT MARK (`) to display the values version.

FIGURE 4-76

The worksheet shows Rodney's Gadgets Annual Income Statement (columns A–C) and Break-Even Analysis (columns E–H):

Revenue			
	Units Sold	554,123	
	Price per Unit	$21.50	
	Total Revenue	$11,913,645	
Fixed Expenses			
	Administrative	$2,550,000	
	Leasing	1,425,000	
	Marketing	1,750,000	
	Salary and Benefits	1,100,000	
	Total Fixed Expenses	$6,825,000	
Variable Expenses			
	Material Cost per Unit	$3.50	
	Total Material Cost	$1,939,431	
	Manufacturing Cost per Unit	$4.55	
	Total Manufacturing Cost	$2,521,260	
	Total Variable Expenses	$4,460,690	
Summary			
	Total Expenses	$11,285,690	
	Operating Income	$627,954	

Break-Even Analysis

Units	Revenue	Expenses	Income
	$11,913,645	$11,285,690	$627,954
300,000	6,450,000	9,240,000	(2,790,000)
325,000	6,987,500	9,441,250	(2,453,750)
350,000	7,525,000	9,642,500	(2,117,500)
375,000	8,062,500	9,843,750	(1,781,250)
400,000	8,600,000	10,045,000	(1,445,000)
425,000	9,137,500	10,246,250	(1,108,750)
450,000	9,675,000	10,447,500	(772,500)
475,000	10,212,500	10,648,750	(436,250)
500,000	10,750,000	10,850,000	(100,000)
525,000	11,287,500	11,051,250	236,250
550,000	11,825,000	11,252,500	572,500
575,000	12,362,500	11,453,750	908,750
600,000	12,900,000	11,655,000	1,245,000
625,000	13,437,500	11,856,250	1,581,250
650,000	13,975,000	12,057,500	1,917,500
675,000	14,512,500	12,258,750	2,253,750
700,000	15,050,000	12,460,000	2,590,000

Table 4-8	Annual Income Data	
TITLE	**CELL**	**ITEM**
Units Sold	C4	554,123
Price per Unit	C5	$21.50
Administrative	C8	$2,550,000
Leasing	C9	$1,425,000
Marketing	C10	$1,750,000
Salary and Benefits	C11	$1,100,000
Material Cost per Unit	C14	$3.50
Manufacturing Cost per Unit	C16	$4.55

In the Lab

13. Determine the operating income for the data in Table 4-9. Print the worksheet for each data set. You should get the following Operating Income results in cell C21: Data Set 1 = $3,933,000; Data Set 2 = $952,500; and Data Set 3 = ($3,562,500).

Table 4-9	Operating Income Data			
TITLE	CELL	DATA SET 1	DATA SET 2	DATA SET 3
Units Sold	C4	815,000	610,000	725,000
Price per Unit	C5	$21.00	$22.00	$19.50
Material Cost per Unit	C14	$3.50	$2.75	$11.00
Manufacturing Cost per Unit	C16	$4.30	$6.50	$4.00

Cases and Places

The difficulty of these case studies varies:
◗ are the least difficult; ◗◗ are more difficult; and ◗◗◗ are the most difficult.

1 ◗ If you know the fixed expenses, the price per unit, and the expense (cost) per unit, you can calculate the number of units you must sell to break even (break-even point). You are a spreadsheet consultant and have been hired by b-Toys (Baby Toys) to create a data table that analyzes the break-even point for prices between $1.00 and $7.25 in increments of $0.25. The following formula determines the break-even point:

Break-Even Point = Fixed Expenses / (Price per Unit − Expense per Unit)

Assume Fixed Expenses = $12,500,000; Price per Unit = $2.50; and Expense per Unit = $1.95.

Enter the data and formula into a worksheet and then create the data table. Use the Price per Unit as the input cell and the break-even value as the result. For a price per unit of $3.25, the data table should show a break-even point of 9,615,385 units.

2 ◗ After visiting with several mortgage companies, Juanita Wright has decided she wants to take out her mortgage with First Bank. She will pay monthly payments over a period of 25 years. Before she finalizes the mortgage, Juanita wants to know her monthly payment and how much she actually will pay for the house including interest. Create a worksheet based on the information provided by Juanita. The cost of the house is $225,500.00; the interest is 8.35% for 25 years. She plans to make a $25,000.00 down payment.

Cases and Places

3 ▶▶ Katiana Guadalupe, president of Rosamar Construction, recently purchased a new payloader. Katiana wants a worksheet that uses a financial function (SLN) to show the payloader's straight-line depreciation and a formula to determine the annual rate of depreciation. Straight-line depreciation is based on an asset's initial cost, how long it can be used (called useful life), and the price at which it eventually can be sold (called salvage value). Katiana has supplied the following information: Cost = $64,551; Salvage = $15,250; Life = 5 years; and Annual Rate of Depreciation = SLN / Cost.

Katiana is not sure how much she will be able to sell the payloader for in 5 years. Create a data table that shows straight-line depreciation and annual rate of depreciation for salvage from $11,000 to $20,000 in $500 increments. Use Help to learn more about the SLN function.

4 ▶▶ Bernetha and Baakari's dream for their two-year old daughter, Chanel, is that one day she will attend their alma mater, Purdue University. For the next 15 years, they plan to make monthly payment deposits to a long-term savings account at a local bank. The account pays 5.25% annual interest, compounded monthly. Create a worksheet for Bernetha and Baakari that uses a financial function to show the future value (FV) of their investment and a formula to determine the percentage of the college's tuition saved. Bernetha and Baakari have supplied the following information: Out of State Annual Tuition = $50,000; Rate (per month) = 5.25% / 12; Nper (number of monthly payments) = 15 * 12; Pmt (payment per period) = $400; and percentage of Tuition Saved = FV / Tuition for Four Years.

Bernetha and Baakari are not sure how much they will be able to save each month. Create a data table that shows the future value and percentage of tuition saved for monthly payments from $175 to $775, in $50 increments. Insert a clip art file and assign it a hyperlink to the HTML file, Pay-Less Financial Services.htm, on the Data Disk.

5 ▶▶ Your sister Alice and her husband Pat have decided to save for the down payment on a home, after living for years with your parents. Pat's cousin, Bill, who works for the local telephone company, promises them he can get the pair an annual interest rate of 9.55% on their savings through a special company program. Pat would like you to create a worksheet that determines how much they have to save each month so that in eight years the value of the account is $32,500. Hint: Use the FV function with a monthly savings of $150. Then use the Goal Seek command to determine the monthly savings amount. The Goal Seek command should yield a result of $226.81 per month savings to reach their goal of $32,500 in eight years.

6 ▶▶▶ Wellington University is offering its faculty a generous retirement package. Professor Skye Paris has accepted the proposal, but before moving to his retirement home near Yellowstone National Park, he wants to settle his account with the school credit union. Professor Paris has three years remaining on a five-year camper loan, with an interest rate of 10.25% and a monthly payment of $452.00. The credit union is willing to accept the present value (PV) of the loan as a payoff. Develop an amortization schedule that shows how much Professor Paris must pay at the end of each of the five years. Include the beginning and ending balance, the amount paid on the principal and the interest paid for years two through five. Because he has already paid for the first year, determine only the ending balance (present value) for year one.

Microsoft Excel 2002

Creating, Sorting, and Querying a Worksheet Database

You will have mastered the material in this project when you can:

OBJECTIVES

- Create a worksheet database
- Add computational fields to a database
- Use the VLOOKUP function to look up a value in a table
- Change the range assigned to a named database
- Use a data form to display records, add records, delete records, and change field values in a worksheet database
- Sort a worksheet database on one field or multiple fields
- Display automatic subtotals
- Use a data form to find records that meet comparison criteria
- Filter data to display records that meet comparison criteria
- Use the advanced filtering features to display records that meet comparison criteria
- Apply database functions to generate information about a worksheet database
- Print a database

Calculating the Costs of Retirement

Building a Stronger Foundation

In 1935, the Social Security Act was enacted into law, and its passage provided many American workers the comfort that Social Security benefits would provide a solid economic foundation after their retirement. Today, many Americans are worried that this foundation is beginning to erode. Currently, the Social Security system now takes in more taxes than it pays out in benefits to retirees. The excess taxes are diverted to a trust fund designed to serve as a reservoir of benefits. Beginning in 2016, as the baby-boom generation retires in increasingly greater numbers, analysts have warned that the flow will be reversed; Social Security will pay out more benefits than it receives in taxes, and benefits will begin to be paid directly out of the trust fund. Eventually, the trust fund will be drained and incoming taxes will provide less than three quarters of the total benefits owed to retirees. In May 2001, the President established a Congressional committee to study how the Social Security system could be preserved and strengthened in the years to come. Committee members were entrusted with the awesome task to determine how to avoid raising Social Security payroll taxes to unacceptable levels, while at the same time guaranteeing that retirement benefits do not decrease, let alone disappear.

The Social Security program was created during the Great Depression to address economic security fears. Today, 95 percent of Americans are protected by the program, and nearly one in five receives Social Security benefits. More than 90 percent of senior citizens receive these funds. In addition, more than 15 million Americans of all ages receive Social Security disability and survivors benefits as compensation for losing a source of family income when severe injury or death strikes.

Since the inception of the Social Security program, more than $4.5 trillion have been paid into the system, and more than $4.1 trillion have been dispersed. Benefits generally are based on the amount a worker has contributed to the program during his or her career.

The Social Security Administration maintains a database that has a record for every person with a Social Security number. Similar to the GPS Golf Cart Distributorship Database you will create in this Excel project, the SSA database has records that contain fields to store such data as Social Security number, last name, first name, gender, birth date, length of time the worker contributed Social Security funds, wages, date of death, date of disability, and birth date of widow or widower.

The data in these fields can be analyzed in computations, just as you will learn to do in this Excel project. The SSA uses the data to manage its trust fund by predicting demands for benefits. By sorting records based on birth date, it can determine people who will reach retirement age each year and the amount of benefits they will draw. Using these figures, the SSA realizes that without taking any action, in 2015 the interest and tax revenues generated from the trust funds will be insufficient to meet these retirees' financial demands. If the agency then begins drawing on the trust fund principal, which is expected to grow to $4 trillion by 2016, that principal will be exhausted by the year 2038, according to current projected estimates.

At anytime, you can request an official Social Security Statement issued by the Social Security Administration. This Statement reviews your complete earnings history, including the total Social Security taxes you and your employers have paid. In addition, the Statement estimates the benefits you and your family may qualify for when you retire. Also available at Social Security Online are online calculators that can estimate your potential Social Security benefits based on different retirement dates and income earnings that you supply. You also can choose to download a calculation program, called the Social Security Benefit Calculator, which can provide a very precise estimate of your expected Social Security retirement benefits. For details, visit Social Security Online at www.ssa.gov.

Microsoft Excel 2002

Creating, Sorting, and Querying a Worksheet Database

PROJECT

5

C A S E   P E R S P E C T I V E

GPS Golf Cart, Inc. developed the first golf carts with global positioning system (GPS) technology in the late 1980s. The GPS technology allows golfers to find their exact position on the course relative to the green, bunkers, water hazards, and sand traps. The system beams the golf cart's exact longitude and latitude back and forth to GPS satellites orbiting the earth.

Clarissa Baldwin, who is the general manager for GPS Golf Cart, oversees one dozen distributors spread equally among six states: Arizona, California, Massachusetts, Nevada, New Jersey, and New York.

Clarissa plans to use Excel 2002 to create, maintain, and query a worksheet database containing data about the GPS Golf Cart's distributors.

Clarissa has assigned you the challenge of creating the database of distributors and demonstrating how to sort and query the database using Excel 2002's database capabilities.

Introduction

A **worksheet database**, also called a **database**, or **list**, is an organized collection of data. For example, a list of friends, a list of students registered for a class, club membership, and an instructor's grade book are databases. In these cases, the data related to a person is called a **record**, and the data items that make up a record are called **fields**. In a database of distributors, each one would have a separate record; some of the fields in the records might be company name, state, start date, age, and quota. A database record also can include formulas and functions. A field in a database that contains formulas or functions is called a **computational field**. A computational field displays results based on other fields in the database.

A worksheet's row-and-column structure can be used to organize and store a database (Figure 5-1). Each row of a worksheet can be used to store a record and each column to store a field. Additionally, a row of column titles at the top of the worksheet can be used as **field names** that identify each field.

Once you enter a database into a worksheet, you can use Excel to: (1) add and delete records; (2) change the values of fields in records; (3) sort the records so they display in a different order; (4) determine subtotals for numeric fields; (5) display records that meet comparison criteria; and (6) analyze data using database functions. This project illustrates all six of these database capabilities.

Project Five — GPS Golf Cart Distributorship Database

From your meeting with Clarissa Baldwin, you have determined the following needs, source of data, and calculations.

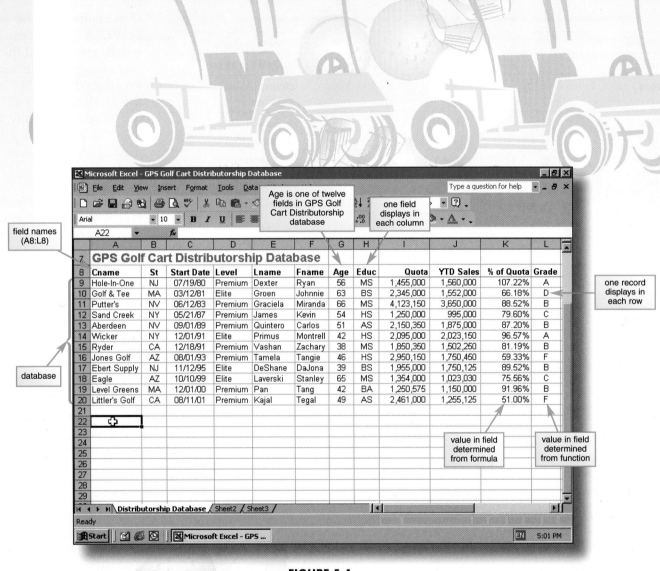

FIGURE 5-1

Needs: Create a distributorship database (Figure 5-1). The field names, columns, types of data, column widths, and field descriptions are shown in Table 5-1 on the next page. Because Clarissa will use the database online as she travels to visit the distributors, it is important that it be readable and that the database is visible on the screen. Therefore, some of the column widths listed in Table 5-1 are determined from the field names and not the maximum length of the data. The last two fields (located in columns K and L) use a formula and function based on data within each record.

Source of Data: Clarissa will supply the distributors' data required for the database.

Calculations: The last two fields in the database in columns K and L are determined as follows:

% of Quota in column K = YTD Sales / Quota
Grade in column L = VLOOKUP function

Table 5-1 GPS Golf Cart Distributorship Database Column Information

COLUMN TITLES (FIELD NAMES)	COLUMN IN WORKSHEET	TYPE OF DATA	COLUMN WIDTH	DESCRIPTION
Cname	A	Text	11.00	Company name
St	B	Text	5.00	State
Start Date	C	Date	10.00	Distributor start date
Level	D	Text	8.00	Quality of distributor
Lname	E	Text	9.00	Last name of owner of distributor
Fname	F	Text	7.00	First name of owner of distributor
Age	G	Numeric	5.00	Age of owner
Educ	H	Text	5.00	Education of owner
Quota	I	Numeric	11.00	Distributor's annual quota
YTD Sales	J	Numeric	11.00	Distributor's year-to-date sales
% of Quota	K	YTD Sales / Quota	11.00	Percent of annual quota met
Grade	L	VLOOKUP Function	6.00	Grade indicates how well sales are going for distributor

The VLOOKUP function will be used to display the grades in column L based on the table in columns N and O in Figure 5-2. The DAVERAGE function will be used to find the average age of Elite and Premium distributors in the database (range Q5:T6 in Figure 5-2). Finally, the DCOUNT function will be used to count the number of distributors who have a grade of F (range Q7:T7 in Figure 5-2). These two functions require that you set up a criteria area (range Q1:S3) to tell Excel what items to average and count.

Excel's Database Capabilities

Even though Excel is not a true database management system, such as Access or Oracle, it does give you many of the same basic capabilities as these dedicated systems. For example, in Excel you can create a database; add, change, and delete data in the database; employ computational fields; sort data in the database; query the database; and create forms and reports.

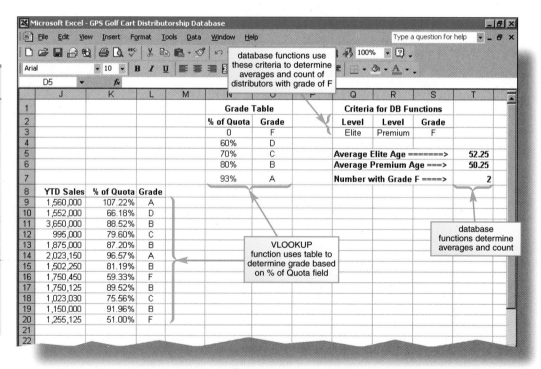

FIGURE 5-2

Starting and Customizing Excel

Perform the following steps to start and customize Excel. For additional information on resetting the toolbars and menus, see Appendix C.

TO START AND CUSTOMIZE EXCEL

1 Click the Start button on the Windows taskbar, point to Programs on the Start menu, and then click Microsoft Excel on the Programs submenu.

2 If the Excel window is not maximized, double-click its title bar to maximize it.

3 If the New Workbook task pane displays, click the Show at startup check box at the bottom of the task pane to remove the check mark and then click the Close button in the upper-right corner to close the task pane.

4 If the Language bar displays, click its Minimize button.

5 If the Standard and Formatting toolbars display on one row, click the Toolbar Options button on the right side of either toolbar and then click Show Buttons on Two Rows in the Toolbar Options list.

The Excel window with the Standard and Formatting toolbars on two rows displays as shown in Figure 5-2.

Once the Excel window opens, steps 3 through 5 close the task pane, minimize the Language bar, and ensure that the Standard and Formatting toolbars display on two rows.

Creating a Database

The three steps to creating a database in Excel are: (1) set up the database; (2) assign a name to the range containing the database; and (3) enter the data into the database. These steps are similar to what you would do with a traditional database package, such as Access. The following pages illustrate these three steps for creating the GPS Golf Cart Distributorship database.

Setting Up a Database

Setting up the database involves entering field names in a row in the worksheet and changing the column widths so the data will fit in the columns. Follow these steps to change the column widths to those specified in Table 5-1, to change the height of row 8 to 15 points to emphasize this row and to enter and format the database title and column titles (field names). The following steps also change the name of Sheet1 to Distributorship Database and save the workbook using the file name GPS Golf Cart Distributorship Database.

Although Excel does not require a database title to be entered, it is a good practice to include one on the worksheet to show where the database begins. With Excel, you usually enter the database several rows below the top. These blank rows will be used later to query the database.

TO SET UP A DATABASE

1 Use the mouse to change the column widths as follows: A = 11.00, B = 5.00, C = 10.00, D = 8.00, E = 9.00, F = 7.00, G = 5.00, H = 5.00, I = 11.00, J = 11.00, K = 11.00, and L = 6.00.

2 Click cell A7 and then enter GPS Golf Cart Distributorship Database as the worksheet database title.

More About

Setting Up the Database

Leave several rows empty above the database on the worksheet to set up a criteria area for querying the database. Some spreadsheet specialists also leave several columns to the left empty, beginning with column A, for additional worksheet activities. A range of blank rows or columns on the side of a database is called a moat of cells.

Microsoft **Excel 2002**

3 With cell A7 selected, click the Font Size box arrow on the Formatting toolbar and then click 14 in the Font list. Click the Bold button on the Formatting toolbar. Click the Font Color button on the Formatting toolbar to change the font color to red.

4 Enter the column titles in row 8 as shown in Figure 5-3. Change the height of row 8 to 15.00.

5 Select the range A8:J8. Click the Bold button on the Formatting toolbar. Right-click the selected range and then click Format Cells on the shortcut menu. Click the Border tab. Click the Color box arrow in the Line area and then click Red (column 1, row 3) on the Color palette. Click the light border style in the Style box (column 1, row 7). Click the Underline button on the left side of the Border area. Click the OK button.

6 Click column heading B to select the entire column. Hold down the CTRL key and click column headings C, G, H, and L. Click the Center button on the Formatting toolbar so that all future entries in columns B, C, G, H, and L will be centered.

7 Right-click column heading C. Click Format Cells on the shortcut menu. When the Format Cells dialog box displays, click the Number tab, click Date in the Category list box, and then click 03/14/01 in the Type box. Click the OK button.

8 Click column heading I. Drag through column heading J to select both columns. Click the Comma Style button on the Formatting toolbar. Click the Decrease Decimal button on the Formatting toolbar twice so that all future numeric entries in columns I and J will display using the Comma style with zero decimal places. Click cell A10 to deselect columns I and J.

9 Double-click the Sheet1 tab at the bottom of the screen. Type `Distributorship Database` as the sheet name. Press the ENTER key. Right-click the tab, click Tab Color, click Red (column 1, row 3), and then click the OK button.

10 Click the Save button on the Standard toolbar. When the Save As dialog box displays, type `GPS Golf Cart Distributorship Database` in the File name text box. Click the Save in box arrow, click 3½ Floppy (A:), and then click the Save button in the Save As dialog box.

The worksheet displays as shown in Figure 5-3.

Automatic Formatting

When you are entering a column or row list, the Extend List Format feature of Excel automatically formats new entries added to the end of a list to match the format of the rest of the list. For this to execute properly, the format must appear in at least three of the five last rows (or columns) preceding the new row (or column). To toggle this feature off, click Options on the Tools menu, click the Edit tab, click the Extend List Formats and Formulas check box to remove the check mark, and then click the OK button.

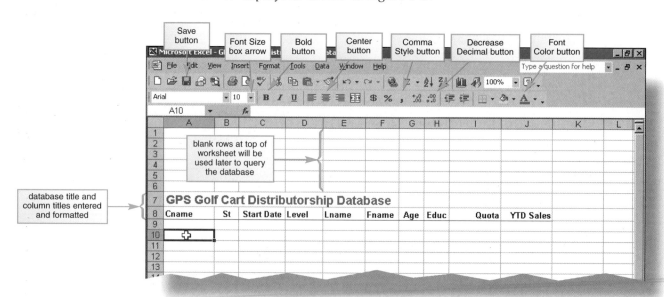

FIGURE 5-3

Compare the column titles in row 8 in Figure 5-1 on page E 5.05 with Figure 5-3. In Figure 5-3, the two computational fields, % of Quota and Grade, are not included in columns K and L. These two fields will be added after the data is entered for the 12 distributors. In Excel, computational fields that depend on data in the database usually are entered after the data has been entered.

Naming a Database

Although Excel usually can identify a **database range** when you invoke a database-type command, assigning the name Database to the range eliminates any confusion when commands are entered to manipulate the database. Thus, you first assign the range A8:J9 to the name Database by selecting the range and typing Database in the Name Box on the left side of the formula bar. The range assigned to the name Database includes the column titles (row 8) and one blank row (row 9) below the column titles. The blank row is for expansion of the database. As records are added using a data form, Excel automatically expands the named range Database to include the last record. Later, when the database is expanded to include the two computational fields, % of Quota and Grade, the name Database will be redefined to encompass the new fields in columns K and L.

Perform the following steps to name the database.

TO NAME THE DATABASE

1 Select the range A8:J9. Click the Name Box in the formula bar and then type Database as the name for the selected range.

2 Press the ENTER key.

The worksheet displays as shown in Figure 5-4.

Using the Name Box in the formula bar to name a range is a useful tool for many worksheet tasks. For example, if you name a cell or range of cells that you select often, you then can select the cell or range of cells by clicking the name in the Name Box list.

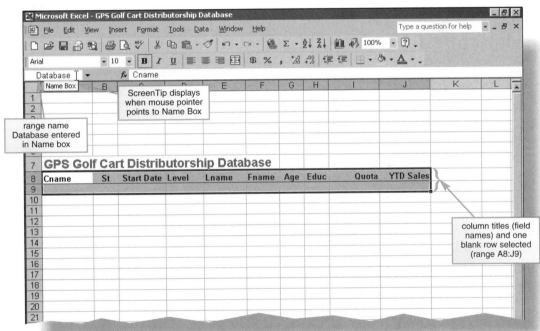

FIGURE 5-4

Entering Records into the Database Using a Data Form

The next step is to use a data form to enter the distributors' records. A **data form** is an Excel dialog box that lists the field names in the database and provides corresponding boxes in which you enter the field values. The steps on the next page add the distributors' records to the database. As indicated earlier, the computational fields in columns K and L will be added after the data is in the database.

More About

Naming Ranges

An alternative to using the Name box in the formula bar to name a cell or range of cells is to use the Define command. To access the Define command, point to Name on the Insert menu and then click Define on the Name submenu.

More About

Names

If you delete columns or rows from the range defined as Database, Excel automatically adjusts the range of the name Database.

Microsoft **Excel 2002**

Steps To Enter Records into a Database Using a Data Form

1 **Click cell A9 to deselect the range A8:J9. Click Data on the menu bar and then point to Form.**

The Data menu displays (Figure 5-5).

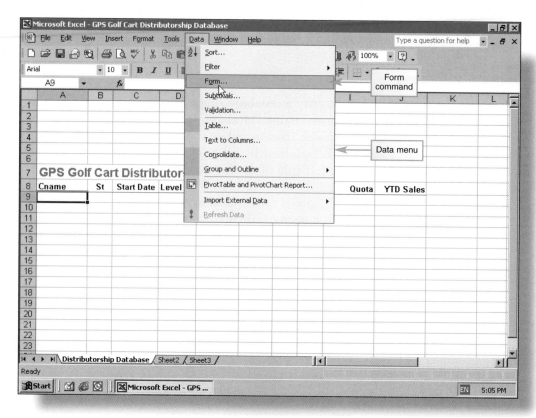

FIGURE 5-5

2 **Click Form.**

Excel displays the data form (Figure 5-6) with the sheet name Distributorship Database on the title bar. The data form automatically includes the field names and corresponding text boxes for entering the field values. Excel selects the field names in the range A8:J8 because they comprise the top row in the range named Database.

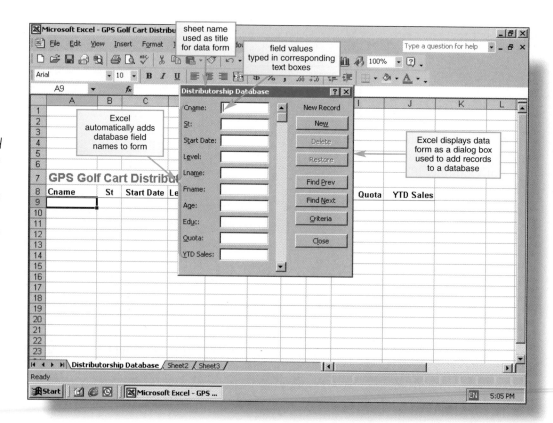

FIGURE 5-6

3 Enter the first distributor's record into the data form as shown in Figure 5-7. Use the mouse or the TAB key to move the insertion point down to the next text box. If you make a mistake, use the mouse or the SHIFT+TAB keys to move the insertion point to the previous text box in the data form to edit the entry. Point to the New button.

The first record displays in the data form (Figure 5-7).

FIGURE 5-7

4 Click the New button. Type the second distributor's record into the data form as shown in Figure 5-8. Point to the New button.

Excel adds the first distributor's record to row 9 in the database range on the worksheet. The second distributor's record displays in the data form (Figure 5-8).

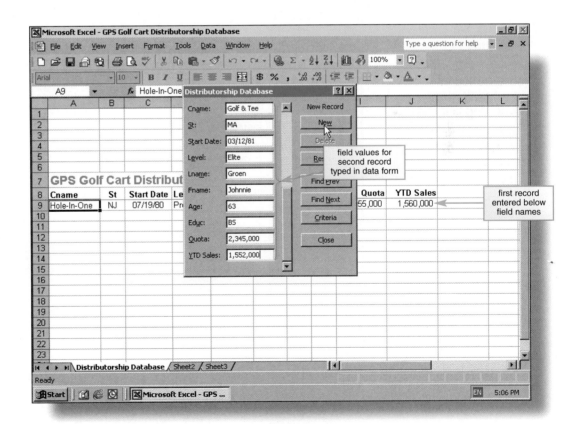

FIGURE 5-8

5 Click the New button to enter the second distributor's record. Use the data form to enter the next nine records in rows 11 through 19, as shown in Figure 5-1 on page E 5.05. Type the last distributor's record into the data form as shown in Figure 5-9. Point to the Close button.

Excel enters the distributorship records into the database range as shown in Figure 5-9. The last record displays in the data form.

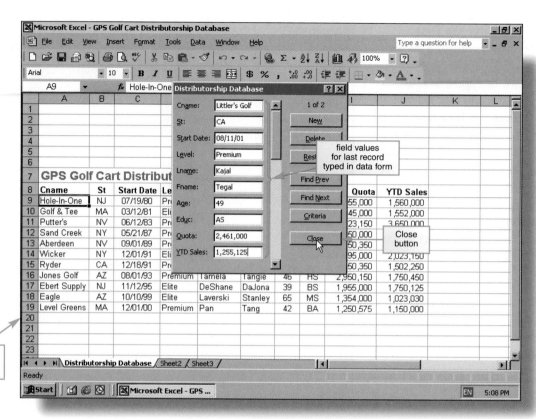

FIGURE 5-9

6 Click the Close button to complete the record entry. Click the Save button on the Standard toolbar to save the workbook using the file name, GPS Golf Cart Distributorship Database.

The data form closes and Excel enters the last distributorship record in row 20 of the database. The GPS Golf Cart Distributorship Database displays (Figure 5-10).

	Cname	St	Start Date	Level	Lname	Fname	Age	Educ	Quota	YTD Sales
8	Cname	St	Start Date	Level	Lname	Fname	Age	Educ	Quota	YTD Sales
9	Hole-In-One	NJ	07/19/80	Premium	Dexter	Ryan	56	MS	1,455,000	1,560,000
10	Golf & Tee	MA	03/12/81	Elite	Groen	Johnnie	63	BS	2,345,000	1,552,000
11	Putter's	NV	06/12/83	Premium	Graciela	Miranda	66	MS	4,123,150	3,650,000
12	Sand Creek	NY	05/21/87	Premium	James	Kevin	54	HS	1,250,000	995,000
13	Aberdeen	NV	09/01/89	Premium	Quintero	Carlos	51	AS	2,150,350	1,875,000
14	Wicker	NY	12/01/91	Elite	Primus	Montrell	42	MS	2,095,000	2,023,150
15	Ryder	CA	12/18/91	Premium	Vashan	Zachary	38	MS	1,850,350	1,502,250
16	Jones Golf	AZ	08/01/93	Premium	Tamela	Tangie	46	HS	2,950,150	1,750,450
17	Ebert Supply	NJ	11/12/95	Elite	DeShane	DaJona	39	BS	1,955,000	1,750,125
18	Eagle	AZ	10/10/99	Elite	Laverski	Stanley	65	MS	1,354,000	1,023,030
19	Level Greens	MA	12/01/00	Premium	Pan	Tang	42	BA	1,250,575	1,150,000
20	Littler's Golf	CA	08/11/01	Premium	Kajal	Tegal	49	AS	2,461,000	1,255,125

all records entered in GPS Golf Cart Distributorship Database

FIGURE 5-10

You also could create the database by entering the records in columns and rows as you would enter data into any worksheet and then assign the name Database to the range (A8:J20). The data form was illustrated here because it is considered to be a more accurate and reliable method of data entry. It also automatically extends the range of the name Database to include any new records.

Moving from Field to Field in a Data Form

You can move from field to field in a data form using the TAB key, or you can hold down the ALT key and press the key that corresponds to the underlined letter in the name of the field to which you want to move. An underlined letter in a field name is called an **access key**. Thus, to select the field titled Level in the form in Figure 5-9, you would hold down the ALT key and press the E key (ALT+E), because E is the access key for the field name, Level.

Adding Computational Fields to the Database

The next step is to add the computational fields % of Quota in column K and Grade in column L. Then the name Database must be changed from the range A8:J20 to A8:L20 so it includes the two new fields.

Adding New Field Names and Determining the % of Quota

The first step in adding the two new fields is to enter and format the two field names in cells K8 and L8, and then enter the first % of Quota formula in cell K9. The formula for the % of Quota in cell K9 is YTD Sales / Quota or =J9 / I9. Once the formula is entered in cell K9, the formula must be copied to the range K10:K20 as shown in the following steps.

More About

The Watchdog

Excel always is watching what you are doing. If you enter the data into the database as you entered worksheets in past projects, you will notice Excel entering data automatically for you, based on the data entered into the column. For example, in the Educ column in Figure 5-11, if you type the letter H in cell H21, Excel will display HS in the cell. To toggle this feature off, click Options on the Tools menu, click the Edit tab, click the Enable AutoComplete for cell values check box to remove the check mark, and then click the OK button. You can also right-click an empty cell under a list of items in a column and click the Pick From List command on the shortcut menu. Excel will display a list of items in the column from which you can select to assign to cell H21.

Steps To Enter New Field Names and the % of Quota Formula

1 Select cell K8. **Type** % of Quota **as the new field name. Select cell L8 and then type** Grade **as the new field name. Click cell J8. Click the Format Painter button on the Standard toolbar. Drag through cells K8:L8. Select cell K9, type** =J9 / I9 **as the formula, and then click the Enter box in the formula bar.**

The new field names display in cells K8 and L8, and the result of the % of Quota formula displays in cell K9 (Figure 5-11).

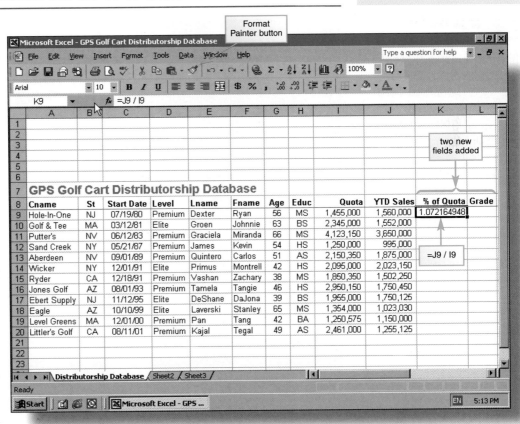

FIGURE 5-11

2 **With cell K9 selected, click the Percent Style button on the Formatting toolbar. Click the Increase Decimal button on the Formatting toolbar twice.**

The % of Quota in cell K9 displays using the Percent style format with two decimal places (Figure 5-12). The 107.22% indicates that Hole-In-One's sales have exceeded their quota.

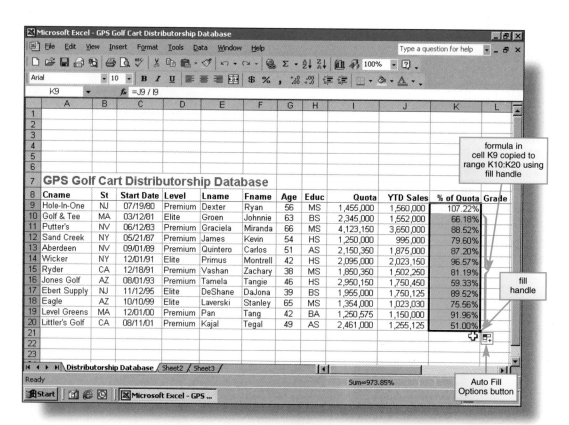

FIGURE 5-12

3 **With cell K9 selected, drag the fill handle down through cell K20.**

The % of Quota displays for each distributorship (Figure 5-13).

FIGURE 5-13

The entries in the % of Quota column give the user an immediate evaluation of where each distributor's YTD Sales stand in relation to their annual quota. Many people, however, dislike numbers as an evaluation tool. Most prefer simple letter grades, which when used properly can group the distributors in the same way an instructor groups students by letter grades. Excel contains functions that allow you to assign letter grades based on a table, as explained in the next section.

Using Excel's VLOOKUP Function to Determine Letter Grades

Excel has several lookup functions that are useful for looking up values in tables, such as tax tables, discount tables, parts tables, and grade scale tables. The two most widely used lookup functions are the HLOOKUP and VLOOKUP functions. Both functions look up a value in a table and return a corresponding value from the table to the cell assigned the function. The **HLOOKUP function** is used when the table direction is horizontal or across the worksheet. The **VLOOKUP function** is used when a table direction is vertical or down the worksheet. The VLOOKUP function is by far the most often used, because most tables are vertical, as is the table in this project.

The grading scale in this project (Table 5-2) is similar to one that your instructor uses to determine your letter grade. In Table 5-2, any score greater than or equal to 93% equates to a letter grade of A. Scores of 80 and less than 93 are assigned a letter grade of B, and so on.

The VLOOKUP function requires that the table indicate only the lowest score for a letter grade. Furthermore, the table entries must be in sequence from lowest score to highest score. Thus, the entries in Table 5-2 must be resequenced for use with the VLOOKUP function so they appear as in Table 5-3. The general form of the VLOOKUP function is:

=VLOOKUP(search argument, table range, column number)

The VLOOKUP function searches the leftmost column of a table (called the **table arguments**). In Table 5-3, the table arguments are the percents. The VLOOKUP function uses the % of Quota value (called the **search argument**) in the record of a distributor to search the leftmost column for a particular value and then returns the corresponding value from the specified column (called the **table values**). In this example, the table values are the grades in the second or rightmost column.

For the VLOOKUP function to work correctly, the table arguments must be in ascending sequence, because the VLOOKUP function will return a table value based on the search argument being less than or equal to the table arguments. Thus, if the % of Quota value is 79.60% (fourth record in database), then the VLOOKUP function returns a grade of C, because 79.60% is greater than or equal to 70% and less than 80%.

The steps on the next page show how to enter the table elements in Table 5-3 in the worksheet and use the VLOOKUP function to determine the letter grade for each distributorship based on the company's % of Quota value.

More About

Lookup Functions

Lookup functions are powerful, useful, and interesting in the way they work. For additional information on lookup functions, enter vlookup in the Ask a Question box on the menu bar.

Table 5-2 Typical Grade Table

% OF QUOTA	GRADE
>=93%	A
80% to < 93%	B
70% to < 80%	C
60% to < 70%	D
0 to < 60%	F

Table 5-3 Typical Grade Table Modified for VLOOKUP Function

% OF QUOTA	GRADE
0	F
60%	D
70%	C
80%	B
93%	A

To Create a Lookup Table and Use the VLOOKUP Function to Determine Letter Grades

Steps

1 Click cell N1 and then enter Grade Table as the table title. Click the Bold button on the Formatting toolbar. Drag through cell O1 and then click the Merge and Center button on the Formatting toolbar. Click cell N2. Enter the column titles and table entries in Table 5-3 on the previous page in the range N2:O7. Select column N and increase its width to 10.00. Click cell L8. Click the Format Painter button on the Standard toolbar. Drag through the range N2:O2. Select the range N3:O7 and click the Center button on the Formatting toolbar. Click cell L9 to deselect the range N3:O7.

The table displays as shown in Figure 5-14.

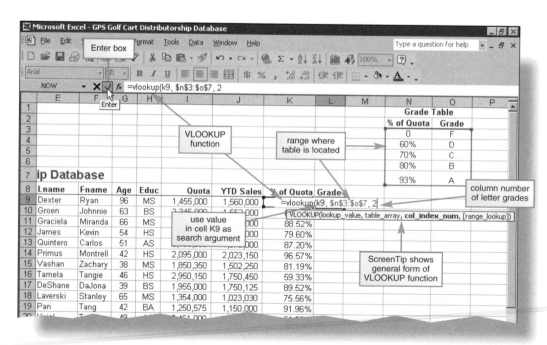

FIGURE 5-14

2 Type =vlookup (k9, n3:o7, 2 in cell L9 and then point to the Enter box in the formula bar.

The VLOOKUP function displays in the cell and in the formula bar (Figure 5-15). In this case, cell K9 is the search argument; n3:o7 is the table range; and 2 is the column number in the table range.

FIGURE 5-15

3 **Click the Enter box.**

The VLOOKUP function returns to cell L9 a grade of A for a % of Quota value in cell K9 of 107.22% (Figure 5-16).

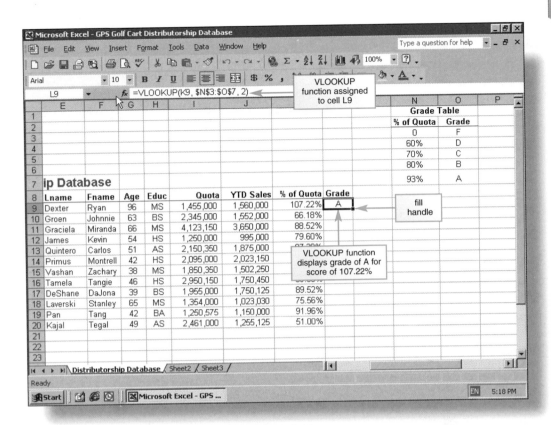

FIGURE 5-16

4 **With cell L9 selected, drag the fill handle through cell L20 to copy the function to the range L10:L20.**

The VLOOKUP function returns the grades shown in column L from the table of grades in columns N and O for the corresponding % of Quota values in column K (Figure 5-17). The Auto Fill Options button displays.

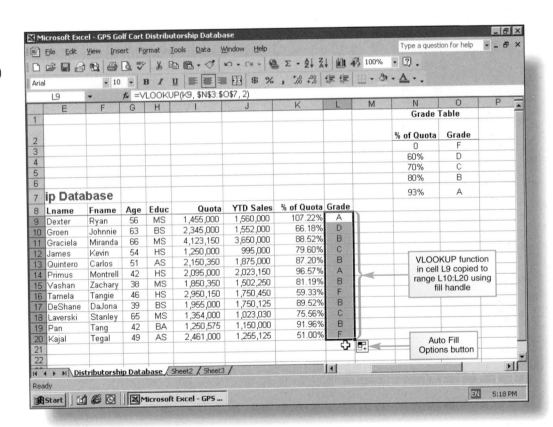

FIGURE 5-17

5 **Select cell A22 to deselect the range L9:L20. Scroll down until row 7 is at the top of the window.**

The entries for the GPS Golf Cart Distributorship database are complete (Figure 5-18).

FIGURE 5-18

As shown in Figure 5-18, any % of Quota value in column K below 60 returns a grade of F in column L. Thus, the eighth record (Jones Golf) receives a grade of F because its % of Quota value is 59.33%. A percent of 60 is required to move up to the next letter grade. The next to the last record (Level Greens) receives a grade of B because its % of Quota value is 91.96%, which is equal to or greater than 80% and less than 93%.

From column L in Figure 5-17 on the previous page, you can see that the VLOOKUP function is not searching for a table argument that matches the search argument exactly. The VLOOKUP function begins the search at the top of the table and works downward. As soon as it finds the first table argument greater than the search argument, it returns the previous table value. For example, when it searches the table with the fourth record (Sand Creek), it determines the % of Quota is less than 80% in the first column in the table and returns the grade of C from the second column in the table, which actually corresponds to 70% in the table. The letter grade of F is returned for any value greater than or equal to 0 (zero) and less than 60. A score less than 0 (zero) returns an error message (#N/A) to the cell assigned the VLOOKUP function.

It is most important that you use absolute cell references ($) for the table range ($N$3:$O$7) in the VLOOKUP function (see the entry in the formula bar shown in Figure 5-16 on the previous page) or Excel will adjust the cell references when you copy the function down through column L in Step 4. This will cause unexpected results in column L.

Redefining the Name Database

The final step in adding the two computational fields to the database is to redefine the name Database. Recall that it originally was defined as the range A8:J9 and it expanded automatically to the range A8:J20 by adding records through the use of the data form. To tie the two new fields to the database, the name Database must be redefined as the range A8:L20. The following steps show how to redefine the range assigned to a name.

More About

The VLOOKUP Function

A score that is outside the range of the table causes the VLOOKUP function to return an error message (#N/A) to the cell. For example, any % of Quota score less than zero in column K of Figure 5-18 would result in the error message being assigned to the corresponding cell in column L.

| Steps | **To Redefine the Name Database** |

1 **Click Insert on the menu bar. Point to Name and then point to Define on the Name submenu.**

The Insert menu and Name submenu display (Figure 5-19).

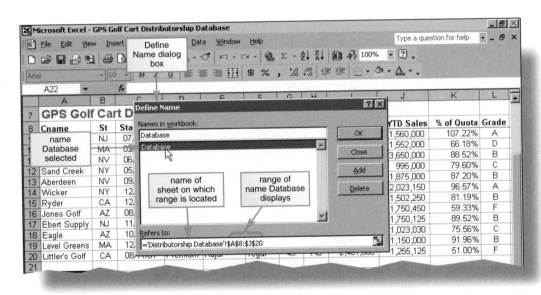

FIGURE 5-19

2 **Click Define. When the Define Name dialog box displays, click Database in the Names in workbook list.**

The Define Name dialog box displays with the name Database selected (Figure 5-20). The Refers to box at the bottom of the dialog box indicates the range assigned to the name Database.

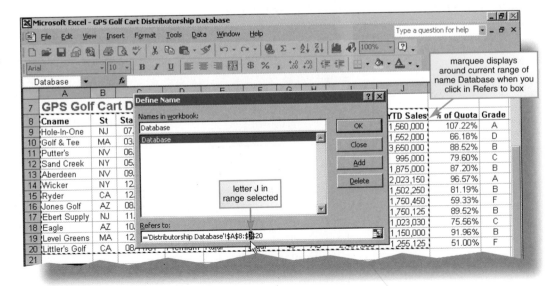

FIGURE 5-20

3 **Drag across the letter J in the Refers to box to select the letter J.**

Excel displays a marquee around the original range assigned to the name Database (Figure 5-21).

FIGURE 5-21

4 Type the letter L to replace the letter J in the Refers to box. Point to the OK button.

The new range in the Refers to box encompasses the two new fields in column K and L (Figure 5-22).

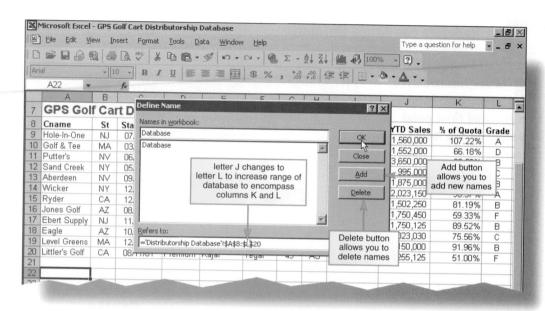

FIGURE 5-22

5 Click the OK button. Click the Name Box box arrow on the left side of the formula bar and then click the name Database.

Excel selects the new range (A8:L20) assigned to the name Database (Figure 5-23).

6 Select cell A21 to deselect the range A8:L20. Click the Save button on the Standard toolbar to save the workbook.

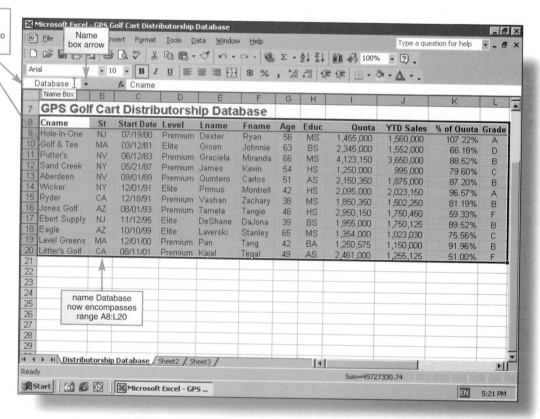

FIGURE 5-23

other_ways

Other Ways

1. Press ALT+I, N, D
2. In Voice Command mode, say "Insert, Name, Define, Database, [enter new range], OK"

Not only can you use the Define Name dialog box in Figure 5-22 to redefine names, you also can use it to define new names through the use of the **Add button,** and you can delete names through the use of the **Delete button.** As shown in Figure 5-23, names are useful in a workbook to select ranges quickly to manipulate them.

Guidelines to Follow When Creating a Database

When you create a database in Excel, you should follow some basic guidelines, as listed in Table 5-4.

Table 5-4 Guidelines for Creating a Database

DATABASE SIZE AND WORKBOOK LOCATION

1. Do not enter more than one database per worksheet.

2. Maintain at least one blank row between a database and other worksheet entries.

3. Do not store other worksheet entries in the same rows as your database.

4. Define the name, Database, as the database range.

5. A database can have a maximum of 256 fields and 65,536 records on a worksheet.

COLUMN TITLES (FIELD NAMES)

1. Place column titles (field names) in the first row of the database.

2. Do not use blank rows or rows with dashes to separate the column titles (field names) from the data.

3. Apply a different format to the column titles and the data. For example, bold the column titles and display the data below the column titles using a regular style.

4. Column titles (field names) can be up to 32,767 characters in length. The column titles should be meaningful.

CONTENTS OF DATABASE

1. Each column should have similar data. For example, company start date should be in the same column for all companies.

2. Format the data to improve readability, but do not vary the format of the data in a column.

Using a Data Form to View Records and Change Data

At anytime while the worksheet is active, you can use the **Form command** on the Data menu to display records, add new records, delete records, and change the data in records.
When a data form is opened initially, Excel displays the first record in the database. To display the seventh record as shown in Figure 5-24, press the ENTER key, the DOWN ARROW key, or click the Find Next button until the seventh record displays. Each time you

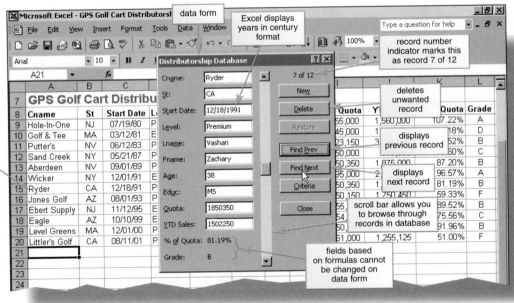

FIGURE 5-24

click the **Find Next button,** Excel advances to the next record in the database. If necessary, you can use SHIFT+ENTER, the UP ARROW key, or the **Find Prev button** to go back to a previous record. You also can use the vertical scroll bar in the middle of the data form to move between records.

To change data in a record, you first display it on a data form. Next, you select the fields to change. Finally, you use the DOWN ARROW key or the ENTER key to confirm or enter the field changes. If you change field values on a data form and then select the Find Next button to move to the next record without entering the field changes, these changes will not be made.

To add a new record, click the **New button** in the data form. Excel automatically adds the new record to the bottom of the database and increases the range assigned to the name Database. To delete a record, you first display it on a data form and then click the **Delete button.** Excel automatically moves all records below the deleted record up one row and appropriately redefines the range of the name Database.

Sorting a Database

The data in a database is easier to work with and more meaningful if the records are arranged sequentially based on one or more fields. Arranging records in a specific sequence is called **sorting.** Data is in **ascending sequence** if it is in order from lowest to highest, earliest to most recent, or alphabetically from A to Z. For example, the records in the GPS Golf Cart Distributorship database were entered in order from the earliest start date to the most recent start date. Thus, the database shown in Figure 5-25 is sorted in ascending sequence by start date. Data is in **descending sequence** if it is sorted from highest to lowest, most recent to earliest, or alphabetically from Z to A.

You can sort data by clicking the **Sort Ascending button** or **Sort Descending button** on the Standard toolbar or by clicking the **Sort command** on the Data menu. If you are sorting on a single field (column), use one of the Sort buttons on the Standard toolbar. If you are sorting on multiple fields, use the Sort command on the Data menu. If you use a button to sort, make sure you select a cell in the field on which to sort before you click the button. The field or fields you select to sort the records are called **sort keys.** The first sort example reorders the records by company name in ascending sequence.

Sorting the Database in Ascending Sequence by Company Name

Follow these steps to sort the records in ascending sequence by company name.

More About

Sorting

Excel uses the following order of priority: numbers from smallest to largest positive, (space), special characters, text, blanks. For example, the order is: 0 1 2 3 4 5 6 7 8 9 (space) ! " # $ % & ( ) * , . / : ; ? @ [\ ] ^ _ ` { | } ~ + < = > A B C D E F G H I J K L M N O P Q R S T U V W X Y Z (blanks).

More About

Sorting Hidden Columns and Rows

When you sort rows, hidden rows are not moved, but the data in hidden columns is sorted. It is recommended that you unhide any hidden rows and columns before you sort.

Steps To Sort a Database in Ascending Sequence by Company Name

1 Click cell A9 and then point to the Sort Ascending button on the Standard toolbar (Figure 5-25).

cell selected in column on which to sort

	A	B	C	D	E	F	G	H	I	J	K	L
7	**GPS Golf Cart Distributorship Database**											
8	**Cname**	**St**	**Start Date**	**Level**	**Lname**	**Fname**	**Age**	**Educ**	**Quota**	**YTD Sales**	**% of Quota**	**Grade**
9	Hole-In-One	NJ	07/19/80	Premium	Dexter	Ryan	56	MS	1,455,000	1,560,000	107.22%	A
10	Golf & Tee	MA	03/12/81	Elite	Groen	Johnnie	63	BS	2,345,000	1,552,000	66.18%	D
11	Putter's	NV	06/12/83	Premium	Graciela	Miranda	66	MS	4,123,150	3,650,000	88.52%	B
12	Sand Creek	NY	05/21/87	Premium	James	Kevin	54	HS	1,250,000	995,000	79.60%	C
13	Aberdeen	NV	09/01/89	Premium	Quintero	Carlos	51	AS	2,150,350	1,875,000	87.20%	B
14	Wicker	NY	12/01/91	Elite	Primus	Montrell	42	HS	2,095,000	2,023,150	96.57%	A
15	Ryder	CA	12/18/91	Premium	Vashan	Zachary	38	MS	1,850,350	1,502,250	81.19%	B
16	Jones Golf	AZ	08/01/93	Premium	Tamela	Tangie	46	HS	2,950,150	1,750,450	59.33%	F
17	Ebert Supply	NJ	11/12/95	Elite	DeShane	DaJona	39	BS	1,955,000	1,750,125	89.52%	B
18	Eagle	AZ	10/10/99	Elite	Laverski	Stanley	65	MS	1,354,000	1,023,030	75.56%	C
19	Level Greens	MA	12/01/00	Premium	Pan	Tang	42	BA	1,250,575	1,150,000	91.96%	B
20	Littler's Golf	CA	08/11/01	Premium	Kajal	Tegal	49	AS	2,461,000	1,255,125	51.00%	F

FIGURE 5-25

2 Click the Sort Ascending button.

Excel sorts the distributorship database in ascending sequence by company name (Figure 5-26).

records sorted in ascending sequence by company name

	A	B	C	D	E	F	G	H	I	J	K	L
7	**GPS Golf Cart Distributorship Database**											
8	**Cname**	**St**	**Start Date**	**Level**	**Lname**	**Fname**	**Age**	**Educ**	**Quota**	**YTD Sales**	**% of Quota**	**Grade**
9	Aberdeen	NV	09/01/89	Premium	Quintero	Carlos	51	AS	2,150,350	1,875,000	87.20%	B
10	Eagle	AZ	10/10/99	Elite	Laverski	Stanley	65	MS	1,354,000	1,023,030	75.56%	C
11	Ebert Supply	NJ	11/12/95	Elite	DeShane	DaJona	39	BS	1,955,000	1,750,125	89.52%	B
12	Golf & Tee	MA	03/12/81	Elite	Groen	Johnnie	63	BS	2,345,000	1,552,000	66.18%	D
13	Hole-In-One	NJ	07/19/80	Premium	Dexter	Ryan	56	MS	1,455,000	1,560,000	107.22%	A
14	Jones Golf	AZ	08/01/93	Premium	Tamela	Tangie	46	HS	2,950,150	1,750,450	59.33%	F
15	Level Greens	MA	12/01/00	Premium	Pan	Tang	42	BA	1,250,575	1,150,000	91.96%	B
16	Littler's Golf	CA	08/11/01	Premium	Kajal	Tegal	49	AS	2,461,000	1,255,125	51.00%	F
17	Putter's	NV	06/12/83	Premium	Graciela	Miranda	66	MS	4,123,150	3,650,000	88.52%	B
18	Ryder	CA	12/18/91	Premium	Vashan	Zachary	38	MS	1,850,350	1,502,250	81.19%	B
19	Sand Creek	NY	05/21/87	Premium	James	Kevin	54	HS	1,250,000	995,000	79.60%	C
20	Wicker	NY	12/01/91	Elite	Primus	Montrell	42	HS	2,095,000	2,023,150	96.57%	A

FIGURE 5-26

Sorting a Database in Descending Sequence by Company Name

Follow the steps on the next page to sort the records in descending sequence by company name.

Other Ways

1. On Data menu click Sort, select field in Sort by list, click Ascending, click OK button
2. Press ALT+D, S
3. Select cell in column to sort, in Voice Command mode, say "Sort Ascending"

TO SORT A DATABASE IN DESCENDING SEQUENCE BY COMPANY NAME

1   If necessary, click cell A9 to select it.

2   Click the Sort Descending button on the Standard toolbar.

Excel sorts the distributorship database in descending sequence by company name (Figure 5-27).

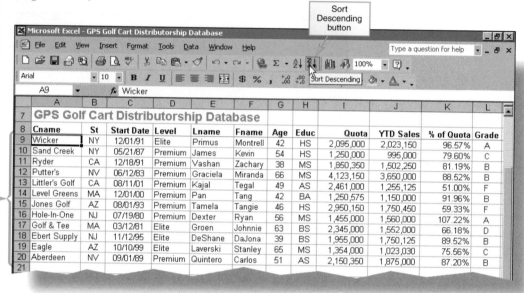

records sorted in descending sequence by company name

FIGURE 5-27

Returning a Database to Its Original Order

When you design a database, it is good practice to include a field that allows you to return the database to its original order. In the case of the GPS Golf Cart Distributorship database, the records were entered in sequence by start date. Follow these steps to return the records back to their original order in ascending sequence by start date.

TO RETURN A DATABASE TO ITS ORIGINAL ORDER

1   Click cell C9.

2   Click the Sort Ascending button on the Standard toolbar.

Excel sorts the GPS Golf Cart Distributorship database in ascending sequence by start date. The database displays in its original order (Figure 5-28).

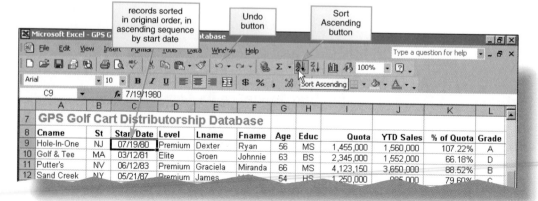

records sorted in original order, in ascending sequence by start date

Undo button

Sort Ascending button

FIGURE 5-28

You also can undo a sort operation by performing one of the following actions: (1) click the Undo button on the Standard toolbar; or (2) click the Undo Sort command on the Edit menu. If you have sorted the database more than once, you can click the Undo button multiple times to undo the previous sorts.

Sorting a Database on Multiple Fields

Excel allows you to sort on a maximum of three fields in a single sort operation. For instance, the sort example that follows uses the Sort command on the Data menu to sort the GPS Golf Cart Distributorship database by quota (column I) within education (column H) within level (column D). The Level and Educ fields will be sorted in ascending sequence; the Quota field will be sorted in descending sequence.

The phrase, sort by quota within education within level, means that the records first are arranged in ascending sequence by level (Premium and Elite). Within level, the records are arranged in ascending sequence by education (MS, BS, AS, and HS). Within education, the records are arranged in descending sequence by the distributor's quota.

In this case, level is the **major sort key** (Sort by field), education is the **intermediate sort key** (first Then by field), and quota is the **minor sort key** (second Then by field).

Follow these steps to complete the multiple-field sort using the Sort command on the Data menu.

 Steps To Sort a Database on Multiple Fields

1 **With a cell in the database active, click Data on the menu bar and then point to Sort.**

The Data menu displays (Figure 5-29).

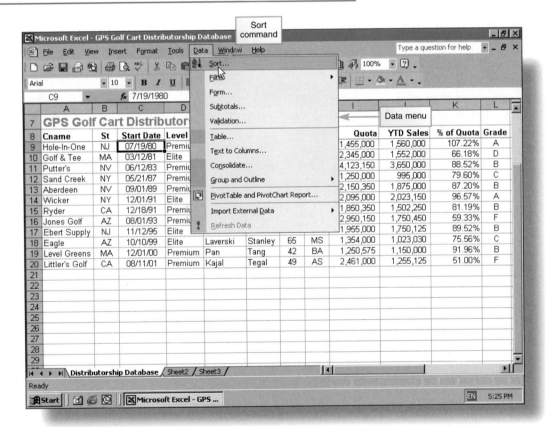

FIGURE 5-29

2 **Click Sort. When the Sort dialog box displays, click the Sort by box arrow and then point to Level.**

Excel selects the database on the worksheet, and the Sort dialog box displays. The Sort by list includes the field names in the database (Figure 5-30).

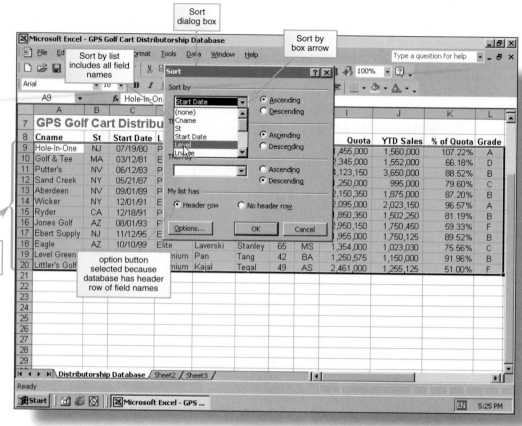

FIGURE 5-30

3 **Click Level. Click the first Then by box arrow and then click Educ. Click the second Then by box arrow and then click Quota. Click Descending in the second Then by area. Point to the OK button.**

The Sort dialog box displays (Figure 5-31). The database will be sorted by quota within education within level.

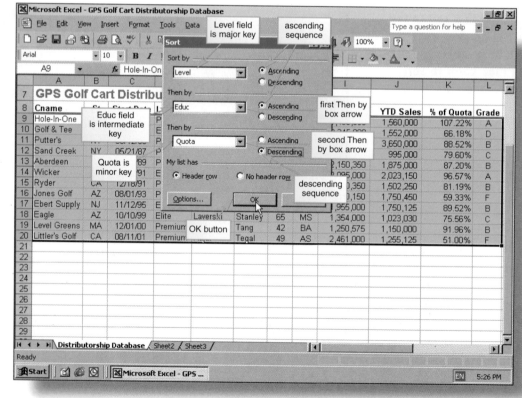

FIGURE 5-31

4 **Click the OK button.**

Excel sorts the GPS Golf Cart Distributorship database by quota within education within level as shown in Figure 5-32.

5 **When you are finished viewing the sorted database and with cell C9 selected, click the Sort Ascending button to sort the database into its original sequence.**

FIGURE 5-32

As shown in Figure 5-32, Excel sorts the records in ascending sequence by level in column D. Within each level, the records are in ascending sequence by the education codes in column H. Finally, within the education codes, the records are sorted in descending sequence by the quotas in column I. Remember, if you make a mistake in a sort operation, you can return the records to their original order by clicking the Undo button on the Standard toolbar.

Because Excel sorts the database using the current order of the records, the previous example could have been completed by sorting on one field at a time using the Sort buttons on the Standard toolbar, beginning with the minor sort key.

Sorting a Database on More than Three Fields

To sort on more than three fields, you must sort the database two or more times. The most recent sort takes precedence. Hence, if you plan to sort on four fields, you sort on the three least important keys first and then sort on the major key. For example, if you want to sort on last name (Lname) within grade (Grade) within state (St) within level (Level), you first sort on Lname (second Then by column) within Grade (first Then by column) within St (Sort by column). After the first sort operation is complete, you sort on the Level field by clicking one of the cells in the Level column and then clicking the Sort Ascending button or Sort Descending button on the Standard toolbar.

Displaying Automatic Subtotals in a Database

Displaying **automatic subtotals** is a powerful tool for summarizing data in a database. Excel requires that you sort the database only on the field on which you want subtotals to be based, and then use the **Subtotals command** on the Data menu. When the Subtotal dialog box displays, you select the subtotal function you want to use.

Other Ways

1. Click cell in minor field column, click Sort Descending button, click cell in intermediate field column, click Sort Ascending button, click cell in major field, click Sort Ascending button

2. Press ALT+D, S

3. In Voice command mode, say "[select cell in minor field column], Sort Descending, [select cell in intermediate field column], Sort Ascending, [select cell in major field column], Sort Ascending"

More About

Sort Options

You can sort left to right across rows by clicking the Options button (Figure 5-30) and then clicking Sort left to right in the Orientation area. You also can click the Case sensitive check box, which would sort lower-case letters ahead of the same capital letters for an ascending sort.

Sort Algorithms

Numerous sort algorithms are used with computers, such as the Insertion sort, Selection sort, Bubble sort, Shaker sort, and Shell Sort. For additional information on sort algorithms, visit the Excel 2002 More About Web page (scsite.com/ex2002/more.htm) click Sort Algorithms.

The field on which you sort prior to invoking the Subtotals command is called the **control field**. When the control field changes, Excel displays a subtotal for the numeric fields you select in the Subtotal dialog box. For example, if you sort on the St field and request subtotals for the Quota and YTD Sales fields, then Excel recalculates the subtotal and grand total each time the St field changes to a new state. The most common subtotal used with the Subtotals command is the SUM function, which displays a sum each time the control field changes.

In addition to displaying subtotals, Excel also creates an outline for the database. The following steps show you how to display subtotals for the Quota field and YTD Sales field by state.

Steps To Display Subtotals in a Database

1 **Select cell B9. Click the Sort Ascending button on the Standard toolbar.**

The GPS Golf Cart Distributorship database displays in ascending sequence by state (Figure 5-33).

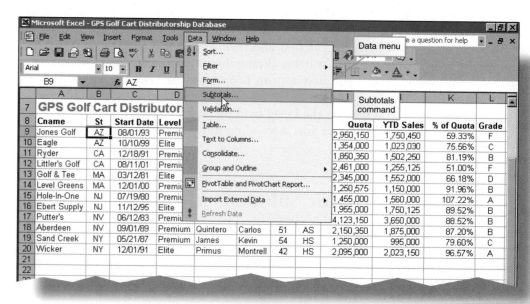

FIGURE 5-33

2 **Click Data on the menu bar and then point to Subtotals.**

The Data menu displays (Figure 5-34).

FIGURE 5-34

3 **Click Subtotals. When the Subtotal dialog box displays, click the At each change in box arrow and then click St. If necessary, select Sum from the Use function list. Click the Quota and YTD Sales check boxes in the Add subtotal to list. Point to the OK button.**

The Subtotal dialog box displays (Figure 5-35). The At each change in box contains the St field. The Use function box contains Sum. In the Add subtotal to box, both Quota and YTD Sales are selected.

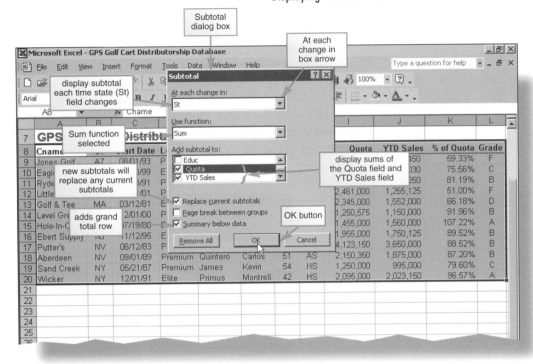

FIGURE 5-35

4 **Click the OK button. If number signs (#) display in row 27, select columns I and J and then double-click the right boundry of column heading J.**

Excel inserts seven new rows in the GPS Golf Cart Distributorship database. Six of the new rows contain Quota and YTD Sales subtotals for each state (Figure 5-36). The seventh new row displays grand totals for the Quota and YTD Sales fields. Excel also outlines the database, which causes the right-most column to be outside the window.

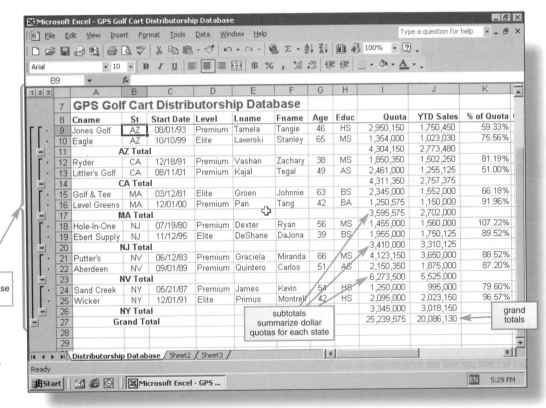

FIGURE 5-36

Other Ways

1. In Voice Command mode, say "[select cell in column to sort], Sort Ascending, Data, Subtotals, [select subtotal characteristics], OK"

As shown in Figure 5-36 on the previous page, Excel has added six subtotal rows and one grand total row to the database. The names for each subtotal row are derived from the state names, which display in bold. Thus, in cell B11 of row 11 the text, AZ Total, names the Quota and YTD Sales totals for Arizona.

In Figure 5-35 on the previous page, the Use function box contains Sum, which instructs Excel to sum the fields selected in the Add subtotal to list. Additional functions are available by clicking the Use function box arrow. The frequently used subtotal functions are listed in Table 5-5.

Table 5-5 Frequently Used Subtotal Functions	
SUBTOTAL FUNCTION	DESCRIPTION
Sum	Sums a column
Count	Counts the number of entries in a column
Average	Determines the average of numbers in a column
Max	Determines the maximum value in a column
Min	Determines the minimum value in a column

Zooming Out on a Worksheet and Hiding and Showing Detail Data in a Subtotaled Database

The following steps show how to use the Zoom box on the Standard toolbar to reduce the magnification of the worksheet so that all fields display. The steps also illustrate how to use the outline features of Excel to display only the total rows.

Steps To Zoom Out on a Worksheet and Hide and Show Detail Data in a Subtotaled Database

1 **Click the Zoom box on the Standard toolbar. Type** 90 **and then press the ENTER key. Select columns I and J. Double-click the right boundary of column heading J to ensure the grand totals display in row 27. Select cell B9 to deselect the range I and J.**

Excel reduces the magnification of the worksheet so that all columns in the database display (Figure 5-37).

FIGURE 5-37

2 Click the row level 2 symbol on the left side of the screen.

Excel hides all detail rows and displays only the subtotal and grand total rows (Figure 5-38).

3 Click the row level 3 symbol on the left side of the screen to display hidden detail rows. Click the Zoom box arrow on the Standard toolbar and then click 100% in the list.

Excel displays the worksheet in normal size (Figure 5-36 on page E 5.29).

4 Change the width of columns I and J back to 11.00.

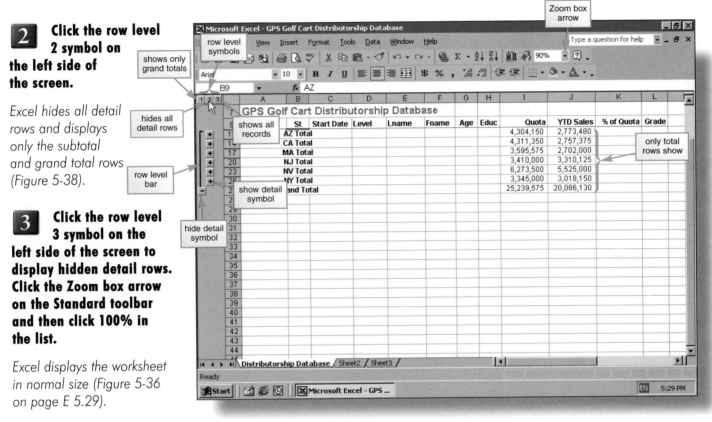

FIGURE 5-38

By utilizing the **outlining features** of Excel, you quickly can hide and show detail data. As described in Step 2, you can click the **row level symbols** to expand or collapse the worksheet. Row level symbol 1 hides all rows except the Grand Total row. Row level symbol 2 hides the detail records so the subtotal and grand total rows display as shown in Figure 5-38. Row level symbol 3 displays all rows.

The minus and plus symbols to the left on the row level bar in Figure 5-38 are called the show detail symbol (+) and hide detail symbol (-). If you click the **show detail symbol** (+), Excel displays the hidden detail records. If you click the **hide detail symbol** (-), Excel hides the detail records within the row level bar. The **row level bar** indicates which detail records will be hidden if you click the corresponding hide detail symbol.

You do not have to display subtotals to outline a worksheet. You can outline any worksheet by using the **Group and Outline command** on the Data menu.

Removing Subtotals from the Database

You can remove subtotals and the accompanying outline from a database in two ways: you can click the Undo button on the Standard toolbar, or you can click the **Remove All button** in the Subtotal dialog box. The steps on the next page show how to use the Remove All button to remove subtotals from a database.

More About

Outlining

When you hide data using the outline feature, you can chart the resulting rows and columns as if they were adjacent to one another. Thus, in Figure 5-38 you can chart the quotas by state as an adjacent range, even though they are not in adjacent rows when the worksheet displays in normal form.

Steps **To Remove Subtotals from a Database**

1 **Click Data on the menu bar and then click Subtotals. When the Subtotal dialog box displays, point to the Remove All button.**

Excel selects the database, and the Subtotal dialog box displays (Figure 5-39).

2 **Click the Remove All button.**

Excel removes all subtotal and total rows and the outline from the database so it displays as shown previously in Figure 5-33 on page E 5.28.

FIGURE 5-39

 Ways

1. Press ALT+D, B, ALT+R
2. In Voice Command mode, say "Data, Subtotals, Remove All"

As shown in the previous sections, Excel makes it easy to add and remove subtotals from a database. Thus, you can generate quickly the type of information that database users need to help them make decisions about products or a company's direction.

Before proceeding to the next section, complete the following steps to sort the GPS Golf Cart Distributorship database into its original order in ascending sequence by start date.

TO SORT THE DATABASE BY START DATE

1 Click cell C9.

2 Click the Sort Ascending button on the Standard toolbar.

The records in the GPS Golf Cart Distributorship database are sorted in ascending sequence by start date.

More *About*

Outlining

Use of the Group and Outline command on the Data menu is especially useful with large worksheets where the user can get lost in the sea of numbers. Outlining allows the user to hide the detail records to reduce the complexity of the worksheet.

Finding Records Using a Data Form

Once you have created the database, you might want to view records that meet only certain conditions, or comparison criteria. Comparison criteria are one or more conditions that include the field names and entries in the corresponding boxes in a data form. Displaying records that pass a test is called querying the database. For example, you can instruct Excel to find and display only those records that pass the test:

Level = Premium **AND** Age >= 48 **AND** Quota > 1,400,000 **AND** Grade = B

You use the same relational operators (=, <, >, >=, <=, and <>) to enter comparison criteria on a data form that you used to formulate conditions in IF functions. For a record to display in the data form, it must pass *all four parts* of the test. Finding records that pass a test is useful for viewing specific records, as well as maintaining the database. When a record that passes the test displays in the data form, you can change the field values or delete it from the database.

To find records in the database that pass a test comprised of comparison criteria, you can use the Find Prev and Find Next buttons together with the **Criteria button** in the data form. The following steps illustrate how to use a data form to find records that pass the test described above.

Steps **To Find Records Using a Data Form**

1 **Click Data on the menu bar and then click Form. When the data form displays, point to the Criteria button.**

The first record in the GPS Golf Cart Distributorship database displays in the data form (Figure 5-40).

FIGURE 5-40

2 **Click the Criteria button in the data form.**

Excel clears the field values in the data form and displays a data form with blank text boxes.

3 **Type** Premium **in the Level text box,** >=48 **in the Age text box,** >1,400,000 **in the Quota text box, and** B **in the Grade text box. Point to the Find Next button.**

The data form displays with the comparison criteria entered as shown in Figure 5-41.

FIGURE 5-41

4 **Click the Find Next button.**

Excel immediately displays the third record in the database because it is the first record that meets the comparison criteria (Figure 5-42). Putter's owner is 66 years old, her company has a Quota of $4,123,150, and her company received a grade of a B. The first two records in the database failed to meet one or more of the four criteria.

5 **Use the Find Next and Find Prev buttons to display the other record in the database that passes the test (Aberdeen). When you are finished displaying the record, click the Close button in the data form.**

FIGURE 5-42

1. Press ALT+D, O
2. In Voice Command mode, say "Data, Form, Criteria, [enter criteria], Find Next"

Two records in the database pass the test: record 3 (Putter's) and record 5 (Aberdeen). Each time you click the **Find Next button,** Excel displays the next record that passes the test. You also can use the **Find Prev button** to display the previous record that passed the test. If you click the Find Next button and the record displaying does not change, then no subsequent records in the database meet the criteria.

In Figure 5-41 on the previous page, no blank characters display between the relational operators and the values. As you enter comparison criteria, remember that leading or trailing blank characters have a significant impact on text comparisons.

You also should note that Excel is not **case-sensitive.** That is, Excel considers uppercase and lowercase characters in a comparison criterion to be the same. For example, the lowercase letter b is the same as uppercase letter B.

Using Wildcard Characters in Comparison Criteria

If you are querying on text fields, you can use **wildcard characters** to find records that contain certain characters in a field. Excel has two wildcard characters, the question mark (?) and the asterisk (*). The **question mark** (?) represents any single character in the same position as the question mark. For example, if the comparison criteria for Lname (last name) is =Quin?ero, then any last name must have the following to pass the test: Quin as the first four characters, any fifth character, and the letters ero as the last three characters. In this database, only Quintero (record 5 in row 13) passes the test.

An **asterisk** (*) can be used in a comparison criteria to represent any number of characters in the same position as the asterisk. Gr*, *i, Pr*s, are examples of valid text entries with the asterisk wildcard character. Querying the Lname field with Gr* means all text that begins with the letters Gr. Groen (record 2 in row 10) and Graciela (record 3 in row 11) pass the test (see Figure 5-25 on page E 5.23). Querying the Lname field with *i, means all text that ends with the letter i pass the test. Only Laverski (record 10 in row 18) passes the test. Querying the Lname field with Pr*s, means all text that begins with the letters Pr and ends with the letter s pass the test. Only Primus (record 6 in row 14) passes the test.

Using Computed Criteria

Using **computed criteria** to query a database involves using a formula in comparison criteria. For example, using the computed criterion > Quota / 100000 in the Age field in a data form finds all records whose Age field is greater than the corresponding Quota field divided by 100000.

More *About*

Wildcard Characters

If you want to search for a wildcard character (* or ?), precede the wildcard character with a tilde (~). For example, the criteria, mo10~?, finds mo10? and mo~*10 finds mo*10.

Filtering a Database Using AutoFilter

An alternative to using a data form to find records that meet comparison criteria is to use AutoFilter. Whereas the data form displays only one record at a time, **AutoFilter** displays all records that meet the criteria as a subset of the database. AutoFilter hides records that do not pass the test, thus displaying only those that pass the test.

To apply AutoFilter to a database, use the **Filter command** on the Data menu and the **AutoFilter command** on the **Filter submenu.** Excel responds by adding **AutoFilter arrows** that are arrows added directly to the cells containing the field names at the top of the database (row 8). Clicking an arrow displays a list of all the items in the field (column). If you select an item from the list, Excel immediately hides records that do not contain the item. The item you select from the list is called the **filter criterion.** If you then select a filter criterion from a second field, Excel displays a subset of the first subset.

The following steps show how to use AutoFilter to display those records in the GPS Golf Cart Distributorship database that pass the following test:

Level = Premium **AND** St = CA

Steps | To Apply AutoFilter to a Database

1 **Select any cell in the database. Click Data on the menu bar. Point to Filter on the Data menu and then point to AutoFilter on the Filter submenu.**

The Data Menu and the Filter submenu display (Figure 5-43).

FIGURE 5-43

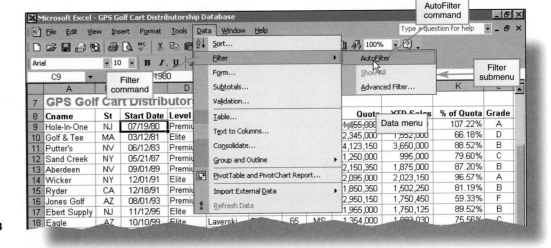

2 **Click AutoFilter.**

AutoFilter arrows display to the right of each field name in row 8 (Figure 5-44).

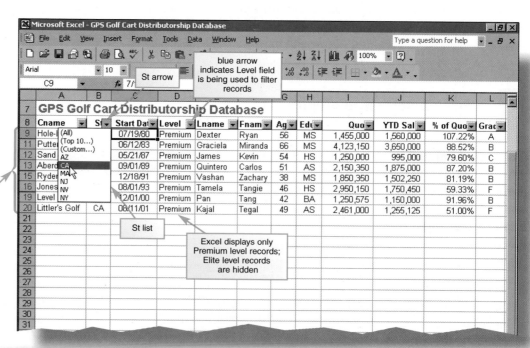

FIGURE 5-44

3 **Click the Level arrow and then point to Premium in the Level list.**

A list of the entries in the Level field displays (Figure 5-45). The entries (All), (Top 10…), and (Custom…) are found in every AutoFilter list. When you first click AutoFilter on the Filter submenu, the filter criteria for each field in the database is set to All. Thus, all records display.

FIGURE 5-45

4 **Click Premium. Click the St arrow and then point to CA in the list.**

Excel hides all records representing Elite level distributors, so that only records representing Premium level distributors display (Figure 5-46). The St list displays.

FIGURE 5-46

5 **Click CA.**

Excel hides all records representing Premium level distributors who do not live in California. As shown in Figure 5-47, only two records pass the filter criteria Level = Premium AND St = CA. Row headings 15 and 20 display in blue indicating the two rows are the result of a filtering process.

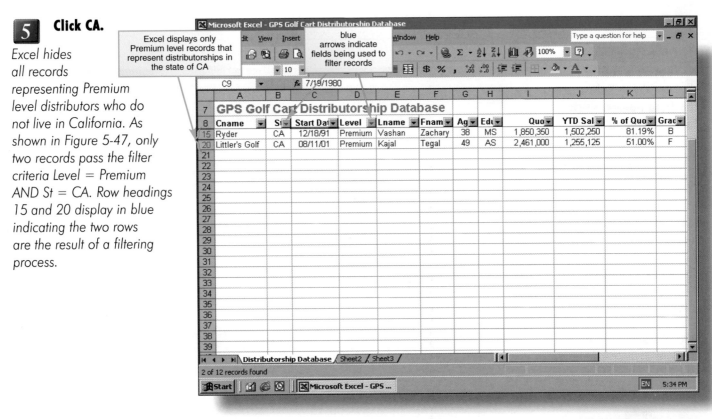

FIGURE 5-47

When you select a second filter criterion, Excel adds it to the first. Hence, in the case of the previous steps, each record must pass two tests to display as part of the final subset of the database. Other important points regarding AutoFilter include the following:

▸ When AutoFilter is active, Excel displays the AutoFilter arrows used to establish the filter and the row headings of the selected records in blue.
▸ Select a cell within the database prior to invoking AutoFilter.
▸ If a single cell is selected prior to applying AutoFilter, Excel assigns arrows to all field names in the database. If you select certain field names, Excel assigns arrows to only the selected field names.
▸ To remove a filter criteria for a single field, select the All option from the list for that field.
▸ If you plan to have Excel determine automatic subtotals for a filtered database, apply AutoFilter first and then apply Subtotals because Excel does not recalculate after selecting the filter criteria.

Removing AutoFilter

The AutoFilter command on the Filter submenu is like a **toggle switch.** That is, if you click it once, Excel adds the AutoFilter arrows to the field names in the database. If you click it again, Excel removes the arrows from the field names and displays all records in the database. If you want to keep the arrows but display all the records, click the **Show All command** on the Filter submenu.

The steps on the next page show how to display all records and remove the AutoFilter arrows from the field names by clicking AutoFilter on the Filter submenu.

Other Ways

1. Press ALT+D, F, F
2. In Voice Command mode, say "Data, Filter, AutoFilter, [select criteria]"

More About

Protected Worksheets

The Sort, Subtotals, and AutoFilter commands are unavailable if the worksheet or workbook is protected.

Microsoft Excel 2002

Steps | To Remove AutoFilter

1 **Select a cell in the database below one of the field names. Click Data on the menu bar. Point to Filter and then point to AutoFilter on the Filter submenu.**

The Data menu and Filter submenu display (Figure 5-48).

2 **Click AutoFilter.**

All the records in the GPS Golf Cart Distributorship database display. The arrows to the right of the field names in row 8 disappear.

Other Ways

1. Press ALT+D, F, F
2. In Voice Command mode, say "Data, Filter, AutoFilter"

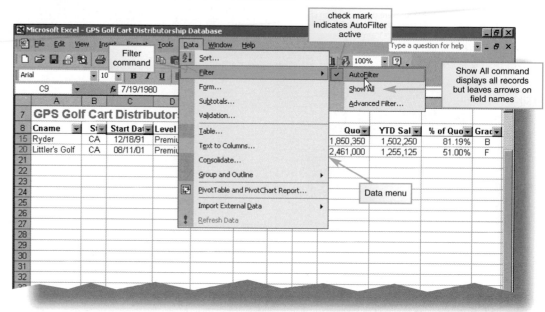

FIGURE 5-48

Entering Custom Criteria with AutoFilter

One of the options available in all of the AutoFilter lists is (Custom...). The (**Custom...**) option allows you to select custom criteria, such as multiple options or ranges of numbers. The following steps show how to enter custom criteria to display records in the database that represent distributors whose ages are in the range 46 to 55 inclusive ($46 \leq Age \leq 55$).

Steps | To Enter Custom Criteria

1 **Select cell A9. Click Data on the menu bar. Point to Filter and then click AutoFilter on the Filter submenu. Click the Age arrow and then point to (Custom...) in the Age list.**

The Age list displays (Figure 5-49).

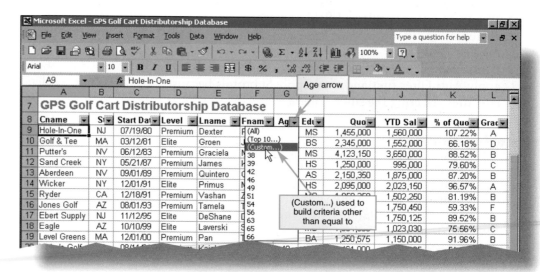

FIGURE 5-49

2 Click (Custom...). When the Custom AutoFilter dialog box displays, click the top left box arrow and then click is greater than or equal to. Type 46 in the top right box. Click the bottom left box arrow and then click is less than or equal to. Type 55 in the bottom right box. Point to the OK button.

The Custom AutoFilter dialog box displays (Figure 5-50). The And option button is selected by default.

FIGURE 5-50

3 Click the OK button.

The records in the database that represent distributors whose ages are between 46 and 55 inclusive display (Figure 5-51). Records that represent distributors whose ages are not between 46 and 55 inclusive are hidden.

4 After viewing the records that meet the custom criteria, point to Filter on the Data menu, and then click AutoFilter to display all the records in the database.

FIGURE 5-51

As shown in Figure 5-50, you can click the And option button or the Or option button to select the AND or the OR operator. The **AND operator** indicates that both parts of the criteria must be true; the **OR operator** indicates that only one of the two must be true. Use the AND operator when the custom criteria is continuous over a range of values, such as Age between 46 *AND* 55 inclusive ($46 \le Age \le 55$). Use the OR operator when the custom criteria is not continuous, such as Age less than or equal to 46 *OR* greater than or equal to 55 ($46 \ge Age \ge 55$).

As indicated at the bottom of the Custom AutoFilter dialog box in Figure 5-50, you can use wildcard characters to build custom criteria just as you can with data forms.

Using a Criteria Range on the Worksheet

Rather than using a data form or AutoFilter to establish criteria, you can set up a **criteria range** on the worksheet and use it to manipulate records that pass the comparison criteria. Using a criteria range on the worksheet involves two steps:

1. Create the criteria range and name it Criteria.
2. Use the Advanced Filter command on the Filter submenu.

Creating a Criteria Range on the Worksheet

To set up a criteria range, you first copy the database field names to another area of the worksheet. If possible, copy the field names above the database, in case the database is expanded downward or to the right in the future. Next, you enter the comparison criteria in the row immediately below the field names you just copied to the criteria range. You then use the Name Box in the formula bar to name the criteria range Criteria. The following steps show how to set up a criteria range in the range A2:L3 to find records that pass the test:

Level = Elite AND Age > 40 AND Grade ≥ C

A grade greater than or equal to C alphabetically means that distributorships with grades of C, D, and F pass the test.

> **More About**
>
> ### The AND and OR Operators
>
> AND means each and every one of the comparison criteria must be true. OR means only one of the comparison criteria must be true.

Steps To Set Up a Criteria Range on the Worksheet

1 Select the range A7:L8. Click the Copy button on the Standard toolbar. Select cell A1. Press the ENTER key to copy the contents on the Office Clipboard to the destination area A1:L2. Change the title in cell A1 to Criteria Area. Enter Elite in cell D3. Enter >40 in cell G3. Enter >=C in cell L3.

The worksheet displays as shown in Figure 5-52.

FIGURE 5-52

2 Select the range A2:L3. Click the Name box in the formula bar and then type Criteria as the range name. Press the ENTER key.

Excel defines the name Criteria to be the range A2:L3.

As you set up a criteria range, remember the following important points:

1. To ensure the field names in the criteria range are spelled exactly the same as in the database, copy and paste the database field names to the criteria range as shown in the previous set of steps.

2. The criteria range is independent of the criteria set up in a data form.

3. If you include a blank row in the criteria range (for example, rows 2 and 3 and the blank row 4), all records will pass the test.

4. You can print the criteria range by clicking Criteria in the Name Box list and then printing the selection.

Filtering a Database Using the Advanced Filter Command

The **Advanced Filter command** is similar to the AutoFilter command, except that it does not filter records based on comparison criteria you select from a list. The Advanced Filter command instead uses the comparison criteria set up in a criteria range (A2:L3) on the worksheet. Follow these steps to apply an Advanced Filter to display the records in the database that pass the test established in Figure 5-52 (Level = Elite and Age >40 and Grade ≥ C).

 To Apply an Advanced Filter to a Database

1 **Click Data on the menu bar. Point to Filter and then point to Advanced Filter on the Filter submenu.**

The Data menu and Filter submenu display (Figure 5-53).

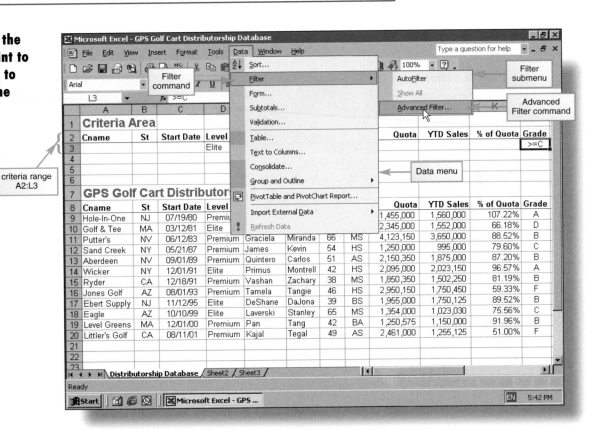

FIGURE 5-53

Click Advanced Filter. When the Advanced Filter dialog box displays, point to the OK button.

The Advanced Filter dialog box displays (Figure 5-54). In the Action area, the Filter the list, in-place option button is selected automatically. Excel automatically selects the database (range A8:L20) in the List range box, because it is named Database. Excel also selects the criteria range (A2:L3) in the Criteria range box, because the name Criteria was earlier assigned to the range A2:L3.

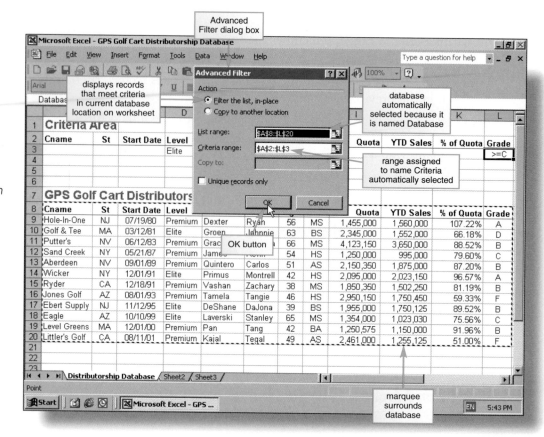

FIGURE 5-54

3 **Click the OK button.**

Excel hides all records that do not meet the comparison criteria, leaving only two records on the worksheet (Figure 5-55). Golf & Tee and Eagle are the only two distributors that are designated as Elite, older than 40, and have a grade of C, D, or F.

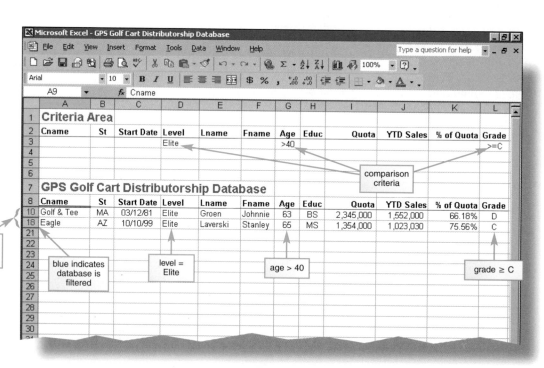

FIGURE 5-55

Other Ways

1. Press ALT+D, F, A

2. In Voice Command mode, say "Data, Filter, Advanced Filter, [select options], OK"

Like the AutoFilter command, the Advanced Filter command displays a subset of the database. The primary difference between the two is that the Advanced Filter command allows you to create more complex comparison criteria, because the criteria range can be as many rows long as necessary, allowing for many sets of comparison criteria.

To display all the records in the database, complete the following steps.

TO DISPLAY ALL RECORDS IN THE DATABASE

1 Click Data on the menu bar and then point to Filter.

2 Click Show All on the Filter submenu.

All the records in the database display.

Extracting Records

If you select the **Copy to another location option button** in the Action area of the Advanced Filter dialog box (Figure 5-54), Excel copies the records that meet the comparison criteria to another part of the worksheet, rather than displaying them as a subset of the database. The location where the records are copied is called the **extract range**. The extract range is set up much like the criteria range was set up earlier. Once the records that meet the comparison criteria in the criteria range are **extracted** (copied to the extract range), you can manipulate and print them as a group.

Creating an Extract Range and Extracting Records

To create an extract range, copy the field names of the database to an area on the worksheet, preferably well below the database range. Next, name this range Extract by using the Name Box in the formula bar. Finally, use the Advanced Filter command to extract the records. The steps on the next page show how to set up an extract range below the GPS Golf Cart Distributorship database and extract records that meet the following criteria, as entered in the Criteria area:

Level = Elite AND Age > 40 AND Grade $\geq$ C

Steps **To Create an Extract Range on the Worksheet and Extract Records**

1 **Select range A7:L8. Click the Copy button on the Standard toolbar. Select cell A24. Press the ENTER key to copy the contents on the Office Clipboard to the destination area A24:L25. Change the title in cell A24 to** Extract Area. **Select the range A25:L25. Type the name** Extract **in the Name box in the formula and then press the ENTER key. Select any cell. Click Data on the menu bar. Point to Filter and then point to Advanced Filter.**

The Data menu and the Filter submenu display (Figure 5-56). On the worksheet, the name Extract is assigned to only the field names in row 25. When the records are extracted, Excel automatically will copy the records to the rows below the range named Extract.

2 **Click Advanced Filter. When the Advanced Filter dialog box displays, click Copy to another location in the Action area. Point to the OK button.**

The Advanced Filter dialog box displays (Figure 5-57). Excel automatically assigns the range A8:L20 to the List range box because it is named Database. Excel automatically assigns the range named Criteria (A2:L3) to the Criteria range box and the range named Extract (A25:L25) to the Copy to box because they were named Criteria and Extract, respectively.

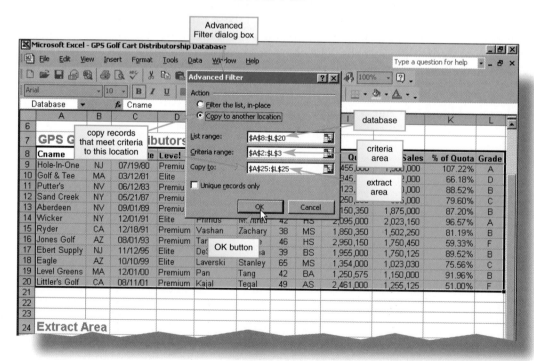

FIGURE 5-56

FIGURE 5-57

3 **Click the OK button.**

Excel copies any records that meet the comparison criteria in the criteria range (see Figure 5-55 on page E 5.42) from the database to the extract range (Figure 5-58).

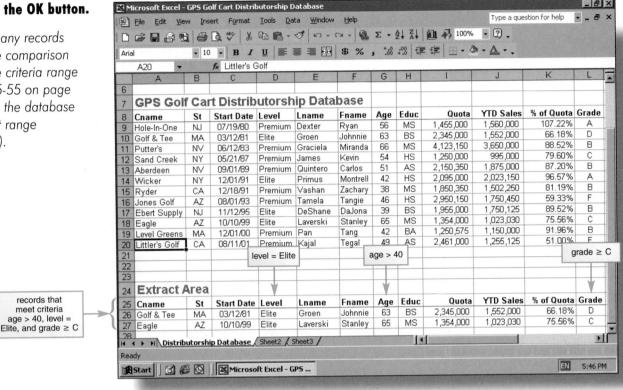

FIGURE 5-58

When you set up the extract range, you do not have to copy all of the field names in the database to the proposed extract range. Instead, you can copy only those field names you want, and they can be in any order. You also can type the field names rather than copy them, although this method is not recommended.

When you invoke the Advanced Filter command and select the Copy to another location option button, Excel clears all the cells below the field names in the extract range. Hence, if you change the comparison criteria in the criteria range and invoke the Extract command a second time, Excel clears the previously extracted records before it copies a new set of records that pass the new test.

In the previous example, the extract range was defined as a single row containing the field names (range A25:L25). When you define the extract range as just one row, any number of records can be extracted from the database; Excel will expand the extract range to include all rows below the first row (row 25) to the bottom of the worksheet, if needed. The alternative is to define an extract range with a fixed number of rows. If you define a fixed-size extract range, however, and if more records are extracted than there are rows available, Excel displays a dialog box with a diagnostic message indicating the extract range is full.

More about Comparison Criteria

The way you set up the comparison criteria in the criteria range determines the records that will pass the test when you use the AutoFilter command. The sections on the next page describe examples of different comparison criteria.

> ## More *About*
>
> ### The Criteria Area
>
> When you add items in multiple rows to a criteria area, you must redefine the range of the name Criteria before you use it. To redefine the name Criteria, delete the name using the Create command. To access the Create command, point to Name on the Insert menu and then click Create on the Name submenu. The Delete button in the Define Name dialog box allows you to delete names. Next, select the new Criteria area and name it Criteria using the Name box.

A Blank Row in the Criteria Range

If the criteria range contains a blank row, it means that no comparison criteria have been defined. Thus, all records in the database pass the test. For example, the blank row in the criteria range shown in Figure 5-59 means that all records will pass the test.

FIGURE 5-59

Using Multiple Comparison Criteria with the Same Field

If the criteria range contains two or more entries under the same field name, then records that pass either comparison criterion pass the test. For example, based on the criteria range shown in Figure 5-60, all records that represent distributors that work in AZ OR CA will pass the test.

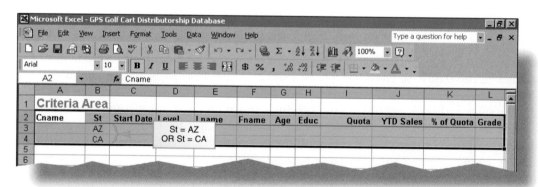

FIGURE 5-60

If an AND operator applies to the same field name (Age > 50 AND Age < 55), then you must duplicate the field name (Age) in the criteria range. That is, add the field name Age to the right of Grade (cell M2) and then adjust the range assigned to the name Criteria by using the Name command on the Insert menu.

Comparison Criteria in Different Rows and Under Different Fields

When the comparison criteria under different field names are in the same row, then records pass the test only if they pass all the comparison criteria. If the comparison criteria for the field names are in different rows, then the records must pass only one of the tests. For example, in the criteria range shown in Figure 5-61, distributors who are at the Premium level (Level = Premium) OR distributor owners who hold a Masters degree (Educ = MS) pass the test.

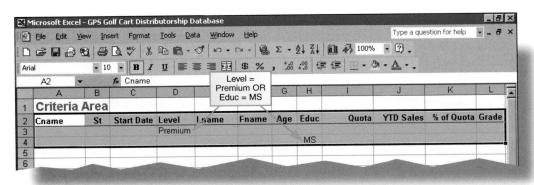

FIGURE 5-61

Using Database Functions

Excel has 12 database functions that you can use to evaluate numeric data in a database. One of the functions is called the DAVERAGE function. As the name implies, you use the **DAVERAGE function** to find the average of numbers in a database field that pass a test. This function serves as an alternative to finding an average using the Subtotals command on the Data menu. The general form of the DAVERAGE function is:

=DAVERAGE(database, "field name", criteria range)

where database is the name of the database, field name is the name of the field in the database, and criteria range is the comparison criteria or test to pass.

Another often used database function is the DCOUNT function. The **DCOUNT function** will count the number of numeric entries in a database field that pass a test. The general form of the DCOUNT function is:

=DCOUNT(database, "field name", criteria range)

where database is the name of the database, field name is the name of the field in the database, and criteria range is the comparison criteria or test to pass.

In the following steps the DAVERAGE function is used to find the average age of the owners of Elite level distributorships and the average age of the owners of Premium level distributorships in the database. The DCOUNT function is used to count the number of distributorship records that have a grade of F. The first step sets up the criteria areas that are required by these two functions.

> **More About**
>
> **Database Functions**
>
> Database functions are useful when working with lists of data, such as the one in this project. Remembering the function arguments and their order within parentheses is not easy. Thus, it is recommended that you use the Insert Function button in the formula bar to assign a database function to your worksheet.

TO USE THE DAVERAGE AND DCOUNT DATABASE FUNCTIONS

1 Click cell Q1 and enter Criteria for DB Functions as the criteria area title. Select the range Q1:S1 and click the Merge and Center button on the Formatting toolbar. Click the Bold button on the Formatting toolbar.

2 Select cell Q2 and enter Level as the field name. Select cell R2 and enter Level as the field name. Select cell S2 and enter Grade as the field name. Select cell L8. Click the Format Painter button on the Standard toolbar. Drag through the range Q2:S2. Enter Elite in cell Q3 as the code for Elite level distributors. Enter Premium in cell R3 as the code for Premium level distributors. Enter F in cell S3 as the grade.

3 Enter Average Elite Age = = = = = = = => in cell Q5. Enter Average Premium Age = = => in cell Q6. Enter Number with Grade F = = = = > in cell Q7.

4 Click cell T5. Enter the database function =daverage(database, "Age", Q2:Q3).

5   Click cell T6. Enter the database function =daverage(database, "Age", R2:R3).

6   Click cell T7. Enter the database function =dcount(database, "Age", S2:S3) in cell T7.

7   Select the range Q5:T7 and click the Bold button on the Formatting toolbar.

Excel computes and displays the average age of the Elite level distributors in the database (52.25) in cell T5, the average age of the Premium level distributors in the database (50.25) in cell T6, and a count of the distributorships who have a grade of F (2) in cell T7 (Figure 5-62).

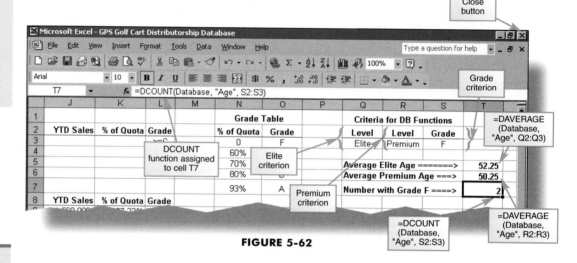

FIGURE 5-62

In Figure 5-62, the first value in the DCOUNT function, database, refers to the database defined earlier in this project (range A8:L20). The second value "Age" identifies the field on which to compute the average. The third value, S2:S3, is the criteria range for the grade count. In the case of the DCOUNT function, it is required that you select a numeric field to count. Excel requires that you surround the field name Age with quotation marks unless the field has been assigned a name through the Name Box in the formula bar.

Other database functions that are similar to the functions described in previous projects include the DMAX, DMIN, and DSUM functions. For a complete list of the database functions, click the Insert Function box in the formula bar. When the Insert Function dialog box displays, select Database in the Or select a category list. The database functions display in the Select a function box. If you click a database function name, Excel displays a description of the function above the OK button in the dialog box.

Printing the Worksheet and Saving the Workbook

To print the worksheet on one page and save the workbook, follow the steps below.

TO PRINT THE WORKSHEET AND SAVE THE WORKBOOK

1   Click File on the menu bar and then click Page Setup. Click the Page tab.

2   Click Landscape in the Orientation area. Click Fit to in the Scaling area.

3   Click the Print button. When the Print dialog box displays, click the OK button.

4 Click the Save button on the Standard toolbar to save the workbook using the file name, GPS Golf Cart Distributorship Database.

The worksheet prints on one page in landscape orientation (Figure 5-63).

Criteria Area

Cname	St	Start Date	Level	Lname	Fname	Age	Educ	Quota	YTD Sales	% of Quota	Grade
			Elite			>40					>=C

Grade Table

% of Quota	Grade
0	F
60%	D
70%	C
80%	B
93%	A

Criteria for DB Functions

Level	Level	Grade
Elite	Premium	F

Average Elite Age ========>   52.25
Average Premium Age ===>   55.25
Number with Grade F ====>   2

GPS Golf Cart Distributorship Database

Cname	St	Start Date	Level	Lname	Fname	Age	Educ	Quota	YTD Sales	% of Quota	Grade
Hole-In-One	NJ	07/19/80	Premium	Dexter	Ryan	96	MS	1,455,000	1,560,000	107.22%	A
Golf & Tee	MA	03/12/81	Elite	Groen	Johnnie	63	BS	2,345,000	1,552,000	66.18%	D
Putter's	NV	06/12/83	Premium	Graciela	Miranda	66	MS	4,123,150	3,650,000	88.52%	B
Sand Creek	NY	05/21/87	Premium	James	Kevin	54	HS	1,250,000	995,000	79.60%	C
Aberdeen	NV	09/01/89	Premium	Quintero	Carlos	51	AS	2,150,350	1,875,000	87.20%	B
Wicker	NY	12/01/91	Elite	Primus	Montrell	42	HS	2,095,000	2,023,150	96.57%	A
Ryder	CA	12/18/91	Premium	Vashan	Zachary	38	MS	1,850,350	1,502,250	81.19%	B
Jones Golf	AZ	08/01/93	Premium	Tamela	Tangie	46	HS	2,950,150	1,750,450	59.33%	F
Ebert Supply	NJ	11/12/95	Elite	DeShane	DaJona	39	BS	1,955,000	1,750,125	89.52%	B
Eagle	AZ	10/10/99	Elite	Laverski	Stanley	65	MS	1,354,000	1,023,030	75.56%	C
Level Greens	MA	12/01/00	Premium	Pan	Tang	42	BA	1,250,575	1,150,000	91.96%	B
Littler's Golf	CA	08/11/01	Premium	Kajal	Tegal	49	AS	2,461,000	1,255,125	51.00%	F

Extract Area

Cname	St	Start Date	Level	Lname	Fname	Age	Educ	Quota	YTD Sales	% of Quota	Grade
Golf & Tee	MA	03/12/81	Elite	Groen	Johnnie	63	BS	2,345,000	1,552,000	66.18%	D
Eagle	AZ	10/10/99	Elite	Laverski	Stanley	65	MS	1,354,000	1,023,030	75.56%	C

FIGURE 5-63

Quitting Excel

The project is complete. To quit Excel, follow the steps below.

TO QUIT EXCEL

1 Click the Close button on the right side of the title bar.

2 If the Microsoft Excel dialog box displays, click the No button.

More About

Printing

To print individual sections of the worksheet, click the Name box and then click the name of the section (Criteria, Database, or Extract) you want to print. On the File menu, click Print. When the Print dialog box displays, click Selection in the Print what area, and then click the OK button.

CASE PERSPECTIVE SUMMARY

The GPS Golf Cart Distributorship database created in this project will allow Clarissa Baldwin, the general manager, to generate information that will help her make decisions regarding the distributors that sell the GPS golf carts. She can sort the database to get different views, use a data form to display and change records, generate subtotals, and query the database using a data form, the Filter command, or the AutoFilter command. She also can use the database functions to generate additional information about the distributors.

Project Summary

In this project, you learned how to create, sort, and filter a database. Creating a database involves assigning the name, Database, to a range in the worksheet. You then can add, change, and delete records in the database through a data form. Sorting a database can be achieved using the Sort Ascending and Sort Descending buttons on the Standard toolbar or by using the Sort command on the Data menu.

Once a database is sorted, you can use the Subtotals command on the Data menu to generate subtotals that display within the database range. Filtering a database involves displaying a subset of the database or copying (extracting) records that pass a test. Finally, this project showed you how to use database functions and lookup functions.

What You Should Know

Having completed this project, you now should be able to perform the following tasks:

▶ Apply an Advanced Filter to a Database *(E 5.41)*

▶ Apply AutoFilter to a Database *(E 5.35)*

▶ Create a Lookup Table and Use the VLOOKUP Function to Determine Letter Grades *(E 5.16)*

▶ Create an Extract Range on the Worksheet and Extract Records *(E 5.44)*

▶ Display All Records in the Database *(E 5.43)*

▶ Display Subtotals in a Database *(E 5.28)*

▶ Enter Custom Criteria *(E 5.38)*

▶ Enter New Field Names and the % of Quota Formula *(E 5.13)*

▶ Enter Records into a Database Using a Data Form *(E 5.10)*

▶ Find Records Using a Data Form *(E 5.33)*

▶ Name the Database *(E 5.09)*

▶ Print the Worksheet and Save the Workbook *(E 5.48)*

▶ Quit Excel *(E 5.49)*

▶ Redefine the Name Database *(E 5.19)*

▶ Remove AutoFilter *(E 5.38)*

▶ Remove Subtotals from a Database *(E 5.32)*

▶ Return a Database to its Original Order *(E 5.24)*

▶ Set Up a Criteria Range on the Worksheet *(E 5.40)*

▶ Set Up a Database *(E 5.07)*

▶ Sort a Database in Ascending Sequence by Company Name *(E 5.23)*

▶ Sort a Database in Descending Sequence by Company Name *(E 5.24)*

▶ Sort a Database on Multiple Fields *(E 5.25)*

▶ Sort the Database by Start Date *(E 5.32)*

▶ Start and Customize Excel *(E 5.07)*

▶ Use the DAVERAGE and DCOUNT Database Functions *(E 5.47)*

▶ Zoom Out on a Worksheet and Hide and Show Detail Data in a Subtotaled Database *(E 5.30)*

Learn It Online

Instructions: To complete the Learn It Online exercises, start your browser, click the Address bar, and then enter scsite.com/offxp/exs.htm. When the Office XP Learn It Online page displays, follow the instructions in the exercises below.

1 Project Reinforcement TF, MC, and SA

Below Excel Project 5, click the Project Reinforcement link. Print the quiz by clicking Print on the File menu. Answer each question. Write your first and last name at the top of each page, and then hand in the printout to your instructor.

2 Flash Cards

Below Excel Project 5, click the Flash Cards link. When Flash Cards displays, read the instructions. Type 20 (or a number specified by your instructor) in the Number of Playing Cards text box, type your name in the Name text box, and then click the Flip Card button. When the flash card displays, read the question and then click the Answer box arrow to select an answer. Flip through Flash Cards. Click Print on the File menu to print the last flash card if your score is 15 (75%) correct or greater and then hand it in to your instructor. If your score is less than 15 (75%) correct, then redo this exercise by clicking the Replay button.

3 Practice Test

Below Excel Project 5, click the Practice Test link. Answer each question, enter your first and last name at the bottom of the page, and then click the Grade Test button. When the graded practice test displays on your screen, click Print on the File menu to print a hard copy. Continue to take practice tests until you score 80% or better. Hand in a printout of the final practice test to your instructor.

4 Who Wants to Be a Computer Genius?

Below Excel Project 5, click the Computer Genius link. Read the instructions, enter your first and last name at the bottom of the page, and then click the Play button. Hand in your score to your instructor.

5 Wheel of Terms

Below Excel Project 5, click the Wheel of Terms link. Read the instructions, and then enter your first and last name and your school name. Click the Play button. Hand in your score.

6 Crossword Puzzle Challenge

Below Excel Project 5, click the Crossword Puzzle Challenge link. Read the instructions, and then enter your first and last name. Click the Play button. Work the crossword puzzle. When you are finished, click the Submit button. When the crossword puzzle redisplays, click the Print button. Hand in the printout.

7 Tips and Tricks

Below Excel Project 5, click the Tips and Tricks link. Click a topic that pertains to Project 5. Right-click the information and then click Print on the shortcut menu. Construct a brief example of what the information relates to in Excel to confirm you understand how to use the tip or trick. Hand in the example and printed information.

online

8 Newsgroups

Below Excel Project 5, click the Newsgroups link. Click a topic that pertains to Project 5. Print three comments. Hand in the comments.

9 Expanding Your Horizons

Below Excel Project 5, click the Articles for Microsoft Excel link. Click a topic that pertains to Project 5. Print the information. Construct a brief example of what the information relates to in Excel to confirm you understand the contents of the article. Hand in the example and printed information.

10 Search Sleuth

Below Excel Project 5, click the Search Sleuth link. To search for a term that pertains to this project, select a term below the Project 5 title and then use the Google search engine at google.com (or any major search engine) to display and print two Web pages that present information on the term. Hand in the printout.

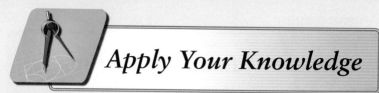

Apply Your Knowledge

1 Querying Moriarty's Machine Shop Employee Database

Instructions: Assume that the figures that accompany each of the following six problems make up the criteria range for the Moriarty's Machine Shop Employee database shown in Figure 5-64. Fill in the comparison criteria to select records from the database according to these problems. So that you understand better what is required for this assignment, the answer is given for the first problem. You can open the workbook, Moriarty's Machine Shop, from the Data Disk and use the Filter command to verify your answers.

12	Moriarty's Machine Shop Employee Database					
13	Employee	Dept	Trade	Gender	Age	Seniority
14	France, Phyllis	2	Laborer	F	38	2
15	Friar, Dean	1	Operator	M	43	13
16	Pole, Ty	3	Machinist	M	53	7
17	Washington, Ed	1	Operator	M	35	12
18	Swan, Hayley	2	Laborer	F	31	10
19	Jenkins, Mary	2	Operator	F	27	5
20	Wynn, Louis	1	Machinist	M	42	20
21	Ruiz, Pedro	3	Operator	M	35	6
22	Lee, Sun	1	Laborer	M	58	2
23	McGraw, Sue	3	Operator	F	25	0
24	Possi, Lisa	1	Laborer	F	45	17

Moriarty's Machine Shop / Sheet2 / Sheet3

Ready

Start | Microsoft Excel - Mori...

FIGURE 5-64

1. Select records that represent males who are at least 45 years old.

EMPLOYEE	DEPT	TRADE	GENDER	AGE	SENIORITY
			M	>=45	

2. Select records that represent a Laborer or Machinist.

EMPLOYEE	DEPT	TRADE	GENDER	AGE	SENIORITY

3. Select records that represent male members whose last names begin with the letter W and who work in department 1.

EMPLOYEE	DEPT	TRADE	GENDER	AGE	SENIORITY

4. Select records that represent female members who are at least 31 years old and have less than 10 years of seniority.

EMPLOYEE	DEPT	TRADE	GENDER	AGE	SENIORITY

5. Select records that represent female employees who work in department 1 or have at least 10 years of seniority.

EMPLOYEE	DEPT	TRADE	GENDER	AGE	SENIORITY

6. Select records that represent employees working in departments 1 or 2 who are at least 43 years old.

EMPLOYEE	DEPT	TRADE	GENDER	AGE	SENIORITY

In the Lab

1 Filtering and Sorting the J. Fox & Sons Clothing Sales Representative Database

Problem: You are a part-time work-study student at J. Fox & Sons Clothing, which supplies apparel to retail stores throughout the United States. The national sales force is divided into districts within divisions within regions. The three regions are the Eastern region (1), Midwest region (2), and Western region (3). The director of the Information Systems department has asked you to create a sales representative database (Figure 5-65), run queries against the database, generate various sorted reports, and generate subtotal information.

FIGURE 5-65

Instructions Part 1: Start Excel. Create the database shown in Figure 5-65 using the techniques learned in this project. In particular, enter and format the database title and field names in rows 6 and 7. Name the range A7:K8 Database. Use a data form to enter the data in rows 8 through 20. Enter your name, course number, laboratory assignment (Lab 5-1), date, and instructor name in the range A40:A44. Save the workbook using the file name Fox & Sons Clothing.

Instructions Part 2: Step through each filter exercise in Table 5-6 on the next page and print the results for each in portrait orientation using the Fit to option.

To complete a filter exercise, use the AutoFilter command. Select the appropriate arrow(s) and option(s) in the lists. Use the (Custom...) option for field names that do not contain appropriate selections. After printing the range name Database for each filtered solution, point to Filter on the Data menu and click Show All on the Filter submenu. After the last filter exercise, remove the AutoFilter arrows by clicking AutoFilter on the Filter submenu. You should end up with the following number of records for Filters 1 through 12: 1 = 4; 2 = 1; 3 = 4; 4 = 6; 5 = 4; 6 = 6; 7 = 2; 8 = 3; 9 = 2; 10 = 0; 11 = 1; and 12 = 13. When you are finished querying the database, close the workbook without saving changes.

(continued)

In the Lab

Filtering and Sorting the J. Fox & Sons Clothing Sales Representative Database *(continued)*

Table 5-6	J. Fox & Sons Clothing Sales Representative Database Filter Criteria										
FILTER	**REGION**	**DIVISION**	**DISTRICT**	**REP**	**LNAME**	**FNAME**	**GENDER**	**AGE**	**HIRE DATE**	**EDUC**	**SALES**
1	2	A									
2	1	A	1								
3					Ends with letter r						
4							F				
5								>35 and < 45			
6									Before 4/2/00		
7						Begins with K					
8							F				>6,000,000
9							F	<29			
10								>60			
11	1						M	<39		MA	
12	All	All	All	All	All	All	All	All	All	All	All

Instructions Part 3: Open the workbook Fox & Sons Clothing created in Part 1. Sort the database according to the following six sort problems. Print the database for each sort problem in portrait orientation using the Fit to option. Begin problems 2 through 6 by sorting on the Hire Date field to put the database back in its original order.

1. Sort the database in ascending sequence by region.
2. Sort the database by district within division within region. All three sort keys are to be in ascending sequence.
3. Sort the database by division within region. Both sort keys are to be in descending sequence.
4. Sort the database by representative number within district within division within region. All four sort keys are to be in ascending sequence.
5. Sort the database in descending sequence by sales.
6. Sort the database by district within division within region. All three sort keys are to be in descending sequence.
7. Hide columns J and K by selecting them and pressing CTRL+0 (zero). Print the database. Select columns I and L. Press CTRL+SHIFT+RIGHT PARENTHESIS to display the hidden columns. Close the J. Fox & Sons Clothing Sales Representative database without saving changes.

In the Lab

Instructions Part 4: Open the J. Fox & Sons Clothing Sales Representative database created in Part 1. Sort the database by district within division within region. Select ascending sequence for all three sort keys. Use the Subtotals command on the Data menu to generate subtotals for sales by region (Figure 5-66). Change column A to best fit. Print the range Database. Click row level symbol 1 and print the range Database. Click row level symbol 2 and print the range Database. Click row level symbol 3. Remove all subtotals. Close the workbook without saving changes.

Region	Division	District	Rep	Lname	Fname	Gender	Age	Hire Date	Educ	Sales
1	A	1	3ER	Shiller	Mike	M	38	10/15/01	BA	7,430,285
1	A	3	3ED	Hierich	John	M	42	11/13/98	BA	1,961,815
1	B	2	6YT	Planer	Kim	F	26	09/17/01	MA	8,340,131
1	B	2	5GH	Landers	Phillip	M	32	07/08/03	HS	6,310,321
1	B	3	5PL	Joplin	Fred	M	32	07/15/97	MA	5,912,056
1 Total										29,954,608
2	A	1	6KL	Ruiz	Maria	F	24	12/23/03	BA	7,301,039
2	A	2	6YU	Shewer	Lilly	F	35	04/02/00	HS	4,910,436
2	A	3	2FD	Blue	Rodney	M	37	12/01/92	HS	4,567,103
2	A	3	5HG	April	Kent	M	34	12/15/98	BA	3,251,756
2	B	1	3RU	Groen	Max	M	27	03/06/95	MA	3,919,342
2	B	1	2QA	Fawner	Wanda	F	54	04/12/02	MA	4,010,394
2 Total										27,960,070
3	A	3	1MN	Frontz	Jill	F	29	05/05/00	HS	2,910,651
3	B	2	6TY	Grunkovich	Janie	F	44	10/14/94	BA	8,340,712
3 Total										11,251,363
Grand Total										69,166,041

J. Fox & Sons Clothing Sales Representative Database

FIGURE 5-66

2 Filtering and Sorting the Office XP MOUS Certification Database

Problem: XP Office Temps, Inc. specializes in supplying consultants to companies in need of Office XP expertise. The company uses a database (Figure 5-67 on the next page) that shows whether an employee has MOUS certification for each Office XP application. (For information on MOUS certification, see Appendix E.)

The president, Sandra Peters, has asked you to sort, query, and determine some averages from the database. Carefully label each required printout by using the part number and step. If a step results in multiple printouts, label them a, b, c, and so on.

(continued)

In the Lab

Filtering and Sorting the Office XP MOUS Certification Database *(continued)*

Name	Educ	Yrs	Age	Gender	Word	Excel	Access	PowerPoint	Outlook	Publisher	FrontPage	Count
Rivera, Rosa	MS	4	27	F	Y	Y	N	N	N	Y	Y	4
Rivich, Jill	PhD	2	32	F	Y	N	N	Y	N	Y	Y	4
Herd, Doug	HS	6	25	M	Y	N	Y	Y	N	N	N	3
Boer, Lori	BS	5	31	F	N	Y	Y	Y	N	N	Y	4
Aaron, Emma	AS	2	25	F	N	N	N	N	N	N	N	0
Claus, Nancy	MS	7	45	F	Y	N	N	Y	N	N	Y	3
Koch, Leon	MS	8	33	M	N	N	Y	N	Y	Y	Y	4
Smith, James	HS	1	25	M	Y	Y	Y	N	N	Y	N	4
Rafalski, Mary	MS	5	35	F	Y	N	Y	N	Y	Y	N	4
Ranta, Rebecca	BS	3	26	F	N	N	N	Y	Y	Y	N	3
Tokarz, Alan	PhD	2	34	M	N	Y	Y	N	N	Y	N	3
Wirtz, Wila	HS	12	42	F	N	Y	N	Y	Y	Y	N	4
Tirado, Carlos	BS	9	63	M	Y	N	N	N	Y	N	N	2
Witvot, Jean	AS	21	45	F	N	N	Y	Y	Y	N	Y	4
Steen, Iris	AS	7	43	F	Y	Y	Y	Y	Y	N	N	5
Slabowski, Ed	BS	17	39	M	N	N	N	N	N	N	N	0
Nunez, Emilio	PhD	10	43	M	N	N	N	N	N	N	N	0
Noojin, Maurice	MS	8	35	M	N	N	N	Y	Y	Y	Y	3
Wang, WuJing	HS	6	28	F	Y	Y	Y	Y	N	N	N	4
Brant, Denise	BS	7	49	F	N	Y	Y	N	N	N	N	2
Goodman, Greg	BS	19	59	M	N	N	Y	Y	N	N	Y	3

FIGURE 5-67

Instructions Part 1: Start Excel and perform the following tasks.

1. Open the workbook Office XP MOUS Certification Database from the Data Disk. If you do not have a copy of the Data Disk, see the inside back cover of this book for instructions on downloading it.
2. Complete the following tasks:
   a. Sort the records in the database into ascending sequence by name. Emma Aaron should display first in the database. Jean Witvot should display last. Print the range Database.
   b. Sort the records in the database by age within gender. Select descending sequence for the age and ascending sequence for gender. Denise Brant should be the first record. Print the range Database.
   c. Sort the database by PowerPoint within Excel within Access within Word. Use the Sort Descending button on the Standard toolbar on all fields. Sort first on PowerPoint, then Excel, and finally Word. Those who are MOUS certified in all four applications should display at the top of the database. Print the range Database. Close the workbook without saving it.

Instructions Part 2: Open the workbook Office XP MOUS Certification Database (Figure 5-67). Select a cell within the database range. Use the Form command on the Data menu to display a data form. Use the Criteria button in the data form to enter the comparison criteria for the tasks below. Use the Find Next and Find Prev buttons in the data form to find the records that pass the comparison criteria. Write down and submit the names

In the Lab

of the employees who pass the comparison criteria for items a through d. Close the data form after each query and then reopen it by clicking the Form command on the Data menu. You should end up with the following number of records for items a through d: a = 6; b = 2; c = 1; and d = 2.

a. Find all records that represent specialists who are female and are MOUS certified in Excel.

b. Find all records that represent MOUS certified employees with more than 7 years of experience (Yrs) and who are certified in Publisher and FrontPage.

c. Find all records that represent male MOUS certified employees who are at least 30 years old and are certified in Excel.

d. Find all records that represent MOUS certified employees who have at least 5 years of experience (Yrs) and who are certified in Excel and Outlook.

e. Close and then reopen the data form. All specialists who did not know Publisher were sent to a seminar on the application. Use the Find Next button in the data form to locate the records of these employees and change the Publisher field entry in the data form from the letter N to the letter Y. Make sure you press the ENTER key or press the DOWN ARROW key after changing the letter. Print the range Database. Close the database without saving the changes.

Instructions Part 3: Open the workbook Office XP MOUS Certification Database. Click a cell within the database range. Click Data on the menu bar and then point to Filter. Use the AutoFilter command on the Filter submenu and redo Part 2 a, b, c, and d. Use the Show All command on the Filter submenu before starting items b, c, and d. Print the range Database for each problem. Click AutoFilter on the Filter submenu to remove the AutoFilter arrows. Close the workbook without saving the changes.

Instructions Part 4: Open the workbook Office XP MOUS Certification Database. Add a criteria range by copying the database title and field names (range A9:M10) to range A1:M2 (Figure 5-68). Change cell A1 to Criteria Area and then color the title area as shown in Figure 5-68. Use the Name Box in the formula bar to name the criteria range (A2:M3) Criteria.

Microsoft Excel - Office XP MOUS Certification Database Final												
File Edit View Insert Format Tools Data Window Help												
A11			*fx* Rivera, Rosa									
	A	B	C	D	E	F	G	H	I	J	K	L	M
1	colspan Criteria Area											
2	Name	Educ	Yrs	Age	Gender	Word	Excel	Access	PowerPoint	Outlook	Publisher	FrontPage	Count
3				>30	M								
4													
5													
6													
7													
8													
9	colspan Office XP MOUS Certification Database											
10	Name	Educ	Yrs	Age	Gender	Word	Excel	Access	PowerPoint	Outlook	Publisher	FrontPage	Count
11	Rivera, Rosa	MS	4	27	F	Y	Y	N	N	N	Y	Y	4
12	Rivich, Jill	PhD	2	32	F	Y		N		N		Y	Y	4

FIGURE 5-68

(continued)

In the Lab

Filtering and Sorting the Office XP MOUS Certification Database *(continued)*

Add an extract range by copying the database title and field names (range A9:M10) to range A37:M38 (Figure 5-69). Change cell A37 to Extract Area and then color the title area as shown in Figure 5-69. Use the Name Box in the formula bar to name the extract range (range A38:M38) Extract.

| Microsoft Excel - Office XP MOUS Certification Database Final | | | | | | | | | | | | |

A11 · *fx* Rivera, Rosa

	A	B	C	D	E	F	G	H	I	J	K	L	M
37						**Extract Area**							
38	Name	Educ	Yrs	Age	Gender	Word	Excel	Access	PowerPoint	Outlook	Publisher	FrontPage	Count
39	Koch, Leon	MS	8	33	M	N	N	Y	N	Y	Y	Y	4
40	Tokarz, Alan	PhD	2	34	M	N	Y	Y	N	N	Y	N	3
41	Tirado, Carlos	BS	9	63	M	Y	N	N	N	Y	N	N	2
42	Slabowski, Ed	BS	17	39	M	N	N	N	N	N	N	N	0
43	Nunez, Emilio	PhD	10	43	M	N	N	N	N	N	N	N	0
44	Noojin, Maurice	MS	8	35	M	N	N	N	N	Y	Y	Y	3
45	Goodman, Greg	BS	19	59	M	N	N	Y	Y	N	N	Y	3
46													
47													
48													
49													

FIGURE 5-69

With a cell active in the database range, use the Advanced Filter command on the Filter submenu to extract records that pass the tests in the following items a through e. Print the entire worksheet using landscape orientation and the Fit to option.

a. Extract the records that represent employees who are male and older than 30 (Figure 5-68 on the previous page). You should extract seven records (Figure 5-69).

b. Extract the records that represent female employees who are certified in Excel, but not in Outlook. You should extract four records.

c. Extract the records that represent female employees who are at least 30 years old and are certified in at least four applications. The field Count in column M uses the **COUNTIF function** to count the number of Ys in a record. A count of 4 means the record represents a specialist with expertise in four areas. You should extract six records.

d. Extract the records that represent specialists whose last name begins with the letter S. You should extract three records.

e. Extract the records that represent employees who are certified in three applications or fewer. You should extract 11 records.

f. Save the workbook using the file name Office XP MOUS Certification Database Final. Close the workbook.

In the Lab

Instructions Part 5: Open the workbook Office XP MOUS Certification Database Final created in Part 4. If you did not complete Part 4, then open the Office XP MOUS Certification Database from the Data Disk.

Scroll to the right to display cell O1 in the upper-left corner of the window. Enter the criteria in the range O1:Q3 as shown in Figure 5-70. Enter the row titles in cells O5:O7 as shown in Figure 5-70.

Use the database function DAVERAGE and the appropriate criteria in the range O1:Q3 to determine the average age of the males and females in the range. Use the database function DCOUNT and the appropriate criteria in the range O1:Q3 to determine the record count of those who have expertise in Excel. The DCOUNT function requires that you choose a numeric field in the database to count, such as Age. Print the worksheet in landscape orientation using the Fit to option. Save the workbook using the file name Office XP MOUS Certification Database Final.

FIGURE 5-70

3 Creating and Manipulating the Valley High CC Dance Club Database

Problem: You are a member of the Valley High CC Dance Club, a dance club for young adults. The president has asked for a volunteer to create a database made up of the club's members (Figure 5-71 on the next page). You decide it is a great opportunity to show your Excel skills. Besides including a member's GPA in the database, the president also would like a GPA letter grade assigned to each member.

(continued)

In the Lab

Creating and Manipulating the Valley High CC Dance Club Database *(continued)*

FIGURE 5-71

Instructions Part 1: Perform the following tasks to create the database shown in the range A6:H17 in Figure 5-71.

1. Enter the database title in cell A6 and the column titles in row 7. Define the range A7:G8 as Database. Format the titles as shown in Figure 5-71.

2. Use the Form command on the Data menu to enter the data shown in the range A8:G17.

3. Enter the Grade table in the range J6:K20. In cell H8, enter the function =vlookup(G8, $J$8:$K$20, 2) to determine the letter grade that corresponds to the GPA in cell G8. Copy the function in cell H8 to the range H9:H17.

4. Redefine the name Database as the range A7:H17.

5. Enter your name, course number, laboratory assignment (Lab 5-3), date, and instructor name in the range F20:F24.

6. Save the workbook using the file name Valley High CC Dance Club. Print the worksheet. At the bottom of the printout, explain why the dollar signs ($) are necessary in the VLOOKUP function in Step 3.

In the Lab

Instructions Part 2:   Perform the following tasks:

1. Hide columns G and H by clicking column heading G, dragging through column heading H to select both columns, and then pressing CTRL+0 (zero). Print the worksheet with columns G and H hidden. Unhide columns G and H by clicking column heading F, dragging through column heading I to select the columns adjacent to the hidden columns, and then pressing CTRL+SHIFT+RIGHT PARENTHESIS.
2. Hide rows 15 through 20 by clicking row heading 15, dragging through row heading 20 to select rows 15 through 20, and then pressing CTRL+9. Print the worksheet with rows 15 through 20 hidden. Unhide rows 15 through 20 by clicking row heading 14, dragging through row heading 21 to select the rows adjacent to the hidden rows, and then pressing CTRL+SHIFT+LEFT PARENTHESIS.
3. Close the workbook without saving changes. Then, increment all part numbers on page E 5.61.

Instructions Part 3:   Open the workbook Valley High CC Dance Club. Use a data form to change the following GPAs: 541098 = 3.75; 671029 = 2.10; 910361 = 1.10. Close the data form. The three members' grades should display as B+, C-, and D-, respectively. Print the worksheet. Close the workbook without saving changes.

Instructions Part 4:   Open the workbook Valley High CC Dance Club. Use the Criteria button and the Find text and Find Prev buttons in the data form to display records that meet the following criteria. Print the worksheet and write down the Student IDs of the records that pass the tests.

1. Gender = M; GPA > 4 (Two records pass the test.)
2. Age ≥ 27 (One record passes the test.)
3. Gender = F; Age > 21 (Three records pass the test.)

Close the workbook without saving the changes.

Instructions Part 5:   Open the workbook Valley High CC Dance Club. Sort the database as follows. Print the database after each sort. After completing the third sort, close the workbook without saving the changes.

1. Sort the database in ascending sequence by the Major field (column F).
2. Sort the database by GPA within Gender. Use ascending sequence for both fields.
3. Sort the database by Age within Gender. Use descending sequence for both fields.

Instructions Part 6:   Open the workbook Valley High CC Dance Club. Use the concepts and techniques presented in this project to set up a Criteria area above the database, set up an Extract area below the Grade table, and complete the following extractions. For each extraction, it is important that you select a cell in the database before using the Advanced Filter command. Extract the records that meet the three criteria sets in Part 4 above. Print the worksheet for each criteria set. Extract the records that meet the following criteria: 21 < Age < 30. It is necessary that you add a second field called Age to the immediate right of the Criteria range and redefine the Criteria area to include the new field. Five records pass the final test. Save the workbook with the last criteria set using the file name Valley High CC Dance Club Final.

Cases and Places

The difficulty of these case studies varies:
❘ are the least difficult; ❘❘ are more difficult; and ❘❘❘ are the most difficult.

1 ❘ Clubs, like individuals, may have distinct personalities and characteristics. A database can help reveal a club's idiosyncrasies. Create a Computer Club database from the membership data in Table 5-7. Begin the database title (Computer Club Database) in row 7. Use the column headings as the field names in the database. Print the worksheet. Save the workbook. Print the worksheet after each of the following sorts: (1) sort the database in ascending sequence by last name; (2) sort by major within age within gender (all in descending sequence); and (3) sort the database by class in ascending sequence. With the database sorted by class, display subtotals for the number of credit hours. Print the worksheet. Use a data form to find all female students who have earned more than 65 credit hours towards graduation. Write the number who pass the test at the bottom of the Subtotals printout.

Table 5-7	Computer Club Database						
LNAME	**FNAME**	**STATE**	**MAJOR**	**CLASS**	**AGE**	**GENDER**	**CREDIT HRS**
Sawchak	Sherry	FL	EE	Freshman	30	F	27
Kloan	Jackie	GA	COM	Senior	21	F	112
Kline	Nellie	AK	CIS	Sophomore	25	F	62
Gwoat	Helmut	SC	CS	Junior	21	M	70
Frome	Alice	NC	EET	Junior	19	F	75
Suarez	Rosa	SC	CNT	Freshman	18	F	32
Weeks	Georgia	FL	CIS	Junior	22	F	84
Quartz	Liz	GA	CS	Senior	38	F	120
Nelson	Jim	LA	MET	Junior	29	M	75
Yest	Harry	TX	MET	Sophomore	25	M	64

Cases and Places

2 ▶ You work part-time for El Rancho Community College. The school's Booster Club raises money by selling merchandise imprinted with the school's logo. The Booster Club purchases products from vendors. You have been asked to create an inventory database from the data in Table 5-8. Use the column headings in the table as the field names in the database. Enter the database title El Rancho Booster Club Merchandise Database in cell A6 and enter the database immediately below it. Name the database range, Database. The Amount and Priority fields are computational fields. Amount equals On Hand times Selling Price. The Priority field ranks the items 1 through 4 based on their inventory (on hand). The higher the number, the stronger the possibility that the Booster Club should put the item on sale or market it better. Create a Priority table in the range J1:K7 from the data shown in Table 5-9. Use the VLOOKUP function to determine the rank. Print the worksheet in landscape orientation using the Fit to option. Save the workbook.

Table 5-8   El Rancho Booster Club Merchandise Database

ITEM NO.	DESCRIPTION	ON HAND	COST	SELLING PRICE	VENDOR CODE	AMOUNT	PRIORITY
CA02	Tie	23	2.50	5.00	AGHT		
CK12	Scarf	76	4.25	7.25	DFGE		
HJ14	Wastebasket	12	6.15	11.50	AGHT		
OR12	Coffee Mug	87	1.10	3.25	DFGE		
ST23	Doormat	43	2.10	5.10	DFGE		
TY34	Sunglasses	22	3.20	7.50	BSJA		
UL12	Pillow	12	1.95	3.15	AGHT		
US34	Pennant	87	0.95	1.25	BSJA		
VW34	Ornament	112	1.05	2.25	DFGE		
ZD12	Pen and Pencil	215	3.25	6.50	AGHT		

Table 5-9   Priority Categories

ON HAND	PRIORITY
0	1
25	2
75	3
100	4

3 ▶ Open the database created in Cases and Places Exercise 2. Print the database for each of the following: (a) sort the database in ascending sequence by on hand; (b) sort the database by amount (descending) within priority (ascending); and (c) sort the database in ascending sequence by vendor code. With the database sorted by vendor code, use the Subtotals command to determine amount subtotals for each vendor code. Print the range Database with the subtotals. Use row level symbol 2 to display only subtotals. Print the range Database.

Cases and Places

4 ▶ Open the database created in Cases and Places Exercise 2. Use the concepts and techniques described in this project to filter (query) the database using the AutoFilter and Show All commands on the Filter submenu. Print the worksheet for each of the following independent queries: (1) priority equal to 3; (2) on hand greater than 75; (3) vendor code equals DFGE and priority code three or greater; and (4) selling price greater than 5.00. The number of records that display are: (1) 3; (2) 5; (3) 3; and (4) 5.

5 ▶▶ Open the database created in Cases and Places Exercise 1. Use the concepts and techniques presented in this project to create a Criteria area and an Extract area. Use the Advanced AutoFilter command to extract records. Print the Extract area for each of the following: (1) males; (2) females; (3) males older than 21; (4) CS majors with fewer than 100 credit hours; (5) females less than 21 years old; (6) female juniors; and (7) students between the ages of 19 and 21, inclusive. The number of records that display are: (1) 3; (2) 7; (3) 2; (4) 1; (5) 2; (6) 2; and (7) 3.

6 ▶▶ Open the database created in Cases and Places Exercise 1. Use the concepts and techniques presented in this project to determine the average age of females, the average age of males, and the average number of credit hours accumulated by students from GA. Count the number of students that are juniors.

7 ▶▶▶ You work for the classified ads section of your local newspaper. Your editors have decided to introduce a new service in which readers can call the office and inquire if a particular house is being advertised. The editors have assigned this task to you. Begin by creating a database with fields for the house for sale, age, year, price, location, and elementary school. Then enter 15 ads in today's newspaper. If any information is missing, enter NA (not available). Test the project by performing queries.

Microsoft Excel 2002

Creating Templates and Working with Multiple Worksheets and Workbooks

You will have mastered the material in this project when you can:

OBJECTIVES

- Create and use a template
- Utilize custom format codes
- Define, apply, and remove a style
- Add a worksheet to a workbook
- Create formulas that use 3-D references
- Consolidate data within the same workbook
- Draw a 3-D Cylinder chart
- Use WordArt to create a title
- Create and modify lines and objects
- Add comments to cells
- Add a header or footer to a workbook
- Change the page margins
- Insert a page break
- Use the Find and Replace commands
- Search for files on disk
- Create and use a workspace file
- Consolidate data by linking workbooks

Building a Solid Foundation
Tools That Help Businesses Grow

The American entrepreneurial spirit has resulted in the creation of many innovative products and businesses. Characterized by a willingness to take risks and work long, hard hours, many individuals every year start their own businesses with the dream of turning a good idea into a financial opportunity. In 1997, more than 880,000 new small businesses were created, and in 1998 that number almost reached 900,000. Currently, 21 million Americans are engaged in some kind of entrepreneurial enterprise. In many cases, the effort to find a more efficient or simplified way to perform a difficult task has laid the foundation for a great business prospect. That is how it all began for Chester Carlson, inventor of the photocopier.

In 1938, Carlson worked as a patent analyzer for an electrical component maker. In this capacity he was required to spend numerous hours reviewing highly technical documents and drawings. Then he prepared the paperwork and applications submitted to the U.S. Patent and Trademark Office to register the company's inventions and ideas. It was during this time that Carlson developed his idea of an automated copying process. The patent office required multiple copies, which he had to duplicate manually, and redrawing the copies took hours. With his experience and technical expertise, Carlson went to work to find a better alternative.

His research led to the development of a copying technique based on photoconductivity, whereby some materials change their electrical properties when exposed to light. He received a patent for his new copying process, called electrophotography. In 1944, Carlson changed the name to xerography, a term derived from the Greek words for dry and writing. He sold his rights to a company that coined the word, Xerox, as the trademark for the new invention. The copier and the words, xerography (to describe the process) and Xerox (to identify the product), were introduced simultaneously in 1948. Today, Xerox, The Document Company, continues to develop and market innovative products in the document-imaging industry.

Of course, a good idea is just one half of the equation that results in a thriving business. Every good idea needs to be nurtured by careful financial management. Thankfully, help is just a Web site away. CCH Incorporated has been providing legal, tax, and business information to American and international businesses since 1913. The company now offers its expertise to small business owners via a Web site, the CCH Business Owner's Toolkit, that provides numerous solutions especially suited for smaller businesses, including worksheet templates that can be downloaded without charge. From balance sheets to daily cash flow, from bank

reconciliations to customer account statements, each worksheet template offers a low-cost means to keep your business on a solid financial footing. By customizing the templates and consolidating the data contained in the different worksheets, you can create an Excel workbook that provides a single source of financial information for your small business.

Similarly, in Project 6 you will create templates that will allow the different divisions of Grand Enterprises Incorporated to enter data about assets, liabilities, and shareholders' equity in separate Excel spreadsheets. The templates will include formulas and formatting that make the worksheets easy to use. Using the data provided by the divisions, you then can consolidate the data in a new worksheet to create the Statement of Financial Condition for Grand Enterprises Incorporated.

Small businesses are anything but small. Approximately 53 percent of the private workforce is employed by a small business, and small business sales constitute 47 percent of all sales nationwide. The continued health and well being of this vital component of the American economy requires that small business owners manage income and expenses wisely, as the key to unlocking the potential of a good idea is careful financial management.

Microsoft Excel 2002

Creating Templates and Working with Multiple Worksheets and Workbooks

PROJECT

6

CASE PERSPECTIVE

Soon after graduating from college, Rodney Jefferson began selling restaurant equipment for a local supplier. Five years later, with financial help from his parents and relatives he opened his own restaurant equipment supply company using his garage as his office and warehouse. Rodney called his company Grand Enterprises Incorporated, or GEI.

Within 10 years, through hard work and clever deals, GEI grew from a garage operation to a multimillion dollar company selling restaurant equipment throughout the United States. Currently, GEI has three divisions, Western, Central, and Eastern. Each division develops its own annual Statement of Financial Condition in January for the previous year and submits it to the company's accounting firm, which in the past consolidated them into one summary for the entire company using paper, pencil, and calculator.

As the chief spreadsheet developer for the accounting firm, you have been asked to use Excel to create a Statement of Financial Condition for each division, a consolidated Statement of Financial Condition, and a 3-D Cylinder chart that compares the assets for the entire company (Figure 6-1).

Introduction

Many business-type applications, such as the one described in the Case Perspective, require data from several worksheets in a workbook to be summarized on one worksheet. In the case of GEI, data comes in from three different divisions. If you place each division's financial data on a worksheet in a workbook, you can click the sheet tabs at the bottom of the Excel window to move from worksheet to worksheet, or division to division. You can enter formulas on one worksheet that reference cells contained on the other worksheets, which allows you to summarize worksheet data. The process of summarizing data included on multiple worksheets on one worksheet is called **consolidation**.

Another important concept is the use of a template. A **template** is a special workbook you can create and then use as a pattern to create new, similar workbooks or worksheets. A template usually consists of a general format (worksheet title, column and row titles, and numeric format) and formulas that are common to all the worksheets. For example, in the GEI workbook, the worksheets for each of the three divisions and the company worksheet are identical (Figure 6-1), except for the data. One way to create the workbook is first to create a template, save it, and then copy it as many times as necessary to a workbook.

Several other techniques are introduced in this project, including using dummy data, custom format codes, creating a format style, adding comments to a cell, headers and footers, using WordArt to create a title, using the Find and Replace commands, searching for files, creating a workspace file, and linking workbooks.

(a) Central Division Worksheet

(b) Western Division Worksheet

(c) Eastern Division Worksheet

consolidate data on one worksheet

3-D Cylinder chart compares company asset allocation

Western Division, Central Division sheet, and Eastern Division assets, liabilities, and stockholders' equity consolidated in one worksheet

Consolidated tab

(d) Consolidated Worksheet

(e) 3-D Cylinder Chart

3-D Cylinder Chart tab

FIGURE 6-1

Project Six — Grand Enterprises Incorporated Statement of Financial Condition

Based on the requirements of GEI, you can determine the following workbook specifications:

Needs: The workbook will require four worksheets and one chart sheet — one for each of the three divisions, a summary worksheet for the company, and a chart on a separate sheet that compares the company's assets (Figure 6-1 on the previous page).

Because the three divisions have the same assets, liabilities and shareholders' equity text entries, the three Statements of Financial Condition are identical, except for the dollar amounts. A template (Figure 6-2) will be created and then copied to the worksheets in the same workbook.

Source of Data: The Statements of Financial Condition from the three divisions.

Calculations: Use the SUM function to determine the total assets, total liabilities, total shareholders' equity, and the total liabilities and shareholders' equity in column C of each of the four worksheets shown in Figure 6-1. Use the SUM function to determine the totals for each asset, liability, and shareholders' equity on the Consolidated sheet (Figure 6-1d).

Graph Requirements: Include a 3-D Cylinder chart on a separate chart sheet that compares the consolidated assets.

A **Statement of Financial Condition**, such as the four shown in Figure 6-1, is a report showing the status of a corporation's assets, liabilities, and shareholders' equity on a given date. An **asset** is any property owned by the corporation. For example, in Figure 6-1a, the Statement of Financial Condition for the Western division lists the following assets: Cash ($54,738,210), Receivables ($43,946,587), Supplies ($17,283,491), Equipment ($32,918,713), Land ($13,019,283), and Other Assets ($3,910,456).

A **liability** is an amount owed by a corporation to its creditors. The Statement of Financial Condition for the Western division in Figure 6-1a lists the following liabilities: Notes Payable ($43,719,321), Accounts Payable ($32,459,873), Income Tax Payable ($15,612,711), and Miscellaneous Liabilities ($1,291,056).

Shareholders' equity represents the ownership interest of the shareholders of the corporation. On the Statement of Financial Condition for the Western division shown in Figure 6-1b, the shareholders' equity consists of the Common Stock ($56,819,432) sold by the corporation, and the Retained Earnings ($15,914,347), which is income retained by the Western division.

Starting and Customizing Excel

Perform the following steps to start and customize Excel. Once the Excel window opens, Steps 3 through 5 close the task pane, minimize the Language bar, and ensure that the Standard and Formatting toolbars display on two rows.

TO START AND CUSTOMIZE EXCEL

1 Click the Start button on the Windows taskbar, point to Programs on the Start menu, and then click Microsoft Excel on the Programs submenu.

2 If the Excel window is not maximized, double-click its title bar to maximize it.

3 If the New Workbook task pane displays, click the Show at startup check box at the bottom of the task pane to remove the check mark and then click the Close button in the upper-right corner to close the task pane.

4 If the Language bar displays, click its Minimize button.

5 If the Standard and Formatting toolbars display on one row, click the Toolbar Options button on the right side of either toolbar and then click Show Buttons on Two Rows in the Toolbar Options list.

An empty workbook displays in the Excel window. The Standard and Formatting toolbars on two rows display as shown in Figure 6-2.

If your toolbars display differently than those shown in Figure 6-2, see Appendix D for additional information on resetting the toolbars and menus.

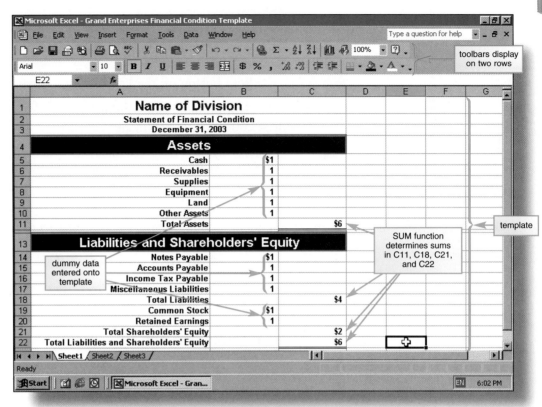

FIGURE 6-2

Creating the Template

Learning how to use templates is important, especially if you plan to use a similar worksheet design or layout for several worksheets or workbooks. In Project 6, for instance, the four worksheets in the workbook (Figure 6-1) are nearly identical. Thus, the first step in building the Statement of Financial Condition workbook is to create and save a template that contains the labels, formulas, and formats used on each of the sheets.

Once the template is saved on disk, you can use it every time you begin developing a similar workbook. Because templates help speed and simplify their work, many Excel users create a template for each application on which they work. Templates can be simple — possibly using a special font or worksheet title — or more complex — perhaps utilizing specific formulas and format styles, such as the template for Project 6.

To create a template, you follow the same basic steps used to create a workbook. The only difference between developing a workbook and a template is the way you save the file.

Changing the Font to Bold and Changing the Column Widths of the Template

The first step in this project is to change the font style of the entire template to bold and adjust the column widths as follows: columns A = 40.00 and B and C = 15.00. Perform the steps on the next page to apply this formatting.

More About

Templates

Templates are most helpful when you need to create several similar or identical workbooks. They help reduce work and ensure consistency. Templates can contain: (1) text and graphics, such as a company name and logo; (2) formats and page layouts; and (3) formulas or macros.

TO BOLD THE FONT AND CHANGE THE COLUMN WIDTHS IN THE TEMPLATE

1 Click the Select All button immediately above row heading 1 and to the left of column heading A.

2 Click the Bold button on the Formatting toolbar. Click column heading A.

3 Drag the right boundary of column heading A to the right until the ScreenTip, Width: 40.00 (285 pixels), displays.

4 Click column heading B. Drag through to column heading C. Drag the right boundary of column heading C to the right until the ScreenTip, Width: 15.00 (110 pixels), displays. Click cell A1 to deselect columns B and C.

Excel assigns the Bold font style to all cells in the worksheet. Column A has a width of 40.00 and columns B and C have a width of 15.00.

Entering the Template Title and Row Titles

The following steps enter the worksheet titles in cells A1, A2, and A3 and the row titles in the range A4:A22.

TO ENTER THE TEMPLATE TITLE AND ROW TITLES

1 With cell A1 selected, type Name of Division and then press the DOWN ARROW key.

2 Type Statement of Financial Condition and then press the DOWN ARROW key.

3 Type 12/31/2003 and then press the DOWN ARROW key.

4 Enter the row titles in the range A4:A22 as shown in Figure 6-3. Cell A12 has no row title.

The template title and row titles display in column A as shown in Figure 6-3.

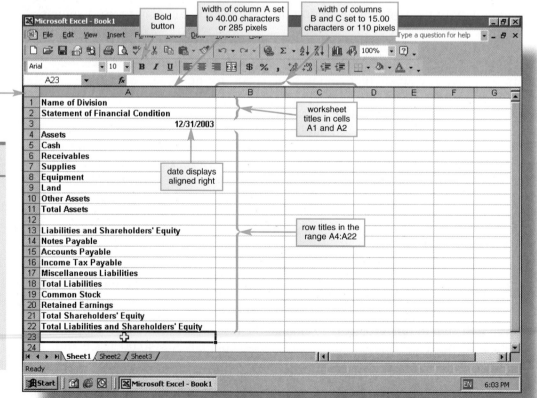

FIGURE 6-3

Entering Dummy Data in the Template

When you create a template, you should use **dummy data** in place of actual data to verify the formulas in the template. Selecting simple numbers such as 1 for each of the dollar amounts allows you to check quickly to see if the formulas are generating the proper results. In the template in Project 6, dummy data is used for the dollar amounts in column B. The following steps enter the dummy data in column B.

TO ENTER DUMMY DATA IN THE TEMPLATE

1 Select cell B5.
Type 1 and click the Enter box on the formula bar. With cell B5 selected, drag the fill handle through cell B10.

2 Select cell B14.
Type 1 and click the Enter box on the formula bar. With cell B14 selected, drag the fill handle through cell B17.

3 Select cell B19.
Type 1 and press the DOWN ARROW key. Type 1 and click the Enter box on the formula bar.

The template displays as shown in Figure 6-4.

FIGURE 6-4

In this example, the integer 1 is used as dummy data because the only formulas involve the use of the SUM function. Depending on the application, you may want to select dummy data that tests the limits of the formulas in the template.

Determining Totals

In a Statement of Financial Condition, the total assets (row 11) must agree exactly with the total liabilities and stockholders' equity (row 22). In the template, the following totals are determined:

    (1) total assets in row 11 equal the sum of the assets in the range B5:B10
    (2) total liabilities in row 18 equal the sum of the liabilities in the range B14:B17
    (3) total shareholders' equity in row 21 equals the sum of the common stock and retained earnings in the range B19:B20
    (4) total liabilities and shareholders' equity in row 22 equals the sum of the total liabilities and total shareholders' equity in cells C18 and C21.

Perform the steps on the next page to determine these four totals.

More About

Dummy Numbers

As you develop more sophisticated workbooks, it will become increasingly important that you create good test data to ensure your workbooks are error-free. The more you test a workbook, the more confident you will be in the results generated. Select test data that tests the limits of the formulas.

Steps **To Determine Totals**

1 **Click cell C11. Click the AutoSum button on the Standard toolbar. Drag through the range B5:B10. Point to the Enter box on the formula bar.**

The SUM function displays in cell C11 and in the formula bar (Figure 6-5). A marquee surrounds the range B5:B10.

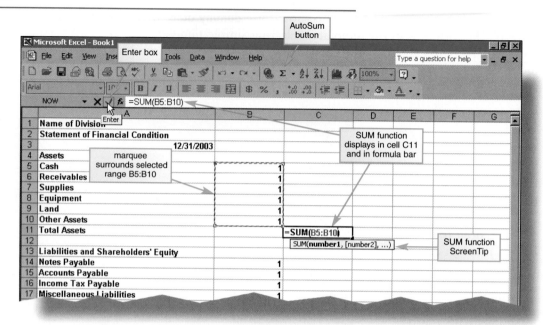

FIGURE 6-5

2 **Click the Enter box. Click cell C18 and then click the AutoSum button on the Standard toolbar. Drag through the range B14:B17 and then click the Enter box on the formula bar. Click cell C21 and then click the AutoSum button on the Standard toolbar. Drag through the range B19:B20 and then click the Enter box on the formula bar. Click cell C22 and then click the AutoSum button on the Standard toolbar. Point to the Enter box on the formula bar.**

The total assets (6) displays in cell C11 (Figure 6-6). The total liabilities (4) displays in cell C18. The total stockholders' equity (2) displays in cell C21. The SUM function displays in cell C22 and in the formula bar. Excel automatically selects the nonadjacent range C21 and C18 to sum.

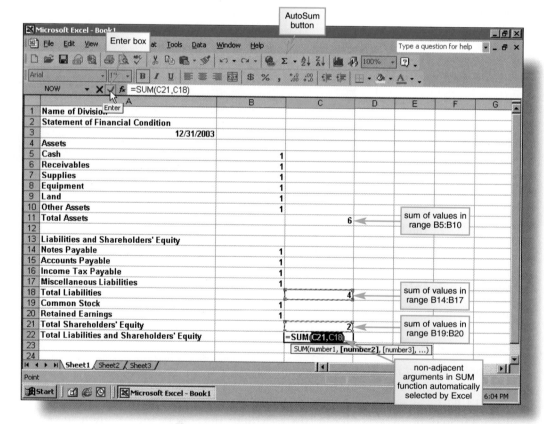

FIGURE 6-6

3   **Click the Enter box.**

The total liabilities and shareholders' equity displays in cell C22 (Figure 6-7).

	A	B	C	D	E	F	G
	C22	▼	*fx* =SUM(C21,C18)				
1	Name of Division						
2	Statement of Financial Condition						
3		12/31/2003					
4	Assets						
5	Cash	1					
6	Receivables	1					
7	Supplies	1					
8	Equipment	1					
9	Land	1					
10	Other Assets	1					
11	Total Assets		6				
12							
13	Liabilities and Shareholders' Equity						
14	Notes Payable	1					
15	Accounts Payable	1					
16	Income Tax Payable	1					
17	Miscellaneous Liabilities	1					
18	Total Liabilities		4				
19	Common Stock	1					
20	Retained Earnings	1					
21	Total Shareholders' Equity		2				
22	Total Liabilities and Shareholders' Equity		6				
23							
24							

sum of values in cells C18 and C21

Sheet1 / Sheet2 / Sheet3 /

Ready

Start   Microsoft Excel - Book1   EN   6:04 PM

FIGURE 6-7

In the previous examples of the SUM function in this book, the arguments were comprised of a range of cells. As you can see in cell C22 of Figure 6-6, the arguments in the SUM function can be individual cells separated by commas. In this case the SUM function is determining the sum of the values in the noncontiguous cells C21 and C18. Excel automatically selected these two cell references as the arguments in the SUM function when the AutoSum button was clicked based on the cell contents surrounding cell C22.

Saving the Template

Saving a template is just like saving a workbook, except that you select Template in the Save as type box in the Save As dialog box. The steps on the next page save the template on drive A using the file name Grand Enterprises Financial Condition Template.

Other Ways

1. Click Insert Function button in formula bar, select SUM in Select a Function list, click OK button, select range, click OK button

2. On Insert menu click Function, select SUM in Select a function list, click OK button, select range, click OK button

3. Press ALT+EQUAL SIGN (=)

4. Type =, click Function box arrow in formula bar, click SUM

5. In Voice Command mode, say "AutoSum, Sum, Enter"

More About

File Extensions

If the MS-DOS extension .xlt shows in your title bar following the file name, it means that the option to omit the MS-DOS extension is not selected on the View sheet in the Options dialog box in Explorer. You display the Options dialog box in Explorer by clicking View on the menu bar, and then clicking Options.

Steps **To Save a Template**

1   **Click the Save button on the Standard toolbar. When the Save As dialog box displays, type** Grand Enterprises Financial Condition Template **in the File name text box. Click the Save as type box arrow and then click Template in the list. Click the Save in box arrow and then click 3½ Floppy (A:). Point to the Save button in the Save As dialog box.**

The Save As dialog box displays (Figure 6-8).

2   **Click the Save button.**

Excel saves the template on the floppy disk in drive A. The new file name displays on the title bar as shown in Figure 6-9.

FIGURE 6-8

Other **Ways**

1. On File menu click Save As, type file name, click Template in Save as type list, select drive or folder, click Save button

2. Press CTRL+S, type file name, click Template in Save as type list, select drive or folder, click Save button

3. In Voice command mode, say "Save, [type desired file name], Save as type, Template, Save in, [select drive or folder], Save"

Formatting the Template

The next step is to format the template so it displays as shown in Figure 6-9. As you format the template, keep in mind that each of the sheets for which the template will be used contains the same basic formats; the formats, therefore, are assigned to the template. Formats that are not common to all the worksheets are added once the workbook is created from the template. The following list summarizes the steps required to format the template.

1. Center worksheet titles in cells A1:A3 across columns A through C. Worksheet title in cell A1 changed to 16-point Arial dark red font.
2. Center two category titles in cells A4 and A13 across columns A through C. Font in cells changed to 16-point Arial white with gray background and thick red outline.
3. Right-align row titles in ranges A5:A11 and A14:A22.
4. Change the height of row 12 to 3.75 points.
5. Assign the Comma style format with zero decimal places to the ranges B6:B10 and B15:B17, and cell B20.
6. Assign the Custom style format $#,##0_);[Blue]($#,##0) to cells B5, C11, B14, C18, B19, C21, and C22.
7. Assign double bottom borders to cells C11 and C22.
8. Create a custom format style and assign it to the date in cell A3.

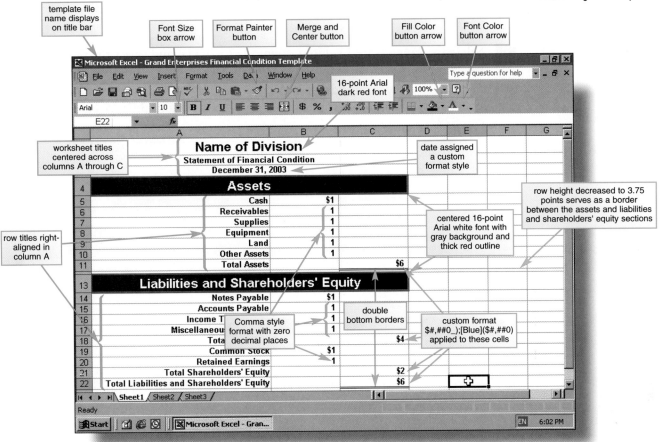

FIGURE 6-9

Formatting the Template Titles

The following steps add the first four formats in the list at the bottom of the previous page to the template.

TO FORMAT THE TEMPLATE TITLES

1 Click cell A1. Click the Font Size box arrow on the Formatting toolbar and then click 16. Click the Font Color button arrow on the Formatting toolbar and then click Dark Red (column 1, row 2) on the Font Color Palette. Select the range A1:C1. Click the Merge and Center button on the Formatting toolbar.

2 Select the range A2:C2 and then click the Merge and Center button on the Formatting toolbar. Select the range A3:C3 and then click the Merge and Center button on the Formatting toolbar.

3 Click cell A4. Click the Font Size box arrow on the Formatting toolbar and then click 16. Select the range A4:C4 and then click the Merge and Center button on the Formatting toolbar. Click the Fill Color button arrow on the Formatting toolbar and then click Gray – 80% (column 8, row 1) on the Fill Color palette. Click the Font Color button arrow on the Formatting toolbar and then click White (column 8, row 5) on the Font Color palette. Right-click cell A4, click Format Cells on the shortcut menu, click the Border tab, click the Color box arrow, click Red (column 1, row 3) on the Color palette, click the heavy border (column 2, row 6) in the Style box, click the Outline button, and then click the OK button.

4 With cell A4 selected, click the Format Painter button on the Standard toolbar. Click cell A13 to assign the formats of cell A4 to cell A13.

5 Select the range A5:A11. Hold down the CTRL key and select the nonadjacent range A14:A22. Click the Align Right button on the Formatting toolbar.

6 Point to the lower boundary of the row heading 12 on the left side of the window and drag up until the ScreenTip reads Height: 3.75 (5 pixels). Select cell E22.

The template displays as shown in Figure 6-10.

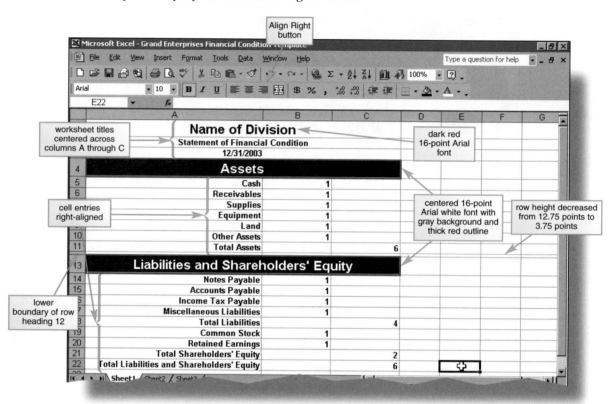

FIGURE 6-10

When you increase the font size in cells A1, A4, and A13, Excel automatically increases the heights of row 1, 4, and 13 so the tallest letter will display properly in the cell.

Assigning a Comma Style Format to Nonadjacent Ranges

The following steps assign the Comma Style format with zero decimal places to the nonadjacent ranges B6:B10 and B15:B17, and cell B20.

TO ASSIGN A COMMA STYLE FORMAT TO NONADJACENT RANGES

1 Select the range B6:B10. Hold down the CTRL key, select the range B15:B17, and then select cell B20.

2 Click the Comma Style button on the Formatting toolbar.

3 Click the Decrease Decimal button twice on the Formatting toolbar.

The dummy numbers in the ranges B6:B10, B15:B17, and B20 display slightly offset from the right borders of their cells indicating the Comma Style format has been assigned to these cells (Figure 6-11). Later, when real data is entered into these cells, the numbers will display with commas when appropriate.

More About

Copying

To copy the contents of a cell to the cell directly below it, click in the target cell and press CTRL+D. If the cell you copy contains a formula, the formula is copied using the relative addresses.

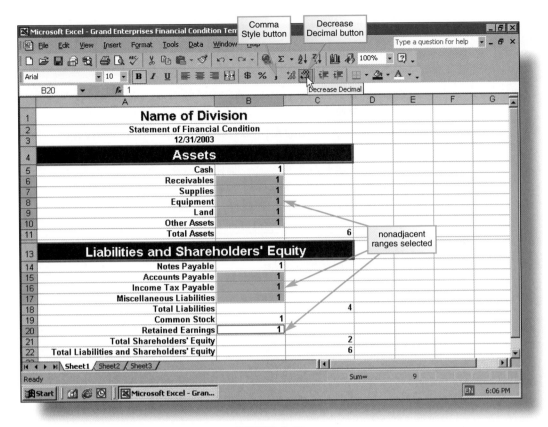

FIGURE 6-11

Creating and Assigning a Customized Format Code

Every format style listed in the Category list box on the Number sheet in the Format Cells dialog box has a format code assigned to it. A **format code** is a series of format symbols (Table 6-1 on the next page) that defines how a format displays. To view the entire list of format codes that come with Excel, select Custom in the Category list box. Before you begin to create your own format codes or modify a customized format code, you should understand their makeup. As shown below, a format code can have up to four sections: positive numbers, negative numbers, zeros, and text. Each section is divided by a semicolon.

$$\$*\#,\#\#0.00;\ [\text{Blue}]\#,\#\#0.00;\ 0.00;\ \text{"The answer is "}@$$

| for positive numbers | for negative numbers | for zero numbers | for text |

A format code need not have all four sections. For most applications, a format code will have only a positive section and possibly a negative section.

The next step is to create and assign a customized Currency style to the nonadjacent cells B5, C11, B14, C18, B19, C21, and C22. To assign a customized Currency style, you select the Custom category in the Format Cells dialog box, select a format code close to the one you want to create, and then modify or customize it. Perform the steps on the next page to create and assign a customized format code. The last step draws a bottom double border on cells C11 and C22.

More About

Creating Customized Formats

Each format symbol within the format code has special meaning. Table 6-1 on the next page summarizes the more frequently used format symbols and their meanings. For additional information on creating format codes, type `create a custom number format` in the Ask a Question box and then click the Create or delete a custom number format link.

Table 6-1 Format Symbols in Format Codes

FORMAT SYMBOL	EXAMPLE OF SYMBOL	DESCRIPTION
# (number sign)	###.##	Serves as a digit placeholder. If more digits are to the right of the decimal point than are number signs, Excel rounds the number. Extra digits to the left of the decimal point are displayed.
0 (zero)	0.00	Functions like a number sign (#), except that if the number is less than 1, Excel displays a zero in the ones place.
. (period)	#0.00	Ensures a decimal point will display in the number. The placement of symbols determines how many digits display to the left and right of the decimal point.
% (percent)	0.00%	Displays numbers as percentages of 100. Excel multiplies the value of the cell by 100 and displays a percent sign after the number.
, (comma)	#,##0.00	Displays comma as a thousands separator.
( )	#0.00;(#0.00)	Displays parentheses around negative numbers.
$ or + or −	$#,##0.00; ($#,##0.00)	Displays a floating sign ($, +, or −).
* (asterisk)	$*##0.00	Displays a fixed sign ($, +, or −) to the left in the cell followed by spaces until the first significant digit.
[color]	#.##;[Red]#.##	Displays the characters in the cell in the designated color. In the example, positive numbers display in the default color, and negative numbers display in red.
" " (quotation marks)	$0.00 "Surplus"; $-0.00 "Shortage"	Displays text along with numbers entered in a cell.
_ (underscore)	#,##0.00_)	Skips the width of the character that follows the underline.

Steps ## To Create and Assign a Custom Format Code

1 **Select cell B5. Hold down the CTRL key and select cells C11, B14, C18, B19, C21, and C22. Right-click one of the selections and then point to Format Cells on the shortcut menu.**

The shortcut menu displays (Figure 6-12).

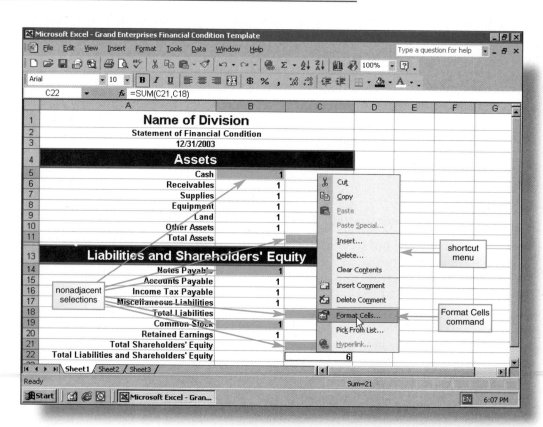

FIGURE 6-12

PROJECT 6

2 **Click Format Cells. When the Format Cells dialog box displays, click the Number tab, click Custom in the Category list. Scroll down and click $#,##0_);[Red]($#,##0) in the Type list. In the Type text box, change the word Red to Blue. Point to the OK button.**

The Format Cells dialog box displays as shown in Figure 6-13. The Custom format has been modified to display negative numbers in blue. Excel displays a sample of the first number in the selected range in the Sample area.

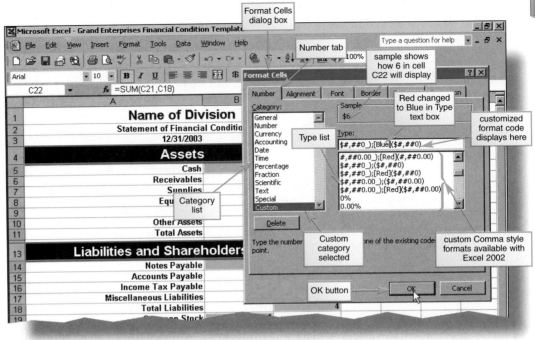

FIGURE 6-13

3 **Click the OK button. Select cell C11. Hold down the CTRL key and select cell C22. Click the Borders button arrow on the Formatting toolbar. Click Bottom Double Border (column 1, row 2) on the Borders palette.**

The dummy numbers in cells B5, C11, B14, C18, B19, C21, and C22 display with a dollar sign appended to their left side (Figure 6-14). The totals in cells C11 and C22 display with double bottom borders.

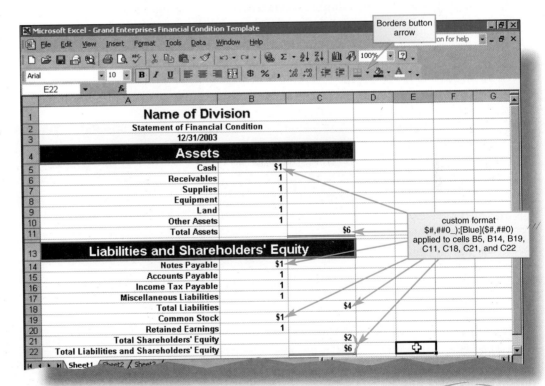

FIGURE 6-14

When you create a new custom format code, Excel adds it to the bottom of the Type list in the Numbers sheet in the Format Cells dialog box to make it available for future use.

Other Ways

1. Press CTRL+1 or on Format menu click Cells, click Number tab, click Custom in Category list, [select desired format and modify], click OK button

2. In Voice Command mode, say "Format, Cells, Number, Custom, [select desired format and modify], OK"

Table 6-2	Styles Available with All Workbooks
STYLE NAME	**DESCRIPTION**
Normal	Number = General; Alignment = General, Bottom Aligned; = Arial 10; Border = No Borders; Patterns = No Shading; Protection = Locked
Comma	Number = (*#,##0.00);_(*(#,##0.00);_(*"-"_);_(@_)
Comma(0)	Number = (*#,##0_);_(*(#,##0)_(*"-"_);_(@_)
Currency	Number = ($#,##0.00_);_($*(#,##0.00);_($*"-"??_);_(@_)
Currency(0)	Number = ($#,##0_);_($*(#,##0);_($*"-"_);_(@_)
Percent	Number = 0%

Creating and Applying a Style

A **style** is a group of format specifications that are assigned to a style name. Excel comes with the styles described in Table 6-2. You can modify the styles in Table 6-2 or create your own styles if you wish.

Using the **Style command** on the Format menu, you can create and then assign a style to a cell, a range of cells, a worksheet, or a workbook in the same way you assign a format using the buttons on the Formatting toolbar. In fact, the Currency Style button, Comma Style button, and Percent Style button assign the Currency, Comma, and Percent styles in Table 6-2, respectively. Excel assigns the **Normal style** to all cells when you open a new workbook.

With the Style command, you also can delete styles and merge styles from other workbooks. You add a new style to a workbook or merge styles when you plan to use a group of format specifications over and over.

The following steps create a new style called Date by modifying the existing Normal style. The new Date style will include the following formats: Number = March 14, 2001; Alignment = Horizontal Center and Vertical Center; and Font = Arial 10, Bold.

Steps **To Create a New Style**

1 **Click Format on the menu bar and then point to Style.**

The Format menu displays as shown in Figure 6-15.

FIGURE 6-15

2 **Click Style. When the Style dialog box displays, drag through Normal in the Style name box and then type** Date **as the new style name. Point to the Modify button.**

The Style dialog box displays with the new style name Date (Figure 6-16).

FIGURE 6-16

3 Click the Modify button. When the Format Cells dialog box displays, click the Number tab, click Date in the Category list, and then click March 14, 2001 in the Type list. Point to the Alignment tab.

The Format Cells dialog box displays (Figure 6-17). The Format Cells dialog box contains a tab for each check box in the Style dialog box.

FIGURE 6-17

4 Click the Alignment tab. Click the Horizontal box arrow and then click Center. Click the Vertical box arrow and then click Center. Point to the OK button.

The Alignment sheet in the Format Cells dialog box displays as shown in Figure 6-18.

FIGURE 6-18

5 **Click the OK button. Click Font, Border, Patterns, and Protection to deselect the check boxes in the Style Includes area. Point to the Add button.**

The Style dialog box displays the formats assigned to the Date style (Figure 6-19).

6 **Click the Add button to add the new style to the style list available with this template. Click the Close button.**

The new style Date becomes part of the list of styles available with the template.

FIGURE 6-19

You can define a new style or modify a current style using any format available on the six sheets in the Format dialog box (Figure 6-18 on the previous page). It is not unusual for spreadsheet specialists to create several styles for use in a workbook.

Applying a Style

In earlier steps, cell A3 was assigned the date 12/31/2003. This project calls for centering the date and displaying it as December 31, 2003. To accomplish this task, the following steps assign the Date style created in the previous set of steps to cell A3.

To Apply a Style

1 **Click cell A3. Click Format on the menu bar and then click Style. When the Style dialog box displays, click the Style name box arrow and then click Date in the list. Point to the OK button.**

The Style dialog box displays (Figure 6-20).

FIGURE 6-20

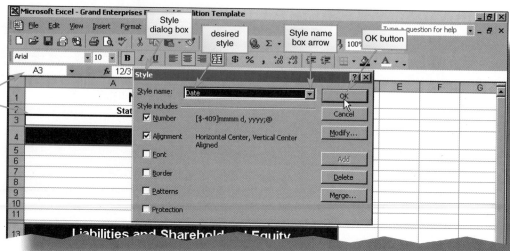

2 **Click the OK button.**

Excel assigns the Date style to cell A3 (Figure 6-21).

FIGURE 6-21

Keep in mind the following additional points concerning styles:

1. If you assign two styles to a range of cells, Excel adds the second style to the first, rather than replacing it.
2. Do not delete the default styles that come with Excel because some of the buttons on the toolbars are dependent on them.
3. You can merge styles from another workbook into the active workbook through the use of the Merge button in the Style dialog box. You must, however, open the workbook that contains the desired styles before you use the Merge button.
4. The six check boxes in the Style dialog box (Figure 6-20) are identical to the six tabs in the Format Cells dialog box (Figure 6-18 on page E 6.19).

Spell Checking, Saving, and Printing the Template

With the formatting complete, the next step is to spell check the template, save it, and then print it.

TO SPELL CHECK, SAVE, AND PRINT THE TEMPLATE

1 Click cell A1. Click the Spelling button on the Standard toolbar. Change any misspelled words.

2 Click the Save button on the Standard toolbar.

3 Click the Print button on the Standard toolbar. Click the Close button on the template title bar.

Excel saves the template using the file name, Grand Enterprises Financial Condition Template, prints the template, and finally closes the template.

Other Ways

1. Press ALT+O, S
2. In Voice Command mode, say "Format, Style, [select style name], OK"

More About

Normal Style

The Normal style is the format style that Excel initially assigns to all cells in a workbook. If you change the Normal style, Excel applies the new format specifications to all cells that are not assigned another style.

More About

The XLSTART Folder

You could replace your default workbook template with the new template you create; the new template then becomes the basis for all new workbooks. All you need to do is give the template the name Book.xlt and save it in the XLSTART folder. (The XLSTART folder is in different places on different systems; use the Find feature of Windows to locate where it is on your system.)

Alternative Uses of Templates

Before continuing and using the template to create the Grand Enterprises 2003 Financial Condition workbook, you should be aware of some additional uses of templates. If you click the **New command** on the File menu, the **New Workbook task pane** displays on the right side of the screen (Figure 6-22). The New Workbook task pane includes a General Templates link. The **General Templates link** displays the **Templates dialog box**, which includes a default Excel template icon titled Workbook. The template associated with this icon contains the defaults that you see whenever you start Excel and it displays the Book1 workbook.

You can save a template to a special template folder that displays whenever you select Templates as the file type when you save. For example, if the Save in location had not been changed in Figure 6-8 on page E 6.12, the Grand Enterprises Financial Condition Template would have been saved to this special template folder rather than drive A. The template then would have displayed in the Templates dialog box in Figure 6-22, and you could have selected it to start a new workbook.

If you save a formatted template in this special folder using the file name Book, Excel uses it as the default blank Workbook template every time you start with a blank workbook. Thus, you easily can change the appearance and formats of the blank workbook that displays whenever you start Excel. You can even add text, such as as a company logo.

More About

Opening a Workbook at Startup

You can instruct Windows to open a workbook (or template) automatically when you turn on your computer by adding the workbook (or template) to the Startup folder. Use Explorer to copy the file to the Startup folder. The Startup folder is in the Programs folder, and the Programs folder is in the Start Menu folder.

FIGURE 6-22

Creating a Workbook from a Template

Once you have saved the template on disk, you can begin the second phase of this project: using the template to create the Grand Enterprises 2003 Financial Condition workbook shown in Figure 6-1 on page E 6.05. The following steps open the template Grand Enterprises Financial Condition Template and save it as a workbook using the file name, Grand Enterprises 2003 Financial Condition.

Steps To Open a Template and Save It as a Workbook

1 **With Excel active, click the Open button on the Standard toolbar. When the Open dialog box displays, click the Look in box arrow and then click 3½ Floppy (A:). Click the file name Grand Enterprises Financial Condition Template and then point to the Open button in the Open dialog box.**

The Open dialog box displays as shown in Figure 6-23.

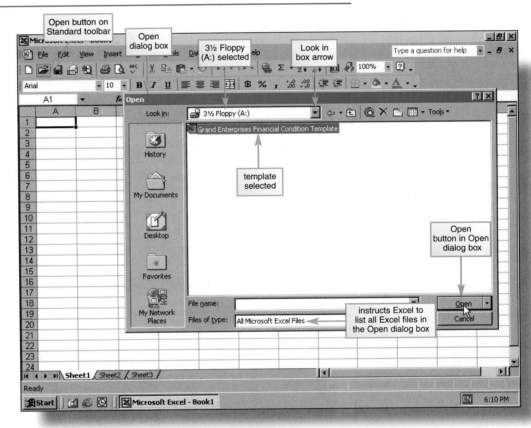

FIGURE 6-23

2 Click the Open button. When the Grand Enterprises Financial Condition Template displays, click Save As on the File menu. When the Save As dialog box displays, type Grand Enterprises 2003 Financial Condition **in the File name box. Click the Save as type box arrow and then click Microsoft Excel Workbook. Click the Save in box arrow and then click 3½ Floppy (A:). Point to the Save button in the Save As dialog box.**

The Save As dialog box displays as shown in Figure 6-24.

3 Click the Save button.

Excel saves the template as a workbook, and the workbook displays on the screen.

FIGURE 6-24

Other Ways

1. Right-click workbook Control-menu icon on menu bar, click Save As on shortcut menu, type file name, select file type, select drive or folder, click OK button

2. Press CTRL+S, type file name, select file type, select drive or folder, click OK button

3. In Voice Command mode, say "File, Save As, [type desired file name], Save as type, Microsoft Excel Workbook, Save in, [select drive or folder], Save"

Excel provides over 30 different file types that you can choose from to save your work. You normally save workbooks using Microsoft Excel Workbook in the Save as type box. You also can save your work in many other formats, such as Web page, template, text, earlier versions of Excel, Lotus 1-2-3, Quattro, and dBase.

Adding a Worksheet to a Workbook

As described earlier, a workbook contains three worksheets by default. You can add worksheets up to a maximum of 255 in a workbook. The Grand Enterprises 2003 Financial Condition workbook requires four worksheets — one for each of the three divisions and one for the company totals. Thus, a worksheet must be inserted in the workbook.

When you insert a worksheet, Excel places its tab to the left of the active tab. To keep the worksheet with the data shown in Figure 6-24 on top or its tab (Sheet1) to the far left, spreadsheet specialists often insert the worksheet between Sheet1 and Sheet2, rather than to the left of Sheet1. Thus, select Sheet2 before adding a worksheet to the workbook. Perform the following steps to add a worksheet to the workbook.

Steps **To Add a Worksheet to a Workbook**

1 **Click the Sheet2 tab at the bottom of the window. Click Insert on the menu bar and then point to Worksheet.**

The Insert menu displays (Figure 6-25).

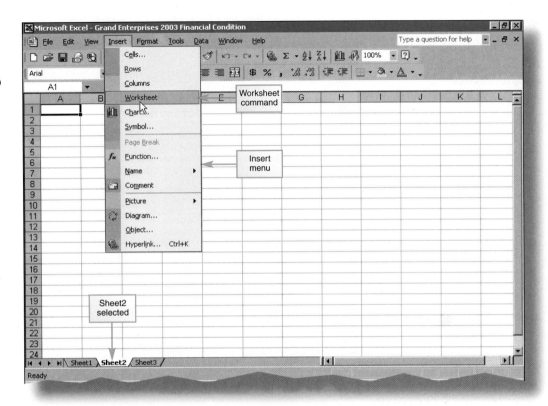

FIGURE 6-25

2 **Click Worksheet.**

Excel adds a fourth worksheet between Sheet1 and Sheet2. Recall that Sheet1 contains the data from the template. As shown on the sheet tab, Sheet4 is the name of the new worksheet (Figure 6-26).

FIGURE 6-26

An alternative to adding worksheets is to change the default number of worksheets before you open a new workbook. To change the default number of worksheets in a blank workbook, click Options on the Tools menu, click the General tab, and change the number in the Sheets in new workbook box. You also can delete a worksheet by right-clicking the tab of the worksheet you want to delete and then clicking Delete on the shortcut menu.

Other **Ways**

1. Press ALT+I, W
2. In Voice Command mode, say "Insert, Worksheet"

Copying the Contents of a Worksheet to Other Worksheets in a Workbook

With four worksheets in the workbook, you can copy the contents of Sheet1 to Sheet4, Sheet2, and Sheet3. Sheet1 eventually will represent the consolidation. Sheet4, Sheet2, and Sheet3 will represent the three divisions.

Steps **To Copy the Contents of a Worksheet to Other Worksheets**

1 **Click the Sheet1 tab to display the data originally added to the template. Click the Select All button and then click the Copy button on the Standard toolbar.**

The template is selected as shown in Figure 6-27. The data on Sheet1 and its formats are copied to the Office Clipboard. A marquee surrounds the Sheet1 worksheet.

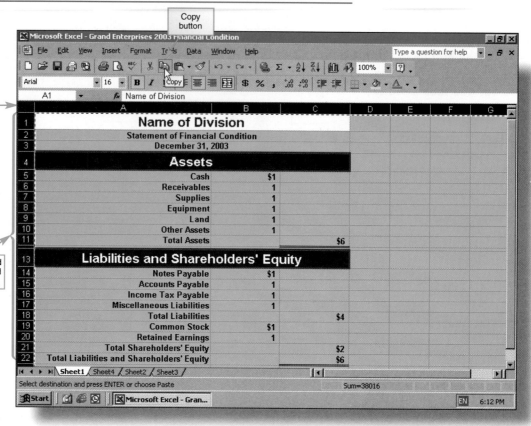

FIGURE 6-27

2 **Click the Sheet4 tab. While holding down the SHIFT key, click the Sheet3 tab so all three blank worksheets in the workbook are selected. Click the Paste button on the Standard toolbar.**

Excel copies the data on the Office Clipboard to Sheet4, Sheet2, and Sheet3. Because multiple sheets are selected, the term [Group] follows the template name on the title bar (Figure 6-28).

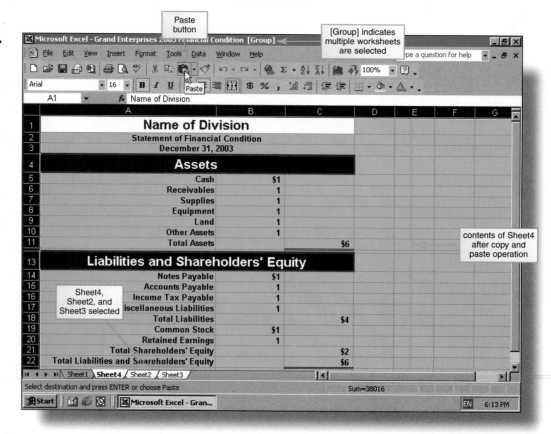

FIGURE 6-28

3 Click the Sheet1 tab. Press the ESC key to remove the marquee surrounding the selection. Hold down the SHIFT key and click the Sheet3 tab. Click cell E22 to select the cell on all four worksheets. Hold down the SHIFT key and click the Sheet1 tab to deselect Sheet4, Sheet2, and Sheet3.

4 Click the Save button on the Standard toolbar.

Excel saves the workbook on drive A using the file name, Grand Enterprises 2003 Financial Condition. Sheet1 is the active worksheet. The four identical worksheets in the workbook display as shown in Figure 6-29.

FIGURE 6-29

Modifying the Western Division Sheet

With the skeleton of the Grand Enterprises 2003 Financial Condition workbook created, the next step is to modify the individual sheets.

The following steps modify the Western Division sheet by changing the sheet name and color, changing the worksheet title, changing the background color of the subtitles, and entering the Western Division financial data.

TO MODIFY THE WESTERN DIVISION SHEET

1 Double-click the Sheet4 tab, type Western Division as the sheet name, and then press the ENTER key. Right-click the Western Division tab, click Tab Color, click Blue (column 6, row 2) in the Format Tab Color dialog box, and then click the OK button.

2 Click cell A1, type Western Division, and then click the Enter box in the formula bar. Click the Font Color button arrow on the Formatting toolbar, and then click Blue (column 6, row 2) on the Font Color palette.

3 Select cell A4. Hold down the CTRL key and click cell A13. Click the Fill Color button arrow on the Formatting toolbar, and then click Blue (column 6, row 2) on the Fill Color palette.

More *About*

The Keyboard Shortcuts

Prefer to use the keyboard over the mouse? If you prefer the keyboard, then use the Ask a Question box to search for keyboard shortcuts. For a list of the shortcut keys and their functions, click the link titled Keyboard shortcuts.

4 Enter the financial data listed in column two in Table 6-3 in the range B5:B20.

5 Click the Save button on the Standard toolbar.

The Western Division worksheet displays as shown in Figure 6-30.

Sheet Tabs

If you right-click a sheet tab, a shortcut menu displays with several commands to modify the workbook. Commands on the shortcut menu allow you to insert a new sheet, delete the active sheet, rename the active sheet, move or copy the active sheet, select all sheets, and color a tab.

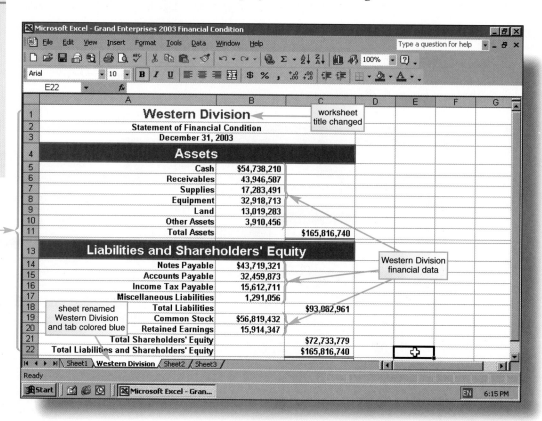

FIGURE 6-30

Table 6-3	Western Division
ASSET	**AMOUNT**
Cash	$54,738,210
Receivables	43,946,587
Supplies	17,283,491
Equipment	32,918,713
Land	13,019,283
Other Assets	3,910,456
LIABILITY AND SHAREHOLDERS' EQUITY	***AMOUNT***
Notes Payable	$43,719,321
Accounts Payable	32,459,873
Income Tax Payable	15,612,711
Miscellaneous Liabilities	1,291,056
Common Stock	56,819,432
Retained Earnings	15,914,347

As you enter the new data, Excel immediately recalculates the formulas on all four worksheets.

Modifying the Central Division Sheet

The following steps modify the Central Division sheet.

TO MODIFY THE CENTRAL DIVISION SHEET

1 Double-click the Sheet2 tab, type Central Division as the sheet name, and then press the ENTER key. Right-click the Central Division tab, click Tab Color, click Red (column 1, row 3) in the Format Tab Color dialog box, and then click the OK button.

2 Click cell A1, type Central Division and then click the Enter box in the formula bar. Click the Font Color button arrow on the Formatting toolbar, and then click Red (column 1, row 3) on the Font Color palette.

3 Select cell A4. Hold down the CTRL key and click cell A13. Click the Fill Color button arrow on the Formatting toolbar, and then click Red (column 1, row 3) on the Fill Color palette.

4 Enter the financial data listed in column two in Table 6-4 in the range B5:B20.

5 Click the Save button on the Standard toolbar.

The Central Division worksheet displays as shown in Figure 6-31.

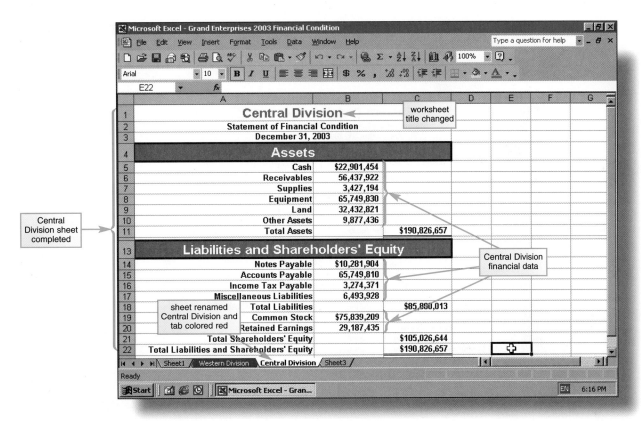

FIGURE 6-31

Modifying the Eastern Division Sheet

As with the Western Division and Central Division sheets, the sheet name, worksheet title, background colors, and data must be changed on the Eastern Division sheet. The following steps modify the Eastern Division sheet.

TO MODIFY THE EASTERN DIVISION SHEET

1 Double-click the Sheet3 tab, type Eastern Division as the sheet name, and then press the ENTER key. Right-click the Eastern Division tab, click Tab Color, click Green (column 4, row 2) in the Format Tab Color dialog box, and then click the OK button.

2 Click cell A1, type Eastern Division and then click the Enter box in the formula bar. Click the Font Color button arrow on the Formatting toolbar, and then click Green (column 4, row 2) on the Font Color palette.

3 Select cell A4. Hold down the CTRL key and click cell A13. Click the Fill Color button arrow on the Formatting toolbar, click Green (column 4, row 2) on the Fill Color palette.

Table 6-4	Central Division
ASSET	**AMOUNT**
Cash	$22,901,454
Receivables	56,437,922
Supplies	3,427,194
Equipment	65,749,830
Land	32,432,821
Other Assets	9,877,436
LIABILITY AND SHAREHOLDERS' EQUITY	**AMOUNT**
Notes Payable	$10,281,904
Accounts Payable	65,749,810
Income Tax Payable	3,274,371
Miscellaneous Liabilities	6,493,928
Common Stock	75,839,209
Retained Earnings	29,187,435

4 Enter the financial data listed in column two in Table 6-5 in the range B5:B20.

5 Click the Save button on the Standard toolbar.

The Eastern Division worksheet displays as shown in Figure 6-32.

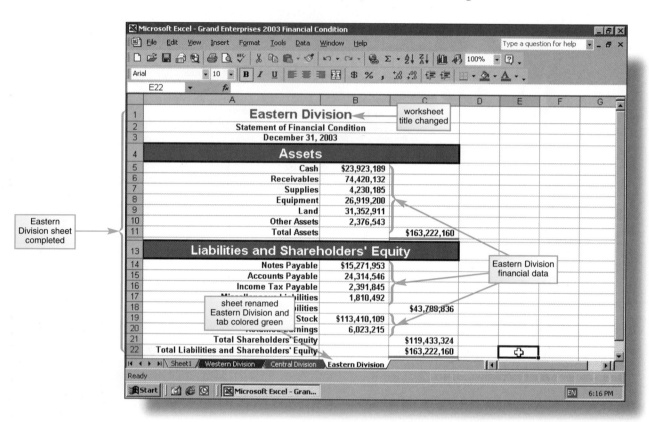

FIGURE 6-32

Table 6-5	Eastern Division
ASSET	**AMOUNT**
Cash	$23,923,189
Receivables	74,420,132
Supplies	4,230,185
Equipment	26,919,200
Land	31,352,911
Other Assets	2,376,543
LIABILITY AND SHAREHOLDERS' EQUITY	**AMOUNT**
Notes Payable	$15,271,953
Accounts Payable	24,314,546
Income Tax Payable	2,391,845
Miscellaneous Liabilities	1,810,492
Common Stock	113,410,109
Retained Earnings	6,023,215

With the three division sheets complete, the next step is to modify Sheet1, which will serve as the consolidation worksheet containing totals of the data on the Western Division, Central Division, and Eastern Division sheets. Because this sheet contains totals of the data, you need to understand how to reference cells in other sheets in a workbook before modifying Sheet1.

Referencing Cells in Other Sheets in a Workbook

To reference cells in other sheets in a workbook, you use the sheet name, which serves as the **sheet reference**, and the cell reference. For example, you refer to cell B5 on the Western Division sheet as shown below.

=Western Division!B5

Using this method, you can sum cell B5 on the three division sheets by selecting cell B5 on the Sheet1 sheet and then entering:

= Western Division!B5 + Central Division!B5 + Eastern Division!B5

A much quicker way to total this is to use the SUM function as follows:

=SUM(Western Division:Eastern Division!B5)

The SUM argument (Western Division:Eastern Division!B5) instructs Excel to sum cell B5 on each of the three sheets (Western Division, Central Division, and Eastern Division). The colon (:) between the first sheet and the last sheet means to include these sheets and all sheets in between, just as it does with a range of cells on a sheet. A range that spans two or more sheets in a workbook, such as Western Division:Eastern Division!B5, is called a **3-D range**. The reference to this range is a **3-D reference**.

A sheet reference, such as Eastern Division!, always is absolute. Thus, the sheet reference remains constant when you copy and paste formulas.

Entering a Sheet Reference

You can enter a sheet reference in a cell by typing it or by clicking the appropriate sheet tab using Point mode. When you click the sheet tab, Excel activates the sheet and automatically adds the sheet name and an exclamation point after the insertion point in the formula bar. Next, click or drag through the cells you want to reference on the sheet.

If the range of cells to be referenced is located on several worksheets (as when selecting a 3-D range), click the first sheet tab and then click the cell or drag through the range of cells. Next, while holding down the SHIFT key, click the sheet tab of the last sheet you want to reference. Excel will include the cell(s) on the end sheets and all the sheets in between.

Modifying the Consolidated Sheet

This section modifies the Consolidated sheet by changing the sheet name, tab color, worksheet title, and entering the SUM function in each cell in the range B5:B10, B14:B17, and B19:B20. The SUM functions will determine the totals for the three divisions. Cell B5 on the Consolidated sheet, for instance, will equal the sum of the Cash assets for the Western Division, Central Division, and Eastern Division in cells Western Division!B5, Central Division!B5, and Eastern Division!B5. Before determining the totals, perform the following steps to change the sheet name, tab color, and worksheet title.

TO RENAME A SHEET, COLOR ITS TAB, AND CHANGE THE WORKSHEET TITLE

1 Double-click the Sheet1 tab, type `Consolidated` as the sheet name, and then press the ENTER key. Right-click the Consolidated tab, click Tab Color, click Gray – 80% (column 8, row 1) in the Format Tab Color dialog box, and then click the OK button.

2 Click cell A1 and then type `Grand Enterprises Incorporated` as the worksheet title. Click the Enter box.

The Consolidated sheet displays with new titles on the sheet tab and in cell A1.

The steps on the next page use 3-D references to sum the total Cash assets for the company in cell B5 and then copy the SUM function to the other 11 categories in column B.

More About

3-D References

If you are adding numbers on noncontiguous sheets, hold down the CTRL key rather than the SHIFT key when selecting the sheets.

More About

Drilling an Entry

An interesting technique, called drilling an entry, can be useful when working with multiple sheets in a workbook. Drilling an entry means that you select multiple sheets and then enter a number, text, or formula into a cell. Excel will duplicate the entry in the same cell on all selected sheets.

Microsoft **Excel** 2002

Steps **To Enter and Copy 3-D References**

1 With the **Consolidated sheet active, click cell B5 and then click the AutoSum button on the Standard toolbar.**

The SUM function displays without a selected range (Figure 6-33).

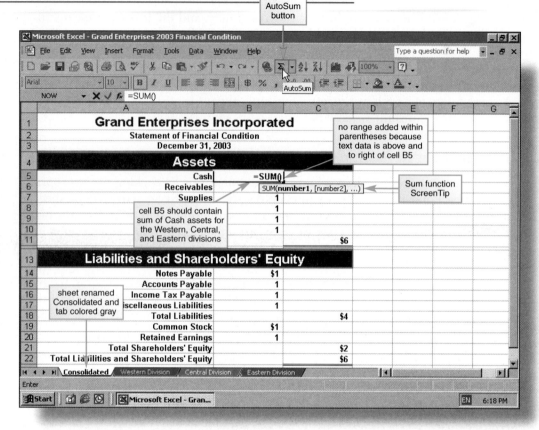

FIGURE 6-33

2 Click the Western **Division tab and then click cell B5. While holding down the SHIFT key, click the Eastern Division tab. Point to the Enter box in the formula bar.**

A marquee surrounds cell Western Division!B5 (Figure 6-34). All four sheet tabs are selected; the Western Division tab displays in bold because it is the active sheet. The SUM function displays in the formula bar.

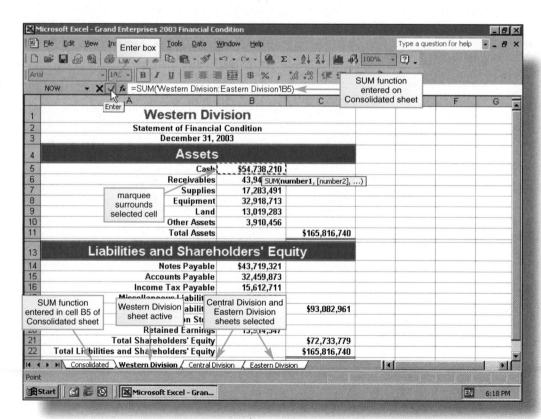

FIGURE 6-34

3 **Click the Enter box.**

The SUM function is entered in cell Consolidated!B5 and the Consolidated sheet becomes the active sheet. The sum ($101,562,853) of the cells Western Division!B5, Central Division!B5, and Eastern Division!B5 displays in cell B5 of the Consolidated sheet. The SUM function assigned to cell B5 displays in the formula bar (Figure 6-35).

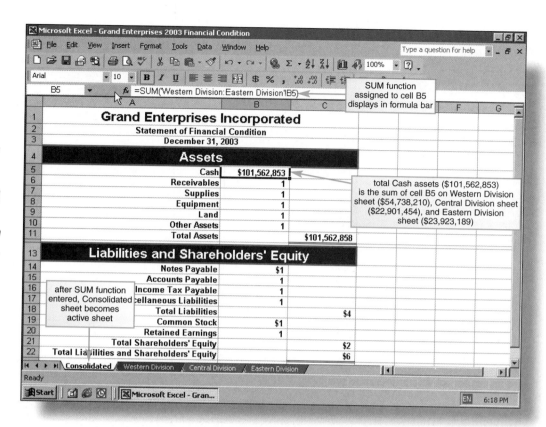

FIGURE 6-35

4 **With cell B5 active, click the Copy button on the Standard toolbar.**

A marquee surrounds cell B5 indicating that its contents have been placed on the Office Clipboard (Figure 6-36).

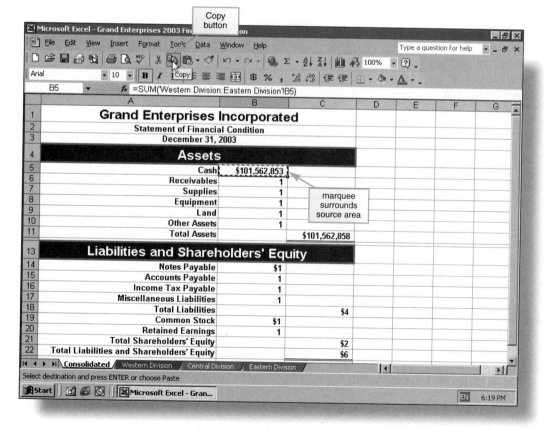

FIGURE 6-36

5 **Select the range B6:B10. Hold down the CTRL key and select the nonadjacent ranges B14:B17 and B19:B20. Click the Paste button arrow on the Standard toolbar. Point to Formulas on the Paste menu.**

The Consolidated sheet displays as shown in Figure 6-37.

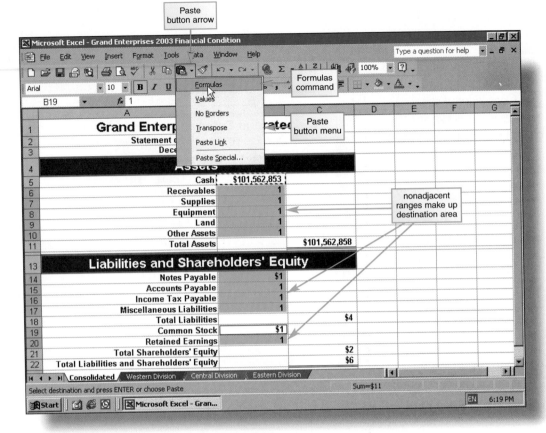

FIGURE 6-37

6 **Click Formulas.**

Excel pastes the SUM function to the ranges B6:B10, B14:B17, and B19:B20. It does not paste the format of cell B5 (Figure 6-38). The Consolidated sheet is complete.

7 **Click the Save button on the Standard toolbar to save the Grand Enterprises 2003 Financial Condition workbook.**

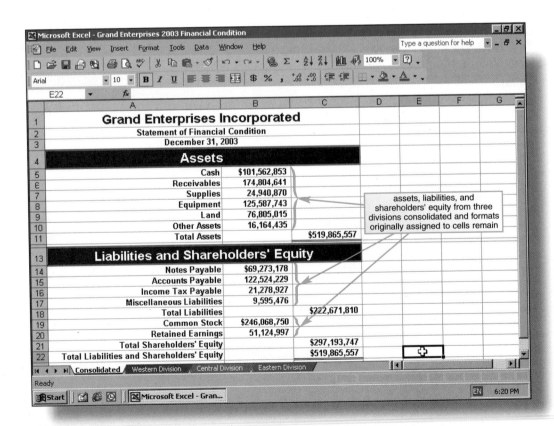

FIGURE 6-38

The cell reference (B5) in the SUM function in the formula bar in Figure 6-35 on page E 6.33 is relative (no dollar signs). Thus, when Excel pastes the SUM function into the destination areas in column B, it changes the cell reference in the SUM function from cell B5 to the cell reference that corresponds to the cell to which the function is being copied. To see how these cell references change, click the cells in the destination areas in column B.

If you click the Paste button on the Standard toolbar to complete the paste operation, rather than using the Formulas option as shown in Figure 6-37, then the Currency Style format assigned to cell B5 also will be copied to the destination areas. By using the Formulas option on the Paste menu, Excel copies the SUM function, but not the format of the source area as shown in Figure 6-38. As shown in this example, the Formulas option on the Paste menu is useful when you already have the desired formats assigned to the destination area. Table 6-6 summarizes the options available on the Paste menu shown in Figure 6-37.

Table 6-6	Paste Menu Options
OPTION	**DESCRIPTION**
Formulas	Paste the formulas from the source area, but not the formats.
Values	Paste the value of the formula from the source area, but not the formulas or formats.
No Borders	Paste the formula and formats from the source area, except for borders.
Transpose	Paste the formula and formats from the source area, but transpose the columns and rows. For example, if you are summing numbers in a column in the source area, then Excel will sum numbers in a row in the destination area.
Paste Link	Paste the cell reference of the source area in the destination area.
Paste Special	Displays the Paste Special dialog box that allows you to choose what you want pasted from the source area to the destination area.

Drawing the 3-D Cylinder Chart

The 3-D Cylinder chart is similar to a 3-D Bar chart in that it can be used to show trends or illustrate comparisons among items. The 3-D Cylinder chart in Figure 6-39, for example, compares the company's allocation of assets. WordArt is used to draw the curved chart title 2003 Assets. A text box and arrow are used to highlight the greatest asset.

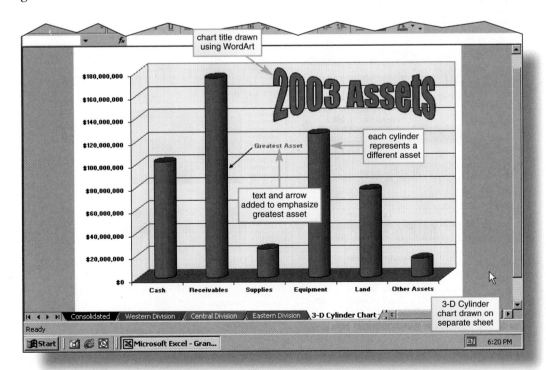

FIGURE 6-39

The following steps create the 3-D Cylinder chart.

Steps To Draw a 3-D Cylinder Chart

1 **With the Consolidated sheet active, select the range A5:B10. Click the Chart Wizard button on the Standard toolbar. When the Chart Wizard - Step 1 of 4 - Chart Type dialog box displays, click Cylinder in the Chart type list. If necessary, click Column with a cylindrical shape (column 1, row 1) in the Chart sub-type area. Point to the Next button.**

The Chart Wizard - Step 1 of 4 - Chart Type dialog box displays as shown in Figure 6-40. The range selection displays behind the dialog box.

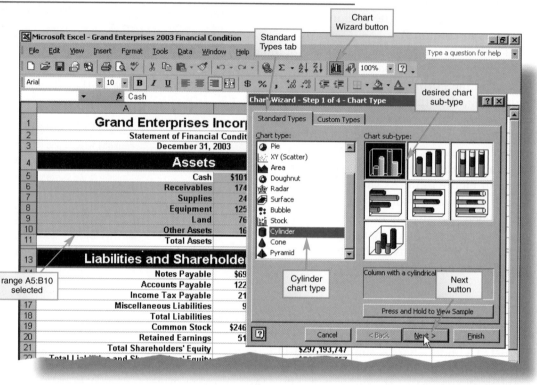

FIGURE 6-40

2 **Click the Next button. When the Chart Wizard - Step 2 of 4 - Chart Source Data dialog box displays, point to the Next button.**

The Chart Wizard - Step 2 of 4 - Chart Source Data dialog box displays with a sample of the 3-D Cylinder chart and the data range selection (Figure 6-41). A marquee surrounds the data range on the Consolidated sheet. Because the range is down the sheet, Excel automatically determines the data range is in columns.

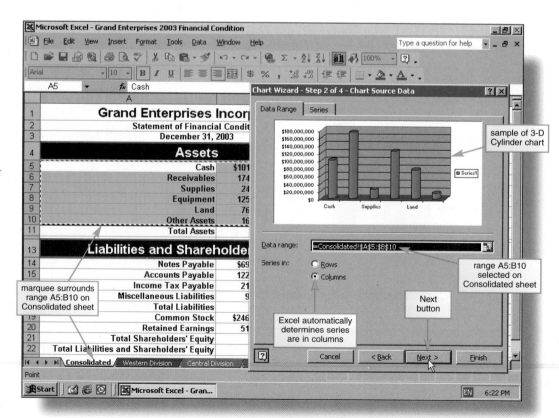

FIGURE 6-41

3 **Click the Next button. When the Chart Wizard - Step 3 of 4 - Chart Options dialog box displays, click the Legend tab. Click Show legend to deselect it so the legend does not display with the chart. Point to the Next button.**

The Chart Wizard - Step 3 of 4 - Chart Options dialog box displays (Figure 6-42). Excel redraws the preview of the chart without the legend.

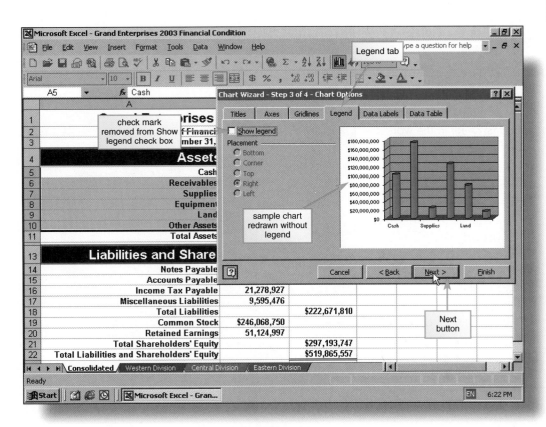

FIGURE 6-42

4 **Click the Next button. When the Chart Wizard - Step 4 of 4 - Chart Location dialog box displays, click As new sheet. Point to the Finish button.**

The Chart Wizard - Step 4 of 4 - Chart Location dialog box displays (Figure 6-43). Because the As new sheet option button is selected, the chart will be drawn on a separate chart sheet.

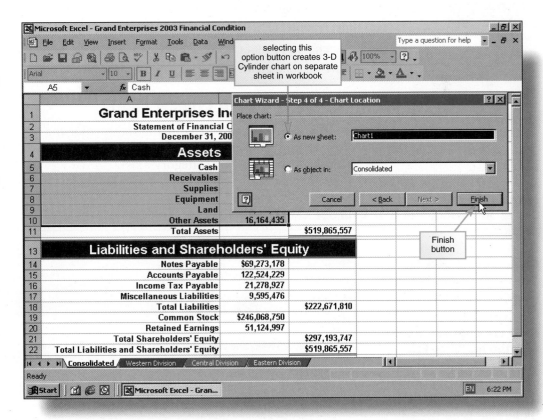

FIGURE 6-43

5 Click the Finish button.

Excel draws the 3-D Cylinder chart. The chart sheet, which is named Chart1, is inserted as the first sheet in the workbook (Figure 6-44).

FIGURE 6-44

The 3-D Cylinder chart compares the six consolidated assets. You can see from the chart that the greatest asset is Receivables and that the Other Assets is the least asset.

Formatting the 3-D Cylinder Chart

The following steps rename the sheet, color the tab, move the sheet, change the color of the cylinders and the wall behind the cylinders, and format the y-axis (values axis) and x-axis (category axis).

Steps To Format the 3-D Cylinder Chart

1 Double-click the Chart1 tab and then

type 3-D Cylinder Chart **as the sheet name. Press the ENTER key. Right-click the tab, click Tab Color on the shortcut menu, and then click Light Yellow (column 3, row 5). Click the OK button. Drag the 3-D**

FIGURE 6-45

Cylinder Chart sheet tab to the right of the Eastern Division sheet tab.

The 3-D Cylinder Chart tab displays as shown in Figure 6-45.

2 **Click the wall behind the cylinders, click the Fill Color button arrow on the Formatting toolbar, and then click Light Yellow (column 3, row 5). Click one of the Cylinders to select all the Cylinders, click the Fill Color button arrow on the Formatting toolbar, and then click Red (column 1, row 3). Click the x-axis, click the Bold button on the Formatting toolbar, click the Font Size box arrow on the Formatting toolbar, and then click 12. Click the y-axis, click the Bold button on the Formatting toolbar, click the Font Size box arrow on the Formatting toolbar, and then click 12. Click outside the chart area.**

The 3-D Cylinder chart displays as shown in Figure 6-46.

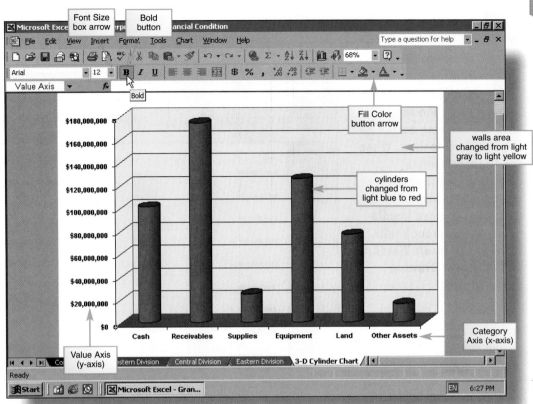

FIGURE 6-46

Adding a Chart Title Using the WordArt Tool

Earlier, you learned how to add a chart title by using the Chart Wizard and how to format it using the Formatting toolbar. This section shows you how to add a chart title and create special text formatting effects using the WordArt tool. The **WordArt tool** allows you to create shadowed, skewed, rotated, and stretched text on a chart sheet or worksheet. The WordArt design is called an **object**. You start the WordArt tool by clicking the WordArt button on the Drawing toolbar. Perform the steps on the next page to add a Chart title using the WordArt tool.

Other Ways

1. Right-click chart item, click Format [chart item] on shortcut menu, select formats, click OK button

Steps **To Add a Chart Title Using the WordArt Tool**

1 With the 3-D Cylinder Chart sheet displaying on the screen, click the Drawing button on the Standard toolbar. When the Drawing toolbar displays, dock it at the bottom of the screen by dragging its move handle below the workbook tabs. Point to the Insert WordArt button on the Drawing toolbar.

The Drawing toolbar displays at the bottom of the screen (Figure 6-47).

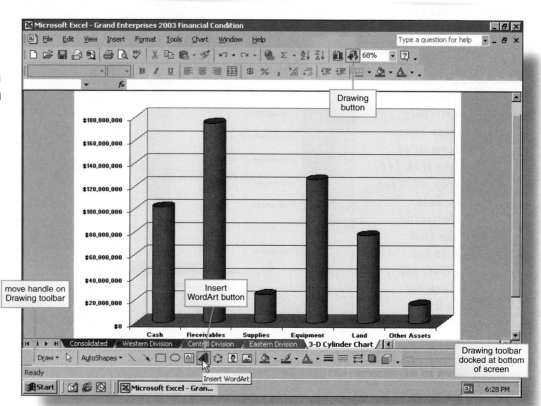

FIGURE 6-47

2 Click the Insert WordArt button. When the WordArt Gallery dialog box displays, click the design in column 4, row 1 in the Select a WordArt style area. Point to the OK button.

The WordArt Gallery dialog box displays (Figure 6-48).

FIGURE 6-48

3 **Click the OK button. When the Edit WordArt Text dialog box displays, type** 2003 Assets **as the title of the 3-D Cylinder chart. Point to the OK button.**

The Edit WordArt Text dialog box displays (Figure 6-49). 2003 Assets will be the chart title.

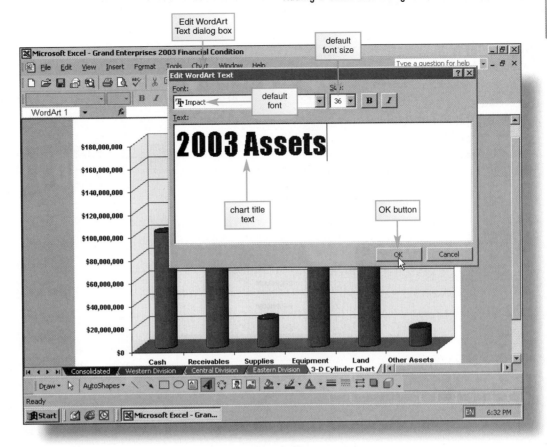

FIGURE 6-49

4 **Click the OK button.**

The WordArt object (2003 Assets) displays in the middle of the chart sheet (Figure 6-50). The WordArt toolbar displays.

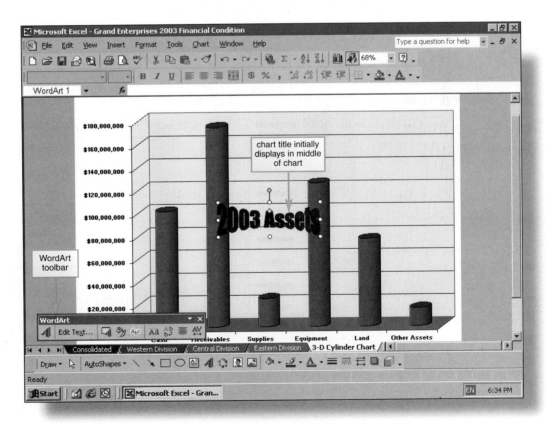

FIGURE 6-50

5 Point to the center of the WordArt object and drag it above the cylinders in the chart and then drag the sizing handles to resize it as shown in Figure 6-51.

The handles (small circles) surrounding the WordArt object indicates it is selected (Figure 6-51).

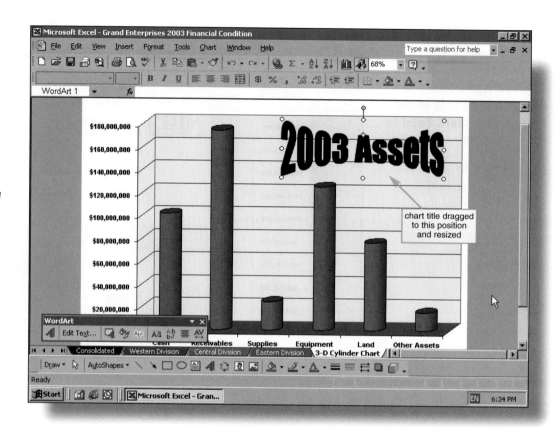

FIGURE 6-51

6 With the WordArt object selected, click the Fill Color button on the Formatting toolbar to change the color to red.

The color of the WordArt object changes to red (Figure 6-52). Even though the title appears to consist of text, the chart title is an object. Thus, you use the Fill Color button, rather than the Font Color button, to change the color of the object.

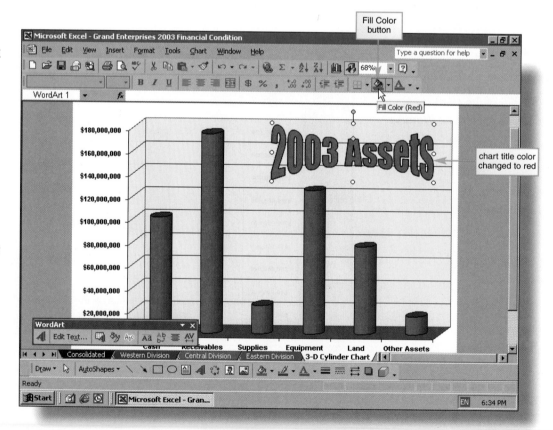

FIGURE 6-52

7 **Click outside the chart area.**

Excel hides the WordArt toolbar. The chart title is complete (Figure 6-53).

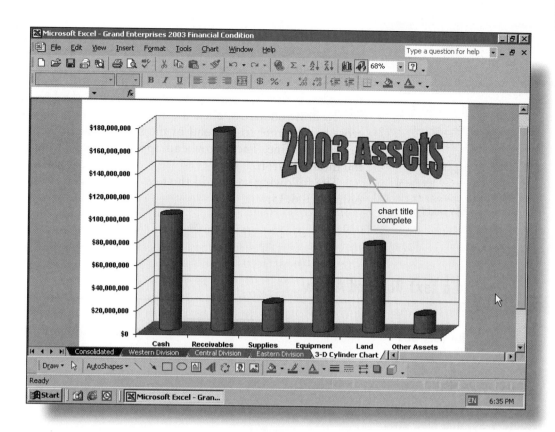

FIGURE 6-53

Once you add a WordArt object to your workbook, you can use the WordArt toolbar (Figure 6-52) to edit it. Anytime you select the WordArt object, the WordArt toolbar should display. If it fails to display, right-click any toolbar and click WordArt on the shortcut menu. The buttons on the WordArt toolbar and their functions are described in Table 6-7.

Adding a Text Box and Arrow to the Chart

A text box and arrow can be used to annotate (callout or highlight) other objects or elements in a worksheet or chart. For example, in a worksheet, you may want to annotate a particular cell or group of cells by adding a text box and arrow. In a chart, you may want to emphasize a column or slice of a Pie chart.

A **text box** is a rectangular area of variable size in which you can add text. You use the sizing handles to resize a text box in the same manner you resize an embedded chart or a WordArt object. If the text box has the same color as the background, then the text appears as if it was written freehand, because the box itself does not show. An **arrow** allows you to connect an object, such as a text box, to an item that you want to annotate.

Table 6-7	Buttons on the WordArt Toolbar	
BUTTON	**NAME**	**FUNCTION**
	Insert WordArt	Starts the WordArt tool
Edit Te_x_t...	Edit Text	Edits text
	WordArt Gallery	Displays the WordArt Gallery dialog box
	Format WordArt	Formats the WordArt object
Abc	WordArt Shape	Changes the shape of an object
Aa	WordArt Same Letter Heights	Switches between the same and different letter heights in an object
Ab b↵	WordArt Vertical Text	Changes the design from horizontal to vertical
≡	WordArt Alignment	Changes the alignment of an object
AV ↔	WordArt Character Spacing	Changes the character spacing in an Spacing object

To draw a text box, click the Text Box button on the Drawing toolbar. Move the cross hair pointer to one corner of the desired location and drag to the diagonally opposite corner. Once the mouse pointer changes to a cross hair, you also can click the upper-left corner of the desired location and Excel will draw a box that you can resize later. To enter text within the box, click the box and begin typing.

To draw an arrow, click the Arrow button on the Drawing toolbar. Move the cross hair pointer to one end of the line you want to draw. Drag the mouse pointer to draw the line. The arrowhead appears at the end of the line where you released the mouse button.

The following steps add the text box and arrow shown previously in Figure 6-39 on page E 6.35.

Steps ## To Add a Text Box and Arrow

1 **Click the Text Box button on the Drawing toolbar. Point to the upper-left corner of the planned text box location (Figure 6-54) and then drag the cross hair to the lower-right corner. With the insertion point active in the text box, type** Greatest Asset **as the text. Drag through the text. Click the Font Size box arrow on the Formatting toolbar and click 12. Click the Bold button on the Formatting toolbar. Click the Font Color button arrow on the Formatting toolbar. Click Red (column 1, row 3) on the Font Color palette.**

The text box displays as shown in Figure 6-54.

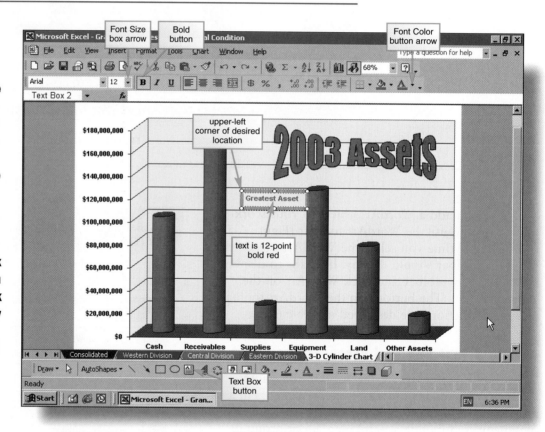

FIGURE 6-54

2 Click the Arrow button on the Drawing toolbar. Point immediately to the left of the letter G in Greatest in the text box. Drag the arrow to the cylinder representing Receivables. Release the mouse button.

The arrow points to the cylinder representing Receivables (Figure 6-55).

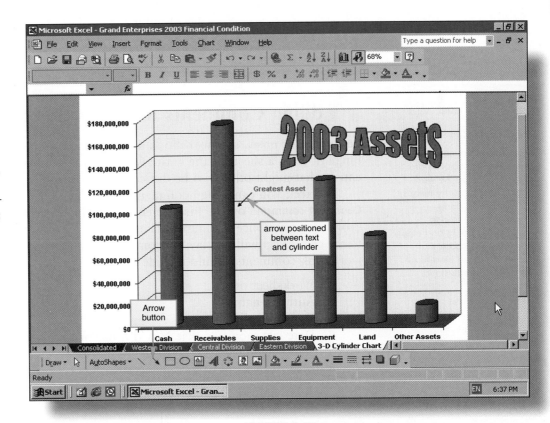

FIGURE 6-55

3 Click the Drawing button on the Standard toolbar to hide the Drawing toolbar.

The 3-D Cylinder chart is complete (Figure 6-56).

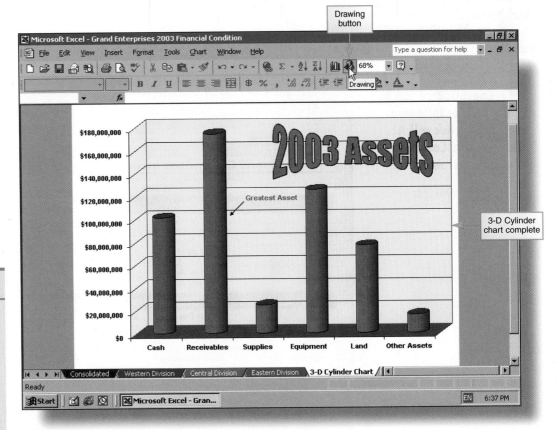

FIGURE 6-56

Other **Ways**

1. On Insert menu point to Picture, click WordArt, select desired style, click OK button, enter text, click OK button

2. Press ALT+I, P, W select desired style, click OK button, enter text, click OK button

3. In Voice Command mode, say "Drawing, Insert WordArt, [select desired style], OK, [enter text], OK"

Besides text boxes, you can use the AutoShapes button on the Drawing toolbar to draw more eloquent callouts, such as flowchart symbols, stars and banners, and balloons that are similar to those used to display words in a comic book.

Adding Comments to a Workbook

Comments, or **notes**, in a workbook are used to describe the function of a cell, a range of cells, a sheet, or the entire workbook. Comments are used to identify entries that might otherwise be difficult to understand.

In Excel, you can assign comments to any cell in the worksheet using the **Comment command** on the Insert menu or the **Insert Comment command** on the shortcut menu. Once a comment is assigned, you can read the comment by pointing to the cell. Excel will display the comment in a **comment box**. In general, overall workbook comments should include the following:

1. Worksheet title
2. Author's name
3. Date created
4. Date last modified (use N/A if it has not been modified)
5. Template(s) used, if any
6. A short description of the purpose of the worksheet

The following steps assign a workbook comment to cell A1 on the Consolidated sheet.

Steps **To Assign a Comment to a Cell**

1 **Click the Consolidated tab to display the Consolidated sheet. Right-click cell A1. Point to Insert Comment on the shortcut menu.**

The shortcut menu displays (Figure 6-57).

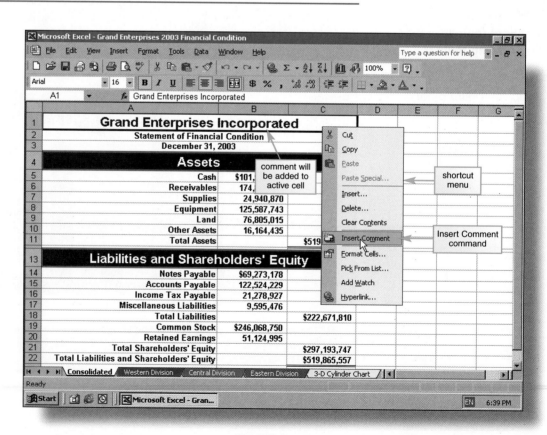

FIGURE 6-57

2 **Click Insert Comment. When the comment box displays, drag the lower-right handle to resize the comment box as shown in Figure 6-58.**

Excel adds a small red triangle, called a comment indicator, to cell A1. A small black arrow attached to the comment box points to the comment indicator.

3 **Enter the comment shown in Figure 6-58 in the comment box. Select the entire comment and click the Bold button. Click after the last period in the comment.**

The comment displays as shown in Figure 6-58.

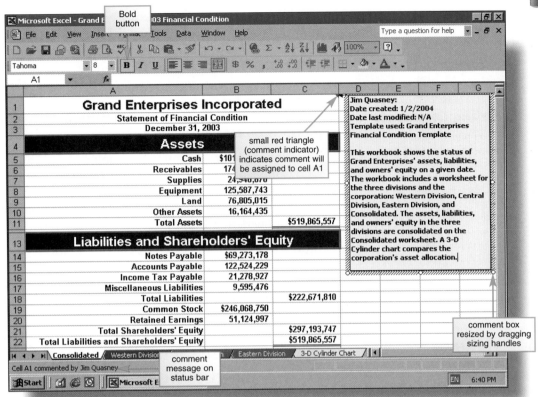

FIGURE 6-58

4 **Click cell E22 and then point to cell A1.**

The comment box displays (Figure 6-59).

5 **Click the Save button on the Standard toolbar to save the workbook.**

FIGURE 6-59

Other Ways

1. On Insert menu click Comment

2. Press ALT+I, M

3. In Voice Command mode, say "Insert, Comment"

The **comment indicator** in the upper-right corner of cell A1 indicates the cell has a comment associated with it. To read the comment, point to the cell and the note will display on the worksheet. To edit the comment, right-click the cell and then click **Edit Comment** on the shortcut menu, or click the cell and then press SHIFT+F2. To delete the comment, right-click the cell and then click **Delete Comment** on the shortcut menu.

If you incorporate comments in a worksheet, you have three options regarding their display on the worksheet:

1. None — do not display the comment indicator or comment
2. Comment indicator only — display the comment indicator, but not the comment unless you point to it
3. Comment & indicator — display both the comment indicator and comment at all times

You select one of the three by clicking Options on the Tools menu and making your selection in the Comments area on the View sheet. If you choose None, then the comment will not display when you point to the cell with the comment. Thus, it becomes a hidden comment.

Printing Comments

You can print comments assigned to cells as follows: click File on the menu bar, click Page Setup on the File menu, click the Sheet tab, click the Comments arrow, and click where you want the comments printed in relation to the worksheet printout.

Templates

Applying page setup characteristics to a template will not work because they are not part of the pasted worksheets. Thus, the page setup characteristics assigned to a template will apply to only the first sheet in a workbook created by copying the template to multiple worksheets in the workbook.

Adding a Header, Changing the Margins, and Printing the Workbook

A **header** is printed at the top of every page in a printout. A **footer** is printed at the bottom of every page in a printout. By default, both the header and footer are blank. You can change either so information, such as the workbook author, date, page number, or tab name, prints at the top or bottom of each page.

Sometimes you will want to change the margins to increase or decrease the white space surrounding the printed worksheet or chart. The default **margins** in Excel for both portrait and landscape orientation are set to the following: Top = 1"; Bottom = 1"; Left = .75"; Right = .75". The header and footer are set at .5" from the top and bottom, respectively. You also can center a printout horizontally and vertically.

Changing the header and footer and changing the margins are all part of the **page setup**, which defines the appearance and format of a page. To change page setup characteristics, select the desired sheet(s) and click the **Page Setup command** on the File menu. Remember to select all the sheets you want to modify before you change the headers, footers, or margins, because the page setup characteristics will change only for selected sheets. The headers and footers for chart sheets must be assigned separately from worksheets.

As you modify the page setup, remember that Excel does not copy page setup characteristics when one sheet is copied to another. Thus, even if you assigned page setup characteristics to the template before copying it to the Grand Enterprises 2003 Financial Condition workbook, the page setup characteristics would not copy to the new sheet. The following steps use the Page Setup dialog box to change the headers and margins and center the printout horizontally.

To Change the Header and Margins and Center the Printout Horizontally

1 **If necessary, click the Consolidated tab to make it active. While holding down the SHIFT key, click the Eastern Division sheet tab. Click File on the menu bar and then point to Page Setup.**

Excel displays the File menu (Figure 6-60). The four worksheet tabs at the bottom of the window are selected. The 3-D Cylinder Chart sheet is not selected.

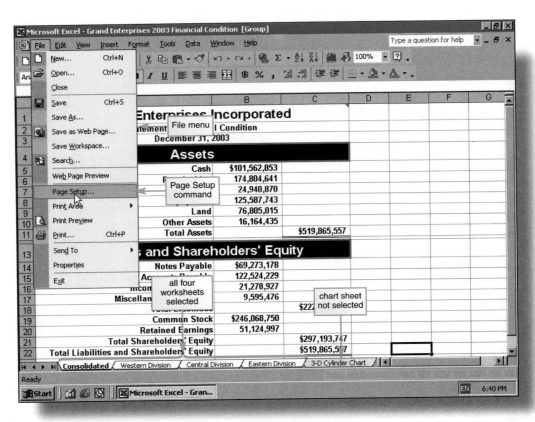

FIGURE 6-60

2 **Click Page Setup. When the Page Setup dialog box displays, click the Header/Footer tab. Point to the Custom Header button.**

The Page Setup dialog box displays (Figure 6-61). The entry (none) indicates that the headers and footers are blank.

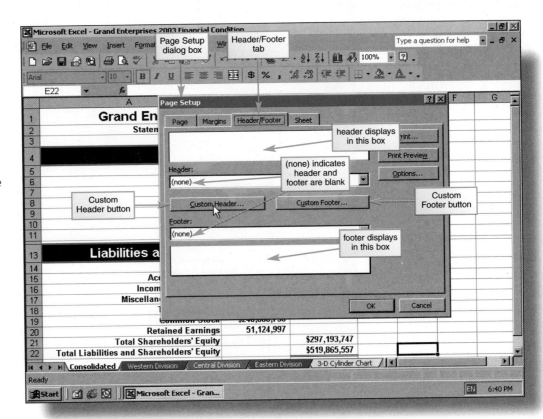

FIGURE 6-61

Microsoft **Excel 2002**

3 **Click the Custom Header button.** When the Header dialog box displays, click the Left section text box. Type Jose Rich and then press the ENTER key. Type 2003 Financial Condition and then click the Center section text box. Click the Tab button. Click the Right section text box. Type Page and then press the SPACEBAR. Click the Page Number button and then press the SPACEBAR. Type of and then press the SPACEBAR. Click the Total Pages button. Point to the OK button in the Header dialog box.

The Header dialog box displays with the new header (Figure 6-62).

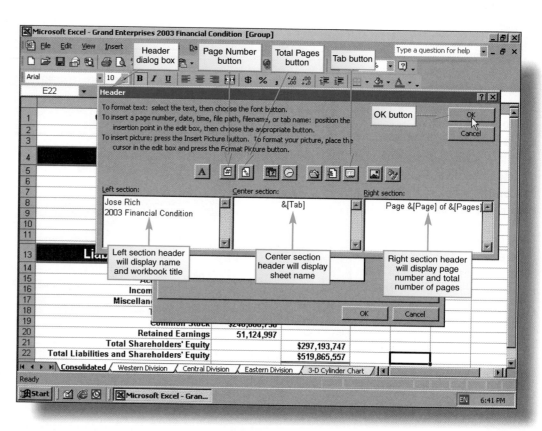

FIGURE 6-62

4 **Click the OK button. When the Page Setup dialog box displays, point to the Margins tab.**

The Header/Footer sheet in the Page Setup dialog box displays as shown in Figure 6-63.

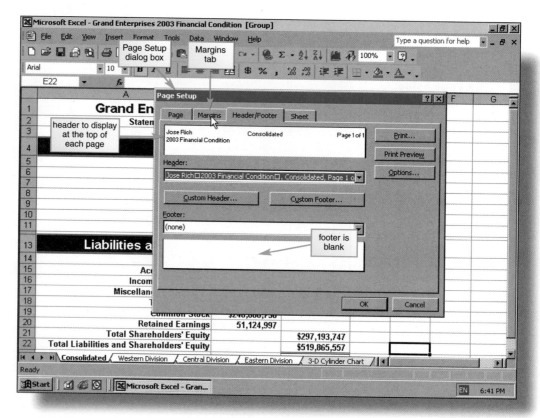

FIGURE 6-63

5 **Click the Margins tab. Click the Top box and then type** 1.5 **to change the top margin to 1.5". Click Horizontally in the Center on page area to center the worksheet on the page. Point to the Print Preview button.**

The Margins sheet in the Page Setup dialog box displays as shown in Figure 6-64.

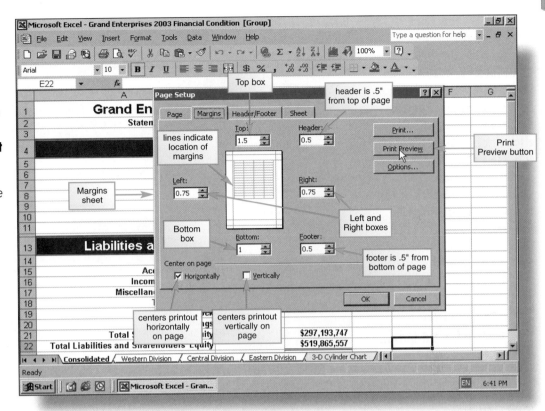

FIGURE 6-64

6 **Click the Print Preview button in the Page Setup dialog box to preview the workbook.**

The Consolidated sheet displays as shown in Figure 6-65. Although difficult to read, the header displays at the top of the page. While the mouse pointer is a magnifying glass, you can click the page to get a better view.

7 **Click the Next button and Previous button on the Print Preview toolbar to preview the other pages. After previewing the printout, click the Close button on the Print Preview toolbar.**

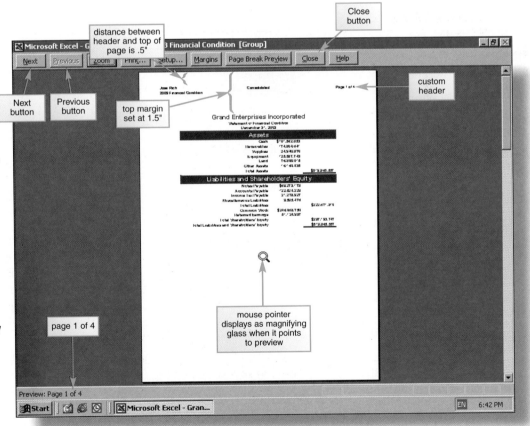

FIGURE 6-65

8 **With the Print Preview window closed, click the 3-D Cylinder Chart tab. On the File menu, click Page Setup. When the Page Setup dialog box displays, click the Header/Footer tab, click the Header box arrow, and select the header entered earlier for the worksheets. Point to the OK button.**

The Header/Footer sheet in the Page Setup dialog box displays as shown in Figure 6-66.

FIGURE 6-66

9 **Click the OK button.**

Excel assigns the same header entered for the worksheets to the 3-D Cylinder Chart sheet.

10 **Click the Consolidated tab. Click the Save button on the Standard toolbar to save the latest changes to the workbook using the file name, Grand Enterprises 2003 Financial Condition.**

Table 6-8 Buttons in the Header or Footer Dialog Box

BUTTON	NAME	CODE	FUNCTION
A	Font	None	Displays the Font dialog box
#	Page	&[Page]	Inserts a page number
	Number of Pages	&[Pages]	Inserts total number of pages
	Date	&[Date]	Inserts the system date
	Time	&[Time]	Inserts the system time
	Path	&[Path]&[File]	Inserts the path and file name
	File	&[File]	Inserts the file name of the workbook
	Tab	&[Tab]	Inserts the tab name
	Picture	&[Picture]	Inserts a picture
	Format Picture	None	Displays the Format Picture dialog box

Other **Ways**

1. On View menu click Header and Footer
2. Press ALT+F, U, H or ALT+V, H
3. In Voice Command mode, say "View, Header and Footer, Custom Header, [enter headings], OK, OK"

When you click a button in the Header dialog box (Figure 6-62 on page E 6.50), Excel enters a code (similar to a format code) into the active header section. A code such as &[Page] instructs Excel to insert the page number. Table 6-8 summarizes the buttons, their codes, and their functions in the Header or Footer dialog boxes.

Printing All the Worksheets in the Workbook

The following steps print all five sheets in the workbook by selecting all the sheets before clicking the Print button on the Standard toolbar.

TO PRINT THE WORKBOOK

1 Ready the printer.

2 Click the Consolidated tab if necessary. While holding down the SHIFT key, click the 3-D Cylinder Chart tab.

3 Click the Print button on the Standard toolbar.

4 Hold down the SHIFT key and click the Consolidated tab to deselect all the sheets but the Consolidated sheet.

The workbook prints as shown in Figures 6-67a and 6-67b on the next page.

Printing Nonadjacent Worksheets in a Workbook

Situations can occur that require non-adjacent sheets in a workbook to be printed. To select non-adjacent sheets, select the first one and then hold down the CTRL key and click the nonadjacent sheets. The following steps show how to print the nonadjacent Consolidated, Central Division, and 3-D Cylinder Chart sheets.

TO PRINT NONADJACENT SHEETS IN A WORKBOOK

1 With the Consolidated sheet selected, hold down the CTRL key and click the Central Division tab and then click the 3-D Cylinder Chart tab.

2 Click the Print button on the Standard toolbar.

3 Hold down the SHIFT key and click the Consolidated tab to deselect the Central Division and 3-D Cylinder Chart sheets.

The Consolidated sheet, Central Division sheet and 3-D Cylinder Chart sheet print. These three pages are shown in Figures 6-67a and 6-67b on the next page.

One problem that beginning students have is trying to determine how to select and deselect sheets. Table 6-9 summarizes how to select and deselect sheets.

Table 6-9 Summary of How to Select and Deselect Sheets	
TASK	**HOW TO CARRY OUT TASK**
Select adjacent sheets	Select the first sheet by clicking its tab and then hold down the SHIFT key and click the tab at the other end of the list of adjacent tabs.
Select nonadjacent sheets	Select the first sheet by clicking its tab and then hold down the CTRL key and click the tabs of the remaining sheets you want to select.
Multiple sheets selected and you want to select a sheet that is selected, but not active (tab name not in bold)	Click the tab of the sheet you want to select.
Multiple sheets selected and you want to select the active	Hold down the SHIFT key and click the tab sheet (tab name in bold) of the active sheet.

(a) Worksheets

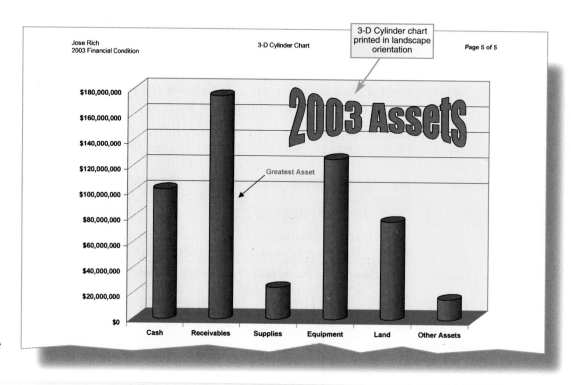

(b) 3-D Cylinder Chart

FIGURE 6-67

Page Breaks

When you print a worksheet or use the Page Setup command, Excel inserts **page breaks** that show the boundaries of what will print on each page. These page breaks are based upon the margins selected in the Margins sheet in the Page Setup dialog box and the type of printer you are using. If the view Page breaks option is on, then dotted lines will display showing the boundaries of each page. For example, the dotted line in Figure 6-68 shows the right boundary of the first page. If the dotted line does not show on your screen, then on the Tools menu click Options. When the Options dialog box displays, click the View tab (Figure 6-71 on Page E 6.57). When the View sheet displays, click Page breaks in the Window options area, and then click the OK button.

You can insert horizontal page breaks in a worksheet at the top of any row to control how much of a worksheet prints on a page. This is especially useful if you have a worksheet that is several pages long and you want certain parts of the worksheet to print on separate pages. For example, say you had a worksheet comprised of 10 departments in sequence and each department had many rows of information. If you wanted each department to begin on a new page, then inserting page breaks would satisfy the requirement.

To insert a horizontal page break, you select a cell in the row that you want to print on the next page and then you invoke the **Page Break command** on the Insert menu. There is no Excel command that inserts or removes a vertical page break, although you can change the margins to adjust the vertical page breaks. Excel displays a dotted line to indicate the beginning of a new page. To remove a page break, you select a cell in the row immediately below the dotted line that indicates the page break you want to remove, and then you invoke the **Remove Page Break command** on the Insert menu.

The following steps show how to insert a page break between rows 11 and 12 and then remove the same page break.

More About

Page Break Preview

You can get a better view of page breaks by clicking the Print Preview button on the Standard toolbar and then clicking the Page Break Preview button at the top of the Preview window.

Steps **To Insert and Remove a Page Break**

1 **Click cell A12. Click Insert on the menu bar and then point to Page Break.**

The Insert menu displays (Figure 6-68).

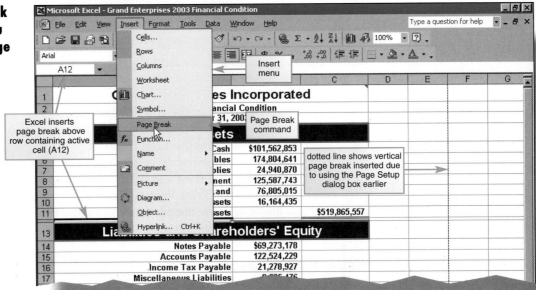

FIGURE 6-68

2 **Click Page Break.**

Excel draws a dotted line above row 12 indicating a page break (Figure 6-69).

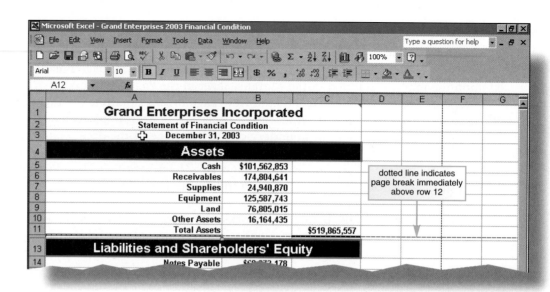

FIGURE 6-69

3 **If necessary, click cell A12. Click Insert on the menu bar and then point to Remove Page Break.**

The Insert menu displays (Figure 6-70).

4 **Click Remove Page Break to remove the page break.**

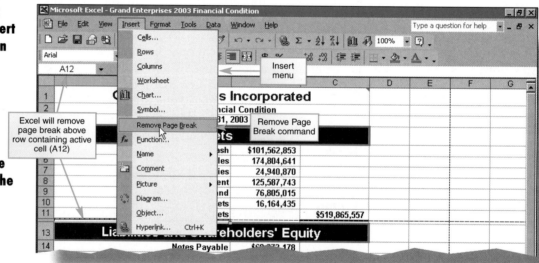

FIGURE 6-70

Other **Ways**

1. Click Print Preview button on Standard toolbar, click Page Break Preview button, click OK button, drag page breaks
2. Select cell in row, press ALT+I, B
3. Select cell in row, in Voice Command mode, say "Insert, Page Break"

You can select any cell in the row immediately below where you want a page break or where you want to remove a page break. You also can select the row heading. The Page Break command on the Insert menu changes to Remove Page Break when you select a cell immediately below a page break symbol.

An alternative to using the Page Break command on the Insert menu to insert page breaks is to click the Print Preview button on the Standard toolbar and then click the **Page Break Preview button**. Once the Page Break preview displays, you can drag the blue boundaries, which represent page breaks, to new locations.

Hiding Page Breaks

Page breaks can be annoying, especially to users who have no interest in where pages break. The following steps show how to hide page breaks so they do not display on your screen.

To Hide Page Breaks

1 **On the Tools menu click Options. When the Options dialog box displays, click the View tab. Click Page breaks to remove the check mark from the check box in the Window options area. Point to the OK button.**

The Options dialog box displays (Figure 6-71).

FIGURE 6-71

2 **Click the OK button.**

Excel hides page breaks (Figure 6-72).

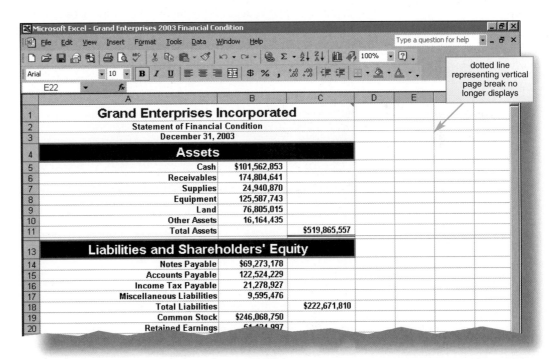

FIGURE 6-72

You can select additional options in the Options dialog box that will change the look and feel of Excel. Many of the changes you can make in the Options dialog box are machine-dependent. That is, these options will affect only the computer on which they are changed.

Other Ways

1. Press ALT+T, O, K

2. In Voice Command mode, say "Tools, Options, View, [select Page breaks], OK"

Microsoft **Excel 2002**

The Find and Replace Commands

The **Find command** on the Edit menu is used to locate a string. A **string** can be a single character, a word, or a phrase. The **Replace command** on the Edit menu is used to locate and replace a string with another string. The Find and Replace commands are not available for a chart sheet.

Both the Find and Replace commands display the **Find and Replace dialog box**. The Find and Replace dialog box has two variations. One version displays minimal options, while the other version displays all the options. When you invoke the Find or Replace command, Excel displays the same one used the last time either command was invoked.

The Find Command

The following steps show how to locate the string, Supplies, (cell A7) in the four worksheets: Consolidated, Western Division, Central Division, and Eastern Division. The Find and Replace dialog box that displays all the options will be used to customize the search to include the entire workbook, match case, and match entire cell contents. **Match case** means that the cell contents must match the word exactly the way it is typed. **Match entire cell contents** means that the string cannot be part of another word or phrase. Unlike the Spelling command, which starts the spell checker at the active cell and works downward, the Find and Replace commands always begin at cell A1, regardless of the location of the active cell.

 To Find a String

1 **With the Consolidated sheet active, click Edit on the menu bar and then point to Find.**

The Edit menu displays (Figure 6-73).

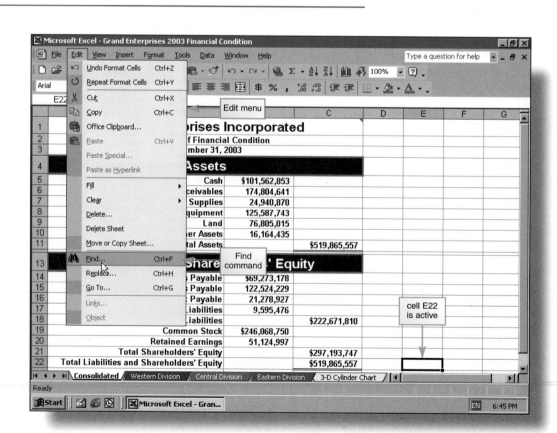

FIGURE 6-73

2 **Click Find. When the initial Find and Replace dialog box displays, point to the Options button.**

The initial Find and Replace dialog box displays. The two greater than signs pointing to the right on the Options button indicate that additional options are available (Figure 6-74).

3 **Click the Options button. When the Find and Replace dialog box displays with additional options, type** Supplies **in the Find what text box. Click the Within box arrow and then click Workbook. Click the Match case and Match entire cell contents check boxes. Click the Find Next button.**

The Find and Replace dialog box with additional options displays as shown in Figure 6-75. Excel begins the search at cell A1 on the Consolidated sheet and makes cell A7 the active cell (Figure 6-75) because it is the first cell to match the search string.

4 **Continue clicking the Find Next button to find the string, Supplies. Click the Close button in the Find and Replace dialog box to terminate the process and close the Find and Replace dialog box.**

FIGURE 6-74

FIGURE 6-75

Other Ways

1. Press CTRL+F
2. In Voice Command mode, say "Edit, Find"

The Format button in the Find and Replace dialog box in Figure 6-75 on the previous page allows you to fine-tune the search by adding formats, such as bold, font style, and font size to the string. The **Within box** options include Sheet and Workbook. The **Search box** indicates whether the search will be done downward through rows or across columns. The **Look in box** allows you to select Values, Formulas, or Comments. If you select Values, Excel will look only in cells that do not have formulas. If you select Formulas, Excel will look in all cells. If you select Comments, it will look only in comments. If you place a check mark in the **Match case check box**, Excel will locate only cells in which the string is in the same case. For example, supplies is not the same as Supplies. If you place a check mark in the **Match entire cell contents check box**, Excel will locate only the cells that contain the string and no other characters.

If the Find command does not find the string you are searching for, it displays a dialog box indicating it has searched the selected worksheets without success.

The Replace Command

The **Replace command** is similar to the Find command, except that the search string is replaced by a new string. You can use the Find Next and Replace buttons to find and replace the string one occurrence at a time, or you can replace the string in all locations at once by clicking the Replace All button. The following steps show how to replace Supplies with Goods using the Replace All button.

To Replace a String with Another String

1 **Click the Consolidated tab. Click Edit on the menu bar and then click Replace. When the Find and Replace dialog box displays, if necessary click the Options button to display the Find and Replace dialog box with additional options. Type** Supplies **in the Find what text box and** Goods **in the Replace with text box. Click the Within box arrow and then click Workbook. Click the Match case and Match entire cell contents check boxes. Point to the Replace All button.**

The Find and Replace dialog box displays as shown in Figure 6-76.

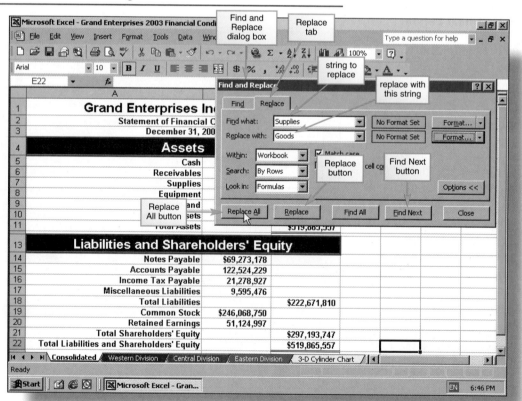

FIGURE 6-76

2 **Click the Replace All button.**

Excel replaces the string, Supplies, with the replacement string, Goods (cell A7) throughout the four worksheets in the workbook. It does not replace the string Supplies on the 3-D Cylinder Chart sheet. Excel displays the Microsoft Excel dialog box indicating four replacements were made (Figure 6-77).

3 **Click the OK button in the Microsoft Excel dialog box. Click the Close button in the Find and Replace dialog box.**

FIGURE 6-77

Closing the Workbook

The following steps close the Grand Enterprises 2003 Financial Condition workbook without saving changes.

TO CLOSE THE WORKBOOK

1 Click the Close button on the right side of the workbook title bar.

2 When the Microsoft Excel dialog box displays, click the No button.

Excel closes the Grand Enterprises 2003 Financial Condition workbook without saving changes. The empty workbook Book1 displays.

Other Ways

1. Press CTRL+H
2. In Voice Command mode, say "Edit, Replace"

Consolidating Data by Linking Workbooks

Earlier in this project, the data from three worksheets were consolidated onto another worksheet in the same workbook using 3-D references. An alternative to this method is to consolidate data from worksheets in other workbooks. Consolidating data from other workbooks also is referred to as linking. A link is a reference to a cell or range of cells in another workbook. In this case, the 3-D reference also includes a workbook name. For example, the following 3-D reference pertains to cell B5 on the Western Division sheet in the workbook GEI Western Division located on drive A.

'A:\[GEI Western Division.xls]Western Division'!B5

location   workbook name   sheet name   cell reference

The single quotation marks surrounding the location, workbook name, and sheet name are required if any spaces are in any of the three names. If the workbook you are referring to is in the same folder as the active workbook, the location (A:\) is not necessary. The brackets surrounding the workbook name are required.

To illustrate linking cells between workbooks, the Consolidated, Western Division, Central Division, and Eastern Division worksheets from the workbook created earlier in this project are on the Data Disk in separate workbooks as described in Table 6-10. In the workbook names in Table 6-10, the GEI stands for Grand Enterprises Incorporated. The division workbooks contain the division data, but the GEI Consolidated workbook does not include any consolidation. The consolidation of data from the three division workbooks will be completed later in this section.

Table 6-10 Workbook Names	
WORKSHEET IN GRAND ENTERPRISES 2003 FINANCIAL CONDITION	SAVED USING THE WORKBOOK NAME
Consolidated	GEI Consolidated
Western Division	GEI Western Division
Central Division	GEI Central Division
Eastern Division	GEI Eastern Division

The remaining sections of this project are divided into demonstrating how to search for the four workbooks in Table 6-10 on drive A, creating a Workspace from the four workbooks, and finally consolidating the data from the three division workbooks into the GEI Consolidated workbook.

Searching for and Opening Workbooks

Excel has a powerful search tool that you can use to locate workbooks (or any file) stored on disk. You invoke the search tool by clicking the **Search button** on the Standard toolbar. The Search button displays the **Basic Search task pane**. If you display the directory of the Data Disk you would see the four workbooks listed in Table 6-10. The following steps, however, show you how to search for workbooks when you cannot remember exactly the name of the file or its location. In this example, the string GEI (the first three characters in the workbook names) will be used to locate the files.

Steps **To Search for and Open Workbooks**

1 **With Excel active, click the Search button on the Standard toolbar. When the Basic Search task pane displays, type** GEI **in the Search text text box. Click the Search in box arrow. If necessary, click the plus sign to the left of Everywhere and click the plus sign to the left of My Computer. Click 3½ Floppy (A:) to select it. If necessary, click any other folder that has a check mark. Click the Search in box arrow to close the Search in list.**

The Basic Search task pane displays on the right side of the screen as shown in Figure 6-78.

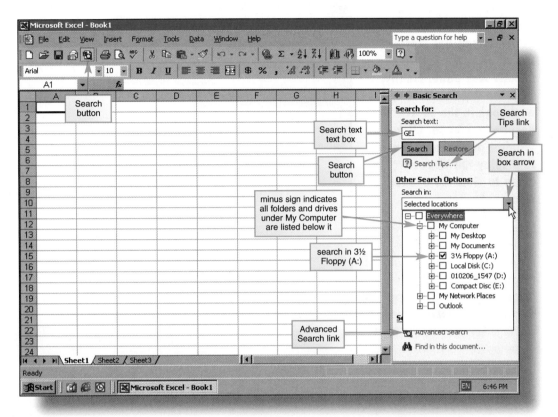

FIGURE 6-78

2 **Click the Search button in the Basic Search task pane.**

Excel displays the Search Results task pane, listing the four workbooks described earlier in Table 6-10 (Figure 6-79).

FIGURE 6-79

3 One at a time, click the three division workbooks (GEI Central Division, GEI Eastern Division, and GEI Western Division) in the Search Results task pane. Finally, click the GEI Consolidated workbook in the Search Results task pane. Click Window on the menu bar to display the Window menu to view the opened workbooks.

Excel opens the four workbooks. The last workbook clicked in the Search Results task pane displays. The names of the four workbooks display on the Window menu with a check mark to the right of the active workbook (Figure 6-80).

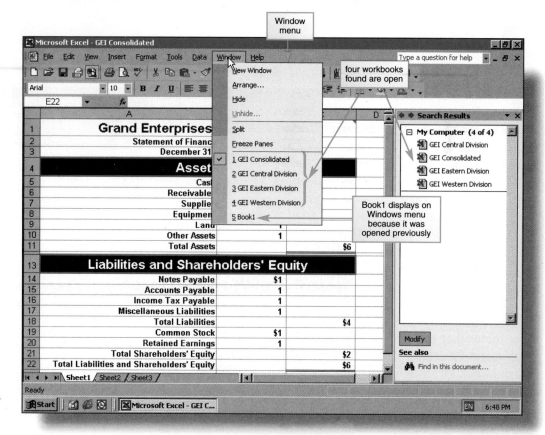

FIGURE 6-80

Other Ways

1. Click Open button on Standard toolbar, click Search on Tools menu in Open dialog box
2. On File menu click Search
3. Press ALT+F, H
4. In Voice Command mode, say "Search"

At the bottom of the Basic Search task pane in Figure 6-78 on the previous page is an Advanced Search link. The **Advanced Search link** allows you to add conditions to customize the file search. For additional information on advanced searching, click the **Search Tips link** in the Basic Search task pane (Figure 6-78), click the Contents tab in the Microsoft Help window, double-click Managing Files in the Contents area, double-click Finding Files in the Contents area, click About search conditions and values.

Creating a Workspace File

If you plan to consolidate data from other workbooks, it is recommended that you first bind the workbooks together using a workspace file. A **workspace file** saves information about all the workbooks that are open when you invoke the **Save Workspace command** on the File menu. A workspace file does not actually contain the workbooks, but rather the information required to open them, such as file names, which one of the files was displaying at the time of the save, and other display settings. Once you save a workspace file, you can open all the associated files by opening the workspace. The following steps show how to create a workspace file from the files opened in the previous set of steps.

Steps: To Create a Workspace File

1 **With the files shown on the Windows menu in Figure 6-80 opened, click Window on the menu bar and then click Book1 to activate it. On the File menu, click Close to close the Book1 workbook.**

Excel closes Book1 so that only the first four workbooks shown on the Window menu in Figure 6-80 are open.

2 **Click Window on the menu bar and then, if necessary, click GEI Consolidated to activate it. Click File on the menu bar and then point to Save Workspace.**

The GEI Consolidated workbook displays, and the File menu displays (Figure 6-81).

3 **Click Save Workspace. Type** GEI Workspace **in the File name box, click the Save in box arrow, and then click 3½ Floppy (A:). Point to the Save button in the Save Workspace dialog box.**

The Save Workspace dialog box displays (Figure 6-82), which is identical to the Save As dialog box used in previous projects, except for the name of the dialog box. Excel automatically chooses Workspaces as the file type in the Save as type box.

FIGURE 6-81

FIGURE 6-82

4 **Click the Save button. Click the Close button on the title bar to quit Excel.**

Excel saves the file names of the workbooks open, of the workbooks displaying, and other display settings. The Excel window closes.

Other Ways

1. Press ALT+F, W
2. In Voice Command mode, say "File, Save Workspace"

More About

Workspace Files

A workspace file saves display information about open workbooks, such as window sizes, print areas, screen magnification, and display settings. Workspace files do not contain the workbooks themselves.

Once you save the workspace you can open the workbooks one at a time as you did in the past, or you can open all of the associated workbooks by opening the workspace. When you invoke the Open command, a workspace file name displays in the Open dialog box the same as any workbook file name.

Consolidating the Data

The following steps show how to open the workspace file GEI Workspace and consolidate the data from the three division workbooks into the GEI Consolidated workbook.

TO CONSOLIDATE DATA BY LINKING WORKBOOKS

1. Start Excel as described on page E 6.06. Click the Open button on the Standard toolbar. When the Open dialog box displays, click the Look in box arrow and then click 3½ Floppy (A:). Double-click GEI Workspace to open the four associated workbooks listed in Table 6-10 on page E 6.62 and activate GEI Consolidated. Double-click the GEI Consolidated window title bar to maximize it, if necessary.

2. Select cell B5. Click the AutoSum button on the Standard toolbar. Click Window on the menu bar and then click GEI Western Division. Click cell B5. Delete the dollar signs ($) in the reference to cell B5 in the formula bar. Click immediately after B5 in the formula bar and then press the COMMA key.

3. Click Window on the menu bar and then click GEI Central Division. Click cell B5. Delete the dollar signs ($) in the reference to cell B5 in the formula bar. Click immediately after B5 in the formula bar and then press the COMMA key.

4. Click Window on the menu bar, and then click GEI Eastern Division. Click cell B5. Delete the dollar signs ($) in the reference to cell B5 in the formula bar. Click the Enter box.

5. With cell B5 active in the GEI Consolidated workbook, click the Copy button on the Standard toolbar. Select the range B6:B10. Hold down the CTRL key and select B14:B17 and B19:B20. Click the Paste button arrow on the Standard toolbar and then click Formulas.

6. Click the Save button on the Standard toolbar. If a dialog box displays, select Overwrite changes. Click the OK button. Click the Print button on the Standard toolbar.

The consolidated Statement of Financial Condition for Grand Enterprises Incorporated displays as shown in Figure 6-83. Excel prints the worksheet.

GEI Consolidated workbook

SUM function with file names, sheet names, and cell references

B5   =SUM('[GEI Western Division.xls]Sheet1'!B5,'[GEI Central Division.xls]Sheet1'!B5,'[GEI Eastern Division.xls]Sheet1'!B5)

1	**Grand Enterprises Incorporated**
2	Statement of Financial Condition
3	December 31, 2003
4	**Assets**
5	Cash $101,562,853
6	Receivables 174,804,641
7	Supplies 24,940,870
8	Equipment 125,587,743
9	Land 76,805,015
10	Other Assets 16,164,435
11	Total Assets $519,865,557
13	**Liabilities and Shareholders' Equity**
14	Notes Payable $69,273,178
15	Accounts Payable 122,524,229
16	Income Tax Payable 21,278,927
17	Miscellaneous Liabilities 9,595,476
18	Total Liabilities $222,671,810
19	Common Stock $246,068,750
20	Retained Earnings 51,124,997
21	Total Shareholders' Equity $297,193,747

Sum of values in cell B5 in three workbooks

SUM function copied to nonadjacent ranges B6:B10, B14:B17, and B19:B20 using Formulas command on Paste button menu

FIGURE 6-83

It is necessary that you remember these two important points about using the SUM function across workbooks. First, as you build the SUM function for cell B5, the cell reference inserted by Excel each time you click a cell in a workbook is an absolute cell reference ($B$5). You must edit the formula and change these to relative cell references because the SUM function later is copied to the nonadjacent ranges B6:B10, B14:B17, and B19:B20. If the cell references are left as absolute, then the copied function always would refer to cell B5 in the three workbooks no matter where you copy the SUM function. Second, because the three cells being summed in this example are not adjacent to one another, the cell references must be separated by commas in the SUM function.

Updating Links

Later, if you open the GEI Consolidated workbook by itself, also called the **dependent workbook**, Excel will ask you whether you want to update the links. The linked workbooks are called the **source workbooks**. If the source workbooks are not open, Excel will display a dialog box that will give you the option to update the links. In the latter case, Excel reads the data in the source workbooks on disk and recalculates formulas in the dependent workbook, but it does not open the source workbooks.

If the three source workbooks are open along with the dependent workbook as in the previous set of steps, Excel updates the links (recalculate) automatically in the GEI Consolidated workbook when a value changes in any one of the source workbooks.

Closing All Workbooks at One Time and Quitting Excel

To close all four workbooks at one time and quit Excel, complete the following steps.

TO QUIT EXCEL AND CLOSE ALL WORKBOOKS AT ONE TIME

1 Hold down the SHIFT key, click File on the menu bar, and then click the Close All command.

2 If the Microsoft Excel dialog box displays, click the No button.

3 Click the Close button on the right side of the Microsoft Excel title bar.

CASE PERSPECTIVE SUMMARY

Rodney Jefferson is sure to be pleased with many aspects of the workbook developed in this project. The use of multiple sheets, for example, allows for better organization of the data, while the 3-D Cylinder chart makes it easy to pinpoint the greatest asset. Perhaps the best aspect of the way the workbook is used, however, is the use of the template: Rodney can use the template in the future to add more divisions to the existing workbook or create new, similar workbooks.

Project Summary

This project introduced you to creating and using a template, customizing formats, creating styles, changing chart types, drawing and enhancing a 3-D Cylinder chart using WordArt, and annotating using text boxes and arrows. You also learned how to reference cells in other sheets and add comments to a cell. To enhance a print-out, you learned how to add a header and footer and to change margins. Finally, you learned how to add and remove page breaks, use the Find and Replace commands, search for files on disk, create a workspace file, and link cell entries from external workbooks.

What You Should Know

Having completed this project, you now should be able to perform the following tasks:

- Add a Chart Title Using the WordArt Tool *(E 6.40)*
- Add a Text Box and Arrow *(E 6.44)*
- Add a Worksheet to a Workbook *(E 6.25)*
- Apply a Style *(E 6.20)*
- Assign a Comment to a Cell *(E 6.46)*
- Assign a Comma Style Format to Nonadjacent Ranges *(E 6.14)*
- Bold the Font and Change the Column Widths in the Template *(E 6.08)*
- Change the Header and Margins and Center the Printout Horizontally *(E 6.49)*
- Close the Workbook *(E 6.61)*
- Consolidate Data by Linking Workbooks *(E 6.66)*
- Copy the Contents of a Worksheet to Other Worksheets *(E 6.26)*
- Create and Assign a Custom Format Code *(E 6.16)*
- Create a New Style *(E 6.18)*
- Create a Workspace File *(E 6.65)*
- Determine Totals *(E 6.10)*
- Draw a 3-D Cylinder Chart *(E 6.36)*
- Enter and Copy 3-D References *(E 6.32)*
- Enter Dummy Data in the Template *(E 6.09)*
- Enter the Template Title and Row Titles *(E 6.08)*
- Find a String *(E 6.58)*
- Format the 3-D Cylinder Chart *(E 6.38)*
- Format the Template Titles *(E 6.13)*
- Hide Page Breaks *(E 6.57)*
- Insert and Remove a Page Break *(E 6.55)*
- Modify the Central Division Sheet *(E 6.28)*
- Modify the Eastern Division Sheet *(E 6.29)*
- Modify the Western Division Sheet *(E 6.27)*
- Open a Template and Save It as a Workbook *(E 6.23)*
- Print Nonadjacent Sheets in a Workbook *(E 6.53)*
- Print the Workbook *(E 6.53)*
- Quit Excel and Close All Workbooks at One Time *(E 6.67)*
- Rename a Sheet, Color Its Tab, and Change the Worksheet Title *(E 6.31)*
- Replace a String with Another String *(E 6.60)*
- Save a Template *(E 6.12)*
- Search for and Open Workbooks *(E 6.63)*
- Spell Check, Save, and Print the Template *(E 6.21)*
- Start and Customize Excel *(E 6.06)*

Learn It Online

Instructions: To complete the Learn It Online exercises, start your browser, click the Address bar, and then enter scsite.com/offxp/exs.htm. When the Office XP Learn It Online page displays, follow the instructions in the exercises below.

1 Project Reinforcement TF, MC, and SA

Below Excel Project 6, click the Project Reinforcement link. Print the quiz by clicking Print on the File menu. Answer each question. Write your first and last name at the top of each page, and then hand in the printout to your instructor.

2 Flash Cards

Below Excel Project 6, click the Flash Cards link. When Flash Cards displays, read the instructions. Type 20 (or a number specified by your instructor) in the Number of Playing Cards text box, type your name in the Name text box, and then click the Flip Card button. When the flash card displays, read the question and then click the Answer box arrow to select an answer. Flip through Flash Cards. Click Print on the File menu to print the last flash card if your score is 15 (75%) correct or greater and then hand it in to your instructor. If your score is less than 15 (75%) correct, then redo this exercise by clicking the Replay button.

3 Practice Test

Below Excel Project 6, click the Practice Test link. Answer each question, enter your first and last name at the bottom of the page, and then click the Grade Test button. When the graded practice test displays on your screen, click Print on the File menu to print a hard copy. Continue to take practice tests until you score 80% or better. Hand in a printout of the final practice test to your instructor.

4 Who Wants to Be a Computer Genius?

Below Excel Project 6, click the Computer Genius link. Read the instructions, enter your first and last name at the bottom of the page, and then click the Play button. Hand in your score to your instructor.

5 Wheel of Terms

Below Excel Project 6, click the Wheel of Terms link. Read the instructions, and then enter your first and last name and your school name. Click the Play button. Hand in your score to your instructor.

6 Crossword Puzzle Challenge

Below Excel Project 6, click the Crossword Puzzle Challenge link. Read the instructions, and then enter your first and last name. Click the Play button. Work the crossword puzzle. When you are finished, click the Submit button. When the crossword puzzle redisplays, click the Print button. Hand in the printout.

7 Tips and Tricks

Below Excel Project 6, click the Tips and Tricks link. Click a topic that pertains to Project 6. Right-click the information and then click Print on the shortcut menu. Construct a brief example of what the information relates to in Excel to confirm you understand how to use the tip or trick. Hand in the example and printed information.

8 Newsgroups

Below Excel Project 6, click the Newsgroups link. Click a topic that pertains to Project 6. Print three comments. Hand in the comments to your instructor.

9 Expanding Your Horizons

Below Excel Project 6, click the Articles for Microsoft Excel link. Click a topic that pertains to Project 6. Print the information. Construct a brief example of what the information relates to in Excel to confirm you understand the contents of the article. Hand in the example and printed information to your instructor.

10 Search Sleuth

Below Excel Project 6, click the Search Sleuth link. To search for a term that pertains to this project, select a term below the Project 6 title and then use the Google search engine at google.com (or any major search engine) to display and print two Web pages that present information on the term. Hand in the printouts to your instructor.

online

Apply Your Knowledge

1 Consolidating Data in a Workbook

Instructions Part 1: Follow the steps below to consolidate the four weekly payroll worksheets on the Month Totals worksheet in the workbook Monthly Payroll (Figure 6-84). At the conclusion of the Part 1 instructions, the Month Totals worksheet should display as shown in the lower screen in Figure 6-84.

1. Open the workbook Monthly Payroll from the Data Disk. See the inside back cover of this book for instructions for downloading the Data Disk or see your instructor for information on accessing the files required in this book.

2. One by one, click the first four tabs and review the weekly payroll totals. Click the Month Totals tab.

3. Determine the monthly totals by using the SUM function and 3-D references to sum the hours worked in cell B20. Copy cell B20 to B20:C23. Copy only the formulas using the Formulas option on the Paste button menu.

4. Save the workbook using the file name, Monthly Payroll 1.

5. Select all five worksheets. Use the Page Setup command to add a header that includes your name and course number in the Left section, the computer laboratory exercise number (Apply 6-1) in the Center section, and the system date and your instructor's name in the Right section. Add the page number and total number of pages to the footer. Center all worksheets on the page and print gridlines. Preview and print the five worksheets. Click the Month Totals tab to select the sheet. Save the workbook with the new page setup using the same file name as in Step 4.

Instructions Part 2: If Excel is active, quit Excel and then start Excel. Use the Search button on the Standard toolbar to find all Excel workbooks on drive A (the Data Disk) that include the string EMP. Open the five files, close any other files, display the EMP Monthly Payroll workbook, and save a workspace file on drive A using the file name, EMP Workspace. Close all files.

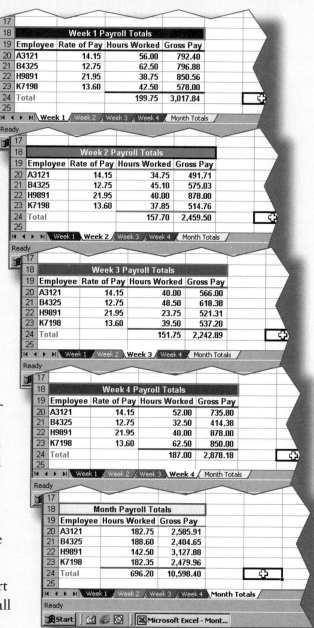

FIGURE 6-84

Open the workspace file EMP Workspace and maximize the workbook window as described in Step 1 on page E 6.66. Consolidate the data in the four weekly payroll workbooks into the range B20:C23 in the workbook EMP Monthly Payroll. Save the workbook using the same name. Close all files. Open EMP Week 1 from the Data Disk and change the hours worked for employee A3121 to 60. Save and close the workbook. Open the workspace EMP Workspace. The gross pay total should be 10,655.00 with the change made to EMP Week 1. Print the five workbooks.

In the Lab

1 Creating a Template for Why Weight Fitness Center

Problem: After working out between classes for several months at Why Weight Fitness Center, the manager asked you if you wanted a job answering the telephone at their main office. Once you were on the job, your immediate supervisor learned about your Excel skills and she asked you to create a template (Figure 6-85) for management to use when they create new Excel workbooks.

Instructions: Start Excel and perform the following steps to create a template.

1. With the Book1 workbook opened, change the font of all cells to 12-point Arial bold. Increase all row heights to 18.00. *Hint:* Click the Select All button to make these changes.

2. Use the Style command on the Format menu to create the format style called Comma (4) as shown in Figure 6-85. Display the Comma style, change the name in the Style name box from Comma to Comma (4), and use the Modify button to

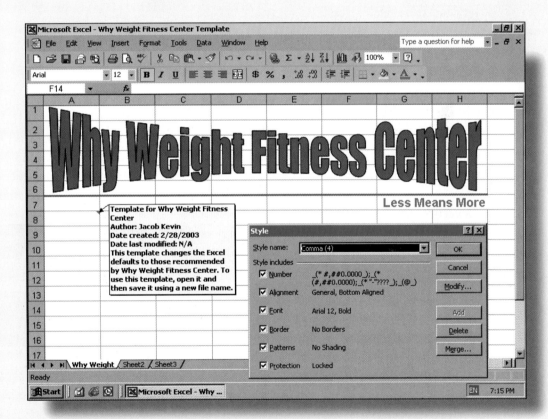

FIGURE 6-85

change the decimal places to 4 and the font to Arial 12, Bold. Create the custom format $#,##0.00_);[Green]($#,##0.00) and assign it to all the cells in the worksheet.

3. Add a comment to cell A8 to identify the template and its purpose, as shown in Figure 6-85. Include your name as the author. Add a fourth worksheet. Delete the Sheet2 worksheet.

4. Use WordArt to create the title shown in the range A1:H6. Use the style in column 4, row 1 of the WordArt Gallery dialog box. Change the color of the title to green. Draw a thick green bottom border across the range A6:H6. Add the subtitle in cell G7.

5. Enter your name, course, computer laboratory assignment (Lab 6-1), date, time, and instructor's name as the header. Add a page number as the footer.

6. Use the Save As command to save the template, selecting Template in the Save as type list. Save the template using the file name, Why Weight Fitness Center Template.

(continued)

In the Lab

Creating a Template for Why Weight Fitness Center *(continued)*

7. Print the template and comment. To print the comment, click the Sheet tab in the Page Setup dialog box. Click the Comments box arrow and then click At end of sheet. The comment will print on a separate sheet. After the comment prints, deselect printing the comment by clicking the Comment box arrow in the Sheet tab in the Page Setup dialog box and then clicking (None).
8. Close the template and then reopen it. Save the template as a regular workbook using the file name Why Weight Fitness Center. Close the workbook.

2 Using a Template to Create a Multiple-Sheet Workbook

Problem: Something for Everyone is a company that specializes in unique gifts for children. The company has outlets in three cities — New York, Chicago, and Los Angeles — and a corporate office in Toledo. All of the outlets sell their products via mail, phone, walk-in, and the Web. Every year, the corporate officers in Toledo use a template to create a year-end sales analysis workbook. The workbook contains four sheets, one for each of the three outlets and one for the company totals. The Consolidated sheet displays as shown in Figure 6-86.

The template is on the Data Disk. See the inside back cover of this book for instructions for downloading the Data Disk or see your instructor for information on accessing the files required in this book. Sally Panda, the company's accountant, has asked you to use the template to create the year-end sales analysis workbook.

Instructions Part 1: Perform the following tasks.

1. Open the template, Something for Everyone Template, from the Data Disk. Save the template a workbook using the file name Something for Everyone. Make sure Microsoft Excel Workbook is selected in the Save as type list.

FIGURE 6-86

In the Lab

2. Add a worksheet to the workbook between Sheet1 and Sheet2 and then paste the contents of Sheet1 to the three empty sheets. Save the workbook using the file name, Something for Everyone.

3. From left to right, rename the sheet tabs Consolidated, New York, Chicago, and Los Angeles. Color the tabs brown, blue, green, and plum, respectively. On each worksheet, change the subtitle in cell A2 to reflect the city. Use the title Consolidated Net Sales in cell A2 of the Consolidated worksheet. Choose the tab color as the background color for each title area in the range A1:F1. Enter the data in Table 6-11 onto the three city sheets.

Table 6-11 Something for Everyone Sales Data		NEW YORK	CHICAGO	LOS ANGELES
Mail	Sales	4,143,756	3,692,100	3,930,715
	Returns	752,320	450,195	618,779
Phone	Sales	2,347,412	1,945,302	723,814
	Returns	423,187	219,625	210,509
Walk-in	Sales	1,291,840	1,856,225	697,612
	Returns	315,675	419,415	116,711
Web	Sales	3,107,442	2,617,995	4,297,296
	Returns	337,435	524,219	384,217

4. On the Consolidated worksheet, use the SUM function, 3-D references, and copy and paste capabilities of Excel to total the corresponding cells on the three city worksheets. First, compute the sum in cell B4 and then compute the sum in cell B5. Copy the range B4:B5 to the range C4:E5. The Consolidated worksheet should resemble the top of Figure 6-86. Save the workbook.

5. Create an embedded Cylinder chart in the range A8:G25 on the Consolidated worksheet by charting the range A3:E5. Select the Bar with a cylindrical shape type chart. Do not include a chart title. Reduce the font size of the labels on both axes to 8-point bold so the chart displays correctly in the range A8:G25. Use the chart colors shown in Figure 6-86. Use the WordArt button on the Drawing toolbar to add the chart title (column 2, row 1 in the WordArt Gallery). Add the text box and arrow as shown in Figure 6-86. Save the workbook.

6. Select all four sheets. Change the header to include your name, course, computer laboratory exercise (Lab 6-2), date, and instructor's name. Change the footer to include the page number and total pages. Use the Fit to option in the Page Setup dialog box to make sure the worksheets each print on one page in portrait orientation. Print the worksheets using the Black and white option. Add the comment shown in cell G1 in Figure 6-86. Preview and then print the entire workbook, including the comment. Save the workbook with the new page setup characteristics.

Instructions Part 2: The following corrections were sent in: (a) New York Walk-in Sales 1,152,810; (b) Chicago Web Returns 625,115; (c) Los Angeles Mail Sales 3,625,638. Enter these corrections. The Company Total Net Sales should equal $25,334,219. Print all the worksheets. Do not print the comment. Place a page break above row 7 on the Consolidated worksheet. Print the Consolidated worksheet. Close the workbook.

(continued)

In the Lab

Using a Template to Create a Multiple-Sheet Workbook *(continued)*

Instructions Part 3: Select all the worksheets in the Something for Everyone workbook and do the following:

1. Select cell A1 on the Consolidated worksheet. Use the Find command to locate all occurrences of the word Sales in the workbook. You should find 12 occurrences of the word Sales.

2. Click Match entire cell contents in the Find dialog box. (Click the Options button to display the desired check box, if necessary.) Use the Find command to find all occurrences of the word Sales. You should find four occurrences.

3. Use the Replace command to replace the word, Web, with the acronym, WWW, on all four sheets. Print all four sheets. Do not save the workbook.

3 Returning Real-Time Stock Quotes to the Stock Portfolio Worksheet

Problem: You have been investing in the stock market for the past few years and you maintain a summary of your stock market investments in an Excel workbook (Figure 6-87a). Each day you go through the Business section of the newspaper and manually update the current prices in column F to determine the value of your equities. You recently heard about the Web query capabilities of Excel and have decided to use them to update your stock portfolio automatically.

Instructions: Perform the following steps to have Web queries automatically update the current price in column F and the major indices in the range B12:B15 of Figure 6-87a.

1. Start Excel and open the workbook Stock Portfolio on the Data Disk. See the inside back cover of this book for instructions for downloading the Data Disk or see your instructor for information on accessing the files required in this book. After reviewing the Stock Portfolio worksheet on your screen, you should notice that it lacks current prices in column F and the major indices in the range B12:B15.

2. Click Sheet2 and then click cell A1. Click Data on the menu bar, point to Import External Data, and then click Import Data on the Import External Data submenu. When the Select Data Source dialog box displays, double-click MSN MoneyCentral Investor Stock Quotes. When the Import Data dialog box displays, click the OK button. When the Enter Parameter Value dialog box displays, click the Investment Analysis tab at the bottom of the screen and drag through the range B3:B10. Click the check box. Use this value/reference for future refreshes. The Enter Parameter Value dialog box should display as shown in Figure 6-87b. Click the OK button. The Web query should return a worksheet with real-time stock quotes to the Stock Quotes worksheet similar to the one shown in Figure 6-87c. Rename the Sheet2 tab Stock Quotes.

3. Click the Investment Analysis tab. Click cell F3. Type = (equal sign). Click the Stock Quotes tab. Click cell D4 (the last price for Pfizer). Press the ENTER key. Use the fill handle to copy cell F3 to the range F4:F10. You now should have current prices for the stock portfolio that are the same as the last prices on the Stock Quotes worksheet in column D. Click cell A16 and save the workbook using the file name, Stock Portfolio Final.

In the Lab

(a) Investment Analysis Worksheet in Stock Portfolio Workbook

(b) Enter Parameter Value Dialog Box

(d) Major Indices

(c) Real-Time Stock Quotes

FIGURE 6-87

4. Click Sheet3 and then click cell A1. Click Data on the menu bar, point to Import External Data, and then click Import Data on the Import External Data submenu. When the Select Data Source dialog box displays, double-click MSN MoneyCentral Investor Major Indices. When the Import Data dialog box displays, click the OK button. Rename the Sheet3 tab Major Indices. A worksheet similar to the one shown in Figure 6-87d should display.

(continued)

In the Lab

Returning Real-Time Stock Quotes to the Stock Portfolio Worksheet *(continued)*

5. Click the Investment Analysis tab. Click cell B12. Type = (equal sign). Click the Major Indices tab. Click cell D4 (the last Dow Jones Industrial Index). Press the ENTER key. Click cell B13. Type = (equal sign). Click the Major Indices tab. Click cell D12 (the last Nasdaq Combined Composite Index). Press the ENTER key. Click cell B14. Type = (equal sign). Click the Major Indices tab. Click cell D16 (the last Russell 2000 Stock Index). Press the ENTER key. Click cell B15. Type = (equal sign). Click the Major Indices tab. Click cell D6 (the last Dow Jones Transportation Index). Press the ENTER key. Click cell A16 and then save the workbook using the file name, Stock Portfolio Final.

6. Select all three worksheets. Use the Page Setup command on the File menu to enter your name, course, computer laboratory assignment (Lab 6-3), date, and instructor name as the header. Add a page number as the footer. Change the top margin to 1.5".

7. Print the three worksheets using the Black and white option in landscape orientation. Use the Fit to option in the Page worksheet on the Page Setup dialog box to print the sheets on one page.

8. With the Investment Analysis worksheet active, click View on the menu bar, point to Toolbars, and then click External Data. If necessary, drag the External Data toolbar to the lower-right corner as shown in Figure 6-87a.

9. Click the Refresh All button on the External Data toolbar (Figure 6-87a). Print the three worksheets.

10. Click the Stock Quotes tab. Use the Zoom box on the Standard toolbar to shrink the view of the worksheet to 65% so it displays in its entirety. Close the workbook without saving changes.

Cases and Places

The difficulty of these case studies varies:
▶ are the least difficult; ▶▶ are more difficult; and ▶▶▶ are the most difficult.

1 ▶ Picture It, Inc. has been a successful full-service photography company for 29 years in San Diego, California. After launching its Web site three years ago, the company has attracted so many clients from Europe that the owners opened a shop in London. The San Diego and London shops' assets last year, respectively, were: cash $298,345 and $332,750; accounts receivable $219,425 and $94,875; marketable securities $256,500 and $89,420; inventory $470,710 and $282,500; and equipment $35,000 and $27,910. The liabilities for each store were: notes payable $38,300 and $36,000; accounts payable $98,650 and $88,455; and income tax payable $75,510 and $32,000. The stockholders' equity was: common stock $971,170 and $588,375 and retained earnings $96,350 and $82,625. Design a template as a balance worksheet to reflect the figures above. Include totals for assets, liabilities, stockholders' equity, and liabilities and stockholders' equity. Use the template to create a balance worksheet for each store and consolidated balance worksheet for the corporation.

2 ▶ Computer Specialists, Inc. has noticed a sharp increase in business since it started a Web site that allows people to order computers and peripheral equipment over the Internet. The chief financial officer (CFO) would like a worksheet representation of the business increases based on the data in Table 6-12.

Create a worksheet for each year and one for the totals, adding a column for quarter totals and a row for item totals. Include the percentage of annual growth (2004 – 2003) / 2003 on the Company Totals worksheet. Add an embedded 3-D Pie chart to the Consolidated worksheet that shows the sales contribution of each quarter to the two-year sales total. Include a header and print the sheets.

Table 6-12 Computer Specialists, Inc. Two-Year Sales History			
	QTR	COMPUTER SYSTEM	PERIPHERALS
2003	1	421,875.75	42,526.45
	2	219,710.00	188,312.25
	3	335,100.10	95,425.55
	4	523,912.90	85,512.70
2004	1	614,750.30	523,630.25
	2	513,341.80	421,733.75
	3	528,521.90	425,333.10
	4	821,715.30	585,545.40

Cases and Places

3 ▶ Star Software Products sells computer software and supplies. Merchandise is divided into six categories based on profit margin: individual application packages (31%), integrated application packages (19%), entertainment software (26%), system software (15%), learning aids (6%), and supplies (3%). Last year's sales data has been collected for the New England region and the Great Lakes region in Table 6-13.

Develop a template that can be used to determine marketing strategies for next year. Include sales, profit margins, profits (sales x profit margin), total sales, total profits, and functions to determine the most and least sales, profit margins, and profits. Use the template to create a worksheet for each region, a consolidated worksheet for the entire company, and a chart on a separate worksheet reflecting the company's profits by category. Before entering the profit margins, select the three sheets so you have to enter the profit margins only once. Excel will drill the numbers through the other sheets. Include a header and print the sheets.

Table 6-13 Last Year's Sales for the New England and Great Lakes Regions	NEW ENGLAND REGION	GREAT LAKES REGION
Individual applications	$156,234	$76,234
Integrated applications	67,134	85,789
Entertainment software	89,320	76,450
System software	76,219	35,598
Learning aids	26,500	43,102
Supplies	45,320	46,356

4 ▶▶ Chesterton's public safety division is comprised of three departments — Fire, Police, and Streets & Sanitation. The departments have submitted figures comparing expenditures this year to anticipated expenditures next year in four categories (Table 6-14). Develop a template that can be used to prepare each department's budget and the division's consolidated total budget within one workbook. Include this year's costs, next year's anticipated costs, and the variance [(anticipated costs — this year's costs) / this year's costs] for each expenditure. Indicate totals where appropriate. Construct an embedded chart on the Public Safety division's worksheet comparing the division's expenditures this year and next.

Table 6-14 Chesterton's Public Safety Division Expenditures	FIRE		POLICE		STREETS AND SANITATION	
	THIS YEAR	NEXT YEAR	THIS YEAR	NEXT YEAR	THIS YEAR	NEXT YEAR
Equipment	$33,675	$35,000	$36,575	$28,000	$43,250	$36,500
Maintenance	$35,300	$30,500	$12,000	$14,500	$14,500	$13,700
Miscellaneous	$21,500	$27,500	$24,850	$21,900	$22,800	$18,500
Salaries and Benefits	$94,300	$109,900	$153,850	$187,000	$66,950	$80,500

Cases and Places

5 ▷▷▷ Video rental stores frequently group the tapes into categories. The popularity of different categories of tapes may vary depending on the day of the week. Visit a video rental store. List six categories of videotapes and the price of renting a tape in each category. Develop a template that can be used to study daily rentals. Include the number of tapes rented in each category, the income from each category, the total number of tapes rented in the six categories, and the total income. Using your template and information gathered from the store's records, produce worksheets showing rental patterns for at least three days. Create a consolidated worksheet based on the dates from the three days, and construct a chart illustrating the consolidated data.

6 ▷▷▷ Meteorologists can use worksheets to summarize weekly weather conditions. For each day of the week, these worksheets might have data on such factors as low temperature, high temperature, median temperature, humidity, and precipitation. Develop a workbook that can be used to study weekly weather conditions for a two-week period. Have at least six factors for each day of the week, and use functions to find weekly averages, highs, and lows where appropriate. Insert the weather data for each week on a separate worksheet. Create a consolidated worksheet based on the two weeks. Include a chart on each of the week's worksheet that illustrates one weather factor.

7 ▷▷▷ Travel agencies book vacations around the world, getting clients to their destinations using a variety of modes of transportation. Visit a travel agency and find out the six most popular travel destinations and the three most popular ways to get there. Create a template that can track travel destinations and transportation mode for a one-week period. Include the prices for each mode of transportation. Use the template to create worksheets that span the period of a month. Create a consolidated worksheet that illustrates the most popular travel destination and the mode of transportation. Add an embedded chart to display this data.

Microsoft Excel 2002

Linking an Excel Worksheet to a Word Document and Web Discussions

CASE PERSPECTIVE

Every Monday, Carmen Chavez, vice president of sales for Tropical Fragrances, sends a memorandum to the sales managers in the organization summarizing the previous week's sales by group and office. She uses Word to produce the memorandum that includes a table of the previous week's sales.

Carmen recently learned of the Object Linking and Embedding (OLE) capabilities of Microsoft Office XP and wants to use them to create the basic memorandum (Figure 1a on the next page) using Word and maintain the previous week's sales on an Excel worksheet (Figure 1b on the next page). Every Monday morning, she envisions sending out the Word document with the updated worksheet (Figure 1c on the next page). Once the link is established, she can update the worksheet each week, modify the date in the memorandum, and then print and distribute a hard copy of the memorandum to the sales managers. She also wants to publish the memorandum to the Web so that the sales representatives can comment on the sales using a discussion server.

Carmen has asked you to handle the details of linking the Excel worksheet to the memorandum and publishing the document to the Web server.

Introduction

With Microsoft Office XP, you can incorporate parts of documents or entire documents, called objects, from one application into another application. For example, you can copy a worksheet created in Excel into a document created in Word. In this case, the worksheet in Excel is called the **source document** (copied from), and the document in Word is called the **destination document** (copied to). Copying objects between applications can be accomplished in three ways: (1) copy and paste; (2) copy and embed; and (3) copy and link.

All of the Microsoft Office applications allow you to use these three methods to copy objects between applications. The first method uses the Copy and Paste buttons. The latter two methods use the Paste Special command on the Edit menu and are referred to as **Object Linking and Embedding**, or **OLE**. Table 1 on page EI 1.03 summarizes the differences among the three methods.

You would use copy and link over the other two methods when an object is likely to change and you want to make sure the object reflects the changes in the source document or if the object is large, such as a video clip or sound clip. Thus, if you link a portion or all of a worksheet to a memorandum, and update the worksheet monthly in Excel, anytime you open the memorandum in Word, the latest updates of the worksheet will display as part of the memorandum as shown on the next page.

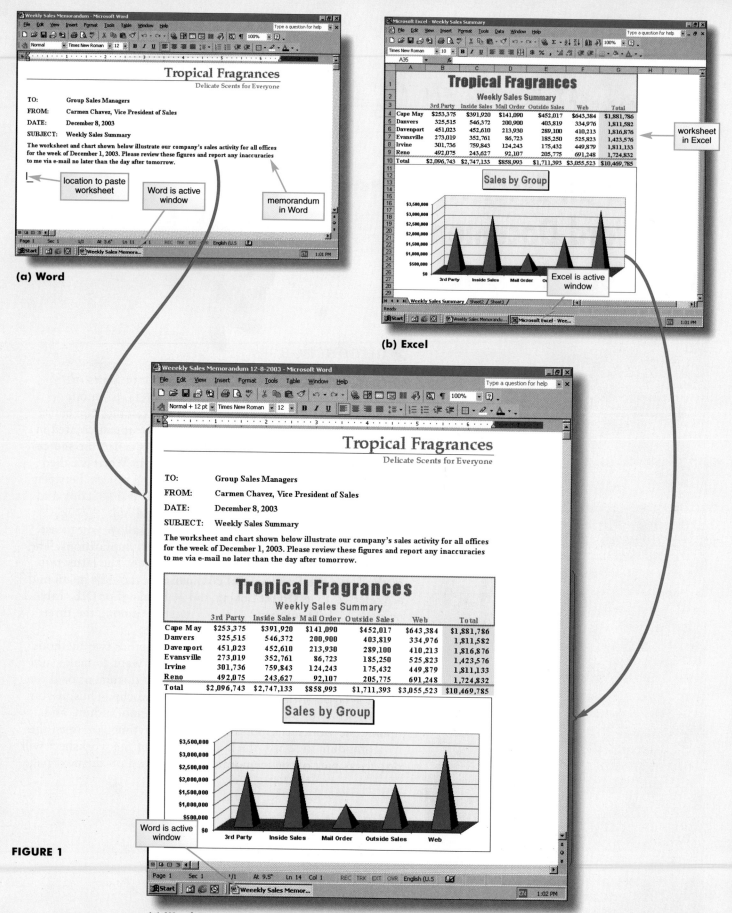

FIGURE 1

(a) Word

(b) Excel

(c) Word Document and Linked Worksheet

Table 1 Three Methods of Copying Objects between Applications

METHOD	CHARACTERISTICS
Copy and paste	The source document becomes part of the destination document. The object may be edited, but the editing features are limited to those in the destination application. An Excel worksheet becomes a Word table. If changes are made to values in the Word table, any original Excel formulas are not recalculated.
Copy and embed	The source document becomes part of the destination document. The object may be edited in the destination application using source editing features. The Excel worksheet remains a worksheet in Word. If changes are made to values on the worksheet with Word active, Excel formulas will be recalculated, but the changes are not updated on the Excel worksheet in the workbook on disk. If you use Excel to change values on the worksheet, the changes will not show in the Word document the next time you open it.
Copy and link	The source document does not become part of the destination document, even though it appears to be part of it. Rather, a link is established between the two documents so that when you open the Word document, the worksheet displays as part of it. When you attempt to edit a linked worksheet in Word, the system activates Excel. If you change the worksheet in Excel, the changes will show in the Word document the next time you open it.

Opening a Word Document and an Excel Workbook

Both the Word document (Weekly Sales Memorandum.doc) and the Excel workbook (Weekly Sales Summary.xls) are on the Data Disk. If you do not have a copy of the Data Disk, see the inside back cover of this book or see your instructor for information on accessing the files required in this book. The first step in linking the Excel worksheet to the Word document is to open both the document in Word and the workbook in Excel as shown in the following steps.

Steps **To Open a Word Document and an Excel Workbook**

1 **Insert the Data Disk in drive A. Click the Start button on the taskbar and then click Open Office document on the Start menu. When the Open Office Document dialog box displays, click the Look in box arrow and then click 3½ Floppy (A:). Double-click the Word file name, Weekly Sales Memorandum. Click the blank line at the bottom of the document.**

The Word window opens, and the Weekly Sales Memorandum displays in Normal View (Figure 2).

FIGURE 2

2 Click the Start button on the taskbar and then click Open Office document on the Start menu. When the Open Office Document dialog box displays, if necessary, click the Look in box arrow and then click 3½ Floppy (A:). Double-click the Excel file name, Weekly Sales Summary.

The Excel window opens, and the Weekly Sales Summary workbook displays (Figure 3). At this point, Word is inactive. Excel is the active window, as shown on the taskbar.

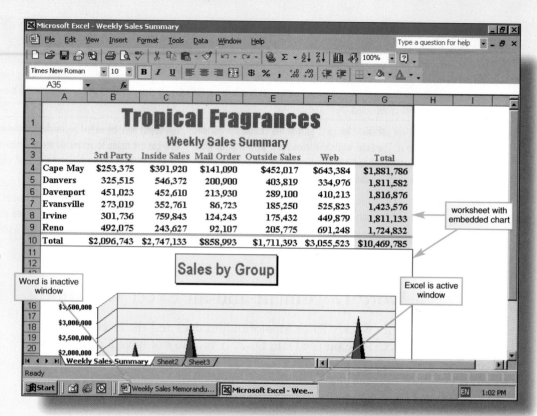

FIGURE 3

More About

Scrap

You can store objects, such as worksheets and pictures, on the desktop, rather than using the Office Clipboard. When you use this technique, the objects are called scrap. To accomplish this task, part of the desktop must be visible behind the window of the source application. Next, point to a border of the object in the source application and right-drag it onto the desktop. When the shortcut menu displays, click Create Scrap Here. Once the object is placed on the desktop, Windows displays it as an icon. Next, activate the destination document and then drag the icon from the desktop to the destination document and drop it where you want it inserted. To delete scrap from the desktop, right-click the scrap icon and then click Delete on the shortcut menu.

With both Word and Excel open, you can switch between the applications by clicking the appropriate program button on the taskbar.

Linking an Excel Worksheet to a Word Document

With both applications running, the next step is to link the Excel worksheet to the Word document as shown in the following steps.

Steps **To Link an Excel Worksheet to a Word Document**

1 **With the Excel window active, select the range A1:G28. Click the Copy button to place the selected range on the Office Clipboard.**

Excel displays a marquee around the range A1:G28 (Figure 4).

FIGURE 4

2 **Click the Weekly Sales Memorandum program button on the taskbar to activate the Word window. Click Edit on the menu bar and then point to Paste Special.**

The Weekly Sales Memorandum document and the Edit menu display on the screen. The insertion point is positioned at the bottom of the document (Figure 5).

FIGURE 5

3 **Click Paste Special. When the Paste Special dialog box displays, click Paste link, and then click Microsoft Excel Worksheet Object in the As list. Point to the OK button.**

The Paste Special dialog box displays (Figure 6).

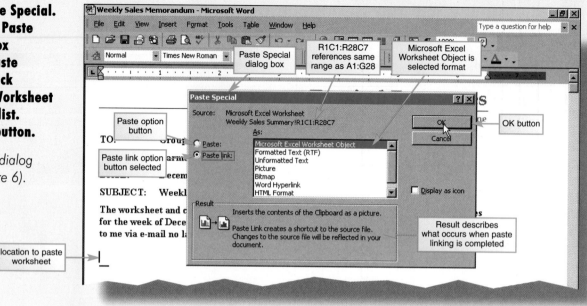

FIGURE 6

4 **Click the OK button.**

The range A1:G28 of the worksheet displays in the Word document beginning at the location of the insertion point (Figure 7).

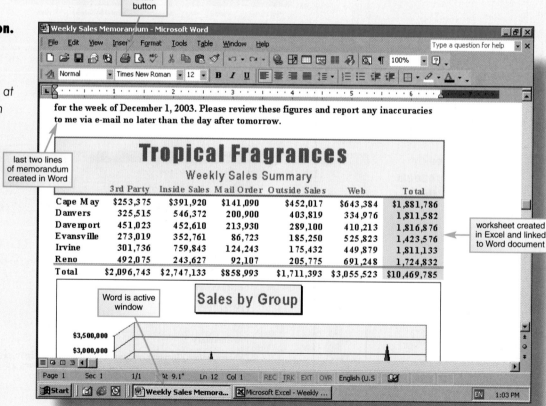

FIGURE 7

The Excel worksheet now is linked to the Word document. If you save the Word document and reopen it, the worksheet will display just as it does in Figure 7. If you want to delete the worksheet, select it and then press the DELETE key. The next section shows how to print and save the memo with the linked worksheet.

Printing and Saving the Word Document with the Linked Worksheet

The following steps print and then save the Word document with the linked worksheet.

More About

Printing

Because the memo and linked worksheet are colorful, they will require additional time and ink in order to print. To speed up printing and save ink, select the Black and White option on the Sheet tab in the Page Setup dialog box.

Steps To Print and Save the Memo with the Linked Worksheet

1 **With the Word window active, click the Print button on the Standard toolbar.**

The memo and the worksheet print as one document (Figure 8).

2 **Click File on the menu bar and then click Save As. Type** Weekly Sales Memorandum 12-8-2003 **in the File name text box. Click the OK button.**

Excel saves the Word document on drive A using the file name, Weekly Sales Memorandum 12-8-2003.doc.

Tropical Fragrances
Delicate Scents for Everyone

TO: Group Sales Managers

FROM: Carmen Chavez, Vice President of Sales

DATE: December 8, 2003

SUBJECT: Weekly Sales Summary

The worksheet and chart shown below illustrate our company's sales activity for all offices for the week of December 1, 2003. Please review these figures and report any inaccuracies to me via e-mail no later than the day after tomorrow.

Tropical Fragrances
Weekly Sales Summary

	3rd Party	Inside Sales	Mail Order	Outside Sales	Web	Total
Cape May	$253,375	$391,920	$141,090	$452,017	$643,384	$1,881,786
Danvers	325,515	546,372	200,900	403,819	334,976	1,811,582
Davenport	451,023	452,610	213,930	289,100	410,213	1,816,876
Evansville	273,019	352,761	86,723	185,250	525,823	1,423,576
Irvine	301,736	759,843	124,243	175,432	449,879	1,811,133
Reno	492,075	243,627	92,107	205,775	691,248	1,724,832
Total	$2,096,743	$2,747,133	$858,993	$1,711,393	$3,055,523	$10,469,785

FIGURE 8

If you quit both applications and reopen Weekly Sales Memorandum 12-8-2003, the worksheet will display in the document even though Excel is not running. Because Word supports object linking and embedding (OLE), it is capable of displaying the linked portion of the Excel workbook without Excel running.

More About

Opening a File

You can open a copy of a workbook, rather than the workbook itself by clicking the arrow to the right of the Open button in the Open dialog box and selecting the Open as Copy command.

Editing the Linked Worksheet

You can edit any of the cells in the worksheet while it displays as part of the Word document. To edit the worksheet, double-click it. If Excel is running, the system will switch to it and display the linked workbook. If Excel is not running, the system will start Excel automatically and display the linked workbook. The following steps show how to change the amount sold by the Outside Sales rep in Evansville (cell E7) from $185,250 to $400,000.

Steps **To Edit the Linked Worksheet**

1 **With the Word window active and the Weekly Sales Memorandum 12-1-2003 document active, double-click the worksheet. When the Excel window becomes active, if necessary double-click the title bar to maximize the window. Click the ESC key to remove the marquee.**

Windows switches from Word to Excel and displays the original workbook, Weekly Sales Summary.

2 **Click cell E7 and then enter** 400000 **as the new value for the Outside sales rep in Evansville.**

Excel recalculates all formulas in the workbook and redraws the 3-D Cone chart (Figure 9).

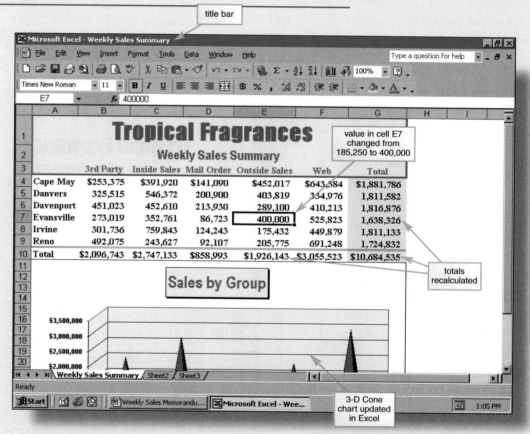

FIGURE 9

3 **Click the Weekly Sales Memorandum 12-1-2003 button on the taskbar.**

Word becomes active. The weekly sales amount for the Outside Sales rep in Evansville, which was 185,250 now is 400,000. New totals display for the Outside Sales reps column, the Evansville total, and the company total (Figure 10).

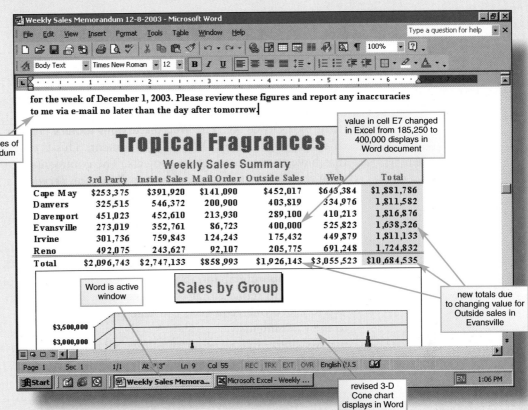

FIGURE 10

As you can see from the previous steps, you double-click a linked object when you want to edit it. Windows will activate the application and display the workbook or document from which the object originated. You then can edit the object and return to the destination application. Any changes made to the object will display in the destination document.

Quitting Word and Excel

If you want the edited changes to the linked workbook to be permanent, you must save the Weekly Sales Summary workbook before quitting Excel. In this feature, the document and modified workbook will not be saved.

TO QUIT WORD AND EXCEL

1 With Excel active, click the Close button on the right side of the title bar to quit Excel. When the Microsoft Excel dialog box displays, click the No button.

2 With Word active, click the Close button on the right side of the title bar to quit Word. When the Microsoft Word dialog box displays, click the No button.

Discussion Servers

When discussion comments are posted to a workbook, document, or Web page, they are not saved in the files themselves. Instead, the comments are saved in a database on the discussion server.

Saving the Word Document as a Web Page and Using a Discussion Server

The Office XP applications include a collaborative feature that allows you and your colleagues to comment online on documents. This is done using the Web discussions feature of Office XP. The **Web discussions feature** enables users to attach comments to a Web page or any Office XP document. This is especially useful in companies that have teams working on projects. The comments that users attach are stored in a database on a discussion server. A **discussion server** is a server that is running Microsoft's SharePoint Portal Server software.

The document being discussed does not have to reside on the discussion server. It can be stored on any Web server. (See Appendix C about saving documents to a Web server.) One way to discuss a Word document with other users is to save it to a Web server, open it on the Web server, click Tools on the menu bar, point to **Online Collaboration**, and then click Web Discussions command. The **Web Discussions command** will request that you log on to a discussion server if you are not already logged on to one. You then can read the comments entered by other users and reply to their comments.

An alternative to using an Office XP document with the Web discussions feature is to save the Office XP document as a Web page. Then, the users can discuss the document without any need for the Office XP application. If you save the document as a Web page, then any user can view the document as a Web page using a browser.

The following steps show how to create a Web page from the Word document created earlier and use the Web discussions feature to comment on it. The comments are made by Jason Rich and Shelly Falcon, employees of Tropical Fragrance.

SharePoint Portal Server

For more information on Microsoft Sharepoint Portal Server software, visit the Excel 2002 More About Web page (scsite.com/ex2002/more.htm) and click SharePoint.

Note: If you plan to do the following steps on your computer, you must have rights to save a Web page to a Web server. In the following example, Tropical Fragrances is a fictitious Web site on a Web server, and you must have access to a discussion server. The Web server and discussion server can be the same server or different servers. See your instructor for details regarding access to a Web server and discussion server.

To Create a Web Page and Use the Web Discussions Feature

Steps **to Enter a Comment**

1 **Start Word and open Weekly Sales Memorandum 12-8-2003 from the Data Disk. On the File menu click Save as Web page. Save the Web page to a Web server in the Weekly Sales folder using the file name WeeklySales12-08-2003. Close Word. Start your browser.**

2 **Display the Web page, www.TropicalFragrances/ WeeklySales/WeeklySales1 2-08-2003.htm. Click the Discuss button on the Standard Buttons toolbar. When the Discussions toolbar displays, click the Insert Discussion about this document button on the Web Discussion toolbar. When the Enter Discussion Text dialog box displays, enter the discussion subject and discussion text as shown in Figure 11. Point to the OK button.**

The Enter Discussion Text dialog box displays as shown in Figure 11.

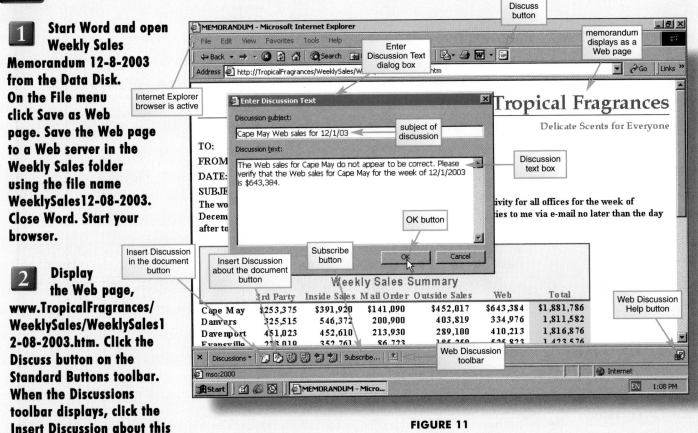

FIGURE 11

3 **Click the OK button.**

A Discussion pane displays in the lower half of the screen (Figure 12). The comment entered in Step 2 displays.

FIGURE 12

In Steps 2 and 3, Jason Rich displays the Web page on the Web server and then makes a comment about the Web page. The comment is added to the database on the discussion server, and it displays in a **Discussion pane** that covers the lower half of the browser window. You can hide the Discussion pane by clicking the **Show/Hide Discussion Pane button** on the Web Discussion toolbar or by clicking the **Discuss button** on the browser's Standard Button toolbar.

Replying to a Comment on a Discussion Server

Once Jason's comment is in the database, his comment will show every time a colleague displays the same Web page while connected to the same discussion server. The following steps show how to reply to Jason's comment using the **Show a menu of actions button** that displays immediately after the comment in the Discussion pane.

Steps **To Reply to a Comment on a Discussion Server**

1 **With the comment shown in Figure 13 in the Discussion pane, click the Show a menu of actions button that displays after the comment. When the shortcut menu displays, point to the Reply command.**

The shortcut menu displays as shown in Figure 13.

FIGURE 13

2 **Click Reply. When the Enter Discussion Text dialog box displays, enter the comment shown in Figure 14. Point to the OK button.**

The Enter Discussion Text dialog box displays as shown in Figure 14.

FIGURE 14

3 **Click the OK button.**

The reply to the first comment displays as shown at the bottom of the Discussion pane (Figure 15).

4 **Right-click the Discussion pane and then click the Print command on the shortcut menu to print the comments. Click the Discuss button on the Standard Buttons toolbar. Click the Close button on the right side of the browser's title bar.**

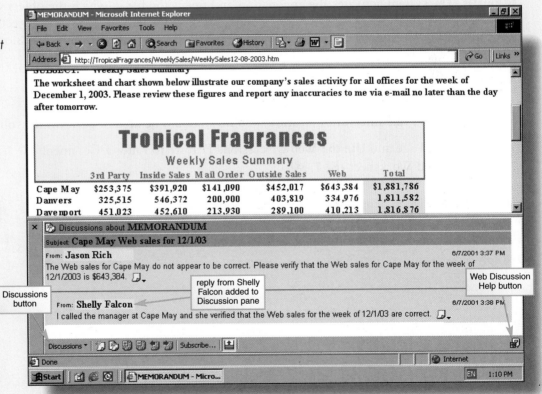

FIGURE 15

The shortcut menu in Figure 13 on page EI 1.12 allows you to reply to, edit, and delete a comment. You can delete and edit a comment only if you are the author. Once someone enters a subject and comment, colleagues usually add comments by clicking the Show a menu of actions button as shown in the previous set of steps.

As you are working in the Discussion pane, it is quite possible that other users will be entering comments at the same time. To display the latest comments, click the **Discussions button** on the left side of the Web Discussion toolbar (Figure 15 on the previous page), and then click **Refresh Discussions**. Additional commands on the Discussions button menu allow you to connect to a discussion server and customize the Discussion pane. For additional information on the Web discussions feature, click the Web Discussion Help button (Figure 15) on the Web Discussion toolbar.

CASE PERSPECTIVE SUMMARY

As the sales for the previous week are sent in from the various offices to Carmen, she updates the Excel workbook. She then opens the Word memorandum from the previous week and modifies the date. After saving the Word document, she prints it and distributes a hardcopy of the updated version to the regional sales managers and publishes the document to a Web server for the sales representatives to view and discuss using a discussion server.

Integration Feature Summary

This Integration Feature introduced you to Object Linking and Embedding (OLE). OLE allows you to bring together data and information that has been created in different applications. When you link an object to a document and save it, only a link to the object is saved with the document. You edit a linked object by double-clicking it. The system activates the application and opens the file in which the object was created. If you change any part of the object and then return to the destination document, the updated object will display. Finally, this Integration Feature introduced you to publishing a document to the Web for discussion purposes.

What You Should Know

Having completed this Integration Feature, you now should be able to perform the following tasks:

▶ Create a Web Page and Use the Web Discussions Feature to Enter a Comment *(EI 1.11)*
▶ Edit the Linked Worksheet *(EI 1.08)*
▶ Link an Excel Worksheet to a Word Document *(EI 1.05)*
▶ Open a Word Document and an Excel Workbook *(EI 1.03)*
▶ Print and Save the Memo with the Linked Worksheet *(EI 1.07)*
▶ Quit Word and Excel *(EI 1.09)*
▶ Reply to a Comment on a Discussion Server *(EI 1.12)*

More About

Microsoft Certification

The Microsoft Office User Specialist (MOUS) Certification program provides an opportunity for you to obtain a valuable industry credential - proof that you have the Excel 2002 skills required by employers. For more information, see Appendix E or visit the Shelly Cashman Series MOUS Web page at scsite.com/offxp/cert.htm.

In the Lab

1 Linking a Sales Summary Worksheet to an Annual Sales Memo

Problem: Your supervisor, Jorge Ramiro, at Wireless Connect, Inc., wants to send out a year-end memo with the previous year's sales by quarter to the sales force. The memo was created in Word. The sales information is on an Excel worksheet. You have been asked to link the worksheet to the Word document.

Instructions Part 1: Perform the following tasks.

1. One at a time, open the document Annual Sales Memorandum and the workbook Quarterly Sales Summary from the Data Disk.
2. Link the range A1:F25 in the Quarterly Sales Summary workbook to the bottom of the Annual Sales Memorandum.
3. Print and then save the document as Annual Sales Memorandum 1-6-04.
4. Double-click the worksheet in the Word document and use the keyboard to increase manually each of the four quarter sales by $200,000. The total sales in cell F4 should be $20,522,369. Activate the Word window and print it with the new values. Close the document and workbook without saving them.

Instructions Part 2: If you have access to a Web server and discussion server, save the document Annual Sales Memorandum 1-6-04 as a Web page. Use Internet Explorer to display the page. Click the Discuss button on the Standard Buttons toolbar and add a comment. Then reply to the comment. Print the comments.

2 Linking an Annual Sales Memo to a Sales Summary Workbook

Problem: Your supervisor, Jorge Ramiro, at Wireless Connect, Inc., has asked you to link the year-end memo to the Excel workbook with the sales information, rather than linking the Excel worksheet to the year-end memo, as was done in the previous exercise.

Instructions Part 1: Complete the following tasks.

1. One at a time, open the document Annual Sales Memorandum and the workbook Quarterly Sales Summary from the Data Disk.
2. With the Excel window active, insert 20 rows above row 1 and then select cell A1. Activate the Word document and copy the entire document. Link the Word document at the top of the worksheet in the workbook, Quarterly Sales Summary. To link, select the Paste link option button in the Paste Special dialog box and then select Microsoft Word Document Object in the As list box.
3. Print the Quarterly Sales Summary sheet and then save the workbook as Quarterly Sales Summary with Memo 1-6-04.
4. With the Excel window active, double-click the linked document and then delete the first sentence in the memo. Activate the Excel window and then print the worksheet with the modified memo. Close the workbook and document without saving them.

Instructions Part 2: If you have access to a Web server and discussion server, save the workbook Quarterly Sales Summary with Memo 1-6-04 as a Web page. Use Internet Explorer to display the page. Click the Discuss button on the Standard Buttons toolbar and add a comment. Then reply to the comment. Print the comments.

Microsoft Excel 2002

Using Macros and Visual Basic for Applications (VBA) with Excel

You will have mastered the material in this project when you can:

O B J E C T I V E S

- Use the Undo button to undo multiple changes
- Use passwords to assign protected and unprotected status to a workbook
- Use the macro recorder to create a macro
- Execute a macro
- Understand Visual Basic for Applications code
- Customize a toolbar by adding a button
- Customize a menu by adding a command
- Add controls to a worksheet, such as command buttons, scroll bars, check boxes, and spin buttons
- Assign properties to controls
- Use VBA to write a procedure to automate data entry into a worksheet
- Understand Do-While and If-Then-Else statements
- Test and validate incoming data
- Explain event-driven programs

Plan Today, Enjoy Tomorrow

Retire in Style

" If you would be wealthy, think of saving as well as getting."
Benjamin Franklin

The good news? Americans now can expect to live longer, healthier lives than ever before. The bad news? Although a current survey indicates that 63 percent of Americans believe they will be able to save enough money to retire comfortably, the number of Americans who no longer share this confidence recently jumped from 10 to 17 percent.

Some experts recommend starting retirement savings with the very first paycheck. But how can you save for retirement when you have tuition payments, a car loan, utility bills, and rent or mortgage payments? The answer is careful planning, starting right now.

Workers are retiring earlier and living longer than ever before. Considering that the average person spends 18 years in retirement, you need to plan for that time early in your career. During your retirement, you will be faced with buying new cars, replacing your appliances, putting a new roof on your home, and needing prescription drugs and hearing aids.

Unfortunately, fewer than half of all American workers have calculated how much money they will need to retire comfortably. Although the number of Americans who devote some portion of their income to retirement savings has increased dramatically in recent years, most Americans are unaware that simply saving is not enough. To save money effectively, you need to calculate how much money you will need after your retirement and implement a retirement savings plan to meet your needs.

At a minimum, a retirement needs calculation should take into account your current annual income, expected retirement age, inflation, your monthly living expenses after retirement, and the types of monthly income you expect to receive after retirement.

The percent of your annual income you devote to retirement savings will vary based on these types of factors, but consider the following example. If your average annual salary is $30,000 a year, and you save 6 percent of your salary each month, or $150, starting at age 30, a 10 percent average annual return on your investments will yield $574,242 by the time you reach age 65. On the other hand, if you do not start saving until age 55, you would realize only $30,983 ten years later.

Although that amount may seem large, consider that inflation also is an important factor. If you spend $25,000 on living expenses the year you retire, you will need $56,000 for these same expenses 20 years later if inflation rises four percent annually.

In this Excel project, you will see just how advantageous retirement plans can be. You will use the Visual Basic for Applications programming language to build the Master Software Employment Retirement Savings Plan worksheet. You then will input current salary, employee investment, employer match, rate of return, and years of service. You will see that regular contributions to this retirement plan for 45 years could yield close to $2 million, even without receiving salary increases.

So where do you start planning for your retirement? The Internet abounds with sites brimming with financial calculators and investment strategies. Begin with the Social Security Administration's site (www.ssa.gov) and find a link to the Social Security Benefits Planner that calculates your potential Social Security payments. Other sites, such as the Administration on Aging (www.aoa.dhhs.gov/retirement), the American Savings Education Council (www.asec.org), and SmartMoney (www.smartmoney.com), have a multitude of interactive tools and worksheets.

No matter your investment strategy, plans today will reap rewards tomorrow. A sound retirement plan can provide you and your family with a firm financial foundation after your retirement.

Microsoft Excel 2002

Using Macros and Visual Basic for Applications (VBA) with Excel

PROJECT

7

C A S E   P E R S P E C T I V E

Louis Pankros is the director of the human resource department for Master Software, a small but growing software provider. One of Louis's main tasks is to convince potential and current employees that Master Software offers excellent benefits.

Master Software's most lucrative benefit is an employee retirement savings plan. This plan is similar to a 401(k) plan. A 401(k) plan is a retirement savings program that allows employees to invest pretax dollars through payroll deductions.

Louis has a planning workbook. Any change to the data causes the planning workbook to recalculate all formulas instantaneously, thus showing the results of investing in the company's employee retirement savings plan.

Louis wants to put the workbook on the company's intranet so potential and current employees easily can determine the financial advantages of the retirement plan. The problem is that without an easy-to-use interface that steps the user through the entry of data, there is too much room for error and confusion. Louis has asked you to use Visual Basic for Applications to create a user-friendly interface for entering data into the workbook in three phases.

Introduction

Before a computer can take an action and produce a desired result, it must have a step-by-step description of the task to be accomplished. The step-by-step description is a series of precise instructions called a **procedure**. A procedure also is called a **program** or **code**. The process of writing a procedure is called **computer programming**. Every Excel command on a menu and button on a toolbar has a corresponding procedure that executes when you click the command or button. **Execute** means that the computer carries out the step-by-step instructions. In a Windows environment, the instructions associated with a task are executed when an event takes place, such as clicking a button, clicking a command, dragging a scroll box, or right-clicking a screen element.

Because a command or button in Excel does not exist for every possible worksheet task, Microsoft has included a powerful programming language called Visual Basic for Applications. The **Visual Basic for Applications** (**VBA**) programming language allows you to customize and extend the capabilities of Excel. Commonly used combinations of tasks can be grouped together using VBA and then reused at a later time. In this project, you will learn how to create macros using a code generator called a **macro recorder**. A **macro** is a procedure composed of VBA code. It is called a macro, rather than a procedure, because it is created using the macro recorder. You also will learn how to add buttons to toolbars and commands to menus and associate these with macros. Finally, you will learn the basics of VBA, including creating the interface, setting the properties, and writing the code.

Project Seven — Master Software Employee Retirement Savings Plan Worksheet

Master Software has determined the following needs and source of data.

Needs: The easy-to-use interface for the employee retirement savings plan workbook will be implemented in three phases:

Phase 1 — Create a macro using the macro recorder that prints the worksheet in portrait orientation using the Fit to option. Assign the macro to a button on the Standard toolbar (Figure 7-1a) and to a command on the File menu so the user can execute the macro by clicking the button or the command.

Phase 2 — Create a button on the worksheet as shown in Figure 7-1a, assign the button properties, and write an associated procedure (Figure 7-1b) that steps the user through entering the required data in the range D5:D10.

Phase 3 — Create an area on the worksheet called Adjustment Center (Figure 7-2 on the next page) that allows the user to enter his or her name and annual salary using a button and the remaining data using scroll bars, a check box, and spin buttons. Verify that the annual salary entered is positive.

Source of Data: The workbook shown in Figure 7-1a, without the button on the worksheet and the button on the toolbar, is available on the Data Disk with the file name Master Software.

(a) Worksheet

(b) Visual Basic for Applications

FIGURE 7-1

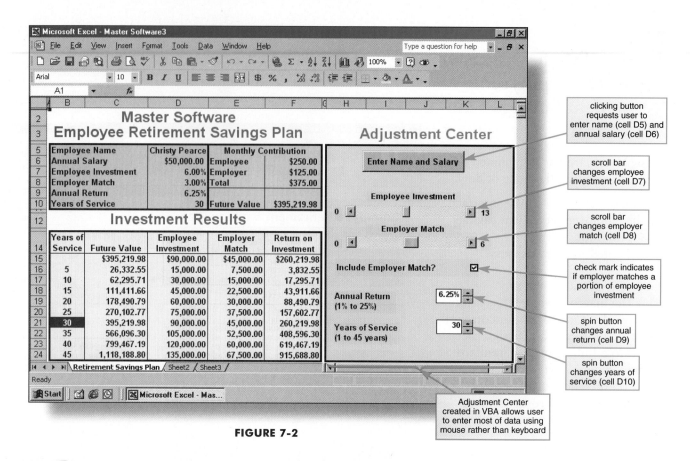

FIGURE 7-2

Starting Excel and Opening a Workbook

Perform the following steps to start Excel, open the workbook Master Software from the Data Disk, and reset the toolbars.

More About

Opening Workbooks

Macros are an easy place for computer virus programmers to hide computer viruses. For this reason, Excel 2002 displays a dialog box whenever you open a workbook that contains a macro. The dialog box requires that you choose to enable or disable the attached macro before it will open the workbook. If you disable the macro and the macro contains a virus, it cannot damage your system. You should enable macros only if you trust the author that created the workbook with the macro.

TO START EXCEL, OPEN A WORKBOOK, AND CUSTOMIZE EXCEL

1 Insert the Data Disk in drive A. See the inside back cover of this book for instructions for downloading the Data Disk or see your instructor for information on accessing the files required in this book.

2 Click the Start button on the taskbar and then click Open Office Document on the Start menu.

3 When the Open Office Document dialog box displays, click the Look in box arrow and then click 3½ Floppy (A:). Double-click Master Software in the Look in list.

4 If the Excel window is not maximized, double-click its title bar to maximize it.

5 If the Language bar displays, click its Minimize button.

6 If the Standard and Formatting toolbars display on one row, click the Toolbar Options button on the right side of either toolbar and then click Show Buttons on Two Rows in the Toolbar Options list.

The Master Software workbook displays in the Excel window (Figure 7-3).

The Retirement Savings Plan worksheet in the Master Software workbook is divided into two parts (Figure 7-3). The top part contains the data (range D5:D10) and the results (range F6:F10). The key cell is F10, which displays the future value of the investment.

The bottom part of the worksheet is a data table that varies the years of service in column B and organizes the results of four formulas in the range C15:F24 — future value (column C), employee investment (column D), employer match (column E), and return on investment (column F). In this worksheet, the return on investment is the future value less the sum of the employee and employer investment.

Many of the buttons on the toolbars are dimmed. When buttons are dimmed and Excel is in Ready mode, then the worksheet is protected. In this case, the cells in the range D5:D10 are unlocked

FIGURE 7-3

so users can enter data, but the rest of the cells in the worksheet are protected and, therefore, cannot be changed. Later in this project, the worksheet will be unprotected so that changes can be made to it.

Gaining Confidence in a Workbook Created by Someone Else

When you modify a workbook created by someone else, such as the Master Software workbook, you should learn as much as you can about the workbook before you modify it. You can learn more about a workbook by doing the following:

1. Press CTRL+ACCENT MARK (`) to display the formulas version to gain an understanding of what formulas and functions are used in the worksheet, and which cells are referenced by the formulas and functions.
2. Use Range Finder or the auditing commands to show which cells are referenced in formulas and functions. You double-click a cell with a formula or function to activate Range Finder.
3. Check which cells are locked and which cells are unlocked. Usually all cells in a workbook are locked, except for those in which you enter data. For example, on the Retirement Savings Plan worksheet in Master Software, only the cells in the range D5:D10 are unlocked.
4. Enter sample data and verify the results.

To illustrate the entry of sample data, the following employee data will be used: Employee Name (cell D5) – Julia Hin; Annual Salary (cell D6) – $76,000.00; Employee Investment (cell D7) – 7.00%; Employer Match (cell D8) – 3.00%; Annual Return (cell D9) – 6.00%; and Years of Service (cell D10) – 35. Before entering the data, select the range D5:D10 so that Excel automatically makes the next cell in the range the active one when you complete a cell entry by pressing the ENTER key.

Perform the steps on the next page to enter the sample data.

More *About*

Retirement Plans

Most employers who make contributions to 401(k) or similar plans require an employee to be vested before the employer matching contributions are granted to the employee. Usually a company requires three to five years of continuous employment before an employee is completely vested. Virtually all 401(k) plans, however, can be transferred from one employer to another.

TO AUTOMATE DATA ENTRY BY SELECTING A RANGE OF CELLS

1 Click cell D5 and then select the range D5:D10. In cell D5 type `Julia Hin` as the employee name and then press the ENTER key.

2 In cell D6 type `76000` as the annual salary and then press the ENTER key.

3 In cell D7 type `7%` as the employee investment and then press the ENTER key.

4 In cell D8 type `3%` as the employer match and then press the ENTER key.

5 In cell D9 type `6%` as the annual return and then press the ENTER key.

6 In cell D10, type `35` as the years of service and then press the ENTER key. Click cell H5 to remove the selection from the range D5:D10.

The worksheet displays with the updated results, including a new future value of $902,316.52 in cell F10 (Figure 7-4).

As shown in Figure 7-4, if Julia Hin earns $76,000 a year and invests 7% of her income a year in the retirement savings plan, then in 35 years her investment will be worth $902,316.52. If she works an additional ten years, then cell C24 shows Julia's investment will be worth an astonishing $1,745,461.99. These future values assume the annual return on the investment will be a conservative 6%. They also assume that Julia will never get a raise, which means the investment could be worth significantly more if she does get raises, because she is investing a percentage of her income, rather than a fixed amount.

Outside of winning the lottery or receiving a large inheritance, a retirement savings plan is the easiest way for a person on a fixed income to legally become a millionaire at some point in his or her lifetime. A significant benefit of the plan is that participants usually do not pay taxes on the money that they invest into the plan.

Once you start drawing funds from the plan, you are required to pay taxes on what you withdraw. Plans usually have penalties for withdrawing funds before you are 59½ years old. For example, you may pay a 10 percent penalty on withdrawals before you are 59½ years old.

As shown in the previous set of steps, when you select a range before entering data, Excel automatically advances one cell downward when you press the ENTER key. If the worksheet consists of multiple columns and you enter the last value in a column, then Excel moves to the top of the next column.

Follow these steps to change the data in the range D5:D10 back to its original values.

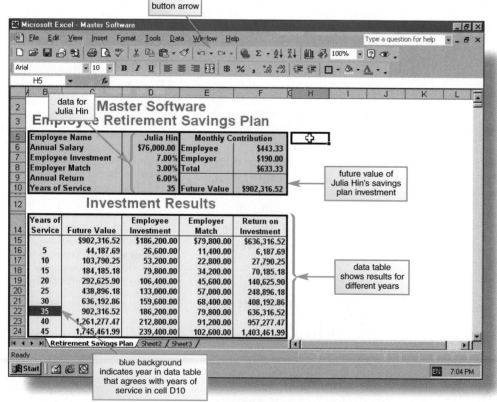

FIGURE 7-4

TO UNDO A GROUP OF ENTRIES USING THE UNDO BUTTON

1 Click the Undo button arrow on the Standard toolbar (Figure 7-4).

2 When the Undo list displays, drag from the top down through Julia Hin and then release the left mouse button. Click cell H5.

Excel changes the range D5:D10 back to its original values and recalculates all formulas and the data table. The Retirement Savings Plan worksheet displays as shown earlier in Figure 7-3 on page E 7.07.

Unprotecting a Password-Protected Worksheet

The Retirement Savings Plan worksheet in the Master Software workbook is protected. When a worksheet is protected, users cannot change data in locked cells or modify the worksheet in any manner. Thus, before modifying the worksheet in the three phases, it must be unprotected. A **password** ensures that users will not unprotect the worksheet by using the Unprotect command. The Retirement Savings Plan worksheet password is planright.

A password, such as planright, can contain any combination of letters, numerals, spaces, and symbols, and it can be up to 15 characters long. Passwords are case-sensitive, so if you vary the capitalization when you assign the password, you must type the same capitalization later when you unprotect the worksheet.

The following steps show how to unprotect the password-protected worksheet.

Steps **To Unprotect a Password-Protected Worksheet**

1 **Click Tools on the menu bar, point to Protection, and then point to Unprotect Sheet on the Protection submenu.**

The Tools menu and Protection submenu display (Figure 7-5).

FIGURE 7-5

2 **Click Unprotect Sheet. When the Unprotect Sheet dialog box displays, type** planright **in the Password text box and then point to the OK button.**

The Unprotect Sheet dialog box displays (Figure 7-6). Excel displays asterisks in place of the password planright so no one can look over your shoulder and copy the password.

3 **Click the OK button.**

Excel unprotects the Retirement Savings Plan worksheet.

FIGURE 7-6

Other Ways

1. Press ALT+T, P, P
2. In Voice Command mode, say "Tools, Protection, Unprotect, [type password] OK"

More About

Password Protection

Excel offers three basic levels of password protection: 1) file level when you save it to disk; 2) workbook level so the window cannot be modified; and 3) worksheet level so locked cells cannot be changed. The first level is available through the Save As command on the File menu. The second and third levels are available through the Protection command on the Tools menu.

With the worksheet unprotected, you can modify the contents of cells regardless of whether they are locked or unlocked. If you decide to password-protect a worksheet, make sure you write down the password and keep it in a secure place. If you lose the password, you cannot open or gain access to the password-protected worksheet.

The Protection submenu shown in Figure 7-5 on the previous page also has a **Protect Workbook command.** The workbook protection level protects the structure and windows of the workbook, but not individual worksheets. Protecting the structure of a workbook means that users cannot add, delete, move, hide, unhide, or rename sheets. Protecting a workbook's windows means users cannot move, resize, hide, unhide, or close the workbook's windows.

Although it is not necessary in this project to unprotect the workbook, you can do so by invoking the Unprotect Workbook command and using planright as the password.

Phase 1 — Recording a Macro and Assigning It to a Toolbar Button and Menu Command

The first phase of this project creates a macro to automate printing the worksheet in portrait orientation using the Fit to option. Recall that the Fit to option ensures that the worksheet will fit on one printed page. The orientation for the printout was set to landscape in Master Software. The planned macro will change the orientation from landscape to portrait and use the Fit to option to force it to fit on one page. It then will reset the print settings back to their original settings.

The purpose of this macro is to give users the option of printing the worksheet in landscape orientation by clicking the Print button on the Standard toolbar or executing the macro to print the worksheet in portrait orientation. Once the macro is created, it will be assigned to a button on the Standard toolbar and a command on the File menu.

Recording a Macro

Excel has a **macro recorder** that creates a macro automatically based on a series of actions you perform while it is recording. As with a video recorder, the macro recorder records everything you do to a workbook over time. The macro recorder can be turned on, during which time it records your activities, and then turned off to stop the recording. Once the macro is recorded, it can be played back, or executed, as often as you want.

It is easy to create a macro. Simply turn on the macro recorder and carry out the steps to be recorded.

1. If necessary, switch from landscape orientation to portrait orientation and from 100% normal size printing to fit to one page.
2. Print the worksheet.
3. Switch from portrait orientation to landscape orientation and from fit to one page to 100% normal size printing.
4. Stop the macro recorder.

What is impressive about the macro recorder is that you actually step through the task as you create the macro. Therefore, you see exactly what the macro will do before you use it.

When you first create the macro, you must name it. The name is used later to reference the macro when you want to execute it. Executing a macro causes Excel to step through all of the recorded steps. The macro name in this project is PrintPortrait. **Macro names** can be up to 255 characters long; they can contain numbers, letters, and underscores; they cannot contain spaces and other punctuation.

Perform the following steps to record the macro.

> **More About**
>
> **The Macro Recorder**
>
> The macro recorder is unforgiving. Once it is turned on, Excel records every action you take. If you make a mistake, you must start over. For this reason, you need to plan carefully from start to finish what you intend to do before you turn the macro recorder on.

To Record a Macro to Print the Worksheet in Portrait Orientation Using the Fit to Option

1 Click Tools on the menu bar. Point to Macro and then point to Record New Macro on the Macro submenu.

The Tools menu and Macro submenu display (Figure 7-7).

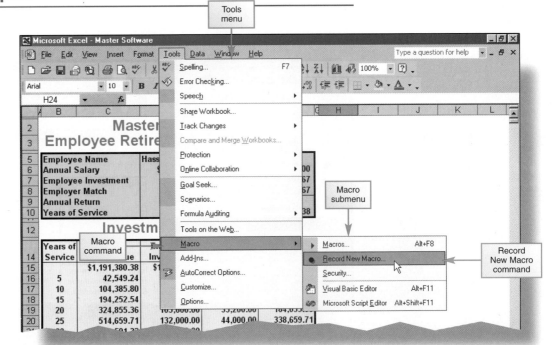

FIGURE 7-7

2 **Click Record New Macro. When the Record Macro dialog box displays, type** PrintPortrait **in the Macro name text box. Type** r **in the Shortcut key text box, and then type** Macro prints worksheet in portrait orientation on one page **in the Description text box. Make sure the Store macro in box displays This Workbook. Point to the OK button.**

The Record Macro dialog box displays as shown in Figure 7-8. The shortcut key for executing the macro is CTRL+R.

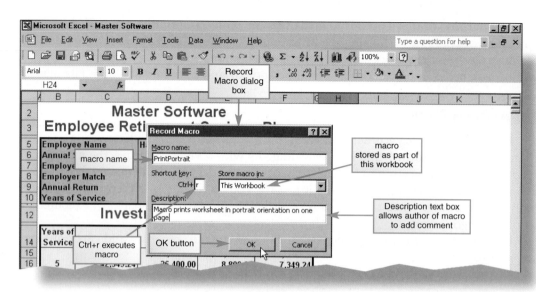

FIGURE 7-8

3 **Click the OK button. If the Stop Recording toolbar does not display, click View on the main menu, then select Stop Recording on the Toolbars submenu.**

The Stop Recording toolbar displays (Figure 7-9). Any task you perform in Excel will be part of the macro. When you are finished recording the macro, clicking the Stop Recording button on the Stop Recording toolbar ends the recording.

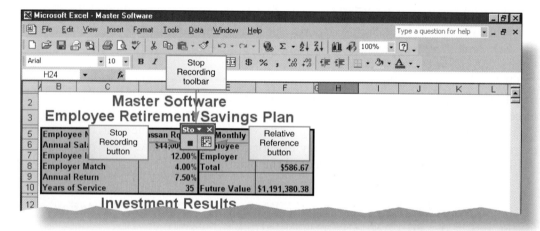

FIGURE 7-9

4 **Click File on the menu bar and then point to Page Setup.**

The File menu displays (Figure 7-10).

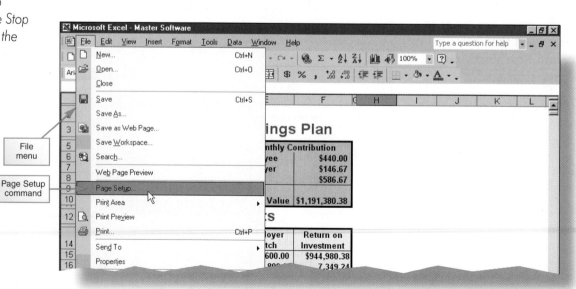

FIGURE 7-10

5 Click Page Setup. When the Page Setup dialog box displays, click the Page tab, click Portrait in the Orientation area if necessary, click Fit to in the Scaling area, and then point to the Print button.

The Page Setup dialog box displays as shown in Figure 7-11.

FIGURE 7-11

6 Click the Print button. When the Print dialog box displays, click the OK button. Click File on the menu bar and then click Page Setup. When the Page Setup dialog box displays, if necessary, click the Page tab, click Landscape in the Orientation area, click Adjust to in the Scaling area, type 100 in the % normal size box, and then point to the OK button.

After the worksheet prints in portrait orientation on one page, the Page Setup dialog box displays as shown in Figure 7-12.

FIGURE 7-12

7 Click the OK button. Point to the Stop Recording button on the Stop Recording toolbar (Figure 7-13).

8 Click the Stop Recording button.

Excel stops recording the worksheet activities and hides the Stop Recording toolbar.

FIGURE 7-13

If you recorded the wrong actions, delete the macro and record it again. You delete a macro by clicking Tools on the menu bar, pointing to Macro on the Tools menu, and then clicking Macros on the Macro submenu. When the Macro dialog box displays, click the name of the macro (PrintPortrait) and then click the Delete button. Finally, record the macro again.

In the Record Macro dialog box (Figure 7-8 on page E 7.12), you select the location to store the macro in the Store macro in box. If you want a macro to be available whenever you use Microsoft Excel, select Personal Macro Workbook in the Store macro in list. This selection causes the macro to be stored in the **Personal Macro Workbook**, which is part of Excel. If you click New Workbook, then Excel stores the macro in a new workbook. Most macros created with the macro recorder are workbook-specific, and thus, are stored in the active workbook.

The following steps protect the Retirement Savings Plan worksheet, save the workbook using the file name Master Software1, and then close the workbook.

TO PASSWORD-PROTECT THE WORKSHEET, SAVE THE WORKBOOK, AND CLOSE THE WORKBOOK

1 Click Tools on the menu bar, point to Protection, and then click Protect Sheet on the Protection submenu. When the Protect Sheet dialog box displays, type planright in the Password text box and then click the OK button. When the Confirm Password dialog box displays, type planright and then click the OK button.

2 Click File on the menu bar and then click Save As. When the Save As dialog box displays, type Master Software1 in the File name text box. Make sure 3½ Floppy (A:) displays in the Save in box and then click the Save button in the Save As dialog box.

3 Click the workbook's Close button on the right side of its menu bar to close the workbook and leave Excel active.

Excel protects the worksheet, saves the workbook to drive A, and closes the Master Software1 workbook.

Opening a Workbook with a Macro and Executing the Macro

A **computer virus** is a potentially damaging computer program designed to affect, or infect, your computer negatively by altering the way it works without your knowledge or permission. Currently, more than 15,000 known computer viruses exist and an estimated 200 more are created each month. The increased use of networks, the Internet, and e-mail has accelerated the spread of computer viruses.

To combat this menace, most computer users run antivirus programs that search for viruses and destroy them before they ever have a chance to infect the computer. Macros are a known carriers of viruses, because of the ease with which a person can add programming code to macros. For this reason, each time you open a workbook with an associated macro, Excel displays a Microsoft Excel dialog box warning that a macro is attached and that macros can contain viruses. Table 7-1 summarizes the buttons users can select from to continue the process of opening a workbook with macros.

Table 7-1	Buttons in the Microsoft Excel Dialog Box When Opening a Workbook with Macros
BUTTONS	**DESCRIPTION**
Disable Macros	Macros are unavailable to the user
Enable Macros	Macros are available to the user to execute
More Info	Opens the Microsoft Excel Help window and displays information on viruses and workbook macros

If you are confident of the source (author) of the workbook and macros, click the Enable Macros button. If you are uncertain about the reliability of the source of the workbook and macros, then click the Disable Macros button. For more information on this topic, click the More Info button.

The following steps open the Master Software1 workbook to illustrate the Microsoft Excel dialog box that displays when a workbook contains a macro. The steps then show how to execute the recorded macro PrintPortrait by using the shortcut key CTRL+R. Recall that the shortcut key was established in Step 2 of the previous set of steps.

Steps **To Open a Workbook with a Macro and Execute the Macro**

1 **With Excel active, click File on the menu bar and then click Open. When the Open dialog box displays, click the Look in box arrow, and then click 3½ Floppy (A:). Double-click the file name Master Software1.**

The Microsoft Excel dialog box displays (Figure 7-14).

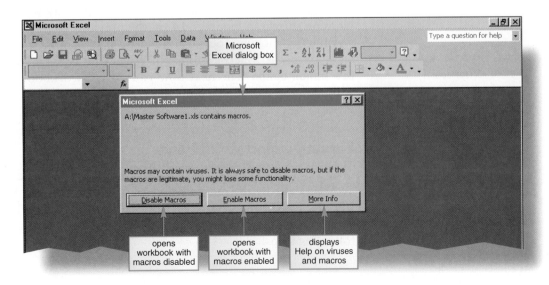

FIGURE 7-14

2 **Click the Enable Macros button.**

When the Retirement Savings Plan worksheet in the Master Software1 workbook displays, press CTRL + R.

Excel opens the workbook Master Software1. The Excel window blinks for several seconds as the macro executes. The report prints as shown in Figure 7-15.

Master Software
Employee Retirement Savings Plan

Employee Name	Hassan Rquibi	Monthly Contribution	
Annual Salary	$44,000.00	Employee	$440.00
Employee Investment	12.00%	Employer	$146.67
Employer Match	4.00%	Total	$586.67
Annual Return	7.50%		
Years of Service	35	Future Value	$1,191,380.38

Investment Results

Years of Service	Future Value	Employee Investment	Employer Match	Return on Investment
	$1,191,380.38	$184,800.00	$61,600.00	$944,980.38
5	42,549.24	26,400.00	8,800.00	7,349.24
10	104,385.80	52,800.00	17,600.00	33,985.80
15	194,252.54	79,200.00	26,400.00	88,652.54
20	324,855.36	105,600.00	35,200.00	184,055.36
25	514,659.71	132,000.00	44,000.00	338,659.71
30	790,501.32	158,400.00	52,800.00	579,301.32
35	1,191,380.38	184,800.00	61,600.00	944,980.38
40	1,773,975.68	211,200.00	70,400.00	1,492,375.68
45	2,620,658.16	237,600.00	79,200.00	2,303,858.16

worksheet printed in portrait orientation using Fit to option

FIGURE 7-15

Other Ways

1. Click Run Macro button on Visual Basic toolbar
2. On Tools menu point to Macro, click Macros, double-click macro name
3. Press ALT+F8, double-click macro name
4. In Voice Command mode, say "Tools, Macro, Macros, [click macro name], OK"

If you are running antivirus software, you may want to turn off the security warning shown in Figure 7-14 on the previous page. You can turn off the security warning by clicking Tools on the menu bar, pointing to Macro, and then clicking Security on the Macros submenu. When the **Security dialog box** displays, click the **Low option button.** The next time you open a workbook that includes a macro, Excel will open the workbook immediately, rather than display the dialog box shown in Figure 7-14.

Viewing a Macro's VBA Code

As described earlier, a macro is comprised of VBA code, which is created automatically by the macro recorder. You can view the VBA code through the Visual Basic Editor. The **Visual Basic Editor** is used by all Office applications to enter, modify, and view VBA code. To view the macro's VBA code, complete the following steps.

Steps To View a Macro's VBA Code

1 **Click Tools on the menu bar. Point to Macro on the Tools menu and then point to Macros on the Macro submenu.**

The Tools menu and Macro submenu display (Figure 7-16).

FIGURE 7-16

2 **Click Macros. When the Macro dialog box displays, click PrintPortrait in the list, and then point to the Edit button.**

The Macro dialog box displays as shown in Figure 7-17.

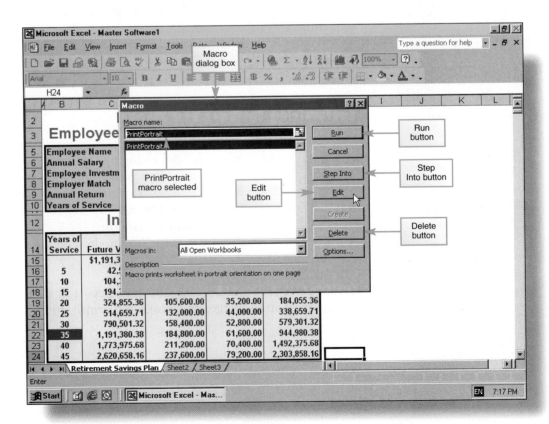

FIGURE 7-17

3 **Click the Edit button.**

The Visual Basic Editor starts and displays the VBA code in the macro PrintPortrait (Figure 7-18). Your screen may display differently depending on how it displayed the last time the Visual Basic Editor was activated.

4 **Scroll through the VBA code. When you are finished, click the Visual Basic Editor Close button on the right side of the title bar.**

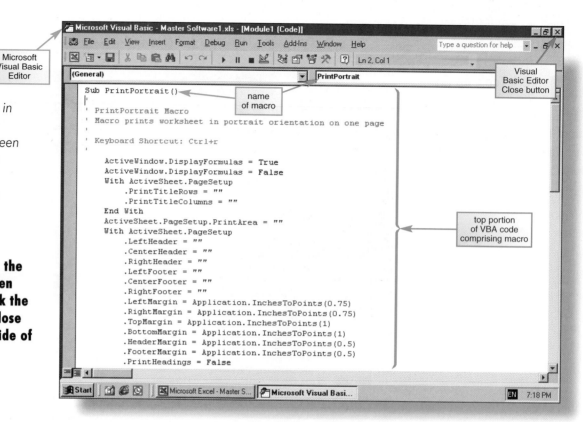

FIGURE 7-18

Other Ways

1. Click Visual Basic Editor button on Visual Basic toolbar
2. Right-click the worksheet tab, click View Code
3. Press ALT+F8, click Edit
4. In Voice Command mode, say "Tools, Macro, Macros, [click macro name], Edit"

More About

The Visual Basic Editor Window

If the window displaying the VBA code appears different than the one shown in Figure 7-18, double-click the Code window's title bar to maximize the window. If the Project window or Properties window displays on the left side of the Visual Basic Editor window, click its Close button.

It is this set of instructions, beginning with line 1 in Figure 7-18 and continuing sequentially to the last line, that is executed when you invoke the macro. By scrolling through the VBA code, you can see that the macro recorder generates a lot of instructions. In this case, 75 lines of code are generated to print the worksheet in portrait orientation using the Fit to option.

Customizing Toolbars and Menus

You can customize toolbars and menus by adding buttons and commands, deleting buttons and commands, and changing the function of buttons and commands. Once you add a button to a toolbar or a command to a menu, you can assign a macro to the button or command. You customize a toolbar or menu by invoking the **Customize command** on the Tools menu. The key to understanding how to customize a toolbar or menu is to recognize that when the Customize dialog box is open, Excel's toolbars and menus are in Edit mode. Edit mode allows you to modify the toolbars and menus.

CUSTOMIZING A TOOLBAR The following steps add a button to the Standard toolbar, change the button image, and assign the PrintPortrait macro to the button.

Steps

To Add a Button to a Toolbar, Assign the Button a Macro, and Use the Button

1 **Click Tools on the menu bar, and then point to Customize.**

The Tools menu displays (Figure 7-19).

FIGURE 7-19

2 **Click Customize. When the Customize dialog box opens, click the Commands tab. Scroll down in the Categories list and then click Macros.**

The Customize dialog box displays as shown in Figure 7-20. The two items in the Command list for the Macro category are Custom Menu Item and Custom Button.

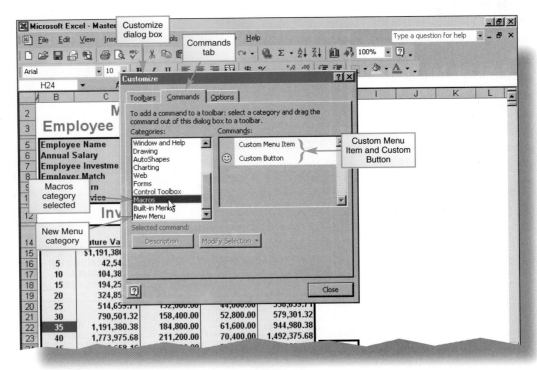

FIGURE 7-20

3   Drag the button with the smiley face image in the Commands list to the right of the Microsoft Excel Help button on the Standard toolbar.

The button with the smiley face image displays next to the Microsoft Excel Help button on the Standard toolbar (Figure 7-21). A heavy border surrounds the button with the smiley face image, indicating Excel is in Edit mode.

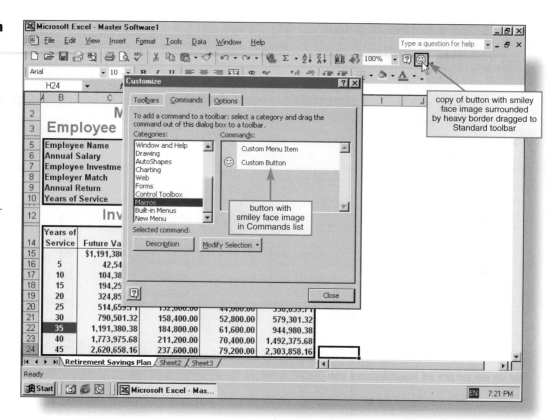

FIGURE 7-21

4   Right-click the button with the smiley face image on the Standard toolbar. When the shortcut menu displays, type Print Portrait in the Name text box. Point to Change Button Image on the shortcut menu. When the Change Button Image palette displays, point to the button with the eye image (row 7, column 4).

Excel displays a palette of button images from which to choose (Figure 7-22).

FIGURE 7-22

5 **Click the button with the eye image. Right-click the button with the eye image on the Standard toolbar and then point to Assign Macro on the shortcut menu.**

Excel replaces the button with the smiley face image on the Standard toolbar with the button with the eye image (Figure 7-23) and the shortcut menu displays.

FIGURE 7-23

6 **Click Assign Macro on the shortcut menu. When the Assign Macro dialog box displays, click PrintPortrait, and then point to the OK button.**

The Assign Macro dialog box displays as shown in Figure 7-24.

FIGURE 7-24

7 **Click the OK button. Click the Close button in the Customize dialog box. Point to the Print Portrait button on the Standard toolbar.**

Excel quits Edit mode. The Print Portrait button displays on the Standard toolbar with the ScreenTip, Print Portrait (Figure 7-25).

8 **Click the Print Portrait button on the Standard toolbar.**

After a few seconds, the worksheet prints in portrait orientation as shown in Figure 7-15 on page E 7.16.

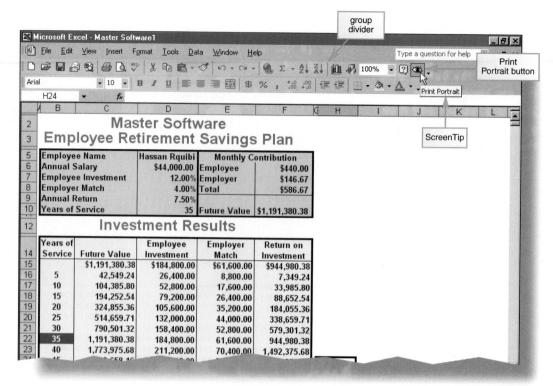

FIGURE 7-25

Other Ways

1. On View menu click Toolbars, click Customize, click Commands tab
2. Right-click toolbar, click Customize on the shortcut menu, click Commands tab
3. Press ALT+V, T, C
4. Click Modify Selection button in Customize dialog box
5. In Voice Command mode, say "Tools, Customize," click the Commands tab

The previous steps illustrate how easy it is in Excel to add a button to a toolbar and assign the button a macro.

Excel includes a complete repertoire of commands for editing buttons on a toolbar as shown on the shortcut menu in Figure 7-23 on the previous page. Table 7-2 briefly describes each of the commands on the shortcut menu.

Table 7-2	Summary of Commands on the Button Shortcut Menu
COMMAND	**DESCRIPTION**
Reset	Changes the icon on the selected button to the original icon and disassociates the macro with the button
Delete	Deletes the selected button
Name	Changes the ScreenTip for a button and changes the command name for a command on a menu
Copy Button Image	Copies the button image to the Office Clipboard
Paste Button Image	Pastes the button image on the Office Clipboard to the selected button
Reset Button Image	Changes the button image back to the original image
Edit Button Image	Allows you to edit the button image
Change Button Image	Allows you to choose a new button image
Default Style;Text Only (Always); Text Only (in Menus); Image and Text	Allows you to choose one of the four styles to indicate how the button should look
Begin a Group	Groups buttons by drawing a vertical line (divider) on the toolbar (see the group divider line in Figure 7-25)
Assign Hyperlink	Assigns a hyperlink to a Web page or Office document to the button
Assign Macro	Assigns a macro to the button

You can add as many buttons as you want to a toolbar. You also can change the image on any button or change a button's function. For example, when in Edit mode (the Customize dialog box is active) you can right-click the Save button on the Standard toolbar and assign it a macro or hyperlink. The next time you click the Save button, the macro will execute or Excel will launch the application associated with the hyperlink, rather than saving the workbook. You reset the toolbars to their installation default by clicking the Toolbars tab in the Customize dialog box, selecting the toolbar in the Toolbars box, and then clicking the Reset button. Because it is so easy to change the buttons on a toolbar, each project in this book begins by resetting the toolbars.

As you add buttons, other buttons on the toolbar will be demoted to the More Buttons box.

CUSTOMIZING A MENU Up to this point, you have been introduced to using a shortcut key and button to execute a macro. Excel also allows you to add commands to a menu. The following steps show how to add a command to the File menu to execute the PrintPortrait macro.

More About

Creating Toolbars

You can create new toolbars and add buttons to it, rather than adding buttons to current toolbars. To create a new toolbar, click the Toolbars tab in the Customize dialog box and then click the New button. You can display the Customize dialog box by right clicking any menu, and then clicking Customize.

To Add a Command to a Menu, Assign the Command a Macro, and Invoke the Command

Steps

1 **Click Tools on the menu bar, and then click Customize. When the Customize dialog box displays, if necessary, click the Commands tab. Scroll down in the Categories box and then click Macros. Click File on the menu bar to display the File menu.**

The Customize dialog box and File menu display as shown in Figure 7-26.

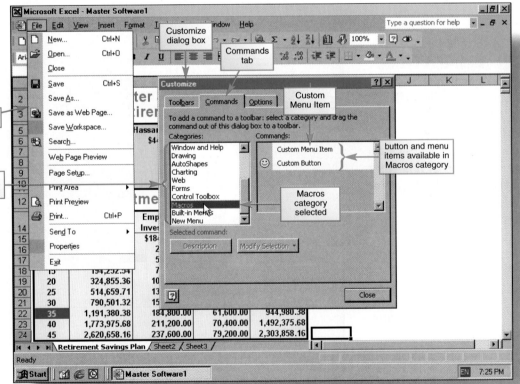

FIGURE 7-26

2 **Drag the Custom Menu Item entry from the Commands list in the Customize dialog box immediately below the Print command on the File menu.**

Excel adds Custom Menu Item to the File menu (Figure 7-27). A heavy border surrounds Custom Menu Item on the File menu, indicating it is in the Edit mode.

FIGURE 7-27

3 **Right-click Custom Menu Item on the File menu and then click the Name text box on the shortcut menu. Type** `Print Po&rtrait   Ctrl+R` **as the new name of this entry on the File menu. Point to Assign Macro on the shortcut menu.**

The shortcut menu displays (Figure 7-28). The ampersand (&) preceding the letter r in Portrait instructs Excel to use the letter r as the access key. The access key is the underlined letter that you can press to invoke the command when the menu displays.

FIGURE 7-28

4 **Click Assign Macro on the shortcut menu. When the Assign Macro dialog box displays, double-click PrintPortrait. Click the Close button at the bottom of the Customize dialog box. Click File on the menu bar and then point to Print Portrait.**

Excel exits Edit mode. The File menu displays with the new command Print Portrait on the menu (Figure 7-29). The underlined letter r in Portrait is the access key.

5 **Click Print Portrait on the File menu.**

After several seconds, the worksheet prints in portrait orientation as shown in Figure 7-15 on page E 7.16.

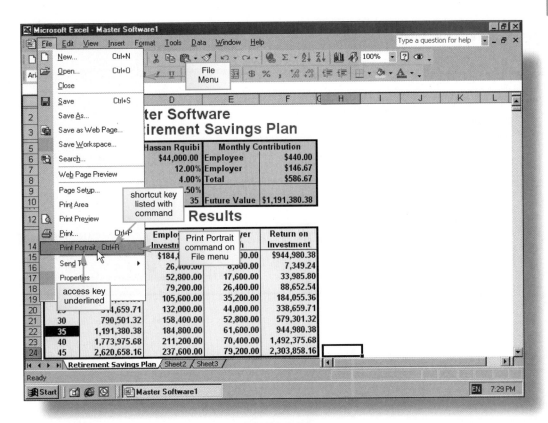

FIGURE 7-29

6 **Click the Save button on the Standard toolbar to save the workbook using the file name Master Software1.**

You have the same customization capabilities with menus as you do with toolbars. All of the shortcut commands described in Table 7-2 on page E 7.22 apply to menus as well. The commands specific to buttons pertain to editing the button image on the left side of a command on a menu.

An alternative to adding a command to a menu is to add a new menu name to the menu bar and add commands to its menu. You can add a new menu name to the menu bar by selecting New Menu in the Categories list of the Customize dialog box (Figure 7-27) and dragging it to the menu bar.

Phase 2 — Creating a Procedure to Automate the Retirement Savings Plan Data Entry

Earlier in this project on page E 7.08, the data for Julia Hin was entered to calculate new future value information. A novice user, however, might not know what cells to select or how much retirement savings plan data is required to obtain the desired results. To facilitate entering the savings plan data, Phase 2 calls for creating a Command Button control (Figure 7-30a on the next page) and an associated procedure (Figure 7-30b on the next page) that steps the user through entering the data using dialog boxes.

Other Ways

1. On View menu click Toolbars, click Customize, click Commands tab
2. Right-click toolbar, click Customize, click Commands tab
3. In Voice Command mode, say "Tools, Customize," click the Commands tab

---

More About

Creating New Menus

You can create an entire new menu on the menu bar by dragging New Menu from the Categories box in the Customize dialog box to the menu bar. You can then add new commands to the new menu using the procedure described in the previous set of steps. You can display the Customize dialog box by right clicking any menu, and then clicking Customize.

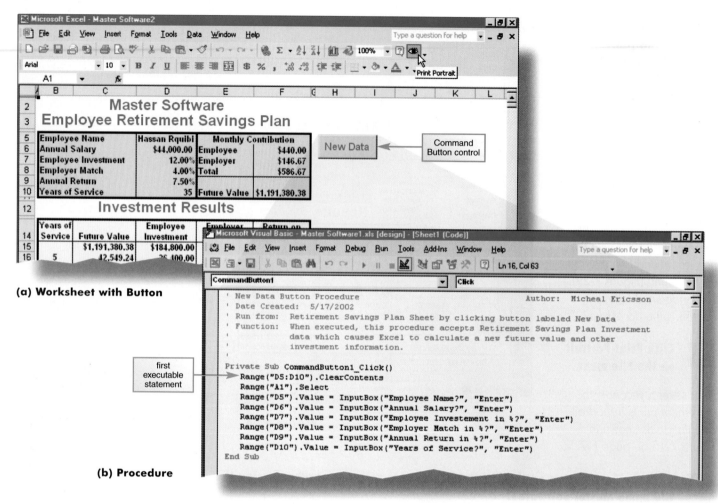

(a) Worksheet with Button

(b) Procedure

first executable statement

FIGURE 7-30

A **Command Button control** is different from a toolbar button in that it is an object you draw on the worksheet. Once you trigger the event by clicking the Command Button control, the instructions in the associated procedure guide the user through entering the required savings plan data in the range D5:D10. The Command Button control also is the user interface. The **user interface** can be as simple as a button and as complex as a series of windows that accept data and display results. The user interface, together with the procedure, is called an **application**. Thus, the name Visual Basic for Applications.

If you step through the procedure (Figure 7-30b) beginning at the line just below Private Sub CommandButton1_Click(), you can see how a procedure methodically steps the user through entering the data in the range D5:D10.

1. The first line clears the range D5:D10.
2. The second line selects cell A1.
3. Lines three through eight accept data for the cells in the range D5:D10, one cell at a time.

Applications are built using the three-step process shown in Figure 7-31: (1) create the user interface; (2) set the properties; and (3) write the VBA code. Before you can create the user interface, the Retirement Savings Plan worksheet in the Master Software1 workbook must be unprotected. The following steps unprotect the worksheet.

FIGURE 7-31

TO UNPROTECT A PASSWORD-PROTECTED WORKSHEET

1 With the Master Software1 workbook open, click Tools on the menu bar, point to Protection, and then click Unprotect Sheet on the Protection submenu.

2 When the Unprotect Sheet dialog box displays, type planright as the password and then click the OK button.

Excel unprotects the worksheet and toolbar buttons become active.

Earlier Excel Version Macros

Some earlier versions of Excel use a language called XLM, rather than VBA, for its macros. Excel 2002 supports both languages. That is, you can execute macros created using XLM. Excel 2002, however, will not allow you to create macros in XLM.

Design Mode

If Excel is in Run mode and you click any control button on the Control Toolbox toolbar, Excel immediately switches to Design mode.

Step 1 – Create the User Interface

The most common way to execute a procedure in Excel is to create a Command Button control. To create the control, click the **Command Button button** on the **Control Toolbox toolbar**. You use the mouse to locate and size the control in the same way you locate and size an embedded chart. You then assign properties and the procedure to the control while Excel is in Design mode.

There are two modes of Visual Basic for Applications within Excel: Design mode and Run mode. **Design mode** allows you to resize controls, assign properties to controls, and enter VBA code. **Run mode** means that all controls are active. That is, if you click a control it triggers the event, and Excel executes the procedure associated with the control. The following steps add a Command Button control to the worksheet.

Steps **To Add a Command Button Control to the Worksheet**

 Right-click a toolbar at the top of the screen. When the shortcut menu displays, click Control Toolbox.

The Control Toolbox toolbar displays.

 Click the Command Button button on the Control Toolbox toolbar. Move the mouse pointer (a cross hair) to the upper-left corner of cell H5. Drag the mouse pointer so the rectangle defining the button area appears as shown in Figure 7-32 and hold.

A light border surrounds the proposed button area in the worksheet (Figure 7-32). When you click the Command Button button, Excel automatically switches to Design mode.

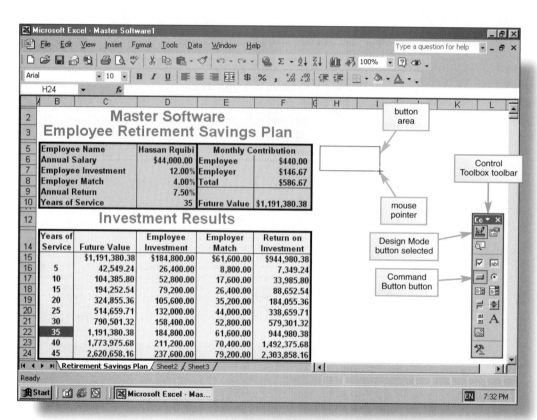

FIGURE 7-32

3 **Release the left mouse button.**

Excel displays the button with the default caption CommandButton1 (Figure 7-33). Because Excel is in Design mode and the button is selected, the button is surrounded by sizing handles.

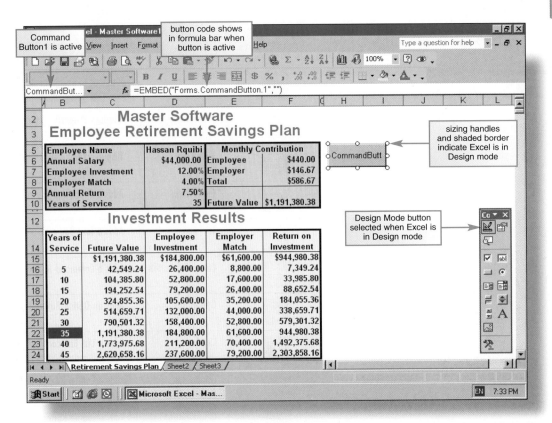

FIGURE 7-33

The Control Toolbox toolbar buttons are summarized in Table 7-3 on the next page. Many of the buttons allow you to add controls to the worksheet that you have worked with previously in Excel, such as check boxes, list boxes, and scroll bars.

Another toolbar that may be helpful as you use Visual Basic for Applications is the **Visual Basic toolbar**. The Visual Basic toolbar is shown in Figure 7-34. You can display the Visual Basic toolbar by right-clicking a toolbar and then clicking Visual Basic on the shortcut menu.

Other Ways

1. Click Design Mode button on Visual Basic toolbar

More About

The User Interface

You can use graphics, such as clip art, rather than a Command Button button to serve as the control that you click to trigger the event.

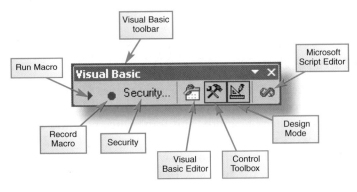

FIGURE 7-34

Table 7-3	Summary of Buttons on the Control Toolbox Toolbar	
BUTTON	**NAME**	**FUNCTION**
	Design Mode	Changes to design mode; Design Mode button changes to Exit Design Mode button when in design mode
	Properties	Displays Properties window
	View Code	Displays VBA code in Visual Basic Editor
	Check Box	Adds a Check Box control
	Text Box	Adds a Text Box control
	Command Button	Adds a Command Button control
	Option Button	Adds an Option Button control
	List Box	Adds a List Box control
	Combo Box	Adds a Combo Box control
	Toggle Button	Adds a Toggle Button control
	Spin Button	Adds a Spin Button control
	Scroll Bar	Adds a Scroll Bar control
	Label	Adds a Label control
	Image	Adds an Image control
	More Controls	Displays a list of additional controls

More Controls

The last button described in Table 7-3 is the More Controls button. If you click this button, nearly 200 additional controls, similar to those in Table 7-3, are available to incorporate in a user interface. The controls will vary depending on the software that is installed on your computer.

Step 2 – Set Properties

A Command Button control has 25 different **properties** (Figure 7-31b on page E 7.27), such as caption (the words on the face of the button), background color, foreground color, height, width, and font. Once you add a Command Button control to a worksheet, you can change any one of the 25 properties to improve its appearance and modify how it works. The steps on the next page change the button's caption, the font size of the caption, and the color of the caption.

Steps **To Set the Command Button Control Properties**

1 **With the Command Button control** selected and Excel in Design mode, click the Properties button on the Control Toolbox toolbar. When the Properties window displays, if necessary, click the Alphabetic tab, click Caption, and then type New Data as the caption. Click ForeColor, click the ForeColor arrow, click the Palette tab, and then point to the color red (column 2, row 3).

Excel displays the Properties window for the Command Button control (Figure 7-35). The Caption property is New Data and the ForeColor Palette sheet displays.

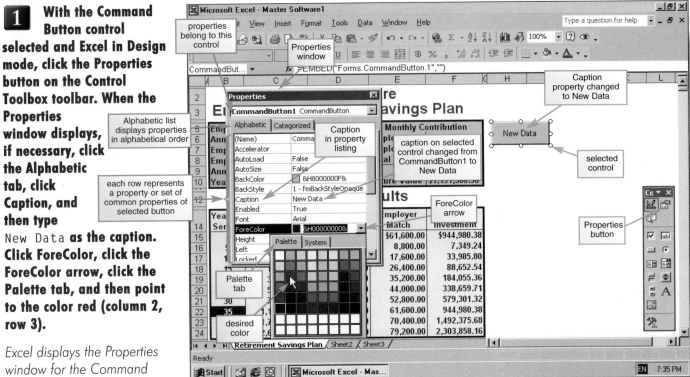

FIGURE 7-35

2 **Click red on the color palette. Click Font in the Properties window and then click the Font button. When the Font dialog box displays, click Bold in the Font style list and 12 in the Size list. Point to the OK button.**

The Properties window and Font dialog box display as shown in Figure 7-36.

FIGURE 7-36

3 **Click the OK button.**

The Command Button control and its Properties window display as shown in Figure 7-37.

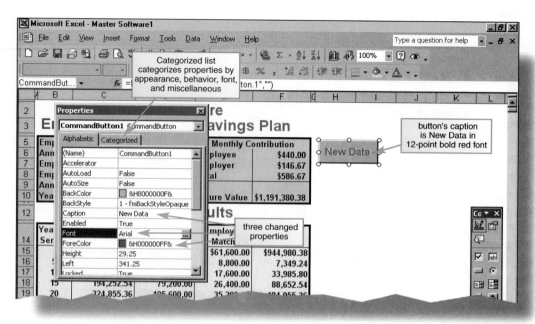

FIGURE 7-37

The Properties window (Figure 7-37) has two tabs, Alphabetic and Categorized. The **Alphabetic list** displays the properties in alphabetical order. The **Categorized list** displays the properties in categories, such as appearance, behavior, font, and miscellaneous.

Depending on the application, you can modify any one of the Command Button control properties shown in Figure 7-35 on the previous page, much like you changed the Caption and Font properties in the previous steps.

Step 3 – Write the VBA Code

The next step is to write and then enter the procedure that will execute when you click the New Data button.

PLANNING A PROCEDURE When you trigger the event that executes a procedure, Excel steps through the Visual Basic statements one at a time, beginning at the top of the procedure. Thus, when you plan a procedure, remember that the order in which you place the statements in the procedure is important because the order determines the sequence of execution.

Once you know what you want the procedure to accomplish, write the VBA code on paper similar to Table 7-4. Then, before entering the procedure into the computer, test it by putting yourself in the position of Excel and stepping through the instructions one at a time. As you do so, think about how it affects the worksheet. Testing a procedure before entering it is called **desk checking** and is an important part of the development process.

Adding comments before a procedure will help you remember its purpose at a later date or help somebody else understand its purpose. In Table 7-4, the first seven lines are comments. **Comments** begin with the word Rem or an apostrophe ('). These comments contain overall documentation and are placed before the procedure, above the Sub statement. Comments have no effect on the execution of a procedure; they simply provide information about the procedure, such as name, creation date, and function. Comments also can be placed in between lines of code or at the end of a line of code as long as the comment begins with an apostrophe (').

Table 7-4 New Data Button Procedure

LINE	VBA CODE
1	' New Data Button Procedure Author: Micheal Ericsson
2	' Date Created: 5/17/2002
3	' Run from: Retirement Savings Plan Sheet by clicking button labeled New Data
4	' Function: When executed, this procedure accepts Retirement Savings Plan
5	' Investment data which causes Excel to calculate a new future
6	' value and other investment information.
7	'
8	Private Sub CommandButton1_Click()
9	Range("D5:D10").ClearContents
10	Range("A1").Select
11	Range("D5").Value = InputBox("Employee Name?", "Enter")
12	Range("D6").Value = InputBox("Annual Salary?", "Enter")
13	Range("D7").Value = InputBox("Employee Investment in %?", "Enter")
14	Range("D8").Value = InputBox("Employer Match in %?", "Enter")
15	Range("D9").Value = InputBox("Annual Return in %?", "Enter")
16	Range("D10").Value = InputBox("Years of Service?", "Enter")
17	End Sub

A procedure begins with a Sub statement and ends with an End Sub statement (lines 8 and 17 in Table 7-4). The **Sub statement** includes the keyword Private or Public followed by the name of the procedure, which Excel determines from the name of the button (CommandButton1), and the event that causes the procedure to execute (Click). **Private** means that the procedure can be executed only from this workbook. **Public** means that it can be executed from other workbooks or programs. Thus, the name of the Command Button control procedure is CommandButton1_Click.

The parentheses following the keyword Click in the Sub statement in line 8 are required. They indicate that arguments can be passed from one procedure to another. Passing arguments is beyond the scope of this project, but the parentheses still are required. The **End Sub statement** signifies the end of the procedure and returns Excel to Ready mode.

The first executable statement in Table 7-4 is line 9, which clears the cells in the range D5:D10. Line 10 selects cell A1 to remove clutter from the screen. One at a time, lines 11 through 16 accept data from the user and assign the data to the cells in the range D5:D10. Each one of the six statements handles one cell each. To the right of the equal sign in lines 11 through 16 is the InputBox function. A **function** returns a value to the program. In this case, the InputBox function displays a dialog box and returns the value entered by the user. For example, in line 11 the InputBox function displays a dialog box with the message, "Employee Name?" When the user responds and enters a name, the InputBox function returns the value entered to the program and assigns it to cell D5.

To enter a procedure, you use the Visual Basic Editor. To activate the Visual Basic Editor, Excel must be in Design mode. With the control selected, you click the **View Code button** on the Control Toolbox toolbar.

The **Visual Basic Editor** is a full-screen editor, which allows you to enter a procedure by typing the lines of VBA code as if you were using word processing software. At the end of a line, you press the ENTER key or use the DOWN ARROW key to move to the next line. If you make a mistake in a statement, you can use the arrow keys and the DELETE or BACKSPACE key to correct it. You also can move the insertion point to previous lines to make corrections.

More About

Entering VBA Comments

If a horizontal line displays between the comment and Sub Statement, press the ENTER key after the last comment to begin a new line. Then press the DELETE key to delete the horizontal line.

Microsoft **Excel 2002**

USING THE VISUAL BASIC EDITOR TO ENTER A PROCEDURE   The following steps activate the Visual Basic Editor and create the procedure for the New Data button.

Steps | **To Enter the New Data Button Procedure**

1   **With Excel in Design mode and the New Data button selected, point to the View Code button on the Control Toolbox toolbar.**

The selected New Data button and Control Toolbox toolbar display as shown in Figure 7-38.

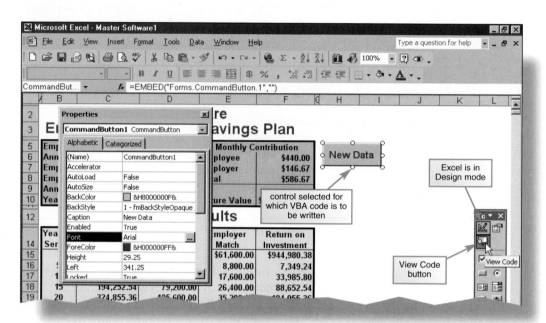

FIGURE 7-38

2   **Click the View Code button. When the Visual Basic Editor starts, if the Project Explorer window displays on the left, click its Close button. Double-click the title bar to maximize the window on the right.**

Excel starts the Visual Basic Editor and opens the Microsoft Visual Basic window (Figure 7-39). The Visual Basic Editor automatically inserts the Sub and End Sub statements and positions the insertion point between the two statements as shown.

FIGURE 7-39

3 **Click to the left of the letter P in the word Private on the first line and press the ENTER key to add a blank line before the Sub statement. Move the insertion point to the blank line and then type the seven comment statements (lines 1 through 7) in Table 7-4 on page E 7.33. Make sure you enter an apostrophe (') at the beginning of each comment line.**

Excel automatically displays the comment lines in green (Figure 7-40).

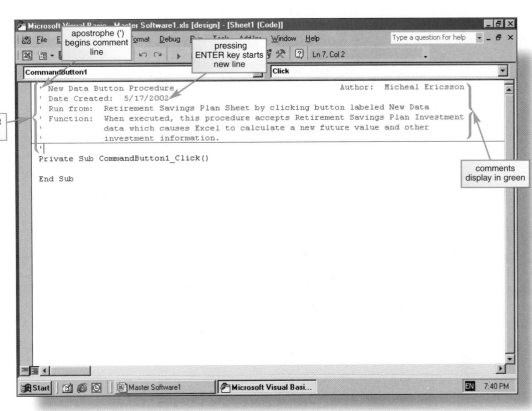

FIGURE 7-40

4 **Position the insertion point on the blank line between the Sub and End Sub statements. Enter lines 9 through 16 in Table 7-4 on page E 7.33. For clarity, indent all lines between the Sub statement and End Sub statement by three spaces.**

The Command Button control procedure is complete (Figure 7-41).

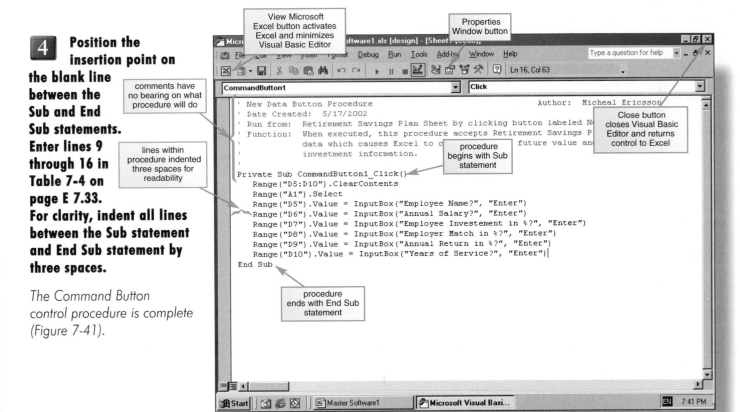

FIGURE 7-41

5 **Click the Close button on the right side of the Microsoft Visual Basic title bar to return to the worksheet. Click the Close button on the right side of the Properties window.**

The worksheet displays as shown in Figure 7-42.

6 **Click the Exit Design Mode button on the Control Toolbox toolbar. Click the Close button on the right side of the Control Toolbox toolbar title bar.**

Excel returns to Run mode, which means if you click the New Data button, Excel will execute the associated procedure.

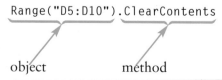

FIGURE 7-42

Two ways exist to return control to the worksheet from the Visual Basic Editor. The Close button on the title bar (Figure 7-41 on the previous page) closes the Visual Basic Editor and returns control to the worksheet. The **View Microsoft Excel button** on the Visual Basic toolbar (Figure 7-41), returns control to Excel, but only minimizes the Visual Basic Editor. If you plan to switch between Excel and the Visual Basic Editor, then use the View Microsoft Excel button, otherwise use the Close button.

Other Ways

1. Click Visual Basic Editor button on Visual Basic toolbar
2. In Design mode, right-click control, click View Code on shortcut menu
3. In Design mode, right-click control, in Voice Command mode, say "View Code"

More About

Printing the VBA Code

To print the VBA code while the Visual Basic Editor is active, click File on the menu bar and then click Print.

More About Visual Basic for Applications

Visual Basic for Applications includes many more statements than those presented here. Even this simple procedure, however, should help you understand the basic composition of a Visual Basic statement. For example, each of the statements within the procedure shown in Figure 7-41 includes a period. The entry on the left side of the period tells Excel which object you want to affect. An **object** can be a cell, a range, a chart, a worksheet, a workbook, a button, or any other control you create on a worksheet. Objects also can be other applications in Windows or parts of other applications. The entry on the right side of the period tells Excel what you want to do to the object. You can place a method or property on the right side of the period. For example, the statement

```
Range("D5:D10").ClearContents
```

object   method

clears the range D5:D10. You use a **method**, such as ClearContents, to change an object's behavior. In this case, the method ClearContents is changing the behavior of the range by deleting its contents.

You previously were shown how to change an object's properties using the Properties window (Figure 7-35 on page E 7.31). The following example shows that you also can change an object's properties during execution of a procedure. The object in this case is a Command Button control.

```
CommandButton1.Caption = "Savings Plan Data"
```

name of control   property

This statement changes the Caption property of the button to Savings Plan Data during execution of the procedure.

The second statement in the procedure in Figure 7-41

```
Range("A1").Select
```

selects cell A1, which, in effect, hides the heavy border that surrounds the active cell. Several of the statements in the procedure also include equal signs. An **equal sign** instructs Excel to make an assignment to a cell. For example, when executed as part of the procedure

```
Range("D5").Value = InputBox("Employee Name?", "Enter")
```

the equal sign instructs Excel to display a dialog box called Enter with the prompt message, Employee Name?, and then assigns cell D5 the value entered by the user in response to the dialog box. Thus, the first argument in the InputBox function is the message to the user and the second argument identifies the dialog box in its title bar.

More About

Running Procedures

Always save a workbook before you execute a procedure in case something unexpected occurs. This is especially true when testing a procedure.

Testing the Retirement Savings Plan Data Entry Procedure

Perform the steps below to enter the following Retirement Savings Plan data: Employee Name (cell D5) – Meg Bell; Annual Salary (cell D6) - $68,500.00; Employee Investment (cell D7) – 9.00%; Employer Match (cell D8) – 4.00%; Annual Return (cell D9) – 8.00%; and Years of Service (cell D10) – 40. Before attempting to enter data using the New Data button, it is important that you exit Design mode and close the Control Toolbox toolbar as indicated in Step 6 of the previous set of steps.

To Enter Retirement Savings Plan Data Using the New Data Button

1 **Click the New Data button. When Excel displays the first Enter dialog box with the prompt message, Employee Name?, type** Meg Bell **in the text box. Point to the OK button.**

Excel clears the range D5:D10 and then selects cell A1. Next, it displays the Enter dialog box shown in Figure 7-43.

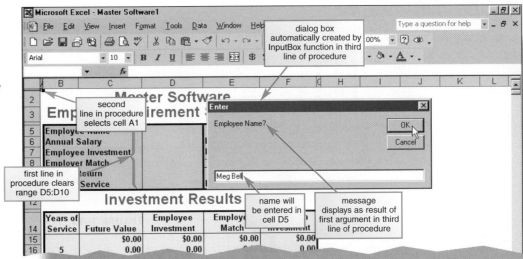

FIGURE 7-43

2 **Click the OK button or press the ENTER key. When Excel displays the next Enter dialog box with the prompt message, Annual Salary?, type** 68500 **in the text box. Point to the OK button.**

Excel assigns the text Meg Bell to cell D5 and displays the second Enter dialog box as shown in Figure 7-44.

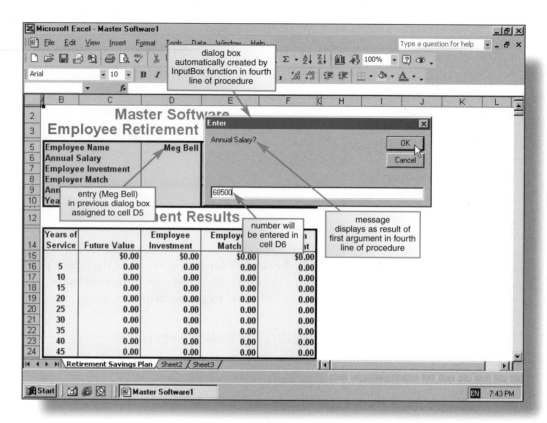

FIGURE 7-44

3 **Click the OK button. When Excel displays the next Enter dialog box with the prompt message, Employee Investment in %?, type** 9% **in the text box, making certain to type the percent (%) sign. Point to the OK button.**

Excel assigns the $68,500.00 to cell D6 and displays the third Enter dialog box as shown in Figure 7-45.

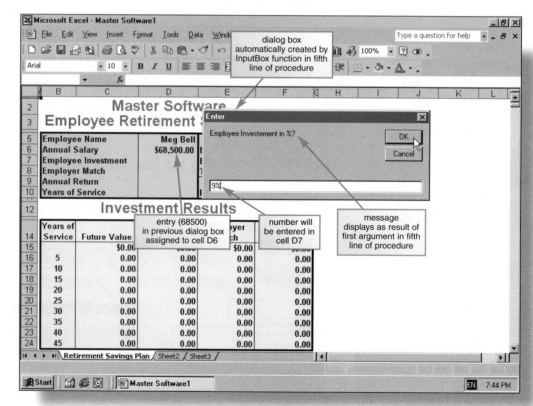

FIGURE 7-45

4 Click the OK button. When Excel displays the next Enter dialog box with the prompt message, Employer Match in %?, type 4% in the text box. Point to the OK button.

Excel assigns the 9.00% to cell D7 and displays the fourth Enter dialog box as shown in Figure 7-46.

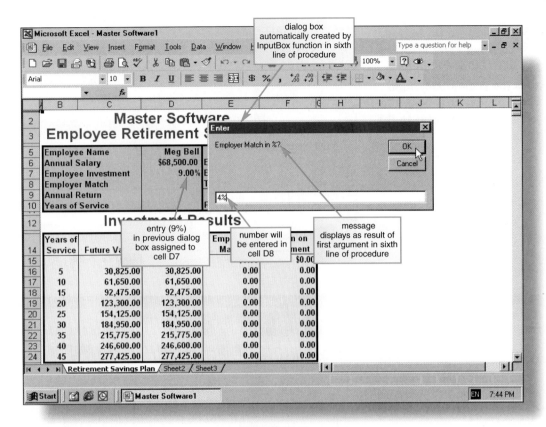

FIGURE 7-46

5 Click the OK button. When Excel displays the next Enter dialog box with the prompt message, Annual Return in %?, type 8% in the text box. Point to the OK button.

Excel assigns 4.00% to cell D8 and displays the fifth Enter dialog box as shown in Figure 7-47.

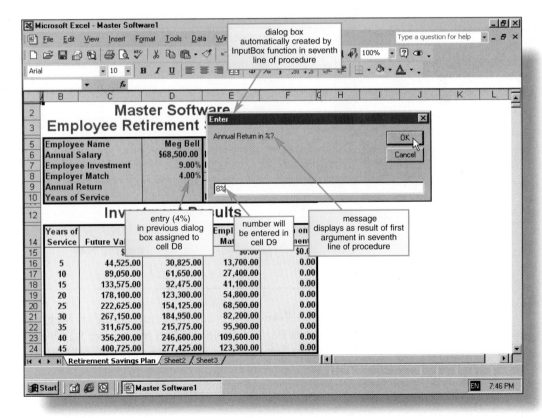

FIGURE 7-47

6 **Click the OK button. When Excel displays the next Enter dialog box with the prompt message, Years of Service?, type** 40 **in the text box. Point to the OK button.**

Excel assigns 8.00% to cell D9 and displays the sixth Enter dialog box as shown in Figure 7-48.

FIGURE 7-48

7 **Click the OK button.**

Excel assigns 40 to cell D10 and displays the results for Meg Bell in the range F6:F10 (Figure 7-49). Excel also recalculates the data table.

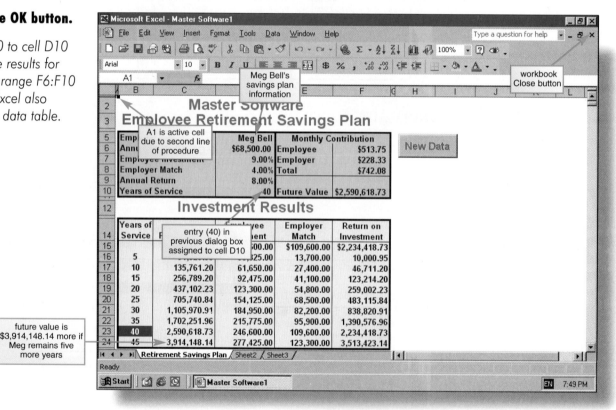

FIGURE 7-49

Figure 7-49 shows that the future value of Meg Bell's investment of $513.75 per month (cell F6) for 40 years is an impressive $2,590,618.73 (cell C23). Meg's total Retirement Savings Plan investment is $246,600.00 (cell D23) and the total employer match is $109,600.00 (cell E23).

Based on this example, you can see the significance of using a VBA to automate the worksheet tasks, especially if the users know little about computers. In this worksheet, each time the user clicks the New Data button, the procedure guides him or her through entering the Retirement Savings Plan data and placing it in the correct cells.

With Phase 2 of this project complete, the final step is to protect the worksheet and save the workbook.

TO PROTECT A WORKSHEET AND SAVE THE WORKBOOK

1 Click Tools on the menu bar, point to Protection, and then click Protect Sheet on the Protection submenu.

2 When the Protect Sheet dialog box displays, type `planright` in the Password text box and then click the OK button. When the Confirm Password dialog box displays, type `planright` and then click the OK button.

3 Click File on the menu bar and then click Save As. When the Save As dialog box displays, type `Master Software2` in the File name text box. Make sure 3½ Floppy (A:) displays in the Save in box and then click the Save button.

4 Click the Close button on the right side of the menu bar to close the Master Software2 workbook.

Phase 2 of this project is complete.

Phase 3 — Creating an Adjustment Center to Automate the Retirement Savings Plan Data Entry

The final phase of this project requires that you add more controls to the worksheet to automate the Retirement Savings Plan data entry. In Phase 2, all of the data was entered using input dialog boxes that displayed one after the other when you triggered the event by clicking the New Data button. This phase uses input dialog boxes for only the name and annual salary. The remaining data (employee investment, employer match, annual return, and years of service) is entered using scroll bars, a check box, and spin buttons.

Consider the Adjustment Center in Figure 7-50. When you click the Enter Name and Salary button, Excel displays input dialog boxes to accept the employee name for cell D5 and the annual salary for cell D6.

The Employee Investment scroll bar immediately below the Enter Name and Salary button allows you to set the employee investment in cell D7. Recall that a scroll bar is made up of three separate areas you can click or drag — the **scroll arrows** on each side that you can click; the **scroll box** between the scroll buttons that you can drag; and the **scroll bar** that you can click that extends from one scroll arrow to the other.

More *About*

Data Validation

The VBA code entered in Step 4 on page E 7.39 does not check the incoming data to be sure it is reasonable. For example, if a user enters a negative value for the Years of Service in Step 6 on the previous page, Excel will calculate an incorrect Future Value. In the next phase of this project, you will learn how to write VBA code that will ensure that unreasonable numbers are rejected. See the VBA code in Figure 7-80 on page E 7.64 for an example.

FIGURE 7-50

Visual Basic for Applications Jobs

Visual Basic for Applications is the most popular programming language used in the computer field today. If you are interested in pursuing a high-paying programmer/analyst career, visit the Excel 2002 Web page (scsite.com/ex2002/more.htm) and click Visual Basic Jobs.

Visual Basic for Applications

To learn Visual Basic for Applications, visit the Excel 2002 Web page (scsite.com/ex2002/more.htm) and click Visual Basic Development Exchange.

The Employee Investment scroll bar has a minimum value of 0% and a maximum value of 13%. When you click one of its scroll arrows, the employee investment percent in cell D7 increases or decreases by 0.5%, depending on which scroll arrow you click. If you click the scroll bar on either side of the scroll box, the employee investment percent in cell D7 increases or decreases by 1%. Finally, you can drag the scroll box to the right or left to increase or decrease the employee investment percent in cell D7.

The Employer Match scroll bar (middle right in Figure 7-50 on the previous page) works the same way, except that the change in the employer match is 0.25% when you click a scroll arrow, and the scroll bar runs from 0% to 6%.

The Include Employer Match? check box in the middle of the Adjustment Center in Figure 7-50 indicates if the Employer Match scroll bar is enabled or disabled. If the check mark is present, then the scroll bar below the check box is enabled. If the check mark is removed, then cell D8 is set equal to 0% and the scroll bar is disabled.

The Annual Return spin button in the lower portion of the Adjustment Center increases or decreases the annual return in cell D9 by 0.25% each time you click a spin button arrow. A **spin button** has two buttons, one to increment and one to decrement the value in the cell with which it is associated. The Years of Service spin button in the lower portion of the Adjustment Center increases or decreases the years of service in cell D10 by one each time you click a spin button arrow.

The following steps open the workbook Master Software1, save it using the file name Master Software3, unprotect the Retirement Savings Plan worksheet, and display the Control Toolbox toolbar.

TO OPEN A WORKBOOK, UNPROTECT A WORKSHEET, AND DISPLAY THE CONTROL TOOLBOX TOOLBAR

1 Click the Open button on the Standard toolbar. When the Open dialog box displays, if necessary, click the Look in box arrow and click 3½ Floppy (A:). Double-click Master Software1 in the list of files. If necessary, click Enable Macros on the Microsoft Excel dialog box.

2 Click File on the menu bar and then click Save As. When the Save As dialog box displays, type `Master Software3` in the File name text box and then click the Save button in the Save As dialog box.

3 Click Tools on the menu bar, point to Protection, and then click Unprotect Sheet on the Protection submenu. When the Unprotect Sheet dialog box displays, type `planright` in the Password text box and then click the OK button.

4 Right-click a toolbar and then click Control Toolbox. Drag the Control Toolbox toolbar to the middle of the window.

Excel opens the workbook Master Software1, saves it using the file name Master Software3, unprotects the Retirement Savings Plan worksheet, and displays the Control Toolbox toolbar.

Step 1 – Create the User Interface

The first step is to create the Adjustment Center user interface shown in Figure 7-50. After creating the light green background for the Adjustment Center in the range H5:L24, the following must be added to it:

1. A Command Button control
2. Two Scroll Bar controls
3. A Check Box control
4. Two Spin Button controls
5. Label controls to identify controls and display data

When you first create a user interface, you position the controls as close as you can to their final location on the screen, and then after setting the properties you finalize the locations of the controls. Therefore, the following steps make no attempt to position the controls exactly in the locations shown in Figure 7-50 on page E 7-41.

Steps **To Add Controls to a User Interface**

1 Select the range H5:L24. Click the Fill Color button arrow on the Formatting toolbar and then click Light Green (column 4, row 5) on the Fill Color palette. Click the Borders button arrow on the Formatting toolbar and then click Thick Box Border (column 4, row 3) on the Borders palette.

2 Click the Command Button button on the Control Toolbox toolbar and then drag the mouse pointer so the control displays as shown in Figure 7-51.

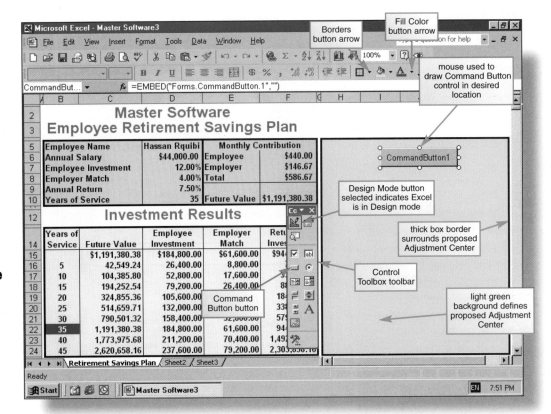

FIGURE 7-51

3 Click the Scroll Bar button on the Control Toolbox toolbar and then move the mouse pointer to approximately the left of cell I12. Drag the mouse pointer so the Scroll Bar control displays as shown in Figure 7-52.

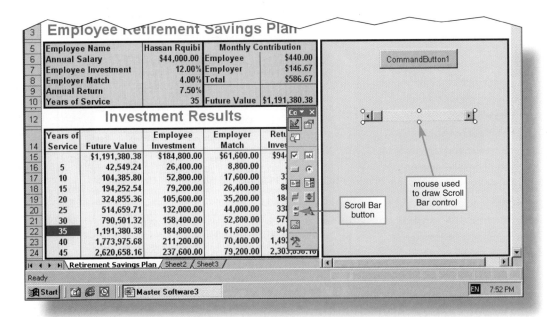

FIGURE 7-52

4 Point to the Scroll Bar control. Hold down the CTRL key and drag a copy of the Scroll Bar control to the location shown in Figure 7-53. It is important that you release the left mouse button before you release the CTRL key.

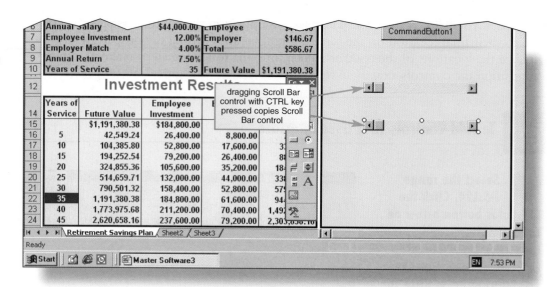

FIGURE 7-53

5 Click the Check Box button on the Control Toolbox toolbar and then move the mouse pointer to the upper-left corner of the location of the Check Box control shown in Figure 7-54. Drag the mouse pointer so the rectangle defining the Check Box control area displays with half of the word CheckBox1 showing.

The check box will be resized after its caption is changed later in this project.

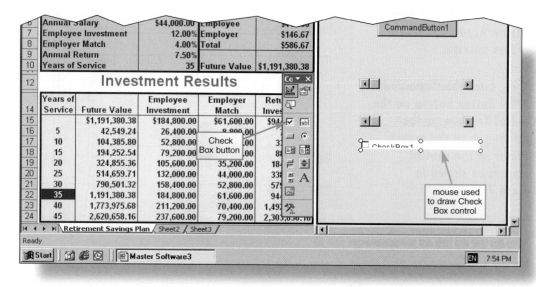

FIGURE 7-54

6 Click the Spin Button button on the Control Toolbox toolbar and then move the mouse pointer to the upper-left corner of the location of the Spin Button control shown in Figure 7-55. Drag the mouse pointer so the rectangle defining the Spin Button control area displays as shown in Figure 7-55.

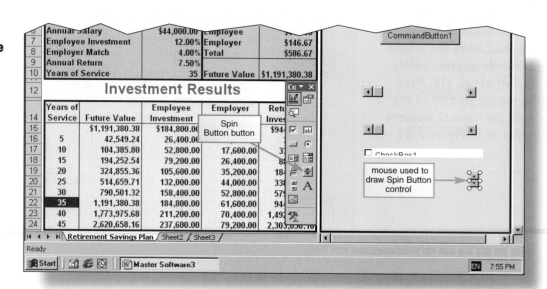

FIGURE 7-55

7 Point to the Spin Button control in the Adjustment Center. Hold down the CTRL key and drag a copy of the Spin Button control to the second location shown in Figure 7-56. It is important that you release the left mouse button before you release the CTRL key.

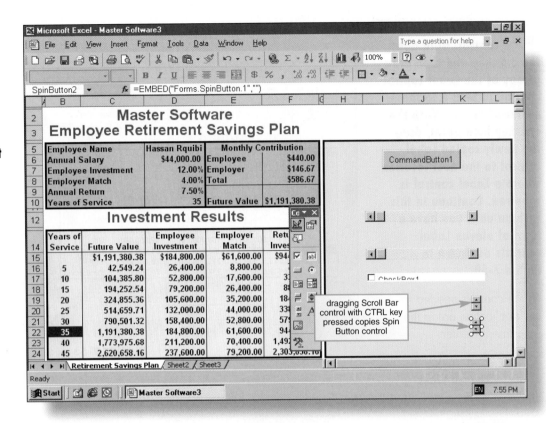

FIGURE 7-56

8 Click the Label button on the Control Toolbox toolbar and then move the mouse pointer to the left of the Scroll Bar control below the CommandButton1 button. Drag the mouse pointer so the rectangle defining the Label control displays as shown in Figure 7-57.

This Label control is used to indicate the lowest value (zero) on the scroll bar.

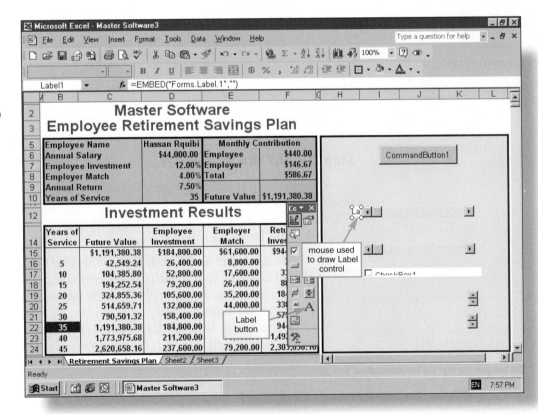

FIGURE 7-57

9 Point to the Label control. Hold down the CTRL key and then drag a copy of the Label control created in Step 8 to the center of cell J3. With the CTRL key held down, drag the newly copied Label control to the next location where a Label control is required. Continue in this fashion until you have a total of eleven Label controls as shown in Figure 7-58.

All the controls needed for this application are in the Adjustment Center.

FIGURE 7-58

Other Ways

1. Select control, click Copy button on Standard toolbar; click Paste button on Standard toolbar
2. Select control, on Edit menu click Copy, on Edit menu click Paste
3. Right-click control, click Copy on shortcut menu, click Paste on shortcut menu
4. Select control, click CTRL+C to copy, click CTRL+V to paste
5. In Voice Command mode, say "Copy" to copy, say "Paste" to paste

When you create a Label control, a caption is associated with it. The Caption property for the first Label control is Label1. For the next Label control you create, the Caption property is Label2, and so on. Because of the size of the Label controls in Figure 7-58, you can see only two characters of the caption, the La.

If you compare Figure 7-58 with 7-50 on page E 7.41, you will notice that except for captions and some minor repositioning of the controls, the Adjustment Center user interface is complete. If you want to delete a control, select it while in Design mode and press the DELETE key. If you want to resize a control, select it while in Design mode and drag its sizing handles. If you want to reposition a control, select it and drag it to its new location.

Step 2 – Set the Properties

The next step is to set the properties for the 16 controls that make up the user interface. The 16 controls best can be seen by referring to Figure 7-50 on page E 7.41 counting the button, labels, scroll bars, check box, and spin buttons. The properties will be set as follows:

1. **Constant Label and Check Box** — Set the BackColor property of the Label controls that identify other controls and the Check Box control to light green so it agrees with the light green background of the user interface. Set the Font property to Bold. Set the Caption property and Text Align property for each Label control that identifies another control. Increase the font size of the Adjustment Center title to size 18.

2. **Command Button** — Change the Caption property to Enter Name and Salary and resize the button so the entire caption shows.

3. **Employee Investment Scroll Bar** — Change the Name property to scrEmployeeInvest, the SmallChange property to 50 (0.5%), the LargeChange property to 100 (1%), the Min property to 0 (0%), and the Max property to 1300 (13%).

4. **Employer Match Scroll Bar** — Change the Name property to scrEmployerMatch, the SmallChange property to 25 (0.25%), the LargeChange property to 100 (1%), the Min property to 0 (0%), and the Max property to 600 (6%).

5. **Employer Match Check Box** — Change the Name property to chkEmployerMatch and the Caption property to Include Employer Match?. Resize the check box so the new caption displays. Change the SpecialEffect to fmButtonEffectFlat. Change the alignment to fmAlignLeft.

6. **Annual Return Spin Button** — Change the Name property to spnAnnualReturn, the SmallChange property to 25 (0.25%), the Min property to 0 (0%), and the Max property to 10000 (100%).

7. **Years of Service Spin Button** — Change the Name property to spnYearsofService, the SmallChange property to 1, the Min property to 1, and the Max property to 45.

8. **Annual Return Label** — Change the Name property to lblAnnualReturn, the Caption property to 5%, the Font property to Bold, the TextAlign property to align right, and the BorderStyle property to single.

9. **Years of Service Label** — Change the Name property to lblYearsofService, the Caption property to 10, the Font property to Bold, the TextAlign property to align right, and the BorderStyle property to single.

More About

Determining Properties

It is best to have all of your properties determined before you sit down at the computer. Using a grid, or graph paper, is often the best way to layout a screen by hand and set properties such as height, width, and location. Other properties should be determined in this manner, as well. Often, this design is detailed in a formal document called a functional specification, which is reviewed and approved by users of the finished worksheet.

Excel automatically assigns the first Command Button control the name CommandButton1. If you create a second Command Button control, Excel will call it CommandButton2, and so on. In the controls just listed, some will have their Name property changed as indicated, while others will not. Usually, you do not change the Name property of Label controls that identify other controls in the user interface. On the other hand, controls that are referenced in the VBA code should be given names that help you recall the control. Table 7-5 summarizes the controls whose Name property will be changed because they will be referenced in the VBA code.

The name of a control, such as scrEmployeeInvest, must begin with a letter, cannot exceed 255 characters, and cannot have a space, period, exclamation point, or the characters @, &, $, or #. You should develop a naming convention of your own and then use it consistently to name controls. In this book, the first three characters of the name identify the type of control. For example: scr stands for scroll bar; chk stands for check box; and spn stands for spin button. Following the three characters are words that identify what the control is controlling. In this case, scrEmployeeInvest is a scroll bar controlling the value in cell D7, the Employee Investment. You also must make sure that the names are unique in an application, because duplicate names are not allowed.

Table 7-5 Referenced Controls and Their Names	
CONTROL	**NAME**
Employee Investment Scroll Bar	scrEmployeeInvest
Employer Match Scroll Bar	scrEmployerMatch
Employer Match Check Box	chkEmployerMatch
Annual Return Spin Button	spnAnnualReturn
Years of Service Spin Button	spnYearsofService
Annual Return Label	lblAnnualReturn
Years of Service Label	lblYearsofService

SETTING THE CONSTANT LABELS AND CHECK BOX PROPERTIES When you create a Label control, it has a white background. If the Label control identifies another control, the background color is changed so it becomes part of the user interface background. If the Label control is going to display a value that varies, the background is left white. The following steps use the SHIFT key to select all the Label controls that identify other controls and the Check Box control so that the BackColor property can be changed for all selected items at once. The Font property of the selected controls also is changed to bold. After the BackColor and Font are changed, then each Label control is selected and the properties are set.

Steps ## To Set Properties of the Constant Label Controls and Check Box Control

1 **With Excel in Design mode, click the Label control in the top-right of the user interface. Hold down the SHIFT key and then one at a time click the Label controls that will remain constant and the Check Box control (right of Figure 7-59). Release the SHIFT key. Click the Properties button on the Control Toolbox toolbar. When the Properties window opens, click BackColor, click the BackColor arrow, if necessary, click the Palette tab, and then point to light green in the list.**

The selected Label controls, the Check Box control, and the Properties window display as shown in Figure 7-59.

FIGURE 7-59

2 **Click light green. Click Font in the Properties window and then click the Font button arrow. When the Font dialog box displays, click Bold in the Font style list and then point to the OK button.**

The Properties window and Font dialog box display as shown in Figure 7-60. The selected Label controls and Check Box control have a light green background.

FIGURE 7-60

3 **Click the OK button. Click anywhere in the Adjustment Center area to deselect the Label controls and Check Box control. Click the Label control to the left of the Employee Investment scroll bar. Click Caption in the Properties window and then type 0 as the caption. Click TextAlign in the Properties window, click the TextAlign box arrow, and then click 2 - fmTextAlignCenter.**

The Label control to the left if the top scroll bar is selected and the Properties window displays its properties as shown in Figure 7-61.

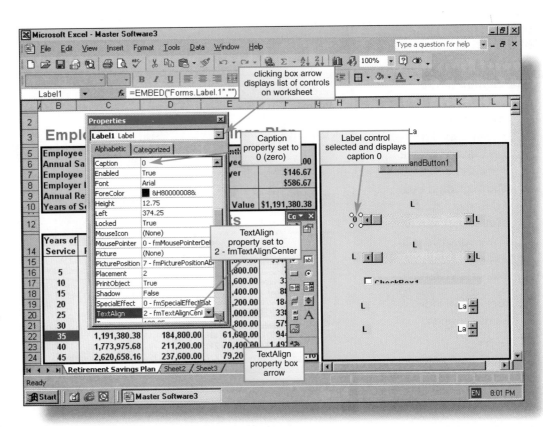

FIGURE 7-61

4 **Click the Label control to the right of the Employee Investment scroll bar. Click Caption in the Properties window and then type 13 as the caption. Click TextAlign in the Properties window, click the TextAlign arrow, and then click number 2 - fmTextAlignCenter. If necessary, resize the Label control so the caption 13 is visible.**

The Properties window for the selected Label control displays as shown in Figure 7-62.

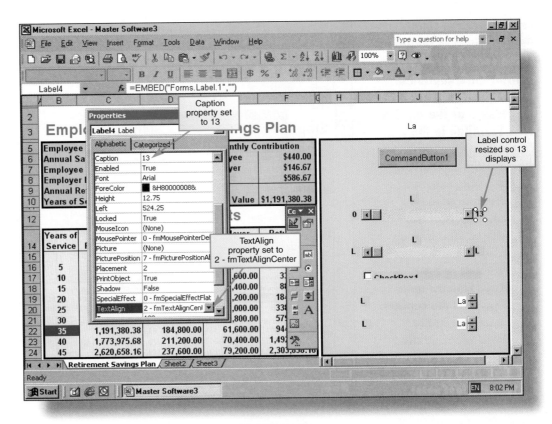

FIGURE 7-62

5 **Click the Label control under the Command Button control. Click Caption in the Properties window and then type** Employee Investment **as the caption. Click TextAlign in the Properties window. Click the TextAlign box arrow and then click 2 - fmTextAlignCenter. Resize the Label control so the caption Employee Investment is visible.**

The Properties window displays as shown in Figure 7-63.

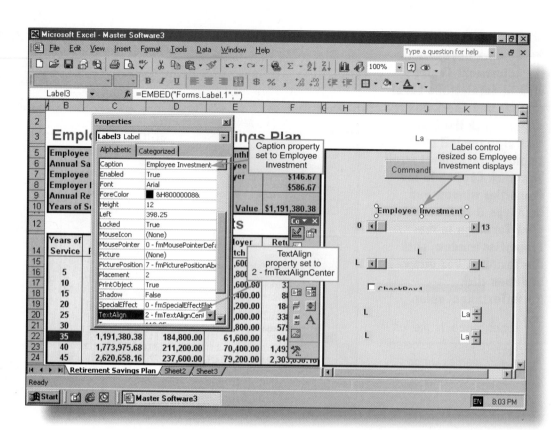

FIGURE 7-63

6 **Click the Label control to the left of the second Scroll Bar control. Click Caption in the Properties window and then type** 0 **as the caption. Click TextAlign in the Properties window, click the TextAlign box arrow, and then click number 2 - fmTextAlignCenter. Click the Label control on the right side of the second Scroll Bar control. Click Caption in the Properties window and then type** 6 **as the caption. Click TextAlign in the Properties window, click the TextAlign box arrow, and then click number 2 - fmTextAlignCenter.**

The Properties window for the selected Label control displays as shown in Figure 7-64.

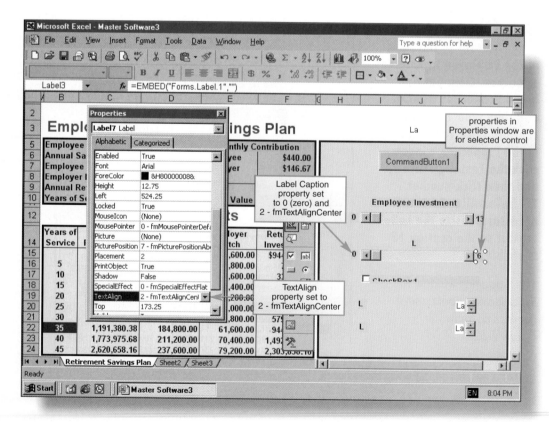

FIGURE 7-64

7 Click the Label control above the Adjustment Center area. Click Caption in the Properties window and then type Adjustment Center as the caption. Click TextAlign in the Properties window, click the TextAlign box arrow, and then click 2 - fmTextAlignCenter. Click Font in the Properties window and then click the Font button. When the Font dialog box displays, click 18 in the Size list and then click the OK button. Resize the Label control so the caption displays in its entirety.

The Properties window for the selected Label control displays as shown in Figure 7-65.

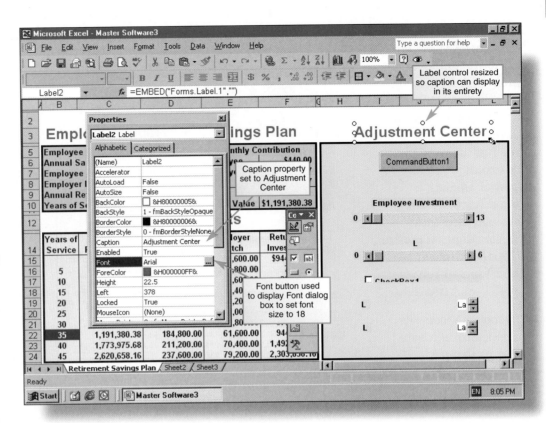

FIGURE 7-65

8 Click the Label control below the upper Scroll Bar control. Click Caption in the Properties window and then type Employer Match as the caption. Click TextAlign in the Properties window, click the TextAlign box arrow, and then click number 2 - fmTextAlignCenter. Resize the Label control so the caption displays in its entirety. Click the Label control to the left of the top Spin Button control. Click Caption in the Properties window and then type Annual Return (1% to 25%) as the caption. Click TextAlign in the Properties window, click the TextAlign box arrow, and then, if necessary, click number 1 - fmTextAlignLeft. Resize the Label control so the caption Annual Return (1% to 25%) is visible.

FIGURE 7-66

The Properties window for the selected Label control displays as shown in Figure 7-66.

9 **Click the Label control to the left of the lower Spin Button control. Click Caption in the Properties window and then type** Years of Service (1 to 45 years) **as the caption. Click TextAlign in the Properties window, click the TextAlign box arrow, and then click 1 - fmTextAlignLeft. Resize the Label control so the caption Years of Service (1 to 45 years) is visible.**

The Properties window for the selected Label control displays as shown in Figure 7-67.

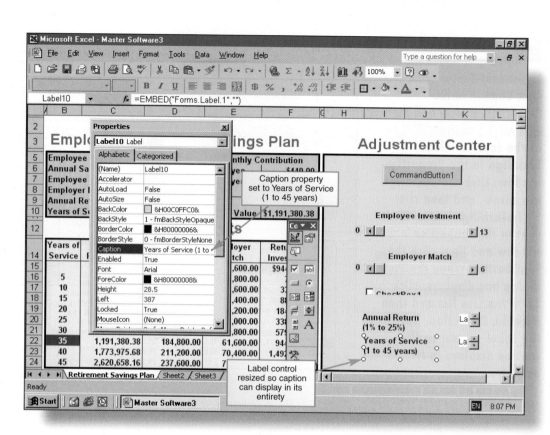

FIGURE 7-67

Every control has its own set of properties. When you select multiple controls as in Step 1 on page E 7.48, then Excel displays only those properties that are common to the controls selected.

SETTING THE COMMAND BUTTON CONTROL PROPERTIES The next step is to change the caption on the Command Button control from CommandButton1 to Enter Name and Salary, and resize it so the caption on the button displays in its entirety, as shown in the following step.

Steps To Set the Command Button Control Properties

1 With Excel in Design mode, click the Command Button control in the Adjustment Center. Click Caption in the Properties window and then type Enter Name and Salary as the caption. Drag one of the sizing handles surrounding the Command Button control so that the caption displays in its entirety.

The button and its properties display as shown in Figure 7-68.

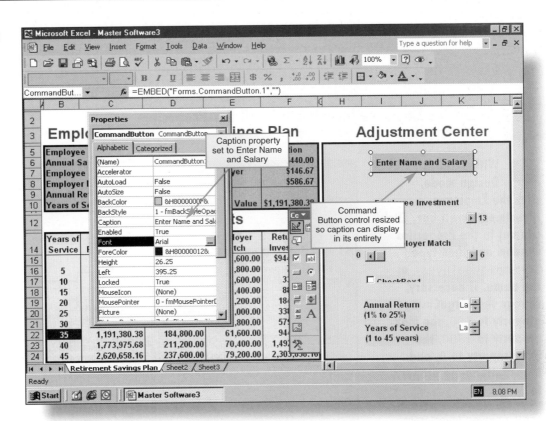

FIGURE 7-68

As you can see from the Properties window shown in Figure 7-68, a Command Button control has many different properties. One that may interest you that is not used in this project is the MousePointer property. If you click MousePointer in the Properties window and then click the MousePointer arrow, you will see several mouse pointers listed, many that you are familiar with from your experiences in Excel. If you change the MousePointer property, the mouse pointer will change when you point to the button. You can choose from the Hour Glass, I-beam, arrow, and cross.

SETTING THE EMPLOYEE INVESTMENT SCROLL BAR PROPERTIES The next step is to set the Employee Investment Scroll Bar properties. The function of this Scroll Bar control is to assign cell D7 a value. When you use a control, such as a scroll bar, you must set the Min and Max properties. The **Min property** is the least value the control can register. The **Max property** is the maximum value the control can register. You also have to set the SmallChange and LargeChange values. The **SmallChange property** is the value the control will change by each time you click the scroll arrow. The **LargeChange** property is the value the control will change by each time you click the scroll bar.

You can assign only whole numbers for these four properties. This increases the complexity of the VBA code because the cell in question must be assigned a decimal number. Thus, to assign the cell the maximum value 0.13 (13%), you actually must set the Maximum property to 1300, and then later in the VBA code divide by 10000 to assign the cell a value of 0.13.

Perform the following step to set the Employee Investment Scroll Bar properties.

 Steps To Set the Employee Investment Scroll Bar Properties

1 **With Excel in Design mode, click the Employee Investment scroll bar. Click (Name) in the Properties window and then type** scrEmployeeInvest **as the name. If necessary, change the LargeChange property to** 100**, the Max property to** 1300**, the Min property to** 0**, and the SmallChange property to** 50**.**

The Employee Investment scroll bar Properties window displays as shown in Figure 7-69.

FIGURE 7-69

The Max Property

One of the more difficult concepts to understand about scroll bars is why the Max property is set to such a large number (600 in Figure 7-70), when the maximum value of the scroll bar is only 6% (.06). The two reasons are (1) the Max property can be set equal to only a whole number; and (2) the large number allows you to assign reasonable increments to the SmallChange and LargeChange properties of the scroll bar.

Excel automatically will determine how far to move the scroll button on the scroll bar when you click the scroll button (small change) and when you click the scroll boxes (large change) from the four numeric values entered in Step 1.

SETTING THE EMPLOYER MATCH SCROLL BAR PROPERTIES The next step sets the Employer Match Scroll Bar properties. The property settings are similar to those assigned to the Employee Investment scroll bar. Once the VBA code is written, this scroll bar will assign a value to cell D8.

To Set the Employer Match Scroll Bar Properties

1 **With Excel in design mode, click the Employer Match scroll bar. Click (Name) in the Properties window and then type** scrEmployerMatch **as the name. Change the LargeChange property to** 100**, the Max property to** 600**, the Min property to** 0**, and the SmallChange property to** 25**.**

The Employer Match scroll bar Properties window displays as shown in Figure 7-70.

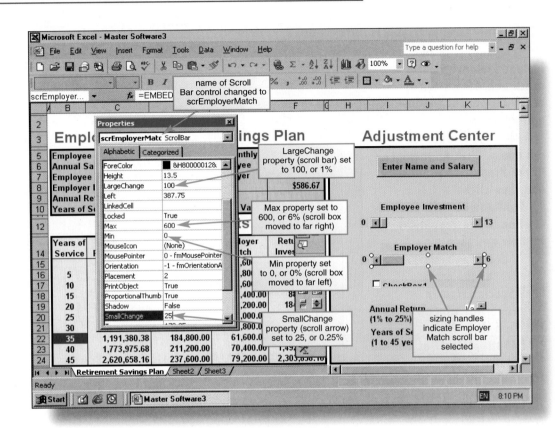

FIGURE 7-70

SETTING THE EMPLOYER MATCH CHECK BOX PROPERTIES The Employer Match check box enables or disables the Employer Match Scroll Bar control. If the Employer Match check box contains a check mark, then the Employer Match scroll bar is enabled and it can be used to change the value in cell D8. If the check box is empty, then the Employer Match Scroll Bar control is disabled. The VBA code will enable or disable the Scroll Bar based on the check box status. The following step sets the Include Employer Match check box properties.

More About

Properties

Many properties, such as the Value property (Figure 7-71), can be only one of two states — True or False. If it is True, the property is turned on. If it is False, the property is turned off. For example, assigning the Value property the value True, means that the check mark will display in the Employer Match check box.

Steps **To Set the Employer Match Check Box Properties**

1 **With Excel in Design mode, click the Include Employer Match check box. Click (Name) in the Properties window and then type** chkEmployerMatch **as the name. Click Alignment in the Properties window and then click 0 - fmAlignmentLeft. Click Caption in the Properties window and then type** Include Employer Match? **as the caption. Click SpecialEffect in the properties window and then click 0 - fmButtonEffectFlat. Click Value in the Properties window and then type** True. **Resize the Check Box control so the caption Include Employer Match? is visible.**

The Include Employer Match check box Properties window displays as shown in Figure 7-71.

FIGURE 7-71

Setting the Value property to True inserts a check mark in the Include Employer Match check box.

SETTING THE ANNUAL RETURN AND YEARS OF SERVICE SPIN BUTTON PROPERTIES   The Annual Return spin button increments or decrements the value in cell D9 by 0.25%. The Years of Service spin button increments or decrements the value in cell D10 by one. With a spin button, the up arrow increases the value, and the down arrow decreases the value. The Label controls to the left of the Spin Button controls (Figure 7-71) indicate the values assigned to the associated cells. The Min, Max, and SmallChange properties must be set. The SmallChange property indicates the change each time you click an arrow.

The following steps set the properties for the Annual Return and Years of Service spin buttons.

Steps **To Set Properties for Annual Return and Years of Service Spin Buttons**

1 **With Excel in Design mode, click the Annual Return spin button. Click (Name) in the Properties window and then type** spnAnnualReturn **as the name. If necessary, change the Max property to** 10000, **the Min property to** 0, **and the SmallChange property to** 25.

The Annual Return Spin Button Properties window displays as shown in Figure 7-72.

FIGURE 7-72

2 **Click the Years of Service spin button. Click (Name) in the Properties window and then type** spnYearsofService **as the name. Change the Max property to** 45, **the Min property to** 1, **and the SmallChange property to** 1.

The Years of Service Spin Button Properties window displays as shown in Figure 7-73.

FIGURE 7-73

The least value the Annual Return spin button can be set to is 0 (0%). The greatest value is 10000 (100%). Once the VBA code is written, each time you click a button, the annual return in cell D9 will change by 0.25%. At this point in the project, no relationship exists between the Annual Return spin button and cell D9. This relationship will be established later in the VBA code. A similar relationship will be established between the Years of Service spin button and cell D10.

SETTING THE LABEL CONTROL PROPERTIES FOR THE ANNUAL RETURN AND YEARS OF SERVICE SPIN BUTTONS   The Label controls to the left of the two Spin Button controls will be used to display the values of their respective spin buttons. Thus, when you click one of the Annual Return spin buttons, the new value will display in the Label control next to the spin button as well as in cell D9. The following steps set the Name property, Caption property, and TextAlign property for the two Label controls to the left of the Spin Button controls.

To Set the Label Control Properties for the Annual Return and Years of Service Spin Buttons

Steps

1 With Excel in Design mode, click the Label control to the left of the Annual Return spin button. Click (Name) in the Properties window and then type `lblAnnualReturn` as the name. Click Caption in the Properties window and then type 5% as the caption. Change the Font property to bold. Change the TextAlign property to 3 - fmTextAlignRight. Resize the Label control as shown in Figure 7-74.

The Annual Return Spin Button Label Properties window displays as shown in Figure 7-74.

FIGURE 7-74

2 **Click the Label control to the left of the Years of Service Spin Button control. Click (Name) in the Properties window and then type** `lblYearsofService` **as the name. Change the Font property to bold. Click Caption in the Properties window and then type** 10 **as the caption. Change the TextAlign property to 3 - fmTextAlignRight. Resize the Label control as shown in Figure 7-75.**

The Years of Service Spin Button Label Properties window displays as shown in Figure 7-75.

FIGURE 7-75

3 **Click the Close button on the right side of the Properties window title bar.**

The Adjustment Center displays as shown in Figure 7-76.

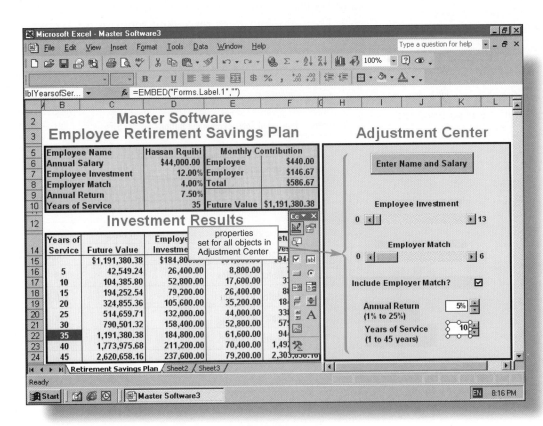

FIGURE 7-76

Microsoft Script Editor

The Microsoft Script Editor allows you to develop complex Web pages that interact with your company's data, whether the data is in Excel or a database. The Script Editor generates what are called Active Server Pages. These Web pages contain both HTML and program code. For more information, click Tools, point to Macro, and click Microsoft Script Editor. When the Microsoft Script Editor opens click Help on the menu bar, and then click Contents on the Help menu.

Later in the VBA code, the Label controls will be set equal to the corresponding Spin Button controls through the use of the names. For example, the VBA statement

```
lblAnnualReturn = spnAnnualReturn.Value / 10000 & "%"
```

assigns the value of the Annual Return Spin Button control divided by 10000 to its corresponding Label control. The & "%" appends a percent sign to the number that displays in the Label control.

FINE-TUNING THE USER INTERFACE After setting the properties for all the controls, you can fine-tune the size and location of the controls in the Adjustment Center. With Excel in Design mode, you have three ways to reposition a control:

1. Drag the control to its new location.
2. Select the control and use the arrow keys to reposition it.
3. Select the control and set the control's Top and Left properties in the Properties window.

To use the third technique, you need to know the distance the control is from the top of row 1 (column headings) and the far left of column A (row headings) in points. Recall that a point is equal to 1/72 of an inch. Thus, if the Top property of a control is 216, then the control is 3 inches (216/72) from the top of the window.

You also can resize a control in two ways:

1. Drag the sizing handles.
2. Select the control and set the control's Height and Width properties in the Properties window.

As with the Top and Left properties, the Height and Width properties are measured in points. Table 7-6 lists the exact points for the Top, Left, Height, and Width properties of each of the controls in the Adjustment Center.

The following steps resize and reposition the controls in the Adjustment Center using the values in Table 7-6.

Table 7-6 Exact Locations of Controls in Adjustment Center				
CONTROL	**TOP**	**LEFT**	**HEIGHT**	**WIDTH**
Enter Name and Salary Command Button	50.25	381	26.25	123.75
Adjustment Center Label	19.5	377.25	22.5	165
Employee Investment Label	99	386.25	14.25	119.75
Employee Investment Scroll Bar	116.25	360.75	14.25	157.5
Employee Investment 0 Label	116.25	348	13.5	6.75
Employee Investment 13 Label	116.25	524.25	13.5	14.25
Employer Match Label	138	386.25	14.25	114.75
Employer Match Check Box	179.25	348	21.75	174.75
Employer Match Scroll Bar	153	360.75	14.25	157.5
Employer Match 0 Label	153	348	13.5	6.75
Employer Match 6 Label	153	524.25	13.5	6.75
Annual Return Label	218.25	348	27	75
Annual Return Spin Button	215.25	502.5	18	13.5
Annual Return Label	215.25	471	18	31.5
Years of Service Label	255.75	348	27	79.75
Years of Service Spin Button	252	502.5	18	13.5
Years of Service Label	252	471	18	31.5

Steps To Resize and Reposition the Controls in the Adjustment Center

1 Click the Properties button on the Control Toolbox toolbar. Drag the Properties window to the left side of the Excel window. Click the Enter Name and Salary button. Change its Top, Left, Height, and Width properties to those listed in Table 7-6.

The Name and Salary Command Button control Properties window displays as shown in Figure 7-77.

FIGURE 7-77

2 One at a time, select the controls and change their Top, Left, Height, and Width properties to those listed in Table 7-6. Close the Properties window and then deselect the Years of Service (1 to 45 years) label by clicking cell A1.

The Adjustment Center displays as shown in Figure 7-78.

3 Click the Save button on the Standard toolbar.

Excel saves the workbook using the file name Master Software3.

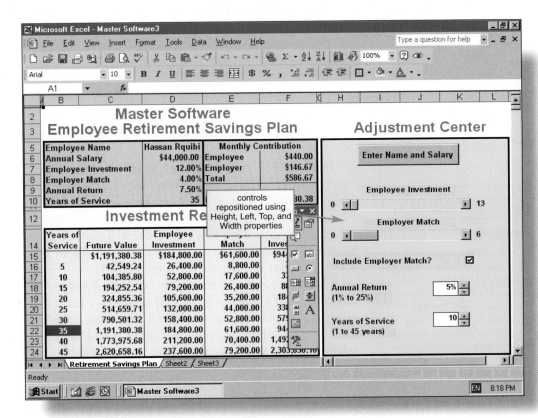

FIGURE 7-78

Step 3 — Write the Code

The next step is to write a procedure for each of the following six controls: (1) Enter Name and Salary Button; (2) Employee Investment Scroll Bar; (3) Include Employer Match Check Box; (4) Employer Match Scroll Bar; (5) Annual Return Spin Button; and (6) Years of Service Spin Button.

NAME AND SALARY BUTTON PROCEDURE   The function of the Enter Name and Salary button is to accept the employee name and annual salary. It also assigns values to the Scroll Bar controls and Spin Button controls, which in turn resets the values in the range D7:D10. The Name and Salary Button procedure is shown in Table 7-7.

Table 7-7	Enter Name and Salary Button Procedure
LINE	**VBA CODE**
1	' Name and Salary Button Procedure Author: Micheal Ericsson
2	' Date Created: 5/17/2002
3	' Run from: Employee Retirement Savings Plan Model Sheet by clicking button
4	' labeled Enter Name and Salary
5	' Function: This procedure initializes the scroll bars and spin buttons,
6	' clears the range D5:D6, selects cell A1, accepts the employee
7	' name (cell D5) and annual salary (cell D6), and validates the
8	' annual salary before assigning it to cell D6.
9	'
10	Private Sub CommandButton1_Click()
11	scrEmployeeInvest = 100
12	scrEmployerMatch = 0
13	spnAnnualReturn = 500
14	spnYearsofService = 10
15	Range("D5:D6").ClearContents
16	Range("A1").Select
17	Range("D5").Value = InputBox("Employee Name?", "Enter")
18	AnnualSalary = InputBox("Annual Salary?", "Enter")
19	Do While AnnualSalary <= 0
20	AnnualSalary = InputBox("Annual salary must be > zero.", "Please Re-enter")
21	Loop
22	Range("D6").Value = AnnualSalary
23	End Sub

In Table 7-7, lines 1 through 9 are comments and have no bearing on the execution of this procedure. Comments help you remember the function of a procedure. Lines 10 and 23 identify the beginning and end of the procedure. Lines 11 through 14 initialize the Scroll Bar controls and Spin Buttons controls by assigning values to their names. Line 15 clears cells D5 and D6 in preparation to receive the employee name and annual salary. Line 16 selects cell A1 so the heavy border surrounding the active cell does not clutter the screen.

Line 17 accepts the employee name and assigns it to cell D5. Lines 18 through 22 accept and validate the annual salary to ensure it is greater than zero. The annual salary is accepted in line 18. Line 19 is called a **Do-While statement**. It tests to see if the annual salary accepted in line 18 is less than or equal to zero. If the annual salary is less than or equal to zero, line 20 displays an error message and requests that the user re-enter the annual salary. The **Loop statement** in line 21 transfers control back to the corresponding Do-While statement in line 19, which tests the annual salary again.

More About

Looping

VBA has several statements that allow you to loop through a series of statements. They are the Do-While or Do-Until, which loops while or until a condition is True; For-Next, which uses a counter to repeat statements a specified number of times; and For Each-Next, which repeats a group of statements for each object in a collection.

The VBA code in lines 19 through 21 is called a **loop**. If the variable Annual Salary is greater than zero, then the Do-While statement in line 19 transfers control to line 22, which assigns the value of AnnualSalary to cell D6. Line 23 halts execution of the procedure and returns Excel to Ready mode.

The variable AnnualSalary first was used in line 18. A **variable** is a location in the computer's memory whose value can change as the program executes. You create variables in VBA code as you need them. In this case, a variable is needed to hold the value accepted from the user in lines 18 and 20. Variable names follow the same rules as control names (see page E 7.47).

The following steps enter the Enter Name and Salary Button procedure shown in Table 7-7.

Steps **To Enter the Enter Name and Salary Button Procedure**

1 With Excel in design mode, click the View Code button on the Control Toolbar toolbar (Figure 7-38 on page E 7.34). Click the Object box arrow at the top of the window and then click CommandButton1 in the alphabetical list.

The Visual Basic Editor starts. When the CommandButton1 control is selected, the Visual Basic Editor displays the Sub and End Sub statements for the procedure and positions the insertion point between the two statements (Figure 7-79).

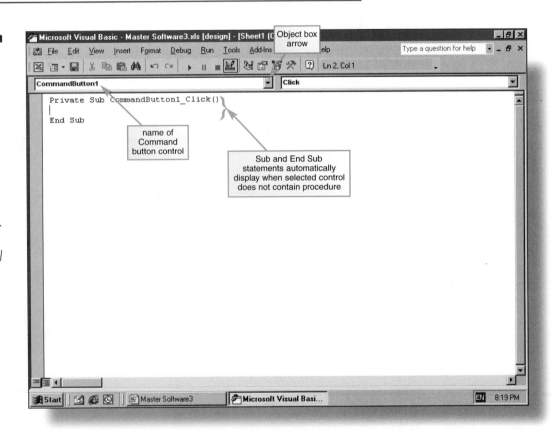

FIGURE 7-79

2 **Click before the P in Private and then press the ENTER key. Enter the lines 1 through 9 in Table 7-7 on page E 7.62. Click the blank line between the Sub and End Sub statements. Enter lines 11 through 22 in Table 7-7.**

The Name and Salary Button procedure displays as shown in Figure 7-80.

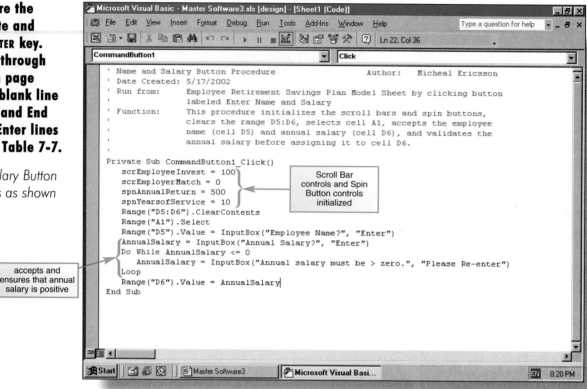

FIGURE 7-80

EMPLOYEE INVESTMENT SCROLL BAR PROCEDURE The Employee Investment Scroll Bar procedure assigns the value of the scroll bar to cell D7. The procedure is shown in Table 7-8.

Table 7-8	Employee Investment Scroll Bar Procedure
LINE	**STATEMENT**
1	' Employee Investment Scroll Bar Procedure Author: Micheal Ericsson
2	' Date Created: 5/17/2002
3	' Run from: Employee Retirement Savings Plan Model Sheet by clicking the
4	' scroll bar labeled Employee Investment
5	' Function: This procedure assigns the value of the Employee Investment scroll
6	' bar to cell D7.
7	'
8	Private Sub scrEmployeeInvest_Change()
9	Range("D7").Value = scrEmployeeInvest.Value / 10000
10	End Sub

In Table 7-8, the first seven lines are comments. Lines 8 and 10 define the beginning and end of the procedure. Line 9 assigns the value of the Scroll Bar control (scrEmployeeInvest) divided by 10000 to cell D7. Recall that the scroll bar was assigned a Max property of 1300, which is equivalent to 130,000%. Thus, the value of scrEmployeeInvest must be divided by 10000 to assign the correct percentage value to cell D7. The following steps enter the Employee Investment Scroll Bar procedure shown in Table 7-8.

Steps **To Enter the Employee Investment Scroll Bar Procedure**

1 **With the Visual Basic Editor active, click the Object box arrow at the top of the window and then click scrEmployeeInvest.**

The Visual Basic Editor displays the Sub and End Sub statements for this procedure and positions the insertion point between the two statements.

2 **Enter the VBA code shown in Table 7-8.**

The Employee Investment Scroll Bar procedure displays as shown in Figure 7-81.

FIGURE 7-81

EMPLOYER MATCH CHECK BOX PROCEDURE As with the other procedures, the Employer Match Check Box procedure executes only when you click the check box. If the check box is checked, then the name of the check box (chkEmployerMatch) is equal to the logical value True. If the check box is unchecked, then the name of the check box is equal to the logical value False. Adding a check mark or removing a check mark triggers the event that executes the Employee Match Check Box procedure shown in Table 7-9.

Table 7-9 Employer Match Check Box Procedure

LINE	STATEMENT
1	' Employer Match Check Box Procedure Author: Micheal Ericsson
2	' Date Created: 5/17/2002
3	' Run from: Employee Retirement Savings Plan Model Sheet by clicking check box
4	' labeled Employer Match
5	' Function: This procedure assigns the value of the Employer Match scroll bar
6	' or 0 (zero) to cell D8.
7	'
8	Private Sub chkEmployerMatch_Click()
9	If chkEmployerMatch.Value = True Then
10	Range("D8").Value = scrEmployerMatch.Value / 10000
11	Else
12	scrEmployerMatch = 0
13	Range("D8").Value = 0
14	End If
15	End Sub

In Table 7-9 on the previous page, lines 1 through 7 are comments. Lines 8 and 15 define the beginning and end of the procedure. Lines 9 through 14 include an If-Then-Else statement. An **If-Then-Else statement** represents a two-way decision with action specified for each of the two alternatives. The computer never executes both the true and false alternatives. It selects one or the other.

If the logical test (chkEmployerMatch = True) is true in line 9 of Table 7-9, then line 10 is executed and cell D8 is set equal to scrEmployerMatch divided by 10000. If the logical test is false, then lines 12 and 13 are executed. Line 12 sets the scroll box to zero percent (0%), and line 13 sets cell D8 equal to zero percent (0%). The following steps enter the code.

To Enter the Employer Match Check Box Procedure

1 **With the Visual Basic Editor active, click the Object box arrow at the top of the window and then click chkEmployerMatch.**

The Visual Basic Editor displays the Sub and End Sub statements for this procedure and positions the insertion point between the two statements.

2 **Enter the VBA code shown in Table 7-9.**

The Employer Match Check Box procedure displays as shown in Figure 7-82.

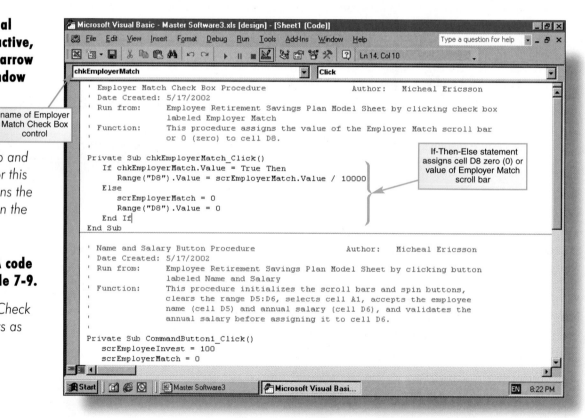

name of Employer Match Check Box control

If-Then-Else statement assigns cell D8 zero (0) or value of Employer Match scroll bar

FIGURE 7-82

EMPLOYER MATCH SCROLL BAR PROCEDURE   The Employer Match Scroll Bar procedure executes whenever you use the Scroll Bar control below the check box. The Scroll Bar control is active only when the Employer Match Check Box control is checked. The Scroll Bar control event assigns the value of scrEmployerMatch to cell D8. The Employer Match Scroll Bar procedure is shown in Table 7-10.

In Table 7-10, line 10 in the If-Then statement assigns the value of the scroll bar (scrEmployerMatch) divided by 10000 to cell D8. This statement, however, is executed only if the logical test in line 9 (chkEmployerMatch =True) is true. Thus, the Employer Match Check Box control determines whether the Scroll Bar control is active. The following steps enter the code.

Table 7-10 Employer Match Scroll Bar Procedure

LINE	STATEMENT
1	' Employer Match Scroll Bar Procedure Author: Micheal Ericsson
2	' Date Created: 5/17/2002
3	' Run from: Employee Retirement Savings Plan Model Sheet by clicking the
4	' scroll bar labeled Employer Match
5	' Function: This procedure assigns the value of the Employer Match scroll bar
6	' to cell D8.
7	'
8	Private Sub scrEmployerMatch_Change()
9	If chkEmployerMatch.Value = True Then
10	Range("D8").Value = scrEmployerMatch.Value / 10000
11	End If
12	End Sub

Steps To Enter the Employer Match Scroll Bar Procedure

1 **With the Visual Basic Editor active, click the Object box arrow at the top of the window and then click scrEmployerMatch.**

The Visual Basic Editor displays the Sub and End Sub statements for this procedure and positions the insertion point between the two statements.

2 **Enter the VBA code shown in Table 7-10.**

The Employer Match Scroll Bar procedure displays as shown in Figure 7-83.

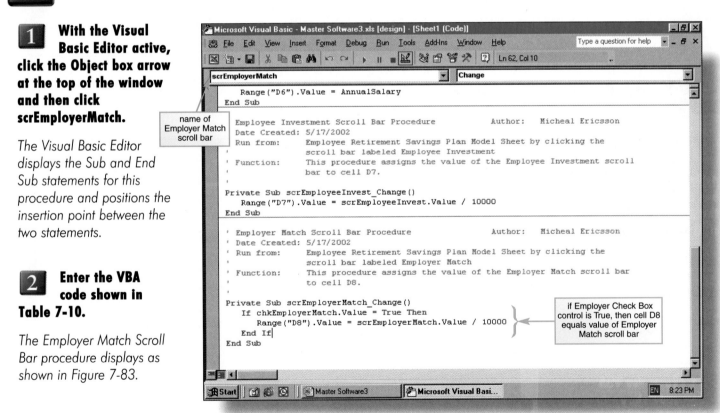

FIGURE 7-83

ANNUAL RETURN SPIN BUTTON PROCEDURE   The Annual Return Spin Button procedure executes whenever you click one of it buttons. Its function is to set the percent value in cell D9 and in the corresponding Label control. Recall that you set the SmallChange property to 25, which when divided by 10000 equals 0.25%. The Annual Return Spin Button Control procedure is shown in Table 7-11.

Table 7-11 Annual Return Spin Button Procedure

LINE	STATEMENT
1	' Annual Return Spin Button Procedure Author: Micheal Ericsson
2	' Date Created: 5/17/2002
3	' Run from: Retirement Savings Plan Model Sheet by clicking the spin
4	' button labeled Annual Return
5	' Function: This procedure assigns the value of the Annual Return spin button
6	' to cell D9.
7	'
8	Private Sub spnAnnualReturn_Change()
9	lblAnnualReturn = spnAnnualReturn.Value / 100 & "%"
10	Range("D9").Value = spnAnnualReturn.Value / 10000
11	End Sub

In Table 7-11, line 9 uses the names of the two controls to assign the value of the Spin Button control to the Label control. In this case, spnAnnualReturn is divided by 100 because a percent should display as a whole number percent in the Label control. The & "%" at the end of line 9 appends a percent sign to the value. Line 10 assigns the value of spnAnnualReturn divided by 10000 to cell D9. The following steps enter the code.

Steps To Enter the Annual Return Spin Button Procedure

1 **With the Visual Basic Editor active, click the Object box arrow at the top of the window and then click spnAnnualReturn.**

The Visual Basic Editor displays the Sub and End Sub statements for this procedure and positions the insertion point between the two statements.

2 **Enter the VBA code shown in Table 7-11.**

The Annual Return Spin Button procedure displays as shown in Figure 7-84.

FIGURE 7-84

YEARS OF SERVICE SPIN BUTTON PROCEDURE The Years of Service Spin Button procedure determines the value assigned to cell D10 and in the corresponding Label control and is executed by Excel when the user clicks one of the buttons making up the spin button control. The procedure is shown in Table 7-12.

Table 7-12	Years of Service Spin Button Procedure
LINE	STATEMENT
1	' Years of Service Spin Button Procedure Author: Micheal Ericsson
2	' Date Created: 5/17/2002
3	' Run from: Employee Retirement Savings Plan Model Sheet by clicking the spin
4	' button labeled Years of Service
5	' Function: This procedure assigns the value of the Years of Service spin
6	' button to cell D10.
7	'
8	Private Sub spnYearsofService_Change()
9	lblYearsofService = spnYearsofService
10	Range("D10").Value = spnYearsofService
11	End Sub

In Table 7-12, line 9 assigns spnYearsofService (value of the Spin Button control) to the corresponding Label control. Line 10 assigns the value of spnYearsofService to cell D10. The following steps enter the code.

 Steps **To Enter the Years of Service Spin Button Procedure**

1 **With the Visual Basic Editor active, click the Object box arrow at the top of the window and then click spnYearsofService.**

The Visual Basic Editor displays the Sub and End Sub statements for this procedure and positions the insertion point between the two statements.

2 **Enter the VBA code shown in Table 7-12.**

The Years of Service Spin Button procedure displays as shown in Figure 7-85.

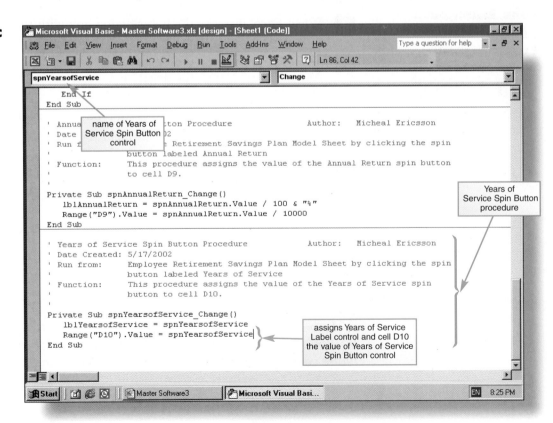

FIGURE 7-85

The VBA code is complete. The following steps close the Visual Basic Editor, quit Design mode, protect the worksheet, and save the workbook. Before closing the Visual Basic Editor, you should verify your code by comparing it with Figures 7-80 through 7-85 on pages E 7.64 through E 7.69.

TO CLOSE THE VISUAL BASIC EDITOR, PROTECT THE WORKSHEET, AND SAVE THE WORKBOOK

1 Click the Close button on the right side of the Visual Basic Editor title bar.

2 When the Excel window displays, click the Exit Design Mode button on the Control Toolbox toolbar. Close the Control Toolbox toolbar.

3 Click Tools on the menu bar, point to Protection, and then click Protect Sheet. When the Protect Sheet dialog box displays, type planright in the Password to unprotect sheet text box. Verify the password when prompted by clicking OK.

4 Click the Save button on the Standard toolbar to save the workbook using the file name Master Software3.

Testing the Controls

The final step is to test the controls in the Adjustment Center. Use the following data: Employee Name – Christy Pearce; Annual Salary (cell D6) – $50,000.00; Employee Investment (cell D7) – 6%; Employer Match (cell D8) – 3%; Annual Return (cell D9) – 6.25%; and Years of Service (cell D10) – 30.

TO TEST THE CONTROLS IN THE ADJUSTMENT CENTER USER INTERFACE

1 Click the Enter Name and Salary button in the Adjustment Center.

2 When Excel displays the Enter dialog box with the prompt message, Employee Name?, type Christy Pearce as the employee name.

3 When Excel displays the Enter dialog box with the prompt message, Annual Salary?, type the negative number -50000 as the annual salary.

4 When Excel displays the Enter dialog box with the prompt message, Annual salary must be >= to zero, type 50000 as the annual salary.

5 Use the includeEmployee Investment scroll bar to change the value in cell D7 to 6%.

6 Click the Include Employer Match check box if it does not have a check mark.

7 Use the Employer Match scroll bar to change the value in cell D8 to 3%.

8 Click the Annual Return spin button arrows to change the value in cell D9 to 6.25%.

9 Click the Years of Service spin button arrows to change the value in cell D10 to 30.

The future value of Christy Pearce's Retirement Savings Plan investment is $395,219.98 as shown in cell F10 of Figure 7-86. If she changes her years of service to 45 years, the Retirement Savings Plan investment is worth $1,118,188.80 (cell C24). Both future value amounts assume she will never get a raise.

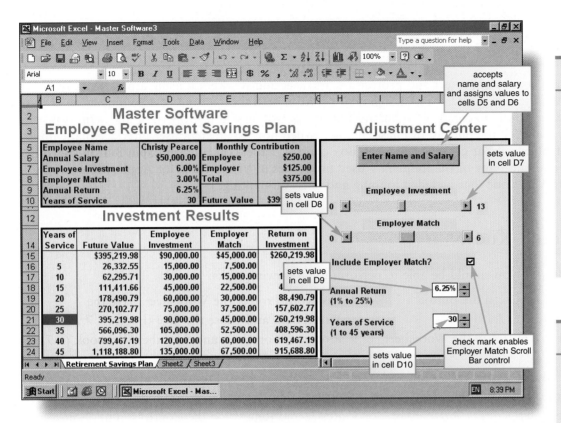

FIGURE 7-86

If the controls in the Adjustment Center do not work as indicated here, then unprotect the worksheet, display the Control Toolbox toolbar, click the Design Mode button on the Control Toolbox toolbar, and check the controls' properties and VBA code.

Quitting Excel

The project is complete. To quit Excel, follow the steps below.

TO QUIT EXCEL

1. Click the Close button on the right side of the title bar.

2. If the Microsoft Excel dialog box displays, click the No button.

3. If you wish to reset the toolbar and File menu to remove the items added in this project, click Tools on the menu bar, and then click Customize. When the Customize dialog box displays, click the Reset my usage data button, and then click the Yes button.

CASE PERSPECTIVE SUMMARY

With the three workbooks developed in this project, Louis Pankros can post the new workbook to the intranet as you complete each phase. The final phase, Master Software3, includes the easy-to-use Adjustment Center that allows the user to enter any reasonable Retirement Savings Plan data with ease and quickly determine the future value of the investment.

Project Summary

In this project, you learned how to unprotect and protect a worksheet and workbook using a password. In Phase 1, you learned how to record a macro and assign it to a button on a toolbar and to a command on a menu. In Phase 2, you learned how to create a Command Button control, assign it properties, and write VBA code that executes when you click the button. In Phase 3, you learned how to create a user interface made up of a Command Button control, Scroll Bar controls, a Check Box control, Label controls, and Spin Button controls. In this phase, you learned about many of the frequently used properties in Visual Basic for Applications. You also learned how to write VBA code that included looping and decision-making.

What You Should Know

Having completed this project, you should be able to perform the following tasks:

- Add a Button to a Toolbar, Assign the Button a Macro, and Use the Button *(E 7.19)*
- Add a Command Button Control to the Worksheet *(E 7.28)*
- Add a Command to a Menu, Assign the Command a Macro, and Invoke the Command *(E 7.23)*
- Add Controls to a User Interface *(E 7.43)*
- Automate Data Entry by Selecting a Range of Cells *(E 7.08)*
- Close the Visual Basic Editor, Protect the Worksheet, and Save the Workbook *(E 7.70)*
- Enter Retirement Savings Plan Data Using the New Data Button *(E 7.37)*
- Enter the Annual Return Spin Button Procedure *(E 7.68)*
- Enter the Employee Investment Scroll Bar Procedure *(E 7.65)*
- Enter the Employer Match Check Box Procedure *(E 7.66)*
- Enter the Employer Match Scroll Bar Procedure *(E 7.67)*
- Enter the Enter Name and Salary Button Procedure *(E 7.63)*
- Enter the New Data Button Procedure *(E 7.34)*
- Enter the Years of Service Spin Button Procedure *(E 7.69)*
- Open a Workbook with a Macro and Execute the Macro *(E 7.15)*
- Open a Workbook, Unprotect a Worksheet, and Display the Control Toolbox Toolbar *(E 7.42)*
- Password-Protect the Worksheet, Save the Workbook, and Close the Workbook *(E 7.14)*
- Protect a Worksheet and Save the Workbook *(E 7.41)*
- Quit Excel *(E 7.71)*
- Record a Macro to Print the Worksheet in Portrait Orientation Using the Fit to Option *(E 7.11)*
- Resize and Reposition the Controls in the Adjustment Center *(E 7.61)*
- Set Properties for the Annual Return and Years of Service Spin Buttons *(E 7.57)*
- Set Properties of the Constant Label Controls and Check Box Control *(E 7.48)*
- Set the Command Button Control Properties *(E 7.31, E 7.53)*
- Set the Employee Investment Scroll Bar Properties *(E 7.54)*
- Set the Employer Match Check Box Properties *(E 7.56)*
- Set the Employer Match Scroll Bar Properties *(E 7.55)*
- Set the Label Control Properties for the Annual Return and Years of Service Spin Buttons *(E 7.58)*
- Start Excel, Open a Workbook, and Customize Excel *(E 7.06)*
- Test the Controls in the Adjustment Center User Interface *(E 7.70)*
- Undo a Group of Entries Using the Undo Button *(E 7.09)*
- Unprotect a Password-Protected Worksheet *(E 7.09, E 7.27)*
- View a Macro's VBA Code *(E 7.17)*

Learn It Online

Instructions: To complete the Learn It Online exercises, start your browser, click the Address bar, and then enter scsite.com/offxp/exs.htm. When the Office XP Learn It Online page displays, follow the instructions in the exercises below.

1 Project Reinforcement TF, MC, and SA

Below Excel Project 7, click the Project Reinforcement link. Print the quiz by clicking Print on the File menu. Answer each question. Write your first and last name at the top of each page, and then hand in the printout to your instructor.

2 Flash Cards

Below Excel Project 7, click the Flash Cards link. When Flash Cards displays, read the instructions. Type 20 (or a number specified by your instructor) in the Number of Playing Cards text box, type your name in the Name text box, and then click the Flip Card button. When the flash card displays, read the question and then click the Answer box arrow to select an answer. Flip through Flash Cards. Click Print on the File menu to print the last flash card if your score is 15 (75%) correct or greater and then hand it in to your instructor. If your score is less than 15 (75%) correct, then redo this exercise by clicking the Replay button.

3 Practice Test

Below Excel Project 7, click the Practice Test link. Answer each question, enter your first and last name at the bottom of the page, and then click the Grade Test button. When the graded practice test displays on your screen, click Print on the File menu to print a hard copy. Continue to take practice tests until you score 80% or better. Hand in a printout of the final practice test to your instructor.

4 Who Wants to Be a Computer Genius?

Below Excel Project 7, click the Computer Genius link. Read the instructions, enter your first and last name at the bottom of the page, and then click the Play button. Hand in your score to your instructor.

5 Wheel of Terms

Below Excel Project 7, click the Wheel of Terms link. Read the instructions, and then enter your first and last name and your school name. Click the Play button. Hand in your score to your instructor.

6 Crossword Puzzle Challenge

Below Excel Project 7, click the Crossword Puzzle Challenge link. Read the instructions, and then enter your first and last name. Click the Play button. Work the crossword puzzle. When you are finished, click the Submit button. When the crossword puzzle redisplays, click the Print button. Hand in the printout.

7 Tips and Tricks

Below Excel Project 7, click the Tips and Tricks link. Click a topic that pertains to Project 7. Right-click the information and then click Print on the shortcut menu. Construct a brief example of what the information relates to in Excel to confirm you understand how to use the tip or trick. Hand in the example and printed information.

8 Newsgroups

Below Excel Project 7, click the Newsgroups link. Click a topic that pertains to Project 7. Print three comments. Hand in the comments to your instructor.

9 Expanding Your Horizons

Below Excel Project 7, click the Articles for Microsoft Excel link. Click a topic that pertains to Project 7. Print the information. Construct a brief example of what the information relates to in Excel to confirm you understand the contents of the article. Hand in the example and printed information to your instructor.

10 Search Sleuth

Below Excel Project 7, click the Search Sleuth link. To search for a term that pertains to this project, select a term below the Project 7 title and then use the Google search engine at google.com (or any major search engine) to display and print two Web pages that present information on the term. Hand in the printouts to your instructor.

online

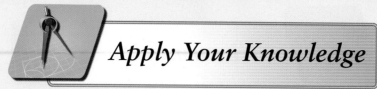

Apply Your Knowledge

1 Creating Macros and Customizing Menus and Toolbars

Instructions: Start Excel and perform the following tasks.

1. Open the workbook Whitewater Plumbing (Figure 7-87a) from the Data Disk. See the inside back cover of this book for instructions for downloading the Data Disk or see your instructor for information on accessing the files required in this book.

2. Reset the toolbars to their installation settings (see Step 6 on page E 7.06).

3. Unprotect the worksheet. The password is dripdrip.

4. Enter your name, course, laboratory assignment number (Apply 7-1), date, and instructor name in the range A11:A15.

5. Use the Record New Macro command to create a macro that prints the range A2:B8. Call the macro PrintNameAndRate, use the shortcut CTRL+N, change the name of the author in the Description box to your name, and store the macro in this workbook. When the Stop Recording toolbar displays, do the following: (a) select the range A2:B8; (b) click File on the menu bar, and then click Print; (c) click the Selection option in the Print what area of the Print dialog box; (d) click the OK button; and (e) click the Stop Recording button on the Stop Recording toolbar. If the Stop Recording toolbar does not display, click View on the main menu, then select Stop Recording on the Toolbars submenu.

6. Press ALT+F8 to display the Macro dialog box. Run the PrintNameAndRate macro. Press ALT+F8 to display the Macro dialog box a second time. Select the PrintNameAndRate macro and then click the Edit button. When the Visual Basic Editor displays the macro, click File on the menu bar and then click Print. Hand in both printouts to your instructor.

7. Add a button to the Standard toolbar (Figure 7-87a) and a command to the File menu (Figure 7-87b). Assign the button and command the PrintNameAndRate macro.

8. Run the macro as follows: (a) click the button you added to the Standard toolbar; (b) on the File menu, click the Print Name and Rate command; and (c) press CTRL+N. Hand in the three printouts to your instructor.

9. Protect the worksheet. Use the first six characters of your last name as the password. Save the workbook using the file name Whitewater Plumbing1.

10. Reset the toolbars to their installation settings (see Step 6 on page E 7.06).

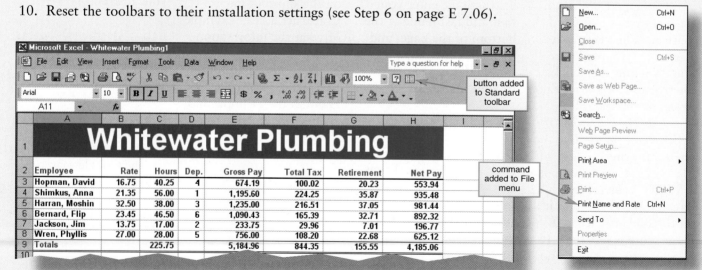

(a) Worksheet

(b) File Menu

FIGURE 7-87

In the Lab

1 Automating a Mortgage Worksheet

Problem: Holiday Mortgage specializes in mortgages for local vacation properties. The president, Eliza Harrison, has asked you to automate the entry of mortgage data into a Mortgage Analysis worksheet.

Instructions Part 1: Start Excel and perform the following tasks.

1. Open the Holiday Mortgage workbook from the Data Disk. See the inside back cover of this book for instructions for downloading the Data Disk or see your instructor for information on accessing the files required in this book.
2. Reset the toolbars to their installation settings (see Step 3 on page E 7.71).
3. Unprotect the Mortgage Analysis worksheet. The password is norent.
4. Display the Control Toolbox toolbar. Click the Command Button button on the Control Toolbox toolbar. Draw the button in the range D3:D5 as shown in Figure 7-88a.
5. With the Command Button control selected, click the Properties button on the Control Toolbox toolbar. Change the following properties: (a) Caption = Mortgage Data; (b) Font = Regular; and (c) PrintObject = False.
6. Click the View Code button on the Control Toolbox toolbar. Enter the procedure shown in Figure 7-88b. Check your code carefully. On the File menu, click Print to print the procedure.
7. Close the Visual Basic Editor window. Click the Exit Design Mode button on the Control Toolbox toolbar. Close the Control Toolbox toolbar. Close the Properties window.
8. Enter your name, course, laboratory assignment number (Lab 7-1), date, and instructor name in the range G3:G7.
9. Use the newly created button to determine the monthly payment for the following mortgage data and print the worksheet for each data set: (a) Price = $149,000; Down Payment = $20,000; Interest Rate = 8.25%; and Years = 15; (b) Price = $129,000; Down Payment = $15,000; Interest Rate = 8.75%; and Years = 12. The Monthly Payment for (a) is $1,251.48 and for (b) is $1,281.36.
10. Protect the worksheet. Use the password norent. Save the workbook using the file name Holiday Mortgage Automated and close the workbook.

Instructions Part 2: With the workbook Holiday Mortgage Automated created in Part 1 open, do the following:

1. Unprotect the worksheet. The password is norent.
2. Use the Record New Macro command to create a macro that prints the formulas version of the worksheet. Call the macro PrintFormulas, use the shortcut CTRL+F, change the name of the author in the Description box to your name, and store the macro in this workbook.
3. With the Stop Recording toolbar on the screen, do the following: (a) Press CTRL+ACCENT MARK (`); (b) On the File menu, click Page Setup, click Landscape option, click Fit to option, click the Print button in the Page Setup dialog box, and then click the OK button; (c) Press CTRL+ACCENT MARK (`); (d) On the File menu, click Page Setup, click Portrait option, click Adjust to option, type 100 in the Adjust to box, and then click the OK button; and (e) Click the Stop Recording button on the Stop Recording toolbar.

(continued)

In the Lab

Automating a Mortgage Worksheet (continued)

4. Press ALT+F8 to display the Macro dialog box. Run the PrintFormulas macro. Press ALT+F8 to display the Macro dialog box a second time. Select the PrintFormulas macro and then click the Edit button. When the Visual Basic Editor displays the macro, click File on the menu bar and then click Print. Hand in both printouts to your instructor.

5. Add a button to the Standard toolbar (Figure 7-88a) and a command to the File menu (Figure 7-88c). Assign the button and command the PrintFormulas macro.

6. Run the macro as follows: (a) click the button you added to the Standard toolbar; (b) on the File menu, click the Print Formulas; and (c) press CTRL+F. Hand in the three printouts to your instructor. The button will not print as part of the worksheet because PrintObject was set to False earlier.

7. Do not protect the worksheet because the Print Formulas macro will not work with a protected worksheet. Save the workbook using the file name Holiday Mortgage Automated2 and close the workbook.

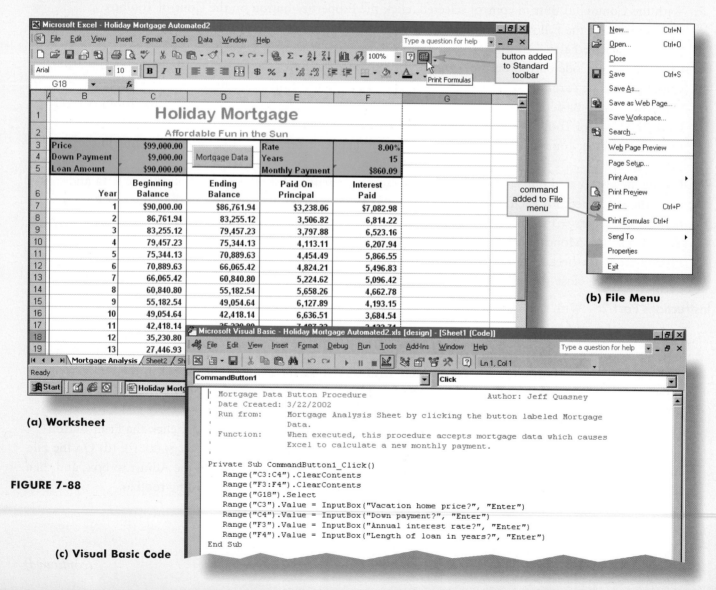

FIGURE 7-88

(a) Worksheet

(b) File Menu

(c) Visual Basic Code

In the Lab

2 Automating a Five-Year Projected Financial Statement

Problem: As the spreadsheet specialist at Executive Chairs, you have been asked to use your Visual Basic for Applications skills to automate the Five-Year Projected Financial Statement worksheet as shown in Figure 7-89. The objective is to simplify data entry for the company's financial analysts. This worksheet projects financial information for a five-year period based on the previous year's sales and additional data. The user interface on the right side of the screen accepts the assumptions in the range I6:I10. The numbers in the range B5:F18 are based on these assumptions.

The user interface has two buttons, one spin button, and three scroll bars. The Reset Assumptions button resets the assumptions as follows: (a) cell I6 = 50,000; (b) cell I7 = $355.00; (c) I8 = 10%; (d) I9 = 5%; and (e) I10 = 60%. The Chairs Sold in 2002 button accepts and ensures the units sold in 2002 is greater than zero and then assigns it to cell I6. The Unit Cost spin button changes the unit cost in cell I7. The Annual Sales Growth scroll bar changes the annual sales growth in cell I8. The Annual Price Decrease scroll bar changes the annual price decrease in cell I9. The Margin scroll bar changes the margin in cell I10.

FIGURE 7-89

Instructions: Start Excel and complete the following tasks.

1. Open the Executive Chairs workbook from the Data Disk. See the inside back cover of this book for instructions for downloading the Data Disk or see your instructor for information on accessing the files required in this book.
2. Reset the toolbars to their installation settings (see Step 3 on page E 7.71).
3. Unprotect the Financial Statement worksheet. The password is chairs.

(continued)

In the Lab

Automating a Five-Year Projected Financial Statement *(continued)*

4. Color the background of the range A19:I23 turquoise (column 5, row 4 on the Fill Color palette). Draw a thick box border (column 4, row 3 on the Borders palette) around the range A19:I23.

5. Display the Control Toolbox toolbar. Use the concepts and techniques developed in this project to add the 17 controls shown on the bottom of Figure 7-89.

6. Modify the properties of the 17 controls as described in Table 7-13.

Table 7-13   Controls and Their Properties

CONTROL	NAME	CAPTION	BACK COLOR	FONT	TEXT ALIGN	WORD WRAP	SPECIAL EFFECT	MAX	MIN	SMALL CHG	LARGE CHG
Reset Assumptions Button	btnReset	Reset Assumptions		8-point bold		True					
Chairs Sold in 2002 Button	btnChairsSold	Chairs Sold in 2002		8-point bold							
Unit Cost Label		Unit Cost	Turquoise	8-point bold	Right						
Unit Cost Spin Button	spnUnitCost							100000	0	100	
Unit Cost Spin Button Label		$320.00		10-point bold	Right		Sunken				
All three 0 Labels		0	Turquoise	8-point bold	Center						
All three 100 Labels		100	Turquoise	8-point bold	Center						
Annual Sales Growth Label		Annual Sales Growth	Turquoise	8-point bold	Center						
Annual Sales Growth Scroll Bar	scrAnnualSalesGrowth							10000	0	25	100
Annual Price Decrease Label		Annual Price Decrease	Turquoise	8-point bold	Center						
Annual Price Decrease Scroll Bar	scrAnnualPriceDecrease							10000	0	25	100
Margin Label		Margin	Turquoise	8-point bold	Center						
Margin Scroll Bar	scrMargin							10000	0	25	100

In the Lab

7. Enter your name, course, laboratory assignment number (Lab 7-2), date, and instructor name in the range H12:H16. Save the workbook using the file name Executive Chairs Automated.

8. The Reset Assumptions Button procedure resets the assumptions as follows:

```
Range("I6").Value = 50000
spnUnitCost = 35000
scrAnnualSalesGrowth = 1000
scrAnnualPriceDecrease = 500
scrMargin = 6000
Range("I10").Select
```

9. The Chairs Sold in 2002 Button procedure accepts and validates the number of chairs sold in 2002 in cell I6 as follows:

```
ChairsSold = InputBox("Chairs Sold in 2002?", "Enter")
Do While ChairsSold <= 0
    ChairsSold = InputBox("Chairs Sold in 2002 must be > zero.", "Please Re-enter")
Loop
Range("I6").Value = ChairsSold
```

10. The Unit Cost Spin Button procedure enters the unit cost in the Unit Cost Spin Button Label control and in cell I7 as follows:

```
lblUnitCost = Format$(spnUnitCost.Value / 100, "currency")
Range("I7").Value = spnUnitCost.Value / 100
```

The Format$ function in the first line formats the result that will display in the Unit Cost Spin Button Label control to include a floating dollar sign and two decimal positions to the right of the decimal.

11. The Annual Sales Growth Scroll Bar procedure changes the annual sales growth in cell I8 as follows:

```
Range("I8").Value = scrAnnualSalesGrowth.Value / 10000
```

12. The Annual Price Decrease Scroll Bar procedure and the Margin Scroll Bar procedure work in a fashion similar to the Annual Sales Growth scroll bar, except that they assign values to cells I9 and I10, respectively.

13. Click the Microsoft Excel button on the taskbar. Click the Exit Design Mode button on the Control Toolbox toolbar. Close the Control Toolbox toolbar. Print the worksheet.

14. Use the newly designed interface to determine the five year projections based on the following assumptions and print the worksheet for each data set: (a) Units Sold in 2002 = 45,000; Unit Cost = $41.70; Annual Sales Growth = 17%; Annual Price Decrease = 4%; and Margin = 58.5% (b) Units Sold in 2002 = 37,000; Unit Cost = $395.00; Annual Sales Growth = 12.5%; Annual Price Decrease = 3.5%; and Margin = 52%. The Net Income for the year 2007 in cell F18 for (a) is $850,389 and for (b) is $3,687,503.

15. Click the Visual Basic Editor button on the taskbar. On the File menu, click Print to print the VBA code. Close the Visual Basic Editor.

16. Protect the worksheet. Use the password, chairs. Click the Save button on the Standard toolbar to save the workbook using the file name Executive Chairs Automated.

In the Lab

3 Automating a Projected Income Statement

Problem: You work in the strategic planning office of E&R, Inc., a local manufacturer. Your boss needs a workbook (Figure 7-90) automated to make it easier for her accountants to use. Because you are taking an advanced Excel course that includes Visual Basic for Applications, she has asked you to automate the data entry in cells D4 (Units Sold); D5 (Price per Unit); D14 (Material Cost per Unit); and D16 (Manufacturing Cost per Unit). All other cells in the worksheet use formulas.

Instructions: Start Excel and complete the following tasks.

1. Open the E&R Inc workbook from the Data Disk. See the inside back cover of this book for instructions for downloading the Data Disk or see your instructor for information on accessing the files required in this book.

2. Reset the toolbars to their installation settings (see Step 3 on page E 7.71).

3. Unprotect the Projected Income Statement worksheet. The password is erinc.

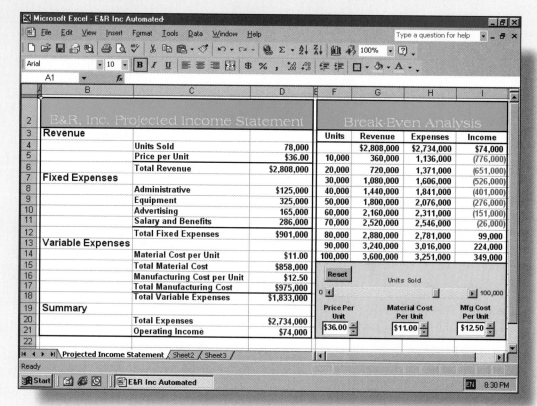

FIGURE 7-90

4. Color the background of the range F15:I21 yellow (column 3, row 4 on the Fill Color palette). Draw a thick box border (column 4, row 3 on the Borders palette) around the range F15:I21.

5. Display the Control Toolbox toolbar. Use the concepts and techniques developed in this project to add the 14 controls shown in the lower-right corner of Figure 7-90. The Units Sold scroll bar should assign a value to cell D4. The Price Per Unit spin button should assign a value to cell D5. The Material Cost Per Unit spin button should assign a value to cell D14. The Mfg Cost Per Unit spin button should assign a value to cell D16.

6. Modify the properties of the 14 controls as described in Table 7-14.

In the Lab

Table 7-14 Controls and Their Properties

CONTROL	NAME	CAPTION	BACK COLOR	FONT	TEXT ALIGN	WORD WRAP	SPECIAL EFFECT	MAX	MIN	SMALL CHG	LARGE CHG
Reset Button	btnReset	Reset		8-point bold							
0 Label		0	Yellow	8-point bold	Center						
Units Sold Label		Units Sold	Yellow	8-point bold	Center						
100,000 Label		100,000	Yellow	8-Point bold	Center						
Units Sold Scroll Bar	scrUnitsSold							100000	0	100	1000
Price Per Unit Label		Price Per Unit	Yellow	8-point bold	Center	True					
Price Per Unit Spin Button	spnPrice							9999	0	10	
Price Per Unit Spin Button Label		$36.00		10-point bold	Right		Sunken				
Material Cost Per Unit Label		Material Cost Per Unit	Yellow	8-point bold	Center	True					
Material Cost Per Unit Spin Button	spnMaterialCost							9999	0	10	
Material Cost Per Unit Spin Button Label		$11.50		10-point bold	Right		Sunken				
Mfg Cost Per Unit Label		Mfg Cost Per Unit	Yellow	8-point bold	Center	True					
Mfg Cost Per Unit Spin Button	spnMfgCost							9999	0	10	
Mfg Cost Per Unit Spin Button Label		$12.50		10-point bold	Right		Sunken				

7. Enter your name, course, laboratory assignment number (Lab 7-3), date, and instructor name in the range B23:B27. Save the workbook using the file name E&R Inc Automated.

8. The Reset Button procedure should set the Units Sold scroll bar (scrUnitsSold) to 78000; the Price Per Unit Spin Button (spnPrice) to 40000; the Material Cost Per Unit (spnMaterialCost) to 10000; and the Mfg Cost Per Unit (spnMfgCost) to 10000. It also should select cell A1.

9. The Units Sold Scroll Bar procedure should assign the value of the scroll bar (scrUnitsSold) to cell D4. For example,

```
Range("D4").Value = scrUnitsSold.Value
```

(continued)

In the Lab

Automating a Projected Income Statement *(continued)*

10. The Price Per Unit Spin Button procedure should assign the value of spnPrice / 100, formatted to the Currency style, to the Price Per Unit Spin Button Label control. It also should assign the value of spnPrice / 100 to cell D5. For example,

```
lblPrice = Format$(spnPrice.Value / 100, "currency")
Range("D5").Value = spnPrice.Value / 100
```

The Format$ function in the first line formats the result that will display in the Price Per Unit Spin Button Label control to include a floating dollar sign and two decimal positions to the right of the decimal. The value assigned to cell D5 will display in the same format because the cell was formatted to the Currency style as part of the normal worksheet formatting.

11. The Material Cost Per Unit Spin Button procedure should assign the value of spnMaterialCost / 100, formatted to the Currency style, to the Material Cost Per Unit Spin Button Label control. It also should assign the value of spnMaterialCost / 100 to cell D14. For example,

```
lblMaterialCost = Format$(spnMaterialCost.Value / 100, "currency")
Range("D14").Value = spnMaterialCost.Value / 100
```

12. The Mfg Cost Per Unit Spin Button procedure should assign the value of the spnMfgCost / 100, formatted to the Currency style, to the Mfg Cost Per Unit Spin Button Label control. It also should assign the value of spnMfgCost / 100 to cell D16. For example,

```
lblMfgCost = Format$(spnMfgCost.Value / 100, "currency")
Range("D16").Value = spnMfgCost.Value / 100
```

13. Click the Microsoft Excel button on the taskbar. Click the Exit Design Mode button on the Control Toolbox toolbar. Hide the Control Toolbox toolbar. Print the worksheet.

14. Use the newly designed user interface to determine the operating income for the following projections and print the worksheet for each data set: (a) Units Sold = 55,000; Price per Unit = $40.00; Material Cost per Unit = $15.50; and Manufacturing Cost per Unit = $12.00 (b) Units Sold = 70,000; Price per Unit = $42.00; Material Cost per Unit = $11.50; and Manufacturing Cost per Unit = $12.00. The Operating Income in cell D21 for (a) is $213,500 and for (b) is $394,000.

15. Click the Visual Basic Editor button on the taskbar. On the File menu, click Print to print the VBA code. Close the Visual Basic Editor.

16. Protect the worksheet. Use the password, erinc. Click the Save button on the Standard toolbar to save the workbook using the file name E&R Inc Automated.

Cases and Places

The difficulty of these case studies varies:
▶ are the least difficult; ▶▶ are more difficult; and ▶▶▶ are the most difficult.

1 ▶ Open the workbook MaxGlass from the Data Disk. Create a Command Button control below the Assumptions box. Change the button's caption to Assumptions. Write a procedure for the Command Button control that accepts data for each of the five assumptions in the range B21:B25. Print the Forecast worksheet. Print the Command Button control procedure. Use the Assumptions button to enter the following data sets and then print the worksheet for each data set: (a) Manufacturing = 43%; R & D = 9%; Marketing = 18%; Corporate = 17%; Commissions = 12%. (b) Manufacturing = 35%; R & D = 6%; Marketing = 20%; Corporate = 18%; Commissions = 15%. The Total Net Income in cell E18 for (a) is $59,299.10 and for (b) is $355,794.60. Save the workbook with the name MaxGlass1. Hand in the four printouts to your instructor.

2 ▶ Open the workbook MaxGlass from the Data Disk. Print the Forecast worksheet. Create a macro that prints the cell formulas version of the Forecast worksheet in landscape orientation using the Fit to option. Make sure that the macro resets the Page Setup options before terminating. Execute the macro. Print the macro VBA code. Save the workbook with the name MaxGlass2. Hand in the three printouts to your instructor.

3 ▶ Using a Web search engine, such as Google, type the keywords Visual Basic for Applications. Visit three Web pages that show VBA code solving a problem. Print each Web page. Hand in the three printouts to your instructor.

4 ▶▶ Open the workbook MaxGlass from the Data Disk. Create a well-balanced user interface made up of a Reset button and five scroll bars, one for each of the cells in the range B21:B25. Have the Reset button set the five assumptions to 45%, 8%, 12%, 12%, and 10%, respectively. The scroll bars should range from 0% to 100% and increment by 0.25% (scroll arrows) and 1% (scroll bars). Use the titles in the Assumptions box in the range A21:A25 for the names of the scroll bars. Print the worksheet. Use the interface to enter the data specified in Cases and Places Exercise 1 above. Save the workbook with the name MaxGlass3. Hand in the printout to your instructor.

5 ▶▶▶ Open the workbook Sky Mortgage Analysis from the Data Disk. Modify the procedure associated with the New Mortgage button on the worksheet so that it validates the price, down payment, interest rate, and years as follows: (a) the price must be between $20,000 and $150,000 inclusive; (b) the down payment must be between $2,000 and $150,000 inclusive; (c) the interest rate must be between 4% and 20% inclusive; and (d) the years must be between 1 and 15 inclusive. Print the procedure. Create and enter two sets of valid test data. Print the worksheet for each set. Hand in the three printouts to your instructor.

Cases and Places

6 ▶▶▶ Open the workbook MaxGlass from the Data Disk. Create a well-balanced user interface that allows the user to change the quarter (months) that the workbook is being used for. The first prompt should ask the user to enter which quarter the data is for. After accepting a valid number (1 through 4), the Visual Basic code should update cells A2, B4, C4, and D4 with appropriate labels.

7 ▶▶▶ Open the workbook Sky Mortgage Analysis from the Data Disk. Remove the New Mortgage command button. Create a well-balanced user interface that allows input for the value in the cells C3, C4, C5, C7, and C8. Use at least one text box control, at least one scroll bar control, and at least one spin button control. Use the same validation rules as detailed in Cases and Places Exercise 5 above. Include a text box control that is labeled as the Maximum Requested Monthly Payment. At the end of each procedure that you create for the controls, include a check that determines if the Monthly Payment in cell C9 is greater than the Maximum Requested Monthly Payment. If so, set the font color in the cell to red by using the Visual Basic statement Range("C9").Font.Color = RGB(255, 0, 0). If the value in C9 is less than or equal to the Maximum Requested Monthly Payment, then set the color in cell C9 to black by using the Visual Basic statement Range("C9").Font.Color = RGB(0, 0, 0). The value of cell C9 must be compared to a numeric value. Use the syntax CDBL(txtMaxPayment.Value) to make the Maximum Requested Monthly Payment a numeric value.

Microsoft Excel 2002

PROJECT

8

Formula Auditing, Data Validation, and Complex Problem Solving

You will have mastered the material in this project when you can:

- Use the Formula Auditing toolbar to analyze a worksheet
- Trace precedents and dependents
- Add data validation rules to cells
- Use trial and error to solve a problem on a worksheet
- Use goal seeking to solve a problem
- Use Excel's Solver to solve a complex problem
- Password-protect a workbook file
- Use Excel's Scenario Manager to record and save different sets of what-if assumptions and the corresponding results
- Create a Scenario Summary of scenarios
- Create a Scenario PivotTable
- Set and change the properties of a workbook

Sustaining the Hungry
Spreadsheet Solutions for Food Distribution

Across America, many dedicated people have joined together to end hunger. In soup kitchens and food banks, at churches and local community centers, approximately one out of every ten Americans seeks help from these committed individuals every year. Nearly half of those seeking assistance are children, and almost 40 percent include households where the primary providers are employed but do not earn enough money to buy the basic foods they need.

Although difficult to comprehend, it is estimated that 30 million Americans are in danger of going hungry. In large part, these families and individuals are helped through the efforts of America's Second Harvest, the nation's largest domestic hunger-relief organization. Corporate donors, local businesses, and individuals provide surplus food to the food banks, which then is distributed to more than 50,000 charitable agencies. A network of more than 200 food banks serves all 50 states and Puerto Rico, and distributes more than 1.5 billion pounds of donated food and groceries each year.

One of Second Harvest's food banks is the Greater Chicago Food Depository. The Food Depository collects donated surplus food from wholesale food manufacturers, produce growers and distributors, food store chains, and restaurants. After gathering the food, Food depository drivers deliver the provisions to warehouses where the products are distributed later to charitable food pantries, soup kitchens, and shelters throughout the Chicago area.

With the huge distribution of food each year, employees needed a more efficient method of keeping track of these goods than using manual methods. Given the ease with which Excel can audit and analyze data, the Food Depository developed Excel worksheets, similar to the worksheets developed in this project.

In Project 8, the management of Northland Instrument Distributors requires an Excel spreadsheet that can analyze complex data in order to provide practical solutions for managing shipments of its products to wholesalers around the country. In the project, you will learn to use Excel's capabilities to evaluate various constraints imposed by both shipping companies and by the management at Northland Instrument Distributors. The formulas will help you determine the most economical combination of products that can be shipped, given the allowable maximum weight and available space on a limited number of trucks.

The Food Depository uses Excel worksheets to organize, tabulate, and summarize hundreds of pallets and thousands of pounds of food shipped each

week to its warehouses. Last year alone, employees at the Food Depository needed to coordinate the distribution of 32.4 million pounds of food, valued at more than $54 million, which they estimate to be the equivalent of 67,000 meals a day, 365 days a year. Excel worksheets help to ensure that distribution centers receive food deliveries just when they need it, which in turn helps to minimize food surpluses at warehouses.

As inventory arrives at a warehouse, employees can enter the quantity and type of delivered items, which facilitates the instant analysis of storage and distribution needs. If items arrive in a damaged or disarrayed state, employees also can enter this information in the spreadsheet so that these items are not included inappropriately in the count of available inventory. Workers can generate reports, study the worksheets to determine their needs, prepare for the amounts of food expected to arrive the following day, and survey how much warehouse space is needed to ensure sufficient room for the products.

Whether your needs are large or small, Excel delivers spreadsheet solutions that improve productivity.

Microsoft Excel 2002

Formula Auditing, Data Validation, and Complex Problem Solving

CASE PERSPECTIVE

Shipping costs comprise a significant portion of expenses for many small businesses. Northland Instrument Distributors receives large shipments of musical instruments from manufacturers, which it then distributes to musical instrument wholesalers around the country. To ship its goods, the company purchases extra space on trucks from trucking firms. Before the company makes a shipment to a particular city, it contacts trucking firms asking whether they have spare capacity on trucks going to that city. Typically, the company receives weight and volume limitations to which they must adhere if they are to ship goods on the truck. As the assistant shipping manager, you are required to prepare a worksheet that will select the most economical mix of products to fill the space on a truck. In addition, you must maximize the company's profit on each shipment.

Marsha Gresham, your manager, has given you a list of products, their dimensions, and weight. You also have the profit per instrument that the company can make on each item. Both Marsha and the trucking companies also want documentation that shows the requirements have been satisfied.

Introduction

This project introduces you to formula auditing a worksheet, data validation, and solving complex problems. Formula auditing allows you to check both the cells being referenced in a formula and the formulas that reference a cell. Formula auditing a worksheet is helpful especially when you want to learn more about a workbook created by someone else or you want to verify the formulas in a newly created workbook.

Data validation allows you to define cells in such a way that only certain values are accepted. This feature also lets you display a prompt message when the user selects the cell and an error message if the user attempts to enter a value outside of a valid range that you define.

The majority of this project introduces you to solving complex problems that involve changing values of cells to arrive at a solution, while abiding by constraints imposed on the changing values. The worksheet in Figure 8-1a on page E 8.06 shows the details of the shipping requirements for this project as described in the Case Perspective. Columns B, C, and D each refer to one of the three instrument types currently in stock, Guitars, Keyboards, and Tubas, that must ship. The row titles in rows 4 through 7 in column A refer to the characteristics of each instrument, such as Item Volume in Cubic Feet, Item Weight in Pounds, Profit per Item, and Amount in Stock. Row 9 is where you enter the number of each instrument to ship. In this case, the number of instruments must be more than one and less than the number in stock. Once you enter the shipment number of each instrument in cells B9, C9, and D9, Excel determines the results of the suggested shipment in rows 11 through 13, Total Shipment Volume, Total Shipment Weight, and Total Shipment Profit. The objective is to maximize the profit while filling up as much of the truck as possible. The constraints given for the current truck under consideration for the shipment are in cells B16 and B17.

The only way to solve some problems is to keep trying different data, in this case varying the number of each instrument to ship, until you are satisfied with the solution. This process is called trial and error. Often, you can use trial and error to solve a problem on your own. Other times, so many possible solutions exist to a problem, that the best way to solve the problem is to use a computer. Excel provides you with tools to solve such problems. One of these tools is Solver. **Solver** allows you to specify up to 200 different cells that can be adjusted to find a solution to a problem. It also lets you place constraints on the variables. A **constraint** is a limitation on the possible values that a cell can contain. Once you define the constraints and instruct Solver what to look for, it will try many possible solutions until it finds the best one.

In Figure 8-1b on the next page, the values of cells B9, C9, and D9 have been modified by Solver to find the best combination of instruments to ship on a particular truck. When Solver finishes solving a problem, you can instruct it to create an Answer Report. An Answer Report (Figures 8-1c and 8-1e on page E 8.07) shows the answer that Solver found, the values that were manipulated by Solver to find the answer, and the constraints that were used to solve the problem.

Excel's **Scenario Manager** is a what-if analysis tool that allows you to record and save different sets of what-if assumptions used to forecast the outcome of a worksheet model. You will use Scenario Manager to manage two different sets of Solver data. Figure 8-1d on the next page shows a scenario where accordions have been substituted for guitars as an instrument available to ship. Scenario Manager also allows you to create reports that summarize the scenarios on your worksheet. Figure 8-1f on page E 8.07 shows a Scenario Summary and Scenario PivotTable that concisely report the differences in the two scenarios in Figures 8-1b and 8-1d.

More About

Constraints

The constraints of a problem are the rules that you must follow to solve a given problem. You even may add constraints to cells that are not referenced in the formulas you are solving. Solver will modify these types of cells to meet the constraints, but they will not affect the solution. For example, you can change row or column headers, or worksheet headers to better explain to the user the results of a Solver solution.

Project Eight — Northland Instrument Distributors Weekly Shipping Worksheet

To create the Northland Instrument Distributors weekly shipping worksheet, you determine the following needs and source of data.

Needs: The Macon Trucking Company has a truck leaving today that is making a delivery very close to the Northland's East Coast distribution center. The truck has spare space that Macon Trucking would like to fill. You are to determine the best mix of items to ship that includes at least one of each item, because that is what the distribution center on the East coast requires. The shipment must fit within the constraints of the current truck under consideration: 400 cubic feet and 600 pounds. When determining the best mix of products to ship, you must maximize the profit to Northland while operating within the constraints that the trucking company has placed on you.

Finally, reports need to be generated for the trucking company that indicate the volume and weight constraints have been met. In addition, a second shipment that includes accordions must be analyzed and compared with the shipment that includes guitars.

More About

The Solver Add-In

If you do not have Solver installed on your computer, see your instructor about obtaining the Microsoft Office XP CD-ROMs. To install the Solver Add-In, use the Add-Ins command on the Tools menu, check the Solver option box, and then follow the instructions.

(b) Solution with Guitars

(a) Worksheet without a Solution

(d) Solution with Accordians

FIGURE 8-1

(c) Answer Report with Guitars

(e) Answer Report with Accordians

(f) Scenario Summary and Scenario PivotTable of Solutions

Source of Data: The workbook shown in Figure 8-1a on page E 8.06 is available on the Data Disk with the file name, Northland Instrument Distributors.

Starting Excel and Opening a Workbook

Perform the following steps to start Excel, reset the toolbars, and open the workbook Northland Instrument Distributors from the Data Disk.

TO START EXCEL, OPEN A WORKBOOK, AND CUSTOMIZE EXCEL

1 Insert the Data Disk in drive A. See the inside back cover of this book for instructions for downloading the Data Disk or see your instructor for information on accessing the files required in this book.

2 Click the Start button on the Windows taskbar and then click Open Office Document.

3 When the Open Office Document dialog box displays, click the Look in box arrow and then click 3½ Floppy (A:). Double-click Northland Instrument Distributors in the Look in list.

4 If the Excel window is not maximized, double-click its title bar to maximize it.

5 If the Language bar displays, click its Minimize button.

6 If the Standard and Formatting toolbars display on one row, click the Toolbar Options button on the right side of either toolbar and then click Show Buttons on Two Rows in the Toolbar Options list.

The Weekly Shipment Worksheet displays in the Excel window (Figure 8-2).

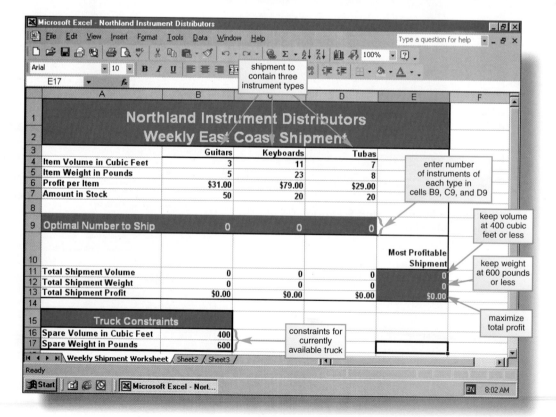

FIGURE 8-2

The Weekly Shipment Worksheet shown in Figure 8-2 consists of information for three types of instruments. Rows 4 through 7 show the information for each type of instrument. Row 9 contains the optimal combination of instruments, which is the information that needs to be determined in this project. Rows 11 through 13 show the totals for each instrument based on the number of instruments entered in the range B9:D9. As cells B9, C9, and D9 change, the values in the range B11:D13 are updated. Finally, the grand totals for the entire shipment are calculated in the range E11:E13. The goals are to keep the total volume of the shipment (cell E11) less than or equal to 400 (cell B16), keep the total weight of the shipment (cell E12) less than or equal to 600 (cell B17), and maximize the total profit made on the shipment (cell E13).

The current worksheet displays guitars as one of the instruments. One of the requirements is to create shipments within the constraints for both guitars and accordions. Therefore, the information in column B needs to be modified later in the project to reflect the volume, weight, profit, and stock of accordions.

Formula Auditing

The term **formula auditing** refers to the practice of proving the correctness of a worksheet. The **Formula Auditing toolbar** supplies several tools that you can use to analyze the formulas in a worksheet.

Formula auditing is useful both for analyzing a complex worksheet and for finding the source of errors that may occur in your worksheet. Excel provides visual auditing tools that display cues to help you understand the worksheet. These cues take the form of tracer arrows and circles around worksheet cells. **Tracer arrows** are blue arrows that point from cell to cell and let you know what cells are referenced in a formula in a particular cell. Tracer arrows display red when one of the cells referenced contains an error.

Displaying the Formula Auditing Toolbar

When you want to audit a worksheet, you can display the Formula Auditing toolbar. The Formula Auditing toolbar contains buttons that allow you to trace the details of a formula or locate the source of errors in a worksheet. To display the Formula Auditing toolbar, complete the steps on the next page.

More About

Auditing

Auditing is a very important job function in corporations and government. For more information about auditing, visit the Excel 2002 More About Web page (scsite.com/ex2002/more.htm) and then click Auditing.

Steps **To Display the Formula Auditing Toolbar**

1 **Click Tools on the menu bar, point to Formula Auditing, and then point to Show Formula Auditing Toolbar on the Formula Auditing submenu.**

The Tools menu and Formula Auditing submenu display (Figure 8-3).

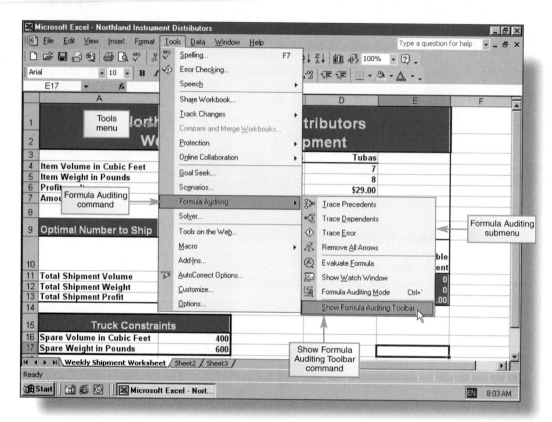

FIGURE 8-3

2 **Click Show Formula Auditing Toolbar.**

The Formula Auditing toolbar displays (Figure 8-4). Excel displays the Formula Auditing toolbar on the screen in the same location and with the same shape as it displayed the last time it was used.

Other Ways

1. Right-click Standard or Formatting toolbar, click Formula Auditing
2. Press ALT+T, U, S
3. In Voice Command mode, say "Tools, Formula Auditing, Show Formula Auditing Toolbar"

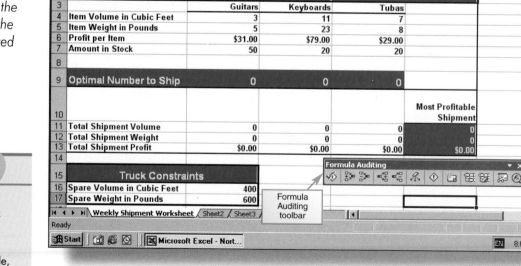

FIGURE 8-4

Tracing Precedents with the Formula Auditing Toolbar

A formula that relies on other cells for a computation is said to have precedents. **Precedents** are cells that are referenced in a formula. For example, if you assign cell A5 the formula =A1+A2, then cells A1 and A2 are precedents of cell A5. Tracing precedent cells shows you how a particular cell is calculated. Often a precedent cell has precedents itself. For instance, in the previous example, if you assign cell A1 the formula =B1+B2, then cell A1, which is a precedent of cell A5, also has precedents. Excel also allows you to trace the precedents of precedents; however, you can audit only one cell at a time. That is, Excel does not allow you to audit ranges. The following steps show the precedent cells for the total profit of the best shipment in cell E13.

 Steps **To Trace Precedents**

1 **Click cell E13 and then click the Trace Precedents button on the Formula Auditing toolbar.**

Excel draws an arrow across the range B13:E13.

2 **Click the Trace Precedents button again.**

Excel draws arrows indicating the precedents of cells B13:D13 (Figure 8-5).

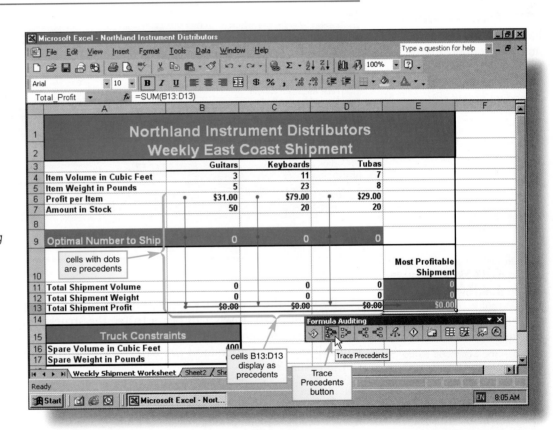

FIGURE 8-5

The arrows in Figure 8-5 have arrowheads on cells that are traced, and dots on cells that are direct precedents of the cells with arrowheads. For example, cell B13 is a precedent of cell E13, the total profit cell, and B13 has precedents above it in cells B6 and B9. As you click the Trace Precedents button, you can visually follow the levels of precedents through the worksheet.

Other **Ways**

1. On Tools menu point to Formula Auditing, click Trace Precedents
2. Press ALT+T, U, T
3. In Voice Command mode, say "Tools, Formula Auditing, Trace Precedents"

Removing Precedent Arrows with the Formula Auditing Toolbar

After understanding the precedents of a particular cell, you can remove the precedent arrows one level at a time, as shown in the steps on the next page.

Steps **To Remove the Trace Precedent Arrows**

1 **Click the Remove Precedent Arrows button on the Formula Auditing toolbar.**

Excel removes the arrows across the range B6:D9, the last level of precedent arrows added.

2 **Click the Remove Precedent Arrows button on the Formula Auditing toolbar again.**

Excel removes the remaining precedent arrows (Figure 8-6).

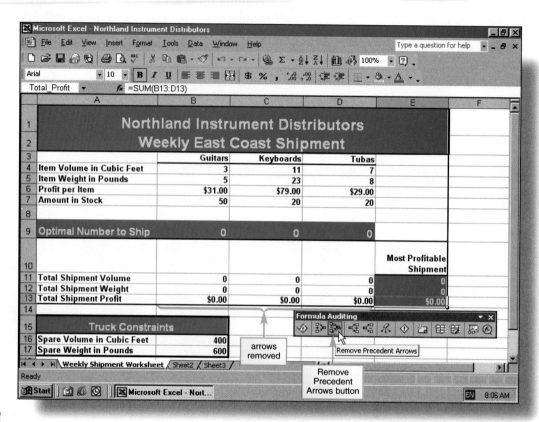

FIGURE 8-6

By using the Trace Precedents and Remove Precedent Arrows buttons in combination, you slowly can begin to see the structure of the worksheet that is hidden in the formulas within the cells. By doing more analysis, you can assure yourself that you understand the worksheet and that no obvious errors are apparent to the casual viewer.

Tracing Dependents with the Formula Auditing Toolbar

A cell is a **dependent** if it is referenced in a formula in another cell. Often, it is useful to find out where a cell is being used in a worksheet to perform subsequent calculations. In other words, you can discover which cells in the worksheet use the cell in question. The following steps trace the dependents of the optimal number of guitars to ship in cell B9.

Steps To Trace Dependents

1 **Click cell B9 and then click the Trace Dependents button on the Formula Auditing toolbar.**

Excel draws arrows to cells B11, B12, and B13.

2 **Click the Trace Dependents button once more.**

Excel draws arrows indicating the remaining dependents of cell B9 (Figure 8-7).

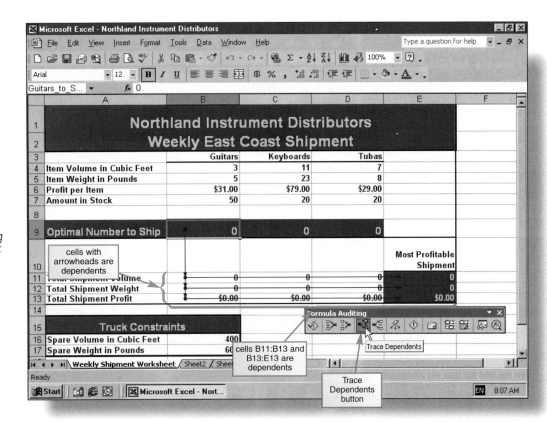

FIGURE 8-7

Figure 8-7 indicates that cells B11, B12, and B13 depend on cell B9. Subsequently, the range E11:E13 depends on those cells. Clearly, before any results can be computed in the range E11:E13, cell B9 must have a value.

Removing All Arrows with the Formula Auditing Toolbar

When you have finished auditing the worksheet with the Formula Auditing toolbar, the easiest way to clear all of the trace arrows is to use the Remove All Arrows button on the Formula Auditing toolbar, as shown in the steps on the next page.

Other Ways

1. On Tools menu point to Auditing, click Trace Dependents
2. Press ALT+T, U, D
3. In Voice Command mode, say "Tools, Formula Auditing, Trace Dependents"

Steps **To Remove the Trace Dependent Arrows**

1 **Click the Remove All Arrows button on the Formula Auditing toolbar.**

Excel removes all of the trace dependent arrows (Figure 8-8).

2 **Click the Close button on the right side of the Formula Auditing toolbar to close it.**

FIGURE 8-8

1. On Tools menu point to Auditing, click Remove All Arrows
2. Press ALT+T, U, A
3. In Voice Command mode, say "Tools, Formula Auditing, Remove All Arrows"

Sometimes, a cell has precedents or dependents on other worksheets or in other workbooks. In this case, Excel draws a dashed arrow to an icon of a worksheet to indicate that the precedent or dependent is outside of the current worksheet. If you click the dashed arrow and the workbook that contains the precedent or dependent is open, Excel displays the Go To dialog box that allows you to navigate to that location.

Figure 8-9 shows the buttons of the Formula Auditing Toolbar. Table 8-1 summarizes the buttons on the Formula Auditing Toolbar.

FIGURE 8-9

The **Trace Error button** is used when you see an error in a cell and want to trace the source of the error. If you see an error in a cell, including #DIV/0!, #NAME?, #NA, #NULL!, #NUM!, #REF!, and #VALUE!, the Trace Error button will display red tracer arrows to inform you of the precedents of the cell that contains the error. You then can inspect the precedent cells to see if you can determine the cause of the error and correct it. The **Error Checking button** will search the current worksheet for any errors and then display the Error Checking dialog box to help you take corrective action.

The **New Comment button** allows you to place comments in cells so that you can make notes to yourself or to others about questionable data in the worksheet. For example, if you are auditing someone else's worksheet and you believe that a cell should be the precedent of a particular cell, you can make a note that will display when the other user opens the worksheet. Comments are discussed further in Project 9.

The **Circle Invalid Data button** and **Clear Validation Circles button** are used in combination with Excel's data validation capability discussed in the next section. If a cell contains data validation parameters and the current data in the cell is outside of those validation criteria, the Circle Invalid Data button draws a circle around the cell. The Clear Validation Circles button is used to clear these circles.

The **Show Watch Window button** displays the Watch Window. The **Watch Window** allows you to monitor cells and formulas as you work on a worksheet. The **Evaluate Formula button** displays the **Evaluate Formula dialog box**, which allows you to debug or understand complex formulas in a worksheet, much in the manner that programmers debug source code. See Project 7 in this book for a more in-depth discussion of programming in Excel.

Table 8-1	Summary of Buttons on the Formula Auditing Toolbar	
BUTTON	**NAME**	**FUNCTION**
	Error Checking	Checks the entire worksheet for errors.
	Trace Precedents	Draws tracer arrows from the cells that affect the formula in the current cell.
	Remove Precedent Arrows	Removes tracer arrows from one level of dependents on the active worksheet.
	Trace Dependents	Draws tracer arrows to the cells that use the current cell in their formula.
	Remove Dependent Arrows	Removes tracer arrows from one level of dependents on the active worksheet.
	Remove All Arrows	Removes all tracer arrows drawn with the Trace Precedents and Trace Dependents buttons.
	Trace Error	If the active cell contains an error value, draws tracer arrows to the cells that may be causing the error value to appear.
	New Comment	Attaches a comment to the active cell.
	Circle Invalid Data	Draws circles around the cells that contain values outside of the limits defined through the Validation command on the Data menu.
	Clear Validation Circles	Clears the circles drawn by the Circle Invalid Data button.
	Show Watch Window	Shows a window that displays cells and their formulas that you select to monitor.
	Evaluate Formula	Allows you to debug complex formulas by monitoring the formula step by step.

Data Validation, Trial and Error, and Goal Seek

Often, it is necessary to limit the values that should be placed in a particular cell. Excel allows you to place limitations on the values of cells by using data validation. **Data validation** restricts the values that may be entered into a cell by the worksheet user. Excel allows you to determine the restrictions placed on data entered into a cell, set an input message that the user will see when selecting the cell, and set an error message that displays when a user violates the restrictions placed on the cell. By implementing these features, you limit the possibilities for error on a worksheet by giving the user as much information as possible about how to use the worksheet properly.

One important aspect of Excel's data validation is that the rules apply only when the user enters data into the cell manually. That is, if a cell is calculated by a formula or set in a way other than direct input by the user, Excel does not check the validation rules.

More *About*

Validation Circles

Validation circles display in red to indicate that these cells contain error values. Excel will display a maximum of 256 invalid data circles at a time.

Data Validation

If you have the Office Assistant turned on, Data Validation input and error messages will be displayed as part of the assistant. Input and error messages can be up to 255 characters in length.

Adding Data Validation to Cells

Recall from the Needs section for this project on page E 8.05, shipment amounts must be whole numbers and at least one of each type of instrument must be included in each shipment, but no more than are in stock of each type of instrument. By examining the worksheet, you can see that cells B9, C9, and D9 must have these restrictions. Data validation is added to cells by using the **Validation command** on the Data menu.

Perform the following steps to add data validation to cells B9, C9, and D9.

 To Add Data Validation

1 Select the range B9:D9. Click Data on the menu bar and then point to Validation.

The Data menu displays (Figure 8-10).

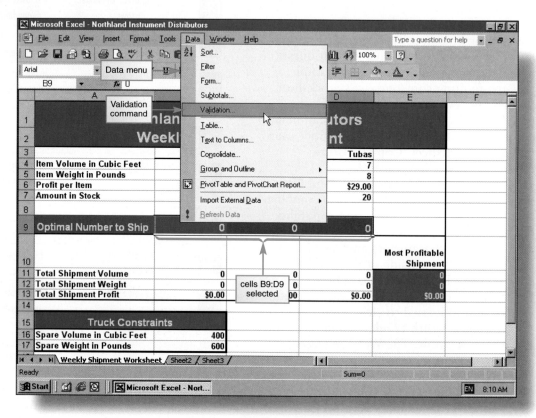

FIGURE 8-10

2 **Click Validation. When the Data Validation dialog box displays, click the Allow box arrow and then click Whole number. Click the Data box arrow and then, if necessary, click between. Type** 1 **in the Minimum box. Select the Maximum box and click cell B7. Point to the Input Message tab.**

The Data Validation dialog box displays (Figure 8-11).

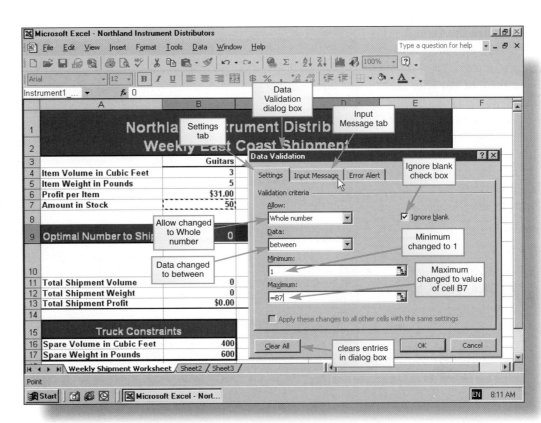

FIGURE 8-11

3 **Click the Input Message tab and then type** Items to Ship **in the Title text box. Type** Enter the number of items to include in this shipment. The number must be greater than zero and less than or equal to the number of items in stock. **in the Input message box. Point to the Error Alert tab.**

The Input Message sheet displays (Figure 8-12).

FIGURE 8-12

4 **Click the Error Alert tab and then type** Input Error in Shipment **in the Title text box. Type** You must enter a whole number that is between zero and the number of items in stock. **in the Error message text box. Point to the OK button.**

The Error Alert sheet displays (Figure 8-13).

5 **Click the OK button.**

FIGURE 8-13

 Other **Ways**

1. Press ALT+D, L
2. In Voice Command mode, say "Data, Validation"

When the user selects one of the cells in the range B9:D9, Excel displays the input message defined in Figure 8-12 on the previous page. When the user enters a value other than 1 through the amount in stock in cells B9:D9, the error message defined in Figure 8-13 displays.

Excel allows several types of validation to be done in the Validation criteria area shown in Figure 8-11 on the previous page. Table 8-2 shows the various criteria types available in the Validation criteria.

TABLE 8-2 Types of Validation Criteria Allowed	
ALLOW	**MEANING**
Any value	Allows the user to enter anything in the cell. Use if you simply want to display an input message.
Whole number	Allows whole numbers in a specific range. Use the Data box to specify how the validation takes place.
Decimal	Allows decimal numbers in a specific range. Use the Data box to specify how the validation takes place.
List	Specifies a range where a list of valid values can be found.
Date	Allows a range of dates.
Time	Allows a range of times.
Text length	Allows a certain length text string to be input. Use the Data drop-down list to specify how the validation takes place.
Custom	Allows you to specify a formula that will validate the data entered by the user.

The Ignore blank check box should be cleared if you want to require that the user enter data in the cell. By leaving the Ignore blank check box selected, Excel allows the user to select the cell, and then leave the cell with no data being entered.

Using Trial and Error to Solve a Complex Problem

Trial and error refers to the practice of adjusting cells in a worksheet manually to try to find a solution to a problem. In the Weekly Shipment Worksheet, you could adjust cells B9, C9, and D9 until the criteria for volume and weight are met. While many combinations of possible values exist, you could try keeping one or two of the values constant while adjusting the others.

Trial and error is more than just guessing. Because you understand the constraints on the problem and the goals, you use logic to make subsequent trials better than the previous. For example, if you increase the number of keyboards by five and it causes the total weight of the shipment to exceed 600 pounds, you may instead try to increase the number of keyboards by one to see if that keeps the totals within the constraints.

The following steps illustrate using trial and error to solve a problem.

Validation Types

When using the Custom validation type, you can use a formula that evaluates to either true or false. If the value is false, data may not be entered in the cell by the user. Suppose, for example, you have a cell that contains an employee's salary. If the salary is zero, which indicates the employee no longer is with the company, you may want to prohibit the user from entering a percentage in another cell that contains the employee's raise for the year.

Steps **To Use Trial and Error to Attempt to Solve a Complex Problem**

1 **Click cell B9 and type** 60 **as the number of guitars to ship and then press the ENTER key. Point to the Retry button.**

The Input Error in Shipment dialog box displays (Figure 8-14), because 60 is outside the limits of acceptable values for this cell. The Items to Ship ScreenTip displays because cell B9 is selected.

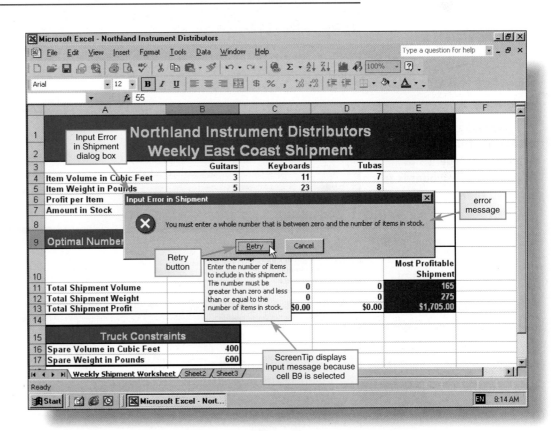

FIGURE 8-14

2 **Click the Retry button. Type** 47 **as the number of guitars to ship in cell B9. Click cell C9 and type** 18 **as the number of keyboards to ship. Click cell D9, type** 18 **as the number of tubas to ship and then press the ENTER key.**

Excel displays the new values and updates the totals in the range B11:E13 as shown in Figure 8-15. The value of 465 in cell E11 indicates that the maximum volume for the shipment of 400 cubic feet (cell B16) has been exceeded.

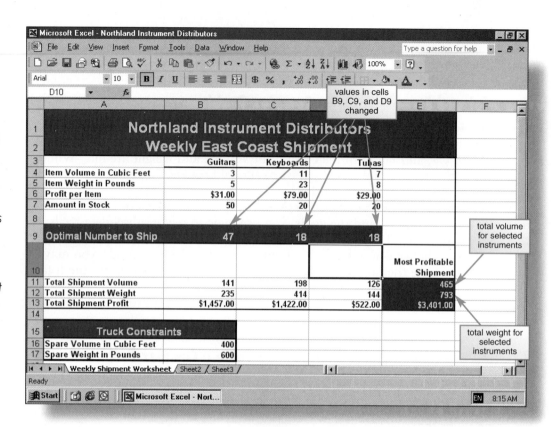

FIGURE 8-15

3 **Click cell B9 and type** 35 **as the number of guitars to ship. Click cell C9, type** 15 **as the number of keyboards to ship, and then press the ENTER key.**

Excel displays the recalculated values for the worksheet (Figure 8-16). The value of 664 in cell E12 indicates that the maximum weight of 600 pounds has been exceeded.

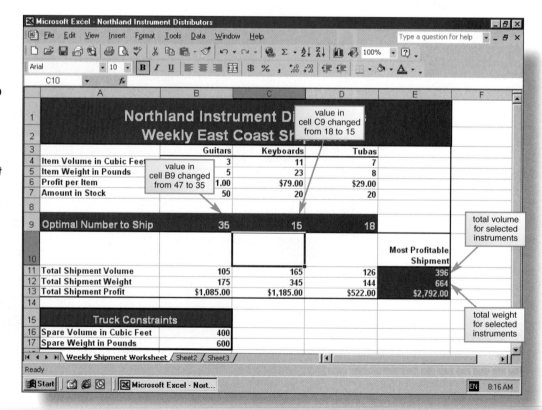

FIGURE 8-16

Trial and error can be used on simple problems in many cases. Trial and error, however, has many limitations. The Weekly Shipment Worksheet has three cells (B9, C9, and D9) that can be adjusted to solve the problem. Because each cell can contain a value between 1 and the amount in stock, many different combinations are possible that you could try, many of which may give the proper volume and weight to the shipment. The biggest drawback to using trial and error in this situation is that you must maximize the profit while meeting the other conditions. It is difficult to determine by casual observation if the profit has been maximized. Rather than using trial and error to test all possible shipment combinations and see which one produces the most profit while meeting the truck constraints, Excel provides other tools to help solve problems where cells can contain a number of values.

Goal Seeking to Solve a Complex Problem

If you know the result you want a formula to produce, you can use **goal seeking** to determine the value of a cell on which a formula depends. In the Weekly Shipment Worksheet, the total volume for the shipment is one result that can be sought by varying the number of one of the instruments. Goal seeking takes trial and error one step further by automatically changing the value of a cell until a single criteria is met in another cell. In this case, suppose you suspect that by varying the number of tubas, you can achieve the goal of 400 cubic feet for the shipment. In doing this, you hope that the other constraints of the problem also are satisfied.

The following steps show how goal seek can be used to alter the number of tubas to keep the total volume at less than or equal to 400 cubic feet.

More About

Goal Seeking

Goal seeking is a methodology in which you know what value you want a formula in a cell to result in but you do not know the value to place in a cell that is involved in the formula. You can goal seek by changing the value in a cell that is used indirectly in the formula.

Steps **To Use the Goal Seek Command to Attempt to Solve a Complex Problem**

1 **Click cell E11, the cell that contains the total volume for the shipment. Click Tools on the menu bar and then point to Goal Seek.**

The Tools menu displays (Figure 8-17).

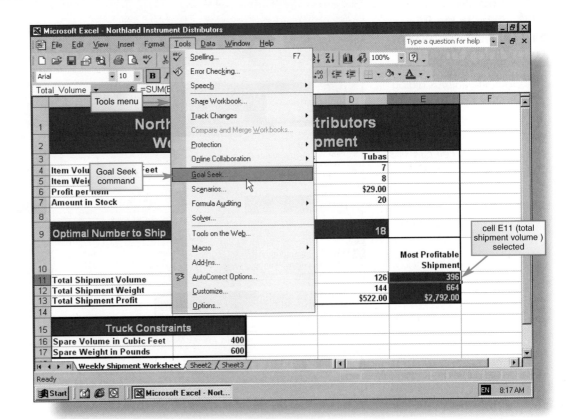

FIGURE 8-17

2 **Click Goal Seek.**

The Goal Seek dialog box displays. The Set cell box is assigned the cell reference of the active cell in the worksheet (cell E11) automatically.

3 **Click the To value text box. Type** 400 **and then click the By changing cell box. Click cell D9 on the worksheet. Point to the OK button.**

The Goal Seek dialog box displays as shown in Figure 8-18. A marquee displays around cell D9.

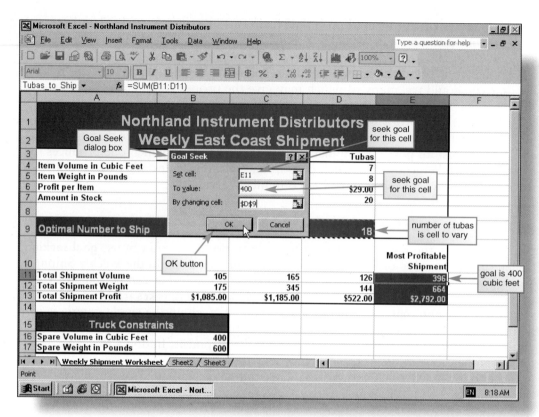

FIGURE 8-18

4 **Click the OK button. Point to the OK button in the Goal Seek Status dialog box.**

The Goal Seek Status dialog box displays as shown in Figure 8-19. Excel changes the number in cell D9 to 19, and the value in cell E11 is updated to 400. The dialog box indicates that Excel found a solution and shows that the target value has been met.

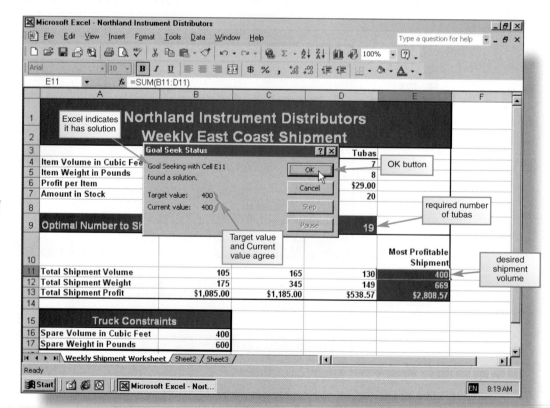

FIGURE 8-19

5 **Click the OK button. Click cell E17 to deselect cell E11.**

The Goal Seek Status dialog box closes, and Excel displays the updated worksheet (Figure 8-20).

	A	B	C	D	E	F
1		Northland Instrument Distributors				
2		Weekly East Coast Shipment				
3		Guitars	Keyboards	Tubas		
4	Item Volume in Cubic Feet	3	11	7		
5	Item Weight in Pounds	5	23	8		
6	Profit per Item	$31.00	$79.00	$29.00		
7	Amount in Stock	50	20	20		
8						
9	Optimal Number to Ship	35	15	19		
10					Most Profitable Shipment	
11	Total Shipment Volume	105	165	130	400	
12	Total Shipment Weight	175	345	149	669	
13	Total Shipment Profit	$1,085.00	$1,185.00	$538.57	$2,808.57	
14						
15	Truck Constraints					

number of instruments are within acceptable range

shipment volume meets requirement

total profit

shipment weight does not meet requirement

FIGURE 8-20

Other Ways

1. Press ALT+T, G
2. In Voice Command mode, say "Tools, Goal Seek"

Goal seeking assumes you can change the value of only one cell referenced directly or indirectly. In this example, to change the total volume in the shipment to 400 cubic feet, the number of tubas must change to 19. This assumes that the numbers of other instruments shipped do not change.

The value of 19 in cell D9 is actually a decimal value, but is formatted as a whole number. Goal Seeking disallows placing a whole number constraint on a changing cell. This is yet another reason that Goal Seeking may not be the best way to solve this particular problem.

As you learned previously, you do not have to reference directly the cell to vary in the formula or function. The total volume is calculated as a sum of the cells in the range B11:D11. The formula does not include a direct reference to the number of tubas in cell D9. Because the total volume of tubas is dependent on the number of tubas shipped, however, Excel is able to goal seek on the total volume of the shipment by varying the number of tubas.

The total volume for the shipment (cell E11) and the total weight for the shipment (cell E12) may satisfy the requirements of the trucking company. Still, you have no way of knowing whether the constraint of maximizing profit (cell E13) has been achieved. Your manager requires that total profit be maximized while satisfying the weight and volume limitations of the trucking company. Surely, other combinations of the three instruments satisfy the shipping requirements and produce total profit that is maximized.

Using Solver to Solve Complex Problems

Solver allows you to solve complex problems where a number of variables can be changed in a worksheet in order meet a goal in a particular cell. As just stated, goal seeking allows you to change only one cell, and trial and error requires too much uncertainty and time to solve complex problems adequately.

Solver uses a technique called linear programming to solve problems. **Linear programming** is a complex mathematical process used to solve problems that include

More About

Linear Programming

For more information about linear programming, visit the Excel 2002 More About Web page (scsite.com/ex2002/more.htm) and then click Linear Programming.

multiple variables and the minimizing or maximizing of result values. Solver essentially tries as many possible combinations of solutions as it can. On each attempt to solve the problem, Solver checks to see if it has found a solution.

Figure 8-21a shows the results of using Solver on the Weekly Shipment Worksheet. Cells B9, C9, and D9 are called the changing cells. **Changing cells** are those cells that will be modified by Solver to solve the problem. The total profit in cell E13 serves as the **target cell**, which means that Solver will attempt to meet some criteria (maximize profit) in this cell by varying the changing cells. **Constraints** are the requirements that have been placed on certain values in the problem. For example, the total volume of the shipment must not exceed 400 cubic feet (cell B16), and the total weight of the shipment must not exceed 600 pounds (cell B17).

Figure 8-21b shows a Solver Answer Report. An **Answer Report** is

(a) Result of Using Solver

(b) Solver Answer Report

FIGURE 8-21

a worksheet that displays the results of a Solver calculation in a concise format. The report satisfies the requirement to document the results of the shipment analysis.

Using Solver to Find the Optimal Combination of Instruments

The Tools menu contains the **Solver command**, which starts Solver. If the Solver command does not display on the Tools menu, then you must use the Add-Ins command on the Tools menu to add it. The cell that is the target for Solver is the total profit cell, E13. The goal is to maximize the value in that cell. The cells that can be changed by Solver to accomplish this goal are cells B9, C9, and D9, which contain the number of each instrument type. The constraints are summarized in Table 8-3.

The following steps show how to use Solver to solve the Weekly Shipment Worksheet within the given constraints.

TABLE 8-3	Additional Constraints for Solver	
CELL	OPERATOR	CONSTRAINT
B9	<=	Value of cell B7
B9	>=	1
B9	int	
C9	<=	Value of cell C7
C9	>=	1
C9	int	
D9	<=	Value of cell D7
D9	>=	1
D9	int	
E11	<=	Value of cell B16
E12	<=	Value of cell B17

Steps **To Use Solver to Find the Optimal Combination**

1 **Click Tools on the menu bar and then point to Solver.**

The Tools menu displays (Figure 8-22).

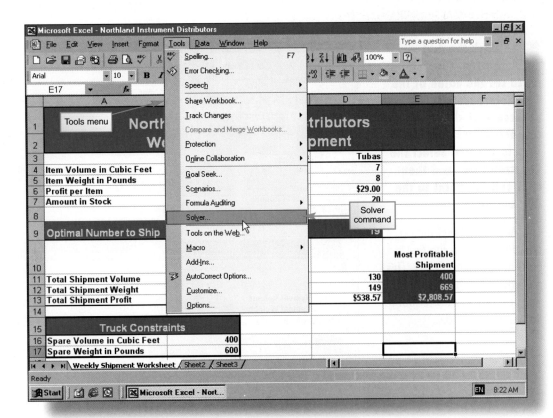

FIGURE 8-22

2 **Click Solver.
When the Solver
Parameters dialog box
displays, click cell E13 to
set the target cell. Click
the By Changing Cells
box and select the range
B9:D9. Point to the Add
button.**

Excel displays the *Solver
Parameters dialog box* as
shown in Figure 8-23. The
Set Target Cell box displays
cell E13.

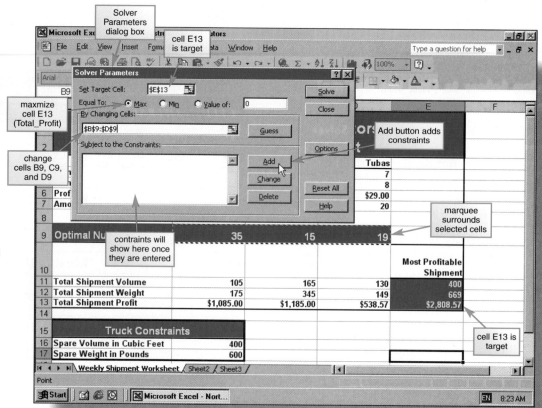

FIGURE 8-23

3 **Click the Add
button. Click cell
B9 to set the value of the
Cell Reference box. If
necessary, click the middle
box arrow and then select
<= in the list. Select the
Constraint box and then
click cell B7. Point to the
Add button.**

The *Add Constraint dialog
box* displays with the first
constraint (Figure 8-24). This
constraint means that cell B9
must be less than or equal to
the value in cell B7.

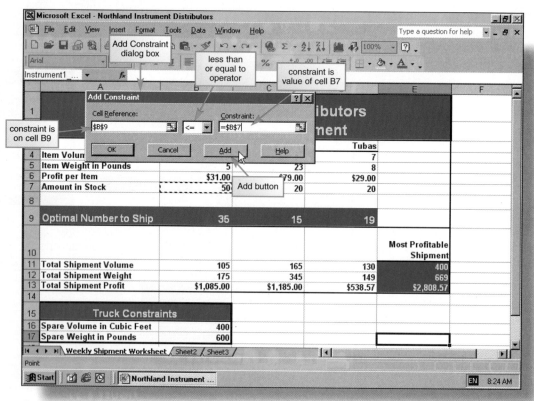

FIGURE 8-24

4 **Click the Add button. Click cell B9 to set the value of the Cell Reference box. Click the middle box arrow and then select >= in the list. Type 1 in the Constraint box and then point to the Add button.**

The values for the second constraint display (Figure 8-25). This constraint means that cell B9 must be greater than or equal to 1.

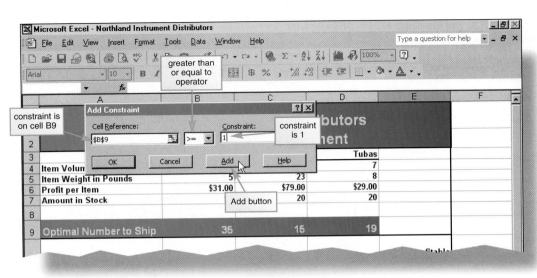

FIGURE 8-25

5 **Click the Add button. Click cell B9 to set the value of the Cell Reference box. Click the middle box arrow and then select int in the list. Point to the Add button.**

The values for the third constraint display (Figure 8-26). This constraint means that cell B9 must be assigned an integer.

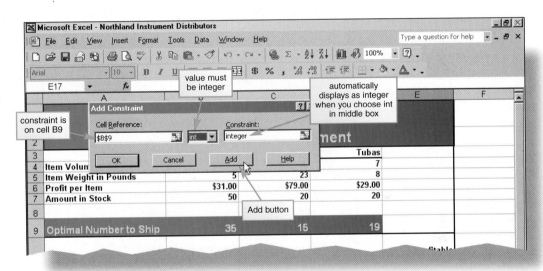

FIGURE 8-26

6 **Click the Add button. Enter the remaining constraints shown in Table 8-3 on page E 8.25 beginning with the constraints for cell C9. When finished with the final constraint, click the OK button in the Add Constraint dialog box. When the Solver Parameters dialog box redisplays, point to the Options button.**

Excel displays all of the constraints in the Subject to the Constraints list (Figure 8-27).

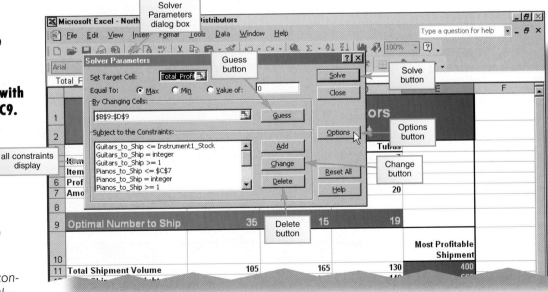

FIGURE 8-27

7 **Click the Options button. When the Solver Options dialog box displays, click Assume Linear Model. Point to the OK button.**

The Solver Options dialog box displays (Figure 8-28).

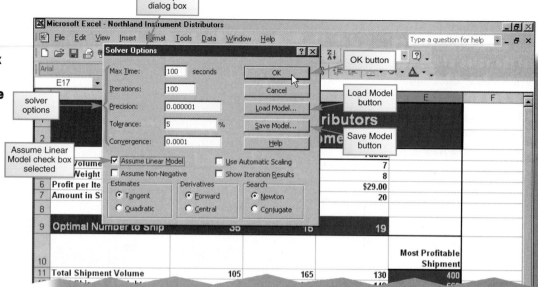

FIGURE 8-28

8 **Click the OK button. When the Solver Parameters dialog box redisplays, click the Solve button.**

The Solver Results dialog box displays. Excel indicates that it has found a solution to the problem as shown in Figure 8-29.

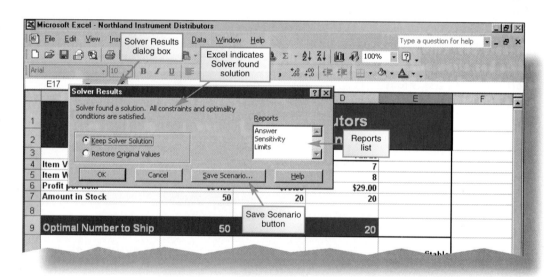

FIGURE 8-29

9 **Select Answer in the Reports list and then point to the OK button.**

The Solver Results dialog box displays as shown in Figure 8-30.

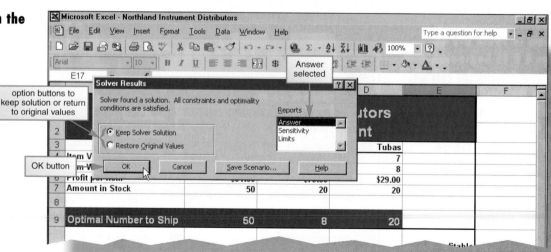

FIGURE 8-30

10 Click the OK button.

Excel displays the values found by Solver and recalculates the totals (Figure 8-31). All of the constraints of the problem have been satisfied.

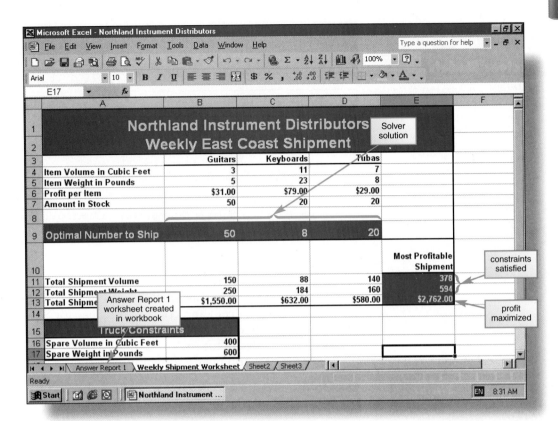

FIGURE 8-31

Other Ways

1. Press ALT+T, V
2. In Voice Command mode, say "Tools, Solver"

Figure 8-31 shows that all of the constraints in the problem have been satisfied. The profit is $2,762.00 for the shipment, which is the only solution thus far that both meets the constraints and maximizes profit.

When adding constraints, as shown in Figure 8-24 on page E 8.26, Solver allows you to enter a cell reference followed by an operator. If the operator is <=, >= or =, you enter the constraint value in the **Constraint cell box**. The constraint can be a value or a cell reference. The other valid operators are **int**, for an integer value, or **bin**, for cells that contain only one of two values, such as yes/no or true/false.

Rather than selecting the range B9:D9 as the changing cells in Step 2 clicking the **Guess button** in the Solver Parameters dialog box (Figure 8-27 on page E 8.27) would have Solver try to determine which cells affect the target cell. The button works much the same way as the Trace Precedents button does on the Formula Auditing toolbar. Solver searches the formula in the target cell to determine which cells are precedents of the target cell and then adds these cells to the **By Changing Cells box** for you. The Guess button is not always accurate, however, which then would require a change to the cells selected by Solver.

The **Change button** and **Delete button** in the Solver Parameters dialog box in Figure 8-27 allow you to edit the constraints that display in the Subject to the Constraints list.

The Solver Options dialog box in Figure 8-28 contains several technical parameters that allow you to configure the inner workings of Solver. Many of the other parameters are beyond the scope of this discussion. Usually, you already have the information for a problem that lets you determine which parameters you need to vary. Table 8-4 on the next page shows the meaning of some of the parameters that you may use from time to time.

More About

Solver Parameters

Sometimes Solver will give you a message telling you that the target cell values do not converge. This means that Solver can meet all of the constraints, but the target value, such as the Total Profit in cell E13 in Figure 8-31, can be increased or decreased indefinitely. Usually, this means that you have not specified enough constraints.

Solver Models

A model is a collection of the data in the target cell, changing cells, and constraints. When you save a model, Excel does not save the solution itself. The solution can be saved separately by using the Save Scenario option in the Solver Results dialog box shown in Figure 8-29 on page E 8.28. When saving a model, the data is saved in an area you select in a worksheet. You should note carefully where you save models, because Excel does not label or mark the model in any way.

Solver Scenarios

When you click the Save Scenario button in the Solver Results dialog box, Solver creates a record of the values of the changing cells that solved the problem. You can name this result and then be able to recall it in the future. It is important to note that the target cell value is not changed, just the changing cells' values.

Other Solver Reports

The Sensitivity Report shows how sensitive the Solver solution is to changes in the constraints and the target cell. The Limits Report shows the upper and lower values that the changing cells can have and still solve the problem given the constraints. Both of these reports are generated as separate worksheets in the current workbook, the same way the Answer Report is.

TABLE 8-4 Commonly Used Solver Parameters in the Solver Options Dialog Box

PARAMETER	MEANING
Max Time	The total time that Solver should spend trying different solutions expressed in seconds.
Iterations	The number of different combinations of possible answer values that Solver should try.
Tolerance	Instructs Solver how close it must come to the target value in order to consider the problem to be solved. For example, if the target value is 100 and the Tolerance is 5%, then 95 is an acceptable answer.
Assume Linear Model	If selected, assume that this problem is linear in nature. That is, the changing values have a proportional effect on the value of the target cell.
Assume Non-Negative	If selected, for all changing cells that do not have constraints on them, Solver should keep these numbers positive.

Excel saves the current Solver parameters automatically. Only the most recent parameters are saved. If you want to use new values in Solver and want to save the target cell, changing cell, and constraint values for Solver, the **Load Model button** and **Save Model button** in the Solver Options dialog box allow you to save the values and then reuse them in the future.

The **Save Scenario button** shown in Figure 8-29 on page E 8.28 allows you to save the results of Solver in a separate area in your workbook. Scenarios are discussed in detail later in this project.

When using Solver, two other issues must be kept in mind. First, some problems do not have solutions. The constraints may be constructed in such a way that an answer cannot be found that satisfies all of the constraints. Second, sometimes multiple answers solve the same problem. Solver does not indicate when this is the case, and you will have to use your own judgment to determine if this is the case. As long as you are confident that you have given Solver all of the constraints for a problem, however, all answers should be equally valid.

Viewing a Solver Answer Report

The **Solver Answer Report** summarizes the problem that you have presented to Solver. It shows the original and final values of the target cell along with the original and final values of the cells that Solver adjusted to find the answer. Additionally, it lists all of the constraints that you imposed on Solver.

The Answer Report documents that a particular problem has been solved correctly. Because it lists all of the relevant information in a concise format, you use the Answer Report to make certain that you have entered all of the constraints and allowed Solver to vary all the cells necessary to solve the problem. You also can use the report to reconstruct the Solver model in the future.

Perform the following steps to view the Solver Answer Report.

Steps **To View the Answer Report**

1 **Click the Answer Report 1 tab at the bottom of the window.**

The Solver Answer Report displays (Figure 8-32).

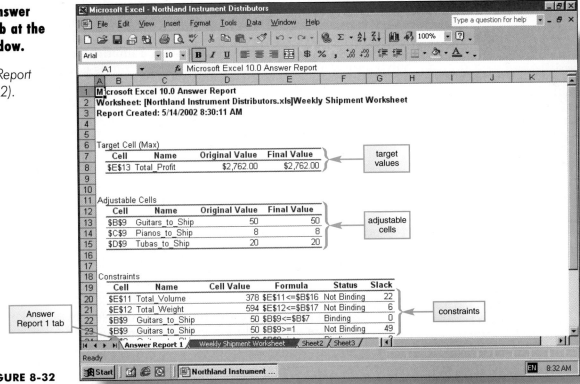

FIGURE 8-32

2 **Double click the Answer Report 1 tab and type** Optimal Shipment Answer Report1 **as the worksheet name. Select cell A1. Right click the Optimal Shipment Answer Report1 tab and then click Tab Color on the shortcut menu. Select the color red in column 1, row 3 on the Color palette and then click the OK button. Drag the tab to the right of the Weekly Shipment Worksheet tab. Use the down scroll arrow to scroll down to view the remaining cells of the Answer Report.**

The tab shows the new worksheet name, and the remainder of the Answer Report displays (Figure 8-33).

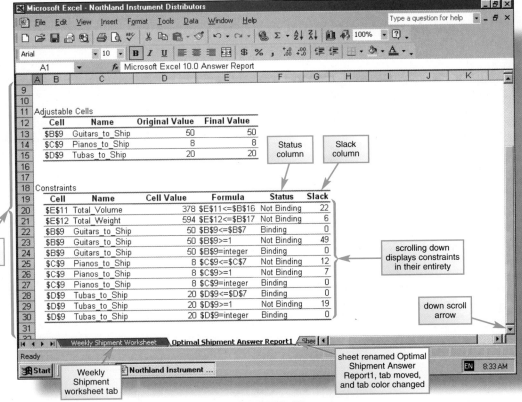

FIGURE 8-33

More About

Answer Reports

The slack value in the Answer Report tells you where you may have some flexibility in the answer that Solver has found. The less slack that a changing cell has, the less you can change it and still meet the constraints of the problem. Slack tells you where you still have options in the Solver answer.

More About

File Protection

Once you have protected your workbook with a password, it is important to write the password down or memorize it for future reference. Once you have saved the file with a password, it always will be a password-protected file; no way exists to bypass the requirement for a password.

Figure 8-33 on the previous page displays additional information about the constraints that you placed on the problem and how the constraints were used to solve the problem. Column F, the **Status column**, indicates whether the constraint was binding or not. A constraint that is **binding** is one that limited the final solution in some way. For example, the total number of guitars to ship is binding because the solution maximizes the amount of guitars that are in stock. No more guitars could possibly be shipped. A constraint that is **not binding** is one that was not a limiting factor in the solution that Solver provided. The total weight of the shipment is not binding because the solution could have had more weight if necessary to meet the other constraints.

Column G, the **Slack column**, shows the difference between the value in the cell in that row and the limit of the constraint. Cell G20 shows that the slack for the Total_Volume is 22. This means that the solution contains 22 fewer cubic feet of items than the maximum allowed in the constraints. Cells that are binding have zero slack.

Saving the Workbook with Passwords

Excel allows you to protect your data at the worksheet level, workbook level, and file level. At the worksheet level, you protect cells. At the workbook level, you protect the Excel window. Both of these levels of protection are available through the Protection command on the Tools menu as described in Project 7. The highest level of protection is file protection. **File protection** lets you assign a password to a workbook for users who are allowed to view the workbook and a separate password for users who are permitted to modify the workbook. Recall that a password is case-sensitive and can be up to 15 characters long.

File protection is performed when Excel saves a workbook. Even though you are the workbook creator, you will be prompted for the passwords when you open the workbook later. The following steps save the workbook with passwords.

Steps **To Save the Workbook with Passwords**

1. **Click the Weekly Shipment Worksheet tab at the bottom of the window. Click File on the menu bar and then click Save As. Type** Northland Instrument Distributors2 **in the File name box and, if necessary, click 3½ Floppy (A:) in the Look in list. Click the Tools button in the Save As dialog box and then point to General Options.**

The Save As dialog box and Tools menu display (Figure 8-34).

FIGURE 8-34

2 **Click General Options. Type** maxprofit **in the Password to open text box. Type** maxprofit **in the Password to modify text box. Point to the OK button.**

The *Save Options dialog box* displays. Excel displays asterisks in place of the password, *maxprofit*, in both instances so that no one is able to see the password you typed (Figure 8-35).

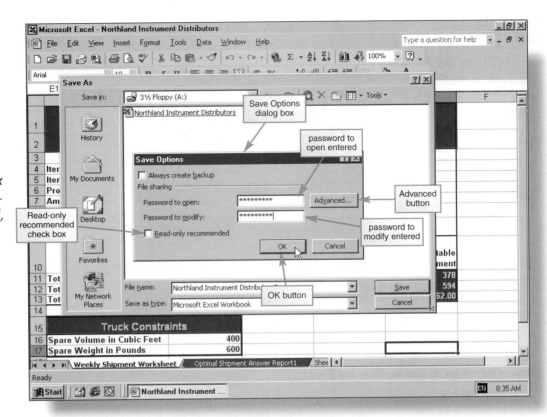

FIGURE 8-35

3 **Click the OK button and type** maxprofit **in the Reenter password to proceed text box. Point to the OK button.**

The *Confirm Password dialog box* displays. Again, Excel displays asterisks in place of the password, *maxprofit* (Figure 8-36).

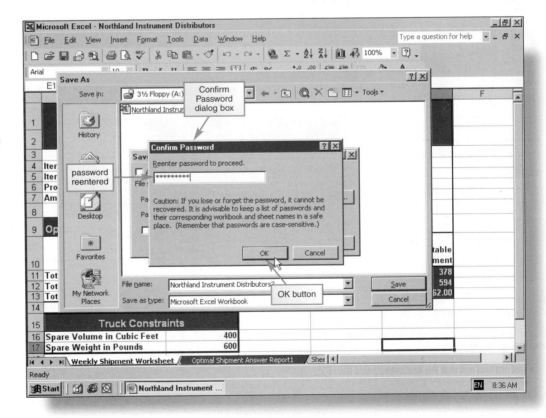

FIGURE 8-36

4 **Click the OK button and type** maxprofit **in the Reenter password to modify text box. Point to the OK button.**

The Confirm Password dialog box displays for the password to modify the workbook (Figure 8-37).

FIGURE 8-37

5 **Click the OK button and then point to the Save button in the Save As dialog box (Figure 8-38).**

6 **Click the Save button.**

Excel saves the password protected file on the floppy disk in drive A.

FIGURE 8-38

1. With Save As dialog box open, press ALT+L, G
2. With Save As dialog box open, in Voice Command mode, say "Tools, General Options"

More About

Read-Only

You can save a file and recommend read-only access to others who open the worksheet. This is not a guarantee that the user will follow the recommendation. To ensure that the worksheet truly is read-only, use a file password and keep it to yourself.

The workbook now is protected with a password, and when a user opens the workbook, Excel will prompt for a password to view the workbook. If the user enters the correct password, Excel prompts for the password to modify the workbook. At this point, the user may choose to open the workbook as read-only, meaning that the user can only view the contents of the workbook and not modify the workbook. The **Read-only recommended check box** shown in Figure 8-35 on the previous page allows you to notify users who open your workbook that it is best to open the workbook as read-only. The **Advanced button** shown in Figure 8-35 allows you to select a method for encrypting the file. **Encryption** allows you to store the file in a secure manner so that malicious users cannot view or alter the contents of your file without a great deal of effort.

Using Scenario Manager to Analyze Data

Excel's **Scenario Manager** allows you to record and save different sets of what-if assumptions (data values) called scenarios. For example, each different shipment being analyzed (guitars or accordions) can be considered a scenario. A shipment containing guitars and meeting the other constraints is the first scenario. The second scenario consists of a shipment that contains accordions, which has different volume, weight, profit, and amount in stock. Each set of values in these examples represents a what-if assumption. The primary uses of Scenario Manager are to:

1. Create different scenarios with multiple sets of changing cells
2. Build summary worksheets that contain the different scenarios
3. View the results of each scenario on your worksheet

The remainder of this project shows how to use Scenario Manager for each of the three uses listed above. Once you create the scenarios, you can instruct Excel to build the summary worksheets, including a Scenario Summary and a Scenario PivotTable.

Saving the Current Data as a Scenario

The current data on the worksheet consists of the Guitars scenario and contains the values that correctly solve one of the problems presented. These values can be saved as a scenario that can be accessed later or compared side by side with other scenarios. The following steps create the Accordion scenario using the **Scenarios command** on the Tools menu.

More About

Scenario Manager

Worksheets are used primarily for what-if analysis. You enter values into cells, and instantaneously the results change in the dependent cells. As you continue to change values in the key cells, you lose the previous results. If you want to go back, you have to reenter the data. Scenario Manager allows you to store the different sets of values (called scenarios) so you can redisplay them easily with a few clicks of the mouse. Each scenario can have up to 32 sets of changing cells.

Steps **To Save the Current Data as a Scenario**

1 **Click Tools on the menu bar and point to Scenarios.**

The Tools menu displays (Figure 8-39).

FIGURE 8-39

2 **Click Scenarios.
When the Scenario
Manager dialog box
displays, point to the
Add button.**

The *Scenario Manager dialog
box* displays indicating that
no scenarios are defined
(Figure 8-40). It also instructs
you to choose Add to add
scenarios.

FIGURE 8-40

3 **Click the Add
button. When the
Add Scenario dialog box
displays, type** Guitars **in
the Scenario name text box.
Point to the Collapse
Dialog button.**

The *Add Scenario dialog box*
displays (Figure 8-41).

FIGURE 8-41

4 **Click the Collapse Dialog button. When the Add Scenario - Changing cells dialog box displays, click cell B3, hold down the CTRL key, and then click cells B4, B5, B6, B7, B9, C9, D9, B16, and B17. Release the CTRL key. Point to the Collapse Dialog button in the Add Scenario - Changing cells dialog box.**

A marquee displays around the selected cells. Excel assigns the cells to the Changing cells text box (Figure 8-42).

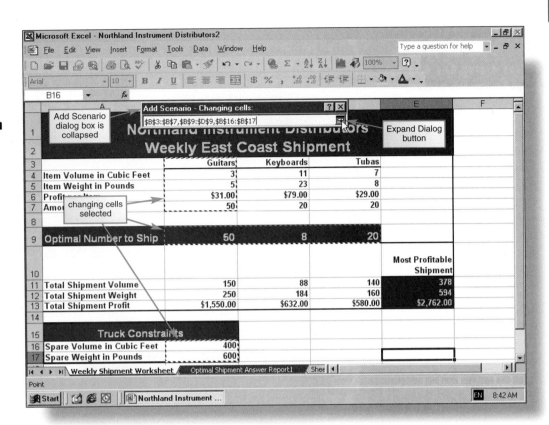

FIGURE 8-42

5 **Click the Expand Dialog button. When the Edit Scenario dialog box displays, point to the OK button.**

The Add Scenario dialog box changes to the Edit Scenario dialog box (Figure 8-43).

FIGURE 8-43

6 **Click the OK button. When the Scenario Values dialog box displays, point to the OK button.**

The Scenario Values dialog box displays. The cell names selected display in a numbered list with their current values (Figure 8-44). Because names were assigned to these cells when the worksheet was created, the cell names, rather than cell references, display in the numbered list.

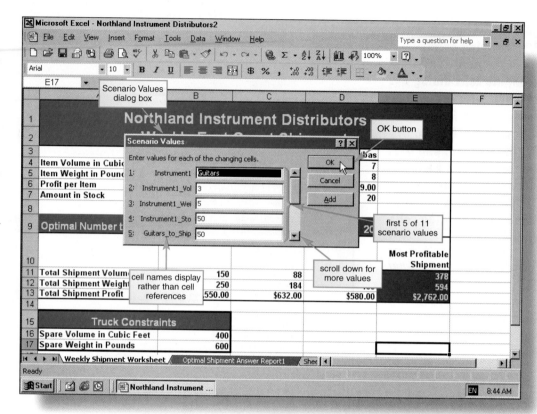

FIGURE 8-44

7 **Click the OK button. When the Scenario Manager dialog box displays, point to the Close button.**

The Guitar scenario displays in the Scenarios list (Figure 8-45). Excel displays the names of the changing cells in the Changing cells text box.

8 **Click the Close button on the Scenario Manager dialog box.**

FIGURE 8-45

Other Ways

1. Press ALT+T, E
2. In Voice Command mode, say "Tools, Scenarios"

Once the scenario has been saved, you can recall it at any time using Scenario Manager. In Figure 8-44, the values of the cells in the Scenario Values dialog box are defaulted to the current changing cells in the worksheet. By changing the text boxes next to the cell names, you can save different values in the scenario from what is shown in the worksheet.

The next step is to change the values on the worksheet to show the data when using accordions as a subsitute for guitars.

Creating a New Scenario

Because the Guitar scenario is saved, you can enter the data for the Accordion scenario directly in the worksheet and then use Solver to solve the Accordion scenario (Figure 8-46a) in the same way that you solved the Guitar scenario. The same constraints apply for both scenarios, so Solver does not require you to reenter all of the constraints. The Answer Report (Figure 8-46b) meets the requirement that you create supporting documentation for your answer. After solving the Accordion scenario, you should save the scenario in the same manner that you saved the Guitar scenario.

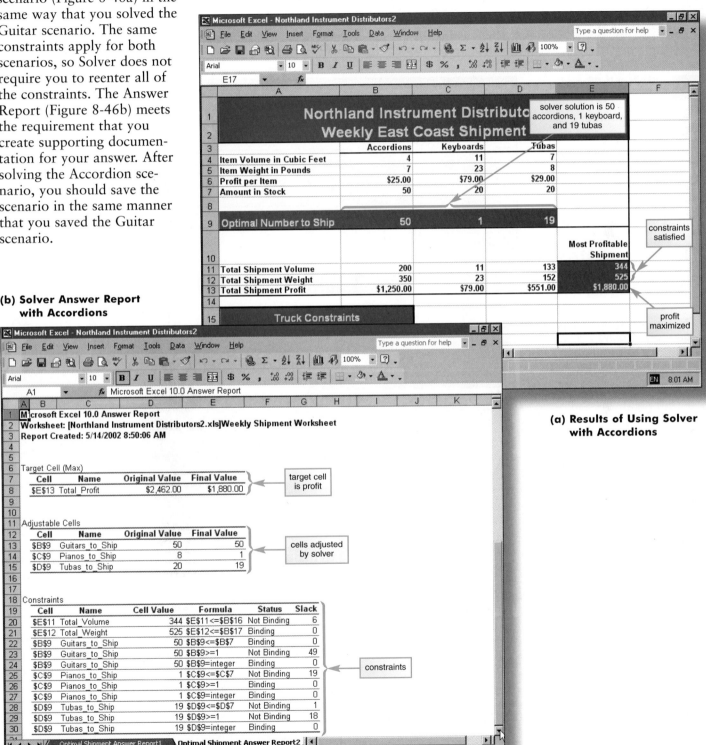

(b) Solver Answer Report with Accordions

(a) Results of Using Solver with Accordions

FIGURE 8-46

The relevant information for the Accordion scenario (Figure 8-46a on the previous page) is that accordions take four cubic feet, weigh seven pounds, contribute $25.00 to profit per item, and 50 are in stock. The truck that is available in the following week for this shipment has 350 cubic feet free and 525 pounds of capacity available. These values must be entered into the appropriate cells before you can use Solver.

Perform the following step to add the data for a new scenario.

Steps **To Add the Data for a New Scenario**

1 **Click cell B3 and type** Accordions **as the column heading. Click cell B4 and type** 4 **as the item volume. Click cell B5 and type** 7 **as the item weight. Click cell B6 and type** 25 **as the profit per item. Click cell B16 and type** 350 **as the spare volume. Click cell B17, type** 525 **as the spare weight, and then click cell E17.**

The Weekly Shipment Worksheet displays with accordions replacing guitars (Figure 8-47).

FIGURE 8-47

Next, Solver must be used to find the optimal combination of instruments that satisfies the constraints and maximizes profit for Northland Instrument Distributors.

Using Solver to Find a New Solution

As was true of the Guitar scenario, the Accordion scenario must be solved before saving it as a scenario. Figure 8-47 shows that the total volume and total weight of the current solution does not satisfy the requirements of the current truck under consideration as shown in cells B16 and B17. It is unknown whether a possible solution to the problem even exists. Solver must be used to make this determination, as shown in the following steps.

Steps To Use Solver to Find a New Solution

1 Click Tools on the menu bar and then point to Solver (Figure 8-48).

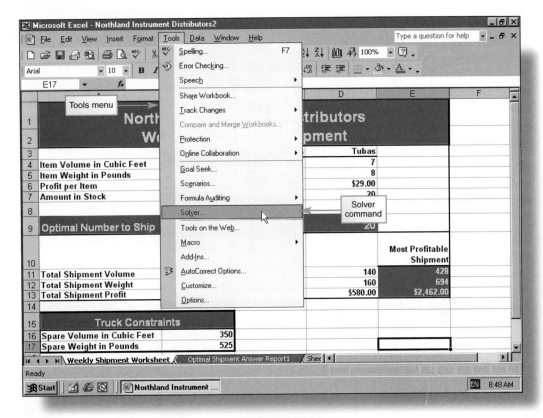

FIGURE 8-48

2 Click Solver. When the Solver Parameters dialog box displays, point to the Solve button.

The Solver Parameters dialog box displays with the previous target cell and constraints (Figure 8-49). Because the constraints remain the same for accordions as they were for guitars, no additional entries are required in the Solver Parameters dialog box.

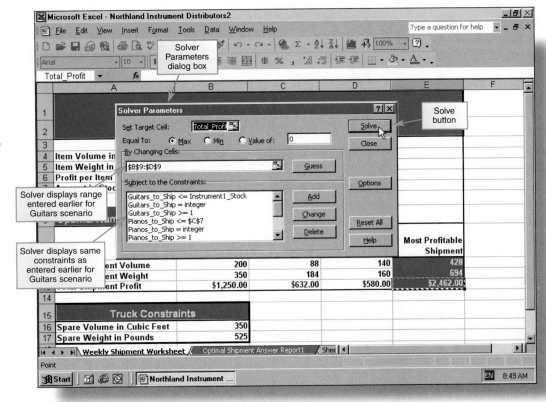

FIGURE 8-49

3 Click the Solve button. When the Solver Results dialog box displays, click Answer in the Reports list. Point to the OK button.

The Solver Results dialog box displays indicating that Solver found a solution to the problem (Figure 8-50).

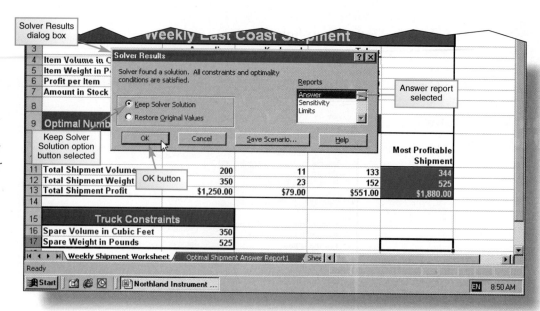

FIGURE 8-50

4 Click the OK button.

The solution displays in the worksheet. The constraints have been satisfied (Figure 8-51).

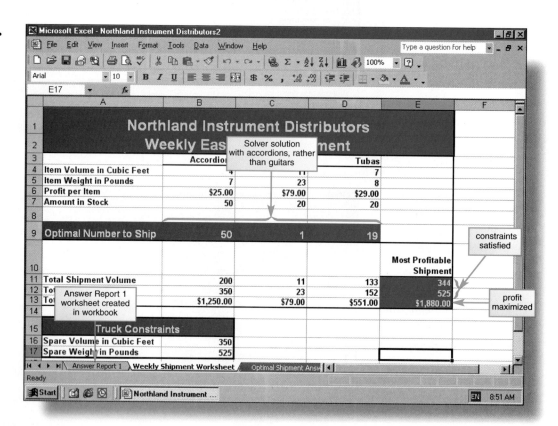

FIGURE 8-51

As shown in Figure 8-51, Solver found a solution that satisfies all of the constraints and maximizes profit. With guitars, the shipment breakdown was 50 guitars, 8 keyboards, and 20 tubas (Figure 8-31 on page E 8.29). With accordions, the shipment breakdown is 50 accordians, 1 keyboard, and 19 tubas (Figure 8-51). The profit for guitars was $2,762.00. The profit for the accordions is $1,880.00.

The next step is to view the Answer Report for the accordion solution that will be presented to the trucking company.

Steps **To View the Second Answer Report**

1 Click the Answer Report 1 tab at the bottom of the window.

The accordion Solver Answer Report displays (Figure 8-52).

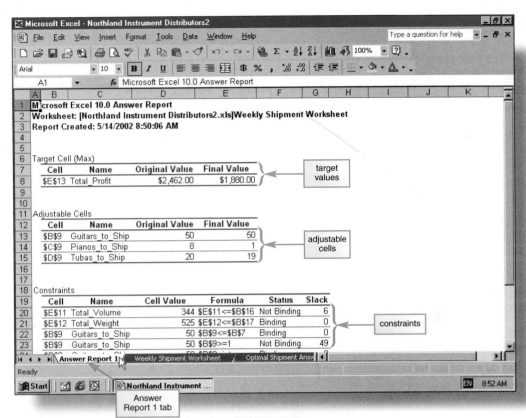

FIGURE 8-52

2 Double click the Answer Report 1 tab and type Optimal Shipment Answer Report2 as the worksheet name. Select cell A1. Right-click the Optimal Shipment Answer Report2 tab and then click Tab Color on the shortcut menu. Select the color yellow in column 3, row 4 on the Color palette and then click the OK button. Drag the tab to the right of the Optimal Shipment Answer Report1 tab. Use the down scroll arrow to scroll down to view the remaining cells of the accordion answer report.

The worksheet is renamed, and the remainder of the answer report for the accordion scenario displays (Figure 8-53).

FIGURE 8-53

Quick Reference

For a table that lists how to complete the tasks covered in this book using the mouse, menu, shortcut menu, and keyboard, see the Excel Quick Reference Summary at the back of this book or visit the Office XP Web page (www.scsite.com/offxp/qr.htm), and then click Microsoft Excel 2002.

The Answer Report indicates that the shipment has six fewer cubic feet of volume than the maximum allowed, and exactly the amount of weight allowed. The shipment is clearly very close to filling the available truck space. Furthermore, the profit on the accordion shipment is far less than that of the guitar shipment.

The next step is to save the accordion solution as a scenario so that it can be referenced in the future.

Saving the Second Solver Solution as a Scenario

The power of Scenario Manager becomes evident when you begin adding scenarios to your worksheet. Multiple scenarios can be compared side by side. Using multiple scenarios on the same worksheet also saves time by recycling the work that you did to create the initial worksheet.

Perform the following steps to save the second Solver solution as a scenario.

Steps ## To Save the Second Solver Solution as a Scenario

1 Click the Weekly Shipment Worksheet tab at the bottom of the window. Click Tools on the menu bar and then point to Scenarios (Figure 8-54).

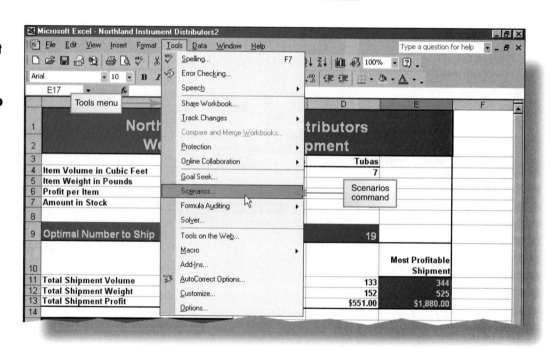

FIGURE 8-54

2 Click Scenarios. When the Scenario Manager dialog box displays, point to the Add button (Figure 8-55).

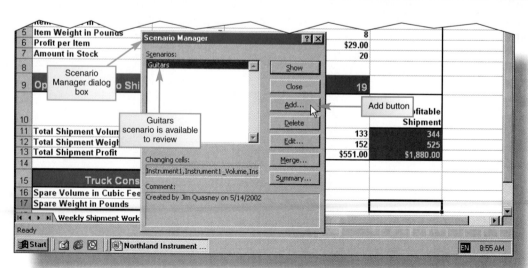

FIGURE 8-55

3 **Click the Add button. Type** Accordions **in the Scenario name text box and then point to the OK button.**

The Add Scenario dialog box displays. The Changing cells box defaults to the previous values used in the Guitars scenario (Figure 8-56).

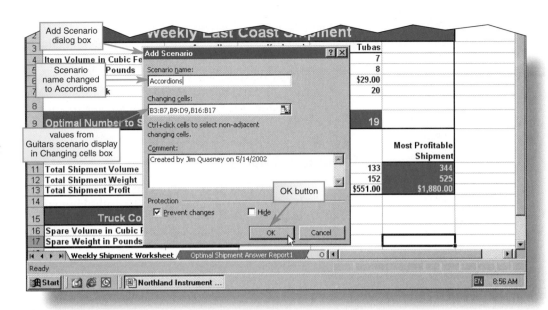

FIGURE 8-56

4 **Click the OK button. When the Scenario Values dialog box displays, point to the OK button.**

The Scenario Values dialog box displays with the values from the worksheet (Figure 8-57).

FIGURE 8-57

5 **Click the OK button. When the Scenario Manager dialog box displays, point to the Close button.**

Accordions displays along with Guitars in the Scenarios list (Figure 8-58). Each name represents a different scenario.

FIGURE 8-58

More About

Showing Scenarios

You can add a list of scenarios to your toolbar by using the Customize command on the Toolbars command in the View menu. Click the Commands tab and select tools. Drag the item named Scenario: with the drop-down arrow up to a toolbar. You then can quickly switch between scenarios on your worksheet.

The Accordion scenario now can be recalled using Scenario Manager. Figure 8-57 on the previous page shows the list of changing cells for the scenario. Instead of entering the data in the worksheet, you simply could enter values here for adding new scenarios. Because Solver is needed to find a solution to the scenario, however, the values were entered on the worksheet first.

The next step is to use Scenario Manager to show the Guitars scenario in the worksheet.

Showing a Scenario

Once a scenario is saved, you use the **Show button** in the Scenario Manager dialog box to display the scenario. The following steps show you how to apply the Guitars scenario created earlier directly to a worksheet.

Steps To Show a Saved Scenario

1 Click Tools on the menu bar and then point to Scenarios (Figure 8-59).

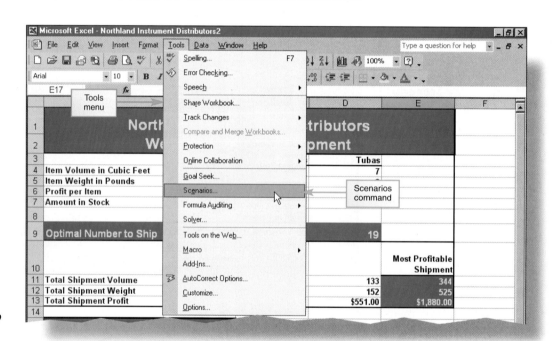

FIGURE 8-59

2 Click Scenarios. When the Scenario Manager dialog box displays, if necessary, select Guitars in the Scenarios list and then point to the Show button (Figure 8-60).

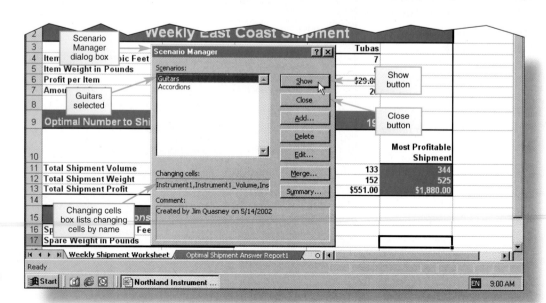

FIGURE 8-60

3 **Click the Show button and then click the Close button.**

Excel displays the data in the worksheet for the Guitars scenario (Figure 8-61).

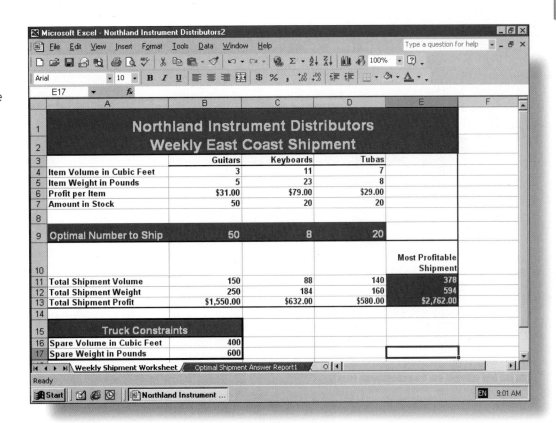

FIGURE 8-61

You can undo the scenario results by clicking the Undo button on the Standard toolbar. If desired, you then can click the Redo button on the Standard toolbar to display the scenario results again. If you had several saved scenarios, you could display each one and then use the Undo and Redo buttons to switch between them.

Scenario Manager is an important what-if tool for organizing assumptions. Using Scenario Manager, you can define different scenarios with up to 32 changing cells per scenario. Once you have entered the scenarios, you can show them one by one, or you can create a Scenario Summary worksheet or a Scenario PivotTable worksheet as described in the next section.

Summarizing Scenarios

This section creates a Scenario Summary worksheet and a Scenario PivotTable worksheet. These concise reports allow you to view and manipulate several what-if situations side by side to assist decision making. The **Scenario Summary worksheet** generated by the Scenario Manager actually is an outlined worksheet (Figure 8-62a on the next page) that you can print and manipulate just like any other worksheet. An **outlined worksheet** is one that contains symbols (buttons) above and to the left, which allows you to collapse and expand rows and columns.

The **PivotTable worksheet** (Figure 8-62b on the next page) generated by the Scenario Manager also is a worksheet that you can print and manipulate like other worksheets. A **PivotTable** is a table that summarizes large amounts of information and can be manipulated to show the data from different points of view. The Scenario PivotTable compares the results of scenarios.

Other Ways

1. Press ALT+T, E, double-click the scenario name
2. In Voice Command mode, say "Tools, Scenario", click the scenario name, say "Show"

More About

Report Manager

Report Manager is an Add-In that allows you to print several scenarios at once. Report Manager is available for download on Microsoft's Web site. Typically, you would need to use the Show command on the Scenario Manager dialog box for each scenario you want to print and then print the worksheet. By using Report Manager, which displays on the View menu, you simply select the scenarios that you want to print; you then can print them all at once.

(a) Scenario Summary Worksheet

(b) Scenario PivotTable Worksheet

FIGURE 8-62

Creating a Scenario Summary Worksheet

The Scenario Summary worksheet in Figure 8-62a displays the total volume, total weight, and total profit for the current worksheet values and the two scenarios. The optimal number of instruments of each type calculated by Solver are shown for shipments that include either guitars or accordions.

Perform the following steps to create a Scenario Summary worksheet.

Steps **To Create a Scenario Summary**

1 **Click Tools on the menu bar and then point to Scenarios (Figure 8-63).**

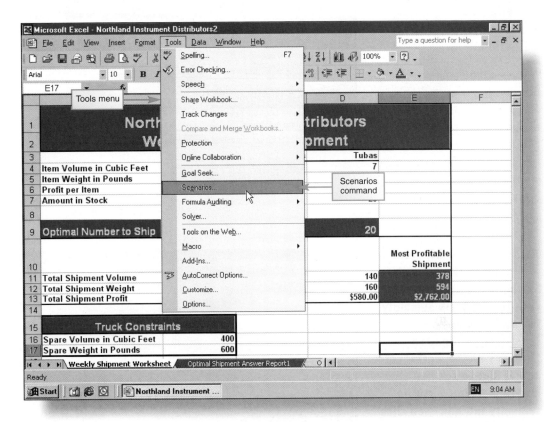

FIGURE 8-63

2 **Click Scenarios. When the Scenario Manager dialog box displays, if necessary, select Guitars, then point to the Summary button.**

The Scenario Manager dialog box displays (Figure 8-64).

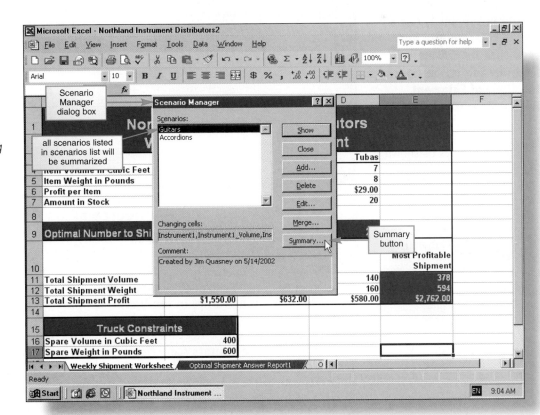

FIGURE 8-64

3 **Click the Summary button. When the Scenario Summary dialog box displays, point to the OK button.**

The Scenario Summary dialog box displays (Figure 8-65). The Scenario summary option button is selected in the Report type area. The dialog box offers the choice of creating a Scenario summary or a Scenario PivotTable report.

FIGURE 8-65

4 **Click the OK button. When the Scenario Summary displays, double-click the Scenario Summary tab and type** Macon Trucking Scenario Summary **as the worksheet name. Right-click the Macon Trucking Scenario summary tab and then click tab color on the shortcut menu. Select the color purple in column 1, row 4 on the color palette and then click the OK button. Drag the tab to the right of the Optimal Shipment Answer Report2 tab.**

The Scenario Summary worksheet displays as shown in Figure 8-66.

FIGURE 8-66

Other **Ways**

1. Press ALT+T, E
2. In Voice Command mode, say "Tools, Scenarios"

Column D in the Scenario Summary worksheet in Figure 8-66 shows the results of the current values in the Weekly Shipment Worksheet, which is the Guitars scenario; columns E and F show the results of the two scenarios. The Scenario Summary worksheet makes it easier to compare the results of the scenarios. For example, in the Guitars scenario, more profit is possible due to the higher profit margin on guitars. Subsequently, Northland Instrument Distributors stands to make a better profit if there is more demand for guitars. Perhaps this indicates how the Northland Instrument Distributors should go about marketing its instruments to its customers.

Working with an Outlined Worksheet

Excel automatically outlines the Scenario Summary worksheet. The outline symbols display above and to the left of the worksheet (Figure 8-66). You click the outline symbols to expand or collapse the worksheet. For example, if you click the **show detail symbol**, Excel displays additional rows or columns that are summarized on the displayed row or column. If you click a **hide detail symbol**, Excel hides any detail rows that extend through the length of the corresponding row level bar or column level bar. You also can expand or collapse a worksheet by clicking the **row level symbol** or **column level symbol** above and to the left of row title 1.

An outline is especially useful when working with large worksheets. To remove an outline, point to Group and Outline on the Data menu and then click Clear Outline on the Group and Outline submenu.

Creating a Scenario PivotTable

Excel also can generate Scenario PivotTables to help analyze and compare the results of multiple scenarios. A **Scenario PivotTable** gives you the ability to summarize the scenario data and then rotate the table's row and column titles to obtain different views of the summarized data. The PivotTable to be created in this project is shown in Figure 8-62b on page E 8.48. The table summarizes the Guitar and Accordion scenarios and displays the result cells for the two scenarios for easy comparison.

PivotTables are powerful data analysis tools because they allow you to view the data in various ways by interchanging or pairing the row and column fields by dragging the buttons located on cells A1, A4, and B3 in Figure 8-62b. The process of rotating the field values around the data fields will be discussed in the next project.

To create the PivotTable shown in Figure 8-62b, perform the following steps.

More About

Outlined Worksheets

You can outline any worksheet by using the Auto Outline command on the Group and Outline submenu. To access outlining features, click Data on the menu bar, point to Group and Outline, and then click Auto Outline on the Group and Outline submenu.

More About

Scenario PivotTables

A Scenario PivotTable is a powerful analysis tool for comparing the results of scenarios when the differences and causes of the differences among scenarios are not completely obvious. You can compare scenarios side by side, perform sorts and filters on the values of the result cells, and rotate rows and columns of the table to gain a different perspective on the results.

Steps **To Create a Scenario PivotTable**

1 **Click the Weekly Shipment Worksheet tab at the bottom of the window. Click Tools on the menu bar and then click Scenarios. When the Scenario Manager dialog box displays, if necessary, select Guitars, then point to the Summary button.**

The Scenario Manager dialog box displays (Figure 8-67).

FIGURE 8-67

2 **Click the Summary button. When the Scenario Summary dialog box displays, click Scenario PivotTable report in the Report type area. Point to the OK button.**

The Scenario Summary dialog box displays as shown in Figure 8-68. The range E11:E13 displays in the Results cells box because these cells were specified the last time this dialog box displayed.

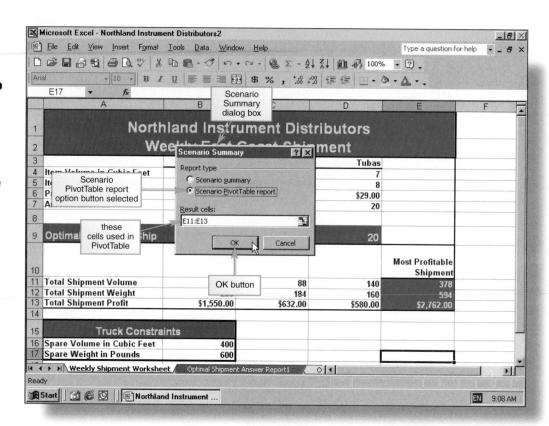

FIGURE 8-68

3 **Click the OK button.**

The Scenario PivotTable worksheet displays with the cell references of the changing values in column A (Figure 8-69). Your worksheet may display differently; you may have to resize the column width of column A if it appears too large. Your worksheet may also have cell names instead of cell references in cells A1 and A4.

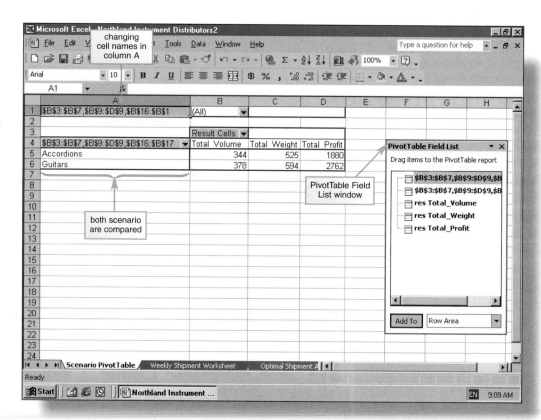

FIGURE 8-69

4 Point to the boundary to the right side of the column A heads and drag to resize the column as shown in Figure 8-70. Double-click the Scenario PivotTable tab and type Macon Scenario PivotTable as the worksheet name. Click cell A8. Right-click the Macon Scenario PivotTable tab and then click Tab Color on the shortcut menu. Select the color green in column 4, row 4 on the Color palette and then click the OK button. Drag the tab to the right of the Macon Trucking Scenario Summary tab.

The Scenario PivotTable displays within the viewable area of the worksheet. The result cells of the two scenarios display in rows 5 and 6, as shown in Figure 8-70.

FIGURE 8-70

5 Click the Save button on the Standard toolbar to save the workbook using the file name, Northland Instrument Distributors2.

Other Ways

1. Press ALT+T, E
2. In Voice Command mode, say "Tools, Scenarios"

Once the PivotTable is created, you can treat it like any other worksheet. Thus, you can print or chart a PivotTable. If you update the data in one of the scenarios, click the **Refresh Data command** on the Data menu. If you show a scenario and merely change values on the scenario worksheet, it is not the same as changing the scenario. If you want to change the data in a scenario, you must use Scenario Manager.

Changing the Properties on a Workbook

Excel allows you to store a variety of information about each workbook. This information collectively is called **workbook properties,** and it is useful when workbooks will be used by many people or if you need to save pertinent data about the purpose of the workbook for future reference.

The Northland Instrument Distributors workbook obviously will be very useful in the future if Macon Trucking or other shipping firms require similar analysis for a shipment. The steps on the next page save relevant information about the Northland Instrument Distributors2 workbook for future reference.

More About

Workbook Properties

Workbook properties can be viewed from Windows Explorer by right-clicking an Excel file and then clicking Properties on the shortcut menu. This makes it easy to determine the contents and purpose of a workbook without opening it. If the user has the View as Web Page option selected in Windows Explorer and the Save preview picture option is selected in the Summary tab, then they can see a preview of the workbook.

Steps **To Change Workbook Properties**

1 **Click the Weekly Shipment Worksheet tab at the bottom of the window. Click File on the menu bar and then point to Properties (Figure 8-71).**

2 **Click Properties. When the Northland Instrument Distributors2 Properties dialog box displays, if necessary, click the Summary tab. Type** Weekly Shipment Worksheet **in the Title text box. Type** Optimal Truck Shipment Calculation **in the Subject text box. Type** Marsha Gresham **in the Manager text box. Type** Shipment planning for East coast shipments for May 2002, week 3. Shipping conditions met for Macon Trucking. **in the Comments text box. Point to the OK button.**

The summary fields display in the Northland Instrument Distributors2 Properties dialog box as shown in Figure 8-72.

3 **Click the OK button.**

4 **Click the Save button on the Standard toolbar to save the workbook using the file name, Northland Instrument Distributors2.**

FIGURE 8-71

FIGURE 8-72

Other **Ways**

1. Press ALT+F, I
2. In Voice Command mode, say "File, Properties"

The **Workbook Properties dialog box** contains other useful information about the workbook. The **General sheet** displays data about the workbook file, including the size of the file, creation date, date modified, and the date the file last was accessed. The **Save preview picture check box** selected on the **Summary sheet** saves an image of the current worksheet that will be visible in the Open dialog box when the file is selected by the user. The **Statistics sheet** displays some of the file data from the General sheet in addition to a record of when the file last was opened and modified.

The **Contents sheet** displays a list of all the worksheets and charts contained in the workbook. This feature allows you to search large workbooks quickly that contain many worksheets and charts when you are looking for a particular worksheet or chart.

The **Custom sheet** allows you to create your own workbook properties. For example, you can add fields such as document number, editor, your telephone number, division, group, owner, or any other field you want to store with the workbook. For each item you define, you can set the data type for the value. Valid data types are Text, Date, Number, and Yes or No.

> **More About**
>
> **Custom Properties**
>
> In addition to using text fields, you can set up custom properties that link to cells in your workbook. For example, you can have a property that contains the value in the total profit cell in the Track Team worksheet.

Quitting Excel

The project is complete. To exit Excel, follow the steps below.

TO QUIT EXCEL

1 Click the Close button on the right side of the title bar.

2 If a Microsoft Excel dialog box displays, click the No button.

CASE PERSPECTIVE SUMMARY

With the two solved scenarios developed in this project, Marsha Gresham is convinced that the company is shipping the best combination of instruments to its customers within the constraints of the shipping method the company has chosen. She also has the confidence that Northland Instrument Distributors is maximizing its profit when making its weekly shipment to the East coast. The worksheet can be used in the future to analyze any potential shipment.

Project Summary

In this project, you learned how to use a number of techniques to approach problem solving, including trial and error, goal seek, and Solver. You learned how to analyze a worksheet using the Formula Auditing toolbar. You learned how to use data validation on cells and inform the user about the validation rules. You also learned how to manage different problems on the same worksheet using Scenario Manager and then summarize the results of the scenarios with a Scenario Summary and a Scenario PivotTable. Finally, you learned how to save a workbook file with passwords and modify the properties of a workbook.

What You Should Know

Having completed this project, you should now be able to perform the following tasks:

▶ Add Data Validation *(E 8.16)*

▶ Add the Data for a New Scenario *(E 8.40)*

▶ Change Workbook Properties *(E 8.54)*

▶ Create a Scenario PivotTable *(E 8.51)*

▶ Create a Scenario Summary *(E 8.49)*

▶ Display the Formula Auditing Toolbar *(E 8.10)*

▶ Quit Excel *(E 8.55)*

▶ Remove the Trace Dependent Arrows *(E 8.14)*

▶ Remove the Trace Precedent Arrows *(E 8.12)*

▶ Save the Second Solver Solution as a Scenario *(E 8.44)*

▶ Save the Current Data as a Scenario *(E 8.35)*

▶ Save the Workbook with Passwords *(E 8.32)*

▶ Show a Saved Scenario *(E 8.46)*

▶ Start Excel, Open a Workbook, and Customize Excel *(E 8.08)*

▶ Trace Dependents *(E 8.13)*

▶ Trace Precedents *(E 8.11)*

▶ Use Solver to Find the Optimal Combination *(E 8.25)*

▶ Use Solver to Find a New Solution *(E 8.41)*

▶ Use the Goal Seek Command to Attempt to Solve a Complex Problem *(E 8.21)*

▶ Use Trial and Error to Attempt to Solve a Complex Problem *(E 8.19)*

▶ View the Second Answer Report *(E 8.43)*

▶ View the Answer Report *(E 8.31)*

Learn It Online

Instructions: To complete the Learn It Online exercises, start your browser, click the Address bar, and then enter scsite.com/offxp/exs.htm. When the Office XP Learn It Online page displays, follow the instructions in the exercises below.

1 Project Reinforcement TF, MC, and SA

Below Excel Project 8, click the Project Reinforcement link. Print the quiz by clicking Print on the File menu. Answer each question. Write your first and last name at the top of each page, and then hand in the printout to your instructor.

2 Flash Cards

Below Excel Project 8, click the Flash Cards link. When Flash Cards displays, read the instructions. Type 20 (or a number specified by your instructor) in the Number of Playing Cards text box, type your name in the Name text box, and then click the Flip Card button. When the flash card displays, read the question and then click the Answer box arrow to select an answer. Flip through Flash Cards. Click Print on the File menu to print the last flash card if your score is 15 (75%) correct or greater and then hand it in to your instructor. If your score is less than 15 (75%) correct, then redo this exercise by clicking the Replay button.

3 Practice Test

Below Excel Project 8, click the Practice Test link. Answer each question, enter your first and last name at the bottom of the page, and then click the Grade Test button. When the graded practice test displays on your screen, click Print on the File menu to print a hard copy. Continue to take practice tests until you score 80% or better. Hand in a printout of the final practice test to your instructor.

4 Who Wants to Be a Computer Genius?

Below Excel Project 8, click the Computer Genius link. Read the instructions, enter your first and last name at the bottom of the page, and then click the Play button. Hand in your score to your instructor.

5 Wheel of Terms

Below Excel Project 8, click the Wheel of Terms link. Read the instructions, and then enter your first and last name and your school name. Click the Play button. Hand in your score to your instructor.

6 Crossword Puzzle Challenge

Below Excel Project 8, click the Crossword Puzzle Challenge link. Read the instructions, and then enter your first and last name. Click the Play button. Work the crossword puzzle. When you are finished, click the Submit button. When the crossword puzzle redisplays, click the Print button. Hand in the printout.

7 Tips and Tricks

Below Excel Project 8, click the Tips and Tricks link. Click a topic that pertains to Project 8. Right-click the information and then click Print on the shortcut menu. Construct a brief example of what the information relates to in Excel to confirm you understand how to use the tip or trick. Hand in the example and printed information.

8 Newsgroups

Below Excel Project 8, click the Newsgroups link. Click a topic that pertains to Project 8. Print three comments. Hand in the comments to your instructor.

9 Expanding Your Horizons

Below Excel Project 8, click the Articles for Microsoft Excel link. Click a topic that pertains to Project 8. Print the information. Construct a brief example of what the information relates to in Excel to confirm you understand the contents of the article. Hand in the example and printed information to your instructor.

10 Search Sleuth

Below Excel Project 8, click the Search Sleuth link. To search for a term that pertains to this project, select a term below the Project 8 title and then use the Google search engine at google.com (or any major search engine) to display and print two Web pages that present information on the term. Hand in the printouts to your instructor.

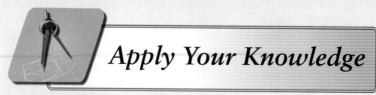

Apply Your Knowledge

1 Determining the Optimal Servings for a Meal

Instructions: Minkus Catering has been asked to create custom meals for a local minor league baseball team. Follow the steps below to use trial and error, and then Solver to find the optimal servings mix that should make up a meal with no more than 400 calories and 20 grams of fat based on the current product costs and prices. The items requested to be included in the meals include potatoes, pork, and carrots. The meal must include at least one serving of each item and no more than four.

Microsoft Excel - Minkus Catering

Minkus Catering
Meal Planning Worksheet

	Potato Dish	Pork Dish	Carrot Dish	Meal Totals
Serving Price	$0.85	$1.20	$0.30	
Serving Cost	$0.55	$0.80	$0.25	
Profit per Serving	$0.30	$0.40	$0.05	
Calories per Serving	77	85	25	
Fat in Grams per Serving	3	5	2	
Optimal Number of Servings	1	3	1	
Total Meal Calories	77	255	25	357
Total Meal Fat in Grams	3	15	2	20
Total Meal Profit	$0.30	$1.20	$0.05	$1.55

FIGURE 8-73

1. Open the workbook Minkus Catering from the Data Disk. If you do not have a copy of the Data Disk, see the inside back cover of this book.
2. Enter your name, course, laboratory assignment number (Apply 8-1), date, and instructor name in the range A15:A19.
3. Using trial and error, enter values in cells B9, C9, and D9 to try to solve the problem.
4. Use Solver to find a solution to the problem so that the profit on the meal is maximized. Allow Solver to change cells B9, C9 and D9. The total calories of the meal should not exceed 400 and the total fat should not exceed 20 grams. The results in B9, C9, and D9 should be integer values. Also, use the Assume Linear Model option in Solver.
5. Instruct Solver to create the Answer Report for your solution. Solver should find the answer as shown in Figure 8-73.
6. Go into the workbook properties on the File menu and enter a title for the workbook of Minkus Catering Custom Meal Workbook. Enter your name in the Author field and your instructor's name in the Manager field.
7. Print the worksheet and the Answer Report 1 worksheet. Hand in the two printouts to your instructor.

In the Lab

1 Gaining Confidence in the Greenback Stock Club Workbook

Problem: You have been given the task of taking over the job of another employee who has retired. Your first task is to learn about some of the Excel workbooks for which you now are responsible.

Instructions: Start Excel and perform the following tasks.

1. Open the BetNet Stock Club workbook from the Data Disk. See the inside back cover of this book for instructions for downloading the Data Disk or see your instructor for information on accessing the files required in this book.

2. Display the Formula Auditing Toolbar. Trace four levels of precedents for cell J14. Trace one level of the precedents for cell G14. Trace one level of the dependents for cell H3. The worksheet should display as shown in Figure 8-74.

FIGURE 8-74

3. Enter your name, course, laboratory assignment number (Lab 8-1), date, and instructor's name in the range A16:G20. Print the worksheet.

4. Remove all trace arrows. Enter the value of zero in cell D5.

5. Use the Trace Error button to trace the error in cell J5. Use the Trace Error button to trace the error in cell J14. Print the worksheet.

6. Select the range D3:D10. Open the Data Validation dialog box. Create a validation rule that forces the user to enter a positive whole number in the cells in the selected range. Clear the Ignore blank check box.

7. Click the Error Alert tab and create an error message with the title `Number of Shares` that contains the message `Enter a positive whole number for the number of shares`. Click the OK button.

8. Reenter the value of zero in cell D5 and press the ENTER key to view the error message. Select Retry and then enter 300 in cell D5. Print the worksheet. Hand in the three printouts to your instructor.

In the Lab

2 Finding the Best Production Mix

Problem: Grouse Products assembles four types of compressors in its factory. Each type of compressor requires a different amount of labor input and a different amount of materials to produce a single compressor. As the production manager, it is your job to determine the best mix of compressors to produce based on the amount of available labor and material for a given week. The company should produce no more than 12 Light Compressor and Medium Compressor units in a week due to a high level of inventory. Due to contractual obligations with a distributor, the company must always produce at least 20 Heavy Compressor units each week. Finally, the company does not wish to produce more than 50 of any item in a week.

Instructions: Start Excel and perform the following tasks.

1. Open the Grouse Products workbook from the Data Disk. If you do not have a copy of the Data Disk, then see the inside back cover of this book.

2. Use Solver to determine the mix of products that maximizes the number of units

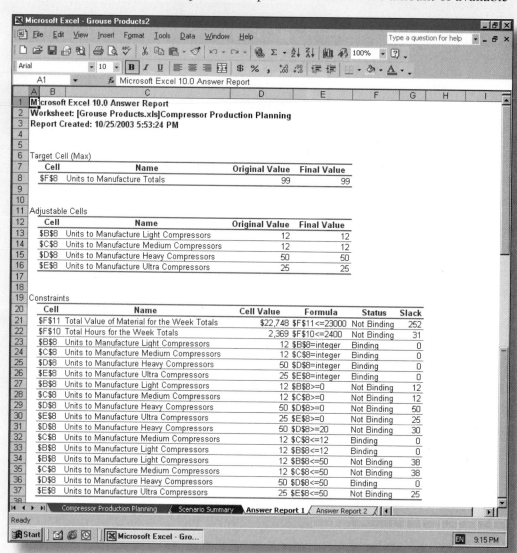

FIGURE 8-75a Answer Report

produced in the week. The total amount of labor hours available in the first week of November is 2,400 hours, and $23,000 worth of materials is available. Use the Assume Linear Model option in Solver. Instruct Solver to create an answer report if it can find a solution to the problem. Figure 8-75a shows the values that Solver should find. If necessary, change the assumptions for the Hours of Labor per Unit in cells B5:E5 to show the values of 15 for Light Compressors, 22 for Medium Compressors, 25 for Heavy Compressors, and 27 for Ultra Compressors.

In the Lab

3. Save the current worksheet as a scenario named November, Week 1. The Changing cells are B5:E6 and B8:E8.

4. Enter your name, course, laboratory assignment number (Lab 8-2), date, and instructor's name in the range A13:A17. Print the worksheet.

5. The company president feels that perhaps the assumptions about how many labor hours it takes to produce certain products is not correct. The new assumptions are that Light Compressors takes 17 labor hours to produce, Medium Compressors takes 15 hours to produce, 31 for Heavy Compressors, and Ultra Compressors takes 25 hours to produce. Enter these new values in the worksheet.

6. Use Solver to find a solution to the problem. Instruct Solver to create an Answer Report if it can find a solution to the problem. Solver should report that the optimal number of units of Light Compressors is 12, of Medium Compressors is 12, of Heavy Compressors is 24, and of Ultra Compressors is 38.

7. Save the current worksheet as a scenario named November, Week 2. Print the worksheet and the Answer Report (Figure 8-75a).

8. Create a Scenario Summary (Figure 8-75b) showing the two scenarios that you have saved in Scenario Manager.

9. Save the workbook with the password, lab8-2, and with the file name, Grouse Products2. Print the Scenario Summary worksheet.

FIGURE 8-75b Scenario Summary

In the Lab

3 Finding the Optimal Advertising Mix

Problem: Your town holds two annual festivals each summer, one in June and one in August. The town manager would like you to help determine how to best promote the events through advertisements in a variety of media. The town board has identified a local newspaper, a local radio station, and the local cable television station as advertising targets. Each type of media claims to be able to target a certain number of individuals in the town's target audience with each advertisement. The town hopes to attract as many people from other local communities as from the town itself. Each media type has a limit on how many advertisements can be placed each month leading up to the festival and the prices vary from month to month.

Instructions: Start Excel and perform the following tasks.

1. Open the Festivals2003 workbook from the Data Disk.
2. Use Solver to determine the best mix of advertising for the festival in the June. The advertising budget for the first festival is $10,500. The newspaper allows a maximum of 14 ads per week, the radio station allows a maximum of 30 advertisement spots per week, and the cable television station allows a maximum of 21 advertisements per week. The costs for the month of June are already in the worksheet. Use the Assume Linear Model option in Solver. Instruct Solver to create an answer report if it can find a solution to the problem. Figure 8-76a shows the values that Solver should find for this situation.
3. Save the current worksheet as a scenario named June 2003 Festival. The Changing cells are B6:D6 and B9:D9.
4. Enter your name, course, laboratory assignment number (Lab 8-3), date, and instructor's name in the range B15:B19. Print the worksheet and the Answer Report.
5. The festival in August is much larger and is allocated a budget of $23,500. Radio advertisements will cost $355 each for that month and cable television advertisements will cost $850 for that week. The cost of newspaper advertisements remains unchanged.
6. Use Solver to solve the problem. Instruct Solver to create an answer report if it can find a solution to the problem. Solver should find that the optimal combination reaches 187,000 people, and includes 14 newspaper advertisements, one radio advertisement, and 20 cable television advertisements.
7. Save the current worksheet as a scenario named August 2003 Festival. Print the worksheet and the Answer Report (Figure 8-76a).
8. Create a Scenario Summary (Figure 8-76b) showing the two scenarios that you have saved in Scenario Manager. Save the workbook with the password, lab8-3, and with the file name, Festivals2003-2. Print the Scenario Summary.

In the Lab

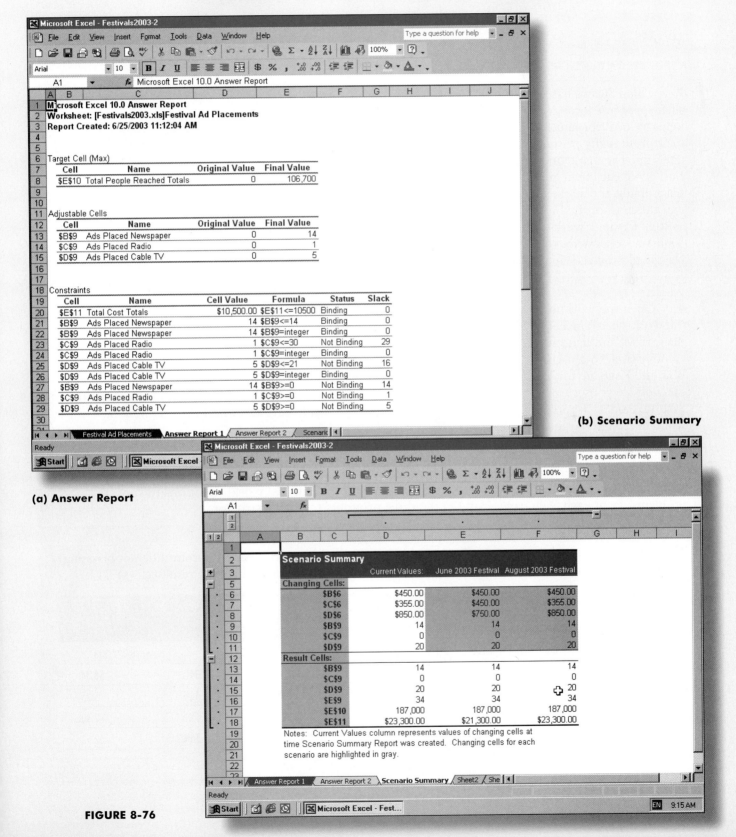

(a) Answer Report

(b) Scenario Summary

FIGURE 8-76

Cases and Places

The difficulty of these case studies varies:
▶ are the least difficult; ▶▶ are more difficult; and ▶▶▶ are the most difficult.

1 ▶ Cillan Snacks has purchased access to 21 square feet of shelf space in a local grocery store to test market two new items to local consumers. Table 8-5 shows the two items, their profitability per item, and how much space each item takes up. The marketing department wants to be sure that at least 15 of each item are on the shelf. If one of the items sells rapidly, the marketing department wants to be certain that the most profitable combination of items is on the shelf as well. Create a worksheet with the necessary information and use Solver to determine the most profitable combination of items to place on the shelves. Create an Answer Report that shows that the constraints have been met. Print the worksheet and Answer Report and hand them in to your instructor.

TABLE 8-5	Snack Marketing Information	
SNACK NAME	PROFIT PER ITEM	SQUARE FEET PER ITEM
Banana Mango Chips	$1.52	.23
Papaya Chips	$1.79	.34

2 ▶ Open the workbook Hyperlink on the Data Disk. Use the Formula Auditing toolbar to learn about the worksheet. Trace 4 levels of precedents for cell H14, the Total Net Income. Print the worksheet with the arrows and hand it in to your instructor. Use Data Validation to limit a user's input on cell B19, the Commission, to a decimal value between 1 and 12. Use Data Validation to limit a user's input on cell B22, the Revenue for Bonus, to a decimal value greater than 5,000,000. Use Data Validation to allow the worksheet user to select a Bonus from a list that ranges from 50,000 to 100,000 in increments of 10,000. Add appropriate input and error messages for all of the data validation rules as well. Save the worksheet as Hyperlink2.

3 ▶ Using a browser search engine, such as Yahoo!, type the keywords Linear Programming. Visit three Web pages that discuss how Linear Programming is used in real world situations to solve business problems. Print each Web page. Hand in the three printouts to your instructor.

4 ▶▶ Open the workbook e-book on the Data Disk. Create four scenarios based on four different planning assumptions outlined in Table 8-6. Create a Scenario Summary that summarizes the result cells of B17, C17, D17, E17, F17, G17, and H17. Print the Scenario Summary worksheet. Hand in the printout to your instructor.

TABLE 8-6				
ASSUMPTION	SCENARIO 1	SCENARIO 2	SCENARIO 3	SCENARIO 4
Units Sold in Year 2002	9,372,859	8,322,338	9,492,016	8,322,338
Unit Cost	$7.23	$7.23	$8.34	$8.34
Annual Sales Growth	5.95%	6.25%	3.45%	5.25%
Annual Price Decrease	3.2%	3.2%	5.5%	2.40%
Margin	40.75%	37.75%	37.75%	42.5%

Microsoft Excel 2002

PROJECT

9

Importing Data, Routing Changes, PivotCharts, PivotTables, and Trendlines

You will have mastered the material in this project when you can:

O B J E C T I V E S

- Import data from a text file
- Import data from an Access database
- Import data from a Web page
- Import data from spreadsheet XML
- Replicate formulas
- Insert, edit, and remove a comment
- Explain collaboration techniques
- Track changes and share a workbook
- Route a workbook to other users
- Accept and reject tracked changes made to a workbook
- Create and format a PivotChart and PivotTable
- Analyze worksheet data using a PivotChart
- Analyze worksheet data using a PivotTable
- Analyze worksheet data using a trendline
- Merge shared workbooks
- Add a trendline to a chart
- Explain the concept of exporting data from a workbook

From Dots and Dashes to the Internet

Electronic Data Transfer
From Morse Code to the Internet

In recent years, daily Internet transactions have become commonplace, making it possible for people to transfer electronically vast amounts of critical business and personal data. Connected to the Web, you can conduct a quick search for any number of online businesses, place orders, and enter your credit card information in a form on a Web page. Within minutes, the data necessary to complete your order is sent to your bank for verification, returned to the e-retailer with authorization codes, and your order is complete.

The first truly successful system for transmitting data electronically was the telegraph, which began operating in England in 1837. The complexity of this system made it impractical to use on a large scale. Not until American inventor Samuel Morse developed a simpler telegraph system that required only a single wire was the telegraph widely used across the United States.

Morse's system enabled an operator to use a device to create or break a flow of electric current between a telegraph machine's battery and its receiver. On the receiving end, the electric current powered an electromagnet that attracted a small armature when a signal was received. The armature produced a series of dots and dashes that could be decoded by a telegraph operator using Morse code, which Morse himself developed.

To create this code, Morse studied a printer's type box to determine the most frequently used letters in English. He assigned these letters the shortest possible patterns of dots and dashes. The letter, e, for instance, is represented by a single dot. The letter, t, is signified by a single dash. In this way, Morse created a code that enabled telegraph operators to send messages across vast distances easily and decode messages reliably.

By 1837, Morse sent a signal across ten miles. Gradually, transmission signals reached greater distances. On May 24, 1844, Morse sent a message over the first official telegraph link, which ran between Baltimore, Maryland, and Washington, D.C. His message simply said, "What hath God wrought!"

Although the Internet has far outpaced the telegraph in terms of its capability of sending and receiving all kinds of data, its basic purpose remains the same: it enables people to send and receive data electronically with a minimum of error.

Today, companies such as Triangle Environmental rely on the Internet to transmit critical business data across the nation. Triangle Environmental field technicians use the company's testing equipment to verify that gas station storage tanks meet federal environmental regulations. Field technicians enter test results into Excel worksheets using notebook computers. When a test is complete, technicians upload the data via a Web page. The data is received and handled by lab technicians who use the data to prepare reports for the state to certify compliance with current regulations. Electronic data transfer is the heart of the company.

In the connected world of the twenty-first century, the ability to use and analyze data from a variety of sources is a necessity, and the Internet has provided an important means to move that data reliably from person to person, place to place.

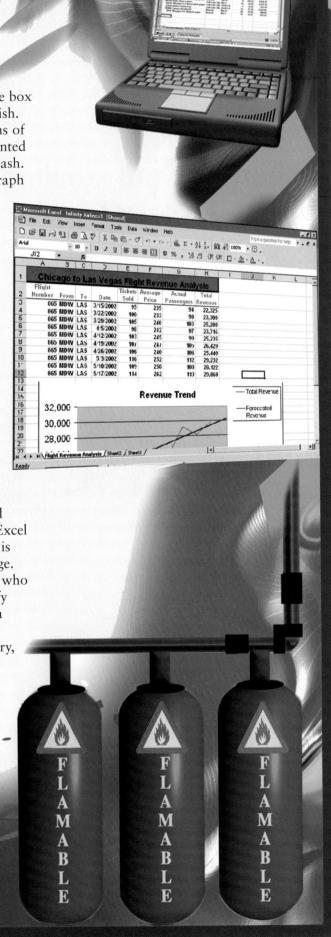

Microsoft Excel 2002

Importing Data, Routing Changes, PivotCharts, PivotTables, and Trendlines

Introduction

In today's diverse business environment, the ability to use and analyze data from a wide variety of sources is a necessity. In this project, you will learn how to **import,** or bring, data from various external sources into an Excel worksheet (Figure 9-1f) and then analyze that data.

Suppose you routinely conduct business with an organization that stores data in text format (Figure 9-1a on page E 9.06) rather than in a workbook. To make use of that data, you first input the data, and then format and manipulate it. Businesses also receive data in various database formats, such as Microsoft Access tables (Figure 9-1b), and from Web pages (Figure 9-1c). Finally, businesses routinely receive data in various XML formats, such as spreadsheet XML (Figure 9-1d).

Businesses often create charts to represent data visually. One way to analyze data visually is through the use of PivotCharts, PivotTables, and trendlines. A **PivotChart** (Figure 9-1g) is an interactive chart that provides the user with ways to graphically analyze data by varying the fields and categories to present different views. For example, if the Curry Foundation wanted to display a pie chart showing percentages of donations from each state, a PivotChart could display that percentage using any field such as total donations for a year or total donations for certain campaign types for a year.

Excel creates and associates a PivotTable with every PivotChart. A **PivotTable** (Figure 9-1h) is an interactive view of worksheet data that gives you the ability to summarize the database and then rotate the table's row and column titles to show different views of the summarized data. An inexperienced user with little knowledge of formulas, functions, and ranges can employ powerful what-if analyses of the data simply by clicking a field from a list of fields in a PivotChart or PivotTable. A **trendline** is a visual way to show how some particular data is changing over time. Excel can overlay a trendline on any chart, including a PivotChart.

Other techniques introduced in this project apply to issues of multiple users of the same workbook, including routing, tracking changes, and comments. If you want several people to look at a workbook and make comments, you can **route** it, or pass the workbook around, electronically. You can **track changes** to a workbook by displaying who changed what data, in which cell, and when. **Comments**, or descriptions, which do not regularly display as part of the worksheet data, can be added to the workbook itself to alert the recipients to special instructions, and later edited or deleted. Workbooks that have been saved and copied to others also can be merged. **Merging** allows you to bring together copies of workbooks that others have worked on independently.

Project Nine — Curry Foundation Analysis

From your meeting with Gene Curry, you have accumulated the following workbook specifications:

Need: Import data from the four states in which the Curry Foundation operates (Figures 9-1a, 9-1b, 9-1c, and 9-1d on the next two pages) into a worksheet containing headings and formulas, but no data (Figure 9-1e on the next page). Once the data is imported, the formulas in cells H3 and I3 must be copied to each row of data (Figure 9-1f on page E 9.07). After the import is complete, the data in the worksheet requires verification by the state coordinators. A PivotChart (Figure 9-1g on page E 9.07) and its associated PivotTable (Figure 9-1h on page E 9.07) allow interactive views of the data from the worksheet.

Source of Data: The four state coordinators for the Curry Foundation will submit data from their respective states via a text file (Minnesota), an Access database (Nevada), a Web page (Georgia), and spreadsheet XML (Oklahoma).

Calculations: The formulas used to calculate average donation per donor in the 2004 and 2003 are in cells H3 and I3 of the worksheet (Figure 9-1d). The formulas divide donation amounts for each year by the number of donor for a particular fund raising campaign each year. After importing the data, the formulas need to be copied down for all rows of data.

Special Requirements: Before creating the PivotChart and PivotTable, route the workbook with the imported data (Figure 9-1f) to the four state coordinators for verification and then accept tracked changes.

Chart Requirements: Create a PivotChart (Figure 9-1g) and associated PivotTable (Figure 9-1h) that analyze donations based on any combination of states and campaigns.

More About

External Data

Imported data that maintains a refreshable link to its external source is called external data. When you use external data, your worksheet also will update whenever a change is made to the original file. You can choose when and how the data is refreshed.

More About

Importing Data

If your system contains only a minimum installation of Excel, the first time you use one of the import features, Excel may attempt to install MSQuery. MSQuery is the supplemental application included in Microsoft Office XP, used to retrieve data from external data sources.

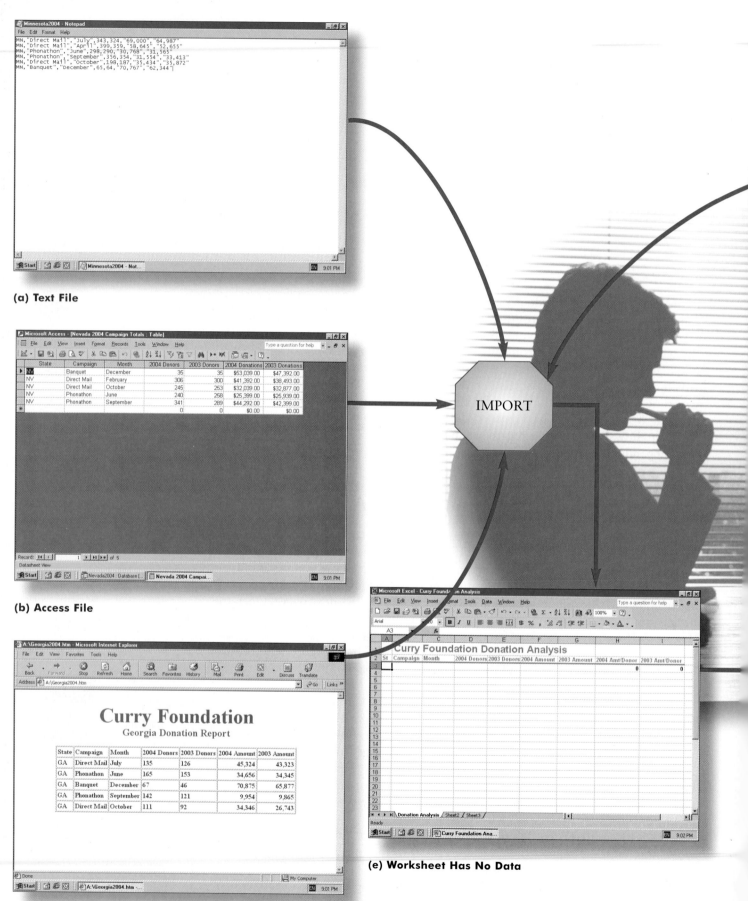

(a) Text File

(b) Access File

(c) HTML File

(e) Worksheet Has No Data

FIGURE 9-1

(h) **PivotTable**

(d) **Spreadsheet XML**

(f) **Data Imported into Worksheet**

(g) **PivotChart**

Starting Excel and Opening a Workbook

Perform the following steps to start Excel, open the empty workbook, Curry Foundation Analysis, from the Data Disk, and reset the toolbars.

TO START EXCEL, OPEN A WORKBOOK, AND CUSTOMIZE EXCEL

1 Insert the Data Disk in drive A. See the inside back cover of this book for instructions for downloading the Data Disk or see your instructor for information on accessing the files required in this book.

2 Click the Start button on the taskbar and then click Open Office Document.

3 When the Open Office Document dialog box displays, click the Look in box arrow and then click 3½ Floppy (A:). Double-click Curry Foundation Analysis in the Look in list.

4 If the Excel window is not maximized, double-click its title bar to maximize it.

5 If the Language bar displays, click its Minimize button.

6 If the Standard and Formatting toolbars display on one row, click the Toolbar Options button on the right side of either toolbar and then click Show Buttons on Two Rows in the Toolbar Options list.

The Curry Foundation Analysis workbook displays in the Excel window (Figure 9-2).

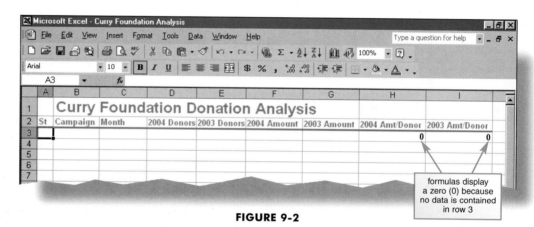

FIGURE 9-2

Table 9-1 Curry Foundation Analysis Data Fields	
NAME OF FIELD	**DATA DESCRIPTION**
St	Standard postal abbreviation for the name of the state in which the office is located
Campaign	The type of fundraising campaign (i.e., Phonathon, Banquet, or Direct Mail)
Month	Month in which the campaign occurred
2004 Donors	Number of donors for this campaign in 2004
2003 Donors	Number of donors for this campaign in 2003
2004 Amount	Total amount in dollars collected for this campaign in 2004
2003 Amount	Total amount in dollars collected for this campaign in 2003
2004 Amt/Donor	Average donation per donor for this campaign (2004 Amount/2004 Donors)
2003 Amt/Donor	Average donation per donor for this campaign (2003 Amount/2003 Donors)

As shown in Figure 9-2, columns A through I have been resized and formatted so the imported data will be readable. Table 9-1 shows a summary of the data fields.

When you import data into a formatted worksheet, Excel formats the incoming data using the formats assigned to the cells as best it can.

Importing Files

Data may come to you from a variety of sources. Even though many users keep data in databases such as Microsoft Access, it is common to receive text files with fields of data separated by commas, especially from mainframe computer users. Also, with the increasing popularity of the World Wide Web, more companies are posting data on the Web. XML quickly is becoming a very popular format for data exchange. The ability to download data from the Web into an Excel worksheet is required. Importing data into Excel, rather than copying and pasting the data, also can create a refreshable link you may use to update data whenever the original file changes.

Importing Text Files

A **text file** contains electronic data created with little or no formatting. Many software applications, including Excel, offer an option to import data from a text file, also called an ASCII text file. **ASCII** stands for the American Standard Code for Information Interchange.

In text files, commas, tabs, or other characters often separate the fields. Alternately, the text file may have fields of equal length in columnar format. Each record usually exists on a separate line. A **delimited file** contains a selected character, such as a comma, to separate data fields. A **fixed width file** contains data fields of equal length in the records. In the case of a fixed width file, a special character need not separate the data fields. During the import process, Excel provides a preview to help you identify the type of text file with which you are working.

The following steps import a comma-delimited text file into the Curry Foundation Analysis workbook using the **Text Import Wizard**. The text file on the Data Disk contains data about fundraising campaigns in Minnesota for 2003 and 2004 (Figure 9-1a on page E 9.06).

More About

Opening a Text File in Excel

If you open a text file, such as Minnesota2004.txt, in Excel, the Text Import Wizard will start automatically. You then could make the same choices shown in the previous set of steps to import the data from the text file. To open a text file in Excel, you must choose Text Files or All Files in the Files of type box in the Open dialog box.

Steps **To Import Data from a Text File into a Worksheet**

---

1 **With the Curry Foundation Analysis worksheet active and the Data Disk in drive A, click cell A3, if necessary. Click Data on the menu bar. Point to Import External Data and then point to Import Data on the Import External Data submenu.**

The Data menu and the Import External Data submenu display (Figure 9-3).

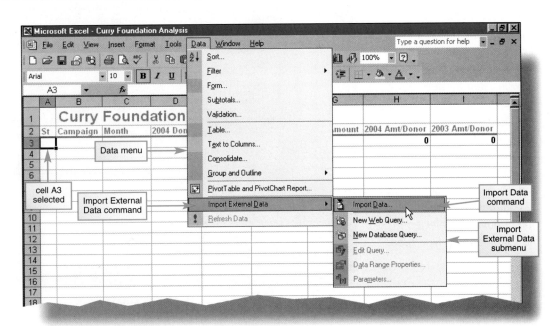

FIGURE 9-3

2 **Click Import Data. When the Select Data Source dialog box displays, click the Look in box arrow, and then click 3½ Floppy (A:). Point to Minnesota2004.**

The files on drive A display (Figure 9-4).

FIGURE 9-4

3 **Double-click Minnesota2004. When the Text Import Wizard - Step 1 of 3 dialog box displays, point to Next button.**

*Excel displays the Text Import Wizard - Step 1 of 3 dialog box (Figure 9-5). The **Text Import Wizard** provides step-by-step instruction on importing text into Excel. The Preview box shows that the data from the file contains one record per line and the fields are separated by commas. The Delimited option button is selected in the Original data type area.*

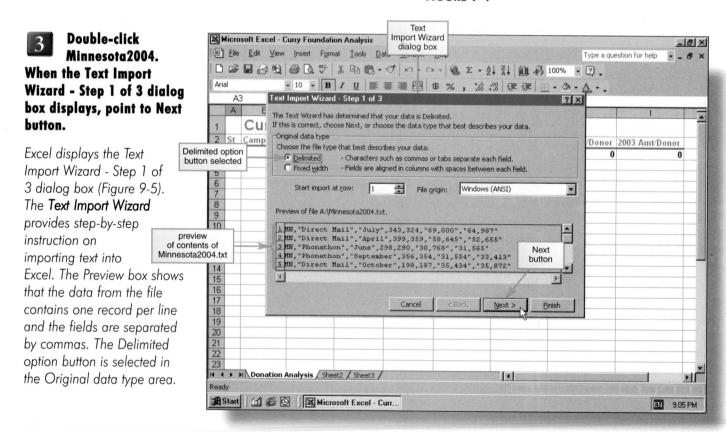

FIGURE 9-5

4 **Click the Next button. When the Text Import Wizard - Step 2 of 3 dialog box displays, click Comma in the Delimiters area. Click Tab in the Delimiters area to clear the check box. Point to the Next button.**

The Data preview area reflects the change (Figure 9-6). Excel correctly shows the fields of data in the Data preview area.

FIGURE 9-6

5 **Click the Next button. When the Text Import Wizard - Step 3 of 3 dialog box displays, point to the Finish button.**

The third dialog box of the Text Import Wizard displays (Figure 9-7). Step 3 allows you to select the format of each column of data. General is the default selection. The Data preview area shows the data separated based on the comma delimiter.

FIGURE 9-7

6 **Click the Finish button. When the Import Data dialog box displays, point to the Properties button.**

The Import Data dialog box displays (Figure 9-8). The Import Data dialog box lets you select the location of the data in the worksheet, as well as providing a way to tailor the data before importing it. Data will be imported beginning at cell A3. A marquee displays around cell A3.

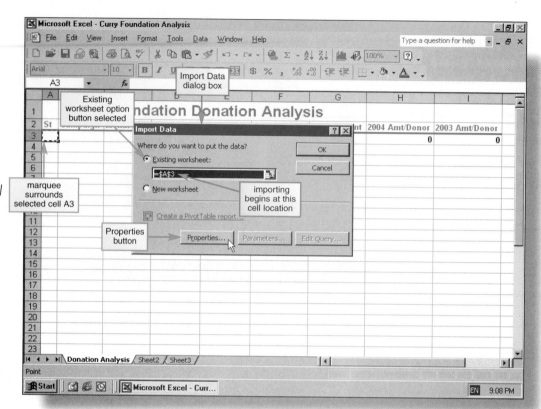

FIGURE 9-8

7 **Click the Properties button. When the External Data Range Properties dialog box displays, click Adjust column width in the Data formatting and layout area to clear the check box. Point to the OK button.**

The External Data Range Properties dialog box displays as shown in Figure 9-9.

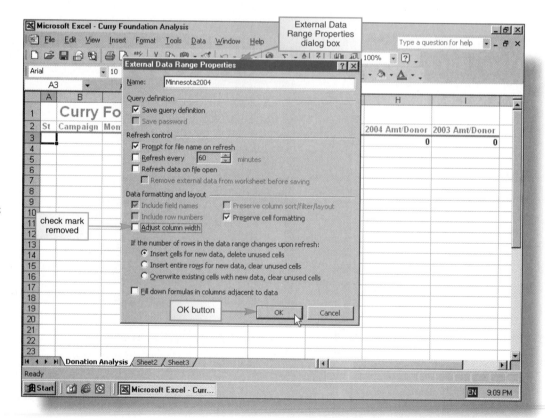

FIGURE 9-9

8 **Click the OK button. When the Import Data dialog box displays, click the OK button. If the External Data toolbar displays on your screen, click its Close button.**

Excel imports the data into the worksheet beginning at cell A3 (Figure 9-10).

FIGURE 9-10

Other Ways

1. Press ALT+D, D, D
2. In Voice Command mode, say "Data, Import External Data, Import Data"

The commas in the last two columns of numbers in the Data preview area (Figure 9-7 on page E 9.11) are not considered to be delimiters because each of these data values was surrounded by quotation marks when the text file was created.

By default, the cell that is active when you perform the text import will become the upper-left cell of the imported range. If you want to import the data to a different location, you can specify the location in the Import Data dialog box (Figure 9-8).

By importing the text file, Excel can **refresh**, or update, the data whenever the original text file changes using the **Refresh Data command** on the Data menu.

Importing Access Tables

When you import data from an Access database, you start by making a query of the data. A **query** is a way to qualify the data you want to import by specifying a matching condition or asking a question of a database. You may choose to import the entire file or only a portion. For example, you can make a query to import only those records that pass a certain test, such as records containing numeric fields greater than a specific amount, or records containing text fields matching a specific value.

The following steps import an entire table from an Access database using the **Query Wizard**. The table in the Access database on the Data Disk contains data about fundraising campaigns in Nevada for 2003 and 2004 (Figure 9-1b on page E 9.06).

More About

Dragging and Dropping a Text File

You also can drag a text file to Excel. Simply drag the file name or the icon from its location to a blank worksheet. You then can format the data easily using the Text to Columns command on the Data menu. The data does not maintain a refreshable link to the text file.

Steps **To Import Data from an Access Table into a Worksheet**

1 **Click cell A9. Click Data on the menu bar, point to Import External Data, and then point to New Database Query.**

The Data menu and the Import External Data sub-menu display (Figure 9-11).

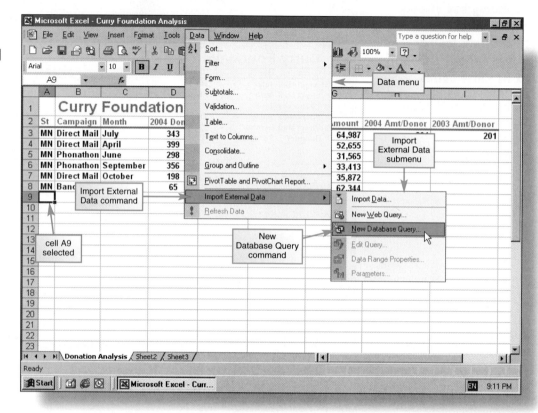

FIGURE 9-11

2 **Click New Database Query. When the Choose Data Source dialog box displays, if necessary, click the Databases tab, and then click MS Access Database* in the list. Point to the OK button.**

The Choose Data Source dialog box displays several database application formats (Figure 9-12). This list may differ on your computer. A check mark displays in the Use the Query Wizard to create/edit queries check box.

FIGURE 9-12

3 Click the OK button. When the Select Database dialog box displays, click the Drives box arrow and then click a. Point to nevada2004.mdb in the Database Name list.

The Select Database dialog box displays (Figure 9-13). Your system may not display the Connecting to data source progress box.

FIGURE 9-13

4 Double-click nevada2004.mdb. When the Query Wizard - Choose Columns dialog box displays, select the Nevada 2004 Campaign Totals table and then point to the Add Table button (Figure 9-14).

The database contains only one table to add to the query, which is listed in the Available tables and columns list.

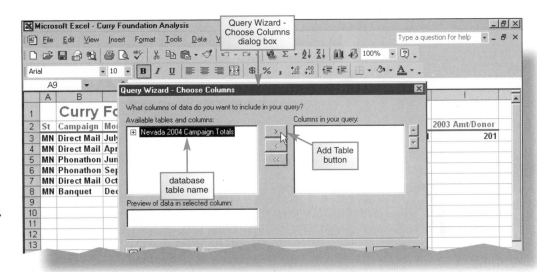

FIGURE 9-14

5 Click the Add Table button and then point to the Next button.

The fields of the Nevada 2004 Campaign Totals table display (Figure 9-15).

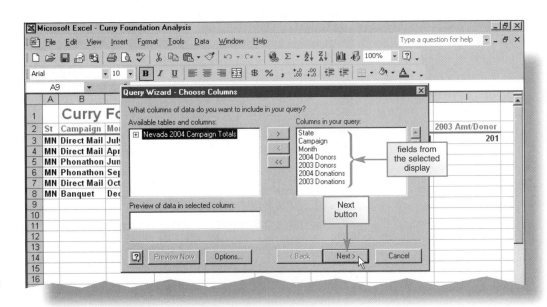

FIGURE 9-15

6 Click the Next button. When the Query Wizard - Filter Data dialog box displays, click the Next button. When the Query Wizard - Sort Order dialog box displays, click the Next button. When the Query Wizard - Finish dialog box displays, point to the Finish button (Figure 9-16).

Because the entire table is being imported without a specific query, clicking the Next button in each of the wizard dialog boxes accepts the preset values.

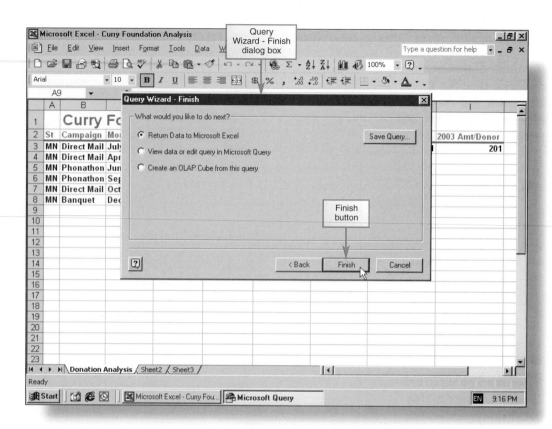

FIGURE 9-16

7 Click the Finish button. When the Import Data dialog box displays, point to the Properties button.

The Import Data dialog box displays (Figure 9-17). Data will be imported beginning at cell A9. A marquee displays around cell A9.

FIGURE 9-17

8 **Click the Properties button. When the External Data Range Properties dialog box displays, click Include field names and Adjust column width in the Data formatting and layout area to clear the check boxes. Point to the OK button.**

The External Data Range Properties dialog box displays (Figure 9-18). With the two check marks removed, Excel will not import the field names or adjust column widths in Excel.

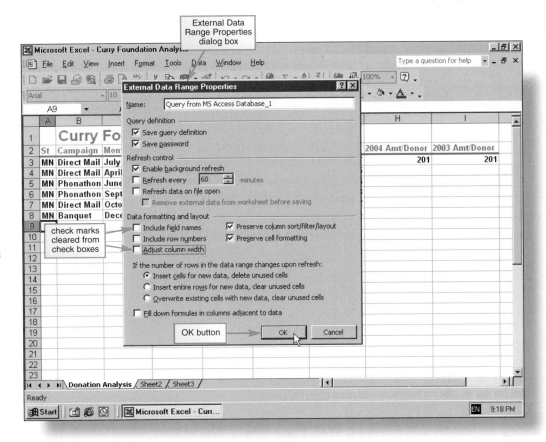

FIGURE 9-18

9 **Click the OK button. When the Import Data dialog box (Figure 9-17) redisplays, click the OK button. If your system displays the External Data toolbar, click its Close button.**

The data imported from the Access database displays in the worksheet (Figure 9-19).

FIGURE 9-19

By default, the cell that is active when you perform the database query becomes the upper-left cell of the imported range. If you want to import the data to a different location, you specify the location in the Returning External Data to Microsoft Excel dialog box (Figure 9-17).

Other Ways

1. Press ALT+D, D, N
2. In Voice Command mode, say "Data, Import External Data, New Database Query"

The Access file, nevada2004.mdb, contains only one table, Nevada 2004 Campaign Totals. The table contains seven fields that correspond to the columns in the worksheet. The Add Table button shown in Figure 9-14 on page E 9.15 added all the columns of data. The second step of the Query Wizard allows you to **filter**, or specify, which records from the database should be included in the result set, using operators such as is-greater-than or begins-with. For example, you can filter the data in the previous example by specifying to import records that have 100 or more donors in 2003.

With the data from Minnesota and Nevada imported, the next step is to import the Georgia data from a Web page.

Importing Data from a Web Page

A Web page uses a file format called HTML. **HTML** stands for **Hypertext Markup Language**, which is a language that Web browsers can interpret. A Web page allows you to import data into preformatted areas of the worksheet. You specify which parts of the Web page you want and how much of the HTML formatting you want to keep.

The next sequence of steps creates a new Web query. You do not have to be connected to the Internet to perform these steps because the Data Disk includes the Web page (Figure 9-1c on page E 9.06).

Steps **To Import Data from a Web Page into a Worksheet**

1 **Click cell A14. Click Data on the menu bar, point to Import External Data, and then point to New Web Query.**

The Data menu and Import External Data submenu display (Figure 9-20).

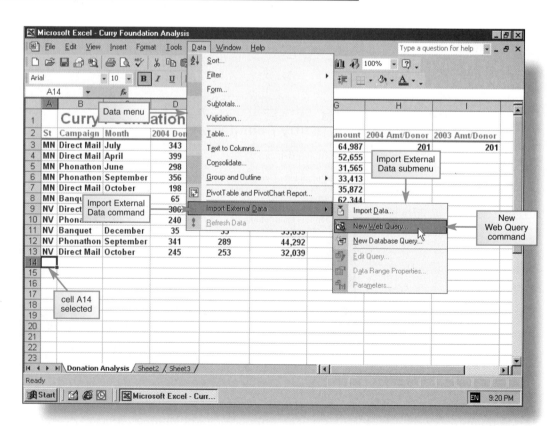

FIGURE 9-20

2 **Click New Web Query. When the New Web Query dialog box displays, type** a:\georgia2004.htm **in the Address box and then click the Go button. Point to the second Select a Table arrow.**

The file location displays in the Address box at the top of the New Web Query dialog box, and the Web page displays in the preview area (Figure 9-21). Excel appends file :// *to the beginning of the address to indicate that the address points to a local file.*

FIGURE 9-21

3 **Click the Select a Table arrow and point to the Import button.**

The table containing the Georgia Donation Report is selected as shown in Figure 9-22.

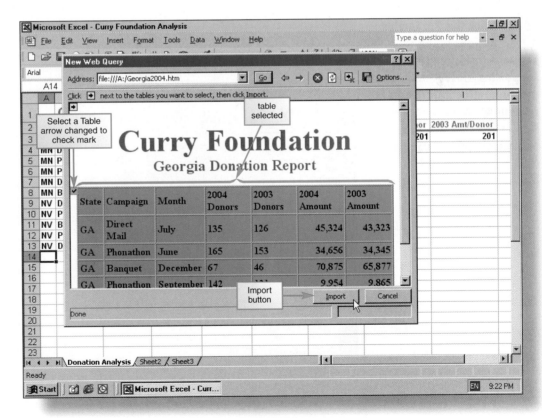

FIGURE 9-22

4 **Click the Import button. When the Import Data dialog box displays, point to the Properties button.**

The Import Data dialog box displays (Figure 9-23). Data will be imported beginning at cell A14. A marquee displays around cell A14.

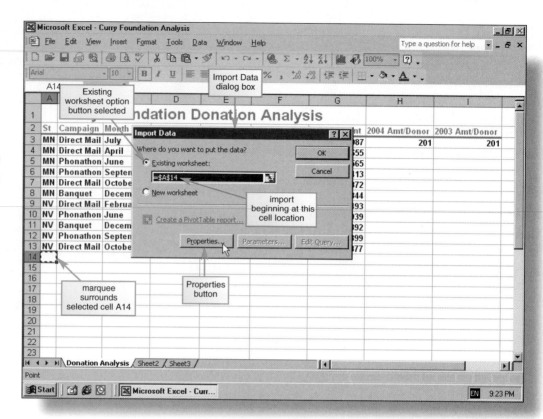

FIGURE 9-23

5 **Click the Properties button. When the External Data Range Properties dialog box displays, click Adjust column width in the Data formatting and layout area to clear the check box and then point to the OK button.**

The External Data Range Properties dialog box displays (Figure 9-24).

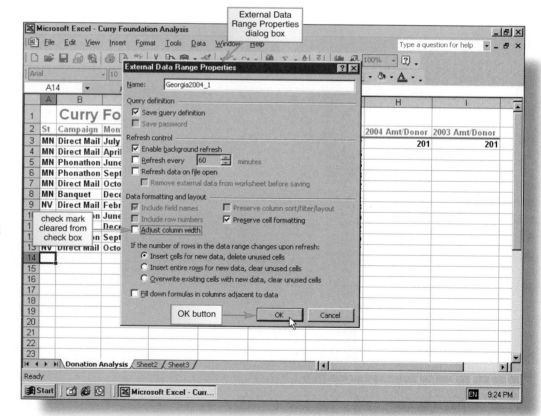

FIGURE 9-24

Step 6

Click the OK button. When the Import Data dialog box displays, click the OK button. If the External Data toolbar displays on your screen, click its Close button.

The data displays in the worksheet (Figure 9-25).

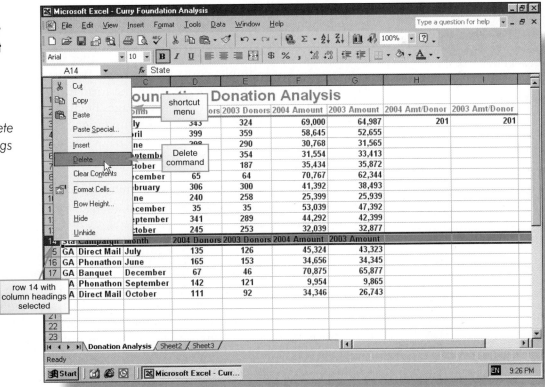

FIGURE 9-25

Step 7

Right-click row heading 14. Point to Delete on the shortcut menu.

The shortcut menu for the selected row displays (Figure 9-26). You will delete these extra column headings from the Web page table.

FIGURE 9-26

8 **Click Delete.**

Excel deletes row 14, which contained the column headings from the Web page (Figure 9-27).

FIGURE 9-27

By default, the cell that is active when you perform the Web query will become the upper-left cell of the imported range. If you want to import the data to a different location, you can specify the location in the Import Data dialog box (Figure 9-23 on page E 9.20).

Using a Web query has advantages over other methods of importing data from a Web page. For example, copying data from Web pages to the Clipboard and then pasting it into Excel does not maintain the formatting. In addition, it is tedious to select just the data you want in a Web page. Finally, copying and pasting does not create a link to the Web page for future updating.

Importing Data from Spreadsheet XML

XML

XML can describe any type of data. Banks use it to transfer financial information among various systems, and graphic artists use it to share multimedia data. The versatility of XML is matched by its simplicity. XML also is being used to make queries over the Web using a common set of rules available to any user. For example, a user can send an XML query to a travel Web site and receive the current information for a specific flight in XML format.

XML is an increasingly popular format for sharing data. **XML** stands for **Extensible Markup Language**, which is a language that is used to encapsulate data and a description of the data in a single file, or **XML file**. **Tags** are used in XML files to describe data items. Industry organizations and companies create standard XML file layouts and tags to describe commonly used types of data. Microsoft has defined a type of XML file called spreadsheet XML. **Spreadsheet XML** is a type of XML file that contains and describes an Excel spreadsheet. In addition to containing the cell data, formulas, formatting, and other information about the workbook also is stored. Other programs and systems that recognize spreadsheet XML can read spreadsheet XML files created by Excel. In addition to spreadsheet XML, any other XML file can be imported into Excel.

An XML file allows you to import data into preformatted areas of the worksheet. You specify which parts of the XML file you want. The next sequence of steps creates a new XML Web query. You do not have to be connected to the Internet to perform these steps because the Data Disk includes the XML file (Figure 9-1c on page E 9.06).

To Import Data from Spreadsheet XML into a Worksheet

1 **Click cell A19.**
Click Data on the
menu bar, point to Import
External Data, and then
point to New Web Query.

The Data menu and Import
External Data submenu
display (Figure 9-28).

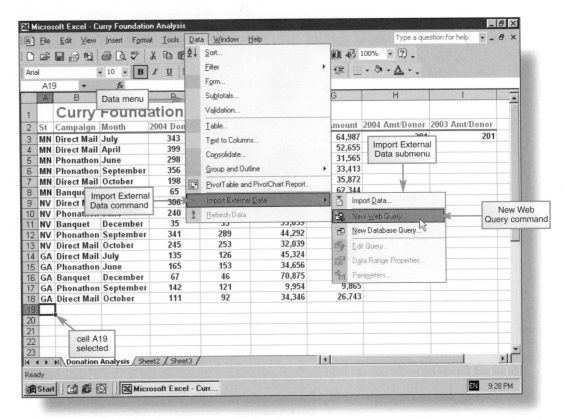

FIGURE 9-28

2 **Click New Web**
Query. When the
New Web Query dialog
box displays, type
`a:\Oklahoma2004.xml`
in the Address box and
then click the Go button.
Point to the Select a
Table arrow.

The file location displays in
the Address box at the top of
the New Web Query dialog
box, and the XML file con-
tents display in the preview
area (Figure 9-29). Excel
appends file :// to the
address to indicate that the
address points to a local file.

FIGURE 9-29

3 **Click the Select a Table arrow and point to the Import button.**

The table containing the Oklahoma 2004 donation XML data is selected as shown in Figure 9-30.

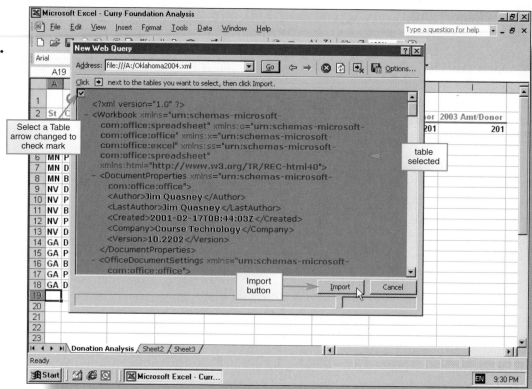

FIGURE 9-30

4 **Click the Import button. When the Import Data dialog box displays, point to the Properties button.**

The Import Data dialog box displays (Figure 9-31). Data will be imported beginning at cell A19. A marquee displays around cell A19.

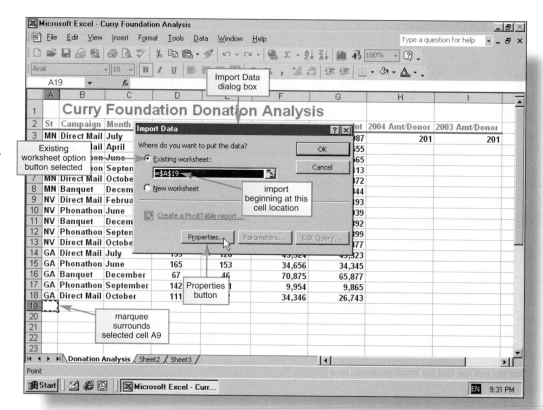

FIGURE 9-31

5 **Click the Properties button. When the External Data Range Properties dialog box displays, click Adjust column width in the Data formatting and layout area to clear the check box and then point to the OK button.**

The External Data Range Properties dialog box displays (Figure 9-32).

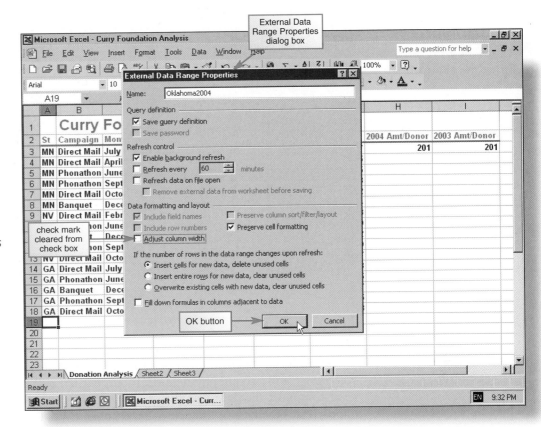

FIGURE 9-32

6 **Click the OK button. When the Import Data dialog box displays, click the OK button. If the External Data toolbar displays on your screen, click its Close button.**

The data displays in the worksheet (Figure 9-33).

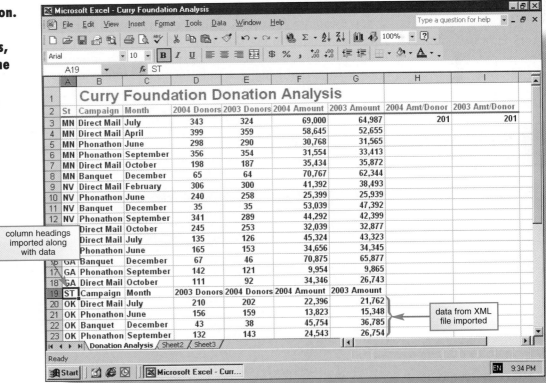

FIGURE 9-33

7 **Right-click row heading 19. Click Delete on the shortcut menu.**

Excel deletes row 19, which contained the column headings from the XML file (Figure 9-34).

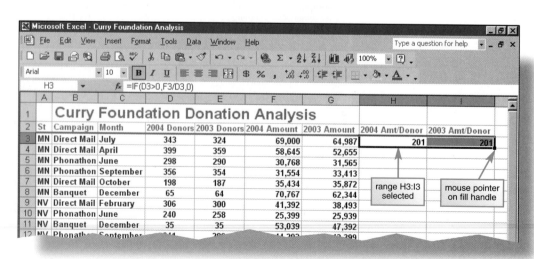

	St	Campaign	Month	2004 Donors	2003 Donors	2004 Amount	2003 Amount
6	MN	Phonathon	September	356	354		33,413
7	MN	Direct Mail	October	198	187	35,434	35,872
8	MN	Banquet	December	65	64	70,767	62,344
9	NV	Direct Mail	February	306	300	41,392	38,493
10	NV	Phonathon	June	240	258	25,399	25,939
11	NV	Banquet	December	35	35	53,039	47,392
12	NV	Phonathon	September	341	289	44,292	42,399
13	NV	Direct Mail	October	245	253	32,039	32,877
14	GA	Direct Mail	July	135	126	45,324	43,323
15	GA	Phonathon	June	165	153	34,656	34,345
16	GA	Banquet	December	67	46	70,875	65,877
17	GA	Phonathon	September	142	121	9,954	9,865
18	GA	Direct Mail	October	111	92	34,346	26,743
19	OK	Direct Mail	July	210	202	22,396	21,762
20	OK	Phonathon	June	156	159	13,823	15,348
21	OK	Banquet	December	43	38	45,754	36,785
22	OK	Phonathon	September	132	143	24,543	26,754
23	OK	Direct Mail	October	202	192	45,233	40,654

row 19 with column headings deleted and all rows moved up

Donation Analysis / Sheet2 / Sheet3 /

Ready   Sum=44570

Start   Microsoft Excel - Curr...   EN   9:35 PM

FIGURE 9-34

Other **Ways**

1. Press ALT+D, D, W

2. In Voice Command mode, say "Data, Import External Data, New Web Query"

As with the other import operations, the cell that is active when you perform the Web query will become, by default, the upper-left cell of the imported range. If you want to import the data to a different location, you can specify the location in the Import Data dialog box (Figure 9-31 on page E 9.24).

Replicating Formulas

The workbook opened at the beginning of this project contained a worksheet title, headings for each column, and formulas in cells H3 and I3 to calculate the average donation per donor for 2004 and 2003. This technique of copying the formulas after completing the import is necessary because the total number of records to be imported usually is unknown. The following steps use the fill handle to copy the formulas. Some spreadsheet specialists refer to copying formulas as **replication**.

Steps **To Replicate Formulas**

1 **Select the range H3:I3 and then point to the fill handle.**

The range H3:I3 is selected (Figure 9-35). The mouse pointer changes to a cross hair when pointing to the fill handle.

Microsoft Excel - Curry Foundation Analysis

File Edit View Insert Format Tools Data Window Help   Type a question for help

Arial   10   B I U $ % , .00 .00   100%

H3   fx =IF(D3>0,F3/D3,0)

	A	B	C	D	E	F	G	H	I
1		**Curry Foundation Donation Analysis**							
2	St	Campaign	Month	2004 Donors	2003 Donors	2004 Amount	2003 Amount	2004 Amt/Donor	2003 Amt/Donor
3	MN	Direct Mail	July	343	324	69,000	64,987	201	201
4	MN	Direct Mail	April	399	359	58,645	52,655		
5	MN	Phonathon	June	298	290	30,768	31,565		
6	MN	Phonathon	September	356	354	31,554	33,413		
7	MN	Direct Mail	October	198	187	35,434	35,872		
8	MN	Banquet	December	65	64	70,767	62,344		
9	NV	Direct Mail	February	306	300	41,392	38,493		
10	NV	Phonathon	June	240	258	25,399	25,939		
11	NV	Banquet	December	35	35	53,039	47,392		
12	NV	Phonathon	September	341	289	44,292	42,399		

range H3:I3 selected

mouse pointer on fill handle

FIGURE 9-35

2 **Drag the fill handle down through row 23.**

Excel copies the two formulas to the range H4:I23 and displays the new values for the Amt/Donor columns (Figure 9-36).

	St	Campaign	Month	2004 Donors	2003 Donors	2004 Amount	2003 Amount	2004 Amt/Donor	2003 Amt/Donor
3	MN	Direct Mail	July	343	324	69,000	64,98?	201	201
4	MN	Direct Mail	April	399	359	58,645	52,65?	147	147
5	MN	Phonathon	June	298	290	30,768	31,56?	103	109
6	MN	Phonathon	September	356	354	31,554	33,41?	89	94
7	MN	Direct Mail	October	198	187	35,434	35,87?	179	192
8	MN	Banquet	December	65	64	70,767	62,34?	1,089	974
9	NV	Direct Mail	February	306	300	41,392	38,49?	135	128
10	NV	Phonathon	June	240	258	25,399	25,93?	106	101
11	NV	Banquet	December	35	35	53,039	47,39?	1,515	1,354
12	NV	Phonathon	September	341	289		42,39?	130	147
13	NV	Direct Mail	October	245	253		32,?7?	131	130
14	GA	Direct Mail	July	135	126		43,32?	336	344
15	GA	Phonathon	June	165	153	34,656	34,34?	210	224
16	GA	Banquet	December	67	46	70,875	65,87?	1,058	1,432
17	GA	Phonathon	September	142	121	9,954	9,86?	70	82
18	GA	Direct Mail	October	111	92	34,346	26,74?	309	291
19	OK	Direct Mail	July	210	202	22,396	21,76?	107	108
20	OK	Phonathon	June	156	159	13,823	15,34?	89	97
21	OK	Banquet	December	43	38	45,754	36,78?	1,064	968
22	OK	Phonathon	September	132	143	24,543	26,75?	186	187
23	OK	Direct Mail	October	202	192	45,233	4??	224	212

formulas in range H3:I3 copied to range H4:I23

Donation Analysis / Sheet2 / Sheet3

Ready — Sum=14,997

Start — Microsoft Excel - Curr... — EN 9:37 PM

FIGURE 9-36

Recall that when you copy, or replicate, a formula, Excel adjusts the cell references so the new formulas contain references corresponding to the new locations. It then performs calculations using the appropriate values. If you want an exact copy without replication, you must hold down the CTRL key while dragging the fill handle. Holding down the SHIFT key while dragging the fill handle inserts new cells rather than over-writing the existing data.

Saving the Workbook with a New File Name

Perform the following steps to save the workbook with the file name Curry Foundation Analysis1.

TO SAVE THE WORKBOOK WITH A NEW FILE NAME

1 Click File on the menu bar and then click Save As.

2 When the Save As dialog box displays, type `Curry Foundation Analysis1` in the File name text box.

3 If necessary, click 3½ Floppy (A:) in the Save in list.

4 Click the Save button in the Save As dialog box.

Excel saves the workbook on the Data Disk in drive A using the file name, Curry Foundation Analysis1.

Exporting Structured Data from Excel

In addition to importing data, Excel allows you to export data in a variety of formats. Exporting is the process of saving data in a format that can be read by another application, such as a database program or a word processor. You export data by

Other Ways

1. Click Copy button on Standard toolbar, click Paste button on Standard toolbar
2. On Edit menu click Copy, on Edit menu click Paste
3. Press CTRL+C, press CTRL+V
4. Click Copy on shortcut menu, click Paste on shortcut menu
5. In Voice Command mode, say "Copy," select destination area, in Voice Command mode, say "Paste"

More About

Replicating Formulas

The External Date Range Properties dialog box includes a check box labeled Fill down formulas in columns adjacent to data. You can use this check box as an alternative to replicating formulas when importing data.

Importing External Data

Excel assigns a name to each external data range. You can view these names by clicking the Name box arrow in the formula bar. External data ranges from text files are named with the text file name. External data ranges from databases are named with the name of the query. External data ranges from Web queries are named with the name of the Web page from which the data was retrieved.

Selecting External Data

If you want to view which part of your spreadsheet is imported, or if you want to format or delete an external data range, click the arrow next to the Name box on the formula bar, and then click the external data range name.

using the Save As command on the File menu. The Save as type box on the Save As dialog box allows you to specify the format of the exported data. Some commonly used formats are tab delimited text, comma delimited text, and spreadsheet XML. Often, data is exported for use on other computer systems, such as mainframe computers.

If you wish to export the Curry Foundation Donation Analysis worksheet to a tab delimited text file in order to send to the Curry Foundation's accounting firm, you select Save As on the File menu. Select Text (Tab delimited) in the Save as type box, and click the OK button.

Preparing the Workbook for Routing

The next step is to add a routing comment and then verify the accuracy of the data by routing it to the state coordinators for review.

Inserting Comments

Comments are used to describe the function of a cell, a range, a sheet, or an entire workbook, or they may be used to clarify entries that might otherwise be difficult to understand. Multiple users or people reviewing the workbook often use comments to communicate suggestions, tips, and other messages. Gene suspects that the donation amount in cell F12 from Nevada is incorrect, and thus will add a comment to the cell before routing the workbook to the four state coordinators as shown in the following steps.

Steps | **To Insert a Comment**

1 Right-click cell F12. Point to Insert Comment on the shortcut menu.

The shortcut menu displays (Figure 9-37).

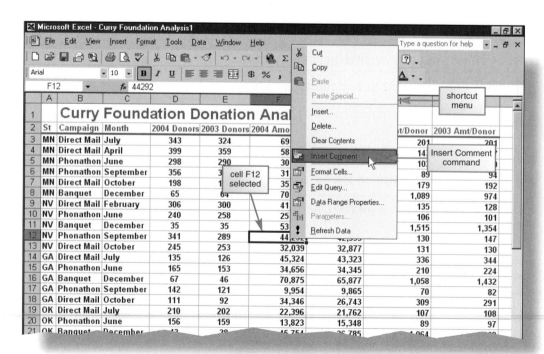

FIGURE 9-37

2 **Click Insert Comment. When the comment box displays, enter the comment as shown in Figure 9-38.**

Excel opens a *comment box* next to the selected cell (Figure 9-38). The insertion point displays in the comment box below the system user name. Your system user name will differ from this figure. Excel adds a small red triangle, called a *comment indicator*, to cell F12. A small black arrow attached to the comment box points to the comment indicator.

3 **Click anywhere outside the comment box and then click the Save button on the Standard toolbar to save the workbook using the file name, Curry Foundation Analysis1.**

FIGURE 9-38

When Excel closes the comment box and returns to the workbook window, the comment disappears from the screen. If you want to redisplay the comment, simply point to the cell containing the red comment indicator.

If you want to print the comments where they display on the sheet, click Comments on the View menu, move and resize the comments as necessary, and then print in the normal way. If you want to print the comments at the end of the worksheet, on the File menu click Page Setup, and then click the Sheet tab. Click At end of sheet in the Comments box.

Collaborating on Workbooks

If you plan to have others edit your workbook or suggest changes, Excel provides four ways to collaborate with others. **Collaborating** means working together in cooperation on a document with other Excel users.

First, you can **distribute** your workbook to others, physically on a disk or through e-mail using the Send To command on the File menu. With the Send To command, you may choose to embed the document as part of the e-mail message or attach the file as an e-mail attachment, which allows recipients of the e-mail message to open the file if the application is installed on their system.

Second, you can **route** your workbook to a list of people who pass it along from one to another on the routing list using e-mail. The Send To command on the File menu includes a Routing Recipient command. A routing slip displays in which you

Other **Ways**

1. On Insert menu click Comment
2. Press ALT+I, M
3. In Voice Command mode, say "Insert, Comment"

More *About*

Collaboration

Another way to collaborate on workbooks is by using an Exchange folder. If you send the workbook to an Exchange folder, others working on the same project have a central location where they can go to locate project information. Because it saves time, this method is preferred if many revisions need to be circulated. Project members can look at what is relevant to them instead of going through numerous project-related e-mails.

More About

Excel's Routing Capability

To e-mail or route a workbook as an attachment in Excel format, you need Excel 2002 and one of the following e-mail programs: Outlook, Outlook Express, Microsoft Exchange Client, Lotus cc:Mail or another compatible program with the Messaging Application Programming Interface (MAPI). To receive a routed workbook, you need Excel 97 or a later version.

can specify e-mail addresses. Excel handles creating the e-mail message with routing instructions. It even reminds people who open the document to pass it along to the next person in the routing list when they are finished.

Third, you can **collaborate** interactively with other people through discussion threads or online meetings. The integration of **NetMeeting** with Microsoft Office XP allows you to share and exchange files with people at different sites. When you start an online meeting from within Excel, NetMeeting automatically starts in the background and allows you to share the contents of your file(s).

Fourth, you can collaborate by sharing the workbook. **Sharing** means more than simply giving another user a copy of your file. Sharing implies that multiple people can work independently on the same workbook at the same time if you are in a networked environment.

With any of the collaboration choices, you should keep track of the changes that others make to your workbook.

Tracking Changes

Tracking changes means that Excel, through the **Track Changes command** on the Tools menu, will display the edited cells with a comment indicating who made the change, when the change was made, and the original value of the cell that was changed. Tracking and sharing work together. When you turn on one, the other is enabled by default. The following steps turn on track changes.

Steps | To Turn on Track Changes

1 **Click Tools on the menu bar, point to Track Changes, and then point to Highlight Changes.**

The Tools menu and the Track Changes submenu display (Figure 9-39).

FIGURE 9-39

2 Click Highlight Changes. When the Highlight Changes dialog box displays, click Track changes while editing. If necessary, clear all of the check boxes in the Highlight which changes area. Point to the OK button.

The Highlight Changes dialog box displays (Figure 9-40). Clicking the Track changes while editing check box also shares the workbook. The When, Who, and Where check boxes and list boxes play no role when you first enable track changes.

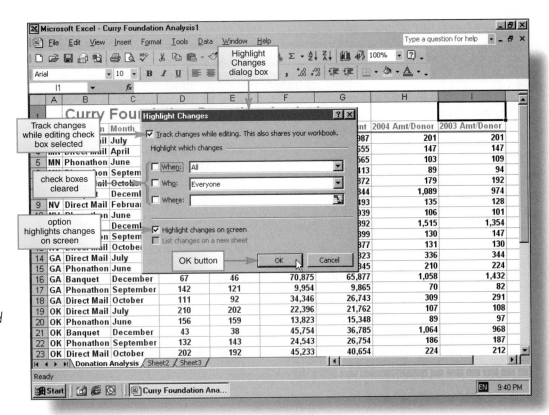

FIGURE 9-40

3 Click the OK button. When the Microsoft Excel dialog box displays asking if you want to continue by saving, click the OK button to save the workbook.

The title bar indicates this workbook is shared (Figure 9-41).

FIGURE 9-41

Other Ways

1. Press ALT+T, T, H
2. In Voice Command mode, say "Tools, Track Changes, Highlight Changes"

Routing the Workbook

The next step is to route the workbook to the four state coordinators for the Curry Foundation. If you are completing this project on a PC, you will be prompted to choose the e-mail addresses of the routing recipients. If you plan actually to execute the routing, substitute the e-mail addresses shown with e-mail addresses from your address book or class. Your return e-mail contact information must be valid as well, in order to round trip the file back to yourself. The term **round trip** refers to sending a document to recipients and then receiving it back at some point in time.

Perform the steps on the next page to route the workbook.

Steps **To Route the Workbook**

1 **Click File on the menu bar, point to Send To, and then point to Routing Recipient.**

The File menu and Send To submenu display (Figure 9-42).

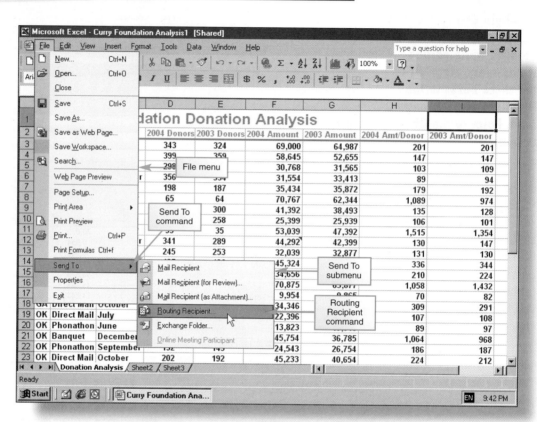

FIGURE 9-42

2 **Click Routing Recipient. If the Choose Profiles dialog box displays, choose your user profile and then click the OK button. If the Check Names dialog box displays, you then may have to add your return address as a new listing to the address book. When the Routing Slip dialog box displays, point to the Address button.**

A routing slip displays that allows you to specify the recipient, subject, and message similar to an e-mail message (Figure 9-43). Your routing slip will display a different name in the From area. If you are working on a networked system, see your instructor or network administrator for the correct e-mail account to use.

FIGURE 9-43

3 **Click the Address button. When the Address Book dialog box displays, click an address in your list, and then click the To button. Repeat the process for three more recipients. Point to the OK button.**

If no addresses display in your address list, you may leave the recipients blank for the purposes of this project. To add new e-mail recipients, you would click the New Contact button and then enter the correct information (Figure 9-44).

FIGURE 9-44

4 **Click the OK button. When the Routing Slip dialog box is visible again, click the Message text box. Type** Please review the attached worksheet and make corrections as necessary. When you are finished reviewing, route to the next recipient. Thank you. **Point to the Route button.**

The Routing Slip dialog box displays the addresses, subject, and message (Figure 9-45).

5 **Click the Route button.**

6 **Click the Save button on the Standard toolbar to save the workbook using the file name Curry Foundation Analysis1. Click the workbook Close button on the menu bar.**

Excel saves a copy of the workbook on the floppy disk and closes the workbook.

FIGURE 9-45

1. Press ALT+F, D, R
2. In Voice Command mode say "File, Send To, Routing Recipient"

More About

Routing Slips

The e-mail addresses you use in the routing slip must be a valid address from your Contacts folder. Your own name and e-mail address must be in the Contacts folder as well, if you want to "round trip" the workbook. To add an address, in the Routing Slip dialog box, click the Address button, and then click the New button in the Address Book dialog box.

In the previous sequence of steps, the e-mail to the first recipient was sent immediately when you clicked the **Route button**. If you had clicked the **Add Slip button** instead of the Route button, then Excel would have asked if it should send the e-mail when the workbook was closed. Figure 9-46 illustrates the e-mail received by the third recipient, Marti Sanchez. A sample message displays and Excel automatically attaches the workbook to the message and inserts instructions to the routing recipients. As each routing recipient receives the e-mail, he or she opens the workbook and looks it over, making changes as necessary. Excel reminds each recipient to forward the workbook to the next person in the list. Excel prompts the last recipient to forward the workbook back to the owner.

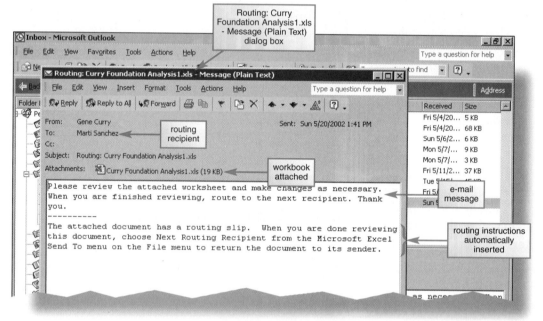

FIGURE 9-46

More About

Shared Workbook Change History

Shared workbooks usually are current, active spreadsheets. Excel maintains a preset change history of 30 days. If you want more time to keep track of changes, you may change the number of days. For example, when you turn on the change history but are not sure exactly when the merge will take place, you can preserve the change history by setting a large number of days to maintain the change history, up to the maximum of 32,767 days.

Excel keeps a **change history** with each shared workbook. In the case of a shared workbook in which you want to track the changes, Excel provides a way for users to make data entry changes, but does not allow them to modify the change history. Click Tools on the menu bar and then point to Protection. In a shared workbook, the only available command on the Protection submenu is **Protect Shared Workbook**. This command displays a dialog box enabling you to protect the change history associated with a shared workbook. Once protected, no one can unprotect, and thereby change, it except the owner.

Reviewing Tracked Changes

Instead of writing suggestions and changes on a printed draft copy, Excel's track changes feature allows users to enter suggested changes directly on the workbook. The owner of the workbook then looks through each change and makes a decision about whether or not to accept it.

Reviewing the Routed Workbook

After a routed workbook has progressed through the entire routing list, it is returned to the owner. Because Highlight Changes was enabled for the Curry Foundation Analysis1 workbook, the file has come back to you with each recipient's changes, corrections, and comments. As the owner, you review those changes and make decisions about whether or not to accept the changes. A tracked workbook named Curry Foundation Analysis2 is stored on the Data Disk. The following steps use this workbook to illustrate reviewing the changes.

Steps ## To Open a Routed Workbook and Review Tracked Changes

1 **With Excel active, click the Open button on the Standard toolbar. When the Open dialog box displays, if necessary click the Look in box arrow and then click 3½ Floppy (A:). Double-click the Curry Foundation Analysis2 workbook. When the workbook displays, click Tools on the menu bar, point to Track Changes, and then point to Highlight Changes.**

The Curry Foundation Analysis2 workbook displays, as do the Tools menu and Track Changes submenu (Figure 9-47).

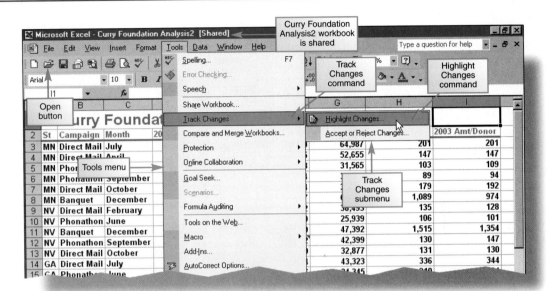

FIGURE 9-47

2 **Click Highlight Changes. When the Highlight Changes dialog box displays, click When to clear the check box. Point to the OK button.**

The Highlight Changes dialog box displays (Figure 9-48). Removing the check mark from the When check box indicates you want to review all changes in the history file.

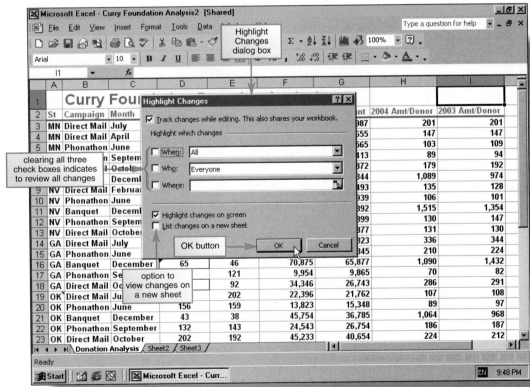

FIGURE 9-48

3 Click the OK button. Click Tools on the menu bar and then click Options. If necessary, click the View tab and then click Comment & indicator in the Comments area. Click the OK button. Point to cell D18.

All comments in the worksheet display. A description of the change made to cell D18 displays (Figure 9-49). Blue triangles represent a data change, and red triangles represent comments.

FIGURE 9-49

4 Click Tools on the menu bar and then click Options. If necessary, click the View tab and then click Comment indicator only in the Comments area. Click the OK button. Click Tools on the menu bar, point to Track Changes, and then point to Accept or Reject Changes.

All comments are hidden. The Tools menu and the Track Changes submenu again display (Figure 9-50).

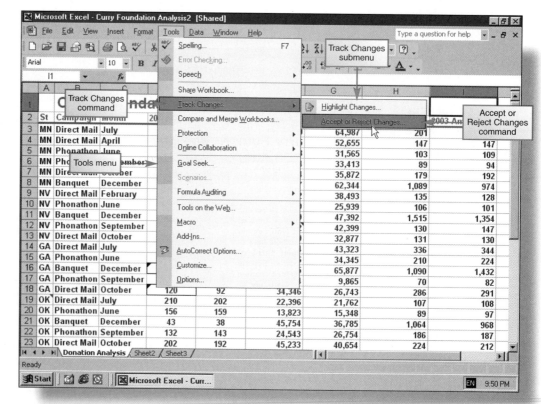

FIGURE 9-50

5 **Click Accept or Reject Changes. When the Select Changes to Accept or Reject dialog box displays, if necessary, clear the check boxes and then point to the OK button.**

The Select Changes to Accept or Reject dialog box allows you to specify the types of changes you want to review (Figure 9-51).

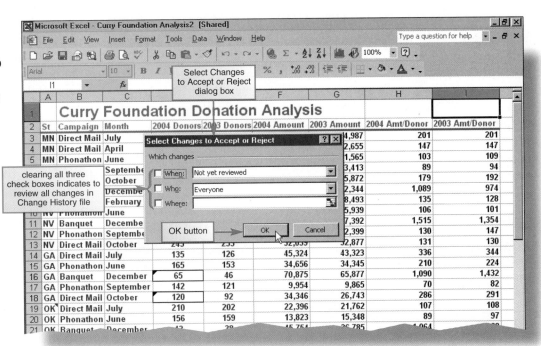

FIGURE 9-51

6 **Click the OK button. When the Accept or Reject Changes dialog box displays Change 1, point to the Accept button.**

One change at a time displays in the Accept or Reject Changes dialog box (Figure 9-52). The cell with the change displays with a marquee. Excel allows you to accept or reject the changes one at a time, or all at once.

7 **Click the Accept button. As each change displays, click the Accept button. Right-click cell A19 and then click Delete Comment on the shortcut menu. Right-click cell F12 and then click Delete Comment on the shortcut menu.**

The process of reviewing and accepting the changes to the workbook is complete.

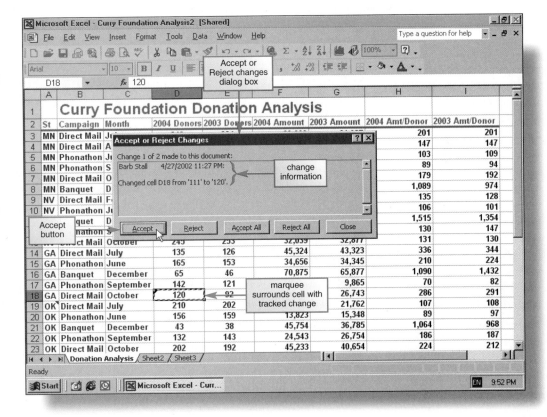

FIGURE 9-52

Table 9-2	Categories of Changes in the Select Changes to Accept or Reject Dialog Box
CHECK BOX	**DESCRIPTION**
When	Select when you want to review changes within a time interval; the four choices are (1) Since I Last Saved; (2) All; (3) Not Yet Reviewed; and (4) Since Date
Who	View changes based on who made them
Where	View changes made to a range of cells

Table 9-3	Buttons in the Accept or Reject Changes Dialog Box
BUTTON	**DESCRIPTION**
Accept	Accepts the current change
Reject	Rejects the current change
Accept All	Accepts all changes
Reject All	Rejects all changes
Close	Closes the Accept or Reject Changes dialog box and terminates the procedure

As shown in Figure 9-51 on the previous page, you can select the category of changes in the change history that you want to accept or reject. Table 9-2 summarizes the three check boxes.

For each tracked change, Excel displays the Accept or Reject Changes dialog box (Figure 9-52 on the previous page) with five buttons from which to choose. Table 9-3 summarizes the five buttons.

With the changes accepted, the following steps save the workbook using a new file name.

TO SAVE THE TRACKED CHANGES IN A WORKBOOK WITH A NEW FILE NAME

1 Click File on the menu bar and then click Save As.

2 When the Save As dialog box displays, type `Curry Foundation Analysis3` in the File name text box.

3 If necessary, click 3½ Floppy (A:) in the Save in list.

4 Click the Save button in the Save As dialog box.

Excel saves the workbook on drive A using the file name, Curry Foundation Analysis3.

The next step is to turn off the track changes feature. Excel denies access to features such as the PivotChart while the workbook is shared. Perform the following steps to turn off track changes, which also automatically turns off sharing and saves the workbook as an exclusive one. That is, it no longer is a shared workbook.

TO TURN OFF TRACK CHANGES

1 Click Tools on the menu bar, point to Track Changes, and then click Highlight Changes.

2 When the Highlight Changes dialog box displays, click Track Changes while editing to clear the check box.

3 Click the OK button in the Highlight Changes dialog box.

4 When the Microsoft Excel dialog box displays asking you to make the workbook exclusive, click the Yes button.

The workbook displays without the word, Shared, on the title bar. Excel disables track changes.

When you turn off track changes, you turn off sharing as well. At the same time, Excel erases the change history. The workbook automatically resaves as an exclusive workbook. An **exclusive workbook** can be opened only by a single user.

The imports and changes complete the Curry Foundation Analysis workbook. The next step is to analyze the data using PivotCharts and PivotTables to better understand the information gathered.

Creating and Formatting PivotCharts and PivotTables

A **PivotChart** is an interactive chart used to analyze data graphically by varying the fields and categories to present different views. After you create a PivotChart, you may view different levels of detail, reorganize the layout of the chart by dragging its fields, or display and hide items in drop-down lists. While you usually create a PivotChart on a separate worksheet in the same workbook containing the data you are analyzing, you can create a PivotChart on the same worksheet as the data.

When you create a PivotChart, Excel creates and associates a PivotTable automatically. A **PivotTable** is an interactive view of worksheet data that gives you the ability to summarize data in the database, and then rotate the table's row and column titles to show different views of the summarized data.

More About

PivotTables

The PivotTable is one of the most powerful analytical tools available in Excel. PivotTables are used to show the relationships among the data in a list or a database. These tables allow you to use drag and drop to examine the data from different views.

Creating a PivotChart

The **PivotChart command** on the Data menu starts the **PivotTable and PivotChart Wizard**, which guides you through creating a PivotChart. The wizard does not modify the data in any way; it simply uses the data to generate information on a new worksheet.

The required PivotChart for this project is shown in Figure 9-53. It summarizes 2003 and 2004 total amounts per donor information by fundraising campaign type within state for the Donation Analysis worksheet. The x-axis displays categories by fundraising campaign within state. The y-axis displays the series values for the total amount per donor for each year. The interactive buttons allow the user to choose which fields to display. The legend displays the color coding for each year.

To create the PivotChart shown in Figure 9-53, perform the steps on the next page.

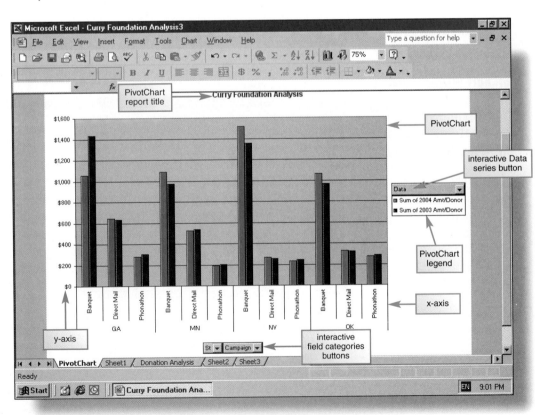

FIGURE 9-53

Steps **To Create a PivotChart**

1 **Scroll to and then click cell A3. Click Data on the menu bar and then point to PivotTable and PivotChart Report (Figure 9-54).**

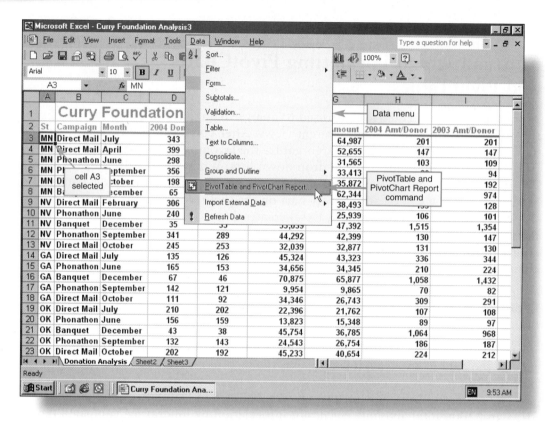

FIGURE 9-54

2 **Click PivotTable and PivotChart Report. When the PivotTable and PivotChart Wizard - Step 1 of 3 dialog box displays, click PivotChart report (with PivotTable report). Point to the Next button.**

The PivotTable and PivotChart Wizard - Step 1 of 3 dialog box displays (Figure 9-55). The Microsoft Excel list or database and the PivotChart report (with PivotTable report) option buttons are selected.

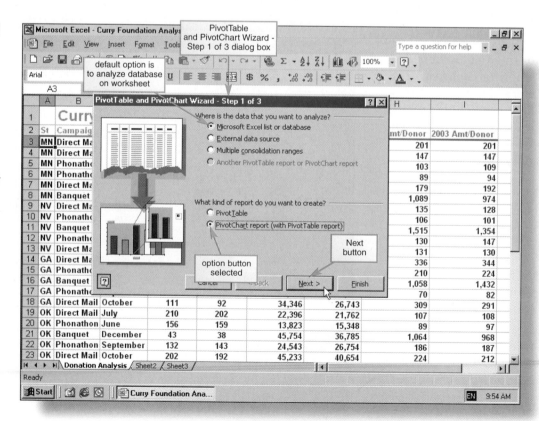

FIGURE 9-55

3 **Click the Next button.**

The PivotTable and PivotChart Wizard - Step 2 of 3 dialog box displays. The range A2:I23 automatically is selected (Figure 9-56). A marquee surrounds the data on the worksheet.

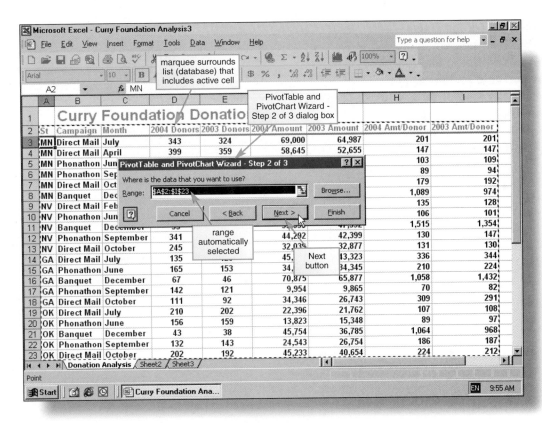

FIGURE 9-56

4 **Click the Next button. When the PivotTable and PivotChart Wizard - Step 3 of 3 displays, if necessary, click New worksheet and then point to the Finish button.**

The wizard will place the chart and table on separate worksheets in the workbook (Figure 9-57).

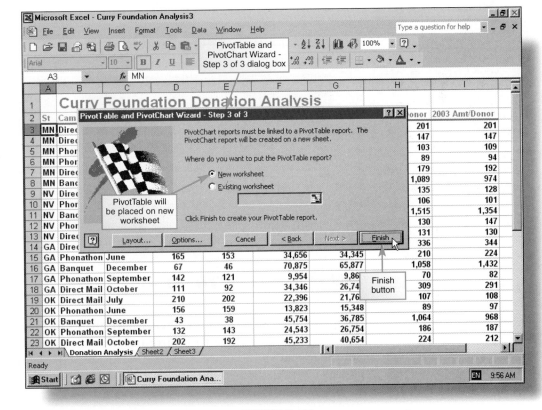

FIGURE 9-57

5 **Click the Finish button. When the PivotChart area and the PivotTable toolbar display, drag the toolbar up and to the right in order to display all areas of the PivotChart.**

The PivotChart displays on a new worksheet (Figure 9-58). The **PivotTable toolbar** *also displays. Fields from the list of data display in the PivotTable Field List window.*

FIGURE 9-58

The four main areas of a PivotChart (Figure 9-58) are described in Table 9-4.

Table 9-4	PivotChart Drop Areas
PIVOTCHART DROP AREA	**DESCRIPTION OF DATA**
Drop Page Fields Here	Data fields that categorize the entire chart
Drop Data Items Here	Data fields plotted on the chart, summarizing the detail of the database cells
Drop Series Fields Here	Multiple data items plotted as a series, summarizing the detail columns of the database cells (y-axis)
Drop Category Fields Here	Data fields to categorize on the x-axis

Adding Data to the PivotChart

The following steps create the PivotChart in Figure 9-53 on page E 9.39 by dropping four fields from the PivotChart Field List window in the PivotChart area: two for the x-axis along the bottom of the chart and two for the data series in the chart. As shown in Figure 9-53, the x-axis displays campaign within state. The y-axis includes the two data fields 2003 Amt/Donor and 2004 Amt/Donor.

Steps **To Add Data to the PivotChart**

1 Drag the St (state) button from the PivotTable Field List window to the Drop Category Fields Here area. Drag the Campaign button from the PivotTable Field List window and drop it to the right of the St (state) button. Point to the 2003 Amt/Donor button.

The State and Campaign field buttons display at the bottom of the chart (Figure 9-59).

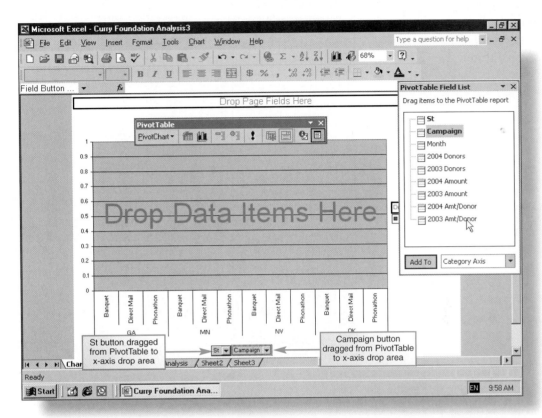

FIGURE 9-59

2 Drag the PivotTable Field List window to the left side of the screen. Drag the 2003 Amt/Donor button to the Drop Data Items Here area in the center of the chart area. Drag the 2004 Amt/Donor button to the same area.

The data fields display in the PivotChart (Figure 9-60). Because multiple fields have been added to the chart, a field Data button displays in the categories area at the bottom of the chart.

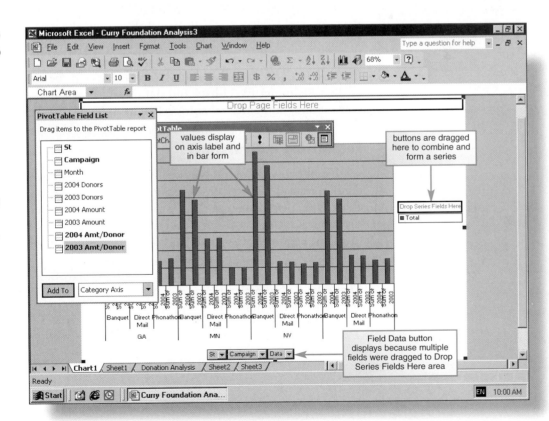

FIGURE 9-60

3 **Drag the Field Data button to the Drop Series Fields Here area.**

The two data fields display stacked (Figure 9-61).

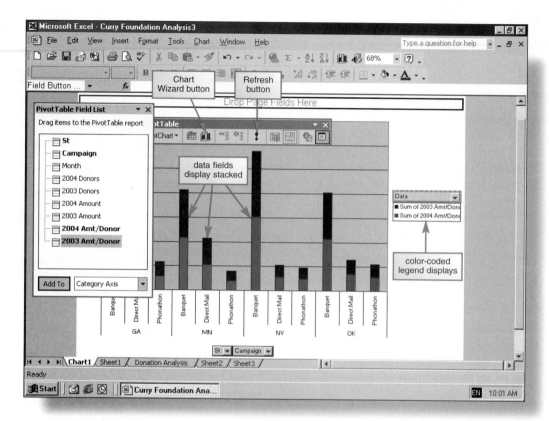

FIGURE 9-61

Regular charts in Excel are linked directly to worksheet cells, which means that when data changes in the worksheet cell, the chart is updated automatically. PivotCharts are not linked to worksheet cells. The PivotTable toolbar contains a Refresh button (Figure 9-61) to update data when it changes on the worksheet. PivotCharts and their associated PivotTables can be based on several different types of data including Excel lists and databases, multiple data ranges that you want to consolidate, and external sources, such as Microsoft Access databases.

Formatting a PivotChart

Excel provides many ways to format PivotCharts. If you are familiar with regular charts, you will find that most formatting processes, such as choosing a chart type, displaying category or axis labels, and inserting titles, are performed the same way in PivotCharts as they are in regular charts.

The default chart type for a PivotChart is a Stacked Column chart. PivotCharts can display any chart type except XY (Scatter), Stock, or Bubble. The following steps change the Curry Foundation PivotChart from a Stacked Column chart to a Clustered Column chart that displays the two-year data side by side, adds a title, and formats the numbers along the y-axis.

Steps **To Change the PivotChart Type and Format the Chart**

1 **Click the Chart Wizard button** (shown in Figure 9-61) on the PivotTable toolbar. When the Chart Wizard - Step 1 of 4 - Chart Type dialog box displays, click the Clustered Column chart in the top row of the Chart sub-type box. Point to the Next button.

The Chart Type dialog box allows you to choose the type of chart and its subtype (Figure 9-62). Clicking the Press and Hold to View Sample button produces a preview.

FIGURE 9-62

2 **Click the Next button. When the Chart Wizard - Step 3 of 4 - Chart Options dialog box displays, if necessary, click the Titles tab. Click the Chart title text box, type** Curry Foundation Analysis **and then point to the Finish button.**

The Chart Options dialog box displays as shown in Figure 9-63.

FIGURE 9-63

3 **Click the Finish button. Right-click any of the numbers along the y-axis on the left side of the PivotChart. Point to Format Axis on the shortcut menu.**

The Chart Wizard closes and the shortcut menu displays (Figure 9-64). Clicking the Finish button accepted the default values for the rest of the Chart Wizard.

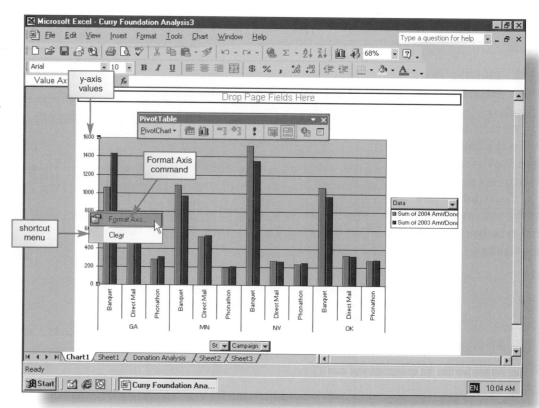

FIGURE 9-64

4 **Click Format Axis. When the Format Axis dialog box displays, click the Number tab, and then click Currency in the Category list. Type 0 in the Decimal places box. Point to the OK button.**

The Format Axis dialog box displays as shown in Figure 9-65.

FIGURE 9-65

5 Click the OK button. Double-click the Chart1 sheet tab at the bottom of the workbook. Type PivotChart and then press the ENTER key to rename the sheet.

The numbers along the y-axis display using the Currency format (Figure 9-66).

6 Click anywhere on the chart to deselect the y-axis. Click the PivotTable toolbar Close button and then click the Save button on the Standard toolbar.

Excel saves the workbook with the PivotChart on drive A.

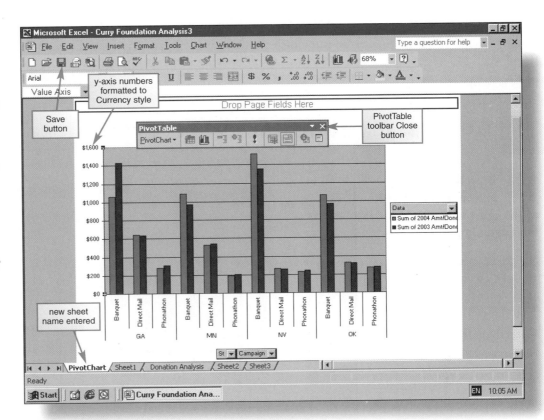

FIGURE 9-66

Other Ways

1. Click PivotChart button on PivotTable toolbar, click Options
2. Click Chart Wizard button on PivotTable toolbar, apply formatting in each wizard step

With the chart completed and formatted appropriately, the chart can be manipulated and the data analyzed in a variety of views.

Changing the View of a PivotChart

With regular charts, you must create one chart for each view of the data summary that you want to see. With a PivotChart, you are able to create a single chart and view the summaries several ways just by using the mouse. The PivotChart provides a powerful interactive summarization of data with the visual appeal and benefits of a chart.

The Curry Foundation PivotChart currently displays the amount per donor for each year within campaign type within state (Figure 9-66).

It is easy to see common trends, such as that banquets seem to have declining amounts given per donor while other event types are increasing in the amount given for each donor. You also can see that in general, Georgia is experiencing better growth than the other states. You may wish to view the data in other ways, such as just looking at one year's worth of information. If you want to compare the data in different combinations, you can use the interactive buttons in the categories area at the bottom of the chart.

Because Minnesota and Oklahoma have similar target audiences for the Curry Foundation fundraising efforts, you might want to view the data and compare only those two states rather than all four. Moving the two data ranges next to each other in the worksheet would be tedious; in the PivotChart, however, you may choose which categories to display by using the interactive buttons at the bottom of the chart.

If you want to isolate two years to compare to one another, for instance, you use the interactive buttons in the series area on the right of the chart.

Perform the following steps to interact with the PivotChart categories and series of data.

Steps **To Change the View of a PivotChart**

1 **Drag the St (state) button at the bottom of the chart to the right of the Campaign button**

Notice the locations are grouped by campaign now, rather than by states (Figure 9-67).

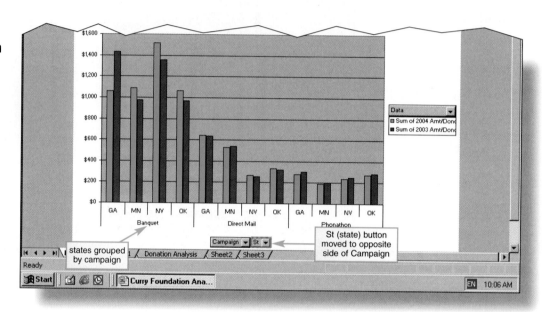

FIGURE 9-67

2 **Click the Data button arrow on the right of the chart. When the list displays, click the check box next to Sum of 2003 Amt/Donor to clear the check box. Point to the OK button.**

The list of fields of data on the chart displays (Figure 9-68).

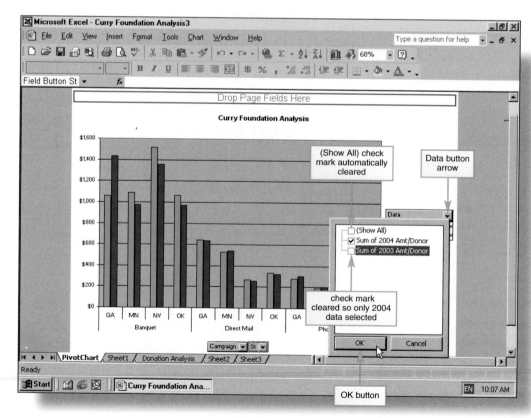

FIGURE 9-68

3 **Click the OK button. Point to the Undo button on the Standard toolbar.**

Only the data for 2004 displays (Figure 9-69). The Sum of 2004 Amt/Donor becomes a field for the entire page.

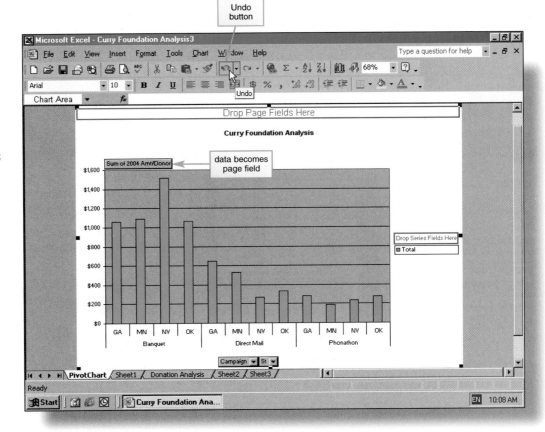

FIGURE 9-69

4 **Click the Undo button on the Standard toolbar. Click the arrow on the St (state) interactive button, click the check boxes for Georgia (GA) and Nevada (NV) to clear them, and then point to the OK button.**

The data fields in the St (state) button display (Figure 9-70). The 2003 data again displays in the PivotChart.

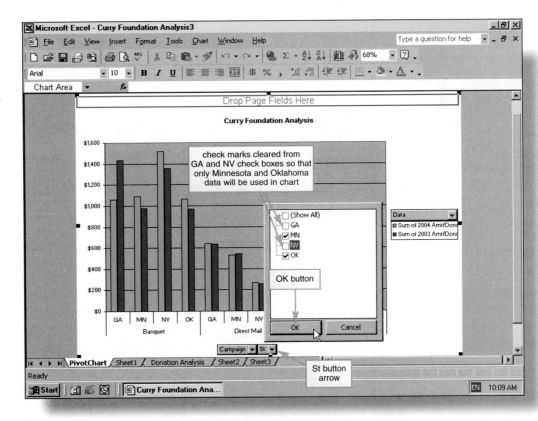

FIGURE 9-70

5 **Click the OK button.**

Only the data for Minnesota and Oklahoma displays (Figure 9-71).

6 **Click the Undo button on the Standard toolbar.**

The data for all states displays (Figure 9-67 on page E 9.48).

FIGURE 9-71

You can employ powerful data summarization techniques using PivotCharts. Choosing which kinds of data best represent trends and comparisons is easy with the interactive buttons on a PivotChart.

PivotChart and PivotTable Relationships

Excel creates and associates a PivotTable on a separate sheet with every PivotChart. A PivotTable (Figure 9-72) is an interactive view of worksheet data that gives you the ability to summarize data and then rotate the table's row and column titles to show different views of the summarized data.

When you change the position of a field in a PivotChart or PivotTable, the corresponding field in the other changes automatically. **Row fields** in a PivotTable correspond to category fields in a PivotChart, while **column fields** in a PivotTable correspond to series fields in charts.

Formatting a PivotTable

When you choose to format a PivotTable, Excel displays samples in the AutoFormat dialog box with various formatting applied to the cells, borders, and numbers. You can choose from colors, patterns, alignments, fonts, and borders, which apply to the entire table. You also may apply any of the wide range of Excel's normal formats to individual cells. The following steps choose a format that contains color and borders to enhance the data.

Steps **To Format a PivotTable**

1 **Double-click the Sheet1 tab at the bottom of the workbook. Type** PivotTable **and then press the ENTER key to rename the sheet. Right-click a toolbar and click PivotTable on the shortcut menu to display the PivotTable toolbar. Point to the Format Report button on the PivotTable toolbar.**

The PivotTable toolbar, created by Excel and associated with the PivotChart, displays (Figure 9-72). If the PivotTable toolbar does not display, right-click the toolbar and click PivotTable.

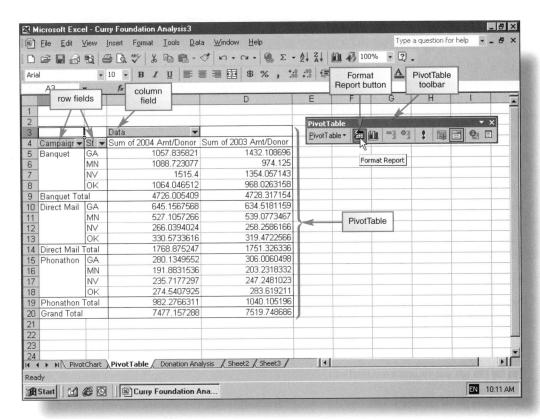

FIGURE 9-72

2 **Click the Format Report button. When the AutoFormat dialog box displays, if necessary, scroll to display Report 6. Click Report 6 and then point to the OK button.**

The AutoFormat dialog box displays report formats you can use to add color and variety to the PivotTable (Figure 9-73).

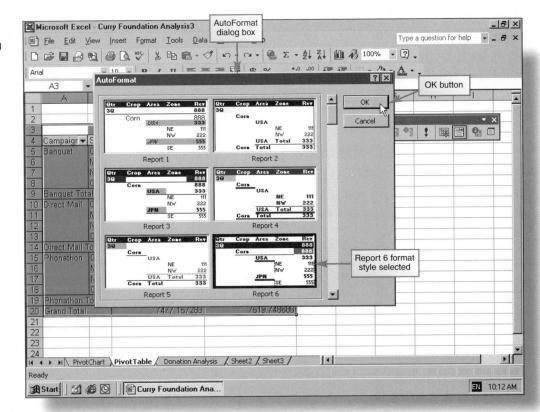

FIGURE 9-73

3 **Click the OK button. Double-click the border between column headings A and B to change column A to best fit. Click the Select All button. Right-click any cell in the table and then click Format Cells on the shortcut menu. When the Format Cells dialog box displays, click Currency in the Category list, type 0 in the Decimal places box, and then click the OK button. Click cell F22 to deselect the worksheet.**

The PivotTable displays as shown in Figure 9-74.

4 **Click the Save button to save the workbook using the file name, Curry Foundation Analysis3.**

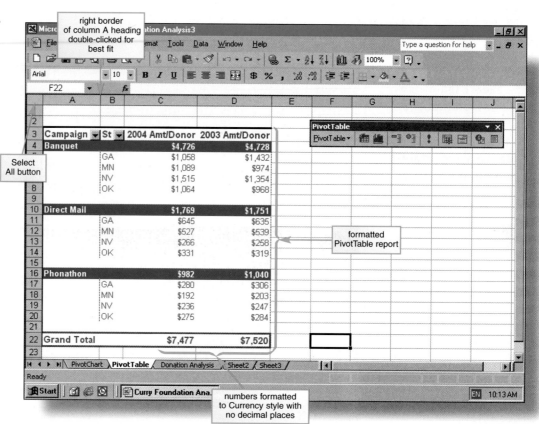

FIGURE 9-74

The AutoFormat dialog box shown in Figure 9-73 on the previous page includes 12 customized formats. Use the scroll box to view the formats that do not display in the dialog box. Each one of these customized formats offers a different look. The one you choose depends on the worksheet you are creating. If you want to remove the format on a PivotTable, you can click None in the list of formats.

Interacting with the PivotTable

Interacting with a PivotTable is as easy as it is with the PivotChart. You can change the way the data fields are summarized, add new fields to the analysis, or you can rotate the row and column fields.

SWITCHING SUMMARY FUNCTIONS   In the Curry Foundation PivotChart, you may have realized that the data created in the chart illustrates the sum of the amount per donor. The fact that more donors are active in Nevada will skew the figures if you just look at the sums. An average might be a better way to compare the campaigns. To change the field setting from sum to average, you simply right-click the field in the PivotTable, click Field Settings on the shortcut menu, and then choose Average in the Summarize by list, as shown in the following steps.

Steps **To Switch Summary Functions in a PivotTable**

1 **Right-click cell C3. Click Field Settings** on the shortcut menu. When the PivotTable Field dialog box displays, click Average in the Summarize by list. Click the OK button.

The numbers in column C change from sums to averages.

2 **Right-click cell D3. Click Field Settings** on the shortcut menu. When the PivotTable Field dialog box displays, click Average in the Summarize by list. Click the OK button.

The numbers in column D change from location sums to location averages (Figure 9-75).

 3 **Click the PivotTable toolbar Close button.**

FIGURE 9-75

Table 9-5 lists the summary functions from which you may choose through the Field Settings command on the shortcut menu to analyze your data in PivotCharts and PivotTables.

CHANGING THE VIEW OF A PIVOTTABLE You can rotate the row and column fields around the data field by dragging the buttons to different locations on the PivotTable. For example, if you drag the St (state) button to the Drop Page Fields Here area at the top of the table (above row 1 in the worksheet), you change the view of the PivotTable, as shown in the steps on the next page.

Table 9-5 Summary Functions for PivotChart and PivotTable Data Analysis	
SUMMARY FUNCTION	**DESCRIPTION**
Sum	Sum values; this is the default function for numeric source data
Count	The number of items
Average	The average of the values
Max	The largest value
Min	The smallest value
Product	The product of the values
Count Nums	The number of rows that contain numeric data
StdDev	An estimate of the standard deviation of all the data to be summarized
StdDevp	The standard deviation of all of the data to be summarized
Var	An estimate of the variance of all of the data to be summarized
Varp	The variance of the data to be summarized

Steps **To Change the View of a PivotTable**

1 **Drag the St button above row 1. Select cell A9.**

Excel displays a new, different view of the PivotTable (Figure 9-76), which is easier to read than the PivotTable shown in Figure 9-75.

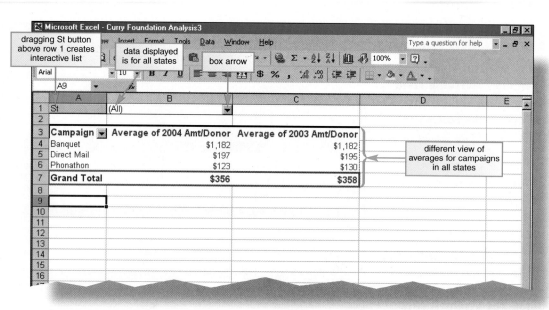

FIGURE 9-76

2 **Click the St box arrow, click MN, and then click the OK button.**

Excel displays the averages for each campaign type in the state of Minnesota (Figure 9-77).

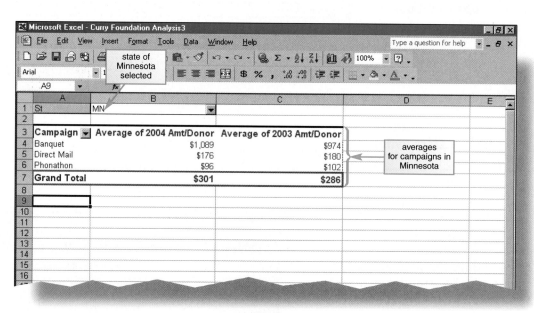

FIGURE 9-77

In Figure 9-76, a box and box arrow display to the right of the St button. Click the box arrow to display the St list box and select specific states whose averages you want to view.

PivotTables are powerful data analysis tools because they allow you to view the data in various ways by interchanging or pairing up the row and column fields. You can print a PivotChart or PivotTable just as you would any other worksheet. If you update the data on the Donation Analysis sheet, click **Refresh Data** on the Data menu or click the **Refresh button** on the PivotTable toolbar to update the corresponding PivotTable and PivotChart.

The donation analysis is complete. To close the Curry Foundation Anaysis3 workbook, follow the step below.

TO CLOSE THE WORKBOOK

1 Click the Curry Foundation Anaysis3 Close window button on the right side of the menu bar.

Merging Workbooks

Instead of tracking all of the changes to a single copy of a workbook, it sometimes is necessary to merge copies of the same workbook. This may be because multiple users are entering data or because new data has come in from a different source. To merge the changes from one workbook into another, both workbooks must satisfy the following requirements:

▶ You must make the original workbook shared, before making copies, and each workbook must be a copy of the same workbook.

▶ When you make copies, track changes or sharing must be turned on (which keeps a change history of the workbook).

▶ The Share Workbook command on the Tools menu displays a dialog box with a tab for recording the number of days to record the change history. Shared workbooks must be merged within that time period.

▶ If you use passwords, all workbooks involved in the merge must have the same password.

▶ When the copies come back, each must have a different file name.

When you have all the copies of the workbook together, you open the copy of the shared workbook into which you want to merge changes from another workbook file on disk. Then, on the Tools menu, click **Merge Workbooks**, which will display choices for you to choose a workbook or workbooks to merge. Not only is the data merged, but if comments are recorded, they display one after another in the given cell's comment box.

If Excel cannot merge the two workbooks, you still can incorporate the information from one workbook into the other, by copying and pasting the information from one workbook to another.

The Curry Foundation maintains historical foundation expense information in a workbook that has been shared and copied to two other members of the staff for review. The Curry Foundation Expenses worksheet also contains a chart that shows total expenses over the past five years. The steps on the next pages merge the changes from the other members of the staff with the original workbook, CurryFoundationExpenses.

More About

Changing PivotTables

At any time while the workbook containing a PivotTable is active, you can click the tab of the sheet containing the PivotTable, and then click PivotTable and PivotChart on the Data menu to display the PivotTable and PivotChart Wizard - Step 3 of 3 dialog box (Figure 9-57 on page E 9.41). Use the Layout button in this dialog box as an alternative to using drag and drop to change the view of the PivotTable.

More About

Merging

If you are not sure of the time period that will elapse before you merge workbooks that you send out for changes, set a large number of days to keep change history. You can set the number of days to be as large as 32,767 days.

More About

Microsoft Certification

The Microsoft Office User Specialist (MOUS) Certification program provides an opportunity for you to obtain a valuable industry credential — proof that you have the Excel 2002 skills required by employers. For more information, see Appendix D or visit the Shelly Cashman Series MOUS Web page at scsite.com/offxp/cert.htm.

Steps **To Merge Workbooks**

1 **Open the file named, CurryFoundationExpenses, from the Data Disk.**

The Curry Foundation Expenses worksheet displays as shown in Figure 9-78. The title bar indicates that the workbook is shared.

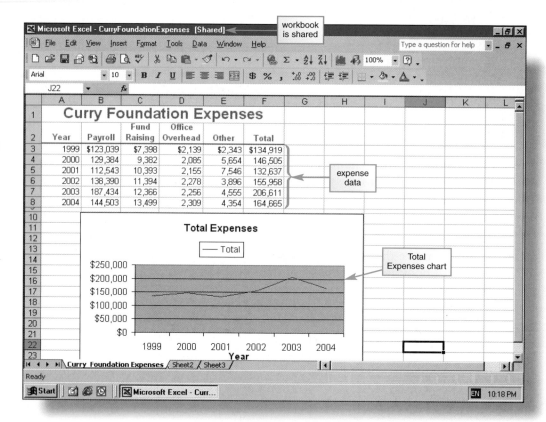

FIGURE 9-78

2 **Click Tools on the menu bar and then point to Compare and Merge Workbooks.**

The Tools menu displays (Figure 9-79).

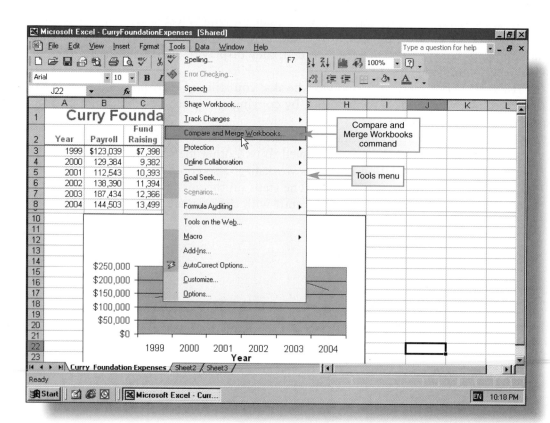

FIGURE 9-79

3 **Click Compare and Merge Workbooks. Click 3½ Floppy (A:), if necessary, in the Look in box. Drag through the workbooks CurryFoundation ExpensesBenny and CurryFoundation ExpensesWanda and then point to the OK button.**

The Select Files to Merge Into Current Workbook dialog box displays. The two workbooks to be merged are selected as shown in Figure 9-80.

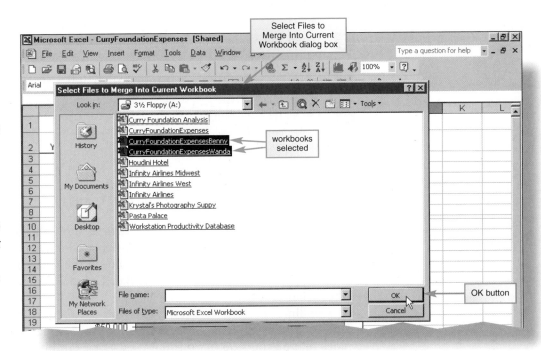

FIGURE 9-80

4 **Click the OK button.**

The workbooks are merged and cells that were changed by Benny and Wanda are changed in the Curry Foundation Expenses worksheet (Figure 9-81).

FIGURE 9-81

Other Ways

1. Press ALT+T, W

2. In Voice Command mode, say "Tools, Compare and Merge Workbooks"

The workbooks have been merged, and the Curry Foundation Expenses worksheet reflects the changes from Benny and Wanda. Excel also updated the Total Expenses historical chart. If Benny and Wanda had changed a common cell with different values, Excel would have prompted you to select which change to keep in the merged workbook.

The next step is to turn off workbook sharing so that the chart can be manipulated.

TO TURN OFF WORKBOOK SHARING AND SAVE THE WORKBOOK

1 Click Tools on the menu bar and then select Share Workbook on the Tools menu.

> **2** When the Share Workbook dialog box displays, clear the check box on the Editing page.
>
> **3** Click the OK button. When the Microsoft Excel dialog box displays, click the Yes button.
>
> **4** Click the Save button on the Standard toolbar.

The workbook no longer is shared.

More About

Trendlines

The R-squared value of a trendline can tell you how accurate the projection may be. Trendlines are most reliable when their R-squared values are at or near 1. When you create a trendline, Excel automatically calculates the R-squared value. You then can display this value on your chart.

Adding a Trendline to a Chart

A **trendline** is used on certain Excel charts to show the general tendency of how data in a chart is changing. Trendlines are calculated automatically and overlaid onto charts using the Add Trendline command on the Chart menu. Excel allows trendlines to be added to Unstacked 2-D Area, Bar, Column, Line, Stock, XY (Scatter), and Bubble charts.

Trendlines become valuable when you use them to project data beyond the values of a data set. This process is called forecasting. **Forecasting** helps predict data values that are outside of your data set. For example, if your data is for a 10-year period and the data shows a trend in that 10-year period, Excel can predict values beyond that period or tell you what the values may have been before that period.

The following steps add a trendline to the Total Expenses chart and predict the total expenses two years beyond the data set.

Steps | **To Add a Trendline to a Chart**

1 Select the chart by clicking the white area around the chart. Click Chart on the menu bar and then point to Add Trendline.

The Chart menu displays (Figure 9-82).

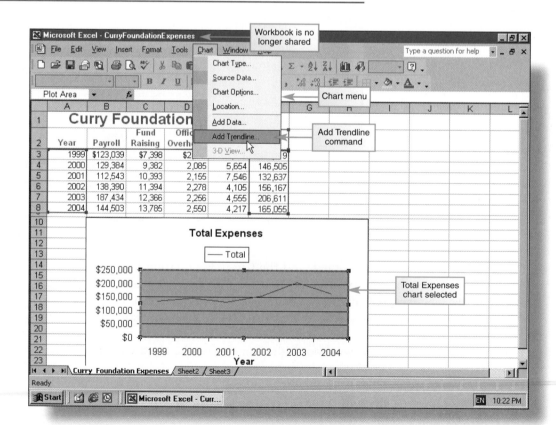

FIGURE 9-82

2 **Click Add Trendline. When the Add Trendline dialog box displays, if necessary, click the Options tab. Click the Forward text box in the Forecast area and type** 2. **Point to the OK button.**

The Add Trendline dialog box displays, and the option is set to forecast two periods forward on the trendline as shown in Figure 9-83.

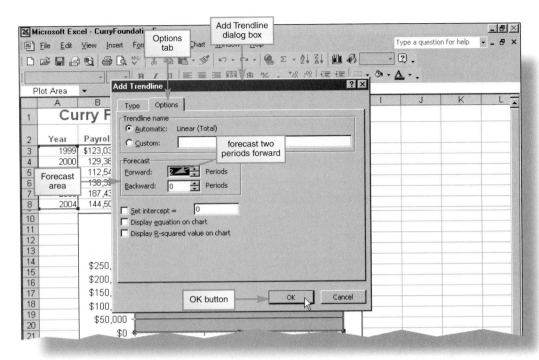

FIGURE 9-83

3 **Click the OK button. Drag the legend sub-title of the chart to the left to align it under the Total Expenses chart title.**

The trendline displays on the chart, and two additional data points are added to the chart to reflect projected values in the years 2005 and 2006 (Figure 9-84).

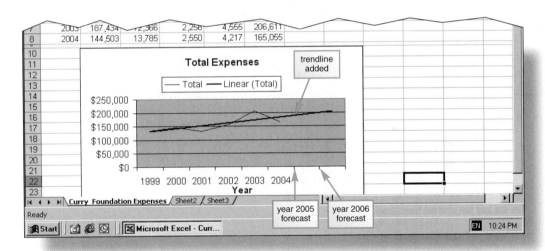

FIGURE 9-84

The **Options tab** (Figure 9-83) allows you to customize the trendline that you are adding to a chart. The Trendline name area allows you to specify a name for the trendline or accept the default name automatically selected by Excel. The Forecast area determines how far before or after your data values to project the trendline on the chart. If the Set intercept checkbox is checked, Excel draws the trendline so that the trendline intercepts the y-axis at the location specified in the Set intercept = box. Excel displays an equation of the form y = mx + b for linear trendlines when the Display equation on chart check box is checked. If another trendline type is being used, Excel displays the corresponding equation for the data being analyzed. When the Display R-squared value on chart check box is checked, Excel displays the statistical correlation of the data values with which the trendline is associated.

Other Ways

1. Select the chart, press ALT+C, R
2. Select the chart, in Voice Command mode, say "Chart, Add Trendline"

Quitting Excel

The project is complete. To quit Excel, follow the steps below.

TO QUIT EXCEL

1 Click the Close button on the right side of the title bar.

2 If the Microsoft Excel dialog box displays, click the No button.

CASE PERSPECTIVE SUMMARY

With the imported data, the PivotChart, and the PivotTable developed in this project, Gene Curry can view and analyze the donation data in a variety of ways. Links to the external data will update automatically when he refreshes his tables. Gene now can prepare his annual report with the knowledge that he has the best data available to him and will be able to better share his vision.

Project Summary

In this project, you learned how to import data in different formats into a worksheet, track changes, route workbooks, and create visual representations of the data in a worksheet. Using a preformatted worksheet, you learned how to import a text file, an Access database, a Web table, and spreadsheet XML. You then learned how to track changes, which also shared the workbook. After routing the workbook to the coordinator from each state, you learned how to accept the changes. You learned how to create interactive PivotChart and PivotTables, format them, and view them in different ways. You learned about sharing and merging workbooks. Finally, you learned how to create a trendline on a chart and use it for what-if analysis.

What You Should Know

Having completed this project, you should be able to perform the following tasks:

- Add a Trendline to a Chart (E 9.58)
- Add Data to the PivotChart (E 9.43)
- Change the PivotChart Type and Format the Chart (E 9.45)
- Change the View of a PivotChart (E 9.48)
- Change the View of a PivotTable (E 9.54)
- Close the Workbook (E 9.55)
- Create a PivotChart (E 9.40)
- Format a PivotTable (E 9.51)
- Import Data from a Text File into a Worksheet (E 9.09)
- Import Data from a Web Page into a Worksheet (E 9.18)
- Import Data from an Access Table into a Worksheet (E 9.14)
- Import Data from Spreadsheet XML into a Worksheet (E 9.23)
- Insert a Comment (E 9.28)
- Merge Workbooks (E 9.56)
- Open a Routed Workbook and Review Tracked Changes (E 9.35)
- Quit Excel (E 9.60)
- Replicate Formulas (E 9.26)
- Route the Workbook (E 9.32)
- Save the Workbook with a New File Name (E 9.27)
- Save the Tracked Changes in a Workbook with a New File Name (E 9.38)
- Start Excel, Open a Workbook, and Customize Excel (E 9.08)
- Switch Summary Functions in a PivotTable (E 9.53)
- Turn off Track Changes (E 9.38)
- Turn off Workbook Sharing and Save the Workbook (E 9.57)
- Turn on Track Changes (E 9.30)

Learn It Online

Instructions: To complete the Learn It Online exercises, start your browser, click the Address bar, and then enter scsite.com/offxp/exs.htm. When the Office XP Learn It Online page displays, follow the instructions in the exercises below.

1 Project Reinforcement TF, MC, and SA

Below Excel Project 9, click the Project Reinforcement link. Print the quiz by clicking Print on the File menu. Answer each question. Write your first and last name at the top of each page, and then hand in the printout to your instructor.

2 Flash Cards

Below Excel Project 9, click the Flash Cards link. When Flash Cards displays, read the instructions. Type 20 (or a number specified by your instructor) in the Number of Playing Cards text box, type your name in the Name text box, and then click the Flip Card button. When the flash card displays, read the question and then click the Answer box arrow to select an answer. Flip through Flash Cards. Click Print on the File menu to print the last flash card if your score is 15 (75%) correct or greater and then hand it in to your instructor. If your score is less than 15 (75%) correct, then redo this exercise by clicking the Replay button.

3 Practice Test

Below Excel Project 9, click the Practice Test link. Answer each question, enter your first and last name at the bottom of the page, and then click the Grade Test button. When the graded practice test displays on your screen, click Print on the File menu to print a hard copy. Continue to take practice tests until you score 80% or better. Hand in a printout of the final practice test to your instructor.

4 Who Wants to Be a Computer Genius?

Below Excel Project 9, click the Computer Genius link. Read the instructions, enter your first and last name at the bottom of the page, and then click the Play button. Hand in your score to your instructor.

5 Wheel of Terms

Below Excel Project 9, click the Wheel of Terms link. Read the instructions, and then enter your first and last name and your school name. Click the Play button. Hand in your score to your instructor.

6 Crossword Puzzle Challenge

Below Excel Project 9, click the Crossword Puzzle Challenge link. Read the instructions, and then enter your first and last name. Click the Play button. Work the crossword puzzle. When you are finished, click the Submit button. When the crossword puzzle redisplays, click the Print button. Hand in the printout.

7 Tips and Tricks

Below Excel Project 9, click the Tips and Tricks link. Click a topic that pertains to Project 9. Right-click the information and then click Print on the shortcut menu. Construct a brief example of what the information relates to in Excel to confirm you understand how to use the tip or trick. Hand in the example and printed information.

online

8 Newsgroups

Below Excel Project 9, click the Newsgroups link. Click a topic that pertains to Project 9. Print three comments. Hand in the comments to your instructor.

9 Expanding Your Horizons

Below Excel Project 9, click the Articles for Microsoft Excel link. Click a topic that pertains to Project 9. Print the information. Construct a brief example of what the information relates to in Excel to confirm you understand the contents of the article. Hand in the example and printed information to your instructor.

10 Search Sleuth

Below Excel Project 9, click the Search Sleuth link. To search for a term that pertains to this project, select a term below the Project 9 title and then use the Google search engine at google.com (or any major search engine) to display and print two Web pages that present information on the term. Hand in the printouts to your instructor.

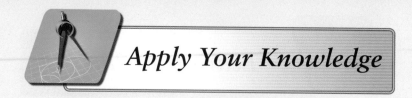

Apply Your Knowledge

1 Merging Workbooks and Creating a Trendline

Instructions: Start Excel and perform the following tasks.

1. Open the workbook, Infinity Airlines, from the Data Disk. See the inside back cover of this book for instructions for downloading the Data Disk or see your instructor for information on accessing the files required in this book. The worksheet displays as shown in Figure 9-85. The worksheet contains revenue information for one of Infinity Airlines flights that departs each week. The worksheet also contains a graph of the total revenue from each week. The workbook is shared.

2. Merge the workbooks Infinity Airlines West and Infinity Airlines Midwest into the Infinity Airlines workbook.

3. Turn off sharing of the workbook. Print the Flight Revenue Analysis worksheet.

4. Add a trendline to the chart on the worksheet. Forecast the total revenue two weeks forward. Resize the chart so the legend and the chart do not overlap. Print the worksheet.

5. Right-click the trendline and then click Format Trendline on the shortcut menu. Click the Options tab and forecast four weeks forward. Resize the chart so the legend and the chart do not overlap. Print the worksheet.

6. Right-click the trendline and then click Format Trendline on the shortcut menu. Click the Options tab and use a custom trendline name of Forecasted Revenue. Forecast eight weeks forward. Resize the chart so the legend and the chart do not overlap. Print the worksheet.

7. Save the workbook as Infinity Airlines1.

FIGURE 9-85

In the Lab

1 Importing Data into an Excel Worksheet

Problem: You work in the strategic planning department for a small chain of fast food restaurants. You have asked each of the regional managers to send you historic data for sales of french fries over the past five years. Each manager has sent the required data, but each is in a different format. The northeast region sent a text file with fields separated by commas. The west region uses an Access database to maintain its data, and queried it, creating a table to send to you. The south region posted its data to the company's intranet site as a Web page. The Midwest region uses spreadsheet XML to communicate its data to other entities.

Instructions: Perform the following tasks.

1. Open the workbook Pasta Palace (Figure 9-86a on the next page) from the Data Disk. See the inside back cover of this book for instructions for downloading the Data Disk or see your instructor for information on accessing the files required in this book.
2. In cell J3, enter the formula =SUM(E3:I3).
3. Click cell A3. From the Data Disk, import the text file, PastaNortheast. It is a comma delimited text file. In step 2 of the Text Import Wizard, click the Comma check box; otherwise accept the default settings. When the Import Data dialog box displays, click the Properties button. When the External Data Range Properties dialog box displays, clear the Adjust the column width check box.
4. Click cell A8. From the Data Disk, import the Access database file, PastaWest. Add all the fields from the West Region French Fries table. Accept all of the default settings. When the Import Data dialog box displays, click the Properties button. When the External Data Range Properties dialog box displays, clear the Adjust the column width and Include field names check boxes.
5. Click cell A13. From the Data Disk, import the HTML file, PastaSouth. Accept the default settings for the New Web Query. When the Import Data dialog box displays, click the Properties button. When the External Data Range dialog box displays, clear the Adjust the column width check box. Manually delete the column headings imported from the HTML file.
6. Click cell A18. From the Data Disk, import the spreadsheet XML file, PastaMidwest. Accept the default settings for the New Web Query. When the Import Data dialog box displays, click the Properties button. When the External Data Range Properties dialog box displays, clear the Adjust the column width check box. Manually delete the column headings imported from the XML file.
7. Replicate the formula from cell J3 to fill the range J4:J23 (Figure 9-87b on the next page). Format all cells with dollar amounts so that they display with a comma, no decimal places, and no currency symbol.
8. Enter your name, course, computer laboratory exercise (Lab 9-1), date, and instructor name in the range A25:A29.
9. On the File menu, click Page Setup. When the Page Setup dialog box displays, click Landscape in the Orientation area on the Page sheet. Print a copy of the worksheet.
10. Save the workbook using the file name, Pasta Palace1.
11. Export the French Fry Analysis worksheet by selecting Save As on the File menu. When the Save As dialog box appears, select Text (Tab delimited)(*.txt) in the Save as type box. Click Save.

(continued)

In the Lab

Importing Data into an Excel Worksheet *(continued)*

(a)

(b)

FIGURE 9-86

2 Routing Workbooks, Tracking Changes, and Inserting Comments

Problem: This problem requires collaboration with two other classmates. Make sure that you can send e-mail to other classmates before completing this exercise.

You work as an assistant in the accounting department of Krystal's Photography Supply. The head of the accounting department has asked you to verify inventory amounts so that she can finish her quarterly reports. To do so, you must ask the warehouse managers to review the numbers that are in the current Inventory Summary worksheet (Figure 9-87).

In the Lab

Instructions: Perform the following tasks:

1. Open the workbook Krystal's Photography Supply from the Data Disk. See the inside back cover of this book for instructions for downloading the Data Disk or see your instructor for information on accessing the files required in this book.

2. Add a comment to cell E6 as shown in Figure 9-87.

3. Track changes to the workbook. On the Tools menu, click Track Changes and then click Highlight Changes. Click Track changes while editing and clear the three check boxes in the Highlight which changes area.

4. Route the workbook to two classmates. On the File menu, point to Send To and then click Routing Recipient. Select the e-mail addresses of two classmates and enter Krystal's Photography Inventory Verification as the Subject. Enter appropriate message text requesting that each classmate add comments to at least one cell and change the contents of two cells. Click the Route button.

5. Ask a classmate to route the workbook to you as well. When you receive the e-mail, print it. Enter comments in at least one cell and change the contents of at least two cells before sending the workbook to the next routing recipient.

6. When you receive your workbook back after it has been routed to all recipients, point to Track Changes on the Tools menu, and then click Accept or Reject Changes. Reject one change and accept all others.

7. Select Page Setup on the File menu. Click the Sheet tab and then select As displayed on sheet in the Comments list box in the Print area. This allows comments to print when you print the worksheet.

8. Enter your name, course, computer laboratory exercise (Lab 9-2), date, and instructor name in the range, B18:B22. Print the worksheet. Save the workbook using the file name, Krystal's Photography Supply1.

FIGURE 9-87

Microsoft Excel - Krystal's Photography Suppy

File Edit View Insert Format Tools Data Window Help

Type a question for help

Arial 10 A18

	Item #	Description	Warehouse	Location	Amount	Cost per Item	Inventory Value
		Krystal's Photography Supply					
		Inventory Summary					
4	3542323	35mm Filmx24 5 pack	Newark	Shelf 11-A	12	11.23	134.76
5	264246	Aluminum tripod	Salt Lake City	Bin 13	31		
6	3456234	Deluxe tripod	Salt Lake City	Bin 2393	18		
7	546344	35mm Filmx36 5 pack	Salt Lake City	Shelf 9-C	27		
8	234543	Leather camera bag	Newark	Bin 33	13		
9	3424354	Digital camera PC connector	Newark	Bin 35	21		
10	2345674	128M memory for digital camera	Salt Lake City	Shelf 12-A	53	199.95	10,597.35
11	975454	Telephoto lens with carrying case	Newark	Bin 12	8	208.54	1,668.32
12	5563782	Basic 35mm camera	Salt Lake City	Bin 9	31	45.65	1,415.15
13	562355	100 pages 5x7 deluxe photo paper	Salt Lake City	Shelf 1-A	7	32.22	225.54
14	234564	Deluxe camera bag	Salt Lake City	Shelf 2-A	15	97.99	1,469.85
15	567865	Camera cleaning kit	Newark	Bin 21	20	15.43	308.60
16	35745	100 pages 5x7 std photo paper	Newark	Bin 9	17	32.67	555.39

Sue Booch: Salt Lake City manager, we are unsure of this number as of the end of the quarter.

Inventory Summary / Sheet2 / Sheet3

Ready

Start Krystal's Photography... EN 10:28 PM

In the Lab

3 Creating a PivotChart Report and Associated PivotTable Report for a Customer Service Database

Problem: You are a quality analyst with the customer service department of the Houdini Hotel. You have been assigned the task of creating a PivotChart and PivotTable from the company's customer complaint database (Figure 9-88a). Records are added to this database whenever a refund is given to a customer due to a complaint. The PivotChart and PivotTable are shown in Figure 9-88b and 9-88c.

Instructions: Perform the following tasks:

1. Open the workbook Houdini Hotel from the Data Disk. See the inside back cover of this book for instructions for downloading the Data Disk or see your instructor for information on accessing the files required in this book.

2. Create the PivotChart shown in Figure 9-88b and PivotTable shown in Figure 9-88c on separate sheets. The PivotChart and PivotTable summarize refund amount information by room number and complaint date. Use the PivotTable and PivotChart Report Wizard to create the PivotChart and associated PivotTable.

3. Add the title shown in Figure 9-88b.

4. Format the y-axis labels to currency with no decimal places.

5. Rename the Chart 1 sheet tab PivotChart. Rename the Sheet1 sheet tab PivotTable.

(a) Worksheet Database

6. Click the PivotChart sheet tab. Drag the Refund button to the Drag Data Items Here area (y-axis). Drag the Room Number and the Date buttons to the Drop Category Fields Here area (x-axis).

7. Select the Customer Complaint Database and PivotTable sheets. Enter your name, course, computer laboratory exercise (Lab 9-3), date, and instructor in the range A21:A25. Hold down the SHIFT key and then click the Customer Complaint Database tab.

8. Print the worksheet, PivotChart, and PivotTable. Save the workbook using the file name, Houdini Hotel1.

9. Click the Date box arrow to deselect the date 7-Jul-2003. Print the PivotChart and PivotTable. Add the 7-Jul-2003 date back in.

10. Remove the Room Number from the x-axis, and add the Manager button to the right of the Date button. Print the PivotChart and PivotTable.

In the Lab

11. Close Houdini Hotel1 without saving changes and then reopen it. Click the PivotTable tab. Drag the buttons to create three different views. Print the PivotTable for each view. Close the workbook without saving changes.

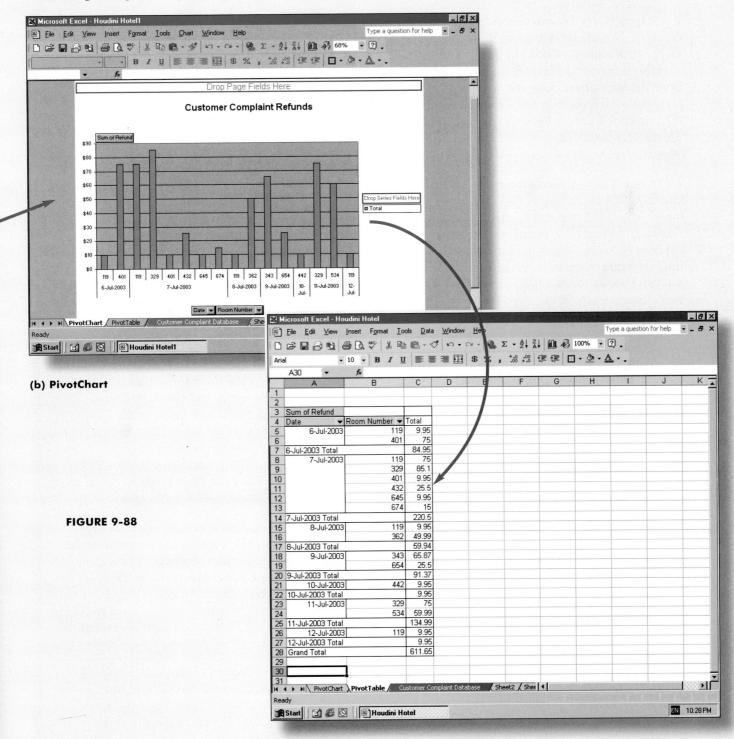

FIGURE 9-88

(b) PivotChart

(c) PivotTable

Cases and Places

The difficulty of these case studies varies:
▶ are the least difficult; ▶▶ are more difficult; and ▶▶▶ are the most difficult.

1 ▶ Open Curry Foundation Analysis from the Data Disk. Import data from the table in the Access database Nevada2004 beginning in row 3. Import the XML file Oklahoma2004 beginning in row 7. Copy the formulas in cell H3 and cell I3 through row 10. Enter your name, course, computer laboratory exercise (Cases and Places 9-1), date, and instructor name in the range A14:A18. Turn on track changes. Print the worksheet. Save the workbook using the file name, Case 9-1. Route the workbook to three classmates. Tell them in the e-mail to respond within a day and make at least two changes each. When the workbook comes back to you, accept the changes. Print the worksheet. Save the workbook using the file name, Case 9-1a.

2 ▶ Open Curry Foundation Analysis from the Data Disk. Import data from the table in the HTML file Georgia2004 beginning in row 3. Import the text file Minnesota2004 beginning in row 7. Copy the formulas in cell H3 and cell I3 through row 10. Enter your name, course, computer laboratory exercise (Cases and Places 9-2), date, and instructor name in the range A14:A18. Share the workbook and allow changes by more than one user. Print the worksheet. Save the workbook using the Save As command on the File menu three times using three different file names: Case 9-2a, Case 9-2b, and Case 9-2c. E-mail the workbooks to three classmates. Tell them in the e-mail to respond within a day and make at least two changes each. When the workbooks come back to you, merge the workbooks. Print the worksheet. Save the workbook using the file name, Case 9-2d.

3 ▶▶ Open the Workstation Productivity Database from the Data Disk. See the inside back cover of this book for instructions for downloading the Data Disk or see your instructor for information on accessing the files required in this book. Develop a PivotChart with the two Unit totals and two Unit Quota amount fields in the Drop Data Items Here area (y-axis) and the Gender and Age fields in the Drop Category Fields Here (x-axis). Include a title and formatted y-axis labels. Enter your name, course, computer laboratory exercise (Cases and Places 9-3), date, and instructor name in the range A17:A21. Save the workbook using the file name, Case 9-3. Print the worksheet, PivotChart, and PivotTable. Display the PivotTable sheet. Drag the buttons to display five different views. Print the PivotTable for each.

4 ▶▶ Golden Arboretum sells medium-sized trees in three different states. The historical sales data for five years is an Access database named GoldenArboretum on the Data Disk. Review the contents of the SalesSummary table in Access. Open a new workbook, add appropriate column headings, add a calculated column for Total Revenue per Unit, and import the database into Excel. Format the worksheet appropriately. Create a PivotChart and PivotTable. Print the worksheet. Print the PivotChart and PivotTable for two different views. Create a PivotChart with the Year as the x-axis, and create a trendline on the chart that forecasts three years in the future for one state. Print the PivotChart with the trendline.

5 ▶▶▶ Using your own book collection or one type of book from your collection create a database of the book titles, authors, year of publication, publishers, and subject. Create a PivotChart and PivotTable with year and subject as the x-axis categories and author as data (y-axis). Print the worksheet, PivotChart, and PivotTable. Display the PivotTable sheet. Drag the buttons to display three different views. Print the PivotTable for each.

Microsoft Excel 2002

Creating a PivotTable List Web Page Using Excel

CASE PERSPECTIVE

JetMassage, Inc. sells a water powered personal body massager through infomercials on television in select countries. The company rents several warehouses throughout the world where it stores and ships its product. Sales districts are broken down by warehouse locations, which are located in four countries: the United States, Canada, Mexico, and the United Kingdom.

After receiving complaints from upper management about the high cost of maintaining inventory in many warehouses, Catherine Cay has been keeping an Excel spreadsheet regarding that state of inventory in each warehouse. Catherine needs to analyze this data in a more comprehensive and flexible manner in order to make some critical decisions.

As the spreadsheet specialist at JetMassage, Inc., Catherine has asked you to take warehouse data supplied in a worksheet and make it available to the upper management in an easy-to-use format. From your experience with Excel 2002, you know that you can create interactive Web pages. You also know that PivotTables are an ideal tool for analyzing data. You decide the best solution is to develop an interactive PivotTable list Web page.

Introduction

Excel 2002 allows you to save a workbook, a worksheet, a range of cells, or a chart as a Web page using the Save as Web Page command on the File menu. Excel also allows you to save worksheet data as a PivotTable list. A **PivotTable list** is a Web page that lets you analyze data using your Web browser, rather than Excel. Similar to a PivotTable report, a PivotTable list is an interactive table that allows you to change the view of data, filter data, and create summaries of the data. The difference between the two PivotTables is that a PivotTable report is manipulated in Excel, whereas a PivotTable list is manipulated in your Web browser.

To create a PivotTable list, you start with an Excel workbook (Figure 1a on the next page). You use the Save as Web Page command on the File menu to create the PivotTable list (Figure 1b on the next page). Once you display the PivotTable list in your Web browser, you can change the view of the data as shown in Figures 1c and 1d on the next page. Figure 1c shows the data in Figure 1b summarized by the warehouse's country within Drain. The Drain column is used to indicate that management has decided to close the warehouse and will no longer ship any product to that location. When a warehouse has no more inventory, it is said to be drained, and is subsequently ready to be shut down. Figure 1d illustrates the filtering capabilities of a PivotTable list, showing only the rows that represent all warehouses in the USA except those in the West area. The other records in the list (Figure 1b) are hidden.

For other users to interact with a PivotTable list, they must have the Office Web components installed, and they must be using Microsoft Internet Explorer 4.01 or later. The Office Web components are installed automatically as part of the Office XP installation process.

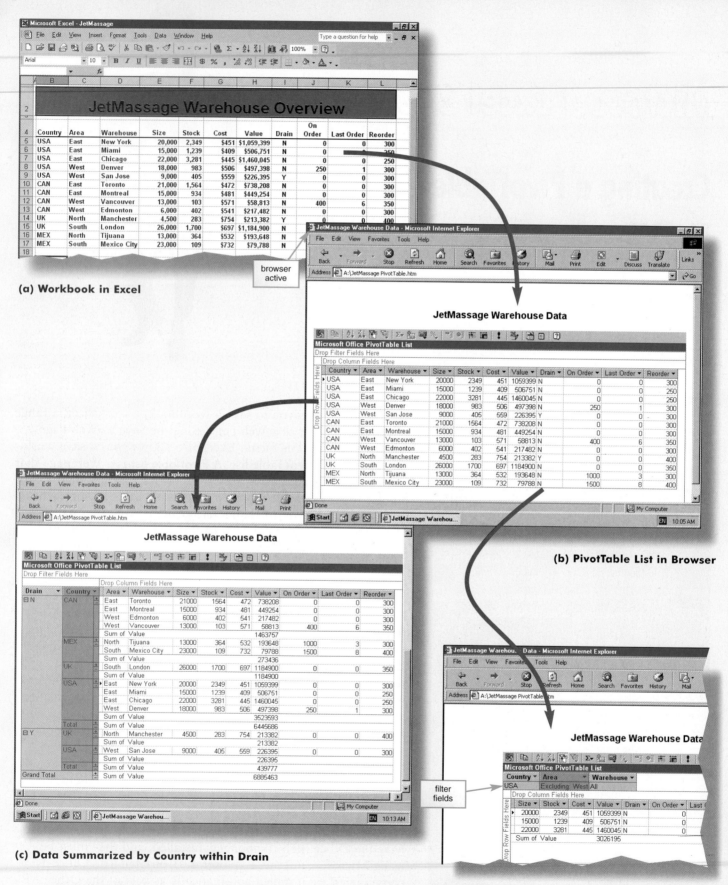

(a) Workbook in Excel

(b) PivotTable List in Browser

(c) Data Summarized by Country within Drain

(d) All Warehouses in the USA Except West Area Display

FIGURE 1

Saving a Worksheet Database as a PivotTable List

The first step in this project is to open the JetMassage workbook (Figure 1a) and save the database in the range B4:L17 as a PivotTable list that can be viewed and manipulated in a browser.

More *About*

PivotTables

For more information on PivotTables, visit the Excel 2002 More About Web page (scsite.com/ex2002/more.htm) and click PivotTables.

Steps **To Save a Worksheet Database as a PivotTable List**

1 **Insert the Data Disk in drive A. Start Excel and then open the workbook JetMassage on drive A. See the inside back cover of this book for instructions for downloading the Data Disk or your instructor for information on accessing the files required in this book. Reset your toolbars as described in Appendix C. Select the range B4:L17. Click File on the menu bar and then point to Save as Web Page.**

The File menu displays (Figure 2).

FIGURE 2

2 **Click Save as Web Page. When the Save As dialog box displays, type** JetMassage PivotTable **in the File name text box and then, if necessary, click the Save in box arrow and click 3½ Floppy (A:). Point to the Publish button.**

The Save As dialog box displays as shown in Figure 3.

FIGURE 3

3 **Click the Publish button. Click the Add interactivity with check box, click the Add interactivity with box arrow, and then click PivotTable functionality. Click the Change button. When the Set Title dialog box displays, type** JetMassage Warehouse Data **in the Title text box. Point to the OK button.**

The Publish as Web Page and Set Title dialog boxes display as shown in Figure 4.

4 **Click the OK button. Click the Publish button in the Publish as Web Page dialog box. Click the Close button on the right side of the Excel title bar. If your browser opens, click the close button on the right side of the browser title bar.**

Excel saves the PivotTable list in HTML (hypertext markup language) format to drive A.

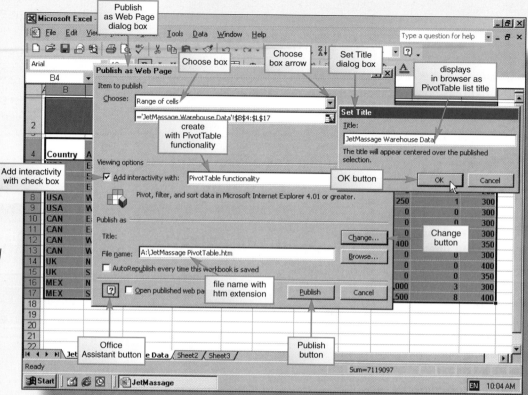

FIGURE 4

More About

PivotTable Lists and Associated Charts

Along with a PivotTable list, you can include a chart that displays the same data graphically. If you display the PivotTable list in your browser and change the view, you will see the same changes in the chart.

If you click the Save button in the Save As dialog box shown in Figure 3 on the previous page, Excel saves the entire workbook as a noninteractive Web page. If you click the Selection: $B$4:$L$17 option button and then click the Save button, Excel saves the selected range B4:L17 as a noninteractive Web page. If you click the Add interactivity check box, then Excel saves the range B4:L17 as an **interactive Web page**. An interactive Web page allows you to change the values in the cells in your browser, but it does not give you the ability to rotate fields the way a PivotTable list does.

When you use the Publish button, you must tell Excel what you want to publish. In Figure 4, the range of cells selected on the worksheet is selected in the Choose list box. In the Viewing options area, once you add a check mark to the Add interactivity with check box, the list box becomes active. The list box gives you two choices — Spreadsheet functionality or PivotTable functionality. The Change button in Figure 4 displays the **Set Title dialog box**, which allows you to add a title to the PivotTable list.

Viewing the PivotTable List Using Your Browser

With the PivotTable list saved as an HTML file, the next step is to view it using your browser, as shown in the following steps.

Steps **To View a PivotTable List Using Your Browser**

1 **Click the Launch Internet Explorer Browser button on the taskbar.**

2 **When the Internet Explorer window displays, type** a:\JetMassage PivotTable.htm **in the Address bar, and then press the ENTER key.**

The PivotTable list, JetMassage PivotTable.htm, displays (Figure 5).

FIGURE 5

The PivotTable list Web page in Figure 5 resembles an Excel worksheet with the column and row structure. The Address bar displays the URL. The title above the columns and rows is the same as the entry made in the Set Title dialog box in Figure 4. The toolbar immediately below the title includes buttons that allow you to complete tasks quickly, such as copy, sort, filter, calculate summaries, and move fields. Figure 6 identifies the buttons on the PivotTable list toolbar.

The area below the toolbar is divided into five areas as shown in Figure 5: (1) data area; (2) data fields; (3) row field area; (4) column field area; and (5) filter field area. The data area contains the data. Each entry in the data area is called an item. The data fields at the top of each column identify the data below them. For example, the Stock data field identifies the amount of product in stock in the same column. Each data field contains a field drop-down arrow that allows you to set up filters to display only records that meet certain criteria. You drag data fields to the row field area on the left side of the PivotTable list and the column field area at the top of the PivotTable list to display different views of the data. You also can drag data fields to the filter field area to display different views of the data using filtering techniques.

FIGURE 6

Undoing PivotTable List Changes

If you make several changes to a PivotTable list and wish to restore it to its original view, quit your browser, launch your browser, and then display the PivotTable list again.

Changing the View of the PivotTable List

This section shows you how to change the view of the PivotTable list by (1) using the field drop-down arrows; (2) adding summary totals; (3) sorting columns of data; (4) dragging data fields to the row field area; and (5) dragging data fields into the filter field area.

Using the Field Drop-Down Arrows to Display Records that Pass a Test

You can use the field drop-down arrows at the right-side of the data fields to hide rows of data that do not pass a test. This allows you to work with a subset of the data. For example, the following steps hide the rows of data representing warehouses remaining open that are displaying in the PivotTable list.

Steps To Use Field Drop-Down Arrows to Display Records that Pass a Test

1 **Click the Drain data field drop-down arrow, click the check box labeled N (for no) to clear the check box, and then point to the OK button.**

A list of the different items in the Drain column of data display as check boxes along with a check box titled All (Figure 7). The N check box does not have a check mark. The AutoFilter button on the toolbar is selected.

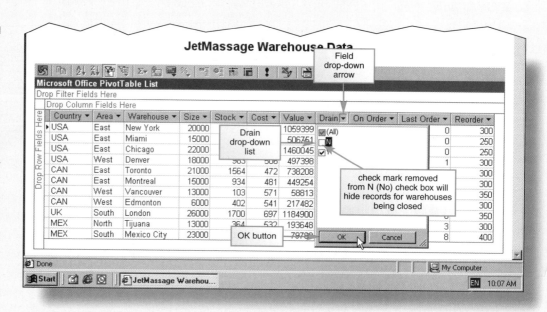

FIGURE 7

2 **Click the OK button. Point to the AutoFilter button.**

Only the rows of data representing warehouses that are closing display (Figure 8). The rows of data representing warehouses to remain open are hidden.

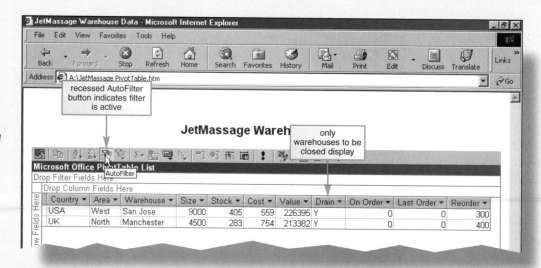

FIGURE 8

3 **Click the AutoFilter button on the toolbar.**

The filter is disabled and all rows of data display (Figure 9).

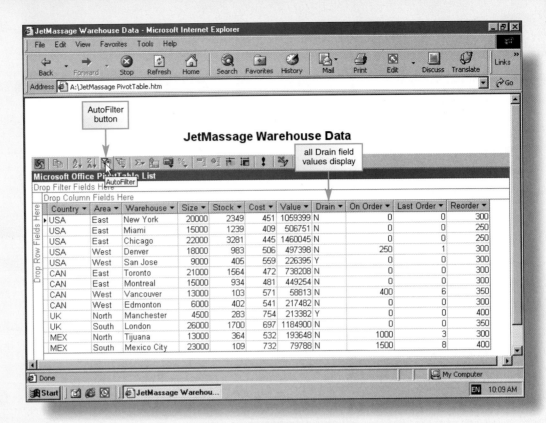

FIGURE 9

When you use a field drop-down arrow to filter the data, the arrow changes to the color blue. It remains blue until you disable the filter using the AutoFilter button or select the All check box in the Drain field drop-down list (Figure 7). You can add additional filters by using other field drop-down arrows. Thus, you can display a subset of a subset. For example, after applying the filter as shown in Figure 8, you can apply a second filter to the Country field that only displays warehouses in the USA. If you disable the filter by clicking the AutoFilter button and then select new filters, the original disabled filter is lost.

Adding Summary Totals

A PivotTable list is more useful if you add summaries to key columns of data. For example, you can add a summary to the Value column in Figure 9. The Value column indicates the total value of the current inventory at a specific warehouse. Nine summary functions are available through the AutoCalc button on the toolbar. The nine **summary functions** are Sum, Count, Min, Max, Average, Standard Deviation, Standard Deviation Population, Variance, and Variance Population. The steps on the next page add the Sum summary function to the Value column of data.

Summary Functions

The type of data in a field determines whether a summary function is available or not. For example, if a field contains dates, then the Sum function is not available. If a field contains text, you cannot use the Sum, Min, or Max function, but you can use Count.

Steps **To Add a Summary Total to a Column of Data**

1 **Click the Value data field to select the entire column. Click the AutoCalc button on the PivotTable list toolbar and point to Sum.**

The PivotTable list displays as shown in Figure 10.

FIGURE 10

2 **Click Sum.**

A grand total displays below the Value column of data (Figure 11).

FIGURE 11

You can select, one at a time, all nine of the summary functions shown in the drop-down list in Figure 10. Each time you select a summary function, a new summary line is added to the summary data area.

Sorting Columns of Data

The data in a PivotTable is easier to work with and more meaningful if you arrange the data sequentially based on one or more fields. The sort routine available with a PivotTable list is similar to Excel in that it sorts the data using the current order of the records. Thus, if you need to sort on more than one column of data, sort the minor field first, progressing to the major field.

The following step sorts the PivotTable list in ascending sequence by the On Order amount.

More About

Sort Order

The order in which numbers, text, and special characters are sorted depends on the source data and your regional settings in the Windows Control Panel.

Steps **To Sort Columns of Data**

1 **Click the On Order data field and then click the Sort Ascending button on the toolbar.**

The data in the PivotTable list is sorted first by country and then the number of items on order at each warehouse (Figure 12).

FIGURE 12

With the data sorted by the On Order value, you now can change the view of the data by moving data fields to the drop areas to change the view of the PivotTable list.

Dragging Data Fields to the Row Field Area

Moving data fields to the drop areas changes the view. The **drop areas** are to the left and above the data area. The steps on the next page drag the Drain and Country data fields to the row field area on the left side of the PivotTable list to generate a new view. The last step returns the PivotTable list to its original view.

More About

Sorting

To undo a sort and return the data to its previous order, click the recessed Sort Ascending or Sort Descending button.

Steps **To Drag Data Fields to the Row Field Area**

1 Drag the Drain data field to the row field area. Drag the Country data field to the row field area and to the right of the Drain field.

The PivotTable list changes dramatically, showing subtotals for each country category and each drain category (Figure 13).

2 When you are finished viewing the PivotTable list, drag the Drain and Country data fields to their original locations in the data area.

FIGURE 13

When you drag a data field to a drop area, the data field is moved rather than copied. Thus, in Figure 13 the data area no longer contains the Drain and Country data fields. They are now in the row field area. In Figure 12 on the previous page, only one total displayed at the bottom of the PivotTable list. In Figure 13, after dragging the two data fields, eight subtotals and one grand total display, and the rows of data are divided into categories based on their respective Drain and Country values.

Dragging Data Fields to the Filter Field Area

Another way to manipulate the view of the PivotTable is to drag data fields to the filter field area at the top of the PivotTable list. When you drag a data field to this drop area, the data field maintains the field drop-down arrow, which allows you to apply a filter to the data. The following steps drag the Country, Area, and Warehouse data fields to the filter field area and then apply a filter.

More About

Dragging Fields to Drop Areas

When you drag a data field to the row field area, each unique data item within the field displays down the rows of the PivotTable list. When you drag a data field to the column field area, each unique data item within the field displays across the columns of the PivotTable list.

Steps To Drag Data Fields to the Filter Field Area and Apply a Filter

1 Drag the Country data field to the filter field area. Drag the Area data field to the right of the Country filter field. Drag the Warehouse data field to the right of the Area filter field.

The PivotTable list displays as shown in Figure 14.

FIGURE 14

2 Click the Country data field drop-down arrow and click check boxes for CAN, MEX, and UK to unselect them. Click the Area data field drop-down arrow and click the check box labeled West.

Only three rows of data display (Figure 15). The remaining rows of data failed to pass the test of belonging to all USA areas except the West.

3 When you are finished viewing the PivotTable list in its current form, click the AutoFilter button on the toolbar to disable the filter. One at a time, drag the three filter fields back to their original position in the data area.

FIGURE 15

More *About*

Microsoft Certification

The Microsoft Office User Specialist (MOUS) Certification program provides an opportunity for you to obtain a valuable industry credential —proof that you have the Excel 2002 skills required by employers. For more information, see Appendix D or visit the Shelly Cashman Series MOUS Web page at scsite.com/offxp/cert.htm.

You could have applied the filters to the data fields in the data area, rather than dragging them to the filter field area. By dragging these fields to the filter field area, however, the rows that pass the test are cleaner and easier to read. For example, you do not have the Country, Area, and Warehouse data fields repeating the same numbers over and over again, as was the case in Figure 7 on page EW 2.06 when the filter was applied to the Drain data field.

Removing Fields and Adding Fields to a PivotTable List

The more data fields you have in a PivotTable list, the more difficult it is to interpret the data. Sometimes it is helpful to remove fields from view temporarily. The following steps show how to remove the Stock data field and then add the field back to the data area.

 To Remove Fields from and Add Fields to a PivotTable List

1 **Click the Field List button on the PivotTable list toolbar to display the PivotTable Field List window. Right-click the Stock data field. When the shortcut menu displays, point to Remove Field.**

The PivotTable Field List window displays a list of all the data fields in the PivotTable list (Figure 16). The Stock data field and its data are selected, and the shortcut menu displays. Most of the commands on the shortcut menu in Figure 16 are the same as the buttons on the toolbar.

FIGURE 16

2 **Click Remove Field.**

The Stock data field and its column of data are hidden. The word, Stock, in the PivotTable Field List window is regular font style, whereas the active data fields are bold in the PivotTable Field List window (Figure 17).

FIGURE 17

3 **Drag the Stock data field from the PivotTable Field List window to its original location between the Size and Cost data fields.**

The Stock data field is added to the data area in the PivotTable list (Figure 18). The word, Stock, now is bold in the PivlotTable Field List window.

FIGURE 18

You can remove (hide) as many data fields as you want from the data area to simplify the PivotTable list. When you add data fields, you can insert them at any location. For example, you could have added the Stock data field anywhere in the data area. You cannot duplicate a data field. That is, the Stock data field can show up only once in the data area.

Besides removing fields and adding fields, you can move data fields from one location in the data area to another by dragging.

Improving the Appearance of a PivotTable List

You can improve the appearance of the PivotTable list through the use of the Property Toolbox button. For example, you can change the font, format numbers, change colors of cells, and align text. You also can increase or decrease the column width by dragging column borders as you did in Excel. Any formatting you do to the PivotTable list remains effective as long as you do not close your browser. Once you close your browser, the formats are lost.

Finally, you can export the PivotTable list to Excel. In Excel, the PivotTable list becomes a PivotTable report. You can format the PivotTable report using Excel's powerful formatting capabilities and then save it as a PivotTable list.

The following step closes your browser.

TO CLOSE YOUR BROWSER

1 Click the Close button on the right side of the browser's title bar.

CASE PERSPECTIVE SUMMARY

Catherine Cay will be pleased with the PivotTable list capabilities. It will serve as the first step towards keeping the management team up to date on warehouse information. The managers and executives will be able to analyze the warehouse data by displaying different views. More importantly, they will be able to analyze the data using their browsers, rather than using Excel.

Web Feature Summary

This Web Feature introduced you to publishing an Excel worksheet as a PivotTable list Web page. You learned how PivotTable lists work and the terms that are used to describe them. You also learned how to enhance a PivotTable list using your browser by adding summaries, filtering data so only rows that pass a test display, sorting, changing the view, and removing and adding data fields.

What You Should Know

Having completed this project, you now should be able to perform the following tasks:

▶ Add a Summary Total to a Column of Data (EW 2.08)

▶ Close Your Browser (EW 2.14)

▶ Drag Data Fields to the Filter Field Area and Apply a Filter (EW 2.11)

▶ Drag Data Fields to the Row Field Area (EW 2.10)

▶ Remove Fields from and Add Fields to a PivotTable List (EW 2.12)

▶ Save a Worksheet Database as a PivotTable List (EW 2.03)

▶ Sort Columns of Data (EW 2.09)

▶ Use Field Drop-Down Arrows to Display Records that Pass a Test (EW 2.06)

▶ View a PivotTable List Using Your Browser (EW 2.05)

In the Lab

1 Creating the Korvin Sales Force PivotTable List

Problem: You are a spreadsheet specialist for Korvin Distributors, a distributor of truck engine parts with a national sales force. You have been asked to make information about the company's sales force available to management on the company's intranet. You decide to use a PivotTable list to distribute information across the company's intranet so that it can be analyzed using a browser.

Instructions: Start Excel and open the workbook, Korvin Distributors, from the Data Disk. If you do not have a copy of the Data Disk, then see the inside back cover of this book. Save the range B4:J14 as a PivotTable list to drive A using the file name, Korvin Distributors PivotTable. Add the title, Korvin Distributors Sales Analysis, as shown in Figure 19 before publishing the Web page. Close Excel and open your browser. Display the PivotTable list by entering a:\Korvin Distributors PivotTable.htm in the Address bar and then print the PivotTable list. Print the PivotTable list for each of the following:

1. Add a total to the Sales column. Sort the PivotTable list on Sales in descending sequence.
2. Sort in ascending sequence Educ within Gender. Drag the Gender data field to the filter field area (Figure 19). Use the Gender drop-down arrow to display rows for all males (M in the Gender field).

FIGURE 19

In the Lab

2 Creating the Ideolix Running Club PivotTable List

Problem: You are a member of a local running club. The members would like to access online the club's database, which includes each member's name, age, gender, zip code, preferred race type, total dues paid, and number of years in the club. You have been asked to use your Excel skills to create a PivotTable list from the database so it can be manipulated remotely using a browser.

Instructions: Start Excel and open the workbook, Ideolix Running, from the Data Disk. If you do not have a copy of the Data Disk, then see the inside back cover of this book. Save the range B4:J17 as a PivotTable list to drive A using the file name, Ideolix PivotTable. Add the title `Ideolix Running Club` as shown in Figure 20 before publishing the Web page. Close Excel and open your browser. Display the PivotTable list by entering the `a:\Ideolix PivotTable.htm` in the Address bar and then print the PivotTable list. Print the PivotTable list for each of the following:

1. Add a total to the Total Dues column. Display only club members who prefer 5k races.
2. Show all Preferred Race Types. Sort in ascending sequence on Preferred Race within Gender. Drag the Gender and Preferred Race data fields to the row field area as shown in Figure 20.

FIGURE 20

APPENDIX A
Microsoft Excel Help System

Using the Excel Help System

This appendix shows you how to use the Excel Help system. At anytime while you are using Excel, you can interact with its Help system and display information on any Excel topic. It is a complete reference manual at your fingertips.

As shown in Figure A-1, you can access Excel's Help system in four primary ways:

1. Ask a Question box on the menu bar
2. Function key F1 on the keyboard
3. Microsoft Excel Help command on the Help menu
4. Microsoft Excel Help button on the Standard toolbar

If you use the Ask a Question box on the menu bar, Excel responds by opening the Microsoft Excel Help window, which gives you direct access to its Help system. If you use one of the other three ways to access Excel's Help system, Excel responds in one of two ways:

1. If the Office Assistant is turned on, then the Office Assistant displays with a balloon (lower-right side in Figure A-1).
2. If the Office Assistant is turned off, then the Microsoft Excel Help window opens (lower-left side in Figure A-1).

① ASK A QUESTION BOX

② KEYBOARD PRESS F1

③ HELP MENU CLICK MICROSOFT EXCEL HELP

Help
- Microsoft Excel Help   F1
- Show the Office Assistant
- What's This?   Shift+F1
- Office on the Web
- Activate Product...
- Lotus 1-2-3 Help...
- Detect and Repair...
- About Microsoft Excel

④ MICROSOFT EXCEL HELP BUTTON ON STANDARD TOOLBAR

Is Office Assistant ON or OFF?

OFF - Display Microsoft Excel Help Window

ON - Display Office Assistant with Balloon

Microsoft Excel Help

Contents | Answer Wizard | Index

- Getting Started with Microsoft Ex
- Microsoft Excel Accessibility
- Installing and Removing Excel
- Managing and Printing Files
- Workbooks and Worksheets
- Data in Worksheets
- Excel and the Web
- External Data
- Analyzing and Managing Data
- Creating and Using Forms
- Creating and Correcting Formula:
- Function Reference
- Drawings and Pictures

Microsoft Excel Help

What's New

Learn about the new features in Microsoft Excel and all Microsoft Off

OfficeUpdateTBD

Visit OfficeUpdateTBD on the web to find additional products, service

Answer Wizard

Learn how to get assistance while you work.

Help Topics
- Accessibility for people with disabilities
- Keyboard shortcuts

What would you like to do?

Type your question here and then click Search.

Options   Search

OFFICE ASSISTANT OFF

OFFICE ASSISTANT ON

FIGURE A-1

Microsoft **Excel 2002**

The best way to familiarize yourself with the Excel Help system is to use it. The next several pages show examples of how to use the Help system. Following the examples are a set of exercises titled Use Help that will sharpen your Excel Help system skills.

Ask a Question Box

The **Ask a Question box** on the right side of the menu bar lets you type questions in your own words, or you can type terms, such as chart, replace, or freeze panes. Excel responds by displaying a list of topics related to the term(s) you entered. The following steps show how to use the Ask a Question box to obtain information on chart types.

To Obtain Help Using the Ask a Question Box

1 **Click the Ask a Question box on the right side of the menu bar, type** chart types, **and then press the ENTER key. When the Ask a Question list displays, point to the About charts link.**

The Ask a Question list displays (Figure A-2). Clicking the See more link displays additional links.

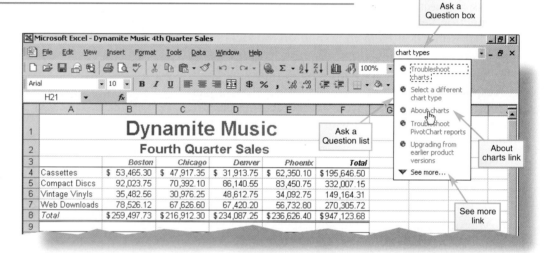

FIGURE A-2

2 **Click About charts. Point to the Microsoft Excel Help window title bar.**

The Microsoft Excel Help window displays information about charts (Figure A-3).

FIGURE A-3

FIGURE A-4

If the Contents sheet is active on the left side of the Microsoft Excel Help window, then Excel opens the book that pertains to the topic for which you are requesting help. In this case, Excel opens the Charts book and the Creating Charts book, which includes a list of topics related to charts. If the information on the right side is not satisfactory, you can click one of the topics in the Contents sheet to display alternative information related to the term, chart type.

As you enter questions and terms in the Ask a Question box, Excel adds them to its list. Thus, if you click the Ask a Question box arrow, a list of previously asked questions and terms will display.

Use the six buttons in the upper-left corner of the Microsoft Excel Help window (Figure A-4) to navigate through the Help system, change the display, and print the contents of the window. Table A-1 lists the function of each of these buttons.

Table A-1 Microsoft Excel Help Toolbar Buttons		
BUTTON	**NAME**	**FUNCTION**
	Auto Tile	Tiles the Microsoft Excel Help window and Microsoft Excel window when the Microsoft Excel Help window is maximized
or	Show or Hide	Displays or hides the Contents, Answer Wizard, and Index tabs
	Back	Displays the previous Help topic
	Forward	Displays the next Help topic
	Print	Prints the current Help topic
	Options	Displays a list of commands

The Office Assistant

The **Office Assistant** is an icon (lower-right side of Figure A-1 on page E A.01) that displays in the Excel window when it is turned on and not hidden. It has dual functions. First, it will respond in the same way the Ask a Question box does with a list of topics that relate to the entry you make in the text box at the bottom of the balloon. The entry can be in the form of a word, phrase, or question written as if you were talking to a human being. For example, if you want to learn more about saving a file, in the balloon text box, you can type any of the following terms or phrases: save, save a file, how do I save a file, or anything similar. The Office Assistant responds by displaying a list of topics from which you can choose. Once you choose a topic, it displays the corresponding information.

Second, the Office Assistant monitors your work and accumulates tips during a session on how you might increase your productivity and efficiency. You can view the tips at anytime. The accumulated tips display when you activate the Office Assistant balloon. Also, if at anytime you see a lightbulb above the Office Assistant, click it to display the most recent tip.

You may or may not want the Office Assistant to display on the screen at all times. You can hide it and then show it at a later time. You may prefer not to use the Office Assistant at all. Thus, not only do you need to know how to show and hide the Office Assistant, but you also need to know how to turn the Office Assistant on and off.

Showing and Hiding the Office Assistant

When Excel initially is installed, the Office Assistant may be off. You turn it on by invoking the **Show the Office Assistant command** on the Help menu. If the Office Assistant is on the screen and you want to hide it, you click the **Hide the Office Assistant command** on the Help menu. You also can right-click the Office Assistant to display its shortcut menu and then click the **Hide command** to hide it. You can move it to any location on the screen. You can click it to display the Office Assistant balloon, which allows you to request Help.

Turning the Office Assistant On and Off

The fact that the Office Assistant is hidden does not mean it is turned off. To turn the Office Assistant off, it must be displaying in the Excel window. You right-click it to display its shortcut menu (right-side of Figure A-5). Next, click Options on the shortcut menu. Invoking the **Options command** causes the **Office Assistant dialog box** to display (left-side of Figure A-5).

FIGURE A-5

The top check box on the **Options sheet** determines whether the Office Assistant is on or off. To turn the Office Assistant off, remove the check mark from the **Use the Office Assistant check box** and then click the OK button. As shown in Figure A-1 on page E A.01, if the Office Assistant is off when you invoke Help, then Excel opens the Microsoft Excel Help window instead of displaying the Office Assistant. To turn the Office Assistant on at a later date, click the Show the Office Assistant command on the Help menu.

Through the Options command on the Office Assistant shortcut menu, you can change the look and feel of the Office Assistant. For example, you can hide the Office Assistant, turn the Office Assistant off, change the way it works, choose a different Office Assistant icon, or view an animation of the current one. These options also are available by clicking the **Options button** that displays in the Office Assistant balloon (Figure A-6).

The **Gallery sheet** in the Office Assistant dialog box (Figure A-5) allows you to change the appearance of the Office Assistant. The default is the paper clip (Clippit). You can change it to a bouncing red happy face (The Dot), a robot (F1), the Microsoft Office logo (Office Logo), a wizard (Merlin), the earth (Mother Nature), a cat (Links), or a dog (Rocky).

Using the Office Assistant

As indicated earlier, the Office Assistant allows you to enter a word, phrase, or question and then responds by displaying a list of topics from which you can choose to display Help. The following steps show how to use the Office Assistant to obtain Help on summing a range.

 To Use the Office Assistant

1 If the Office Assistant is not on the screen, click Help on the menu bar and then click Show the Office Assistant. Click the Office Assistant. When the Office Assistant balloon displays, **type** how do i sum a range **in the text box immediately above the Options button. Point to the Search button.**

The Office Assistant balloon displays as shown in Figure A-6.

FIGURE A-6

2 Click the Search button. When the Office Assistant balloon redisplays, point to the topic, SUM worksheet function.

A new list of links display in the Office Assistant's balloon (Figure A-7).

FIGURE A-7

3 **Click the topic SUM worksheet function.** If necessary, move or hide the Office Assistant so you can view all of the text in the Microsoft Excel Help window.

The Microsoft Excel Help window displays the information on how to use the SUM function (Figure A-8).

4 **Click the Close button on the** Microsoft Excel Help window title bar.

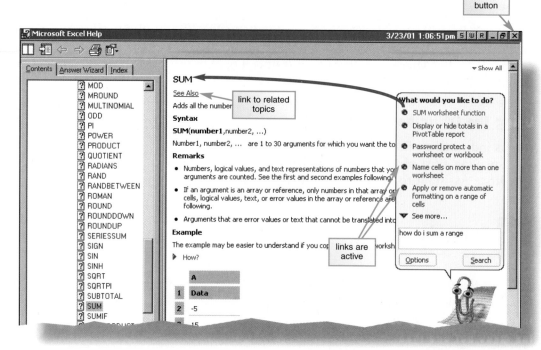

FIGURE A-8

The Microsoft Excel Help Window

If the Office Assistant is turned off and you click the Microsoft Excel Help button on the Standard toolbar, the Microsoft Excel Help window opens (Figure A-9). The left side of this window contains three tabs: Contents, Answer Wizard, and Index. Each tab displays a sheet with powerful look-up capabilities.

Use the Contents sheet as you would a table of contents at the front of a book to look up Help. The Answer Wizard sheet answers your queries the same as the Office Assistant. You use the Index sheet in the same fashion as an index in a book to look up Help. Click the tabs to move from sheet to sheet.

Besides clicking the Microsoft Excel Help button on the Standard toolbar, you also can click the Microsoft Excel Help command on the Help menu, or press the F1 key to display the Microsoft Excel Help window to gain access to the three sheets.

Using the Contents Sheet

The **Contents sheet** is useful for displaying Help when you know the general category of the topic in question, but not the specifics. The following steps show how to use the Contents sheet to obtain information on the AVERAGE function.

TO OBTAIN HELP USING THE CONTENTS SHEET

1 With the Office Assistant turned off, click the Microsoft Excel Help button on the Standard toolbar.

2 When the Microsoft Excel Help window opens, double-click the title bar to maximize the window. If necessary, click the Show button (see Table A-1 on page E A.03) to display the tabs.

3 Click the Contents tab. Double-click the Function Reference book on the left side of the window. Double-click the Statistical Functions book.

4 Click the subtopic AVERAGE below the Statistical Functions book.

Excel displays Help on the subtopic AVERAGE (Figure A-9).

FIGURE A-9

Once the information on the subtopic displays, you can scroll through and read it or you can click the Print button to obtain a printed copy. If you decide to click another subtopic on the left or a link on the right, you can get back to the Help page shown in Figure A-9 by clicking the Back button.

Each topic in the Contents list is preceded by a book icon or question mark icon. A **book icon** indicates subtopics are available. A **question mark icon** means information on the topic will display if you double-click the title. The book icon opens when you double-click the book (or its title) or click the plus sign (+) to the left of the book icon.

Using the Answer Wizard Sheet

The **Answer Wizard sheet** works like the Office Assistant in that you enter a word, phrase, or question and it responds by listing topics from which you can choose to display Help. The following steps show how to use the Answer Wizard sheet to obtain Help on adding conditional formatting to a worksheet.

TO OBTAIN HELP USING THE ANSWER WIZARD SHEET

1 With the Office Assistant turned off, click the Microsoft Excel Help button on the Standard toolbar (see Figure A-6 on page E A.05).

2 When the Microsoft Excel Help window opens, double-click the title bar to maximize the window. If necessary, click the Show button to display the tabs.

3 Click the Answer Wizard tab. Type `conditional formatting` in the What would you like to do? text box on the left side of the window.

4 When a list of topics displays in the Select topic to display list, click the Add, change, or remove conditional formats. Click the Add a conditional format link on the right side of the Microsoft Excel Help window.

Excel displays Help on how to add conditional formatting to a worksheet (Figure A-10 on the next page).

Microsoft **Excel 2002**

FIGURE A-10

If the topic, Add, change, or remove conditional formats, does not include the information you are seeking, click another topic in the list. Continue to click topics until you find the desired information.

Using the Index Sheet

The third sheet in the Microsoft Excel Help window is the Index sheet. Use the **Index sheet** to display Help when you know the keyword or the first few letters of the keyword you want to look up. The following steps show how to use the Index sheet to obtain Help on selecting all the cells in a worksheet.

TO OBTAIN HELP USING THE INDEX SHEET

1 With the Office Assistant turned off, click the Microsoft Excel Help button on the Standard toolbar.

2 When the Microsoft Excel Help window opens, double-click the title bar to maximize the window. If necessary, click the Show button to display the tabs.

3 Click the Index tab. Type select in the Type keywords text box on the left side of the window. Click the Search button.

4 When a list of topics displays in the Choose a topic list, click Select data or cells.

Excel displays Help on how to select cells, including a section on selecting all cells on a worksheet (Figure A-11). When you click the Search button, Excel automatically appends a semicolon to the keyword in the Type keywords text box.

What's This? Command and Question Mark Button • **E A.09**

APPENDIX A

FIGURE A-11

An alternative to typing a keyword in the Type keywords text box is to scroll through the Or choose keywords list (the middle list on the left side of the window). When you locate the keyword you are searching for, double-click it to display Help on the topic. Also in the Or choose keywords list, the Excel Help system displays other topics that relate to the new keyword. As you begin typing a new keyword in the Type keywords text box, Excel jumps to that point in the middle list box. To begin a new search, click the Clear button.

What's This? Command and Question Mark Button

Use the What's This? command on the Help menu or the Question Mark button in a dialog box when you are not sure what an object on the screen is or what it does.

What's This? Command

You use the **What's This? command** on the Help menu to display a detailed ScreenTip. When you invoke this command, the mouse pointer changes to an arrow with a question mark. You then click any object on the screen, such as a button, to display the ScreenTip. For example, after you click the What's This? command on the Help menu and then click the Merge and Center button on the Formatting toolbar, a description of the Merge and Center button displays (Figure A-12 on the next page). You can print the ScreenTip by right-clicking it and then clicking Print Topic on the shortcut menu.

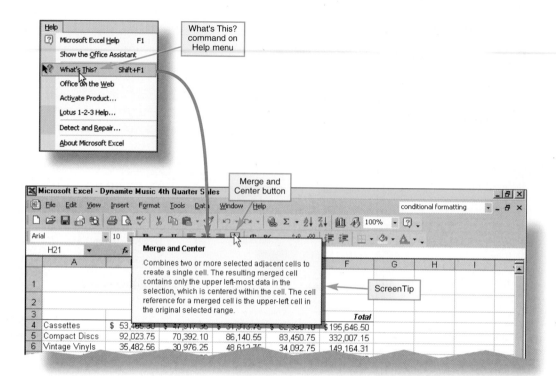

FIGURE A-12

Question Mark Button

In a fashion similar to the What's This? command, the **Question Mark button** displays a ScreenTip. You use the Question Mark button with dialog boxes. It is located in the upper-right corner on the title bar of dialog boxes, next to the Close button. For example, in Figure A-13, the AutoFormat dialog box displays on the screen. If you click the Question Mark button in the upper-right corner of the dialog box and then click one of the previewed formats in the AutoFormat dialog box, an explanation displays. You can print the ScreenTip by right-clicking it and then clicking Print Topic on the shortcut menu.

If a dialog box does not include a Question Mark button, press the SHIFT+F1 keys. This combination of keys displays an explanation or changes the mouse pointer to an arrow with a question mark. You then can click any object in the dialog box to display the ScreenTip.

FIGURE A-13

Office on the Web Command

The **Office on the Web command** on the Help menu displays a Microsoft Web page containing up-to-date information on a variety of Office-related topics. To use this command, you must be connected to the Internet. When you invoke the Office on the Web command, the Assistance Center Home page displays. Read through the links that in general pertain to topics that relate to all Office XP topics. Scroll down and click the Excel link in the Help By Product area to display the Assistance Center Excel Help Articles Web page (Figure A-14). This Web page contains numerous helpful links related to Excel.

Other Help Commands

Four additional commands available on the Help menu are Activate Product, Lotus 1-2-3 Help, Detect and Repair, and About Microsoft Excel. The Lotus 1-2-3 Help command is available only if it was included as part of a custom installation of Excel 2002.

FIGURE A-14

Activate Product Command

The **Activate Product command** on the Help menu lets you activate Excel if it has not already been activated.

Lotus 1-2-3 Help Command

The **Lotus 1-2-3 Help command** on the Help menu offers assistance to Lotus 1-2-3 users switching to Excel. When you choose this command, Excel displays the Help for Lotus 1-2-3 Users dialog box. The instructions in the dialog box step you through the appropriate selections.

Detect and Repair Command

Use the **Detect and Repair command** on the Help menu if Excel is not running properly or if it is generating errors. When you invoke this command, the Detect and Repair dialog box displays. Click the Start button in the dialog box to initiate the detect and repair process.

About Microsoft Excel Command

The **About Microsoft Excel command** on the Help menu displays the About Microsoft Excel dialog box. The dialog box lists the owner of the software and the product identification. You need to know the product identification if you call Microsoft for assistance. The two buttons below the OK button are the System Info button and the Tech Support button. The **System Info button** displays system information, including hardware resources, components, software environment, and applications. The **Tech Support button** displays technical assistance information.

Use Help

1 Using the Ask a Question Box

Instructions: Perform the following tasks using the Excel Help system.

1. Click the Ask a Question box on the menu bar, and then type how do i enter formulas. Press the ENTER key.

2. Click Create a formula in the Ask a Question list. Double-click the Microsoft Excel Help window title bar. Read and print the information. One at a time, click two of the links on the right side of the window to learn about formulas. Print the information. Hand in the printouts to your instructor. Use the Back and Forward buttons to return to the original page.

3. If necessary, click the Show button to display the tabs. Click the Contents tab to prepare for the next step. Click the Close button in the Microsoft Excel Help window.

4. Click the Ask a Question box and press the ENTER key. Click IF worksheet function in the Ask a Question box. When the Microsoft Excel Help window displays, maximize the window. Read and print the information. Click each of the six logical functions in the Logical Functions book in the Contents sheet. Print the information for each. Close the Microsoft Excel Help window.

2 Expanding on the Excel Help System Basics

Instructions: Use the Excel Help system to understand the topics better and answer the questions listed below. Answer the questions on your own paper, or hand in the printed Help information to your instructor.

1. Right-click the Office Assistant. If it is not turned on, click Show the Office Assistant on the Help menu. When the shortcut menu displays, click Options. Click Use the Office Assistant to remove the check mark, and then click the OK button.

2. Click the Microsoft Excel Help button on the Standard toolbar. Maximize the Microsoft Excel Help window. If the tabs are hidden on the left side, click the Show button. Click the Index tab. Type undo in the Type keywords text box. Click the Search button. Click Restore original settings for buttons, commands, or toolbars. Print the information. Click the Hide and then Show buttons. Click the Show All link. Read and print the information. Close the Microsoft Excel Help window. Hand in the printouts to your instructor.

3. Press the F1 key. Click the Answer Wizard tab. Type help in the What would you like to do? text box, and then click the Search button. Click About getting help while you work. Read through the information that displays. Print the information. Click the first two links. Read and print the information for both.

4. Click the Contents tab. Click the plus sign (+) to the left of the Smart Tags book. One at a time, click the first three topics in the Smart Tags book. Read and print each one. Close the Microsoft Excel Help window. Hand in the printouts to your instructor.

5. Click Help on the menu bar and then click What's This? Click the Format Painter button on the Standard toolbar. Right-click the ScreenTip and then click Print Topic on the shortcut menu. Click the Save As command on the File menu. When the Save As dialog box displays, click the Question Mark button on the title bar. Click the Save in box. Right-click the ScreenTip and then click Print Topic. Hand in the printouts to your instructor.

APPENDIX B
Speech and Handwriting Recognition and Speech Playback

Introduction

This appendix discusses how you can create and modify worksheets using Office XP's new input technologies. Office XP provides a variety of **text services**, which enable you to speak commands and enter text in an application. The most common text service is the keyboard. Two new text services included with Office XP are speech recognition and handwriting recognition.

When Windows was installed on your computer, you specified a default language. For example, most users in the United States select English (United States) as the default language. Through text services, you can add more than 90 additional languages and varying dialects such as Basque, English (Zimbabwe), French (France), French (Canada), German (Germany), German (Austria), and Swahili. With multiple languages available, you can switch from one language to another while working in Excel. If you change the language or dialect, then text services may change the functions of the keys on the keyboard, adjust speech recognition, and alter handwriting recognition.

The Language Bar

You know that text services are installed properly when the Language Indicator button displays by the clock in the tray status area on the Windows taskbar (Figure B-1a) or the Language bar displays on the screen (Figure B-1b or B-1c). If the Language Indicator button displays in the tray status area, click it, and then click the **Show the Language bar command** (Figure B-1a). The Language bar displays on the screen in the same location it displayed last time.

You can drag the Language bar to any location in the window by pointing to its move handle, which is the vertical line on its left side (Figure B-1b). When the mouse pointer changes to a four-headed arrow, drag the Language bar to the desired location.

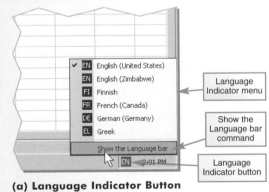

(a) **Language Indicator Button in Tray Status Area on Windows Taskbar and Its Menu**

(b) **Language Bar with Text Labels Disabled**

(c) **Language Bar with Text Labels Enabled**

FIGURE B-1

If you are sure that one of the services was installed and neither the Language Indicator button nor the Language bar displays, then do the following:

1. Click Start on the Windows taskbar, point to Settings, click Control Panel, and then double-click the Text Services icon in the Control Panel window.
2. When the Text Services dialog box displays, click the Language Bar button, click the Show the Language bar on the desktop check box to select it, and then click the OK button in the Language Bar Settings dialog box.
3. Click the OK button in the Text Services dialog box.
4. Close the Control Panel window.

You can perform tasks related to text services by using the **Language bar**. The Language bar may display with just the icon on each button (Figure B-1b) or it may display with text labels to the right of the icon on each button (Figure B-1c). Changing the appearance of the Language bar will be discussed shortly.

Buttons on the Language Bar

The Language bar shown in Figure B-2a contains eight buttons. The number of buttons on your Language bar may be different. These buttons are used to select the language, customize the Language bar, control the microphone, control handwriting, and obtain help.

When you click the **Language Indicator button** on the far left side of the Language bar, the Language Indicator menu displays a list of the active languages (Figure B-2b) from which you can choose. The **Microphone button**, the second button from the left, enables and disables the microphone. When the microphone is enabled, text services adds two buttons and a balloon to the Language toolbar (Figure B-2c). These additional buttons and the balloon will be discussed shortly.

The third button from the left on the Language bar is the Speech Tools button. The **Speech Tools button** displays a menu of commands (Figure B-2d) that allow you to hide or show the balloon on the Language bar; train the Speech Recognition service so that it can better interpret your voice; add and delete words from its dictionary, such as names and other words not understood easily; and change the user profile so more than one person can use the microphone on the same computer.

The fourth button from the left on the Language bar is the Handwriting button. The **Handwriting button** displays the **Handwriting menu** (Figure B-2e), which lets you choose the Writing Pad (Figure B-2f), Write Anywhere (Figure B-2g), or the on-screen keyboard (Figure B-2h). The **On-Screen Symbol Keyboard command** on the Handwriting menu displays an on-screen keyboard that allows you to enter special symbols that are not available on a standard keyboard. You can choose only one form of handwriting at a time.

The fifth button indicates which one of the handwriting forms is active. For example, in Figure B-1a on the previous page, the Writing Pad is active. The handwriting recognition capabilities of text services will be discussed shortly.

The sixth button from the left on the Language bar is the Help button. The **Help button** displays the Help menu. If you click the Language Bar Help command on the Help menu, the Language Bar Help window displays (Figure B-2i). On the far right of the Language bar are two buttons stacked above and below each other. The top button is the Minimize button and the bottom button is the Options button. The **Minimize button** minimizes (hides) the Language bar so that the Language Indicator button displays in the tray status area on the Windows taskbar. The next section discusses the Options button.

Customizing the Language Bar

The down arrow icon immediately below the Minimize button in Figure B-2a is called the Options button. The **Options button** displays a menu of text services options (Figure B-2j). You can use this menu to hide the Speech Tools, Handwriting, and Help buttons on the Language bar by clicking their names to remove the check mark to the left of each button. The Settings command on the Options menu displays a dialog box that lets you customize the Language bar. This command will be discussed shortly. The Restore Defaults command redisplays hidden buttons on the Language bar.

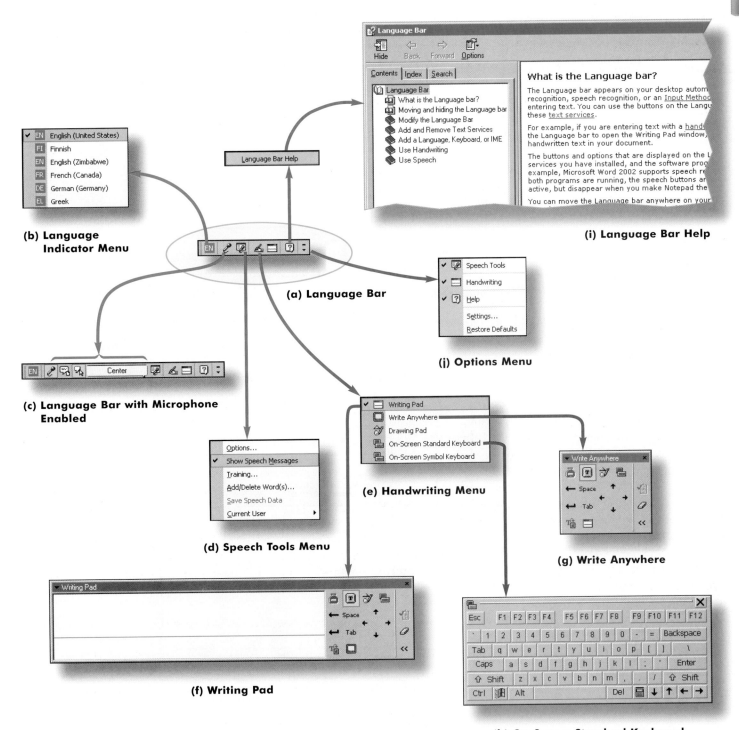

FIGURE B-2

If you right-click the Language bar, a shortcut menu displays (Figure B-3a on the next page). This shortcut menu lets you further customize the Language bar. The **Minimize command** on the shortcut menu minimizes the Language bar the same as the Minimize button on the Language bar. The **Transparency command** toggles the Language bar between being solid and transparent. You can see through a transparent Language bar (Figure B-3b). The **Text Labels command** toggles text labels on the Language bar on (Figure B-3c) and off (Figure B-3a). The **Additional icons in taskbar command** toggles between only showing the Language Indicator button in the tray status area and showing icons that represent the text services that are active (Figure B-3d).

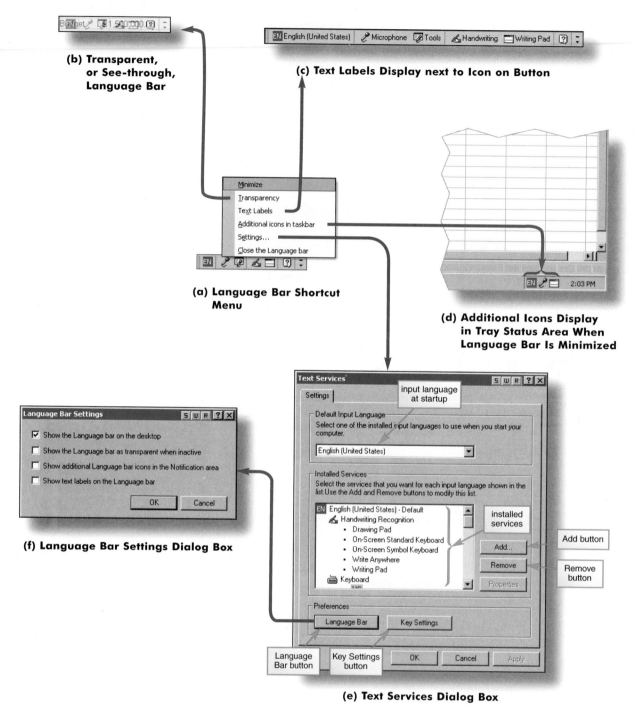

(b) Transparent, or See-through, Language Bar

(c) Text Labels Display next to Icon on Button

(a) Language Bar Shortcut Menu

(d) Additional Icons Display in Tray Status Area When Language Bar Is Minimized

(f) Language Bar Settings Dialog Box

(e) Text Services Dialog Box

FIGURE B-3

The **Settings command** displays the Text Services dialog box (Figure B-3e). The **Text Services dialog box** allows you to select the language at startup; add and remove text services; modify keys on the keyboard; and modify the Language bar. If you want to remove any one of the entries in the Installed Services list, select the entry, and then click the Remove button. If you want to add a service, click the Add button. The Key Settings button allows you to modify the keyboard. If you click the **Language Bar button** in the Text Services dialog box, the **Language Bar Settings dialog box** displays (Figure B-3f). This dialog box contains Language bar options, some of which are the same as the commands on the Language bar shortcut menu described earlier.

The **Close the Language bar command** on the shortcut menu shown in Figure B-3a closes the Language bar and hides the Language Indicator button in the tray status area on the Windows taskbar. If you close the Language bar and want to redisplay it, follow the instructions at the top of page E B.02.

Speech Recognition

The **Speech Recognition service** available with Office XP enables your computer to recognize human speech through a microphone. The microphone has two modes: dictation and voice command (Figure B-4). You switch between the two modes by clicking the Dictation button and the Voice Command button on the Language bar. These buttons display only when you turn on Speech Recognition by clicking the **Microphone button** on the Language bar (Figure B-5). If you are using the Microphone button for the very first time in Excel, it will require that you check your microphone settings and step through voice training before activating the Speech Recognition service.

The **Dictation button** places the microphone in Dictation mode. In **Dictation mode**, whatever you speak is entered as text in the active cell. The **Voice Command button** places the microphone in Voice Command mode. In **Voice Command mode**, whatever you speak is interpreted as a command. If you want to turn off the microphone, click the Microphone button on the Language bar or in Voice Command mode say, "Mic off" (pronounced mike off). It is important to remember that minimizing the Language bar does not turn off the microphone.

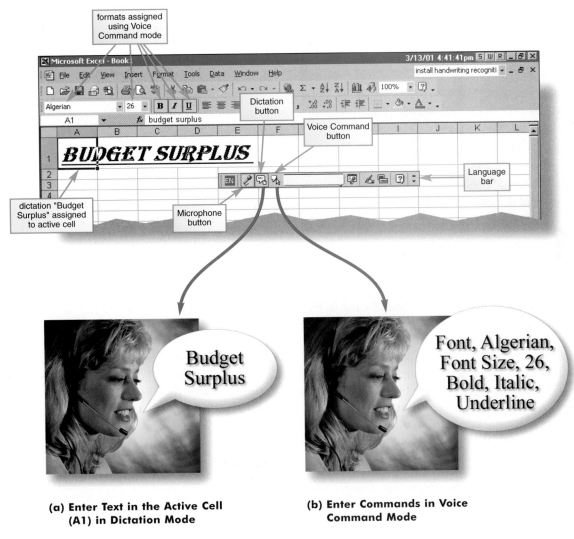

(a) Enter Text in the Active Cell (A1) in Dictation Mode

(b) Enter Commands in Voice Command Mode

FIGURE B-4

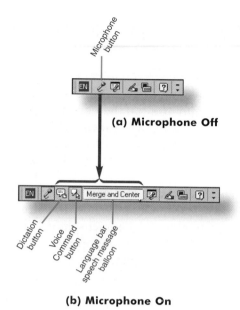

(a) Microphone Off

(b) Microphone On

FIGURE B-5

The **Language bar speech message balloon** shown in Figure B-5b displays messages that may offer help or hints. In Voice Command mode, the name of the last recognized command you said displays. If you use the mouse or keyboard instead of the microphone, a message will appear in the Language bar speech message balloon indicating the word you could say. In Dictation mode, the message, Dictating, usually displays. The Speech Recognition service, however, will display messages to inform you that you are talking too soft, too loud, too fast, or to ask you to repeat what you said by displaying, What was that?

Getting Started with Speech Recognition

For the microphone to function properly, you should follow these steps:

1. Make sure your computer meets the minimum requirements.
2. Install Speech Recognition.
3. Set up and position your microphone, preferably a close-talk headset with gain adjustment support.
4. Train Speech Recognition.

The following sections describe these steps in more detail.

SPEECH RECOGNITION SYSTEM REQUIREMENTS   For Speech Recognition to work on your computer, it needs the following:

1. Microsoft Windows 98 or later or Microsoft Windows NT 4.0 or later
2. At least 128 MB RAM
3. 400 MHz or faster processor
4. Microphone and sound card

INSTALLING SPEECH RECOGNITION   If Speech Recognition is not installed on your computer, start Microsoft Word and then click Speech on the Tools menu.

SETUP AND POSITION YOUR MICROPHONE   Set up your microphone as follows:

1. Connect your microphone to the sound card in the back of the computer.
2. Position the microphone approximately one inch out from and to the side of your mouth. Position it so you are not breathing into it.
3. On the Language bar, click the Speech Tools button, and then click Options (Figure B-6a).
4. When the Speech Properties dialog box displays (Figure B-6b), if necessary, click the Speech Recognition tab.
5. Click the Configure Microphone button. Follow the Microphone Wizard directions as shown in Figures B-6c, B-6d, and B-6e. The Next button will remain dimmed in Figure B-6d until the volume meter consistently stays in the green area.
6. If someone else installed Speech Recognition, click the New button in the Speech Properties dialog box and enter your name. Click the Train Profile button and step through the Voice Training Wizard. The Voice Training Wizard will require that you enter your gender and age group. It then will step you through voice training.

You can adjust the microphone further by clicking the **Settings button** (Figure B-6b) in the Speech Properties dialog box. The Settings button displays the **Recognition Profile Settings dialog box** that allows you to adjust the pronunciation sensitivity and accuracy versus recognition response time.

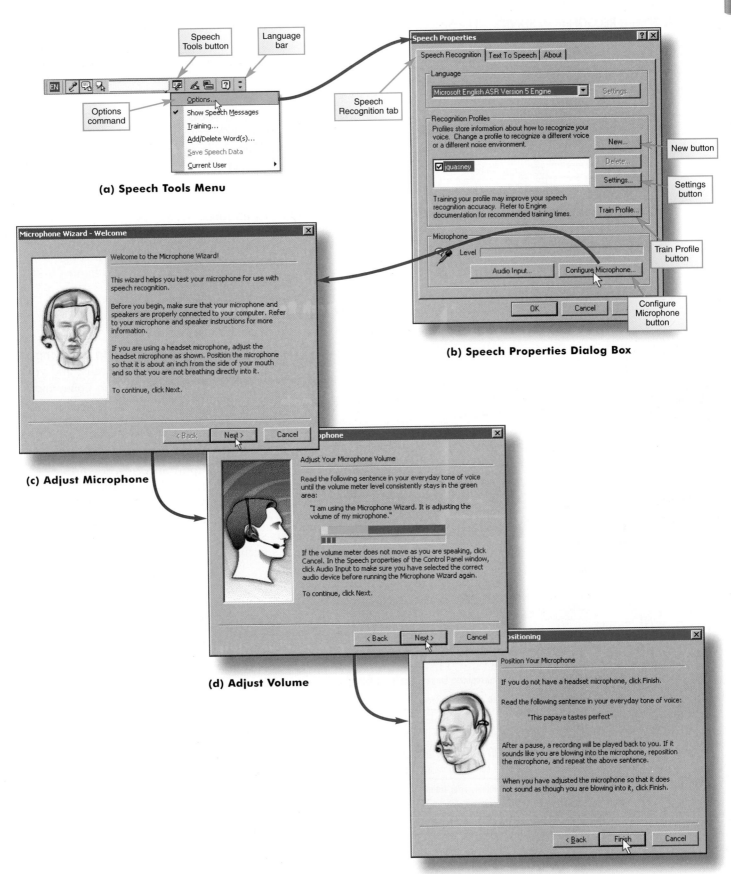

(a) Speech Tools Menu

(b) Speech Properties Dialog Box

(c) Adjust Microphone

(d) Adjust Volume

(e) Test Microphone

FIGURE B-6

TRAIN THE SPEECH RECOGNITION SERVICE The Speech Recognition service will understand most commands and some dictation without any training at all. It will recognize much more of what you speak, however, if you take the time to train it. After one training session, it will recognize 85 to 90 percent of your words. As you do more training, accuracy will rise to 95 percent. If you feel that too many mistakes are being made, then continue to train the service. The more training you do, the more accurately it will work for you. Follow these steps to train the Speech Recognition service:

(a) Speech Tools Menu

(b) Voice Training Dialog Box

FIGURE B-7

1. Click the Speech Tools button on the Language bar and then click Training (Figure B-7a).
2. When the **Voice Training dialog box** displays (Figure B-7b), click one of the sessions and then click the Next button.
3. Complete the training session, which should take less than 15 minutes.

If you are serious about using a microphone to speak to your computer, you need to take the time to go through at least three of the eight training sessions listed in Figure B-7b.

Using Speech Recognition

Speech recognition lets you enter text into a worksheet similarly to speaking into a tape recorder. Instead of typing, you can dictate text that you want to assign to cells, and you can issue voice commands. In **Voice Command mode**, you can speak menu names, commands on menus, toolbar button names, and dialog box option buttons, check boxes, list boxes, and button names. Speech Recognition, however, is not a completely hands-free form of input. Speech recognition works best if you use a combination of your voice, the keyboard, and the mouse. You soon will discover that Dictation mode is far less accurate than Voice Command mode. Table B-1 lists some tips that will improve the Speech Recognition service's accuracy considerably.

Table B-1	Tips to Improve Speech Recognition
NUMBER	**TIP**
1	The microphone hears everything. Though the Speech Recognition service filters out background noise, it is recommended that you work in a quiet environment.
2	Try not to move the microphone around once it is adjusted.
3	Speak in a steady tone and speak clearly.
4	In Dictation mode, do not pause between words. A phrase is easier to interpret than a word. Sounding out syllables in a word will make it more difficult for the Speech Recognition service to interpret what you are saying.
5	If you speak too loudly or too softly, it makes it difficult for the Speech Recognition service to interpret what you said. Check the Language bar speech message balloon for an indication that you may be speaking too loudly or too softly.
6	If you experience problems after training, adjust the recognition options that control accuracy and rejection by clicking the Settings button shown in Figure B-6b on the previous page.
7	When you are finished using the microphone, turn it off by clicking the Microphone button on the Language bar or in Voice Command mode say, "Mic off." Leaving the microphone on is the same as leaning on the keyboard.
8	If the Speech Recognition service is having difficulty with unusual words, then add the words to its dictionary by using the Add/Delete Word(s) command on the Speech Tools menu (Figure B-8a). The last names of individuals and the names of companies are good examples of the types of words you should add to the dictionary.
9	Training will improve accuracy; practice will improve confidence.

The last command on the Speech Tools menu is the Current User command (Figure B-8a). The **Current User command** is useful for multiple users who share a computer. It allows them to configure their own individual profiles, and then switch between users as they use the computer.

For additional information on the Speech Recognition service, click the Help button on the Standard toolbar, click the Answer Wizard tab, and search for the phrase, Speech Recognition.

Handwriting Recognition

Using the Office XP handwriting recognition capabilities, you can enter text and numbers into Excel by writing instead of typing. You can write using a special handwriting device that connects to your computer or you can write on the screen using your mouse. Four basic methods of handwriting are available by clicking the **Handwriting button** on the Language bar: Writing Pad; Write Anywhere; Drawing Pad; and On-Screen Keyboard. The Drawing Pad button is dimmed, which means it is not available in Excel. Although the on-screen keyboard does not involve handwriting recognition, it is part of the Handwriting menu and, therefore, will be discussed in this section.

FIGURE B-8

If your Language bar does not include the Handwriting button (Figures B-1b or B-1c on page E B.01), then for installation instructions click the Help button on the Standard toolbar, click the Answer Wizard tab, and search for the phrase Install Handwriting Recognition.

Writing Pad

To display the Writing Pad, click the Handwriting button on the Language bar and then click Writing Pad (Figure B-9). The **Writing Pad** resembles a note pad with one or more lines on which you can use freehand to print or write in cursive. With the **Text button** enabled, you can form letters on the line by moving the mouse while holding down the mouse button. To the right of the note pad is a rectangular toolbar. Use the buttons on this toolbar to adjust the Writing Pad, select cells, and activate other handwriting applications.

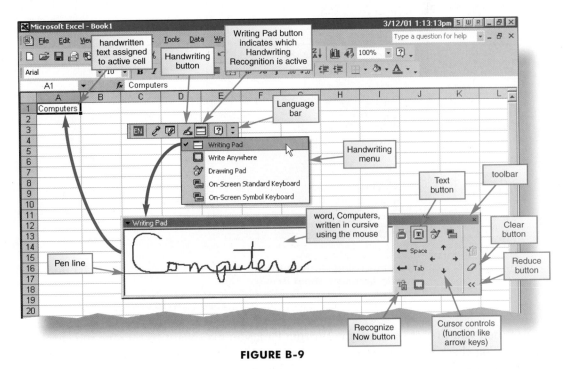

FIGURE B-9

Consider the example in Figure B-9 on the previous page. With cell A1 selected, the word, Computers, is written in cursive on the **Pen line** in the Writing Pad. As soon as the word is complete, the Handwriting Recognition service automatically assigns the word to cell A1.

You can customize the Writing Pad by clicking the **Options button** on the left side of the title bar and then clicking the Options command (Figure B-10a). Invoking the **Options command** causes the Handwriting Options dialog box to display. The **Handwriting Options dialog box** contains two sheets: Common and Writing Pad. The **Common sheet** lets you change the pen color and pen width, adjust recognition, and customize the toolbar area of the Writing Pad. The **Writing Pad sheet** allows you to change the background color and the number of lines that display in the Writing Pad. Both sheets contain a **Restore Default button** to restore the settings to what they were when the software was installed initially.

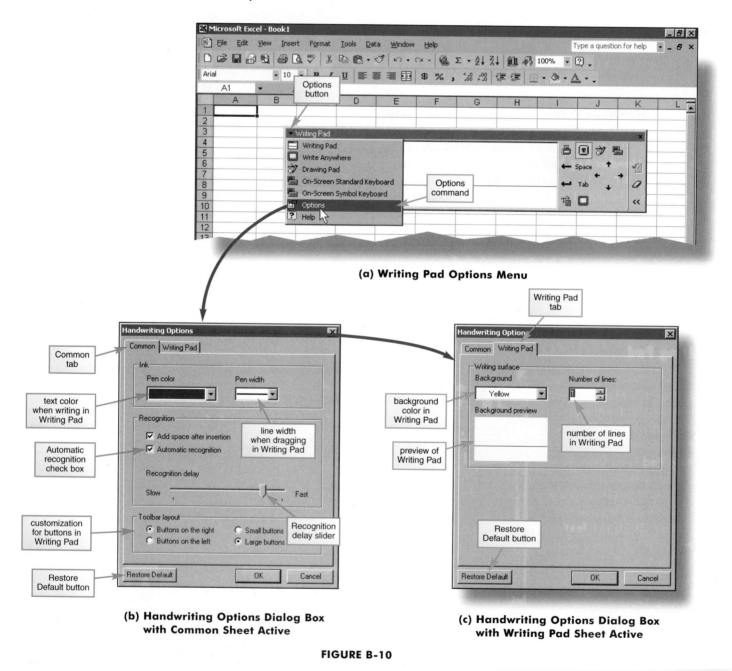

FIGURE B-10

When you first start using the Writing Pad, you may want to remove the check mark from the **Automatic recognition check box** in the Common sheet in the Handwriting Options dialog box (Figure B-10b). With the check mark removed, the Handwriting Recognition service will not interpret what you write in the Writing Pad until you click the **Recognize Now button** on the toolbar (Figure B-9 on the previous page). This allows you to pause and adjust your writing.

The best way to learn how to use the Writing Pad is to practice with it. Also, for more information, click the Help button on the Standard toolbar, click the Answer Wizard tab, and search for the phrase, Handwriting Recognition.

Write Anywhere

Rather than use a Writing Pad, you can write anywhere on the screen by invoking the **Write Anywhere command** on the Handwriting menu (Figure B-11) that displays when you click the Handwriting button on the Language bar. In this case, the entire window is your writing pad.

In Figure B-11, the word, Chip, is written in cursive using the mouse button. Shortly after you finish writing the word, the Handwriting Recognition service interprets it, assigns it to the active cell, and erases what you wrote.

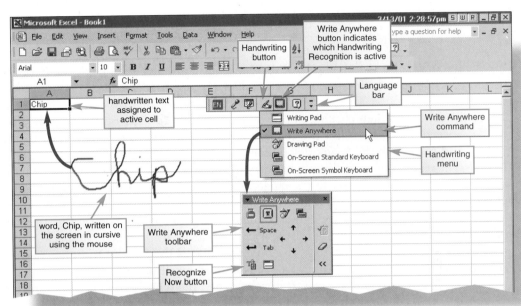

FIGURE B-11

It is recommended that when you first start using the Writing Anywhere service that you remove the check mark from the Automatic recognition check box in the Common sheet in the Handwriting Options dialog box (Figure B-10b). With the check mark removed, the Handwriting Recognition service will not interpret what you write on the screen until you click the Recognize Now button on the toolbar (Figure B-11).

Write Anywhere is more difficult to use than the Writing Pad, because when you click the mouse button, Excel may interpret the action as selecting a cell rather than starting to write. For this reason, it is recommended that you use the Writing Pad.

On-Screen Keyboard

The **On-Screen Standard Keyboard command** on the Handwriting menu (Figure B-12) displays an on-screen keyboard. The **on-screen keyboard** lets you enter data into a cell by using your mouse to click the keys. The on-screen keyboard is similar to the type found on handheld computers.

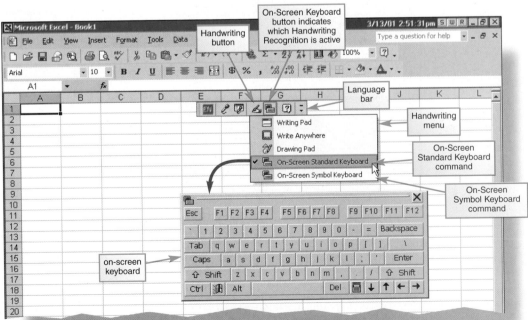

FIGURE B-12

The **On-Screen Symbol Keyboard command** on the Handwriting menu (Figure B-12 on the previous page) displays a special on-screen keyboard that allows you to enter symbols that are not on your keyboard, as well as Unicode characters. **Unicode characters** use a coding scheme capable of representing all the world's current languages.

Speech Playback

With Excel, you can use **speech playback** to have your computer read back the data in a worksheet. To enable speech playback, you use the **Text To Speech toolbar** (Figure B-13). You display the toolbar by right-clicking a toolbar and then clicking Text To Speech on the shortcut menu. You also can display the toolbar by pointing to Speech on the Tools menu and then clicking Show Text To Speech Toolbar on the Speech submenu.

To use speech playback, select the cell where you want the computer to start reading back the data in the worksheet and then click the **Speak Cell button** on the Text To Speech toolbar (Figure B-13). The computer stops reading after it reads the last cell with an entry in the worksheet. An alternative is to select a range before you turn on speech playback. When you select a range, the computer reads from the upper-left corner of the range to the lower-right corner of the range. It reads the data in the worksheet by rows or by columns. You choose the direction you want it to read by clicking the **By Rows button** or **By Columns button** on the Text To Speech toolbar. Click the **Stop Speaking button** or hide the Text To Speech toolbar to stop speech playback.

The rightmost button on the Text To Speech toolbar is the Speak On Enter button. When you click the **Speak On Enter button** to enable it, the computer reads data in a cell immediately after you complete the entry by pressing the ENTER key or clicking another cell. It does not read the data if you click the Enter box on the formula bar to complete the entry. You disable this feature by clicking the Speak On Enter button while the feature is enabled. If you do not turn the Speak On Enter feature off, the computer will continue to read new cell entries even if the toolbar is hidden.

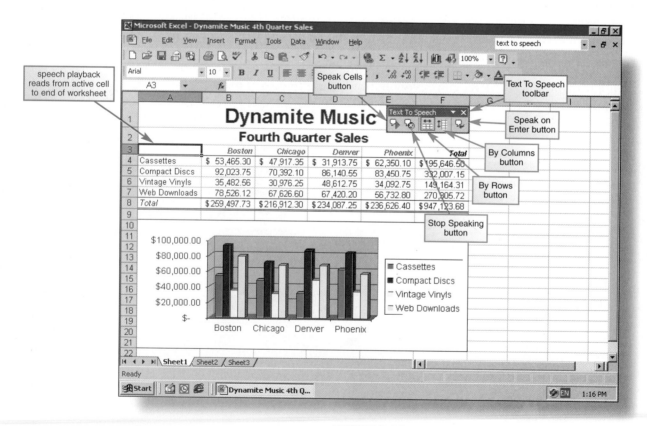

FIGURE B-13

Customizing Speech Playback

You can customize speech playback by double-clicking the **Speech icon** in the Control Panel window (Figure B-14a). To display the Control Panel, point to Settings on the Start menu and then click Control Panel. When you double-click the Speech icon, the Speech Properties dialog box displays (Figure B-14b). Click the Text To Speech tab. The Text To Speech sheet has two areas: Voice selection and Voice speed. The Voice selection area lets you choose between a male and female voice. You can click the Preview Voice button to preview the voice. The Voice speed area contains a slider. Drag the slider to slow down or speed up the voice.

(a) Control Panel Window

(b) Speech Properties Dialog Box

FIGURE B-14

APPENDIX C
Publishing Office Web Pages to a Web Server

With the Office applications, you use the Save as Web Page command on the File menu to save the Web page to a Web server using one of two techniques: Web folders or File Transfer Protocol. A **Web folder** is an Office shortcut to a Web server. **File Transfer Protocol** (**FTP**) is an Internet standard that allows computers to exchange files with other computers on the Internet.

You should contact your network system administrator or technical support staff at your ISP to determine if their Web server supports Web folders, FTP, or both, and to obtain necessary permissions to access the Web server. If you decide to publish Web pages using a Web folder, you must have the Office Server Extensions (OSE) installed on your computer.

Using Web Folders to Publish Office Web Pages

When publishing to a Web folder, someone first must create the Web folder before you can save to it. If you are granted permission to create a Web folder, you must obtain the URL of the Web server, a user name, and possibly a password that allows you to access the Web server. You also must decide on a name for the Web folder. Table C-1 explains how to create a Web folder.

Office adds the name of the Web folder to the list of current Web folders. You can save to this folder, open files in the folder, rename the folder, or perform any operations you would to a folder on your hard disk. You can use your Office program or Windows Explorer to access this folder. Table C-2 explains how to save to a Web folder.

Using FTP to Publish Office Web Pages

When publishing a Web page using FTP, you first must add the FTP location to your computer before you can save to it. An **FTP location**, also called an **FTP site**, is a collection of files that reside on an FTP server. In this case, the FTP server is the Web server.

To add an FTP location, you must obtain the name of the FTP site, which usually is the address (URL) of the FTP server, and a user name and a password that allows you to access the FTP server. You save and open the Web pages on the FTP server using the name of the FTP site. Table C-3 explains how to add an FTP site.

Office adds the name of the FTP site to the FTP locations list in the Save As and Open dialog boxes. You can open and save files using this list. Table C-4 explains how to save to an FTP location.

Table C-1	Creating a Web Folder
1.	Click File on the menu bar and then click Save As (or Open).
2.	When the Save As dialog box (or Open dialog box) displays, click My Network Places (or Web Folders) on the Places Bar. Double-click Add Network Place (or Add Web Folder).
3.	When the Add Network Place Wizard dialog box displays, click the Create a new Network Place option button and then click the Next button. Type the URL of the Web server in the Folder location text box, enter the folder name you want to call the Web folder in the Folder name text box, and then click the Next button. Click Empty Web and then click the Finish button.
4.	When the Enter Network Password dialog box displays, type the user name and, if necessary, the password in the respective text boxes and then click the OK button.
5.	Close the Save As or the Open dialog box.

Table C-2	Saving to a Web Folder
1.	Click File on the menu bar and then click Save As.
2.	When the Save As dialog box displays, type the Web page file name in the File name text box. Do not press the ENTER key.
3.	Click My Network Places on the Places Bar.
4.	Double-click the Web folder name in the Save in list.
5.	If the Enter Network Password dialog box displays, type the user name and password in the respective text boxes and then click the OK button.
6.	Click the Save button in the Save As dialog box.

Table C-3	Adding an FTP Location
1.	Click File on the menu bar and then click Save As (or Open).
2.	In the Save As dialog box, click the Save in box arrow and then click Add/Modify FTP Locations in the Save in list; or in the Open dialog box, click the Look in box arrow and then click Add/Modify FTP Locations in the Look in list.
3.	When the Add/Modify FTP Locations dialog box displays, type the name of the FTP site in the Name of FTP site text box. If the site allows anonymous logon, click Anonymous in the Log on as area; if you have a user name for the site, click User in the Log on as area and then enter the user name. Enter the password in the Password text box. Click the OK button.
4.	Close the Save As or the Open dialog box.

Table C-4	Saving to an FTP Location
1.	Click File on the menu bar and then click Save As.
2.	When the Save As dialog box displays, type the Web page file name in the File name text box. Do not press the ENTER key.
3.	Click the Save in box arrow and then click FTP Locations.
4.	Double-click the name of the FTP site to which you wish to save.
5.	When the FTP Log On dialog box displays, enter your user name and password and then click the OK button.
6.	Click the Save button in the Save As dialog box.

APPENDIX D
Resetting the Excel Toolbars and Menus

Excel customization capabilities allow you to create custom toolbars by adding and deleting buttons and personalize menus based on their usage. Each time you start Excel, the toolbars and menus display using the same settings as the last time you used it. This appendix shows you how to reset the Standard and Formatting toolbars and menus to their installation settings.

Steps | **To Reset the Standard and Formatting Toolbars**

1 **Click the Toolbar Options button on the Standard toolbar and then point to Add or Remove Buttons on the Toolbar Options menu.**

The Toolbar Options menu and Add or Remove Buttons submenu display (Figure D-1).

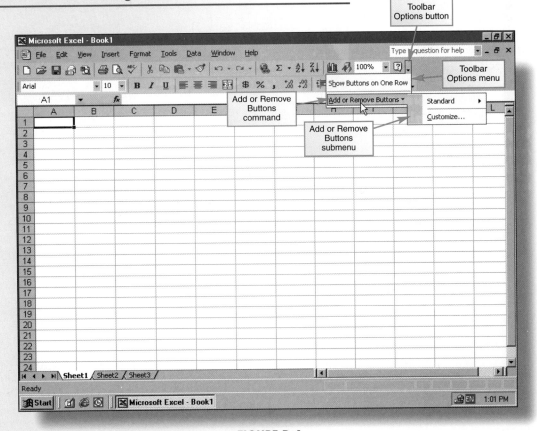

FIGURE D-1

2 **Point to Standard on the Add or Remove Buttons submenu. When the Standard submenu displays, scroll down and then point to Reset Toolbar.**

The Standard submenu displays indicating the buttons and boxes that display on the toolbar (Figure D-2). To remove any buttons, click a button name with a check mark to the left of the name to remove the check mark.

3 **Click Reset Toolbar.**

Excel resets the Standard toolbar to its installation settings.

4 **Reset the Formatting toolbar by following Steps 1 through 3 and replacing any reference to the Standard toolbar with the Formatting toolbar.**

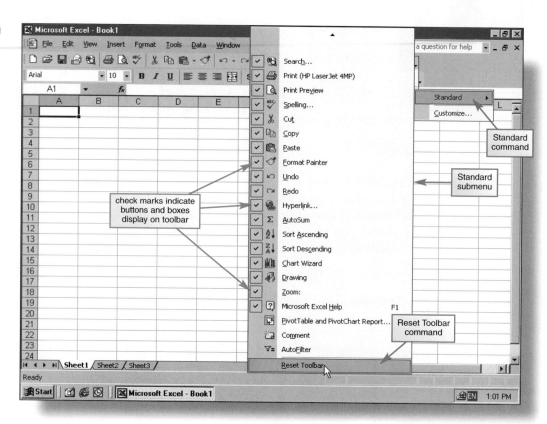

FIGURE D-2

Other Ways

1. On View menu point to Toolbars, click Customize on Toolbars submenu, click Toolbars tab, click toolbar name, click Reset button, click OK button, click Close button

2. Right-click toolbar, click Customize on shortcut menu, click Toolbars tab, click toolbar name, click Reset button, click OK button, click Close button

To Reset Menus

1 **Click the Toolbar Options button on the Standard toolbar and then point to Add or Remove Buttons on the Toolbar Options menu. Point to Customize on the Add or Remove Buttons submenu.**

The Toolbar Options menu and Add or Remove Buttons submenu display (Figure D-3).

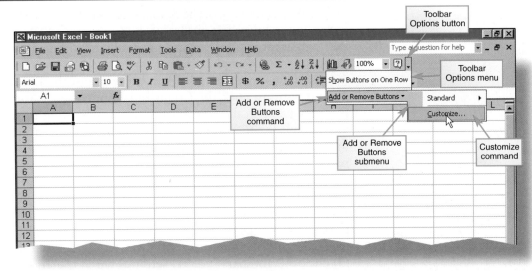

FIGURE D-3

2 **Click Customize. When the Customize dialog box displays, click the Options tab and then point to the Reset my usage data button.**

*The Customize dialog box displays (Figure D-4). The **Customize dialog box** contains three tabbed sheets used for customizing the Excel toolbars and menus.*

3 **Click the Reset my usage data button. When the Microsoft Excel dialog box displays, click the Yes button. Click the Close button in the Customize dialog box.**

Excel resets the menus to the installation settings.

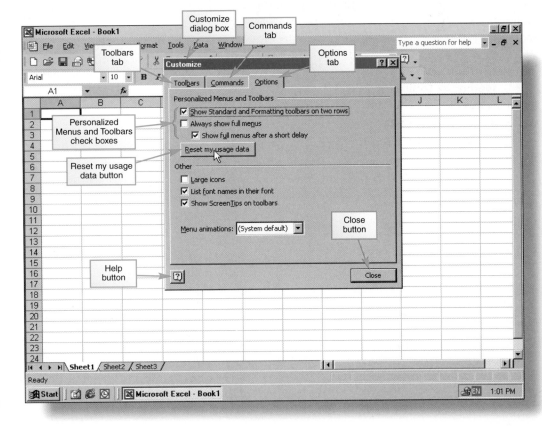

FIGURE D-4

Other Ways

1. On View menu point to Toolbars, click Customize on Toolbars submenu, click Options tab, click Reset my usage data button, click Yes button, click Close button

In the **Options sheet** in the Customize dialog box shown in Figure D-4 on the previous page, you can turn off toolbars displaying on two rows and turn off short menus by removing the check marks from the two top check boxes. Click the **Help button** in the lower-left corner of the Customize dialog box to display Help topics that will assist you in customizing toolbars and menus.

Using the **Commands sheet**, you can add buttons to toolbars and commands to menus. Recall that the menu bar at the top of the Excel window is a special toolbar. To add buttons, click the Commands tab in the Customize dialog box. Click a category name in the Categories list and then drag the command name in the Commands list to a toolbar. To add commands to a menu, click a category name in the Categories list, drag the command name in the Commands list to the menu name on the menu bar, and then, when the menu displays, drag the command to the desired location in the menu list of commands.

In the **Toolbars sheet**, you can add new toolbars and reset existing toolbars. If you add commands to menus as described in the previous paragraph and want to reset the menus to their default settings, do the following: (1) Click View on the menu bar and then point to Toolbars; (2) click Customize on the Toolbars submenu; (3) click the Toolbars tab; (4) scroll down in the Toolbars list and then click Worksheet Menu Bar; (5) click the Reset button; (6) click the OK button; and then (7) click the Close button.

APPENDIX E
Microsoft Office User Specialist Certification Program

What Is MOUS Certification?

The Microsoft Office User Specialist (MOUS) Certification Program provides a framework for measuring your proficiency with the Microsoft Office XP applications, such as Word 2002, Excel 2002, Access 2002, PowerPoint 2002, Outlook 2002, and FrontPage 2002. The levels of certification are described in Table E-1.

Table E-1 Levels of MOUS Certification			
LEVEL	**DESCRIPTION**	**REQUIREMENTS**	**CREDENTIAL AWARDED**
Expert	Indicates that you have a comprehensive understanding of the advanced features in a specific Microsoft Office XP application	Pass any ONE of the Expert exams: Microsoft Word 2002 Expert Microsoft Excel 2002 Expert Microsoft Access 2002 Expert Microsoft Outlook 2002 Expert Microsoft FrontPage 2002 Expert	Candidates will be awarded one certificate for each of the Expert exams they have passed: Microsoft Office User Specialist: Microsoft Word 2002 Expert Microsoft Office User Specialist: Microsoft Excel 2002 Expert Microsoft Office User Specialist: Microsoft Access 2002 Expert Microsoft Office User Specialist: Microsoft Outlook 2002 Expert Microsoft Office User Specialist: Microsoft FrontPage 2002 Expert
Core	Indicates that you have a comprehensive understanding of the core features in a specific Microsoft Office 2002 application	Pass any ONE of the Core exams: Microsoft Word 2002 Core Microsoft Excel 2002 Core Microsoft Access 2002 Core Microsoft Outlook 2002 Core Microsoft FrontPage 2002 Core	Candidates will be awarded one certificate for each of the Core exams they have passed: Microsoft Office User Specialist: Microsoft Word 2002 Microsoft Office User Specialist: Microsoft Excel 2002 Microsoft Office User Specialist: Microsoft Access 2002 Microsoft Office User Specialist: Microsoft Outlook 2002 Microsoft Office User Specialist: Microsoft FrontPage 2002
Comprehensive	Indicates that you have a comprehensive understanding of the features in Microsoft PowerPoint 2002	Pass the Microsoft PowerPoint 2002 Comprehensive Exam	Candidates will be awarded one certificate for the Microsoft PowerPoint 2002 Comprehensive exam passed.

Why Should You Get Certified?

Being a Microsoft Office User Specialist provides a valuable industry credential — proof that you have the Office XP applications skills required by employers. By passing one or more MOUS certification exams, you demonstrate your proficiency in a given Office XP application to employers. With over 100 million copies of Office in use around the world, Microsoft is targeting Office XP certification to a wide variety of companies. These companies include temporary employment agencies that want to prove the expertise of their workers, large corporations looking for a way to measure the skill set of employees, and training companies and educational institutions seeking Microsoft Office XP teachers with appropriate credentials.

The MOUS Exams

You pay $50 to $100 each time you take an exam, whether you pass or fail. The fee varies among testing centers. The Expert exams, which you can take up to 60 minutes to complete, consists of between 40 and 60 tasks that you perform online. The tasks require you to use the application just as you would in doing your job. The Core exams contain fewer tasks, and you will have slightly less time to complete them. The tasks you will perform differ on the two types of exams.

How Can You Prepare for the MOUS Exams?

The Shelly Cashman Series® offers several Microsoft-approved textbooks that cover the required objectives on the MOUS exams. For a listing of the textbooks, visit the Shelly Cashman Series MOUS site at scsite.com/offxp/cert.htm and click the link Shelly Cashman Series Office XP Microsoft-Approved MOUS Textbooks (Figure E-1). After using any of the books listed in an instructor-led course, you will be prepared to take the MOUS exam indicated.

How to Find an Authorized Testing Center

You can locate a testing center by calling 1-800-933-4493 in North America or visiting the Shelly Cashman Series MOUS site at scsite.com/offxp/cert.htm and then clicking the link Locate an Authorized Testing Center Near You (Figure E-1). At this Web site, you can look for testing centers around the world.

Shelly Cashman Series MOUS Web Page

The Shelly Cashman Series MOUS Web page (Figure E-1) has more than fifteen Web sites you can visit to obtain additional information on the MOUS Certification Program. The Web page (scsite.com/offxp/cert.htm) includes links to general information on certification, choosing an application for certification, preparing for the certification exam, and taking and passing the certification exam.

FIGURE E-1

Microsoft Excel 2002 User Specialist Certification Core and Expert Maps

This book has been approved by Microsoft as courseware for the Microsoft Office User Specialist (MOUS) program. After completing the projects and exercises in this book, students will be prepared to take the Core-level and Expert-level Microsoft Office User Specialist Examinations for Microsoft Excel 2002. Table E-2 lists the Microsoft Excel 2002 Core Exam skill sets, activities, page numbers where the activities are demonstrated, and page numbers where the activities can be practiced. Table E-3 lists the Microsoft Excel 2002 Expert Exam skill sets, activities, page numbers where the activities are demonstrated, and page numbers where the activities can be practiced.

Table E-2 Microsoft Excel 2002 MOUS Core Skill Sets, Activities, and Locations in the Book

SKILL SET	ACTIVITY	ACTIVITY DEMONSTRATED IN BOOK	ACTIVITY EXERCISE IN BOOK
I. Working with Cells and Cell Data	A. Insert, delete, and move cells	E 3.16, E 3.18, E 1.32	E 1.57 (Apply Your Knowledge), E 2.70 (In the Lab 1 Step 14), E 3.78 (In the Lab 3 Part 3)
	B. Enter and edit cell data including text, numbers, and formulas	E 1.08, E 1.16, E 1.19, E 1.21, E 1.49, E 1.51, E 2.07, E 2.16-23, E 2.33-38	E 1.58 (In the Lab 1 Steps 1, 10), E 1.60 (In the Lab 2 Step 5), E 2.70 (In the Lab 1 Steps 2-4), E 2.72 (In the Lab 2 Steps 5, 7-9, 13), E 3.70 (In the Lab 1 Step 7), E 3.77-78 (In the Lab 3 Steps 10-15)
	C. Check spelling	E 2.48-50	E 2.70 (In the Lab 1 Step 10), E 2.73 (In the Lab 2 Step 18)
	D. Find and replace cell data and formats	E 1.35-36, E 6.58-61	E 1.59-64, E 6.73 (In the Lab 2 Part 3)
	E. Work with a subset of data by filtering lists	E 5.35-39, E 5.40-47	E 5.53 (In the Lab 1 Part 2), E 5.57 (In the Lab 2 Part 3)
II. Managing Workbooks	A. Manage workbook files and folders	E 1.46, EW 1.06, E 6.62-64	E 1.57 (Apply Your Knowledge), EW 1.16 (In the Lab 1 Step 1)
	B. Create workbooks using templates	E 6.22-24	E 6.71 (In the Lab 1 Step 6), E 6.72 (In the Lab 2 Part 1)
	C. Save workbooks using different names and file formats	E 1.40-44, E 2.24-25, E 2.50, EW 1.06-08, E 6.12, E 6.24, E 6.65	E 1.58 (In the Lab 1 Step 8), EW 1.15-16 (In the Lab 1 Step 1, In the Lab 2 Step 2), E 6.71 (In the Lab 1 Step 6), E 6.72 (In the Lab 2 Steps 4, 6)
III. Formatting and Printing Worksheets	A. Apply and modify cell formats	E 1.28-35, E 2.26-43, E 3.32-43, E 4.07, E 4.09, E 4.36, E 6.12-21	E 1.58-59 (In the Lab 1 Step 5), E 2.68 (Apply Your Knowledge Step 5), E 2.72 (In the Lab 2 Steps 10, 13-15), E 3.69-71 (In the Lab 1 Steps 1-2, 8)
	B. Modify row and column settings	E 3.16-18, E 2.46, E 2.48, E 3.20, E 3.31	E 2.72 (In the Lab 2 Step 10), E 3.70 (In the Lab 1 Step 4), E 3.77 (In the Lab 3 Step 3), E 5.61 (In the Lab 3 Part 2)
	C. Modify row and column formats	E 2.32, E 2.43-48, E 5.08	E 2.70 (In the Lab 1 Steps 6 and 7), E 2.72 (In the Lab 2 Steps 10, 13), E 3.70 (In the Lab 1 Steps 2, 4), E 5.53 (In the Lab 1 Part 1)
	D. Apply styles	E 6.18-21	E 6.71 (Apply Your Knowledge Step 2)
	E. Use automated tools to format worksheets	E 1.33-35	E 1.59 (In the Lab 1 Step 5), E 1.60 (In the Lab 2 Step 5), E 1.61 (In the Lab 3 Step 4)
	F. Modify Page Setup options for worksheets	E 2.54, E 2.57, E 3.57, E 4.44-45, E 6.48-54	E 2.68 (Apply Your Knowledge Steps 8-9), E 2.73 (In the Lab 2 Step 19), E 3.71 (In the Lab 1 Step 10), E 6.70 (Apply Your Knowledge Step 5), E 6.73 (In the Lab 2 Step 6)
	G. Preview and print worksheets and workbooks	E 2.51-58, E 4.44-49, E 6.51, E 6.53	E 2.68 (Apply Your Knowledge Steps 8-9), E 2.70 (In the Lab 1 Steps 9-12), E 2.73 (In the Lab 2 Step 19), E 4.56 (Apply Your Knowledge Step 8), E 6.73 (In the Lab 2 Part 2)

Table E-2 Microsoft Excel 2002 MOUS Core Skill Sets, Activities, and Locations in the Book *(continued)*

SKILL SET	ACTIVITY	ACTIVITY DEMONSTRATED IN BOOK	ACTIVITY EXERCISE IN BOOK
IV. Modifying Workbooks	A. Insert and delete worksheets	E 6.24-25	E 6.71 (In the Lab 1 Step 3), E 6.73 (In the Lab 2 Step 2)
	B. Modify worksheet names and positions	E 3.54-56	E 3.71 (In the Lab 1 Part 2), E 3.74 (In the Lab 2 Step 11), E 3.75 (In the Lab 2 Part 2 Step 6)
	C. Use 3-D references	E 6.30-35, E 6.62, E 6.66-67	E 6.70 (Apply Your Knowledge Step 3, Part 2), E 6.73 (In the Lab 2 Step 4), E 6.75 (In the Lab 3 Step 5)
V. Creating and Revising Formulas	A. Create and revise formulas	E 2.9-13, E 2.17, E 2.22, E 3.25-29, E 4.15-16, E 4.31	E 2.67 (Apply Your Knowledge Steps 1, 4), E 2.70 (In the Lab 1 Step 2), E 2.72 (In the Lab 2 Steps 5-9), E 3.70 (In the Lab 1 Step 7), E 3.74 (In the Lab 2 Step 7), E 4.56 (Apply Your Knowledge Steps 3-5), E 4.57 (In the Lab 1 Step 4), E 4.60 (In the Lab 2 Step 7), E 4.61 (In the Lab 3 Step 4)
	B. Use statistical, date and time, financial, and logical functions in formulas	E 1.23-24, E 1.27-28, E 2.16-24, E 3.22-24, E 3.27-28, E 4.15-16, E 4.31	E 2.70 (In the Lab 1 Step 4), E 2.72 (In the Lab 2 Steps 6-9), E 3.68 (Apply Your Knowledge Steps 1-4), E 3.69-70 (In the Lab 1 Steps 1 and 7), E 4.57 (In the Lab 1 Step 4), E 4.60 (In the Lab 2 Step 7)
VI. Creating and Modifying Graphics	A. Create, modify, position, and print charts	E 1.37-40, E 3.43-54, E 6.35-46, E 6.53-54	E 1.59 (In the Lab 1 Step 6), E 1.60 (In the Lab 2 Step 6), E 1.62 (In the Lab 3 Part 2), E 2.73 (In the Lab 2 Part 2), E 3.75 (In the Lab 2 Part 2)
	B. Create, modify, and position graphics	E 1.39, E 3.52-54, E 6.35-46	E 1.59 (In the Lab 1 Step 6), E 1.60 (In the Lab 2 Step 6), E 1.62 (In the Lab 3 Part 2), E 6.72-73 (In the Lab 2 Step 5)
VII. Workgroup Collaboration	A. Convert worksheets into Web pages	EW 1.04-05, EW 1.06-08, EW 1.10-12	EW 1.15 (In the Lab 1 Step 2), EW 1.16 (In the Lab 2 Part 1 Step 2)
	B. Create hyperlinks	E 4.39-44	E 4.60 (In the Lab 2 Step 10)
	C. View and edit comments	E 6.46-48, EI 1.10-14	E 6.71 (Apply Your Knowledge Step 3), E 6.73 (In the Lab 2 Step 6), EI 1.15 (In the Lab 1 Part 2, In the Lab 2 Part 2)

Table E-3 Microsoft Excel 2002 MOUS Expert Skill Sets, Activities, and Locations in Book

SKILL SET	ACTIVITY	ACTIVITY DEMONSTRATED IN BOOK	ACTIVITY EXERCISE IN BOOK
I. Importing and Exporting Data	A. Import data to Excel	E 9.9, E 9.14, E 9.18, E 9.23	E 9.63 (In the Lab 1)
	B. Export data from Excel	E 9.18, E 9.23, E 9.27	E 9.63 (In the Lab 1, Steps 5-6), E 9.63 (In the Lab 1, Step 11)
	C. Publish worksheets and workbooks to the Web	EW 1.04, Appendix C, EI 1.11, EW 2.03-04	EW 1.15 (In the Lab 1 Step 2), EW 1.16 (In the Lab 2 Part 1 Step 2), EI 1.15 (In the Lab 1 Part 1, In the Lab 2 Part 2), EW 2.15 (In the Lab 1), EW 2.16 (In the Lab 2)
II. Managing Workbooks	A. Create, edit, and apply templates	E 6.07-12	E 6.71 (In the Lab 1 Steps 1-8), E 6.72 (In the Lab 2 Part 1)
	B. Create workspaces	E 6.13-21, E 6.23-24, E 6.64-66	E 6.70 (Apply Your Knowledge Part 2), E 6.71 (In the Lab 1), E 6.72 (In the Lab 2 Part 1)
	C. Use Data Consolidation	E 6.30-35, E 6.62-67, E 9.56	E 6.70 (Apply Your Knowledge Parts 1-2), E 6.73 (In the Lab 2 Step 4), E 9.62 (In the Lab 2)
III. Formatting Numbers	A. Create and apply custom number formats	E 6.15-17	E 6.71 (Apply Your Knowledge Step 2)
	B. Use conditional formats	E 2.40-43, E 4.25-28	E 2.70 (In the Lab 1 Step 8), E 2.72 (In the Lab 2 Step 14), E 4.58 (In the Lab 1 Step 7)
IV. Working with Ranges	A. Use named ranges in formulas	E 4.12-13, E 4.47, E 5.09, E 5.18-20	E 4.56 (Apply Your Knowledge Steps 2-4), E 4.57 (In the Lab 1 Step 4), E 4.61 (In the Lab 3 Step 4)
	B. Use Lookup and Reference functions	E 4.15-16, E 5.15-18, E 5.48	E 4.56 (Apply Your Knowledge Steps 2-4), E 4.57 (In the Lab 1 Step 4), E 4.61 (In the Lab 3 Step 4), E 5.59 (In the Lab 2 Part 5), E 5.60 (In the Lab 3 Step 3), E 5.63 (Cases & Places 2)

Table E-3   Microsoft Excel 2002 MOUS Expert Skill Sets, Activities, and Locations in Book

SKILL SET	ACTIVITY	ACTIVITY DEMONSTRATED IN BOOK	ACTIVITY EXERCISE IN BOOK
V. Customizing Excel	A. Customize toolbars and menus	E 7.18-25	E 7.74 (Apply Your Knowledge), E 7.76 (In the Lab 1 Part 2 Step 5)
	B. Create, edit, and run macros	E 7.19-23, E 7.11-13, E 7.15-18, E 7.63-69	E 7.74 (Apply Your Knowledge), E 7.75-82 (In the Labs 1-3)
VI. Auditing Worksheets	A. Audit formulas	E 8.13	E 8.59 (In the Lab 1 Step 2)
	B. Locate and resolve errors	E 2.25, E 4.52-53, E 8.11	E 2.68 (Apply Your Knowledge Step 6), E 2.70 (In the Lab 1 Step 5), E 4.58 (In the Lab 1 Step 9), E 4.60 (In the Lab 2 Step 13), E 4.62 (In the Lab 3 Step 8), E 8.59 (In the Lab 2 Steps 2, 5)
	C. Identify dependencies in formulas	E 8.12-14	E 8.59 (In the Lab 1 Steps 2, 4)
VII. Summarizing Data	A. Use subtotals with lists and ranges	E 5.27-32	E 5.55 (In the Lab 1 Part 4)
	B. Define and apply filters	E 5.32-39, E 5.40-47	E 5.53 (In the Lab Part 2), E 5.57 (In the Lab Parts 3-4), E 5.61 (In the Lab Parts 4, 6)
	C. Add group and outline criteria to ranges	E 5.30-31	E 5.55 (In the Lab 1 Part 4)
	D. Use data validation	E 8.16-18	E 8.59 (In the Lab 1 Steps 6, 7, 8)
	E. Retrieve external data and create queries	E 9.23-26	E 9.63 (In the Lab 1)
	F. Create Extensible Markup Language (XML) Web queries	E 9.23-26	E 9.63 (In the Lab 1)
VIII. Analyzing Data	A. Create PivotTables, PivotCharts, and PivotTable/PivotChart Reports	E 9.34-39, E 9.51-52	E 9.66 (In the Lab 3)
	B. Forecast values with what-if analysis	E 9.58	E 9.62 (Apply Your Knowledge)
	C. Create and display scenarios	E 8.35-45	E 8.60-63 (In the Lab 2, In the Lab 3)
IX. Workgroup Collaboration	A. Modify passwords, protections, and properties	E 4.49-52	E 4.56 (Apply Your Knowledge Step 9), E 4.58 (In the Lab 1 Step 12), E 4.61 (In the Lab 2 Step 15), E 4.62 (In the Lab 3 Step 10)
	B. Create a shared workbook	E 9.30-31	E 9.64-65 (In the Lab 2)
	C. Track, accept, and reject changes to workbooks	E 9.30-31, E 9.35-37	E 9.64-65 (In the Lab 2)
	D. Merge workbooks	E 9.56-57	E 9.62 (Apply Your Knowledge)

Index

Microsoft
EXCEL 2002
Quick Reference Summary

In Microsoft Excel 2002, you can accomplish a task in a number of ways. The following table provides a quick reference to each task presented in this textbook. The first column identifies the task. The second column indicates the page number on which the task is discussed in the book. The subsequent four columns list the different ways the task in column one can be carried out. You can invoke the commands listed in the MOUSE, MENU BAR, and SHORTCUT MENU columns using Voice commands.

Microsoft Excel 2002 Quick Reference Summary

TASK	PAGE NUMBER	MOUSE	MENU BAR	SHORTCUT MENU	KEYBOARD SHORTCUT
Advanced Filter	E 5.41		Data | Filter | Advanced Filter		ALT+D | F | A
Arrow, Add	E 6.44	Arrow button on Drawing toolbar			
AutoFilter	E 5.35		Data | Filter | AutoFilter		ALT+D | F | F
AutoFormat	E 1.33		Format | AutoFormat		ALT+O | A
AutoSum	E 1.23	AutoSum button on Standard toolbar	Insert | Function		ALT+= (equal)
Bold	E 1.29	Bold button on Formatting toolbar	Format | Cells | Font tab	Format Cells | Font tab	CTRL+B
Borders	E 2.30	Borders button on Formatting toolbar	Format | Cells | Border tab	Format Cells | Border tab	CTRL+1 | B
Center	E 2.32	Center button on Formatting toolbar	Format | Cells | Alignment tab	Format Cells | Alignment tab	CTRL+1 | A
Center Across Columns	E 1.32	Merge and Center button on Formatting toolbar	Format | Cells | Alignment tab	Format Cells | Alignment tab	CTRL+1 | A
Chart	E 1.37	Chart Wizard button on Standard toolbar	Insert | Chart		F11
Clear Cell	E 1.51	Drag fill handle back	Edit | Clear | All	Clear Contents	DELETE
Close All Files	E 6.67		SHIFT+File | Close All		SHIFT+ALT+F | C
Close All Workbooks	E 1.45		SHIFT+File | Close All		SHIFT+ALT+F | C
Close Workbook	E 1.45	Close button on menu bar or workbook Control-menu icon	File | Close		CTRL+W
Color Background	E 2.30	Fill Color button on Formatting toolbar	Format | Cells | Patterns tab	Format Cells | Patterns tab	CTRL+1 | P
Color Tab	E 3.55			Tab Color	
Column Width	E 2.44	Drag column heading boundary	Format | Column | Width	Column Width	ALT+O | C | W
Comma Style Format	E 2.34	Comma Style button on Formatting toolbar	Format | Cells | Number tab | Accounting	Format Cells | Number tab | Accounting	CTRL+1 | N
Command Button	E 7.28	Command Button button on Control Toolbox toolbar			
Comment	E 6.46		Insert | Comment	Insert Comment	ALT+I | M
Conditional Formatting	E 2.40		Format | Conditional Formatting		ALT+O | D

Microsoft Excel 2002 Quick Reference Summary *(continued)*

TASK	PAGE NUMBER	MOUSE	MENU BAR	SHORTCUT MENU	KEYBOARD SHORTCUT
Copy and Paste	E 3.14	Copy button and Paste button on Standard toolbar	Edit | Copy; Edit | Paste	Copy to copy; Paste to paste	CTRL+C; CTRL+V
Custom Formats	E 6.15		Format | Cells | Number tab | Custom	Format Cells | Number tab | Custom	ALT+O | E | N
Currency Style Format	E 2.34	Currency Style button on Formatting toolbar	Format | Cells | Number tab | Currency	Format Cells | Number | Currency	CTRL+1 | N
Cut	E 3.16	Cut button on Standard toolbar	Edit | Cut	Cut	CTRL+X
Data Form	E 5.09		Data | Form		ALT+D | O
Data Table	E 4.18		Data | Table		ALT+D | T
Data Validation, Cell	E 8.16		Data | Validation		ALT+D | L
Date	E 3.22	Insert Function box on formula bar	Insert | Function		CTRL+SEMICOLON
Decimal Place Decrease	E 2.35	Decrease Decimal button on Formatting toolbar	Format | Cells | Number tab | Currency	Format Cells | Number tab | Currency	CTRL+1 | N
Decimal Place Increase	E 2.35	Increase Decimal button on Formatting toolbar	Format | Cells | Number tab | Currency	Format Cells | Number tab | Currency	CTRL+1 | N
Delete Rows or Columns	E 3.18		Edit | Delete	Delete	
Draft Quality	E 4.45		File | Page Setup | Sheet tab		ALT+F | U | S
Drop Shadow	E 3.40	Shadow Style button on Drawing toolbar			
Embed a Clip Art	E 4.39		Insert | Picture | Clip Art		ALT+I | P | C
E-Mail from Excel	E 2.63	E-mail button on Standard toolbar	File | Send To | Mail Recipient		ALT+F | D | A
File Passwords, Saving	E 8.32		File | Save As | Tools | General Options		ALT+F | A | ALT+L | G
Find	E 6.58		Edit | Find		CTRL+F
Fit to Print	E 2.56		File | Page Setup | Page tab		ALT+F | U | P
Folder, New	EW 1.06		File | Save As		ALT+F | A
Font Color	E 1.31	Font Color button on Formatting toolbar	Format | Cells | Font tab	Format Cells | Font tab	CTRL+1 | F
Font Size	E 1.30	Font Size box arrow on Formatting toolbar	Format | Cells | Font tab	Format Cells | Font tab	CTRL+1 | F
Font Type	E 2.28	Font box arrow on Formatting toolbar	Format | Cells | Font tab	Format Cells | Font tab	CTRL+1 | F
Footer	E 6.48		File | Page Setup | Header/Footer tab		ALT+F | U | H
Formula Auditing Toolbar, Display	E 8.10	Right-click any toolbar, click Formula Auditing	Tools | Formula Auditing | Show Formula Auditing Toolbar		ALT+T | U | S
Formula Checker	E 4.52		Tools | Error Checking		ALT+T | K
Formula Palette	E 2.19	Insert Function box on formula bar	Insert | Function		CTRL+A after you type function name
Formulas Version	E 2.56		Tools | Options | View tab | Formulas		CTRL+ACCENT MARK
Freeze Worksheet Titles	E 3.20		Window | Freeze Panes		ALT+W | F
Full Screen	E 1.12		View | Full Screen		ALT+V | U
Function	E 2.20	Insert Function box on formula bar	Insert | Function		SHIFT+F3
Go To	E 1.36	Click cell	Edit | Go To		F5
Goal Seek	E 3.63		Tools | Goal Seek		ALT+T | G
Gridlines	E 4.45		File | Page Setup | Sheet tab		ALT+F | U | S
Header	E 6.48		File | Page Setup | Header/Footer tab		ALT+F | U | H

Microsoft Excel 2002 Quick Reference Summary

TASK	PAGE NUMBER	MOUSE	MENU BAR	SHORTCUT MENU	KEYBOARD SHORTCUT
Help	E 1.52 and Appendix A	Microsoft Excel Help button on Standard toolbar	Help | Microsoft Excel Help		F1
Hide Column	E 2.46	Drag column heading boundary	Format | Column | Hide	Hide	CTRL+0 (zero) to hide CTRL+SHIFT+ RIGHT PARENTHESIS to display
Hide Row	E 2.48	Drag row heading boundary	Format | Row | Hide	Hide	CTRL+9 to hide CTRL+SHIFT+ LEFT PARENTHESIS to display
Hyperlink	E 4.39	Insert Hyperlink on Standard toolbar	Insert | Hyperlink	Hyperlink	CTRL+K
In-Cell Editing	E 1.49	Double-click cell			F2
Import Data from Access Table	E 9.14		Data | Get External Data | New Database Query		ALT+D | D | N
Import Data from Text Fiie	E 9.09		Data | Get External Data | Import Text File		ALT+D | D | T
Import Data from Web Page	E 9.18		Data | Get External Data | New Web Query		ALT+D | D | W
Import Data from Spreadsheet XML	E 9.23		Data | Get External Data | New Web Query		ALT+D | D | W
Insert Rows or Columns	E 3.16		Insert | Rows or Insert | Columns	Insert	ALT+I | R or C
Italicize	E 3.42	Italicize button on Formatting toolbar	Format | Cells | Font tab	Format Cells | Font tab	CTRL+I
Language Bar	E 1.16	Language Indicator button in tray	Tools | Speech | Speech Recognition		ALT+T | H | H
Link	EI 1.04		Edit | Paste Special		ALT+E | S
Link Update	E 6.67		Edit | Links		ALT+E | K
Macro, Execute	E 7.15	Run Macro button on Visual Basic toolbar	Tools | Macro | Macros		ALT+F8
Macro, Record	E 7.11		Tools | Macro | Record New Macro		ALT+T | M | R
Macro, View Code	E 7.17		Tools | Macro | Macros | Edit		ALT+F8
Margins	E 6.48		File | Page Setup | Margins		ALT+F | U | M
Menu, Customize	E 7.23		Tools | Customize | Commands tab	Customize | Commands tab	ALT+T | C | C
Merge Cells	E 1.32	Merge and Center button on Formatting toolbar	Format | Cells | Alignment tab	Format Cells | Font tab | Alignment tab	ALT+O | E | A
Move	E 3.16	Point to border and drag	Edit | Cut; Edit | Paste	Cut; Paste	CTRL+X; CTRL+V
Name Cells	E 1.36, E 4.12	Click Name box in formula bar and type name	Insert | Name | Create or Insert | Name | Define		ALT+I | N | D
Name Cells, Redefine	E 5.18		Insert | Name | Define		ALT+I | N | D
New Workbook	E 1.52	New button on Standard toolbar	File | New		CTRL+N
Open Workbook	E 1.46	Open button on Standard toolbar	File | Open		CTRL+O
Outline a Range	E 4.09	Borders button on Formatting toolbar	Format | Cells | Border tab	Format Cells | Border tab	CTRL+1 | B
Outline a Worksheet	E 5.30		Data | Group and Outline		ALT+D | G | A
Page Break	E 6.55		Insert | Page Break		ALT+I | B
Page Break, Remove	E 6.55		Insert | Remove Page Break		ALT+I | B
Percent Style Format	E 2.39	Percent Style button on Formatting toolbar	Format | Cells | Number tab | Percentage	Format Cells | Number tab | Percentage	CTRL+1 | N
PivotChart, Add Data to	E 9.43	Drag button from PivotTable toolbar to PivotChart			
PivotChart, Change View	E 9.48	Click interactive buttons on PivotChart			

Microsoft Excel 2002 Quick Reference Summary (continued)

TASK	PAGE NUMBER	MOUSE	MENU BAR	SHORTCUT MENU	KEYBOARD SHORTCUT
PivotChart, Create	E 9.40		Data | PivotTable and PivotChart Report		ALT+D | P
PivotChart, Format	E 9.45	Chart Wizard button on PivotTable toolbar	Chart | Chart Type	Chart Type	ALT+C | T
PivotTable, Change View	E 9.54	Drag buttons to different locations on PivotTable			
PivotTable, Format	E 9.51	Format Report button on PivotTable toolbar	Format | AutoFormat	Format Report	ALT+O | A
PivotTable List, Add Fields	EW 2.12	Drag field from PivotTable Field List window			
PivotTable List, Add Summary Totals	EW 2.08	AutoCalc button on toolbar in browser			
PivotTable List, Change View	EW 2.10	Drag data fields to Row Field area in browser			
PivotTable List, Create	EW 2.03		File | Save as Web Page		ALT+F | G
PivotTable List, Filter	EW 2.06	Click field drop-down arrow and remove check marks			
PivotTable List, Remove Field	EW 2.12		Remove Field		
PivotTable List, Sort	EW 2.09	Sort Ascending button or Sort Descending button on toolbar in browser			
Preview Worksheet	E 2.51	Print Preview button on Standard toolbar	File | Print Preview		ALT+F | V
Properties, Set	E 7.31	Properties button on Control Toolbox toolbar			
Print Area, Clear	E 4.46		File | Print Area | Clear Print Area		ALT+F | T | C
Print Area, Set	E 4.45		File | Print Area | Set Print Area		ALT+F | T | S
Print Row and Column Headings	E 4.45		File | Page Setup | Sheet tab		ALT+F | U | S
Print Row and Column Titles	E 4.45		File | Page Setup | Sheet tab		ALT+F | U | S
Print Worksheet	E 2.51	Print button on Standard toolbar	File | Print		CTRL+P
Protect Worksheet	E 4.49		Tools | Protection | Protect Sheet		ALT+T | P | P
Quit Excel	E 1.45	Close button on title bar	File | Exit		ALT+F4
Range Finder	E 2.25	Double-click cell			
Redo	E 1.51	Redo button on Standard toolbar	Edit | Redo		ALT+E | R
Remove Precedent Arrows, Audit	E 8.12	Remove Precedent Arrows button on Auditing toolbar			
Remove Splits	E 3.61	Double-click split bar	Window | Split		ALT+W | S
Rename Sheet Tab	E 2.62	Double-click sheet tab		Rename	
Replace	E 6.60		Edit | Replace		CTRL+H
Rotate Text	E 3.08		Format | Cells | Alignment tab	Format Cells | Alignment tab	ALT+O | E | A
Route Workbook	E 9.32		File | Send To | Routing Recipient		ALT+F | D | R
Row Height	E 2.47	Drag row heading boundary	Format | Row | Height	Row Height	ALT+O | R | E
Save as Web Page	EW 1.06		File | Save as Web Page		ALT+F | G
Save Workbook – New Name	E 1.41		File | Save As		ALT+F | A
Save Workbook – Same Name	E 2.50	Save button on Standard toolbar	File | Save		CTRL+S

Microsoft Excel 2002 Quick Reference Summary

TASK	PAGE NUMBER	MOUSE	MENU BAR	SHORTCUT MENU	KEYBOARD SHORTCUT
Scenario, Add	E 8.35	Add button in Scenario Manager dialog box	Tools | Scenarios		ALT+T | E | ALT+A
Scenario, Show	E 8.46	Show button in Scenario Manager dialog box	Tools | Scenarios		ALT+T | E | ALT+S
Scenario Manager	E 8.35		Tools | Scenarios		ALT+T | E
Scenario PivotTable	E 8.51	Summary button in Scenario Manager dialog box, choose Scenario PivotTable	Tools | Scenarios		ALT+T | E | ALT+U | ALT+P
Scenario Summary	E 8.49	Summary button in Scenario Manager dialog box, choose Scenario summary	Tools | Scenarios		ALT+T | E | ALT+U | ALT+S
Select All of Worksheet	E 1.52	Select All button on worksheet			CTRL+A
Select Cell	E 1.16	Click cell			Use arrow keys
Select Multiple Sheets	E 3.57	CTRL+click tab or SHIFT+click tab		Select All Sheets	
Search for File	E 6.62	Click Search button on Standard toolbar	File | Search		ALT+F | H
Series	E 3.08	Drag fill handle	Edit | Fill | Series		ALT+E | I | S
Shortcut Menu	E 2.28	Right-click object			SHIFT+F10
Solver	E 8.23		Tools | Solver		ALT+T | V
Solver, Solve Problem	E 8.25	Solve button in Solver Parameters dialog box*	Tools | Solver		ALT+T | V | ALT+S
Sort	E 5.22	Click Sort Ascending or Sort Descending button on Standard toolbar	Data | Sort		ALT+D | S
Spell Check	E 2.48	Spelling button on Standard toolbar	Tools | Spelling		F7
Split Cell	E 1.32	Merge and Center button on Formatting toolbar	Format | Cells | Alignment tab	Format Cells | Alignment tab	ALT+O | E | A
Split Window into Panes	E 3.60	Drag vertical or horizontal split box	Window | Split		ALT+W | S
Stock Quotes	E 2.58		Data | Import External Data | Import Data		ALT+D | D | D
Style, Add	E 6.18		Format | Style | Add button		ALT+O | S
Style, Apply	E 6.20		Format | Style		ALT+O | S
Subtotals	E 5.27		Data | Subtotals		ALT+D | B
Subtotals, Remove	E 5.31		Data | Subtotals | Remove All button		ALT+D | B | R
Switch Summary Functions	E 9.53	Field Settings button on PivotTable toolbar		Field Settings	
Task Pane	E 1.08		View | Task Pane		ALT+V | K
Text Box, Add	E 6.43	Text Box button on Drawing toolbar			
Toolbar, Customize	E 7.19		Tools | Customize | Commands tab	Customize | Commands tab	ALT+T | C | C
Toolbar, Dock	E 3.38	Drag toolbar to dock			
Toolbar, Reset	Appendix D	Toolbar Options, Add or Remove Buttons, Customize, Toolbars		Customize | Toolbars	ALT+V | T | C | B
Toolbar, Show Entire	E 1.14	Double-click move handle			
Toolbar, Show or Hide	E 3.38	Right-click toolbar, click toolbar name	View | Toolbars		ALT+V | T
Track Changes, Disable	E 9.38		Tools | Track Changes | Highlight Changes | remove check mark		ALT+T | T | H

Microsoft Excel 2002 Quick Reference Summary (continued)

TASK	PAGE NUMBER	MOUSE	MENU BAR	SHORTCUT MENU	KEYBOARD SHORTCUT
Track Changes, Enable	E 9.30		Tools | Track Changes | Highlight Changes		ALT+T | T | H
Track Changes, Review	E 9.35	Point to blue triangle	Tools | Track Changes | Accept or Reject Changes		ALT+T | T | A
Trendline, Create	E 9.58		Chart | Add Trendline		ALT+C | R
Underline	E 3.42	Underline button on Formatting toolbar	Format | Cells | Font tab	Format Cells | Font tab	CTRL+U
Undo	E 1.52	Undo button on Standard toolbar	Edit | Undo		CTRL+Z
Unfreeze Worksheet Titles	E 3.32		Windows | Unfreeze Panes		ALT+W | F
Unhide Column	E 2.46	Drag column heading boundary to left	Format | Column | Unhide	Unhide	ALT+O | C | U
Unhide Row	E 2.48	Drag row heading boundary down	Format | Row | Unhide	Unhide	ALT+O | R | U
Unlock Cells	E 4.49		Format | Cells | Protection tab	Format Cells | Protection tab	CTRL+1 | SHIFT+P
Unprotect Worksheet	E 4.51		Tools | Protection | Unprotect Sheet		ALT+T | P | P
Visual Basic Editor	E 7.34	View Code button on Control Toolbox toolbar	Tools | Macro | Visual Basic Editor	View Code	ALT+F11
Web Page Preview	EW 1.03-04		File | Web Page Preview		ALT+F | B
WordArt	E 6.39	Insert WordArt button on Drawing toolbar	Insert | Picture | WordArt		ALT+I | P | W
Workbook Properties	E 8.54		File | Properties		ALT+F | I
Workspace File	E 6.64		File | Save Workspace		ALT+F | W
Zoom	E 3.58	Zoom box on Standard toolbar	View | Zoom		ALT+V | Z